Contents

P9-CFH-218

ADMINISTRATIVE REGIONS

1 Alsace
2 Aquitaine
3 Auvergne
4 Bourgogne
5 Bretagne
6 Centre
7 Champagne-
   Ardenne
8 Corse
9 Franche-Comté
10 Ile-de-France
11 Languedoc-
   Roussillon
12 Limousin
13 Lorraine
14 Midi-Pyrénées
15 Nord-
   Pas-de-Calais
16 Basse-Normandie
17 Haute-Normandie
18 Pays de la Loire
19 Picardie
20 Poitou-Charentes
21 Provence-Alpes-
   Côte d'Azur
22 Rhône-Alpes

Fr. an. 1

Principal sights

Conventional signs

Worth a journey ★★★	═══ Motorway or similar	♣ Ruins
Worth a detour ★★	── Main tourist route	⋒ Caves
Interesting ★	● Place described	♦ Prehistoric sight
	✝ Ecclesiastical Building	▲ Miscellaneous sight
	⨯ Castle or château	0 ——— 50 km

Shown on this map are the towns and sights in the alphabetical section of the guide, with the additional sites attached to them, as well as principal resorts.

A number of other places, monuments, historical events and natural sites appear in the guide and may be found in the index.

De   in Deutsch
En   in English
Es   en Español
Fr   en Français
It   in Italiano
Ne   in het Nederlands
Po   em Português

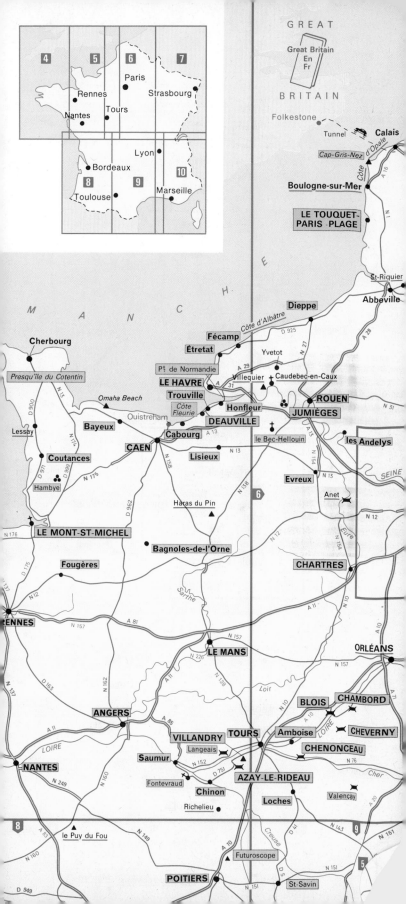

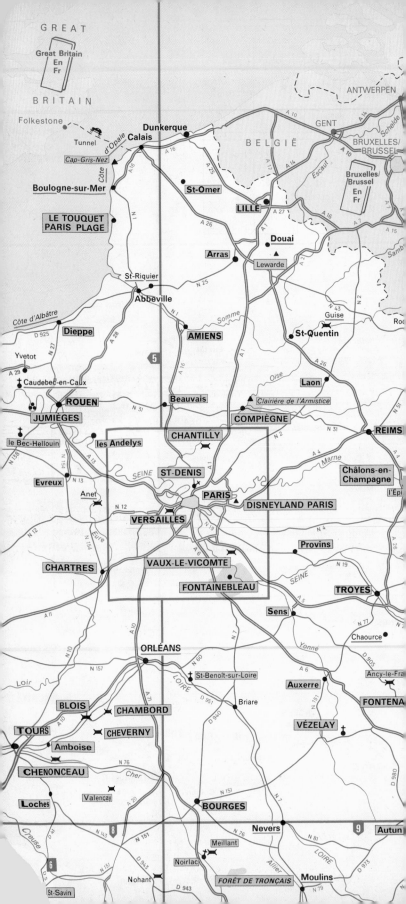

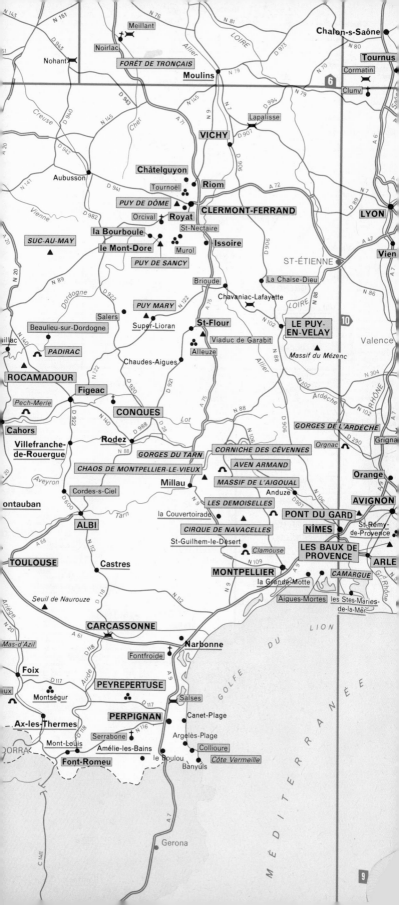

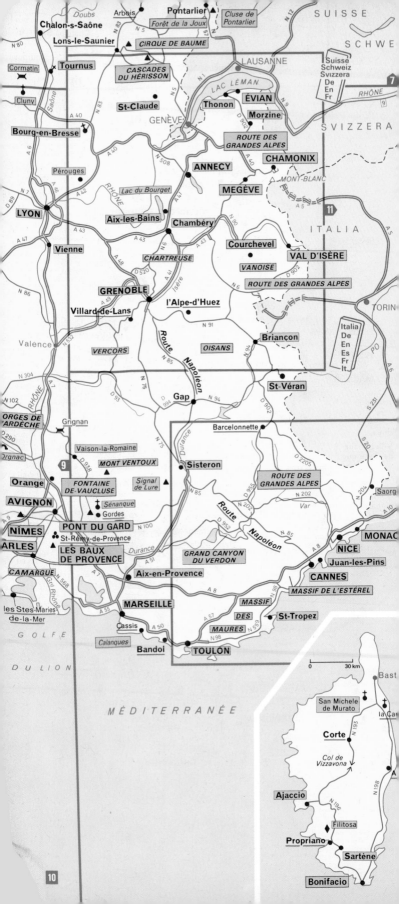

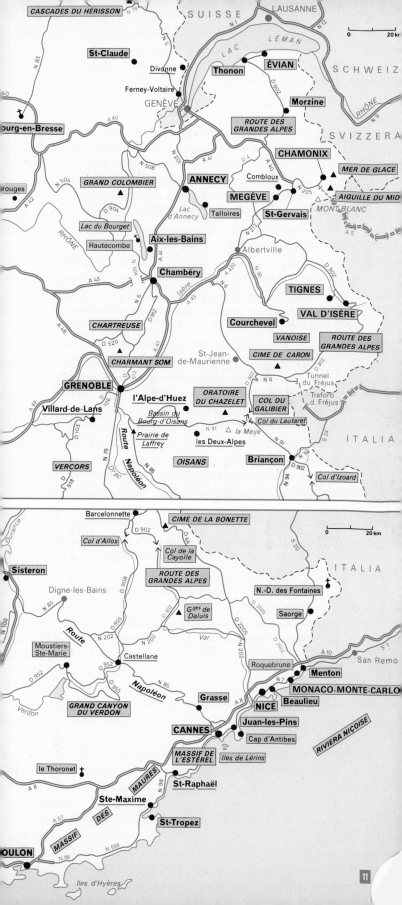

Present-Day France

Although France is ranked among the five leading countries in the world in terms of international trade, it remains a nation with a strong **rural tradition**, even if the number of people employed in farming is on the decline. The French have stayed close to their native land, either by acquiring a cottage in the country or by inheriting a family estate.

For most French people, the qualities associated with this ancestral land are encapsulated in the traditional **village**. The village where one was born, where one has chosen to live or where one spends one's holidays. Leaving aside the differences attributed to climatic conditions and building materials, all villages feature common characteristics: the **main street** (Grand'rue) lined with small shops, the **marketplace**, where local cattle fairs used to be held, and of course the **church**, whose chimes continue to herald the fortunes and misfortunes of the community. Although they see a surge of activity during municipal and trade fairs, French villages lead quiet, peaceful lives most of the year. Only the traditional **café** and the **boules playing ground** echo with the conversations of the locals idly debating on the meaning of life.

Although a series of decentralisation reforms was implemented in 1982, Paris and her nine million inhabitants remain the administrative core of the country, ruling supreme over the provinces.

The seat of political power and an important centre for world trade, "the city of lights" is also a privileged stopover for tourists, on account of its wealth of architectural marvels, its museums and its high cultural standards.

Over the past decades, a number of **regional capitals** have been created, striking a balance between the capital and small country villages. These new urban zones are resolutely turned towards the future and illustrate the thriving activity of the French regions.

This brief description would not be complete without mentioning the **French**. Frequently misunderstood by foreign visitors, believed to be grumpy, unhelpful and unresponsive to outside influences, they are nonetheless always ready to defend their traditions and support a just cause. To those who make the effort of going towards them, the French will always extend a warm, genuine welcome.

Introduction

Landscape

"La France est diversité" France is diversity (Fernand Braudel).

France has a happy location in the European continent – not detached from it like the British Isles, nor projecting far to the west like Iberia, nor set deep in its interior like the countries of Central Europe, yet in touch with the resources and the life of the whole of Western Europe and the seas around it, Atlantic, Channel, Mediterranean and North Sea. These seas together with the other natural frontiers, the Alps and Pyrenees and the River Rhine, define the compact shape of the "hexagon". Within this unified and robust framework there flourishes a geographical identity which is unmistakably French yet of an unrivalled local richness and variety. Less a paradox than a wonderful synthesis, this coexistence of unity and diversity is the work of both Nature and Man.

Geological history – It has been said that the whole of Earth's history – the building of the planet – can be traced within the confines of France. The country's complex geological history starts in the Primary era (600 million years ago), when the Hercynian folding was responsible for the raising up of the great mountain ranges which were the ancestors of today's Massif Central, Armorican Peninsula, Vosges and Ardennes.

In Secondary times (beginning 200 million years ago), the Paris region, Aquitaine, the Rhône and Loire valleys and the southern part of the Massif Central all lay under the sea which gradually filled them with sedimentary deposits.

New mountain ranges reared up in the Tertiary era (beginning 60 million years ago): the Alps, Pyrenees, the Jura and Corsica. The shock-waves of this violent mountain-building were felt far afield, particularly in the Massif Central where great volcanoes erupted.

The Quaternary age (2 million years ago) saw an alternation of warm and cold periods; glaciers advanced and retreated and rivers swelled and shrank, sculpting much of the land surface into its present forms.

Climate and relief – In climatic terms too, France gathers into herself the patterns of the continent as a whole; Atlantic, Continental and Mediterranean influences are all present, contributing decisively to the formation of soils and their mantle of vegetation as well as to the processes which have shaped the geological foundation into the patterns of today's relief.

14

e north of the country is largely composed of great sedimentary basins, scarp
tes) and vale country, drained by slow-flowing rivers like the Seine and the Loire.
the extremities of these lowlands are rugged areas formed of Primary rocks, the
ch eroded granites of Brittany and the gneisses and schists of the Ardennes, and
e higher massifs of the Vosges and the centre. Beyond lie the fertile plains of
uitaine and Languedoc while the corridor carved by the Rhône and Saône links the
rth and south of the country. Finally come the "young" mountains of the Jura, Alps
d Pyrenees; their high peaks and ranges, while forming fine natural frontiers, are
no means impermeable to political, commercial and cultural currents.

e regions of France and their individuality – Few parts of the country are
favourable to human settlement; France is still a largely rural country, with a
atively even spread of population. Great cities and conurbations exist, but beyond

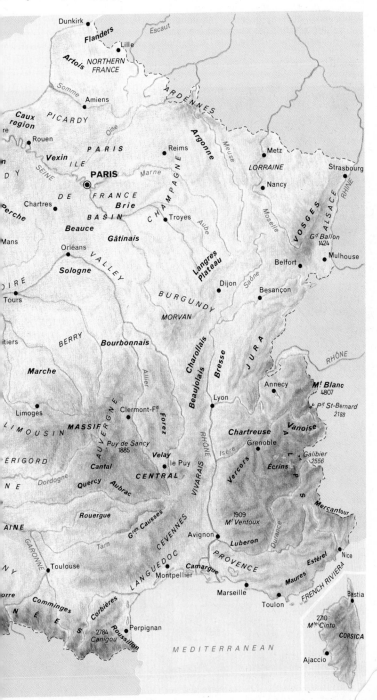

them spreads a spacious countryside, uncrowded but rarely deserted, create
over the centuries by the efforts of its inhabitants, whose collective understandin
of the places where they live is expressed in every detail of the local landscap
The layout of fields, the pattern of crops and woodlands, the grouping of th
population in hamlets, villages and towns, the materials and styles of building, a
combine to proclaim the individuality of the innumerable localities or *pays* whic
themselves contribute to the identity of the larger regions listed belo
and which form the subject of the 24 Michelin regional guides (12 in English

Paris

The presence of a number of islands in the Seine made a convenient crossing poi
here for the prehistoric North-South trade route. Under the Gauls, urba
development was confined to the Île de la Cité, though Roman Lutetia sprea
southwards over today's Latin Quarter. It was the Capetian kings who made Par
their capital, thereby giving it the dominant role in the country's political an
cultural life which it has exercised ever since.

Until modern times, Paris tended to be tightly circumscribed by successive rin
of fortifications (the wall of Philippe Auguste in the 13C, the wall of Charles V
the 14C, and the wall of the Farmers-General in the late 18C), giving the city a muc

The Pyramid at the Louvre

more densely built-up character than, say, London. Within these boundaries, a succession of bold building and planning projects, spread over the centuries, has helped give the city its distinct identity.

Renaissance urbanism was responsible for the layout of the Marais district, centred on the Place des Vosges, where the French town mansion, the *hôtel*, took on its definitive form, while the Baroque sense of drama and movement in the townscape is seen in the grand perspectives opened up on the Invalides, Champ-de-Mars and above all the Champs-Élysées.

Neo-classical monumentality was favoured by Napoleon I in his attempt to make Paris a fittingly Imperial capital, but the greatest planned transformation of all was undertaken in the 19C by Napoleon III and his Prefect, Baron Haussmann, who drove great axial boulevards through the dense web of ancient streets and laid out splendid green spaces like the Bois de Boulogne and the Parc Monceau. In the late 19C and early 20C it was the new institution of the international exhibition which gave the *"Ville Lumière"* some of its most characteristic monuments, the Eiffel Tower, the Grand Palais and Petit Palais, and the Palais de Chaillot.

Under the influence of Le Corbusier and many others, the aesthetics of Parisien architecture have been radically revamped since 1945: UNESCO (1957), the Palais de la Défense (CNIT, 1958), the Maison de la Radio et de la Télévision (1963), the Montparnasse Tower (1973), the Palais des Congrès (1974). This trend was to be confirmed in subsequent years with the building in central Paris of several major landmarks, designed by prominent contemporary architects: the Palais Omnisports de Paris-Bercy (1984), the City of Science and Industry and the Géode Cinema at La Villette (1986), the Opera-Bastille (1989), La Grande Arche at La Défense (1989), the Louvre Pyramid (1989), the Ministry of Finance at Bercy (1990), the Richelieu Wing (1994), an important stage of the "Grand Louvre" projet (1981-1998) and the City of Music at La Villette (1995).

Ile-de-France

This historic region, the kernel from which the French state has grown, is called Île-de-France (literally: Island of France) because of its location between the rivers Seine, Aisne, Oise and Marne. Where its limestone plateaux have been cut into by the rivers, lush valleys have been formed, contrasting with the vast arable tracts of the Beauce, Vexin and Brie. A girdle of greenery surrounds the capital; there are great forests like those of Fontainebleau, Halatte, Chantilly, Ermenonville and Rambouillet, into which merge the landscapes of leisure and pleasure with which the mighty surrounded their châteaux, the parks and gardens of Versailles, Chantilly, Vaux-le-Vicomte... The region's privileged position has left it an exceptional legacy of fine building, ranging from innumerable parish churches to the great monuments of the Gothic dawn, St Denis, Chartres...

From Corot's time, the landscapes of the Île-de-France have moved artists to render their subtleties in paint, the Seine valley above all becoming the great axis of Impressionist activity.

The capital has long burst its bounds to invigorate its region with urban activity of all kinds; its established towns have expanded rapidly to accommodate new populations, aided by new foundations, planned towns like St-Quentin-en-Yvelines, Marne-la-Vallée and Cergy-Pontoise. One indication of the importance of the region in the country's economic life; covering only 2% of the area of France, it now employs 22% of the economically active population.

The Loire valley

This "garden of France" with its abundant horticultural crops, its flowers and its vineyards, has also been called "a homespun cloak with golden fringes", a reference to the contrast between the fertile valleys of the Loire and its tributaries and the low, somewhat bleak plateaux that separate them.

Rising far to the southeast in the Massif Central, France's longest (some 1 000km – 620 miles) river was once a busy waterway, connected as early as 1642 to the Seine basin by the Briare Canal. Many of the towns along its banks bear traces of this former activity, from Gien, rebuilt after its bombing in the Second World War, to Orléans, once the Loire's foremost port, Blois, Tours, Langeais, Saumur... But, as on the Rhône, navigation was never easy, and once the railways came, the Loire was left to its caprices.

Below Gien, the valley opens out and the river describes a great bend partly enclosing the immense heathy tract of the Sologne, rich in game. But it is from Orléans onward that the Loire exercised, and continues to exercise, its greatest attraction; its gentle landscapes and soft light encouraged the kings, courtiers and magnates to build the Renaissance châteaux for which the region is famous, Blois, Chambord, Azay... their elegance and architectural exuberance contrasting with the sterner fortresses of an earlier age like the great castle at Angers. Other building has a distinctive character too, often with white walls of tufa and roofs of slate, while there are trogloditic dwellings, notably around Amboise and Tours.

Brittany

Populated by Celtic settlers who arrived here from Cornwall in the 5C, Brittany retains many affinities with the other Celtic lands fringing the Atlantic. Its identity, quite distinct from that of the rest of France, is expressed in language (Breton, akin to Welsh) and traditions as well as in its landscape.

The province turns its face towards the sea. Its extraordinarily indented coastline, 1 200km – 750 miles long, was given its name **Armor** ("country near the sea") by the Gauls. Its cliffs, reefs, rocky headlands and offshore islands are battered by Atlantic breakers, while its narrow drowned valleys *(abers)* and sandy bays are washed by tides of exceptional range (up to 15m – 49ft).

Much of France's fishing fleet operates from Brittany and there are naval bases, shipyards and commercial harbours too. All around the coast are resorts, some smart (Dinard), some simple.

Inland is the **Argoat** ("country of the wood"), once thickly afforested, now a mixture of *bocage* countryside and wilder landscapes of heath and moor rising to wind-blown granite heights (like Trévezel Rock 384m – 1 229ft) commanding vast prospects. The Montagnes Arrée and Noires mark the natural boundaries of the Lake Guerlédan region and the Châteaulin basin.

The province's long and mysterious past makes itself felt in the abundance of prehistoric remains, menhirs, dolmens, and the great lines of megaliths around Carnac. Granite, outcropping nearly everywhere, distinguishes Breton building, whether in church or chapel, castle or château, harbour wall or humble house, and is used to great effect in the robust and expressive forms of churchyard calvaries.

Normandy

Taking its name from the Norsemen or Normans, this old dukedom extends from the western edge of the Paris Basin towards the Breton peninsula. To many it is reminiscent of southern England, not only in its shared heritage of glorious Norman architecture, but also in the lush, pastoral countryside of the *bocage*, with its small hedged fields, abundant trees and woodlands, apple orchards, sunken lanes and scattered hamlets.

Lower Normandy (Basse-Normandie), like Brittany, is built of old rocks, the sandstones, granites and schists of the Primary era. The Cotentin peninsula projects into the English Channel dividing the Bay of the Seine from the Gulf of St Malo with its dramatic tides washing Mont St-Michel and the rocky Channel Islands (Anglo-Norman Islands in French). To the southeast lies the *bocage* – its hedgebanks offered excellent cover to the German defence in 1944.

On either side of the Seine Valley extends **Upper Normandy** (Haute-Normandie) centred on the historic city of Rouen. To the south is the Pays d'**Auge**, quintessential *bocage* country, famous for its ciders, cheeses and calvados. To the north stretches the vast chalk plain of the Pays de **Caux**, good arable land, bordered by the Channel coast with its white cliffs and hanging valleys.

A diversity of resources has given rise to an exceptional variety in the materials and styles of building; Norman masons fashioned the fine Caen limestone into great ecclesiastical edifices on both sides of the Channel, while humbler structures were built from cob, chalk, pebbles in mortar, brick, timber, shingles and thatch.

Normandy's coast is the nearest to Paris, and while much has changed since Marcel Proust watched Albertine playing at diabolo, its cliffs and beaches continue to attract visitors and holidaymakers.

The North: Flanders, Artois, Picardy

Before the rising sea cut its way through the Straits of Dover at the

Fishing boats, Boulogne

end of the last Ice Age, the chalklands of southern England and the North of France were one; even today the broad fields of the old provinces of **Artois** (capital Arras) and **Picardy** (capital Amiens) recall the English downland, while a gap of only some 30km – 19 miles separates Cap Gris-Nez from the South Foreland and Shakespeare Cliff.

In the claylands of the Pays de Bray, the Vimeux and the Bas Boulonnais is *bocage* countryside, but most of the North's landscapes are open, with few field boundaries to check the view. This high-yielding arable land is broken by a number of valleys like that of the Somme making its way slowly to the sea, its alluvial soils intensively exploited by market gardeners whose tiny plots of land are linked by narrow canals. Many of the towns are sited by these sluggish streams, like Amiens, its superb cathedral a reminder that the region, together with the Île-de-France, was the cradle of Gothic architecture. With few dramatic hills, man-made verticals take on more importance, not only cathedral spires and church towers, but also the bright white concrete water-towers, the volcanic cones of pit-heaps or lines of electricity pylons marching majestically to the horizon. Much of the North is built of brick, from single-storeyed roadside cabin to tall town house, though grander buildings may merit stone.

In close succession along the coast are the ports of Boulogne, Calais and Dunkirk, making this one of France's most important outlets to the sea. As well as chalk and limestone cliffs, there are extensive areas of land reclaimed from the sea, impressive dune systems and fine sandy beaches overlooked by resorts like Le Touquet.

The edges of the chalk country are marked by other, very different landscapes. Northeast is French **Flanders**, consisting largely of polderlands having much in common, including language, with the adjoining Low Countries. Inland is France's "Black country", the *pays noir* of the great coalfield stretching from Béthune to Valenciennes and running into the vast conurbation of a million people formed by Lille-Tourcoing-Roubaix. Further eastward, the green pastures of the more hilly Thierache and Avenois country anticipate the landscapes of the nearby Ardennes. As the Île-de-France is approached, extended wooded tracts appear, like the forest of Compiègne, impressive relics of the Gaulish forest which once extended from the Paris basin to the eastern frontier.

The North is indeed a frontier land, open to the Northern European Plain, an invasion route for successive waves of would-be conquerors, its countryside today studded with the memorials to the victims of two world wars, its place-names redolent of bloody struggles, defeats and victories.

Champagne, Ardennes

The eastern rim of the Paris Basin is formed by an outward-facing series of limestone escarpments pierced by rivers flowing northwest, Marne, Aube, Seine... Around Reims, the steep, sometimes cliff-like slopes of the Côte de l'Île-de-France carry the vineyards which since the days of Dom Pérignon have produced the world's most prestigious sparkling wine. Beyond stretch the sweeping Champagne chalklands, once notorious for their meagre soils, but now, with the use of artificial fertilisers, one of France's most productive agricultural regions. To the east are the Champagne claylands, an area of mostly mixed farming and woodlands, where great artificial lakes, designed to regulate the flow of Seine and Marne, have become important recreational areas. Further eastward still is the Barrois plateau and the escarpment of the Côte des Bars, a favoured site for towns like Bar-le-Duc, Bar-sur-Seine... while to the north, forming a buffer between Champagne and Lorraine, is the vast Argonne forest. The upper valleys of both Marne and Seine lead to an extensive and well-wooded limestone upland, the Plateau de Langres, named after the old fortified town sited on one of its spurs.

The French **Ardennes** form a small part of an ancient massif stretching away into southeastern Belgium and merging with the uplands of the German Eifel. This is one of Europe's most extensive areas of forest, with fine stands of oak and beech as well as conifers, all sheltering abundant game. Sometimes pronounced "impenetrable", the Ardennes have rarely proved a reliable barrier to the passage of armies, least of all in the spring of 1940. Below Charleville-Mézières the meandering Meuse cuts into the plateau, accompanied by a string of industrial towns.

Alsace, Lorraine, Vosges

Alsace forms France's window onto Central Europe. Its capital, Strasbourg, was a free city, part of the Holy Roman Empire, until the days of Louis XIV; together with the other towns and villages along this left bank of the Rhine it has a picturesqueness of decidedly Germanic character. The Rhine itself is both a frontier and, with the Alsace Canal, a great international waterway, flowing through the broad rift valley defined by the Black Forest to the east, the Vosges uplands to the west. The towns avoid the river and its once unpredictable moods; its course leads it through a mysterious and little-frequented landscape of reed swamps, stagnant backwaters and old cut-offs. On the infertile sands and gravels brought down from the Alps grow forests like that of Haguenau, almost 140km² – 54sq miles, 2/7 of which is constituted of Scots pine and the rest of hornbeam, beech and oak. But most of the Alsace countryside wears a cheerful air, particularly when the orchards are in blossom or when the grape-harvest is being collected in the famous vineyards of the foothills, where each eminence seems crowned by some ruined stronghold. Above these lower slopes rise the **Vosges** themselves, their rounded granite summits in the south (the Ballons) contrasting with the more rugged forms of the red sandstone outcropping in the north. The latter is both attractive and easily worked, furnishing building material for many a castle, church or cathedral. In the valleys of these uplands, whose breadth rather than height once hindered communication, are glacial lakes, while the slopes are clad with splendid forests giving way near the summits to rich pastures, the Hautes Chaumes. Laid out for strategic puposes in the First World War, the high-level Route des Crêtes now forms a fine north-south tourist route.

Lorraine owes its name to ancient Lotharingia, central of the three kingdoms into which Charlemagne's inheritance was divided. To the west, the landscape is one of alternating outcrops of limestone and clay, the former giving rise to the escarpments of the Côte de Moselle and Côte de Meuse overlooking these northward-flowing rivers. Eastward to the foot of the Vosges extends the Lorraine plateau, a mixed-farming area of monotonous appearance.

The presence of coal, iron-ore and salt led to the development of heavy industry in adjoining Luxembourg and Saarland as well as in Lorraine (Longwy, Thionville) itself. Fortress towns stud this much-contested province, Bitche, Metz, Verdun...

The Jura

These limestone uplands, part of them in Switzerland, run in a great arc for some 240km – 150 miles from Rhine to Rhône, corresponding roughly to the old province known as the Franche-Comté. The limestones from which they were formed were folded along a northeast-southwest axis into long parallel ridges and valleys by the pressure exerted on them in the Alpine-building period; the exceptionally massive development of the limestone beds (they reach a maximum thickness of some 1 300m – 4 300ft) has led to the term "Jurassic" passing into geological usage for rocks of this age and type (cf the oolitic limestone of the English Cotswolds). Many characteristic features of limestone country occur, like great natural amphitheatres or *cirques* (Cirque de Baume), gorges, caves and chasms, while the regular pattern of valleys and ridges stepping down westwards can be easily appreciated from a number of high viewpoints like the Grand Colombier (1 571m – 5 151ft).

Owing to the high rainfall, extensive forests of beech and oak, firs and spruce (covering 40% of the land surface), and vast upland pastures, this is a verdant landscape. Water is everywhere present, rising from springs and resurgences to feed rushing torrents, spill over spectacular falls (like the Cascades du Hérisson) and fill some seventy lakes. Winters are harsh here, sometimes burying the sturdily-built isolated farmhouses to the eaves of their spreading roofs, and encouraging the development of woodcarving skills during the long months of enforced indoor activity. Woodmanship and forestry have long been supplemented by upland farming (the Jura is famous for its Comté and other cheeses) and at times by other occupations of an industrial character, salt production at Salins and Lons-le-Saunier, clock and watch-making at Besançon, and metal-working, now mostly gone.

The margins of the upland have their own interest; where the westernmost and lowest ridge drops to the Bresse plain is the *Bon Pays*, an attractively variegated countryside including many vineyards, while at the foot of the great cliff falling away from the highest, easternmost ridge towards Geneva and its lake is the Pays de Gex, very much part of the hinterland of the great Swiss city.

Burgundy

Burgundy's unity is based more on history than on geography. Fortunately located on the great trade route linking northern Europe to the Mediterranean, the territory was consolidated in the 15C by the diplomatic skills of its great Dukes; it consists of a number of *pays* of varying character, though its heartland lies in the limestone plateaux stretching eastward from the Auxerre area to the country around the ducal capital, Dijon.

The old dukedom's heritage of Romanesque architecture is outstanding, but the village scene is characteristic too, the colours of the countryside repeated in the warm red roofs and mellow limestone walls of the houses clustered around a modest church made of the same materials.

Towards the east, the elevated land terminates in escarpments dropping down to the wide valley of the Saône. Of these, La Côte is the most renowned, its slopes producing some of the world's finest wines, its centuries of prosperity made manifest in the large and comfortable houses of the wine-growers.

Standing apart from the province and long isolated from the wider world through poor communications, is the **Morvan**, a granite massif of poor soils, lonely farmsteads and scattered hamlets and extensive forests, its highest point being

Haut-Folin (901m – 2 956ft). To the west and north of the Morvan are other pays, the plateaux and hills of the Nivernais stretching away to the Loire, the moorlands and pastures of the Gâtinais and Puisaye, while to the south the lower reaches of the Saône are bordered by the broad Bresse plain, famous for its beef, pork and delicately-fleshed poultry.

Berry, Limousin

Little touched by industrialisation or mass tourism, these two regions seem to represent the quintessence of rural France.

Berry centres on Bourges, which with its great cathedral was once the seat of the French court. The vast limestone plateau which forms the area's heartland was settled as long ago as Neolithic times and is now devoted to large-scale arable farming. In contrast are the intimate *bocage* landscapes of the valleys of the Boischaut, the vines and orchards of the Sancerrois and the Brenne marshlands, a nature reserve of the first importance with innumerable ponds and little sandstone knolls covered in pine and broom.

Limousin is the name of the old province around Limoges forming the northwestern extremity of the Massif Central. Much of it is a quiet countryside of hedgerows, ponds and shady meadows, drained by rivers flowing westwards towards Saintonge and the Dordogne. In contrast is the Montagne, its name derived more from the rigour of its climate than from altitude since nowhere does it rise above 1 000m – about 3 300ft; the Plateau des Millevaches is a thinly-peopled upland, grazed by sheep and cattle, blasted by wind and rain and with a high snowfall. The province's urban pattern is one of old market towns with solid, granite-walled and slate-roofed houses.

The Atlantic Coast: Poitou, Vendée, Charentes

Between the estuaries of the Loire and the Gironde France faces the breezes and breakers of the Atlantic with a generally flat but otherwise fascinatingly varied coastline. There are great marshy tracts like the Marais Breton and above all the Marais Poitevin, low cliffs, vast mud-flats shimmering at low tide and dune systems bordering splendid sandy beaches. Landscapes inland are equally varied. Like Brittany, the **Vendée** has a granite foundation; its *bocage* countryside is one of deep

lanes and scattered farm-steads, while its heaths and moors rise to 295m – 968ft at Puy Crapaud. **Poitou** and **Charentes** are linked by the green valley of the Charente. Low lime-stone plateaux form the characteristic scenery of the region; on the right bank of the river are the vineyards of Cognac, whose product is distilled into the famous spirit, while further north, stretching across the Gate of Poitou, the water-shed between Loire and Charente, are extensive

Taking the ferry, Marais poitevin

tracts of open, almost treeless farmland. In places the limestone forms spurs, good defensive sites for towns like Angoulême.

To the south is the Gironde, the name given to the estuary of the Garonne; its fine beaches extend from Meschers to the Coubre headland.

Off this western coast are a number of islands, each with a distinct identity. **Noirmoutier** is connected to the mainland by a causeway covered at high tide. **Yeu**, further south, has an altogether more Breton character, with a wild, rocky coastline. The holiday island of **Ré** with its saltmarshes is now linked to the mainland by a new road bridge. **Aix**, fortified by Vauban, was where Napoléon spent his last days on French soil, while **Oléron**, France's largest island apart from Corsica, enjoys a remarkably mild climate.

Dordogne: Périgord, Quercy

With its hills, its mature and varied agricultural landscapes, its deciduous woodlands and its mellow stone buildings, this is a welcoming region, not unlike parts of southern England, albeit with a more genial climate and a general atmosphere of good living. Perhaps it is this pleasing synthesis of the familiar and the mildly exotic, more than the traces of the area's long association with the English Crown, that has led to its popularity with visitors from beyond the Channel. Limestone underlies most of the area, in **Périgord** forming extensive plateaux deeply dissected by the Dordogne and other rivers; along the banks grow southern crops like maize, tobacco and sunflowers, as well as grass and cereals and numerous walnut trees. The soil is also suitable for the cultivation of strawberries.

On the higher land there are woodlands of oak and chestnut, and in the Périgord noir, evergreen oaks too. The region is famous for the truffles which grow at the foot of oak trees.

In **Quercy** the thick layers of Jurassic limestone form *causses*, lying at a height of about 300m – 1 000ft, with a sparse cover of juniper, scrubby oaks and carob trees. These sheep-grazed uplands are dissected by dry valleys and spectacular canyons and there are caves and chasms and underground watercourses.

The area has been settled since very early times. Evidence of its attractiveness to prehistoric people extends beyond tools and implements to wall paintings and engravings, low reliefs and decorated bone, ivory and stone. As well as stunning examples of medieval settlement seeming to have grown organically from its site (Rocamadour, St-Cirq-Lapopie), there are numerous reminders of the Anglo-French struggle, from the geometrically planned towns *(bastides)* laid out by both parties to help consolidate their hold on the territory (Monpazier), to rugged strongholds like Beynac and Bonaguil. The medieval and later importance of the towns is expressed in a fine tradition of building in limestone (Sarlat).

Auvergne

The Auvergne forms the core of the **Massif Central**. It is a volcanic landscape, unique in France – its forms range from the classic cones of the Monts Dômes to the rugged shapes of the much eroded Monts Dore and the great Cantal volcano and to the lava flows which seem to have only just cooled into immobility. In the Cézallier area, the streams of lava have piled up on one another to surround the flattened dome of the Signal du Luguet; at La Cheire d'Aydat, the molten torrent has taken on a crystalline pattern, while around St-Flour it has formed the great stretches of upland known locally as *planèzes*. Elsewhere, the lava has filled valley floors, protecting them from the erosion wearing away the hills around and giving rise to the phenomenon of relief inversion (Polignac, Carlat, Gergovie). At Bort-les-Orgues and Le Puy there are curious crystalline formations resembling organ-pipes.

The volcanic activity has created an array of lakes and other water-bodies; at Aydat and Guéry a lava flow has blocked a valley, trapping its waters, while the same effect has been produced at Chambon and Montcineyre by a volcano erupting in the valley itself. Elsewhere, as at Chauvet, the hollows produced by a series of volcanic exposions have filled with water. Lakes have also formed inside a crater (Bouchet, Servière) or within the steep walls of an explosion crater (Gour de Tazenat, Pavin). This great variety of relief makes for fine upland walking country, while the towns and villages of sombre granite have their own allure, heightened by the presence of some of France's finest Romanesque churches. The Auvergne is a mainly agricultural region, the grazing grounds of the higher land complemented by the rich alluvial soils of the series of basins through which the Allier flows northward towards the **Bourbonnais** with its *bocage* countryside of rich pasturelands. Industry is present too, notably at Clermont-Ferrand (Michelin), the provincial capital overlooked from a height of 1 465m – 4 806ft by the old volcano of the Puy de Dôme.

The area is famous for its springs, the spas which have grown up around them (Vichy) and for the bottling and marketing of mineral water.

The Rhône valley

Together with its tributary, the Saône, which joins it at Lyons, this great river has long served as a communications corridor of the first importance, linking northwestern Europe to the Mediterranean. Though its valley seems to divide the ancient uplands to the west from the younger, folded rocks of the Alps to the east, its geological structure is of some complexity; at Vienne and St-Vallier the river carves its way through some of the outermost granitic bastions of the Massif Central, while at Valence it flows between one of the last terraces of the Dauphiné and the limestone ridge of Crussol backing on to the granite mass of the Vivarais. The area around the great city of Lyon itself is marked by centuries of industrial activity. Downstream, the river's course takes it through a succession of narrow gorges and broad basins, where châteaux perched on spurs alternate with an attractive pattern of red-roofed villages set among vineyards (some of them first planted in pre-Roman times) and orchards, though industry is present too. The southern character of the landscape becomes ever more pronounced, olives and evergreen oaks appearing just below Montélimar.

Fed by Alpine thaws, the Rhône's currents could be dangerously swift, its level unpredictable, its bed mobile. Until the incorporation of the Dauphiné, Dromme and the Papal lands around Avignon into the French kingdom, it was a frontier too, further obstacle to easy commerce. Towns tended to develop in pairs, one on the east "foreign" bank, one on the west "French" bank, like Vienne/Ste-Colombe, Valence/St-Péray, Avignon/Villeneuve-lès-Avignon... The very diverse character of the river's banks and the frequency with which it is joined by wide tributaries made it difficult to form a satisfactorily continuous towpath, and later to engineer railway lines. But the Rhône has been tamed; decades of construction (18 dams, 13 power stations and locks) now allow 2 000 tonne barges to reach Lyon. Nevertheless, the improved waterway only carries a fraction of the total traffic using its corridor; it is supplemented by the A6 motorway, two national highways, a main line railway on each bank (one carrying TGV traffic), a gas pipeline, an oil pipeline...

To the west of the river runs an escarpment marking the edge of the Massif Central. Close to the old industrial area centred on St-Étienne is Mont Pilat (1 432m – 4 698ft) offering a number of splendid viewpoints over the Rhône valley (Crêt de l'Oeillon). Southward lie the basalt plateaux of the Velay and the lava flows and limestone country of the Vivarais, cut by the spectacular Ardèche gorges.

Provence and the Rhône delta

The Rhône flows into the sea in the centre of France's Mediterranean coastline, the Midi (South). Here, "the climate has imposed a unifying stamp reflected in both the landscape and the way of life" (J. Sion) and Mediterranean influences are supreme, from the extensive remains of the six centuries of Roman occupation to the traditional triumvirate of wheat, vine and olive alternating with the remnants of the natural forest (evergreen oaks, pines) and the infertile but wonderfully aromatic *garrigues*.

Among the fertile Provençal plains stand the *mas*, shallow-roofed pantiled farmsteads protected from the fierce sun by stone walls with few window openings. Crops and buildings are shielded from the violence of the master-wind from the north, the *mistral*, by serried ranks of cypresses. The plains are flanked by ranges of limestone hills running east-west, including the picturesque Alpilles, the rugged Luberon range and the Vaucluse plateau with its chasms, gorges and great resurgent spring at Fontaine-de-Vaucluse.

The Provençal landscape and the intensity of the light have played a key role in the evolution of modern painting; Mt Ste-Victoire never ceased to fascinate Paul Cézanne, while Arles and the countryside around was made to reflect the tormented spirit of Vincent van Gogh.

The 20 million cubic metres of sand, gravel and silt brought down annually by the the Rhône has created the vast deltaic plain of the **Camargue**, a lonely place of saltmarshes and lagoons, populated by herdsmen and wildfowl. Before it changed its course to join the Rhône, the Durance too flowed directly into the sea through the Lamanon Gap, depositing vast quantities of boulders and pebbles to form the Grande Crau, a stony wasteland scorched by summer sun and blasted by the *mistral* in winter and increasingly invaded by the industries spawned by Marseille, France's great Mediterranean port and second city.

The Rhône at Tain-l'Hermitage

Tarn Gorges: Cévennes, Lower Languedoc

Along the southern edge of the Massif Central stretch the **Grands Causses**, vast limestone tablelands of striking severity. They are laced with corniche roads offering unforgettable views over the deep canyons and gorges hollowed out by the Tarn and its tributaries. Below the surface is a "speleologist's paradise" of caves and chasms, and the endlessly weird forms produced by dissolution and deposition. Where dolomite occurs, weathering has resulted in the fantastic pinnacles and castellations of the rocky chaos known as Montpellier-le-Vieux.

The *causses* are bounded by landscapes of surprising diversity. The lava flows of the Aubrac area have given rise to a countryside of immensely broad horizons, one of France's least populated areas. The **Cévennes**, mostly designated a National Par consist of lowering granite summits overlooking deep and narrow valleys separated by crests *(serres)*, a secret and long impenetrable area which merges southward with the Mediterranean vegetation of the *garrigues*.

The central plain of **Lower Languedoc** (capital: Montpellier) with its vast and highly productive vineyards, is bordered by a chain of brackish lakes, separated from the sea by sandy bars. Old towns like Sète (created in the 17C by Louis XIV) are complemented by planned modern resorts such as La Grande Motte with its modern apartment buildings in ziggurat form.

Far to the southwest, the ancient rocks of the Montagne Noire form the last outpost of the Massif Central. Behind it stretches the varied countryside of the Segalas and the great granite block of the Sidobre.

The Pyrenees

Dividing France from Spain, these mountains, the "most satisfactory of France's frontiers", run some 400km – 250 miles from Atlantic to Mediterranean.

In the west is the **Basque country**, topographically and linguistically distinct, though many of the valleys descending northwards at right angles to the main crestline form *pays* (**Béarn, Bigorre**) with their own character and traditions. Here is spectacular mountain scenery, jagged ridges, great natural amphitheatres streaked with waterfalls, high altitude lakes and rushing torrents, all in contrast to the well-cultivated valley bottoms with their scattering of white houses.

Cirque de Gavarnie

The centre of the range is formed by the splendid Maladetta Massif rising high above the **Comminges** country and the most venerable of the Pyrenees' many spas, Luchon. Northwards, a vast fan-shaped area of ridges and valleys has been formed from glacial debris brought down from the mountains and by subsequent river action. Prolonged westwards by the valleys of the turbulent Adour and its tributaries, this landscape gives way to varied cropland along the course of **Aquitaine's** principal river, the Garonne. Here, the kindly climate and rich alluvial soils have allowed each town to develop its own specialised product, like the plums of Agen, which, dried, become delicious prunes. The ancient English province of **Guyenne** grew up around the confluence of Garonne and Dordogne, an area devoted then as now to the production of the world's most coveted wines. Beyond the provincial capital of Bordeaux, the Garonne widens out into the broad estuary of the Gironde. The Atlantic coast (Côte d'Argent) south of Grave Point at the mouth of the estuary runs in a straight line almost to the Spanish border, interrupted only by the great Bay of Arcachon. Behind the vast sandy beaches rise the highest sand dunes in Europe, while inland are the **Landes**, once an immense, ill-drained waste, now successfully planted with profitable pinewoods.

Among the former statelets of the Pyrenees like the Pays de Foix, Andorra alone preserves its independence. The watershed between Atlantic and Mediterranean is crossed by the Canal du Midi, built as early as 1680 to link sea to ocean. The former capital of Languedoc, Toulouse, is France's sixth largest city, an important industrial centre. All around and northward in the **Albigeois** too, lies rich farming country, the granary of Southern France.

At the Mediterranean extremity of the Pyrenees lies **Roussillon**, France's Catalan province, the often snow-covered peak of Canigou (2 784m – 9 134ft) a symbol to Catalans on both sides of the border. At a lower level lie the upland basins of the Cerdagne and the Capcir, then come the forests and pastures of the Vallespir (Tech valley), the rugged Aspres hills, and finally the plain of Roussillon itself, a great market-garden with its vines and abundant fruit and vegetable crops. The province is bounded to the south by the rocky Côte Vermeille, where the Albères mountains descend to the sea through the Banyuls vineyards and scattered cork oaks clinging to the steep slopes. Few contrasts could be greater than the one between this charmingly irregular coastline with its ancient port-resort of Collioure and the sweeping beaches to the north, backed by the planned modern tourist developments of Languedoc-Roussillon.

The French Alps

Stretching 370km – 230 miles from the Mediterranean to Lake Geneva, the French Alps display all the varieties of mountain scenery, from the sublimity of bare rock and eternal snow to the animation of densely-settled valleys. Nowhere more than among these incomparable mountains does human habitat show such close adaptation to natural conditions. Centuries of endurance and ingenuity have overcome formidable obstacles and brought all possible resources into play, settling not only valley floors, but pushing grazing and cultivation to its highest limits and developing widely-varied local traditions of living and building. Whether grouped sociably in village or hamlet or standing proudly in isolation, the traditional farmhouse combines under a single roof, with a minimum of openings, virtually all the functions of the farm (residence, barn, storage, drying...). Building form, orientation and choice of materials (stone, slate, timber, shingles...) all reflect the resources of the locality, reinforcing a sense of place which is already strong in these valley *pays*.

In modern times the Alps have become a vast playground, welcoming visitors at all seasons to sophisticated resort and remote cabin alike. The mountains have never discouraged communication, rather channelling it through valleys linked by pass routes where necessary. The grandiose works of the railway engineers have been followed by steady improvement of the road network, opening up to the touring motorist such spectacular itineraries as the Route des Grandes Alpes.

The northern boundary of the French Alps and part of the country's frontier with Switzerland is marked by the great sweep of **Lake Geneva**. To the south of the superb lake rise the Alps of Savoy, first the Chablais and Faucigny country, then the famous peaks and glaciers around the great white mountain, Mont-Blanc. Westward lie other graceful stretches of water, Lake Annecy, Le Bourget Lake, still in a mountain setting, but bordered by flower-bedecked resorts and villages and a countryside of human scale, patterned by woodlands, fruit and nut trees, crops and pasture, a landscape in cheerful contrast to the sometimes severe countenance of the higher land.

An important southwest-northeast communication route is formed by the Sub-Alpine Furrow, a broad and prosperous valley in which Grenoble, the metropolis of the Alps, sits at the confluence of Isère and Drac. The latter river and its tributaries rise among the crystalline rocks of the **Écrins** mountains, while the headwaters of the Isère flow through the **Vanoise** massif, with its deep valleys and vast pastures the site of France's first National Park.

The western rampart of the Alps is formed by a succession of massifs, Bauges, **Chartreuse, Vercors...**; the last an extraordinary natural fortress of giddy limestone cliffs.

Beyond Briançon, hard up against the Italian border, the mountains are lit by the strong light of the Mediterranean. Here, among splendid forests of larch and high grazing grounds, settlement reaches its maximum altitude in Europe in villages like St-Véran (2 040m – 6 693ft); the houses exhibit extreme adaptation to rigours of site and climate.

Further south still, the scene is often one of striking severity, bare rock rising from vegetation of increasingly Mediterranean character, the olive tree making its appearance in the middle reaches of the Durance, the main watercourse of the Southern Alps.

The stark summit of Mount Ventoux overlooks the Comtat plain, while eastwards lie the most desolate tracts of the whole Alpine region, the Pre-Alps and high plateaux of Provence; here torrential streams have scored deep gorges like that of the Grand Canyon of the Verdon.

In Upper Provence (Haute-Provence), and particularly in the Maritime Alps which form the backdrop to the French Riviera, the proximity of the Mediterranean world makes itself felt again in the numerous fortified hill-top villages, with their houses of stone, pantiled roofs and fountains splashing in shady squares.

The richness of the natural heritage of the French Alps is reflected in the number of National (Mercantour, Écrins as well as Vanoise) and Regional Parks (Vercors, Queyras) set up to protect these incomparable landscapes and enhance the visitors' experience of them.

The French Riviera

The Riviera's brilliant light, abundant sunshine, exotic vegetation and dramatic combination of sea and mountains have made it a fashionable place of pleasure since its "discovery" in the 19C; it is the archetypal holiday coast against which all others must be measured.

Between Nice and Menton, the Pre-Alps plunge almost sheer into the sea. The coast is densely built up, the resorts linked by triple corniche roads. Further north are the Maritime Alps, dissected by the upper valleys of the Var, Tinée, Vésubie and Roya, and, on the Italian border, the great crystalline massif of the **Mercantour** (Cime du Gélas 3 143m – 10 312ft). To the west of Nice the coast flattens out, forming wide bays with fine beaches.

The bustle of the coast is in contrast to the quieter charm of the interior, with i valleys carpeted in olive groves, its spectacular gorges, and its many hill-villag built to protect the population from the perils which proximity to the coast mig bring. The limestone plateaux of the Provence tableland are separated from the s by two massifs, Esterel and Maures. The jagged rocks of brightly-coloured porphy making up the **Esterel massif** are best appreciated from the coast road leading fro St-Raphaël to Cannes. The Estérel has been largely denuded of its former fores but to the west, the **Maures massif** retains much of its fine cover of pine, cork o; and chestnut. Its coastline has great promontories and narrow tongues of lar extending into the sea, defining wide bays like that of the Gulf of St-Tropez. Offsho are the densely-vegetated Hyères Islands, detached from the mainland in geolo(cally recent times.

The Toulon coast, with its outstanding roadstead, is characterised by vertical clif interrupted by a number of attractive beaches. To the north rise the rugg limestone heights of the Provençal Ranges; Mount Fanon overlooks the great Fren(naval port from an elevation of 584m – 1 916ft.

Corsica

The mountainous "Island of Beauty", the name given to Corsica by the ancie Greeks, lies some 170km – just over 100 miles off the coast of mainland Franc With its intense light, its superbly varied and dramatic coast and its wild and rugg(interior, it is a place of utterly distinct natural identity, enhanced by the successic of peoples who have been attracted here to settle or to rule; these have include megalith builders and mysterious Torreens, Greeks and Romans, Pisans a Genoese, French and British, though the somewhat absurd interlude of t Anglo-Corsican Viceroyalty of 1794-96 seems to have left little trace.

The gulfs of Corsica's west coast are of extraordinary beauty, the jagged headlan and precipitous porphyry cliffs rising from the Golfe de Porto being especia memorable. The Cap Corse promontory prolongs the island's backbone of schist rocks 40 km – 25 miles northwards into the sea. The coastal plains of Bast and Aléria to the east constitute the only substantial areas of flat land; the agricultural prosperity has revived in recent years, largely through the enterpri of resettled *pieds-noirs* from Algeria.

The interior is penetrated by a skeletal network of narrow and winding roads well as by a remarkable metre-gauge railway. Here are villages of tall granite hous overlooking deep gorges, as well as superb forests of oak, Corsican pine and swe chestnut, *garrigue* and *maquis* vegetation. Above the tree line rise the high ba summits, all the more imposing because of their proximity to the sea. Much of inla Corsica is now protected as a Regional Nature Park, through which GR 20, one Europe's finest long-distance footpaths, threads its way.

Les Aiguilles at Bavella and Zonza

Historical table and notes

The great sweep of prehistory has left abundant traces in France, and it is to Frenchmen that much of our knowledge of prehistoric times is due. *See p 150* (ABC of Prehistory).

Ancient times

BC	
5000	Megalithic culture flourishes in Brittany (Carnac), then in Corsica, lasting for over 2 500 years.
8C	Celtic tribes from central Europe arrive in Gaul where they build the fortified settlements known as oppidums.
6DD	Greek traders found a number of cities, including Marseilles, Glanum *(qv)* and Aléria in Corsica.
2C	Celtic culture, which had spread as far as Brittany, gives way to both Germanic and Roman influences. The port of Fréjus, on the Mediterranean coast, is founded in 154 by the Romans as a link on the sea route to their possessions in Spain. By the year 122 they have established themselves at Aix, and four years later at Narbonne.
58-52	Julius Caesar's Gallic Wars. He defeats the Veneti in 56BC *(qv)*, then himself suffers defeat at the hands of Vercingetorix *(qv)* in BC52, though the latter's surrender comes only a few months later.

AD	
1C	During the reign of Augustus Roman rule in Gaul is consolidated and expanded *(p 211)*. Fréjus is converted into a naval base and fortified.
5C	The monasteries set up by St Martin at Ligugé and by St Honorat at Lérins reinforce Christian beliefs and mark the beginning of a wave of such foundations (by St Victor at Marseilles, by St Loup at Troyes, by St Maxime at Riez…).

The Merovingians (418-751)

451	Merovius, king of the Salian Franks (from the Tournai area in present-day Belgium), defeats Attila the Hun *(p 120)*. It is to him that the dynasty owes its name.
476	Fall of the Roman Empire in the West; Gaul occupied by barbarian tribes.
496	Clovis, grandson of Merovius and King of the Franks, is baptised in Rheims.
507	Defeat of the Visigoths under Alaric II at Vouillé *(qv)* by Clovis.
6C	Accompanied by Christian missionaries, settlers from Britain arrive in the Breton peninsulas, displacing the original Celtic inhabitants. But they too are overcome, first by the Franks (in the 9C), then by the Angevins (11C).
732	The Arab armies invading France are defeated at Moussais-la-Bataille *(qv)* by Charles Martel.

The Carolingians (751-986)

751	Pepin the Short has himself elected king by an assembly of magnates and bishops at Soissons, sending the powerless Childeric, last of the Merovingians, to a monastery.
800	Charlemagne is crowned Emperor of the West in Rome.
842	The Strasbourg Oaths.
843	By the Treaty of Verdun, the Carolingian Empire is divided between the sons of Louis I, Charles the Bald receiving the territories to the west, roughly corresponding to modern France.
850	Nominoé *(qv)* wrests eastern Brittany and the Rais country south of the Loire from its Frankish rulers.
910	Foundation of the great abbey at Cluny.
911	By the Treaty of St-Clair-sur-Epte, Charles the Simple and the Viking chief Rollo create the Duchy of Normandy.

The Capetians (987-1789)

The Direct Capetians (987-1328)

987	A descendant of Robert the Strong, Hugh Capet, Duke of "France", ousts Charles of Lorraine and has himself elected. By having his son crowned during his own lifetime, he consolidated his family's rule, which nevertheless does not become truly hereditary until the accession of Philippe Auguste in 1180.

1066	William Duke of Normandy (qv) sets out for the English coast from Dives. His victory over Harold at the Battle of Hastings leads to his coronation as King of England, though technically speaking he is still a vassal of the French king.
1095	The First Crusade is preached at Clermont-Ferrand.
1137	Louis VII weds Eleanor of Aquitaine (qv); the annulment of their marriage 15 years later is a disaster for the dynasty.
	Foundation of the School of Medecine at Montpellier.
1204	Gaillard Castle falls to Philippe Auguste, who goes on to conquer Normandy, Maine, Touraine and Anjou.
1209	Start of the Albigensian Crusade.
1214	Victory at the Battle of Bouvines (qv); for the first time, a genuinely French patriotism appears.
1244	Cathars burnt at the funeral pyre at Montségur.
1270	St Louis (Louis IX) dies aboard ship off Tunis on his way to the Eighth Crusade.

The House of Valois (1328-1589)

The Hundred Years War – 1337-1475. Extending over six reigns, the war was both a political and dynastic struggle between Plantagenets and Capetians over who should rule in France. Accompanied by plague (including the Black Death of 1348) and religious confusion, it was a time of tribulation for the people of France, harrassed as they were by bands of outlaws as well as by the English soldiery.

In 1337, Philippe VI of Valois resisted the claims to his throne made by Edward III of England (the grandson on his mother's side of Philippe le Bel (the Fair). This marked the beginning of the war. Three years after the French defeat at Crécy (qv), Philippe VI purchased the Dauphiné (up to then a territory of the Empire) from its ruler, Humbert II, thereby extending French rule far to the east of the Rhône.

In 1356 King John the Good was defeated by the Black Prince at the Battle of Poitiers (qv). Under Charles V, Du Guesclin succeeded in restoring internal order. But at this point in their conflict, both adversaries were beset by

Royal Seal of Saint Louis

problems of their own, caused in England by the minority of Richard II. In France Charles VI was under age, then affected by madness. The War between Armagnacs and Burgundians began and the Church was torn by the Great Schism (p 84). Following the English victory at Agincourt (qv) and the assassination of John the Fearless of Burgundy at Montereau (qv), the Treaty of Troyes, promising the French crown to the English king, seemed to extinguish any hope of the future Charles VII succeeding.

In 1429, however, after having picked out the king from among the courtiers assembled at Chinon, Joan of Arc recaptured Orléans, thereby preventing Salisbury's army from crossing the Loire and meeting up with the English troops who had been stationed in central and southwestern France following the Treaty of Brétigny in 1360. On 17 July, Charles VII was crowned in Rheims cathedral; in 1436 Paris was freed, followed by Normandy and Guyenne. In 1453, the French victory at Castillon-la-Bataille was the last important clash of arms in the war, which was formally brought to an end by the Treaty of Picquigny (qv).

1515	Accession of François I; Battle of Marignano and the signing of peace in perpetuity with Switzerland.
1520	Meeting of François I and Henry VIII of England at the Field of the Cloth of Gold at Guînes.
1539	The Ordinance of **Villers-Cotterêts (53** 3), one of the bases of French law, is promulgated by François I. Among its 192 articles are ones decreeing the keeping of parish registers of births and deaths, and the compulsory use of French instead of Latin in legal matters. By this time, provincialism was on the way out, supplanted by a truly national consciousness, the outcome of three centuries of shared ordeals and triumphs.
1541	Calvin's *"Institutes of the Christian Religion"* is published. In it, this native Frenchman (born at Noyon) attempts to stem the fissiparious tendencies of the Reformation and to proclaim its universality. Style, structure and significance combine in this work to make it the first great classic of French literature.
1559	Treaty of Le Cateau-Cambrésis (qv).
1560	The Amboise Conspiracy, harbinger of the looming political and religious crisis.

The Wars of Religion – 1562-98. This is the name given to the 36-year long crisis marked by complex political as well as religious conflict. During the latter half of the 16C, the French monarchy was in poor shape to withstand the looming hegemony of Spain, with political life in chaos and debt reaching incredible dimensions. The firm stand taken on religion by Spain and Italy on the one hand and by the Protestant countries on the other was missing in the France of Catherine de' Medici's regency, where both parties jostled for favour and a policy of appeasement applied. The nobility took advantage of the situation, seeking to bolster their power base in the provinces and, under cover of religion, to grasp the reins of government. The Catholic League was formed by the Guise and Montmorency families, supported by Spain and opposed by the Bourbon, Condé and Coligny factions, Huguenots all, with Englishbacking.

Though historians distinguish eight wars separated by periods of peace or relative tranquillity, the troubles were continuous; in the country, endless assassinations, persecutions and general lawlessness, at court, intrigues, volte-faces and pursuit of particular interests. Actual warfare, threatened ever since the Amboise Conspiracy, began at Wassy in 1562, following a massacre of Protestants. The names of Dreux, Nîmes, Chartres, Longjumeau, Jarnac, Montcontour, St-Lô, Valognes, Coutras, Arques, Ivry follow in bloody succession.

The Peace of St-Germain in 1570 showed a general desire for reconciliation, but only two years later came the St Bartholemew's Day Massacre in which some 20 000 Huguenots died.

Fearful of the power enjoyed by Duke Henri of Guise, head of the Catholic League, King Henri III had him assassinated in the château at Blois one cold morning in December 1588, only to be cut down himself by a fanatical monk the following year. This left the succession open for the Huguenot Henry of Navarre, the future Henri IV. By formally adopting the Catholic faith in 1593 and by promulgating the Edict of Nantes in 1598, this able ruler succeeded in rallying all loyal Frenchmen to his standard, putting at least a temporary end to the long-drawn-out crisis.

The Bourbons (1589-1789)

Henri IV – 1589-1610. Though his political manœuvrings and his personal conduct did not endear him to everybody, Henri IV put France's affairs on a firm footing once more, attaching the provinces of Bresse and Bugey to the kingdom and setting great architects like Du Cerceau and Métezeau to work on projects in Paris such as the Place des Vosges and the Louvre Gallery, and La Rochelle and Charleville in the provinces.

Important economic reforms were undertaken, and the king's old Huguenot friend, Maximilien de Béthune, Duke of **Sully** set the nation's finances in order, dug canals and laid out new roads and port facilities.

In 1600, the landowner **Olivier de Serres** published his great work on progressive farming technique *"The Theatre of Agriculture and Field Husbandry"*, supporting Sully in his contention that "tilling and stock-keeping are the two breasts from which France feeds". The king's concern with his people's well-being found expression too in his famous statement "a chicken in the pot every Sunday".

1610	Louis XIII becomes King. The country's trade flourishes with the development of inland ports and there are fine planned expansions to a number of towns (Orléans, La Rochelle, Montargis, Langres). The reign is marked by an aristocratic rebellion, as well as by the pioneering work of St Vincent de Paul in social welfare (hospitals, Sisters of Mercy). In the field of ideas, Descartes publishes his *"Discourse on Method"* (1637), with its reasoning based on systematic questioning *("Cogito, ergo sum")*, a starting point for the intellectual revolution which, amongst other achievements, led to the invention of analytical geometry.
1624	The King's First Minister, Richelieu (1585-1642) is successful in his attempts to reduce the power of a Protestantism over-inclined to seek foreign aid (La Rochelle) or to resist the unification of the kingdom (Montauban, Privas). A few exemplary executions serve to humble the nobility (Montmorency, Cinq-Mars), a process carried further by the demolition of castles. He strengthens France's role in Europe (Thirty Years War) and, in 1635, founds the Academy (Académie française).

Louis XIV – 1643-1715. The 72 years of the Sun King's reign marked both France and Europe with the force of his personality *(p 221 and p 330)*. At the time of his accession, the king was only five years old and Anne of Austria confirmed Mazarin in his role as first minister. Five days later, the French victory at Rocroi (1643) signalled the end of Spanish dominance of Europe's affairs. In 1648, the Peace of Westphalia ended the Thirty Years War, confirmed France's claim to Alsace (apart from Strasbourg and Mulhouse) and established French as the language of diplomacy.

In 1657, while the king looked on, the two-month siege of Montmédy was brought to a triumphant conclusion by La Ferté and Vauban, thereby putting an end to Spanish rule in the Low Countries. In 1662, the king's first year of personal rule

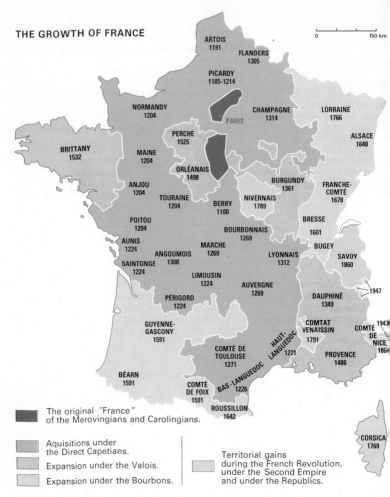

THE GROWTH OF FRANCE

0 ——————— 150 km

ARTOIS
1191

FLANDERS
1305

PICARDY
1185-1214

NORMANDY
1204

CHAMPAGNE
1314

LORRAINE
1766

PARIS

ALSACE
1648

PERCHE
1525

BRITTANY
1532

MAINE
1204

ORLÉANAIS
1498

ANJOU
1204

TOURAINE
1204

BERRY
1100

BURGUNDY
1361

FRANCHE-
COMTÉ
1678

NIVERNAIS
1789

POITOU
1204

BOURBONNAIS
1269

BRESSE
1601

AUNIS
1224

MARCHE
1269

BUGEY

ANGOUMOIS   1308
SAINTONGE
1224

LYONNAIS
1312

SAVOY
1860

LIMOUSIN
1224

AUVERGNE
1269

DAUPHINÉ
1349

1947

PÉRIGORD
1224

GUYENNE-
GASCONY
1591

COMTAT
VENAISSIN
1791

1947

COMTÉ
DE
NICE
186

COMTÉ DE
TOULOUSE
1271

HAUT-
LANGUEDOC
1271

PROVENCE
1486

BÉARN
1591

COMTÉ
DE FOIX
1591

BAS-LANGUEDOC 1226

ROUSSILLON
1642

CORSICA
1769

■ The original "France"
of the Merovingians and Carolingians.

□ Aquisitions under
the Direct Capetians.

□ Expansion under the Valois.

□ Expansion under the Bourbons.

□ Territorial gains
during the French Revolution,
under the Second Empire
and under the Republics.

was crowned by the purchase of the port of Dunkirk, a result of the statesman Lionne's diplomacy; the place became a base for smugglers and for privateers like Jean Bart operating in the service of the king. Anglo-French rivalry for control of the seas *(p 94)* now became the main theme of international politics. In 1678, the Treaty of Nijmegen marked the end of the war with Holland, the giving-up of the Franche-Comté and of 12 strongholds in Flanders by Spain, and the reconquest of Alsace. This was a high point in Louis' reign and in French expansion, insured by Vauban's work in fortifying the country's new frontiers. The politics of religion were not always straightforward; for 20 years, the king was in conflict with the Pope in what was known as the Affair of the Régale; in 1685 came the Revocation of the Edict of Nantes with all its dire consequences, and in 1702, the suppression of the *camisard* revolt *(qv)*. The monarch's later years were clouded by the country's economic exhaustion, though the Battle of Denain in 1712 saved France from invasion by the Austro-Dutch armies and led to the end of the War of the Spanish Succession.

Oriental ventures – In 1664, a century after the voyages of Jean Ango and Jacques Cartier, the French East India Company was revived by Colbert, Louis XIV's great minister of finance.

Louis XIV in his coronation robes by Hyacinthe Rigaud (Louvre Museum)

Two years later he authorised it to set up bases both at **Port-Louis** (where the original East India Company had been) and on waste ground on the far side of the confluence of the Scorff and Blavet rivers. In 1671 the first great merchantman was fitted out for its journey to the East and the new port was given the name of L'Orient in 1671 (**Lorient** in 1830). Anglo-French naval rivalry now began in earnest. Over a period of 47 years the Company put a total of 76 ships into use, which, in the course of their long and often dangerous voyages, would bring back cargoes of spices and porcelain (France alone importing over 12 million items of the latter). The initially fabulous profits eventually declined when the Company became a kind of state enterprise under the control of the bank run by the Scots financier Law. In the end, Lorient moved from a commercial role to a naval one.

1715	Louis XV succeeds to the crown at the age of five; the Duke of Orleans is Regent. The reign is marked by indecision, frivolity and corruption; many of France's colonies (Senegal, Québec, the Antilles, possessions in India) are lost. Internally, however, the country prospers, benefiting from a wise economic policy; the standard of living improves and a long period of stability favours agricultural development (introduction of the potato, artificial extension of grazing lands). Lorraine is absorbed into France in 1766 and Corsica in 1769.
1774	Louis XVI becomes King. Lafayette *(qv)* takes part in the American War of Independence, brought to an end by the Treaty of Versailles in 1783. The spirit of scientific enquiry leads to rapid technological progress, the growth of industry (textiles, porcelain, steam power) and to endeavours such as Lalande's astronomical experiments and the Montgolfier brothers balloon flights at Annonay in 1783.

The French Revolution (1789-99)

The Revolution, opening up the continent of Europe to democracy, was the outcome of the long crisis affecting the Ancien Régime.

Hastened along by the teachings of the thinkers of the Enlightenment as much as by the inability of a still essentially feudal system to adapt itself to new social realities, the Revolution broke out following disastrous financial mismanagement and the emptying of the coffers of the state. The main events unfolded in Paris but their repercussions were felt in the provincial cities (Lyon, Nantes...) as well as in the countryside.

The year 1789 heralded a number of major historical events for France. The Estates General were renamed the National Assembly, the Bastille was stormed, privileges were abolished (night of 4 July) and the Rights of Man were proclaimed. Two years later, in 1791, the king, fleeing with his family, was arrested in Varennes (22 June) and brought back to Paris, where he was suspended from office on 30 September. The following year the **Convention** (1792-1795) was signed while in Valmy (20 September) Kellermann and Dumouriez saved France from invasion by forcing the Prussians to retreat; on 22 September France is proclaimed a one and indivisible Republic. The major landmarks of 1793 were the execution of Louis XVI (21 January), the Vendée revolt, the crushing of the Lyon uprising and the siege of Toulon (July-December). In 1795 France adopted the metric system. In 1799 Napoleon overthrew the **Directory** (9 November) and declared himself First Consul of the Republic. Finally, in 1801, the *Code Napoléon* was promulgated throughout the country.

The Vendée – This is the name given to the Royalist-led but popular uprising in western France in 1793 in reaction to the excesses of the Convention. The *bocage* countryside of much of the area favoured the guerilla warfare waged by the "Whites" (Catholic royalists) against "Blues" (Republicans), who brought in the Alsatian general Kléber. In the winter of 1794 thousands of Whites were executed at Nantes, Angers, Fontenay... while the countryside was ravaged by mobile columns of vengeful soldiery (known as the infernal columns of General Turreau). Still resistance continued, until finally put to an end by the more conciliatory policies of Hoche.

Liberty leading the People by Eugène Delacroix
(Louvre Museum)

Musée du Louvre/R.M.N.

31

The Empire (1804-1815)

1804	On 2 December, Napoleon is crowned Emperor of the French in Notre-Dame by Pope Pius VII. The territorial acquisitions made in the course of the French Revolution now have to be defended against a whole series of coalitions formed by the country's numerous enemies.
1805	Napoleon gives up his planned invasion of England, abandoning the great camp set up at Boulogne for that purpose. The Royal Navy's victory at Trafalgar gives Britain control of the seas, but France's armies win the Battles of Ulm and Austerlitz (Slavkov).
1806	Intended to bring about England's economic ruin, the Continental Blockade pushes France into further territorial acquisitions.
1808	Some of the best French forces bogged down in the Peninsular War.
1812	Napoleon invades Russia. The Retreat from Moscow.
1813	The Battle of Leipzig. The whole of Europe lines up against France. Not even Napoleon's military genius can prevent the fall of Paris and the Emperor's farewell at Fontainebleau (20 April 1814).

The Restoration (1815-1830)

1814	Louis XVIII returns from exile in England.
1815	The Hundred Days (20 March-22 June); the attempt to re-establish the Empire ended by the victory of the Allies at Waterloo. Louis XVIII once more on the throne. France returns to the frontiers of 1792. Talleyrand's efforts at the Congress of Vienna help bring France back into the community of European nations. Execution of Marshal Ney.

The July Monarchy (1830-1848)

1830	Charles X's "Four Ordinances of St Cloud" violate the Constitution and lead to the outbreak of revolution. There follow the "Three Glorious Days" (27, 28 and 29 July) and the flight of the Bourbons. Louis-Philippe becomes King.
1837	France's first passenger-carrying railway is opened between Paris and St-Germain-en-Laye.

Second Republic and Second Empire (1848-70)

1848	On 10 December, Louis Napoléon is elected President of the Republic by universal suffrage.
1851	On 2 December, Louis Napoléon dissolves the Legislative Assembly and declares himself President for a ten-year term.
1852	A plebiscite leads to the proclamation of the Second Empire (Napoleon III).
1855	The World Fair is held in Paris.
1860	Savoy and the county of Nice elect to become part of France.
1869	Freedom of the Press is guaranteed.
1870	War declared on Prussia on 19 July. On 2 September, defeat at Sedan spells the end of the Second Empire. Two days later Paris rises and the Republic is proclaimed. But the way to the capital lies open, and soon Paris is under siege.

The Republic (1870-the present day)

1870	Following the disaster at Sedan, the Third Republic is proclaimed on 4 September.
1871	The Paris Commune (21-28 May). By the Treaty of Frankfurt France gives up all of Alsace (with the exception of Belfort) and part of Lorraine.
1881	Jules Ferry secularises primary education, making it free and, later, compulsory.
1884	Trade unions recognised.
1885	Vaccination in the treatment of rabies (Pasteur). Inauguration of the Eiffel Tower (World Fair).
1894	The Dreyfus Affair divides the country. Forged evidence results in this Jewish General Staff captain being imprisoned for spying.
1897	Clément Ader's heavier-than-air machine takes to the air at Toulouse. Entente Cordiale
1905	Separation of Church and State.
1914	Outbreak of the First World War. On 3 August the German armies attack through neutral Belgium but are thrown back in the Battle of the Marne. Four years of trench warfare follow, a bloody climax being reached in 1916-17 around the fortress city of Verdun, where the German offensive is held, at immense cost in lives on both sides. In 1919 the signing of the Treaty of Versailles brings the First World War to an end.

1934	France is deeply divided; on 6 February, the National Assembly is attacked by right-wing demonstrators. Two years later, Léon Blum forms his Popular Front government.
1939	Outbreak of the Second World War. In June 1940 France is overrun by the German army and Marshal Pétain's government requests an armistice. Much of the country is occupied (the north and the whole of the Atlantic seaboard), but the "French State" with its slogan of "Work, Family, Fatherland" is established at Vichy and collaborates closely with the Germans. France's honour is saved by General de Gaulle's Free French forces, active in many theatres of the war, and by the courage of the men and women of the Resistance. In 1942, the whole country is occupied, and the French fleet scuttles itself at Toulon. In June 1944 the Allies land in Normandy and in the South of France in August. Paris is liberated and the German surrender signed at Rheims on 7 May 1945. This major conflict, which inflamed all continents, is detailed in this guide under the places which it affected most in France.
1947	The Fourth Republic established. Its governments last an average of six months.
1954	Dien Bien Phu falls to the Vietminh. France abandons Indo-China and grants Morocco and Tunisia their independence (1956).
1958	The Algerian crisis leads to the downfall of the Fourth and the establishment of the Fifth Republic under De Gaulle. Civil war is narrowly averted. Nearly all its French population leaves Algeria, which becomes independent in 1962.
1958	The Fifth Republic established. The European Economic Community (EEC) comes into effect. The new constitution inspired by General de Gaulle is voted by referendum.
1962	Referendum establishing that the future President of the Republic be elected by universal suffrage.
1967	Franco-British agreement to manufacture Airbus.
1968	The "events of May"; workers join students in mass protests, roughly put down by riot police. The Gaullists triumph in national elections, but it is a hollow victory and De Gaulle, defeated in the referendum of April 1969, retires to continue writing his memoirs.
1969	Georges Pompidou is elected President (16 June).
1974	Valéry Giscard d'Estaing is elected President (19 May).
1981	François Mitterrand is elected President (10 May). Inauguration of the TGV line between Paris and Lyons (2 h 40 min); Paris-Marseille (1981); and Paris Bordeaux (1990).
1994	Inauguration of the Channel Tunnel (6 May).
1995	Jacques Chirac is elected President (7 May).

PIX, Paris

Charles de Gaulle

The development of art in France from earliest times to the present day

FROM PREHISTORY TO THE GALLO-ROMAN ERA

Prehistory – While stone and bone tools appeared in the Lower Paleolithic period, prehistoric art did not make its entrance until the Upper Paleolithic (350 to 100 centuries BC), and reached its peak in the Magdalenian Period *(see Les Eyzies-de-Tayac for the chronology of prehistoric eras)*. The art of engraved wood and ivory objects together with votive statuettes developed alongside the art of wall decoration as is well illustrated in France by caves in the Dordogne, the Pyrenees, the Ardèche and the Gard. Early artists used pigments with a mineral base for their cave paintings and sometimes took advantage of the natural shape of the rock itself to execute their work in low relief.

The Neolithic revolution (6500 BC), during which populations began to settle, brought with it the advent of pottery as well as a different use of land and a change in burial practices – some megaliths (dolmens and covered passageways) are ancient burial chambers. Menhirs, a type of megalith found in great numbers in Brittany (Carnac and Locmariaquer), are as yet of an unknown origin.

The discovery of metal brought prehistoric civilisation into the Bronze Age (2300-1800 BC) and then into the Iron Age (750-450 BC). Celtic art showed perfect mastery of metalwork as in the tombs of Gorge-Meillet, Mailly-le-Camp, Bibracte and Vix in which the treasures consist of gold torques (necklaces) and other items of jewellery, various coins andbronzeware.

The Gallo-Roman Era and the Early Middle Ages – When the Romans conquered Gaul (2-1C BC), they introduced the technique of building with stone. In cities, the Empire's administrative centres, the centralised power of Rome favoured a style of architecture that reflected its strength and prestige and imposed its culture. Theatres (Orange and Vienne), temples (the Square House or

Head of a neighing horse (Museum of National Antiquities, St-Germain-en-Laye)

Maison Carrée in Nîmes), baths, basilicas and triumphal arches were constructed while the local aristocracy took to building Roman villas with frescoes and mosaics (Vaison-la-Romaine and **Grand**, map 62, fold 2). The presence of the Romans has had a lasting effect on the shape of France in terms of town-planning, roads, bridges and aqueducts (Pont du Gard). Towards the end of the late Empire, official recognition of the Christian church in the year 380 prompted the first examples of Christian architecture, among them the baptistries of **Fréjus**, map 84, fold 8, **Riez**, map 84 fold 5 and Poitiers.

During the great barbarian invasions of the 5C, figurative art, unknown to Germanic peoples, gave place to abstract (intertwining, circular shapes) and animal motifs. The technique of *cloisonné* gold and silverware (Childeric's treasure) became widespread.

Merovingian art (6-8C), a synthesis of styles, included elements of antique, barbarian and Christian art (the Dunes hypogeum near Poitiers and the crypt in **Jouarre**, map 106, fold 24) out of which evolved medieval art.

The **Carolingian Renaissance** (9C) was marked by a great flowering of illuminated manuscripts and ivory-carving (the Dagulf psalter in the Louvre) and by a deliberate return to imperial, antique art forms (Aix-la-Chapelle and the oratory of Germigny-des-Prés).

The altar in churches of the period is sometimes raised above a vaulted area of the chancel known as the crypt which was originally on the same level as the nave (St Germanus of Auxerre and **St-Philibert-de-Grand-Lieu**, map 67, fold 3).

THE ROMANESQUE PERIOD (11-12C)

In the early 11C, after the disturbances of the year 1000 (decadence of the Carolingian dynasty and struggles between great feudal barons), the spiritual influence and power of the Church gave rise to the birth of Romanesque architecture.

The principles of Romanesque architecture – Early Romanesque edifices were characterised by the widespread use of stone vaulting which replaced timber roofs, the use of buttresses and a return to architectural decoration (as in the churches

34

of **St-Martin-du-Canigou,** map 86, fold 17 and St-Bénigne in Dijon). The darkness of the nave was explained by the fact that for structural reasons wide openings could not be cut into the walls supporting the vaulting.

The basilica plan with nave and side aisles, sometimes preceded by a porch, predominated in France although some churches were built to a central plan (the church of **Neuvy-St-Sépulcre,** map 68, fold 19). Depending on the church, the east end might have been flat or have had apsidal chapels ; it was often semicircular with axial chapels (as in the church of **Anzy-le-Duc,** map 69, fold 17) or may have featured radiating chapels. More complex designs combined an ambulatory with radiating chapels (the churches of Conques and Cluny).

The first attempts at embellishment led to a revival of sculptural decoration of which the lintel of St-Genis-les-Fontaines Church is one of the earliest examples. Tympana, archivolts, arch shafts and piers were covered with carvings of a religious or profane nature (as in the illustration of the *Romance of Renart* in the church of St-Ursin in Bourges). Interior decoration consisted mainly of frescoes (the churches of St-Savin-sur-Gartempe and **Berzé-la-Ville,** map 70, fold 11) and carved capitals with the occasional complex theme (as in the chancel capitals in Cluny). The Romanesque decorative style drew largely upon three main models, the Oriental (griffons and imaginary animals) which was spread by the Crusades, the Byzantine (illustrations of Christ in Majesty and a particular style for folds) and the Islamic (stylised foliage and pseudo-Cufic script).

Regional characteristics – The Romanesque style spread throughout France affecting some areas earlier than others and developing special stylistic features according to the region. It first appeared in the south and in Burgundy, reaching the east of France at a much later date.

Romanesque architecture in the **Languedoc** owes much to Toulouse's St-Sernin Basilica, whose tall lantern-tower pierced by ornamental arcading served as a model for many local bell-towers. The sculptures on the Miégeville doorway, completed in 1118, have a distinctive style, with highly expressive folds and a lengthening of the figures which is repeated in Moissac and, to a lesser extent, in **St-Gilles-du-Gard,** map 83, fold 9.

In **Saintonge-Poitou** the originality of the edifices derives from the great height of the aisles which serve to reinforce the walls of the nave and thus lend balance to the barrel vaulting. The gabled façades, flanked by lantern towers, are covered in ornamental arcading with statue niches and low relief (as in the church of Notre-Dame-la-Grande in Poitiers).

In **Auvergne,** the transept crossing is often covered by a dome, buttressed by high, quadripartite vaulting and supported on diaphragm arches. This constitutes an oblong mass which juts out above the roof beneath the bell-tower. The use of lava, a particularly difficult stone to carve, explains the limited sculptural decoration (as in the churches of St-Nectaire, Notre-Dame-du-Port in Clermont-Ferrand and that of Orcival). The tympana lintels are gable-shaped.

The development of the Romanesque in **Burgundy** was strongly influenced by the Abbey of Cluny (now destroyed) with its great chancel with radiating chapels, a double transept and the hint of direct lighting in the nave through slender openings at the base of the barrel vaulting. The churches of Paray-le-Monial and Notre-Dame in La Charité-sur-Loire were built on the Cluniac model.

The basilica of Sainte Madeleine in Vézelay in the north of the Morvan, with its harmonious, simplified church body and its covering of groined vaults, was also to influence churches in the region.

In the **Rhine** and **Meuse** regions, architectural characteristics from the Carolingian era, with an Ottonian influence, tend to prevail. This is borne out by double chancels and transepts (as in Verdun) and a central plan and interior elevation like that of the Palatine Chapel in Aachen (as in Ottmarsheim).

Lastly, until a relatively late date the churches in **Normandy** faithfully retained the custom of a timber roof (as in Jumièges and Bayeux). As stone vaulting was introduced decorative ribs gradually came into use (as in St Stephen's in Caen). The monumental size of the edifices and their harmoniously proportioned façades with two towers, are also typical of the Anglo-Norman Romanesque style.

Apart from these regional features some buildings owe their individuality to their function. The **pilgrimage churches,** for instance, had an ambulatory around the chancel, transept aisles and two aisles on either side of the nave to give pilgrims easy access to the relics they wished to venerate. The main churches of this kind on the way to Santiago de Compostela were St Faith in Conques, St-Sernin in Toulouse, St-Martial in Limoges and St-Martin in Tours (the two latter have since been destroyed).

Romanesque religious art treasures – Liturgical items at the time consisted of church plate, manuscripts, precious fabrics and reliquaries. Church treasure would often include a Virgin in Majesty made of polychrome wood or embossed metal decorated with precious stones.

The blossoming of **Limousin enamelware** marked a great milestone in the history of the decorative arts during the Romanesque period when it was exported throughout Europe. The *champlevé* method consisted of pouring the enamel into a grooved

Tympanum over the central doorway of Autun Cathedral

metal surface of gilded copper. Enamel was used in a number of ways to decorate items ranging from small objects such as crosses, ciboria and reliquaries to monumental works like altars (high altar of **Grandmont**, map 72, fold 8, and items in the Cluny Museum, Paris).

THE GOTHIC PERIOD (12-15C)

Architecture

Transitional Gothic – In about 1140, important architectural innovations in St-Denis Cathedral, such as intersecting ribbed vaulting and pointed arches in the narthex and chancel, heralded the dawn of the Gothic style.

In the late-12C, there were further innovations common to a group of buildings in Ile-de-France and in the north of France. They included ogives and mouldings which extended down from the vaulting into bundles of engaged slender columns around the pillars of great arches. Capitals were simplified, became smaller with time and gradually diminished in importance. New concepts of sculptural decorating, including the appearance of statue-columns, affected building façades. In Sens Cathedral, the rectangular layout of the bays called for sexpartite vaulting with alternating major and minor pillars to support large arches. The major pillars supported three ribs while the minor ones supported a single intermediary rib. Apart from sexpartite vaulting with alternating supports, this early Gothic architecture typical of Sens, Noyon and Laon, was also characterised by a four-storeyed elevation, great arches, tribunes, a triforium and tall bays.

In the years 1180-1200, in Notre-Dame Cathedral in Paris, raised vaults were reinforced by the addition of flying buttresses on the outside of the edifice while inside, alternating supports disappeared. These new measures gave rise to the emergence of a transitional style which led to Lanceolate Gothic.

Lanceolate Gothic – The Gothic style reached its height during the reigns of Philippe Auguste (1180-1223) and St Louis (1226-1270). The rebuilding of Chartres Cathedral from 1210-1230 gave rise to a model for what is known as the Chartres family of cathedrals (Reims, Amiens and Beauvais) which included oblong plan vaulting, a three-storeyed elevation

Interior of Reims Cathedral

(without tribunes) and flying buttresses. The chancel with its double ambulatory and the transept arms with side aisles made for a grandiose interior. The upper windows in the nave were divided into two lancets surmounted by a round opening. The façades were subdivised into three horizontal registers, as in the cathedrals of Laon and Amiens. The doorways were set in deep porches with gables while above them was an openwork rose window with stained glass. A gallery of arches ran beneath the bell-towers.

There are a number of variations of Lanceolate Gothic in France. An example is Notre-Dame Church in Dijon where the ancient section of the sexpartite vaulting has been preserved.

Development of the Gothic style to the 15C – The improvement in vaulting from a technical point of view, in particular the use of relieving arches, meant that the supporting function of walls was reduced and more space could be given over to windows and stone tracery as in St Urban's Basilica in Troyes and the Sainte-Chapelle in Paris (1248). This gave rise to the **High Gothic** style in the north of France from the end of the 13C to the late 14C. (Examples include the chancel in Beauvais Cathedral, Évreux Cathedral and the north transept of Rouen Cathedral.)

Gothic architecture in the centre and south-west of France developed along unusual lines in the late 13C. Jean Deschamps, master mason of Narbonne Cathedral, designed a massively proportioned building in which the vertical upsweep of the lines was interrupted by wide galleries above the aisles. St Cecilia's Cathedral in Albi diverged completely from Gothic models in the north of France through the use of brick and a buttress system inherited from the Romanesque period.

Throughout the 14C, church interiors were filled with sculptural decoration in the form of rood-screens, choir-screens, monumental altarpieces and devotional statues.

As from the late 14C, development of the main principles of Gothic architecture came to a halt but decorative devices grew apace giving rise to the elaborate **Flamboyant Gothic** style with its gables, lancet arches, pinnacles and exuberant foliage. This ornamentation, occasionally referred to as baroque Gothic, also played a part in civil architecture. An example is the Great Hall in the Law Courts at Poitiers, carved by Guy de Dammartin in the last ten years of the 14C. Riom's Sainte-Chapelle, built for the Duke Jean de Berry, is another early example. Flamboyant Gothic in France left its mark on a good number of public and religious edifices (Jacques Cœur Palace in Bourges and the façade of St Maclou Church in Rouen) as well as on liturgical furnishings (the choir-screen and rood-screen in St Cecilia's Cathedral in Albi).

Throughout the Gothic period castle architecture remained faithful to feudal models (Angers Castle, the walled city of Cordes and the mountain fortress of Merle Towers) and did not develop further until the beginning of the Renaissance.

Sculpture, Decorative Arts and Painting

Gothic sculpture – Progress towards naturalism and realism, the humanism of the Gothic style, can be seen in the statuary and sculptural decoration of the time. Statue-columns of doorways in the 12C tended to be more rigidly hieratic but in the 13C took on greater freedom of expression as may be seen in Amiens and Reims (the Smiling Angel). New themes emerged including the Coronation of the Virgin which first appeared in Senlis in 1191 and thereafter became a popular subject.

Stained glass – The four main areas producing stained glass in France in the 12C were St-Denis, Champagne, the west (Le Mans, Vendôme and Poitiers) and a group of workshops in the Rhine area in eastern France. Master glassworkers developed an intense blue-coloured glass known as Chartres blue which was to become famous. The invention of silver yellow in 1300-1310 led to a more translucent enamelled glass with a subtler range of colour.

The combination of stained glass and Gothic architecture gave rise to larger bays – formerly opaque wall space could be opened up and filled with glass thanks to new support systems. The fragility of stained glass explains the fact that there are very few original medieval windows intact today, many have been replaced by copies or later works. The windows of Chartres, Évreux and the Sainte-Chapelle are precious testimonies to the art.

Illumination and painting – The art of illumination reached its peak in the 14C when artists freed from University supervision produced sumptuous manuscripts, including Books of Hours, for private use. Among them were Jean Pucelle (*Les Heures de Jeanne d'Évreux*) and the Limbourg brothers (*Les Très Riches Heures du Duc de Berry*, dating from the early 15C).

Easel painting first made its appearance in France in 1350 (the portrait of John the Good, now in the Louvre, is an example). Italian and more particularly Flemish influences, evident as much in depiction of landscape as in attention to detail, may be seen in works by great 15C artists like **Jean Fouquet, Enguerrand Quarton** and the **Master of Moulins**.

THE RENAISSANCE

Gothic art persisted in many parts of France until the middle of the 16C. In the Loire region, however, there were signs of a break with medieval traditions as early as the beginning of the century.

Italian style and Early Renaissance – Renaissance aesthetics in Lombardy, familiar in France since the military campaigns of Charles VIII and Louis XII at the end of the 15C, at first only affected architectural decoration, through the introduction of motifs from Antiquity such as pilasters, foliage and scallops (as in the tomb of Solesmes, **Château de Gaillon**, map 55, fold 17). Little by little, however, feudal, military and defensive architecture gave way to a more comfortable style of seigniorial residence. The Château de Chenonceau (begun before 1515) and that of Azay-le-Rideau (1518-1527) are examples of this development, particularly in their regular layout, the symmetry of the façades and the beginnings of a new type of architectural decoration. However, it was the great royal undertakings of the time that brought about the blossoming of the Renaissance style in France.

Palatial architecture and decoration under François I (1515-1547) – The Façade des Loges (1520-1524) in the Château de Blois (begun in 1515) is a free replica of the Vatican loggia in Rome. While the castle's irregular fenestration recalls the old medieval style, its great novelty is the preoccupation with Italianate ornamentation. During the reign of François I, the Château de Chambord (1519-1547) which combines French architectural traditions (corner towers, irregular roofs and dormer windows) with innovative elements (symmetrical façades, refined decoration and a monumental internal staircase) served as a model for a good many of the Loire castles including Chaumont, Le Lude and Ussé.

After his defeat at the Battle of Pavia in 1525, François I left his residences in the Loire valley to turn his attention to those in Ile-de-France. In 1527 building began on the Château de Fontainebleau under the supervision of Gilles le Breton.

The Virgin with a Garland by Botticelli

The interior decoration by artists from the **First School of Fontainebleau** was to have a profound influence on the development of French art.

The Italian artist **Rosso** (1494-1540) introduced a new system of decoration to France that combined stuccowork, wood panelling and allegorical frescoes which drew upon humanistic, philosophical and literary references and were painted in acid colours. The Mannerist style, characterised by the influence of antique statuary, a lengthening of lines and overabundant ornamentation, became more pronounced after **Primaticcio** (1504-1570) arrived at the court in 1532.

The influence of this art could be felt until the end of the century in works by sculptors such as **Pierre Bontemps, Jean Goujon** (reliefs on the Fountain of the Innocents in Paris) and **Germain Pilon** (monument for the heart of Henri II in the Louvre) and painters like Jean Cousin the Elder. Court portraitists, on the other hand (**Jean** and **François Clouet** and **Corneille de Lyon**), were more influenced by Flemish traditions.

Henri IV and pre-Classicism – After the Wars of Religion (1560-1598) new artistic trends revived the arts and heralded the dawn of classicism. Monarchical interest in town-planning gave rise to the regular, symmetrical layout of squares (Place des Vosges and Place Dauphine in Paris) and to the harmonisation of the buildings that surrounded them (ground level arcades and brick and stone façades). These were copied in the provinces (Charleville and Montauban) foreshadowing the royal squares of the 17C, France's *Grand Siècle*.

The Fontainebleau style of adornment continued to develop under the auspices of the **Second School of Fontainebleau.** This was made up of all the court painters working during the reign of Henri IV and the regency of Marie de' Medici. The style was further shaped by decoration in other royal palaces including the Tuileries, the Louvre and Château-Neuf in St-Germain-en-Laye. **Toussaint Dubreuil** (1561-1602), **Ambroise Dubois** (1542-1614) and **Martin Fréminet** (1567-1619) continued the Mannerism of Fontainebleau (light effects, half-length figures and a lengthening of perspectives) in their works and at the same time sought greater classicism as well as a revival of themes from contemporary literature (*La Franciade* by Ronsard). In the late 16C, castle architecture took on a new form with a single main building centred around a projecting section flanked by corner pavilions (**Rosny-sur-Seine,** map 106, fold 15, and the Château de Gros-Bois). Right-angled wings were done away with and façades were given a brick facing with stone courses.

During the regency period, the architect Salomon de Brosse (Law Courts in Rennes, Luxembourg Palace in Paris) designed sober, impressive monuments with a clarity of form which contained some of the characteristics of classical architecture.

16C decorative arts – The 16C was a productive period for jewellery-making, in particular for small brooches fastened in the hair or hat and pendants which were used as articles of dress or simply as collector's items. **Étienne Delaune** (1518-1583) was one of the great goldsmiths of the time.

There was rich regional variety in ceramics. Beauvaisis produced famous blue-tinged stoneware. Following the example of Italy, Lyon and Nevers manufactured majolica (glazed and historiated earthenware). The decorative arts in Saintonge were dominated by **Bernard Palissy** (*c* 1510-*c* 1590) who, apart from making a great many plates covered in reptiles, fish and seaweed, all modelled from nature, also decorated the grotto at the Château d'Écouen and that of the Tuileries. Some of his ceramics (nymphs in a country setting) were influenced by engravings from the Fontainebleau School. The technique for painted enamel on copper with permanent colours was developed in Limoges in the 15C during the reign of Louis XV. J.C. Pénicaud and especially **Léonard Limosin** (1501-1575) excelled in the technique. The French court made use of it in portrait painting.

THE 17C

The establishment of French classicism in the early 17C

Architecture – Three architects, **Jacques Lemercier** (*c* 1585-1654), **François Mansart** (1598-1666) and **Louis le Vau** (1612-1670), played an essential part in drawing up the standards for French classical architecture.

J. Lemercier, who built the Château de Rueil, the town of Richelieu and the Église de la Sorbonne in Paris, supported the Italian style which was particularly evident in religious architecture : two-storeyed façades and projecting central sections with columns and triangular pediments. F. Mansart was even more inventive (**Château de Balleroy,** map 54, fold 14, **Château de Maisons-Laffitte** and the Gaston of Orléans Wing in the Château de Blois). From his time on castle plans with a central pavilion and projecting section, architectural decoration that accentuated horizontal and vertical lines, and the use of orders (Doric, Ionic and Corinthian), remained constant features of classical French architecture. Le Vau, who began his career before the reign of Louis XIV by designing town houses (Hôtel Lambert in Paris) for the nobility and the upper middle classes, favoured a grandiose, majestic style of architecture characteristic of Louis XIV classicism (Château de Vaux-le-Vicomte).

Painting – The French school of painting blossomed as a result of **Simon Vouet**'s (1590-1649) return to France in 1627 after a long stay in Rome and the foundation of the Royal Academy of Painting and Sculpture in 1648. References to Italian painting, in particular Venetian (richness of colour) and Roman (dynamism of composition), albeit tempered by a concern for order and clarity, are evident in the work of Vouet and that of his pupil **Eustache le Sueur** (1616-1655).

Musée du Louvre/R.M.N.

Wealth by Vouet (Louvre Museum)

39

Painters such as **Poussin** (1595-1665) and **Philippe de Champaigne** (1602-1674) produced highly intellectual works that drew upon philosophical, historical and theological themes – all emblematic of French classicism.

Other trends in French painting flourished in the first half of the century. The realism of the Italian painter Caravaggio influenced the Toulouse school to which the major artist was **Nicolas Tournier** (1590-post 1660). In Lorraine, **Georges de la Tour** (1593-1652) was deeply affected by Caravaggio's style, notably in the use of light and shade and the portrayal of people from humble blackgrounds. The **Le Nain** brothers, Antoine (*c* 1588-1648), Louis (*c* 1593-1648) and Mathieu (*c* 1607-1677), who painted first in Laon and then in Paris, belonged to a trend known as "painters of reality" that favoured genre scenes, drawing more upon the world of the landed upper middle classes than that of peasant farmers. Their work bore the stamp of Flemish craftsmanship.

Sculpture – Sculpture in the early 17C was influenced by contemporary Italian models. **Jacques Sarrazin** (1588-1660), who studied in Rome, worked in a moderate, classic mode that derived from Antiquity and also drew upon paintings by Poussin (decoration in the Château de Maisons-Laffitte and the tomb of Henri of Bourbon in the Château de Chantilly). François Anguier (Montmorency Mausoleum in the Lycée chapel in Moulins) and his brother Michel (sculptural decoration on the St-Denis gateway in Paris) showed a more baroque tendency in their treatment of dynamism and the dramatic stances of their sculptures.

Versailles classicism

During the reign of Louis XIV (1643-1715) the centralisation of authority and the all-powerful Royal Academy gave rise to an official art that reflected the taste and wishes of the sovereign. The Louis XIV style evolved in Versailles and spread throughout France where it was imitated to a lesser degree by the aristocracy in the late 17C.

The style was characterised by references to Antiquity and a concern for order and grandeur, whether in architecture, painting or sculpture. French resistance to baroque, which had but a superficial effect on French architecture, was symbolised by the rejection of Bernini's projects for the Louvre. One of the rare examples of the style is Le Vau's College of Four Nations (today's Institute of France) which consists of a former chapel with a cupola and semicircular flanking buildings.

In Versailles **Louis le Vau** and later **Jules Hardouin-Mansart** (1646-1708) built a majestic type of architecture: rectangular buildings set off by projecting central sections with twin pillars, flat roofs and sculptural decoration inspired by Antiquity.

Charles le Brun (1619-1690), the leading King's Painter, supervised all the interior decoration (paintings, tapestries, furniture and *objets d'art*), giving the palace remarkable homogeneity. There were dark fabrics and panelling, gilded stuccowork, painted coffered ceilings, and copies of Graeco-Roman statues. The decoration became less abundant towards the end of the century.

In 1662, the founding of the **Gobelins**, the "Royal Manufactory for Crown Furniture", stimulated the decorative arts. A team of painters, sculptors, warp-weavers, marble-cutters, goldsmiths and cabinet-makers worked under Charles le Brun, achieving a high degree of technical perfection. Carpets were made at the Savonnerie in Chaillot. The massive furniture of the period was often carved and sometimes gilded. Boulle marquetry, a combination of brass, tortoiseshell and gilded bronze, was one of the most sumptuous of the decorative arts produced at the time.

Versailles park, laid out by **Le Nôtre** (1613-1700), fulfilled all the requirements of French landscape gardening with its emphasis on rigour and clarity. Its geometrically tailored greenery, long axial perspectives, fountains, carefully designed spinneys and allegorical sculptures reflect the ideal of perfect order and control over nature.

Sculptures were placed throughout the gardens. Many of the works were by the two major sculptors of the time, **François Girardon** (1628-1715) and **Antoine Coysevox** (1640-1720) who drew upon mythology from Antiquity. The work of **Pierre Puget** (1620-1694), another important sculptor, was far more tortured and baroque – an unusual style for the late 17C.

THE 18C

The 18C style in France grew from a reaction against the austerity and grandeur of the Louis XIV style which was considered ill-adapted to the luxurious life and pleasures of the aristocracy and the upper middle classes during the regency of Philippe of Orléans (1715-1723) and the reign of Louis XV (1723-1774).

French rocaille (1715-1750)

Rocaille was an 18C rococo style or ornamentation based on rock and shell motifs.

Architecture – Rocaille architecture, at least on the outside, remained faithful to some of the principles of classical composition – plain buildings with symmetrical façades and projecting central sections crowned by a triangular pediment – but the

The Oval Salon in the Hôtel de Soubise

use of classical orders became less rigid and systematic. The most representative examples of this new type of architecture were town houses such as the Hôtel de Soubise by **Delamair** and Hôtel Matignon by **Courtonne**, both in Paris.

The majestic apartments of the previous century gave way to smaller, more intimate rooms such as boudoirs and studies.

Inside, woodwork, often white and gold, covered the walls from top to bottom (Hôtel de Lassay in Paris and the Clock Room or Cabinet de la Pendule in Versailles). The repertoire of ornamentation included intertwining plant motifs, curved lines, shells and other natural objects. Paintings of landscapes and country scenes were inserted in the woodwork above doors or in the corners of ceilings. **Verberckt,** who worked in Versailles for Louis XV, was an exceptionally skilled interior decorator.

Painting – The generation of painters working at the turn of the century was influenced by Flemish art. Artists such as **Desportes** (1661-1743), **Largillière** (1656-1746) and **Rigaud** (1659-1743) painted sumptuously decorative still lifes and formal portraits. Secular themes including scenes of gallantry *(fêtes galantes)* and fashionable society life became popular. **Watteau** (1684-1721), **Boucher** (1703-1770), **Natoire** (1700-1777) and **Fragonard** (1732-1806) reflected the taste of the day in their elegant genre scenes, some with mythological overtones, of pastoral life and the game of love.

Religious painting was not neglected in spite of these trends. Charles de la Fosse (1636-1716), one of Le Brun's pupils, Antoine Coypel (1661-1722) and especially **Restout** (1692-1768) adapted it to the less stoical ideals of the 18C by stripping it of too strong a dogmatism.

There was a revival in portraiture during the 18C. **Nattier** (1685-1766), official painter of Louis XV's daughters, produced likenesses in mythological guise or half-length portraits which were far less pompous than the usual court picture. The pastellist **Quentin de la Tour** (1704-1788) excelled in portraying his subjects' individual temperament and psychology rather than their social rank by concentrating more on faces than dress and accessories.

The lesser genres (still lifes and landscapes), scorned by the Academy but favoured by the middle classes for the decoration of their homes, blossomed considerably at the time. **Chardin** (1699-1779) painted simple still lifes in muted tones and Flemish-inspired scenes of everyday life, giving them a realistic, picturesque quality.

Sculpture – Baroque influence swept through sculpture in the first half of the century. The **Adam** brothers (Neptune Basin at Versailles), **Coustou** (1677-1746) (Horses of Marly), and **Slodtz** (1705-1764) introduced the style's expressiveness into their work to lend movement and feeling. The main characteristics of baroque were flowing garments, attention to detail and figures shown in action.

In contrast, the contemporary work of **Bouchardon** (1698-1762) who trained in Rome and was therefore influenced by Antique sculpture, tended to be more classical (Fountain in the Rue de Grenelle in Paris).

Decorative arts – The rise of fashionable society brought with it a great need for luxury furniture that matched the style of woodwork inside elegant homes. New types of furniture were created: after commodes (chests of drawers) came writing-desks – upright or inclined –, escritoires, chiffoniers and countless small tables. For the comforts of conversation there were wing-chairs and deep easy chairs. There were also *voyeuses* or conversation chairs (special seats in gaming houses placed behind players to allow spectators to watch) and all manner of sofas and seats on which to recline (couches, lounging-chairs, divans and settees). Curved lines were favoured as were rare and precious materials like exotic woods and lacquered panelling often set off by floral marquetry and finely chased gilded bronze. Among the great rocaille cabinet-markers were Cressent, Joubert and Migeon while the principal seat carpenters of the time were Foliot, Sené and Cresson.

The **Vincennes Porcelain Factory** moved to **Sèvres** in 1756 and produced luxury items of which some were decorated in deep blue known as Sèvres blue. Gilt ornamentation was theoretically only used for royal services. Rocaille gold and silver plate was adorned with reed motifs, crested waves, scroll-work and shells often arranged in asymmetrical patterns. **Thomas Germain** (1673-1748), one of the most prestigious names in the trade, supplied the princely tables of the time.

Neo-classical reaction

The middle of the century brought a reaction against rocaille on moral and aesthetic grounds. The style was considered to be too florid and frivolous, the result of decadence in both morals and the arts. Classical models from Antiquity and the 17C were then deemed the only recourse to revive proper artistic creation.

Architecture – The new style of architecture that emerged was more austere and tended towards the monumental. Sculptural decoration on façades grew more restrained and the Doric order became widespread (Église St-Philippe-du-Roule by J.F. Chardin in Paris). Some buildings, like the Église St. Genevieve (the present-day Panthéon) in Paris by **G. Soufflot** (1713-1780), were direct copies of Antique models. Louis XVI commissioned men like **Victor Louis** (1731-1802) who designed the Bordeaux theatre, **A.T. Brongniart** (1739-1813) and **J.F. Bélanger** (1744-1818) for most of the great architectural undertakings of the time. The philosophical influence of the Englightenment led to a keen interest in the architecture of functional, public buildings such as the Royal Salt-works in Arc-et-Senans by **Claude-Nicolas Ledoux** (1736-1806).

Sculpture – Sculptors distanced themselves from rocaille extravagance by striving towards a natural portrayal of anatomy. E.M. Falconet (1716-1791), P. Julien (1731-1804) and G.C. Allegrain (1710-1795) drew upon Graeco-Roman models for their greatly admired sculptures of female bathers. **J.A. Houdon** (1741-1828), one of the greatest sculptors of the late 18C, made busts of his French and foreign contemporaries (Voltaire, Buffon and Madame Adélaïde for the first and Benjamin Franklin and George Washington for the second) which constitued a veritable portrait gallery. The busts, executed in an extremely realistic manner, many without wigs or articles of dress to detract from the faces, were the culmination of modelled portraiture in France. Houdon also sculpted tombs and mythological statues. **J.B. Pigalle** (1714-1785) maintained the style of sculpture predominant at the beginning of the century that the neo-classical reaction had not managed to stifle entirely (mausoleum of the Marshal de Saxe in the Église St. Thomas in Strasbourg).

Painting – In the 1760s attempts by the Royal Academy to restore a style of painting known as the grand manner encouraged the emergence of new themes such as antique history, civic heroism and 17C tragedies. These were adopted by painters like **J.L. David** (1748-1825), **J.B.M. Pierre** (1714-1789) and **J.F.P. Peyron** (1744-1814). The style drew upon low-reliefs and statuary from Antiquity and followed the principles of composition used by painters like Poussin and other 17C masters.

Works by **J.M. Vien** (1716-1809) and **J.B. Greuze** (1725-1805) showed a less austere approach to painting, with more room for sensibility and emotion, that heralded the romanticism that was to blossom after the Revolution.

Decorative arts – Louis XVI furniture kept some of the characteristics inherited from the beginning of the century such as the use of precious materials and chased gilt bronze ornamentation but curves and sinuous shapes gave way to straight lines. As far as decoration was concerned, while the floral motifs and ribbons of the past were maintained, ovoli friezes, Greek fret-work and fasces were willingly introduced. **René Dubois** (1738-1799) and **Louis Delanois** (1731-1792) initiated the Greek style derived from Antique furniture seen in friezes at Herculaneum and Pompeii. Prestigious artists of the genre included Oeben and Riesener while Carlin followed by Beneman and Levasseur specialised in furniture adorned with plaques of painted porcelain.

At the end of the century new decorative motifs including lyres, ears of corn, wickerwork baskets and hot-air balloons were imported from England.

The technique of hard-paste porcelain that was introduced into France at the beginning of the 1770s, took the lead over soft-paste porcelain in the factory at Sèvres. Figurines of **biscuit** porcelain (white, fired, unglazed pottery) shaped on models by Fragonard, Boucher and other artists, became very popular.

The iconoclasm that prevailed during the **Revolution** marked a break in the history of French art although the neo-classical movement continued into the early 19C. The Louvre opened in 1793 paving the way for many more museums in France.

THE 19C

Art during the First Empire – After his investiture in 1804, Napoleon favoured the emergence of an official style of art by commissioning palace decoration (Tuileries, destroyed in 1870, and Fontainebleau) and paintings that related the great events of the Empire. The artists to benefit from the Emperor's patronage were men like J.L. David and his pupils **A.J. Gros** (1771-1835) and **A.L. Girodet-Trioson** (1767-1824).

Paintings of the time took on new themes derived from the romanticism in contemporary literature, orientalism and an interest in the medieval. National historic anecdotes were painted by artists who, like the troubadours, praised heroic deeds and fine sentiment.

Artistic development in the realm of architecture was less innovative. Napoleon commissioned large edifices commemorating the glory of the *Grande Armée* including Carrousel Arch, the column in Place Vendôme and Madeleine Temple (now a church). The official architects **Percier** (1764-1838) and **Fontaine** (1762-1853) were responsible for the overall supervision of the undertakings, setting models not only for buildings but also for decoration at official ceremonies and guidelines for the decorative arts.

Ambitious town-planning projects like the reconstruction of Lyon were also accomplished under the Empire.

Former royal palaces were refurnished. The style of First Empire furniture derived from the neoclassical with massive, quadrangular, commodes and jewel-cases made of mahogany with gilt bronze plating and Antique decorative motifs. **Desmalter** (1770-1841) was the main cabinet-maker of the imperial court. The sculptors **Chaudet** (1763-1810) and **Cartellier** (1757-1831) supplied models for furniture ornamentation in the neoclassical style which also inspired their statues. After the Egyptian Campaign motifs like sphinxes and lotuses began to appear in the decorative arts.

Restoration and the July Monarchy – Two major trends affected French art between 1815 and 1848. The first was the gradual disappearance of the neoclassical style which, however, still influenced church building (Notre-Dame-de-Lorette and St-Vincent-de-Paul in Paris) and the second was the birth of historicism, a style that fostered regard for past architecture, particularly medieval (Église Notre-Dame in Boulogne-sur-Mer and Marseille Cathedral by Léon Vaudoyer). The trend was furthered by the founding of the *Monuments Historiques* (a body set up for the classification and preservation of the national heritage) in 1830 and the enthusiasm of **Viollet-le-Duc** (1814-1879).

The Second Empire – On the accession of Napoleon III the arts in general were affected by a spirit of **eclecticism**. The Louvre, completed by Percier's disciple **Visconti** (1791-1853) and **H Lefuel** (1810-1880), and the Paris Opera by **Garnier** (1825-1898) were among the greatest undertakings of the century. References to architectural styles of the past (16, 17 and 18C) were present everywhere. Nevertheless, the introduction of new materials like glass and cast-iron (the Gare du Nord by Hittorff and the Église St-Augustine by V Baltard) showed the influence of technological progress and a new rational approach to building.

Baron Haussmann (1809-1891), Prefect of the *département* of the Seine, laid down the principles for a public works programme that was to modernise the capital. Prefect C.M. Vaïsse carried out a similar plan in Lyon.

Academicism reigned over the **painting** of the time. **Cabanel** (1823-1883), **Bouguereau** (1825-1905) and the portraitist **Winterhalter** (1805-1873) drew their inspiration as easily from Antique statuary as from works by 16C Venetian masters or rococo ornamentation. However, **Courbet** (1819-1877), **Daumier** (1808-1879) and **Millet** (1814-1875) formed an avant-garde group that fostered realism in painting with subjects from town and country life.

Ingres (1780-1867) who represented the classical trend, and **Delacroix** (1798-1863), the great romantic painter of the century, were both at the height of their powers. Great architectural projects stimulated the production of **sculpture. Carpeaux** (1827-1875), responsible for the high relief of Dance on the façade of the Paris Opera, transcended the eclecticism of his time by developing a very personal style that was reminiscent of, and not simply a copy of, Flemish, Renaissance and 18C art. **Dubois** (1829-1905), **Frémiet** (1824-1910) and **Guillaume** (1822-1905) were more academic in their approach.

A taste for pastiche prevailed in the decorative arts. The shapes and ornamental motifs of the Renaissance, the 16 and 18C were reproduced on furniture and *objets d'art*. The advent of **industrialisation** affected certain fields. The goldsmith Christofle

(1805-1863) and the bronze founder Barbedienne (1810-1892) made luxury items for the imperial court as well as mass-produced articles for new clients amongst the rich upper middle classes.

Artistic trends in the late 19C – Architecture during the Third Republic was mainly marked by edifices built for Universal Exhibitions held in Paris (the former Trocadero Palace, the Eiffel Tower, the Grand-Palais and the Pont Alexandre III). The pompous style of the buildings with their exotic ornamentation derived from the trend for eclecticism.

In the 1890s **Art Nouveau** architects, influenced by trends in England and Belgium, distanced themselves from the official style of the day. They harmonised decoration on façades with that inside their buildings and designed their creations as a whole – stained glass, tiles, furniture and wall paper. Decoration included plant motifs, stylised flowers, Japanese influences and asymmetrical patterns. **Guimard** (1867-1942) was the main proponent of the style in France (Castel Béranger in Paris and entrances to the capital's metro stations).

The decorative arts followed the Art Nouveau movement with works by the cabinet-maker **Majorelle** (1859-1929) and the glass and ceramics artist **Gallé** (1846-1904) in Nancy.

Gare St-Lazare by Claude Monet (Orsay Museum)

In the field of painting, the **Impressionnists** began exhibiting their work outside official salons in 1874. **Monet** (1840-1926), **Renoir** (1841-1919) and **Pissarro** (1830-1903) breathed new life into the technique and themes of landscape painting by working out of doors, studying the play of light in nature and introducing new subjects drawn from contemporary life. **Manet** (1832-1883) and **Degas** (1834-1917) joined the group temporarily.

Between 1885 and 1890, Neo-Impressionists like **G. Seurat** (1859-1891) and **Signac** (1863-1935) brought the Pointillist (painting with small dots) technique known as divisionism to a climax. The Dutch painter **Van Gogh** (1853-1890) settled in France in 1886. His technique of using pure and expressionist colours with broad swirling brushstrokes coupled with his belief that expression of emotional experience should override impressions of the external world were to have a great influence on early 20C painters. **Cézanne** (1839-1906) and **Gauguin** (1848-1903), who were influenced by primitive and Japanese art, partly dispensed with Impressionism to give more importance to volume. In 1886, seeking new inspiration, Gauguin moved to Pont-Aven, a small town east of Concarneau in Brittany that had often been visited by the painter Corot in the 1860s. Fellow artists **Émile Bernard** and **Paul Sérusier** formed the **Pont-Aven School** that favoured synthetist theories and symbolic subjects which paved the way for the **Nabis**.

Among the Nabis were artists like **Denis** (1870-1943), **Bonnard** (1867-1947) and **Vuillard** (1868-1940) who advocated the importance of colour over shape and meaning.

Sculpture at the end of the century was dominated by the genius of **Rodin** (1840-1917). His expressionistic, tormented, symbolic work stood free from formal academic conventions and was not always understood in his time.

THE 20C

Avant-garde movements up to 1945 – At the beginning of the 20C, proponents of the avant-garde reacted against the many trends of the 19C including the restrictions laid down by official art, academicism in painting and Art Nouveau in architecture.

The **Stijl** movement was characterised in architecture by simple, geometric buildings adorned with sober low-reliefs. One of its most magnificent examples was the Théâtre des Champs-Élysées by the Perret brothers with sculptural decoration by **Bourdelle** (1861-1929). In the field of sculpture, the artists **Maillol** (1861-1944), **Bartholomé** (1848-1928) and **J. Bernard** (1866-1931) opposed Rodin's aesthetic concepts and produced a very different type of art by simplifying their figures, in some cases to the point of schematic representation.

Fauvism was the great novelty at the Autumn Salon of **painting** in 1905. A. Derain (1880-1964), A. Marquet (1875-1947) and M. de Vlaminck (1876-1958) broke up their subject-matter through the vivid and arbitrary use of colour, a technique which was to pave the way for non-figurative painting. After an early period with the Fauvist movement, **Matisse** (1869-1904) went his own way developing a personal style based on the exploration of colour.

A further major avant-garde movement in painting followed on from **Cézanne**'s (1839-1906) structural analysis in which he broke up his subject-matter into specific shapes. The trend was taken up by artists like **Braque** (1882-1963) and **Picasso** (1881-1973) whose exploration led to **Cubism**, a new perception of reality using not what the eye saw but an analytical approach to objects, depicting them as a series of planes, usually in a restricted colour range. The style dominated their work from 1907 to 1914.

Members of the *Section d'Or* (golden section) Cubist group like A. Gleizes, J. Metzinger and F. Léger (his early works) were less revolutionary and more figurative. The main contribution to French cubism in the field of sculpture came from Henri Laurens who was influenced by Braque.

Surrealism breathed new life into the art world in the 1920s and 1930s. It was a subversive art form that created an irrational, dreamlike, fantasy universe. For the first time chance and promptings from the subconscious were integrated into the creative process. **Duchamp** (1887-1968), **Masson** (b 1896), **Picabia** (1879-1953) and **Magritte** (1898-1967) all formed part of the movement.

Artistic creation since 1945 – Abstract art began to affect the field of painting after the Second World War. **Herbin** defined it as the triumph of mind over matter. In 1949 he published *Non-figurative, Non-objective Art (L'Art non figuratif non objectif)* and greatly influenced young artists of the **geometric abstract** art movement. All his works from the 1950s onwards have been one-dimensional patterns of letters and simple geometric shapes painted in pure colours.

The **lyrical abstract** artists focused on the study of colour and texture. **Riopelle** applied his paint with a knife while **Mathieu** applied it directly from the tube. **Soulages**, who was influenced by art from the Far East, produced meditative, expressive work in shades of black. **Nicolas de Stael's** art constituted a link between abstract and figurative in that his abstract compositions were the result of observations of real objects which could sometimes be distinguished in the final work.

Stravinsky Fountain

Some artists like **Fautrier** worked with very thick paint to which they added other materials including sand.

There was an important revival in architecture with **Le Corbusier** (1897-1965) whose buildings fulfilled functional requirements with great clarity of form (Cité Radieuse in Marseille and Ronchamp Chapel).

In the 1960s, **New Realism** *(Nouveau Réalisme),* a form of pop art, with **Pierre Restany** as its leading theoretician, attempted to express the reality of daily life in modern consumer society. Industrial items, the symbols of this society, came under critical scrutiny – they were accumulated, broken up (by the artist **Arman**), compressed and assembled (by **César**) or trapped in glass.

Yves Klein (1928-1962) took his adherence to New Realism a step further in his *Monochromes* by trying to capture and express space, energy and the universal essence of objects. He worked in pure colours and created I.B.K. or International Klein Blue. He rejected formal and traditional values as did **Dubuffet** (1901-1985) who, in 1968, wrote a pamphlet entitled *Asphyxiating Culture (Asphyxiante culture)* which made a stand for permanent revolution, derision and the unexpected. Dubuffet's later paintings and sculptures consisted of puzzles of coloured or black and white units.

Since the 1960s, the problems posed by town-planning have led to a re-evaluation of the relationship between architecture and sculpture and an attempt to reconcile the two arts. Architects and sculptors often work together as in the case of the project by Ricardo Bofill and D. Karavan in Cergy-Pontoise northwest of Paris, and artists are increasingly being asked to modify townscapes (*p 191,* Buren's columns in the Palais Royal in Paris).

The **Support-Surface** movement (**Claude Viallet, Pagès** and **Daniel Dezeuze**) of the 1970s reduced painting to its pure material state by focusing on the support itself or the way the paint was applied. Paintings were removed from their stretchers and cut up, suspended and folded.

The 1980s saw the return of **Figuration** in manifold ways. References to tradition are evident in the work of artists like **Gérard Garouste** and **Jean-Charles Blais**.

The great vitality of contemporary art can be seen in the extremely wide variety of styles and trends favoured by artists today.

The Man Representing Freedom,
a sculpture by César (Place Tolzau in Lyon)

Food and drink

KEY – REGIONAL SPECIALITIES see map overleaf

Aïoli	Garlic mayonnaise
Andouille	Large chitterling sausage
Andouillettes	Chitterling sausages
Angélique	Angelica
Anis	Aniseed confectionery
Asperges	Asparagus
Bergamotes	Orange-flavoured sweets
Berlingots	Humbugs
Bêtises	Hard mints
Beurre blanc	White butter sauce
Bouillabaisse	Seafood stew
Bourride	Fish soup
Brandade	Creamed salt-cod
Cagouilles	Snails
Calissons	Almond and crystallised fruit sweetmeats
Canard au sang	Pressed duck
Cassoulet	Stew with haricot beans and pork rinds
Cedrats confits	Crystallised citrus fruit
Cèpes	Cèpe mushrooms
Charcuterie	Smoked, cured or dried meats
Chipirones	Small cuttlefish, often stuffed
Choucroute	Sauerkraut
Confiseries	Confectionery
Confits	Goose preserved in fat
Crêpes dentelles	Thin pancakes
Dragées	Sugared almonds
Escargots	Snails
Esturgeons	Sturgeon
Far	Flan with prunes
Ficelles picardes	Ham pancakes with mushroom sauce
Foie gras	Goose liver
Fouace	Dough cakes
Fraises	Strawberries
Fruits confits	Crystallised fruit
Galettes	Thick pancakes or waffles
Gâteau d'amandes	Almond cake
Garbure	Meat and vegetable stew
Gratins	Potatoes browned under the grill
Jambon	Ham
Jambon cru des Ardennes	Ardennes cured ham
Kouign-Amann	Cake

Kougelhopf	Plain yeast cake
Lamproies	Lampreys
Macarons	Macaroons
Madeleines	Small sponge cakes
Magrets	Breast of duck
Marrons glacés	Crystallised chestnuts
Massepains	Marzipan cakes
Matelote	Eel stew
Meurette	Wine sauce
Mouclade	Mussel stew
Moutarde	Mustard
Mouton de pré-salé	Salt-pasture lamb
Noix	Nuts
Nougat	Sugar, honey and nut sweetmeat
Nougatine	Caramel syrup and almond sweetmeat
Ortolans	Buntings
Oursins	Sea urchins
Pain d'épice	Spiced honey cake
Pâté d'alouette	Lark paté
Pâté de merle	Blackbird paté
Pauchouse	Fish stew with wine
Pieds de cochon	Pigs' trotters
Piperade	Sweet pepper and tomato omelette
Poulardes	Chickens
Pralines	Caramelised almond confectionery
Pruneaux	Prunes
Quenelles	Poached meat or fish dumplings
Quenelles de brochet	Poached pike dumplings
Quiche (Lorraine)	Beaten egg, cream and bacon flan
Rillettes	Potted pork
Rillons	Potted chopped pork
Saupiquet	Spiced wine sauce
Saucisse de Morteau	Morteau sausage
Saucisson	Dried sausage
Soupe au pistou	Vegetable soup with basil
Touron	Soft almond confectionery
Tourteau fromager	Goats' cheese gateau
Tripes	Tripe
Tripoux	Stuffed tripe
Truffes	Truffles
Volailles	Poultry

Food and drink
REGIONAL SPECIALITIES – PRINCIPAL AREAS OF PRODUCTION
(See the key to regional specialities on the previous page)

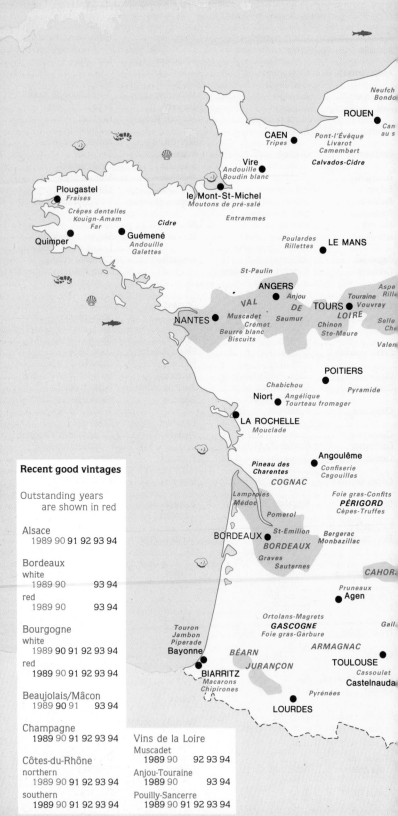

Neufch
Bondo

ROUEN

Can
au s

CAEN
Tripes

Pont-l'Évêque
Livarot
Camembert

Calvados-Cidre

Vire
*Andouille
Boudin blanc*

Plougastel
Fraises

*Crêpes dentelles
Kouign-Amam
Far*

le Mont-St-Michel
Moutons de pré-salé

Cidre

Entrammes

Quimper

Guémené
*Andouille
Galettes*

Poulardes
Rillettes

LE MANS

St-Paulin

ANGERS

Anjou

Aspe
Rill

Touraine

TOURS *Vouvray*

VAL   *DE*   *LOIRE*

Selle
Che

NANTES

*Muscadet
Crémet
Beurre blanc
Biscuits*

Saumur

*Chinon
Ste-Maure*

Valen

POITIERS

Chabichou

Niort

*Angélique
Tourteau fromager*

Pyramide

LA ROCHELLE
Mouclade

Angoulême
*Confiserie
Cagouilles*

*Pineau des
Charentes*

COGNAC

*Lamproies
Médoc*

Foie gras-Confits
PÉRIGORD
Cèpes-Truffes

Pomerol

BORDEAUX
St-Emilion

*Bergerac
Monbazillac*

BORDEAUX

CAHOR

*Graves
Sauternes*

Pruneaux
Agen

Ortolans-Magrets
GASCOGNE
Foie gras-Garbure

Gail

*Touron
Jambon
Piperade*
Bayonne

BÉARN

ARMAGNAC

TOULOUSE
Cassoulet

JURANÇON

Castelnauda

BIARRITZ
*Macarons
Chipirones*

Pyrénées

LOURDES

Recent good vintages

Outstanding years
are shown in red

Alsace
   1989 90 **91 92 93 94**

Bordeaux
white
   1989 90   93 94
red
   1989 90   93 94

Bourgogne
white
   1989 90 **91 92 93 94**
red
   1989 **90 91 92 93 94**

Beaujolais/Mâcon
   1989 **90 91**   93 94

Champagne
   1989 90 **91 92 93 94**

Côtes-du-Rhône
northern
   1989 90 **91 92 93 94**
southern
   1989 90 **91 92 93 94**

Vins de la Loire
Muscadet
   1989 90   92 93 94
Anjou-Touraine
   1989 90   93 94
Pouilly-Sancerre
   1989 90 **91 92 93 94**

Bêtises: Regional speciality
Maroilles: Cheese
BORDEAUX: Wine-producing region
Pomerol: Fine wine
Bière: Other alcoholic products

mentières
Genièvre-Bière

Arras
Maroilles
...ulette d'Avesnes

Cambrai
Bêtises

AMIENS
Ficelles picardes
Macarons

ontdidier
Rollot

Jambon cru
des Ardennes

Biscuits
REIMS

Dragées
Verdun

Epernay
Ste-Menehould
Pieds de cochon

PARIS
Coulommiers
Brie

CHAMPAGNE

Commercy
Madeleines

NANCY
Bergamotes
Macarons

STRASBOURG
Bière
Eaux-de-vie

Quiche

ALSACE
Choucroute
Kougelhopf
Matelote

Fontainebleau

Andouillettes
Troyes
Soumaintrain
Chaource

Géromé

Gérardmer

Munster

Pithiviers
Gateau d'amandes
Pâté d'alouettes

ORLÉANS
...ô-Olivet cendré

Chablis

Langres
Langres

...ottin de
...avignol

Sancerre
Pouilly
Sancerre

Époisses
St-Florentin

Flavigny
Anis

Cassis

DIJON
Pain d'épice
Moutarde

Saucisse de Morteau

Nevers
Nougâtine

Côte de Beaune

BOURGOGNE

Arbois
Cancoillotte
Comté-Morbier
Vacherin

Pontarlier

JURA
Meurette
Gruyère
Septmoncel

Mâcon
Escargots
Saupiquet
Pauchouse

BEAUJOLAIS

BRESSE
Volailles
Quenelles

Fondue
Tomme de Savoie

Pralines
Bleu
Aigueperse

CLERMONT-FERRAND
St-Nectaire
Gaperon

SAVOIE
Beaufort
Reblochon
Persillé

ANNECY
Gratins

LYON
Quenelles de brochet
Charcuterie

Hermitage

Fourme
d'Ambert

Rigotte
de Condrieu

CÔTES

GRENOBLE
Noix

St-Flour
Cantal

St-Marcellin

DAUPHINÉ
Gratins

Aligot

Laguiole

Privas
DU

Montélimar
Nougat

Gap
Massepains

Marrons glacés

Cabécou
Rodez

Tripous

Pélardon
des
Cévennes

RHÔNE

Châteauneuf
du Pape
Berlingots
Bânon

Carpentras

Fruits confits
Soupe de pistou

Bleu des Causses

Millau
Roquefort
Fouace

Brandade
Nimes

Apt
Fruits confits

NICE

Arles
Saucisson

Bourride
Brousse

Aix-en-Provence
Calissons

LANGUEDOC

Frontignan

PROVENCE

VAR
Aïoli
Olives

MARSEILLE
Bouillabaisse
Oursins

CORBIÈRES

ROUSSILLON
Rivesaltes
PERPIGNAN
Banyuls

Pâté de Merles
Cédrats confits

CORSE

Braccio
Niolo

Main tourist routes

NORTH-SOUTH routes

(for east-west routes see following pages)

These are a combination of the most direct and most interesting routes to and from a variety of popular destinations. They can be joined and left at any point.

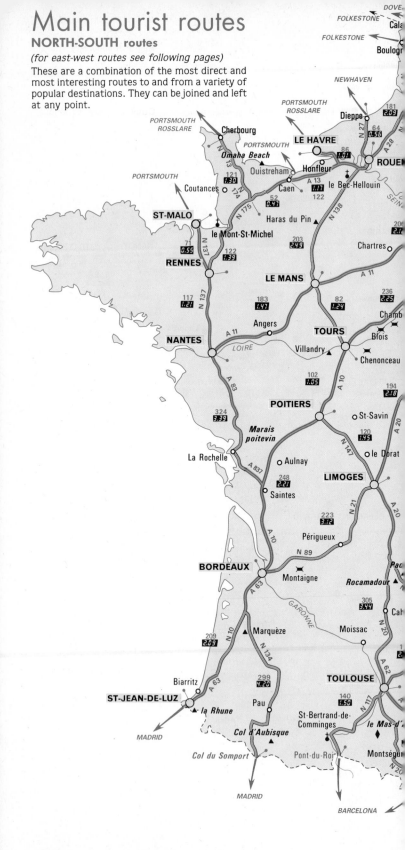

DOVE...
FOLKESTONE · Cala...
FOLKESTONE
Boulogn...
NEWHAVEN
PORTSMOUTH
ROSSLARE
Dieppe
181
2.09
N 27
64
0.56
A 28
PORTSMOUTH
ROSSLARE
Cherbourg
PORTSMOUTH
LE HAVRE
86
1.01
ROUE...
PORTSMOUTH
ROSSLARE
Omaha Beach
Honfleur
N 13
Ouistreham
le Bec-Hellouin
PORTSMOUTH
Coutances
121
1.30
N 174
Caen
A 13
1.11
122
SEIN...
N 175
ST-MALO
52
0.47
Haras du Pin
N 138
200
2.1...
le Mont-St-Michel
203
2.49
Chartres
71
0.55
122
1.39
RENNES
N 137
LE MANS
A 11
117
1.21
183
1.47
82
1.24
236
2.25
N 137
Chamb...
Angers
A 11
TOURS
Blois
NANTES
LOIRE
Villandry
Chenonceau
A 83
102
1.05
A 10
194
2.18
A 20
POITIERS
St-Savin
324
3.39
Marais
poitevin
120
1.45
le Dorat
A 837
N 147
La Rochelle
Aulnay
LIMOGES
248
2.21
Saintes
A 10
N 21
A 20
223
3.12
Périgueux
N 89
BORDEAUX
Pac...
A 63
Montaigne
Rocamadour
GARONNE
305
3.44
Cah...
209
2.09
N 10
Marquèze
Moissac
N 20
A 62
N 134
2...
Biarritz
299
4.20
TOULOUSE
ST-JEAN-DE-LUZ
A 63
140
1.50
N 117
A...
la Rhune
Pau
St-Bertrand-de-
Comminges
le Mas-d'...
MADRID
Col d'Aubisque
Montségu...
Col du Somport
Pont-du-Roi
N 20...
MADRID
BARCELONA

TOURS ○ Tourist centre with good hotel provision and visitor interest.

50

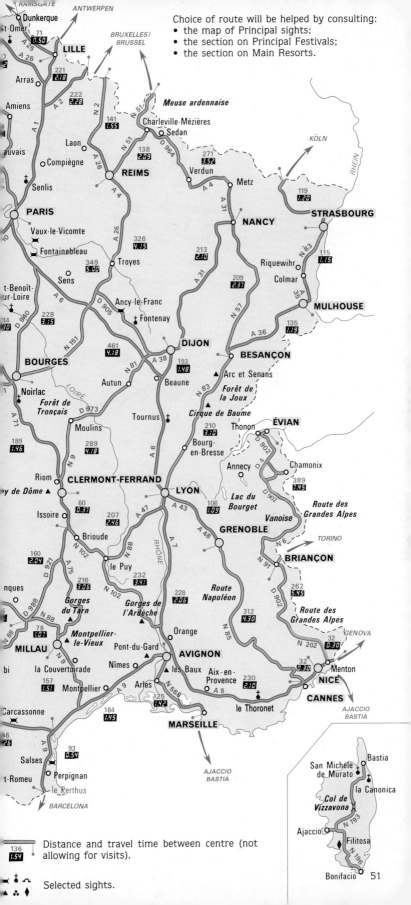

Choice of route will be helped by consulting:
- the map of Principal sights;
- the section on Principal Festivals;
- the section on Main Resorts.

RAMSGATE
ANTWERPEN
t-Omer
Dunkerque
71
0.50
BRUXELLES/
BRUSSEL
LILLE
A 25
A 26
221
2.18
Arras
Meuse ardennaise
KÖLN
222
2.28
Amiens
N 2
141
1.55
Charleville-Mézières
Sedan
RHEIN
A 1
Laon
N 51
138
2.09
271
3.52
Verdun
119
1.20
STRASBOURG
Compiègne
Beauvais
A 26
REIMS
Metz
N 83
Senlis
A 4
A 4
A 31
NANCY
PARIS
Vaux-le-Vicomte
A 26
326
4.15
213
2.10
Riquewihr
115
1.15
Fontainebleau
Troyes
209
2.37
Colmar
A 6
349
5.00
Sens
A 31
MULHOUSE
A 35
t-Benoît-
ur-Loire
D 905
Ancy-le-Franc
N 57
135
1.19
14
30
228
3.15
D 940
Fontenay
DIJON
A 36
N 151
461
4.18
A 38
193
1.48
BESANÇON
BOURGES
N 87
Autun
Beaune
Arc et Senans
Forêt de
la Joux
Noirlac
Forêt de
Tronçais
LOIRE
N 83
ÉVIAN
D 973
Cirque de Baume
Thonon
A 71
Moulins
210
3.10
D 902
289
4.18
Bourg-
en-Bresse
Annecy
Chamonix
389
1.45
189
1.46
N 9
Riom
Lac du
Bourget
D 902
Route des
Grandes Alpes
y de Dôme
CLERMONT-FERRAND
LYON
Vanoise
60
0.37
106
1.09
A 47
A 43
Issoire
207
2.46
A 48
GRENOBLE
N 6
TORINO
Brioude
A 7
BRIANÇON
160
2.04
N 102
le Puy
N 91
D 902
A 75
216
3.06
232
3.41
262
5.45
Route des
Grandes Alpes
D 921
Gorges
du Tarn
N 102
Route
Napoléon
312
4.30
D 988
Gorges de
l'Ardèche
228
2.06
N 85
GENOVA
N 88
78
1.07
Montpellier-
le-Vieux
Orange
32
0.30
N 88
MILLAU
Pont-du-Gard
AVIGNON
32
0.30
Menton
bi
la Couvertoirade
Nîmes
les Baux
Aix-en-
Provence
230
2.10
NICE
157
1.51
Montpellier
Arles
A 8
CANNES
Carcassonne
184
1.45
125
1.42
N 568
le Thoronet
AJACCIO
BASTIA
A 9
MARSEILLE
93
0.54
Salses
AJACCIO
BASTIA
t-Romeu
Perpignan
le Perthus
BARCELONA

136
1.54
Distance and travel time between centre (not
allowing for visits).

Selected sights.

San Michele
de Murato
Bastia
la Canonica
Col de
Vizzavona
Ajaccio
N 193
Filitosa
N 196
Bonifacio

51

Main tourist routes
EAST-WEST routes
(for north-south routes see previous pages)

DOVE
FOLKESTONE
Ca

NEWHAVEN

PORTSMOUTH
ROSSLARE
PORTSMOUTH
ROSSLARE

Cherbourg
Fécamp
Étretat
Diepp
106
1.38
D
Caudebec-en-Ca
PORTSMOUTH
86
1.11
Villequier
Jumièges
A 15
LE HAVRE
ROU

PLYMOUTH
CORK
PORTSMOUTH
Ouistreham
Honfleur
†
le Bec-Hellouin
122
1.33
A 13
N 13
121
1.30
Coutances
Caen
N 175
52
0.47

Roscoff
189
2.19 *Cap Fréhel*
ST-MALO
le Mont-St-Michel
114
1.33
Chartres
203
2.11
BREST
N 12
St-Thégonnec
152
1.32
N 176
Pointe de Pen-Hir
65
0.47
Pointe du Raz
Locronan
Kernascléden
245
2.38
RENNES
LE MANS
A 11
82
1.11
Blois
Cham
Concarneau
N 165
Josselin
N 24
A 81
183
2.19
A 11
N 38
TOURS
A 10
Chever
N
Carnac
298
3.22
Angers
Villandry
Chenonceau
Guérande
N 165
LOIRE
206
2.54
NANTES
Fontevraud
183
2.34
N 149
POITIERS
192
2.37
N 15
Marais poitevin
A 10
St-Savin
LA ROCHELLE
N 11
138
1.37
N 147
119
1.45
LIMOGES
D
N 137
Aulnay
Brouage
Saintes
N 141
141
1.56
ANGOULÊME
180
2.49 *Suc-au-Ma*
Brantôme
D 939
D 47
N 89
Montaigne
les Eyzies-de-Tayac
Sarlat
Pad
BORDEAUX
N 89
D 936
192
3.25
Domme
66
0.50
la Brède
A 62
GARONNE
Rocamado
CAHORS
D
247
2.18
Moissac

TOULOUSE

ST-JEAN-DE-LUZ
166
2.59
PAU
335
4.30
la Rhune
D 918
N 117
la Rhune
N 134
Betharram
N 25
le Mas-d'A
MADRID
St-Jean-Pied-de-Port
Lourdes
Col d'Aubisque
D 918
179
2.38
N 20
Cirque de Gavarnie

BARCELON

52

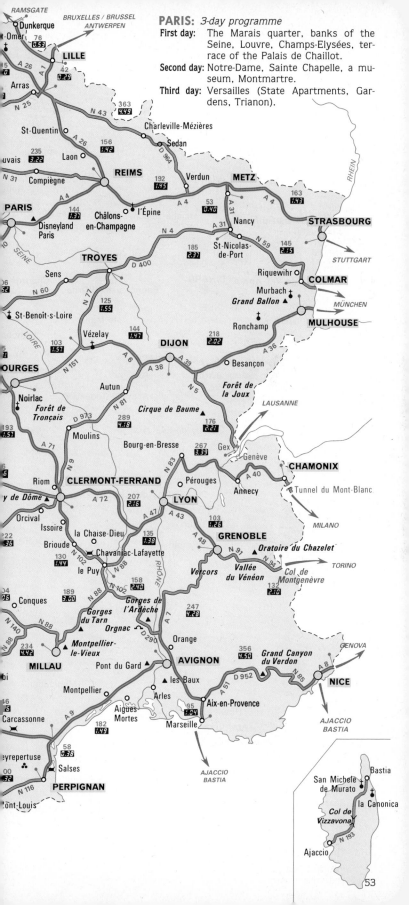

RAMSGATE
BRUXELLES / BRUSSEL
ANTWERPEN

Dunkerque
-Omer 76
0.53

LILLE
42
0.29

A 26
A 1

Arras
N 25

N 43
363
4.49

St-Quentin
A 26
Charleville-Mézières
Sedan
D 964
156
1.42

235
3.22
Laon
192
1.45
Verdun
METZ
163
1.43
STRASBOURG

uvais
N 31
Compiègne
REIMS
A 4
53
0.40
Nancy
A 31
145
2.15
STUTTGART

PARIS
144
1.37
Châlons-en-Champagne
l'Épine
N 4
St-Nicolas-de-Port
185
2.37
N 59
COLMAR

Disneyland
Paris
Riquewihr
Murbach
Grand Ballon
MÜNCHEN

TROYES
D 400
Ronchamp
MULHOUSE

Sens
N 60
125
1.55
144
1.47
218
2.02
RHEIN

St-Benoît-s-Loire
Vézelay
DIJON
A 36

103
1.57
LOIRE
N 151
A 6
A 39
Besançon
Forêt de
la Joux

OURGES
Autun
A 38
N 5

Noirlac
Forêt de
Tronçais
N 81
Cirque de Baume
176
2.21
LAUSANNE

193
1.57
D 973
289
4.18
267
3.39
Gex
Genève
CHAMONIX

Moulins
Bourg-en-Bresse
Annecy
A 40
Tunnel du Mont-Blanc

Riom
CLERMONT-FERRAND
Pérouges
LYON

y de Dôme
A 72
207
2.46
A 47
A 43
103
1.26
GRENOBLE
MILANO

Orcival
Issoire
la Chaise-Dieu
135
1.38
A 48
Oratoire du Chazelet
TORINO

222
Brioude
Chavaniac-Lafayette
N 91
Vallée
du Vénéon
N 94
Col de
Montgenèvre

130
1.44
le Puy
N 102
N 88
Vercors
132
2.10

04
189
3.00
N 102
158
2.40
RHÔNE

Conques
N 88
Gorges de
l'Ardèche
247
4.28

N 140
N 88
Gorges
du Tarn
Orgnac
A 7

234
4.42
Montpellier-
le-Vieux
Orange
356
4.50
Grand Canyon
du Verdon
GENOVA

MILLAU
Pont du Gard
AVIGNON
A 8

Montpellier
les Baux
A 51
D 952
N 85
NICE

bi
Arles
95
1.04
Aix-en-Provence

Carcassonne
A 9
Aigues
Mortes
Marseille
AJACCIO
BASTIA

182
1.49

58
0.38
eyrepertuse
Salses
AJACCIO
BASTIA

00
N 116
PERPIGNAN

ont-Louis

Bastia
San Michele
de Murato
la Canonica

Col de
Vizzavona

N 193

Ajaccio

53

PARIS: *3-day programme*

First day: The Marais quarter, banks of the
Seine, Louvre, Champs-Elysées, terrace of the Palais de Chaillot.

Second day: Notre-Dame, Sainte Chapelle, a museum, Montmartre.

Third day: Versailles (State Apartments, Gardens, Trianon).

Main resorts – Principal festivals

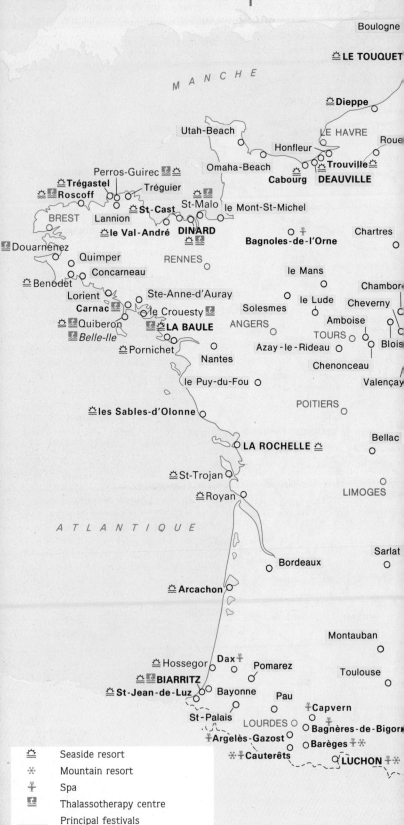

Boulogne

☆ **LE TOUQUET**

M A N C H E

☆ **Dieppe**

Utah-Beach

LE HAVRE

Honfleur   Roue

Omaha-Beach   ☆ **Trouville**

Cabourg   **DEAUVILLE**

Perros-Guirec ☆☆   Chartres

☆ **Trégastel**   Tréguier

☆☆ **Roscoff**

BREST   Lannion   St-Malo   le Mont-St-Michel

St-Cast   ☆ St-Malo

☆ **le Val-André**   ☆ **DINARD**   **Bagnoles-de-l'Orne**

☆ Douarnenez   RENNES   le Mans

Quimper   le Lude   Chambor

Concarneau   Cheverny

☆ Bénodet   Ste-Anne-d'Auray   Solesmes   Amboise

Lorient   le Crouesty ☆   ANGERS   TOURS   Blois

Carnac ☆

☆☆ **Quiberon**   ☆☆ **LA BAULE**   Azay-le-Rideau   Valençay

Belle-Ile   Chenonceau

☆ **Pornichet**   Nantes

le Puy-du-Fou   POITIERS

☆ **les Sables-d'Olonne**

Bellac

LA ROCHELLE ☆

☆ **St-Trojan**   LIMOGES

☆ **Royan**

A T L A N T I Q U E   Sarlat

Bordeaux

☆ **Arcachon**

Montauban

☆ **Hossegor**   Dax ✝   Pomarez   Toulouse

☆☆ **BIARRITZ**   Bayonne   Pau

☆ **St-Jean-de-Luz**   ✝ **Capvern**

St-Palais   LOURDES   ✝ **Bagnères-de-Bigor**

✝ **Argelès-Gazost**   **Barèges** ✝☀

☀✝ **Cauterêts**   **LUCHON** ✝☀

☆	Seaside resort
☀	Mountain resort
✝	Spa
☆	Thalassotherapy centre
	Principal festivals and other events

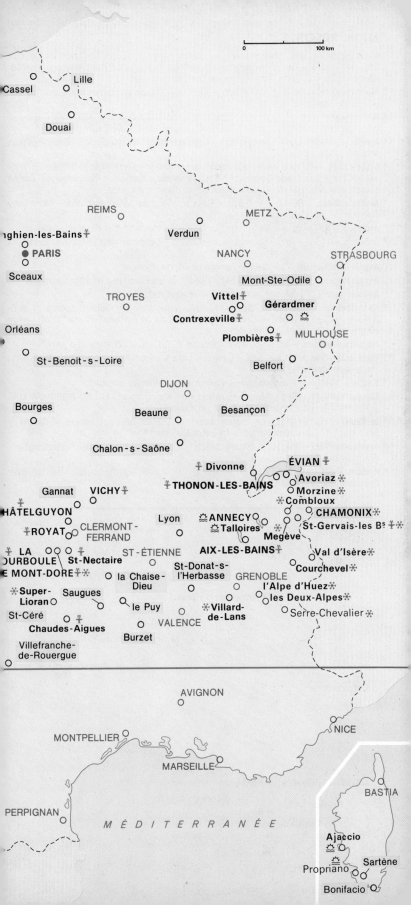

MAIN RESORTS

Most of the resorts listed below have a wide range of accommodation and leisure facilities and are therefore only characterised in terms of their setting or other special features. The figures refer to the Michelin map and fold number.

★★ **Aix-en-Provence.** - 84 3 – *(qv)* – Spa – Casino – 18C spa complex built next to site of Roman baths.

★★ **Aix-les-Bains.** - 74 15 – Spa – Palais de Savoie Casino and Nouveau Casino – prestigious "Season" – Parks – Lakeside esplanade★ – Dr Faure Museum★.

★★ **Ajaccio.** - 90 17 – *(qv)* – Sandy beach – Casino – Place Maréchal-Foch – other beaches around Ajaccio Bay.

★ **L'Alpe-d'Huez.** - 77 6 – Mountain resort with winter sports (1 860-3 350m/6 100-10 990ft) – Lac Blanc Summit★★★ *(by cableway and cable car):* view of Écrins Massif and Mont Blanc – Lake Besson★ *(6.5km – 4 miles).*

★ **Amélie-les-Bains.** - 86 18, 19 – Spa – Casino – Restored Roman baths – Montdony Gorges.

★★★ **Annecy.** - 74 6 – *(qv)* – Swimming in lake – Lakeside★★★ – Riverside walk.

★★ **Arcachon.** - 71 20 – *(qv)* – Sandy beach – Casino – Seafront with views over Arcachon Bay.

Argelès-Gazost. - 85 17 – Spa – Panorama of the Pyrenees.

Argelès-Plage. - 86 20 – Casino – Sandy beach at northern end of Côte Vermeille★★.

★★ **Avoriaz.** - 189 3 – Mountain resort (winter sports).

★ **Ax-les-Thermes.** - 86 15 – Spa – Mountain resort with winter sports (1 400-2 400m/4 590-7 870ft) – Ladres Valley – Bonascre Plateau★ (View★★ of Ariège heights and Andorra mountains).

★ **Bagnères-de-Bigorre.** - 85 16 – Spa – Casino – Salut spa complex and park★.

★★ **Bagnoles-de-l'Orne.** - 60 1 – Spa – Casino – Lake★ – Park★ – Roc-au-Chien Walk★ (in Tessé-la-Madeleine).

★ **Bandol.** - 84 14 – Sandy beach – Casino – Jean-Moulin avenue★.

Barèges. - 85 18 – Spa – Mountain resort with winter sports (1 250-2 350m/4 100-7 710ft) – Lienz Plateau – Font d'Ayré funicular.

★★★ **La Baule.** - 63 14 – *(qv)* – Sandy beach – Thalassotherapy centre – Casino – Seafront★★ – Dryades Park★ – La-Baule-les-Pins★★.

★★ **Beaulieu-sur-Mer.** - 84 10 – Sandy beach – Casino – Villa Kerylos★ (setting★) – Fourmis Bay★.

★ **Bénodet.** - 58 15 – Sandy beach – Casino – Pyramide lighthouse (panorama★ over Cornouaille coast and Glénan islands).

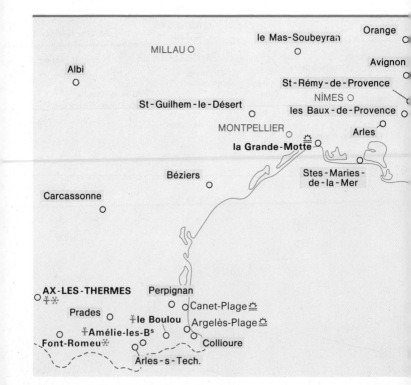

56

Biarritz. – 85 2 – *(qv)* – Sandy beach with rocks – Thalassotherapy centre – Casino – La Perspective viewpoint★★ – St-Martin Point (view★) – Vierge Rock★ – Museum of the Sea★.

Le Boulou. – 86 19 – Spa – Casino – Setting at foot of Albères Mountains.

La Bourboule. – 73 13 – Spa – Fenestre Park★ – Charlannes Plateau.

Cabourg. – 55 2 – Sandy beach – Casino – Marcel-Proust Promenade.

Canet-Plage. – 86 20 – Sandy beach – Casino – Active sports centre.

Cannes. – 84 9 – *(qv)* – Sandy beach – Fleurs Casino, Palm Beach Casino, Casino Municipal) – Boulevard de la Croisette★★ – La Croisette Point★ – Super-Cannes Observatory (panorama★★★) – La Castre Museum★.

Cap-d'Antibes. – 84 9 – Sandy beach with rocks – Round tour★★ – La Garoupe Plateau (panorama★★) – Thuret Gardens★.

Capvern. – 85 9 – Spa – View of Pyrenees.

Cauterets. – 85 17 – Spa – Mountain resort with winter sports (930-2 340m/3 050-7 680ft) – Casino Esplanade – Espagne Bridge★★ – Lutour Valley★ and Falls★★; Jeret Valley★★.

Chamonix. – 74 8, 9 – *(qv)* – Mountain resort with winter sports (1 035-3 842m/3 400-12 604ft) – Setting at foot of Aiguille du Midi with view of Mont-Blanc.

Châtelguyon. – 73 4 – Spa – Casino – Prades Valley★ – Enval Gorge★.

Chaudes-Aigues. – 76 14 – Spa – Source of the River Par – Neighbourhood saints in niches.

La Clusaz. – Mountain resort with winter sports (1 100-2 600m/3 600-8 500ft).

Combloux. – 74 8 – Mountain resort with winter sports (1 000-1 853m/3 280-6 080ft) – View★ of Mont-Blanc.

Contrexéville. – 62 14 – Spa – Casino – La Folie Lake.

Courchevel. – 74 18 – Mountain resort with winter sports (1 300-2 700m/4 260-8 860ft) – Panorama★ – La Saulire *(cableway and cable car):* panorama★★.

Dax. – 78 6, 7 – Spa – Casino – Warm springs – *9km – 6 miles northeast:* Buglose (birthplace of St Vincent de Paul).

Deauville. – 55 3 – *(qv)* – Sandy beach – Summer and Winter Casinos – Boardwalk★ (Promenade des Planches).

Les Deux-Alpes. – 77 6 – Twin winter resorts (L'Alpe-du-Mont-de-Lans and L'Alpe-de-Venosc) with winter sports (1 650-3 560m/5 410-11 680ft) – From L'Alpe-de-Venosc: La Croix viewpoint★ and Cimes viewpoint★ *(by cableway).*

Dieppe. – 52 4 – *(qv)* – Pebble beach – Casino – Boulevard de la Mer (view★) – Boulevard du Maréchal-Foch.

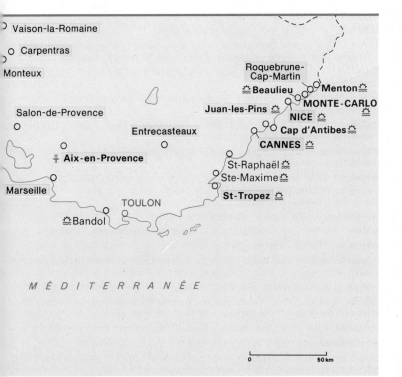

★★★ **Dinard.** – 59 5 – *(qv)* – Sandy beach with rocks – Thalassotherapy centre – Casino – Moulinet Point (view★★) – Grande Plage beach★ – Clair de Lune Promenade★.

★ **Divonne.** – 70 16 – *(qv)* – Spa – Casino – Park.

★ **Douarnenez.** – Thalassotherapy centre.

★ **Enghien.** – 101 5 – Spa – Casino – Lake★.

★★★ **Évian.** – 70 70 – *(qv)* – Spa – Casino – English Garden.

★★ **Font-Romeu.** – 86 16 – Mountain resort with winter sports (1 850-2 204m/6 070-7 230ft) – Casino – Hermitage★ (Camaril★★) – Calvary (panorama★★ over the Cerdagne).

★★ **Gérardmer.** – 62 17 – *(qv)* – Spa – Mountain/forest setting – Winter sports (870-1 130m/2 850-3 710ft) – Lake★.

★ **La Grande-Motte.** – 83 8 – *(qv)* – Sandy beach – Casino – Modern resort architecture.

★ **Hossegor.** – 78 17 – Sandy beach – Casino – Lakeside Promenade★.

★★ **Juan-les-Pins.** – 84 9 – *(qv)* – Sandy beach – Casino: Eden Beach – Fine coastal setting.

★★ **Luchon.** – 85 20 – Spa – Mountain setting with winter sports at Super-Bagnères (1 420-2 260m/4 660-7 420ft) – d'Étigny avenues.

★★★ **Megève.** – 74 7, 8 – *(qv)* – Alpine setting with winter sports (1 067-2 350/3 510-7 710ft) – Casino – Mont d'Arbois *(by cable car):* panorama★★★ over Aravis mountains and Mont-Blanc.

★★ **Menton.** – 84 10, 20 – *(qv)* – Pebble beach – Casino du Soleil – Promenade du Soleil★★ – Carnolès Palace Museum★.

★★ **Le Mont-Dore.** – 73 13 – Spa – Montain resort with winter sports (1 350-1 850m/4 430-6 070ft) – Casino – Promenade des Artistes★ – Salon du Capucin *(funicular).*

★★★ **Monte-Carlo.** – 84 10 – *(qv)* – Sandy beach with rocks – Grand Casino, Casino du Sporting Club, Casino Loews – Museum of Dolls and Automata★.

★★ **Morzine.** – 74 8 – *(qv)* – Mountain setting with winter sports (1 000-2 460m/3 280-8 070ft) – Meeting point of six valleys – Le Pléney cable car: panorama.

★★★ **Nice.** – 84 9, 10 – *(qv)* – Pebble beach – Casino-club.

★ **Perros-Guirec.** – 59 1 – Sandy beach – Thalassotherapy centre – Casino – Le Château Point (view★) – Viewing table (view★) – Douaniers Path★★.

★ **Plombières.** – 62 16 – Spa – Casino – Park designed by Haussmann.

★ **Pornichet.** – 63 14 – *(qv)* – Sandy beach – Casino – Boulevard des Océanides.

★ **Propriano.** – 90 18 – Sandy beach – Valinco Bay★.

Quiberon. – 63 12 – *(qv)* – Sandy beach with rocks – Thalassotherapy centre – Casino – Côte Sauvage★★.

★★★ **La Rochelle.** – 71 12 – *(qv)* – Sandy beach – Casino.

★ **Roscoff.** – 58 6 – *(qv)* – Thalassotherapy centre – Sandy beaches with some pebbles – Aquarium★ – Notre-Dame-de-Kroaz-Betz Church★ (Belfry★, alabaster statues★).

★★ **Royan.** – 71 15 – Sandy beach – Casino *(at Pontaillac)* – Seafront★ – Notre-Dame Church★.

★★ **Royat.** – 73 14 – Spa – Casino – Set among foothills of Monts Dômes – Spa Park and Bargoin Park.

★★ **Les Sables-d'Olonne.** – 67 12 – Sandy beach – Casino de la Plage – Casino des Sports – Remblai promenade★ – Fishermen's quarter.

★★ **St-Cast-le-Guildo.** – 59 5 – Sandy beach – St-Cast Point (view★★) – La Garde Point (view★★).

★★ **St-Gervais.** – 74 8 – Spa – Mountain resort with winter sports (850-2 350m/2 790-7 710ft) – Bettex scenic route★★★ – Eagle's Nest and Bionassay glacier★★ *(Mont-Blanc mountain railway).*

★★ **St-Jean-de-Luz.** – 85 2 – *(qv)* – Sandy beach – Casino.

★★★ **St-Malo.** – 59 6 – *(qv)* – Sandy beach – Thalassotherapy centre – Casino.

★★ **St-Nectaire.** – 73 14 – *(qv)* – Spa.

★ **St-Raphaël.** – 84 8 – Sandy beach – Casino – Sheltered setting at foot of Esterel Massif – Seafront.

St-Trojan. – 71 14 – Sandy beach – Pinetum.

★★ **St-Tropez.** – 84 17 – *(qv)* – Sandy beach – Harbour★ and quaysides – L'Annonciade Museum★★ – View★ from harbour wall – View★ from citadel.

★ **Ste-Maxime.** – 84 17 – Sandy beach – Casino – Panorama★ from semaphore.

★ **Serre-Chevalier.** – 177 18 – Winter sports.

★ **Super-Lioran.** – 76 3 – Mountain resort with winter sports (1 160-1 830m/3 810-6 000ft) – Plomb du Cantal★ *(cable car):* panorama★★.

Talloires. – 77 6 – *(qv)* – Bathing in the lake – Lakeside setting★★★ (Petit Lac d'Annecy).

Thonon. – 70 17 – *Spa.*

Le Touquet-Paris-Plage. – 51 11 – *(qv)* – Sandy beach – La Forêt and Quatre Saisons Casinos – Seafront promenade – Woodland – Lighthouse (view★★).

Trégastel. – 59 1 – Sandy beach – Rocky coastline of the Breton Corniche★ – White Shore (La Grève blanche) footpath★.

Trouville. – 55 3 – Sandy beach – Casino – Corniche road★ – Boardwalk (Promenade des Planches).

Le Val-André. – 59 4 – Sandy beach – Casino – Pléneuf Point★ (View★★) – Promenade de la Guette★.

Val-d'Isère. – 74 19 – *(qv)* – Mountain resort with winter sports (1 850-3 450m/6 070-11 320ft) – Rocher de Bellevarde *(cable car):* panorama★★★ – Tête du Solaise *(cable car):* panorama★★.

Vichy. – 73 5 – *(qv)* – Spa – Élysée Palace Casino, Grand Casino – Sources Park★ – Allier Park★.

Villard-de-Lans. – 77 4 – Mountain resort with winter sports (1 050-2 170m/3 450-7 120ft) – Vercors Regional Park setting – Bourne Gorge★★★.

Vittel. – 62 14 – Spa – Casino – Landscape park★.

Monte-Carlo.

J. Lebar/PIX

59

Sights

ABBEVILLE

Population 23 787
Map p 6 – Michelin map 52 folds 6, 7 or 236 fold 22
Green Guide Flanders, Picardy and the Paris Region
Town plan in the current Michelin Red Guide France

Abbeville's site was once an island in the estuary of the Somme which provided a refuge for local people fleeing from raiding Norsemen. The town itself developed out of an agricultural estate belonging to the abbey of St Riquier and became a market centre for both the Ponthieu plateau north of the Somme and the Vimeux country to the south with its villages hidden among the hedges of the *bocage*.

Beginning and end of the Hundred Years War – The first battle of the Hundred Years War *(qv)* took place in the Forest of **Crécy**, 19km – 12 miles to the north of Abbeville. Here the armies of Philippe VI and Edward III came face to face on 26 August 1346. In spite of its bravery, Philippe's formidable force of cavalry proved no match for Edward's infantry, hardened in battle against the Welsh and Scots and supported by the unrivalled English archers. Primitive cannon appear on the battlefield for the first time, producing more sound and fury than actual damage. The encounter marked a sharp decline in the power and prestige of the Capetian monarchy and a corresponding consolidation of the Plantagenets' position in France; Calais would remain in English hands for another 200 years.

The war was finally brought to an end 129 years later by the Treaty of **Piquigny** *(34km – 19 miles southwest)*. This treaty, uniquely, was proposed, accepted, drawn up and signed (on 29 August 1475) within the space of two days. In mid-June, Edward IV had disembarked at Calais, led by his Burgundian informants to believe that his campaign need be little more than a march past, duly applauded by an enthusiastic local population. In the event, resistance was widespread and effective; to Louis XI, lying in wait for him at Compiègne at the head of a powerful army, Edward made a proposition; for a lump sum of 75 000 crowns to be paid within a fortnight and an annual payment for seven years of 50 000 crowns he might be ready to quit French soil. The deal was done; it was a sign that times had changed, that the ideals of chivalry were giving way to bourgeois values and that the greatest war the feudal world had known could be brought to an end by a monetary transaction.

The beginnings of prehistoric studies – In the middle of the 19C, **Jacques Boucher de Perthes** (1788-1868) put prehistoric studies *(qv)* on a firm basis through his work on the dressed flints found at St Acheul *(26km – 16 miles northeast)* in the valley of the River Authie. His successors proved the flint industry of St Acheul to be of Lower Paleolithic date; its technique of splitting arrowheads like flakes (rather than fashioning them individually from a piece of stone) marks an important stage in the evolution of mankind.

June 1940 – Battle of the Somme – Towards the end of May 1940 the Caubert heights on the south bank of the Somme were taken by rapidly advancing German units who quickly strengthened their natural defences. Although hurriedly thrown together and without other support, General de Gaulle's Fourth Armoured Division launched a counter-attack on 27-29 May, driving deeply into the enemy's lines without however dislodging him completely. By the beginning of June, the sheer weight of the German mechanised forces, the pusillanimous French leadership and growing general panic turned the Battle of France into a rout.

Some 2 000 of Abbeville's ancient dwellings were destroyed during this battle and in later bombing raids. The result of this extensive damage is that the town has acquired a resolutely modern appearance.

> **Collégiale St-Vulfran** – This fine example of the vitality of late Gothic architecture dates from the late 15C when Picardy was rising from the ruins of the Hundred Years War and rediscovering the pleasures of building.
>
> ★ **West Front** – With its gables rising above rose window and tympana, its wealth of statuary, its delicate arcading and flame-like fenestration and balustrading, this is a perfect example of the Flamboyant style at its most opulent. The central doors retain their Renaissance leaves, masterpieces by local carpenters.
>
> ⊙ ►► Château de Bagatelle★ ; Musée Boucher de Perthes★ – prehistory, medieval paintings and sculpture.

In this guide
town plans show the main streets and the way to the sights
local maps show not only the main roads but also the roads recommended in a round tour

Massif de l'AIGOUAL★★★

Map p 9 – Michelin map 80 fold 16 or 240 southeast of fold 10
Green Guide Pyrenees-Languedoc-Tarn Gorges

The immense forces involved in the formation of the Alps in the Tertiary era acted on the ancient granitic foundation of this landscape, uplifting it to form a massif which reaches its highest point at **Mont Aigoual**★★★ (1 567m – 5 141ft). Subsequent erosion, all the more vigorous because of high precipitation and the low elevation of the surrounding country, has created a landscape of long straight ridges cut by deep ravines. These well-watered highlands make a striking contrast to the arid landscapes of the neighbouring *causses* where any rainfall is immediately absorbed by the porous limestone.

From 1875 onwards a massive programme of reafforestation was undertaken by the state; the forest today covers some 14 000ha – 50 square miles. Tree growth is particularly vigorous on the more exposed western slopes. In the last 20 years conifers have been added to the beeches planted in the 19C, and there are sweet chestnuts too, the traditional tree of the Cévennes, growing between altitudes of 600-900m (2 000-3 000ft).

★★★ **Panorama** – From the viewing table at the top of the meteorological station the view extends over the Causses and the Cévennes. In winter it is sometimes possible to see both Mont Blanc and the Maladeta Massif in the Pyrenees, though at other times haze or fog may reduce the extent of the view.

AIGUES-MORTES★★

Population 4 999
Map p 9 – Michelin map 83 fold 8 or 240 fold 23 – Green Guide Provence

Few places evoke the spirit of the Middle Ages as vividly as Aigues-Mortes sheltering behind its ramparts in a landscape of marshland, lakes and salt-pans.

In 1240, Louis IX (St Louis), then 26 years old, was perturbed by the lack of French involvement in the kind of commerce undertaken by the merchant fleets of Pisa and Genoa. He was also very much taken by the idea of a Crusade, but he lacked a Mediterranean port and a French king could not countenance sailing from a foreign harbour (at this time Provence was part of the Holy Roman Empire, Sète did not exist, and Narbonne was silting up). Louis' solution was to buy a site from a priory and grant a charter to the township which began to develop on what up to then had been virtually an island. The new settlement was laid out more or less on the geometrical lines of a bastide and was linked to the sea via an artificial channel.

★★ **Tour de Constance** ⊙ – The tower (1241-49) rests on wooden piles and was intended to be a symbol of royal power as much as a purely military installation. The layout of its elaborate internal defences (staircases, winding passageways, portcullises) is typical of the Capetian dynasty, and its fine walls of Beaucaire limestone stand out boldly against the surrounding sandy landscape. Its turret originally served as a lighthouse, the sea being only 3km – 2 miles away at the time. On 28 August 1248 the king embarked for the Sixth Crusade aboard a fleet of 38 Genoese vessels drawn up in the Grau Louis channel. Twenty-two years later, on 1 July 1270, he set out from here once more, on the Crusade (the Eighth) which, for him, was to prove fatal. St Louis succumbed as the fleet lay off Tunis.

Aigues-Mortes – aerial view

H. Champollion/OUEST FRANCE

★★ **Ramparts** ⊙ – These were never seen by St Louis. They were begun in 1272 on the orders of Philip the Bold and their completion led to Aigues-Mortes becoming the Capetian kingdom's principal Mediterranean harbour.

At the end of the 13C Philip the Fair improved the port and completed the defences, adding 20 massive towers to protect the gateways and provide enfilading fire along the walls themselves.

In the 14C Aigues-Mortes' population totalled 15 000, but its waterways began to silt up and the sea to retreat; the Constance Tower lost its military significance altogether and became a prison, housing Knights Templar and rebel barons; for more than a century after the revocation of the Edict of Nantes in 1665 Huguenots were incarcerated here too.

The silting up of the port and the incorporation of Marseilles into the French kingdom in 1481 helped push Aigues-Mortes into decline and the coup-de-grâce was the founding (17C) and subsequent development of Sète.

AIX-EN-PROVENCE★★

Population 123 842
Map p 10 – Michelin map 84 fold 3 or 245 fold 31 or 246 fold J
Green Guide Provence – Town plan in the current Michelin Red Guide France

From the 4C BC onwards the commercial development of Marseilles and the other Greek cities of the coast had been threatened by the warlike Salian Franks from their capital at Entremont. Finally, in 123BC an appeal for help was made to Rome; a year later Sextius and his legions laid waste to Entremont; the camp he set up a little to the south near some thermal springs (Aquae Sextiae) marks the origin of Aix.

Twenty years later the sway of Rome was threatened by the fierce Cimbrians, a Germanic people capable of chasing the legions from the field of battle. At the same time the Teutons, another Germanic group, were on the move southward, but their attempt to make their way into Italy via the Maritime Alps was frustrated by the Roman general Marius who crushed them in a great battle near the foot of Mount Ste-Victoire to the east of Aix.

LE VIEIL-AIX

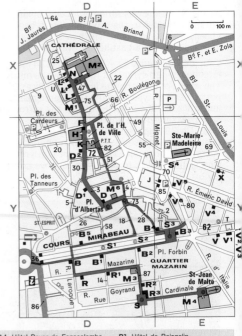

Aquae Sextiae was subsequently destroyed by the Lombards (AD 574) and by Saracens; its deserted buildings served as a quarry for building materials for a good six centuries. In the 12C its fortunes were restored by the Counts of Provence who made it their place of residence. The last and most illustrious of the line was King René (1409-80), Duke of Anjou, Lorraine and Bar, King of Naples, and the ally of Charles VII of France against the English and Burgundians. The enlightened monarch supported literature and the arts and completed Aix' cathedral. Though a benevolent ruler, he was also a strict administrator. Towards the end of his life he made Charles of Maine his heir; Charles however was to die without issue, enabling Louis XI to incorporate Provence into France (1486).

Harsh times intervened; invasion by Imperial troops, feuding, and religious conflict. While the Aix Parliament was putting up a strong resistance to Richelieu's centralising policies, an administrative caste grew and prospered and the peaceful period ushered in by Cardinal Mazarin saw the extension and rebuilding of the city on classical lines; judges, lawyers and rural notables built themselves the sober but distinguished urban residences that contribute so much to the charm of the Old Town (Vieil Aix) today (rusticated doorways, mask and scroll decoration, stucco-work and ornate staircases). The intellectual life fostered by King René continued to flourish and the roll-call of great men who were born or who lived in Aix is a long one. It includes the 17C astronomer Fabri de Peiresc who in 1636 drew the first map of the moon. In the 18C there was the elegant portrait-painter Jean-Baptiste van Loo, Vauvenargues, that most optimistic of moralists, and **Count Mirabeau**, the great orator; the latter, meeting only contempt and rejection from his peers, gained election to the Estates-General in 1789 as a representative, not of the nobility, but of the Third Estate. Finally there is **Paul Cézanne** (1839-1906), one of the founders of modern painting; his many studies of Mount Ste-Victoire are justly renowned. The room devoted to him in Aix' Granet Museum houses amongst other paintings his *Still Life with Sugar-bowl, Nude at the Mirror* and the monumental *Bathers*.

★★ **Vieil Aix** – Elegant 17C-19C mansions with corner statues, pleasant squares and charming fountains combine to give the old town its distinctive character.

★★ **Cours Mirabeau (DY)** – Fountains splash under the canopy of fine plane trees shading this most pleasant of boulevards from the fierce Provençal sun. It was laid out on the line of the 15C ramparts by Mazarin's brother who was also responsible for the construction of the district immediately to the south. This was planned in a systematic way to give the mansions a formal façade to the north and a sunny garden to the south. Aristocratic residences line the south side of the Cours Mirabeau, distinguished by the warm patina of their Rognes stone, their sculptured doorways and their balconies of wrought iron held up by caryatids and atlantes of the school of **Pierre Puget.**

Hôtel Boyer d'Eguilles (DY M⁴) ⊙ – *Natural History Museum* ⊙. Attributed to Puget, it marks the transition from Baroque to Rococo and has a beautiful ironwork staircase of 1678.

Place d'Albertas – The fine hotel of 1724 and fountain of 1745 are complemented by other 18C buildings with soaring first floor pilasters and graceful balconies contrasting with the more robust appearance of the ground floor which has semicircular arches and rusticated stonework.

E. Baret

Place d'Albertas

Hôtel de ville (**DY H**) – The city's traditional centre of administration and justice. Designed by Pierre Pavillon, the building has a façade much divided up by pilasters and entablatures but relieved by an elegant ironwork balcony. The treatment of the **courtyard★** (1671) is on strictly classical lines.

The square was laid out in the 18C. The nearby 16C Clock Tower (Tour de l'Horloge) (**F**) has a bell hung high in a wrought-iron cage.

Cathédrale St-Sauveur ⊘ – The interesting **baptistery★** is of Merovingian date (4C); eight ancient columns, probably from a Roman basilica nearby, have been used to hold up the 18C octagonal cupola crowning the Gallo-Roman structure. In the nave is the **Triptych of the Burning Bush★★**, painted around 1475 by Nicolas Froment; it is one of the masterpieces of the Second School of Avignon, integrating a religious subject, a landscape derived from Italian Quattrocento models, and Flemish decorative elements (precious stones, mirrors, folds of clothing).

The **doorway panels★** of 1500-08 *(masked by false doors)* represent Prophets and Sibyls, and the roof of the delightful **Romanesque Cloisters★** (**N**) ⊘ rests on delicate columns. In the time of the Emperor Augustus this was the site of the Forum of Aquae Sextiae.

Every year, in July and August, the **International Festival of Music and Lyrical Art**, one of the most prestigious events of its kind in Europe, turns the old city of Aix into the capital of music. Since 1948, stunning performances of Mozart's operas have revealed not only new "voices" (Teresa Stich-Randall, Teresa Berganza, Régine Crespin, Luigi Alva) but also budding directors of great talent. The splendid sets are often designed and executed by famous painters of the calibre of G. Whakevitch, Cassandre and Balthus.

The new part of town is rapidly expanding and attracting more and more residents; it has established itself as a city of the arts, a thermal spa and an important centre for industry and the tourist trade.

⊘ ►► Musée des Tapisseries. 17-18C tapestries **M²**; Eglise St-Jean-de-Malte – Nave★; Musée Granet★ **M³** – fine arts and archaeology; Église Ste-Marie-Madeleine – statue of Our Lady★, triptych★; Fondation Vasarely★ ; Fontaine des Quatre dauphins★ **S**.

AJACCIO★★

Population 52 315
Map p 10 – Michelin map 90 fold 17 – Green Guide Corse (in French)
Town plan in the current Michelin Red Guide France

Ajaccio occupies a natural amphitheatre looking out over its splendid bay. The town was founded in 1492 by the Office of St George which governed Corsica on behalf of the Republic of Genoa. Native Corsicans were forbidden residence there until 1553, when, in the course of the first French intervention in the island, it was taken by the legendary military adventurer Sampiero Corso (1498-1567), born in the village of Bastelica 25km – 15 miles to the northeast.

It was here, at 1am on 13 September 1943, that the first Free French forces to land on the territory of France itself were disembarked from the submarine *Casabianca*, under Commander L'Herminier.

Ajaccio's historic importance is due above all to its being the birthplace of Napoleon **Bonaparte**; his extraordinary career not only arose out of the political realities of his time but also changed them decisively. The town continues to revere the memory of its "glorious child prodigy". Born on 15 August 1769, the son of Charles-Marie Bonaparte and Letizia Romolino, he was admitted to the military school at Brienne (Aube) at the age of 10. At 27 he married Josephine Tascher de la Pagerie, the widow of General Beauharnais, before directing the Italian campaign (the Battle of Arcole) and, two years later, the expedition to Egypt. In 1804, taking the title of Napoleon I, he crowned himself Emperor of the French. On 26 August the following year he launched the Grand Army *(Grande Armée)* against Austria from the encampment at Boulogne whence he had threatened England with invasion. By 1807, at the age of 38, he dominated Europe.

It was now, however, that the various coalitions originally formed to resist the French Revolution were turned against the Empire. England was deeply involved in them all, in the colonies and on the high seas as well as in Europe. Though bloated and prematurely aged, Napoleon rose to the challenge, never more formidable than from 1809 on, the years of struggle against the Fifth and Sixth Coalitions. But France and her Emperor were now out of touch with a changed Europe; the ideology of the Revolution, disseminated by France's territorial conquests, had awakened a strong desire for national independence among the peoples of Europe and ranged them against her. The Napoleonic Age was brought to a close on 18 June 1815 by the Battle of Waterloo; the last farewells at Malmaison on 29 June were followed by embarkation aboard the *Bellerophon* at Aix Island on 15 July and by exile on St Helena, where "General Bonaparte" died on 5 May 1821.

★ **Maison Bonaparte**  – The Genoese-style house came into the Bonaparte family's possession in 1743; Napoleon is supposed to have been born on a couch in the antechamber on the first floor. His father's modest earnings and the income from landholdings at Mielli, Egitto, Salines and Sposata did not suffice for a life of luxury. It was Letizia, "a most remarkable woman", who directed the household and who brought up her children with a wise mixture of discipline and tenderness. In May 1793, Bonaparte, loyal to Republican ideas, was forced by the followers of Pascal Paoli to abandon the house; the building was sacked and the adjoining family properties laid waste.

On her return to Ajaccio in 1798, Letizia put the house back in order with the help of her half-brother, Abbot Fesch (a future cardinal). The work was financed in part by a grant from the Directory, in part by sums sent to his brother Joseph by Napoleon (now in Egypt) enabling him to acquire the upper storeys and the adjoining house. On his return from Egypt on 29 September 1799, Bonaparte stopped off at Ajaccio to see the family home. He is supposed to have slept in the alcove on the second floor. After six days he slipped away via a trap-door, never to see his birthplace again.

Bonaparte by David

★★ **Musée Fesch**  – This has France's most important collection of **Italian paintings**★★ outside the Louvre, together with a number of French and Spanish works. Entry to the museum is on the second level, via the main courtyard. Temporary exhibitions are housed here, while on the level above can be seen 15C paintings by Jacopo Sellajo, Lorenzo di Credi, **Bellini** *(Mary with the Infant Jesus)* and **Botticelli** *(Virgin with Garland)*. There are two outstanding works from the 16C: Veronese's **Leda** and the second **Man with Glove** by Titian.

Place Letizia – Napoleon was anxious to have an appropriate setting for the house where he was born. The square was laid out on the site of a number of demolished buildings. There is a bust of the Emperor's son, the "Aiglon" (Eaglet).

Place Maréchal-Foch – This fine square, the focus of Ajaccio's outdoor social life, is shaded by palm trees; its upper part is dominated by a marble statue by Laboureur of Napoleon as First Consul.

Musée Napoléonien  – *First floor of the Town Hall.* Napoleon's baptism certificate (21 July 1771) in Genoese dialect, family pictures, portraits and statues, make a moving display which draws serious historians as well as faithful admirers. Also shown is a bronze cast of a death mask made on St Helena.

ALBI★★★

Population 46 579
Map p 9 – Michelin map 80 fold 11 or 82 fold 10 or 235 fold 23
Green Guide Pyrenees-Languedoc-Tarn Gorges
Town plan in the current Michelin Red Guide France

The whole of Albi, from the bridges spanning the Tarn to the extraordinary cathedral, is made of brick which owes its rosy hue to the clays dug from the river's bed.

At the beginning of the 13C the city was one of the centres of the dualist Cathar doctrine, dubbed the "Albigensian heresy" by a fearful Church. The subsequent "Albigensian Crusade" was directed on the spiritual side by St Dominic; on the ground, armies moved in from north and east to commit the terrible atrocities of Béziers, Carcassonne, Minerve and Lavaur. The Capetian kings took advantage of the troubles, which lasted from 1208 to 1229, to gain a foothold in Languedoc, but the Albigensian heresy itself was only finally stamped out by the Inquisition and the ghastly funeral pyre at Montségur *(qv)*.

★★★ **Cathédrale Ste-Cécile** – Construction of the cathedral, extending over two centuries, began in 1282 at a time when work on the neighbouring Berbie Palace, the bishops' residence, and on that of the Dominicans at Toulouse, was already well advanced. For the bishops, the status of the church was inextricably linked to its temporal power and they therefore gave their cathedral the appearance

CATHÉDRALE STE-CÉCILE

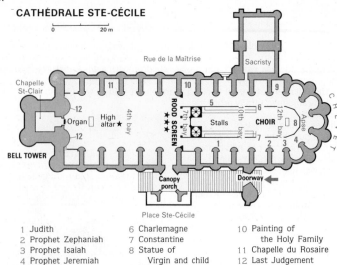

0   20 m

Rue de la Maîtrise

Sacristy

Chapelle St-Clair

ROOD SCREEN

High altar ★

Organ

BELL TOWER

Stalls

CHOIR

Apse

CHEVET

Canopy porch

Doorway

Place Ste-Cécile

1 Judith	6 Charlemagne	10 Painting of
2 Prophet Zephaniah	7 Constantine	the Holy Family
3 Prophet Isaiah	8 Statue of	11 Chapelle du Rosaire
4 Prophet Jeremiah	Virgin and child	12 Last Judgement
5 Esther	9 Chapelle Sainte-Croix	

of a fortress. In the 19C the formidable edifice acquired the three upper stories of its keep-like bell tower, its machicolations and its inspection gallery.

Inside, the perfect simplicity of the single broad nave with its Southern French Gothic side-chapels passes almost unnoticed, such is the exuberance of the Flamboyant decorative scheme. The **rood screen**★★★, one of the few to have survived, is also one of the most sumptuous. In the 15C and 16C all the greater churches possessed such a screen; it separated the clergy, in the choir, from the lay worshippers in the nave; during services readings would be given from its gallery. This example dates from 1485, as does the screen closing off the **choir** ⊙; its arches and gables, columns and arcading all show the extraordinary skill and attention to detail of the craftsmen who worked the white limestone. The naturalistic poses and facial expressions typical of Gothic art are brought here to a fine pitch. Old Testament figures are on the outside, those from the New Testament on the side of the choir, where there are two rows of 66 stalls. The vaults were painted in 1509-12 by Bolognese artists; they repay study with binoculars.

The hallucinatory Last Judgement is a masterpiece of late 15C mural painting; it was unfortunately disfigured by the installation in the 17C of the great organ. But it is nevertheless possible to admire the upper part depicting the Heavenly Kingdom: on the left the Apostles, haloed in gold, and the saints as well as the elect bearing the book of their life held open; on the right the damned, punished by their sin itself.

★ **Palais de la Berbie** ⊙ – The former Bishops' Palace houses the **Toulouse-Lautrec Museum**★★. Henri de Toulouse-Lautrec (1864-1901) was born in Albi at the Hôtel du Bosc and was crippled in early life by two accidents. He is revealed here as one of the great painters of everyday life; his vision of the depravity and decadence of late 19C Paris is communicated with restraint and compassion.

▸▸ Old Town★.

ALERIA★

Population 2 726
Map p 10 – Michelin map 90 fold 6 – Green Guide Corse (in French)

Founded by Greek settlers about 565 BC, Aleria subsequently became a colony, first of Carthage (280 BC), then, following its conquest by Scipio, of Rome (259 BC). The city was thus subjected to Hellenistic, African, and Roman influences; in turn, its own influence extended over much of the Mediterranean. Its end came with the collapse of the Roman Empire; scourged by malaria and sacked by the Vandals, it was abandoned by its own inhabitants at the beginning of the fifth century.

★★ **Musée Jérôme-Carcopino** ⊙ – This museum is housed in the Matra Fortress and named after the Corsican-born historian, an authority on the history and archaeology of Ancient Rome (particularly on Caesar and on Cicero's letters), who was instrumental in reviving the study of the island's archaeology generally and of its ancient capital in particular. The relations Aleria once enjoyed with the world of Classical times are evoked by collections of pottery found both here and in Etruria or Greece. Note especially two Attic drinking vessels (rhytons).

⊙ ▸▸ Aléria excavation site.

AMBOISE★★

Population 10 982
Map p 5 – Michelin map 64 fold 16 and 238 fold 14
Green Guide Châteaux of the Loire – Town plan in the current Michelin Red Guide France

Amboise is a bridge-town, built at the foot of an escarpment already fortified in Gallo-Roman times, on which stand the proud remains of its great château.

★★ **Château** ⊙ – The 15C saw the Golden Age of Amboise. Charles VIII was born here in 1470; from his 22nd year onwards he carried on the work begun by his father, Louis XI. By the time he left on his Italian campaign, work was well in hand on a number of projects: the round towers, the great Gothic roof of the wing overlooking the Loire, and the Flamboyant St Hubert Chapel, which served as an oratory for Anne of Brittany and has particularly fine Flemish door panels. In 1496 Charles returned from Italy, dazzled by what he had seen, and bringing with him not only works of art but a whole retinue of artists, architects (Fra Giocondo and Il Boccadoro), sculptors, cabinet-makers and gardeners.

With these Italians came a taste for Antiquity and a decorative sense unknown at the time in France (doorways resembling triumphal arches, inlaid ceilings, superimposed arches etc). Charles' liking for luxury enhanced the prestige of the monarchy; his promotion of the artistic ideas of the Renaissance was continued by Louis XII and even more by François I, under whom château life became a whirl of princely gaiety with festivals, entertainments, hunting parties... However, this first French château of the Renaissance was destined to disappear; partly demolished by the troops of Louis XIII, it was further dismantled on the orders of Napoleon's Senate. Now it is only known from an engraving by Du Cerceau.

Less than a year after the Treaty of Le Cateau-Cambrésis came the **Amboise Conspiracy**, a bloody precursor of events to follow. Led by La Renaudie, 1 500 Huguenots marched on Blois where, on 15 March 1560, they demanded guarantees of freedom of worship from the young François II. They were in fact planning to seize the King and force him to denounce the Guises, their bitter enemies. But forewarned, the Court fled to Amboise which was easier to defend. As the conspirators began to arrive at the château they were arrested. Savage punishment was meted out; it is even thought that Catherine de' Medici, François II and his young wife Mary Stuart enjoyed the last gasps and grimaces of the condemned swinging from balcony and battlement as an after-dinner entertainment.

★ **Clos-Lucé** ⊙ – It was to this manor house of red brick with stone dressings that François I invited **Leonardo da Vinci** in 1516.

The great Florentine was then 64. At Amboise he neither painted nor taught, devoting himself instead to organising royal festivities, designing a château at Romorantin for Louise of Savoy, François' mother, planning the drainage of the Sologne and amusing himself with mechanical inventions which lack of motive power kept on the drawing-board.

AMIENS★★★

Conurbation 156 120
Map p 6 – Michelin map 52 fold 8 or 236 fold 24
Green Guide Flanders, Picardy and the Paris Region
Town plan in the current Michelin Red Guide France

It was in the middle years of the 4C on a high road near Amiens that a young Roman officer took pity on a beggar freezing in the icy wind. Slicing his cloak in two with his sword, he shared it with the poor wretch. Later ordained, then Bishop of Tours, the former soldier was eventually canonised as St Martin, patron saint of France. Amiens gained its charter in 1117, and in 1477, on the death of Charles the Bold this ancient capital of Picardy became subject to the French Crown. In the 17C its textile industry prospered (Amiens Velvet) largely thanks to Colbert's economic policies. The city suffered in both World Wars, in 1918 during the Ludendorff Offensive, in 1940 during the Battle of France.

The famous names associated with the city include: **Pierre Choderlos de Laclos** (1741-1803), military engineer and author of *Les Liaisons Dangereuses (Dangerous Liaisons)*, Charles Tellier (1828-1913), inventor of refrigeration, **Jules Verne** (1828-1905), born in Nantes, author of *20 000 Leagues under the Sea* and *Around the World in Eighty Days*, **Édouard Branly** (1844-1940), whose radioconductors made wireless telegraphy possible, and Roland Dorgelès (1885-1973), author of *Croix de bois (Cross of Wood)*, a realistic account of trench warfare.

Traditionally, Amiens has always been an important crossroads and a major centre for the arts and the economy. In 1964 it became the seat of a university.

★★★ **Cathédrale Notre-Dame** – The harmonious building was begun in 1220 and completed 68 years later, an achievement made possible by its architect, Robert de Luzarches, who had all the stonework cut to its finished dimensions before it left the quarry, then simply assembled on site.

The cathedral is in Gothic Lanceolate style, with three-storey elevations including a blind triforium in nave and transept. The wonderfully elegant nave is the highest in France (42.5m – 140ft).

At an early date problems arose through water from the Somme penetrating the foundations; movement occurred along the length of the building, evidence of which can be seen in cracks in the nave near the transept. The weight of the vaults aggravated the effect; to remedy it, in the 16C a brace of Toledo steel was inserted into the triforium, heated red-hot, and allowed to cool. For four centuries it has served its purpose admirably. The building was further strengthened by increasing the number of buttresses at the east end and by adding side chapels in the form of double aisles to the nave in order to spread the downward forces as widely as possible.

The famous slender steeple rising above the crossing was built by the master carpenter Cardon in two years (1528-29).

Much of the cathedral's decoration is of very high quality indeed: the sculpture of the west front (including the noble figure of Christ known as the "Beau Dieu"), and the rose windows of the main façade, including the 16C Sea Window (rose de la Mer), of the north transept – the 14C Window of the Winds (rose des Vents), and of the south transept – the 15C Window of Heaven (rose du Ciel). Inside, the wrought-iron choir screen dates from the 18C and the oak choir-stalls from the beginning of the 16C. The third chapel of the north aisle houses a remarkable Romanesque Crucifixion probably influenced by oriental art. Christ's feet are nailed to the Cross separately; clad in a long robe, He wears His royal crown in glory. The figure was carved before the arrival in Paris of the relics of the Passion (including the Crown of Thorns) purchased by St Louis; it thus predates Western awareness of the medical realities of Christ's agony.

⊘ ►► Musée de Picardie★★ – archaeology, painting; Hôtel de Berny★; Hortillonnages★ *(Riverside allotments)*.

Château d'ANCY-LE-FRANC★★

Map p 6 – Michelin map 65 fold 7 or 243 fold 1 – Green Guide Burgundy Jura

Designed by Sebastian Serlio, one of the Italian architects attracted to the French court in 1541 by François I, this **château** ⊘ was begun in 1546 and completed 50 years later for Antoine III of Clermont-Tonnerre. It marks the end of the early, Italian-influenced French Renaissance in all its brilliance.

The exterior gives an impression of great order and dignity, combining a symmetry worthy of Bramante with a masterly handling of spaces and surfaces according to the rules of the Golden Section. The treatment of the courtyard is particularly subtle with its deeply-sunken twin pilasters topped by Corinthian capitals and separating scalloped niches.

The interior is equally fine. The Judith Room has a coffered ceiling painted by a pupil of Primaticcio, Cornelius van Haarlem; There are ancient bindings in the library, secret cabinets from Italy, and a monochrome study of musculature in dell'Abbate's *Battle of Pharsalus* and, in the Arts Salon, oval medallions by Primaticcio representing the Liberal Arts.

Les ANDELYS★★

Population 8 455

Map p 5 – Michelin map 55 fold 17 or 231 fold 24 or 237 folds 2, 3
Green Guide Normandy – Town plan in the current Michelin Red Guide France

The site of Les Andelys commands the Seine valley and the old highway linking Paris and Rouen. Its exceptional strategic value was appreciated by Richard Lionheart, son of Henry II Plantagenet and Eleanor of Aquitaine, Duke of Normandy as well as King of England. In 1196 he decided to break the agreement concluded at Louviers with the king of France and construct the mightiest fortress of the age to protect his possessions from French ambition. Within the year, so legend has it, the great work was complete, and Richard was able to cry aloud "See my fine yearling!".

★★ **Château Gaillard** ⊘ *(3/4 hour)* must certainly have been an impressive sight; with its 17 towers, eight-foot thick walls, its cliff-top site and with three successive rings of defences protecting its keep, it was virtually impregnable. Impregnable that is, save by means of a ruse, and it was in this way that King Philippe Auguste succeeded in taking it in 1274 after a siege of eight months. This victory enabled him to incorporate Normandy, Maine, Anjou and Touraine into the French kingdom. In 1419, four years after Agincourt, Henry V of England took it back. La Hire, companion to Joan of Arc, won it again for France ten years later, only to lose it to Henry once more. It finally passed into French possession under Charles VII in 1449.

ANDLAU *

Population 1 632
Map p 7 – Michelin map 62 fold 9 or 242 fold 27
Green Guide Alsace Lorraine (in French)

Prettily sited among its vineyards, this typical Alsace village has large half-timbered houses with many-dormered steep roofs and windows and balconies decorated with a profusion of flowers.

★ **Church (Église)** – The massive western end of about 1130 has the finest Romanesque sculpture in Alsace. Its 30m – 100ft frieze dating from the middle of the 12C has 40 panels showing biblical themes together with scenes from everyday life.

The **west door★★** is solid, archaic work of great intensity of character; it is decorated with low-relief sculpture of remarkable quality. On either side of the doorway the pilasters carry foliated scrolls and figures of animals and people; the lintel has scenes of the Creation and of the Garden of Eden, while the tympanum shows Christ giving Paul his book and Peter his key.

The **crypt★** dates mostly from the 11C.

12C frieze, Andlau Church

M. Guillard/SCOPE

ANDUZE

Population 2 913
Map p 9 – Michelin map 80 fold 17 or 240 fold 15
Green Guide Pyrenees-Languedoc-Tarn Gorges

Anduze, "the gateway to the Cévennes", commands a narrow valley just below the point where two streams meet to form the river known as the Gardon d'Anduze. The little town once rivalled Alès before the latter's coal mines were developed. Calvinism gained a foothold here in 1557 and Anduze became an important centre of the Huguenot community. It was fortified by the great Protestant leader the Duke de Rohan, who also raised the flood wall along the right bank of the river. Richelieu's centralising policies were no more welcome here than in other Huguenot towns; old resentments were stirred up and the town became a focus of resistance, of sufficient strength for Louis XIII to prefer to attack Alès (in 1629) instead. It was there that he signed the edict confirming the freedom of worship granted at Nantes 31 years earlier. But at the same time the Protestants also lost their status as a political body and thereby their right to fortifications; Anduze's defences were consequently razed to the ground. The town became a rebel supply base at the time of the Camisard uprising at the beginning of the 18C.

EXCURSION

★ **Le Mas Soubeyran** – *7km – 4 miles north; 1 hour*. The tiny hamlet is famous for its role in the history of French Protestantism. It was here on 3 January 1680 that the Camisard leader Roland was born, and it is here, every September, that one of the annual general assemblies of the Protestant Church in France is held.

The Reformation was born when Luther nailed his 95 theses to the church door at Wittenberg in 1517. Calvin's publication of his *Institutes of the Christian Religion* in 1541 and the Synod of La Rochelle in 1559 marked its spread in France. The Amboise Conspiracy and the Wars of Religion demonstrated the depth of the political and religious crisis into which the country had fallen.

The death of Henri IV signalled the start of hard times for the Protestants (imprisonment, galley-slavery, harassment by the military). In 1685 the Revocation of the Edict of Nantes required them to recant; as a result, almost 200 000 of them went into emigration, others staying to practise their creed in secret in the wild Cévennes countryside, the *Désert*. Abbot Chayla's death in a brawl in 1702 at Pont-de-Montvert unleashed the full fury of the law against them, but resistance was strong; the **Camisards** (wearers of white shirts – camiso in Languedoc = shirt) were formed to wage guerrilla war in the *Désert* against

Louis XIV's army. For a while they held their own but repression was ruthlesss, including the destruction of 460 villages and hamlets on the orders of the King, and with the death of Roland in 1704, the rebellion came to an end.

Shorn of their civil status, the Protestants led a clandestine existence from 1724 to 1787, when the Edict of Tolerance was promulgated. The triumph of the idea of Liberty in 1789 finally put the principle of freedom of worship on a firm basis.

★ **Musée du Désert** ⊙ – Here, in Roland's birthplace, are documents, proclamations, decrees, maps, Bibles and other objects reminding us of the Cévennes Protestants' defiant exercise of their faith.

⊙ ►► Bambouseraie de Profance★ (exotic park).

Château d'ANET★

Map p 5 – Michelin map 55 fold 17 or 196 fold 13 or 234 fold 34
Green Guide Normandy

The powerful Diane de Poitiers had been Henri II's mistress for 10 years when, in 1546, she engaged the architect Philibert Delorme to take over the work already begun at Anet. What remains of the **Château** ⊙ (the left wing, chapel, and some ancillary buildings) is essentially his creation.

Aged 34, Delorme had worked in Italy; he had an assertive personality and demanded much of himself. Anet is his only major work to have survived. Completed in 1552, it is the first building in the style of Henri II, but it also anticipates the classical ideals of Mansart in the 17C. Freeing himself from the decorative preoccupations of the Italian masters of the School of Fontainebleau, Delorme was able to conceive of a building as an architectural whole based on the proportions of the Golden Section, with ornament playing a strictly subordinate role. He was responsible for the moat with its corner pavilions, the great roof with its rhythmic sequence of large and small windows and its soberly-designed chimneys, the turrets of the gable walls, the interlaced balustrades and the monumental portal in white stone from Vernon with black marble inlay – black and white were the colours worn by Diane in mourning for her husband. The portal is crowned by a bronze stag at bay.

Inside, there are tapestries woven for Diane and, in the dining room, a huge fireplace with caryatids by Puget and medallions by **Jean Goujon**.

⊙ ►► Chapelle funéraire de Diane de Poitiers – statue★.

ANGERS★★★

Conurbation 206 276

Map p 5 – Michelin maps 63 fold 20 or 64 fold 11, or 232 fold 31
Green Guide Châteaux of the Loire – Town plan in the current Michelin Red Guide France

The Rivers Loir, Sarthe, Mayenne and Oudon flow through a tranquil *bocage* landscape before joining together to form the Maine just above Angers, itself only 8km – 5 miles upstream from the Loire. Two geological systems meet here; the sedimentary rocks of the Paris basin to the east and the schists of the Armorican Massif to the west, the latter quarried since the 12C at nearby Trélazé.

On 9 June 1129, Geoffrey Plantagenet, stepson of Fulk Nerra, married William the Conqueror's grand-daughter, the proud Mathilda, whose inheritance of both Normandy and England made her the most desirable of brides *(qv)*. 23 years later an equally significant marriage took place, that of Henry II, Geoffrey's son, to Eleanor of Aquitaine, the divorced wife of Louis VII. Two months later Henry became King of England, thereby extending the frontiers of the Angevin state to Scotland in the north and the Basque country in the south. By contrast, the Capetian kingdom to the east cut a sorry figure, its capital, Paris, seeming little more than an overgrown village in comparison with Angers.

In 1203, with the 81-year old Eleanor living in retirement at Fontevraud, King Philippe Auguste succeeded in incorporating Anjou into the French kingdom, together with Normandy, Maine, Touraine and Poitou, all territories of John Lackland (the Plantagenets, contrary to feudal law, had effectively allowed these lands to become English possessions). In 1471, King René *(qv)* let Anjou pass into the hands of Louis XI.

Angevin (or Plantagenet) vaulting – This type of vault marks the transition from Romanesque to Gothic in a particularly elegant way. Curved vaults (with the central keystone some 3m – 10ft higher than that of the supporting arches) probably originated in the late 11C domes of Eleanor of Aquitaine's homeland with their quadripartite arches and slender ribs. The characteristic Angevin vault is identifiable by the middle of the 12C, notably in the vaulting of the nave of the **Cathédrale St-Maurice**★★ with its transverse arches with double roll mouldings by Normand le Doué. By the end of the century the vaulting has become lighter; the number of ribs increases, springing from slender columns (as in the choir and transepts of St Maurice). At the beginning of the 13C it reaches its peak of development; lateral support is dispensed with; the structure dissolves into a graceful web of liernes (as in the hospital ward of the former St John's Hospital) resting on a small number of slim columns (as in the early 13C ceiling of the **choir**★★ of the **Église St-Serge**★ ⊘.

Angevin vaulting

Middle of 12C   End of 12C   Beginning of 13C
Cathédrale St-Maurice   Église St-Serge

★★★ **Château** ⊘ – Rebuilt by Louis IX between 1228-38 on the surviving Roman foundations, this splendid example of medieval military architecture was intended to counter any threat arising from the territorial ambitions of the Dukes of Brittany. The site's natural potential for defence is particularly evident where the substantial walls overlook the river; with their 17 towers in alternating courses of dark schist and white freestone they must indeed have constituted a formidable deterrent. The moats were dug in 1485 by Louis XI.

In the reign of Henri III during the Wars of Religion, the towers were reduced in height by Philibert Delorme, the former Abbot of St-Serge, who also formed terraces to give the defenders a clear field of fire.

★★★ **Tenture de l'Apocalypse** – 1375-80. This wonderful tapestry, originally 168m – 550ft long and 5m – 16ft high, is the oldest and most important to have been preserved. According to Jean Lurçat (1892-1966) who discovered it in 1938 and whose artistic career was inspired by it, it is "one of the greatest works of Western art". The 76 extant scenes are closely based on the Apocalypse of St John, and are impressive in their masterly scale, composition and design. Commissioned by the Duke of Anjou Louis I, this superb tapestry was executed by the master weaver **Nicolas Bataille**, most likely in Robert Poinçon's Parisian workshop after cartoons by Hennequin of Bruges; it draws its inspiration from the illuminations of a manuscript belonging to King Charles V.

Apocalypse Tapestry (detail), Angers

H. Champollion/OUEST-FRANCE

★★ **Tenture de la Passion et Tapisseries mille-fleurs** – Located in the Governor's Lodging, the fine collection of Flemish tapestries includes the 16C Lady at the Organ and Penthesilea and above all the three-part Passion of the late 15C with its rich colours and graceful angels carrying the instruments of the Passion.

★ **Hôpital St-Jean** – Founded in 1174 and in use for 680 years, the former hospital now houses the **Musée Jean-Lurçat** ⊘. In the hospital ward with its Angevin vaulting is Lurçat's series of tapestries known as **Le Chant du Monde**★★ (The Song of the World), 10 huge compositions symbolising the contradictions of the modern world. Lurçat's achievement marked the revival of the art of tapestry *(qv)*.

⊘ ►► Maison d'Adam★; Galerie David d'Angers★ – sculpture; Romanesque arcade★★ (in the Prefecture) – Hôtel Pincé★ – Musée Turpin de Crissé: archaeology, Oriental art; La Doutre district★ – Château Pignerolles musée européen de la Communication★.

ANGOULÊME★★

Population 42 876
Map p 8 – Michelin map 72 folds 13, 14 or 233 folds 29, 30
Green Guide Atlantic Coast
Town plan in the current Michelin Red Guide France

From its lofty promontory Angoulême's stately **upper town**★★ (ville haute) overlooks the Anguienne and Charente 70m – 230ft below. The character of the lower town is quite different, busy with paper-making and engineering.

The vain and darkly witty Guez de Balzac (1597-1654), though famous as one of the original members of the *Académie Française* and as a champion of literary French, eventually buried himself away in his native town. Another Balzac, Honoré (1799-1850), added to the city's literary renown when he became a citizen by adoption.

Charles Augustin de Coulomb, born here in 1736, owes his reputation to his having perfected the torsion balance and to his "Law" of 1785 confirming Newton's law of gravitation.

In 1806 a daring exploit was carried out on the city's northern **ramparts;** the 77-year old General Resnier launched himself into the void in a flying-machine of his own invention.

★ **Cathédrale St-Pierre** – Extensively destroyed by the Calvinists, this cathedral was restored in 1634 and again from 1866 onwards by Abadie.

The early 12C statuary of the **west front**★★ is, happily, mostly intact; more elaborate than the other façades typical of the region around Angoulême, its themes include the Ascension (treated as at Cahors) and the Last Judgement.

Particularly noteworthy among the 70 statues and low-reliefs are the superb Christ in Majesty surrounded by the Evangelists, the medallions of saints and the scene of combat inspired by the *Song of Roland (qv)* (lintel of the first doorway to the right).

◌ ►► Centre National de la Bande Dessinée et de l'Image – strip cartoon centre.

ANNECY★★★

Population 49 644
Map p 11 – Michelin map 74 fold 6 or 244 folds 18, 19
Green Guide Alpes du Nord (in French)
Town plan in the current Michelin Red Guide France

Annecy's setting is a perfect composition of lakes and mountains, the meeting point of the Bauges massif to the south and the gentler hilly country stretching northwards towards Geneva. Originally a settlement of lake-dwellers, then a Gallo-Roman township, the city shifted its site in the Middle Ages from Annecy-le-Vieux to the lower slopes of the Semnoz, finally settling under the walls of its castle by the Thiou, whose rapid waters once supplied the motive power for its many mills.

In the 16C Annecy became the regional capital, displacing Geneva, abandoned by its overlords who had tired of the incessant squabbling between Calvinist burghers and diehard Catholics. In the 17C it was the home of **St Francis of Sales**, provost of the cathedral and bitter opponent of the Calvinism which had spread throughout the Chablais area. In 1604 he met St Jeanne de Chantal, widow of Rabutin Chantal, grandmother of Mme de Sévigné, and founder of the Order of the Visitation at Annecy. In what is now the St Francis of Sales Library (Bibliothèque Salésienne) he wrote his *Introduction to a Devout Life*. In 1608, together with Antoine Favre, he founded the *Académie Florimontaine*, 30 years before the *Académie Française*.

★★ **Old Annecy** – *1 1/2 hours*. The picturesque old town spans the Thiou as it runs out from the lake; from its bridges can be seen the highly-folded skyline of Mont Veyrier as well as the **Palais de l'Isle**★ (a former prison which nowadays houses the **musée de l'histoire d'Annecy** ◌, evoking the town's history) rising out of the bed of the stream like the prow of a ship. Rue Ste-Claire with its arcades and gabled houses has kept its 17C appearance.

It was in the courtyard of the Bishops' Palace on a spring morning in 1728 that a meeting took place between Jean-Jacques Rousseau and Mme de Warens.

★★★ **Lake** ◌ – Best seen from the **Avenue d'Albigny**★. Overlooked by the Semnoz, this lovely stretch of water in its glaciated valley site fully deserves its title of "Pearl of the Alps".

◌ ►► Annecy: Jardins de l'Europe★ – arboretum; Château★; Musée de la Cloche★ – 14 to 19C bells – at Sevrier *5km – 3 miles south.*

Annecy

EXCURSION

★★ **Talloires** - This little resort has a most charming **setting**★★★ overlooking the narrows dividing the Grand Lac to the north from the Petit Lac to the south. From the lakeside there are fine views of the Entrevernes Mountain and, nearer at hand, the wooded promontory of the Château de Duingt.

ARBOIS★

Population 3 900
Map p 10 - Michelin map 70 east of fold 4 or 243 fold 30
Green Guide Burgundy Jura

Sited in one of the steep-sided valleys characteristic of the Jura, Arbois is known for its St Just Church, its picturesque Place de la Liberté, its delicate rosé wines, but above all for its connections with **Louis Pasteur** (1822-95), truly one of the greatest figures the human race has produced.

At the age of four Pasteur was brought here from Dole by his father, a tanner. He grew up in Arbois and throughout his life spent his holidays here, surrounded by friends and family.

By the early age of 25, working in his laboratory at the École Normale Supérieure in Paris, he had established the principle of molecular dissymmetry, by 35 the principle of fermentation. At 40 he developed his ideas on asepsis, putting paid to long-held theories of spontaneous reproduction. He went on to study the diseases affecting wine, beer, and silkworms. At 58, he was investigating viruses and vaccines. Finally he isolated the rabies virus and, on 7 July 1885, succeeded in inoculating against it.

By the side of the main road (N83) outside the town can be seen **Pasteur's vine.** This is where he carried out his experiments into fermentation of the grape. In Arbois itself is Pasteur's House, **Maison de Pasteur★** ⊙, originally his father's tannery. It was transformed by the great man into a comfortable middle-class home. Furniture, library, scientific instruments, all evoke Pasteur's restless devotion to the tasks he set himself, even when here on holiday.

ARCACHON★★

Population 11 770
Map p 8 – Michelin map 71 fold 20 or 234 fold 6 – Green Guide Atlantic Coast
Town plan in the current Michelin Red Guide France

The site of Arcachon was no more than a pinewood when, in 1852, the Pereire brothers, who had just bought up the loss-making railway line from Bordeaux to La Teste, had the inspired idea of extending it further seawards. This gave the green light to a building boom and Arcachon was born.

It is both a winter resort, with villas sheltering among the pines, and a place for summer holidays, boasting a fine seafront and the attractive **Boulevard de la Mer★**.

★ **Bassin (bay)** ◎ – Bordered by the resorts of Arcachon, Andernos and the wooded dunes of the Cap Ferret peninsula, this vast bay, with the Île aux Oiseaux (Bird Island) at its centre, extends over an area of 25 000ha – nearly 100 sq miles, four-fifths of which is exposed at low tide. There are great stretches of oyster beds totalling 1 800ha – 4 500 acres in all; the production of oysters was first established here (late 19C) on such a scale owing to the discovery of the process of limewashing tiles and bark in which the oyster brood could be fixed and washed by the tides.

EXCURSION

★★ **Dune du Pilat** – 7.5km – 4.5 miles south. This dune, the highest (114m – 374ft) and longest (2 800m – over 3 000yds) in Europe, is still in the process of formation. On its landward side it drops almost sheer to the pine woodland.

The top of the dune offers the best of all views over the Côte d'Argent (Silver Coast). This long, straight shore with its magnificent sandy beaches and splendid Atlantic rollers runs for 230km – 140 miles from the mouth of the Gironde to the Nivelle. Apart from the harbours at Arcachon and Capbreton, it affords little hospitality to sailors. Every year some 15 cubic metres of sand per linear metre of coastline are deposited by the ocean, building up dunes which in places rival the cliffs of Normandy in height and which, in 1774, swallowed up the church at Soulac. The problem they present was tackled by Bremontier (1738-1809), a Bordeaux engineer, who succeeded in checking the invading dunes on a front of 5km – 3 miles. Their advance was finally stopped during the period of the Restoration (1815-48). The dunes have been responsible for the formation of lakes some distance from the coast but linked to it by channels *(courants)*. The **panorama★★** of the ocean and the local pine forest reveals the romantic aspect of the region, especially at dusk.

ARC-ET-SENANS

Population 1 277
Map p 7 – Michelin map 70 northeast of fold 4 or 243 fold 18
Green Guide Burgundy Jura

Erected between 1775-80, the classical buildings of the former royal salt-works are an extraordinary essay in utopian town planning of the early Industrial Age.

★★ **Saline Royale** ◎ – Only the cross-axis and half the first ring of buildings envisaged by the architect Nicolas Ledoux (1736-1806) were actually completed; what we see today is however enough to evoke the idea of an ideal 18C city. His plan was ambitious; a whole town laid out in concentric circles with the Director's Residence at the centre, flanked by storehouses (Bâtiments des sels), offices and workshops, and extending out to include a church, a market, public baths, recreational facilities... Ledoux' vision makes him one of the forerunners of modern architecture and urban design.

The quality of the architecture is striking; highly original but dignified, it has a pervasive symbolism; not only is there the use of the Director's Residence as a focal point, decorative elements too are exploited like rock formations or the petrified overflow from great urns representing the salt-works' basic resource. Unity of style, use of materials, the arrangement of columns and pediments, all reveal the influence of the 16C Italian architect **Palladio**.

The Michelin Green Guide France

A selection of the most unusual and the most typical sights along the main tourist routes

Gorges de l'ARDÈCHE★★★

Map p 9 – Michelin map 80 fold 9 or 240 fold 8 or 245 fold 14 and 15 or 246 fold 23
Green Guide Provence

The Ardèche rises 1 467m – 4 813ft up in the Mazan Massif to the north of the Col de la Chavade and flows 119km – 67 miles before joining the Rhône. The river is notorious for its spring floods and sudden spates which are capable of increasing its flow by a factor of 3 000 (the spate of 22 September 1890 brought down 28 bridges).

Ardèche plateau – Consisting of the Gras uplands to the north and the Orgnac uplands to the south, the Ardèche plateau contrasts strongly with the high valley and orchard country between Pont-de-Labeaume and Vallon. Its thick beds of much-fissured grey limestone were built up from the sediments deposited in the seas of the Secondary Era. Its surface was exposed and uplifted during the formation of the Alps in Tertiary times and is faulted in places. The vegetation cover consists of scrubby evergreen oaks, box and juniper, and there are jackdaws, shrikes and various birds of prey.

The proximity of the great migration route formed by the Rhône valley meant that prehistoric people came here very early indeed; it may well have been here that the invention of the bow took place, together with the domestication of the dog, the beginnings of agriculture and the making of pottery. The galleries at Orgnac III *(qv)* sheltered auroch-hunters who were probably the contemporaries of Tautavel Man *(see Les Eyzles-de-Tayac)*; at St-Marcel-d'Ardèche there is evidence of the presence of agriculturalists in the warmer times which followed the last Ice Age some 10 000 years ago, and of pastoralists at Vallon-Pont-d'Arc in the Neolithic era. The dolmens and cave-dwellings near St-Remèze date from the Bronze Age.

★★★ **Aven d'Orgnac** – *South bank. See Aven d'ORGNAC.*

★★ **Aven de Marzal** ⊘ – *North bank.* At the bottom of this deep swallow-hole, 130m – 426ft from the surface, the Gallery of Diamonds is made up of glittering crystals of calcite.

In the **Musée du Monde souterrain** is a display of equipment used by the great explorers of these subterranean realms. Nearby, the **Zoo préhistorique** ⊘ another museum featuring reproductions of prehistoric animals attracts many visitors.

Gorges: from Vallon-Pont-d'Arc to Pont-St-Esprit – *47km – 29 miles.* The meanders of the river mark the course it originally followed on the ancient surface of the plateau before cutting down through the rocks as they were uplifted during the Alpine-building Tertiary period. Great sweeps of vertical cliffs, dramatic meanders cut deep into the limestone, and rapids alternating with calm stretches of water combine to form a splendid object lesson in the geography of river formation.

Vallon Pont-d'Arc

Erku/ICONOS

★★ **Pont-d'Arc** – Spanning the full width of the river, the arch of this gigantic natural bridge is 34m – 112ft high and 59m – 194ft wide. In geological terms it is a recent phenomenon, caused by the action of the river, which, helped by the presence of fissures and cavities in the limestone, has succeeded in eroding away the base of a meander.

★★★ **Scenic route** (Haute Corniche) – The road links a number of splendid viewpoints. From the Serre de Tourre can be seen the Pas du Mousse meander, where the river has still to cut through the wooded isthmus; the view from the Morsanne Needles (Aiguilles de Morsanne) gives a good idea of the structure of the plateau as it dips down to the south.

Limestone ridges can be viewed from Gournier, while the rock spires of the Cathedral Rock (Rocher de la Cathédrale) lend this natural monument the appearance of a ruined cathedral.

The Templars' Belvedere (Balcon des Templiers) commands a fine prospect of the Templars' Wall (Mur des Templiers) whose high cliffs (220m – 720ft) dominate the spectacular meander far below. On a rocky spur in the valley stand the ruins of a leper hospital built by the Templars.

ARLES★★★

Conurbation 54 309
Map p 9 – Michelin map 83 fold 10 or 245 fold 28 or 246 fold 26
Green Guide Provence – Town plan in the current Michelin Red Guide France

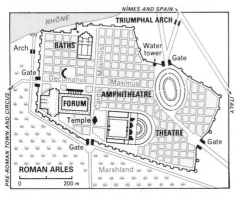

Arles is an important centre of Provençal life, proud of its traditions and famed for both its Roman and its early medieval heritage. It is also France's largest commune covering 77 000 ha – 30 sq miles.

The Rome of the Gauls – The ancient Celtic-Ligurian town was colonised by the Greeks of Marseilles as early as the 6C BC, and went on to play an important role in Roman rule in southern France. Following his victory over the Teutons Marius used his prisoners to dig a canal linking Arles with the sea (much nearer at the time), thus enabling the city to be supplied readily from Rome. Later, at the end of the Gallic Wars, Caesar established a veterans colony; the fleet he used to defeat Marseilles (49BC) was also built here. Subsequently Arles became an important sea and river port.

Under Augustus the city prospered, exploiting its pivotal position in the Roman highway system. Later still it became the administrative and political capital of both parts of Gaul, celebrating its status with many fine buildings.

★★ **Théâtre antique** ⊘ – One of the most important Roman theatre, it dates from the end of the 1C BC. Two fine columns in African breccia and Italian marble still stand elegantly among the ruins. The theatre was quarried for its stone as early as the 5C; in the 9C it was made into a redoubt, subsequently disappearing completely under houses and gardens. It was only excavated in the 19C.

★★ **Arènes** ⊘ – With a capacity of 20 000 spectators, this amphitheatre dates from the reign of Vespasian (c75AD). Its good state of preservation is due to the role it played as a fortress in the 5C and 6C at a time when the Empire was crumbling in the face of the barbarian assault. It was then that its topmost gallery disappeared... if indeed it was ever built. The amp-

The lower gallery of the Roman Amphitheatre, Arles

hitheatre is of later construction and even larger than its counterpart at Nîmes and illustrates clearly the power of the architecture of Antiquity. Hellenistic influence is apparent in the horizontal entablature of the cornices and in the flat slabs which cover the galleries in place of the usual Roman vaults.

★ **Cryptoporticus** ⊘ – *In the basement of the* **Musée d'art chrétien.** These impressive 1C storerooms enabled the forum above to be built on the level in spite of the sloping site.
The sarcophagi in the museum show scenes testifying to the spread of Christianity in the Rhône valley as early as the reign of Constantine (about 350). Those of Imago and of the Hunt are particularly interesting.

★ **Église St-Trophime** – The church was rebuilt from 1080 on. Its **porch**★★ is one of the masterpieces of late 12C Provençal Romanesque. The arrangement of columns and design of the frieze hark back to Roman work like the municipal arch at Glanum *(qv)* and the 4C sarcophagi at nearby Alyscamps and Trinquetaille. The fact that the stone from which the church is built was taken from the Roman Theatre further strengthens a sense of continuity with the Classical past.
The **cloisters**★★ ⊘ were built after 1150 and are renowned for their sculpture. Particularly fine are the corner pillars of the north gallery and the capitals, foliated or decorated with Biblical scenes.

Hôtel de Ville – The classical façade of the Town Hall exemplifies the second phase of the Louis XIV style in architecture. The vestibule on the groond floor has a fine flat **vault**★ (1684) supported by 20 columns along the walls. It is the work of Hardouin-Mansart and the details of its construction used to be an object-lesson to journeymen on their way around France. Note particularly the groins, some curved, some out of true, and also the perfect stonework of the arches.

⊘ ►► Arles: Musée d'Art païen★ – ancient art; Musée d'Art chrétien★★ – Museon Arlaten★ – Provençal culture and traditions; Musée Réattu★ – paintings, Picasso Bequest★; Palais Constantin★ – largest baths in Provence; Alyscamps★ – necropolis.

EXCURSION

★★ **Camargue** – The immense alluvial plain of 95 000ha – 367sq miles is the product of the interaction of the Rhône and Mediterranean and the winds. This most original area is divided into three distinct regions: a cultivated region north of the delta, saltmarshes near **Salin-de-Giraud** and to the west of the Petit Rhône, and the nature reserve to the south.
An exceptional variety of flora and fauna – there are 300 bird species including the famous flamingoes – contributes to the fragile ecological balance of the nature reserve.
The traditional image of the Camargue is associated with the herds *(manades)* of sheep, white horses and agile black bulls and the horsemen *(gardians)*. Although **Arles**★★★, **Aigues-Mortes**★★ *(qv)* and **Les Saintes-Maries-de-la-Mer**★ *(qv)* are the main attractions of the Camargue, a visit to three centres is recommended as an introduction to the fascinating world of the Camargue Regional Nature Park.

⊘ ►► Musée camarguais at Pont de Rousty; Camargue Information Centre at Ginès; Pont de Grau Parc Ornithologique – bird sanctuary.

ARRAS★★

Conurbation 79 607
Map p 6 – Michelin map 53 fold 2 or 236 fold 15
Green Guide Flanders, Picardy and the Paris Region
Town plan in the current Michelin Red Guide France

The Abbey of St-Vaast formed the nucleus around which the capital of Artois grew in the Middle Ages. Between the 12C and the 14C it gained various municipal privileges from the Counts of Artois encouraging an economy based on corn, cloth and money-changing. The city prospered; poetic and literary societies thrived in which Arras' notables could enjoy hearing themselves lampooned by minstrels and entertainers. In the 15C, Artois passed into the hands of the Dukes of Burgundy, ensuring steady orders until *c*1460 for its tapestry industry whose products treated profane subjects with a high degree of realism.
Arras' civic pride was symbolised by the construction of its Town Hall, **Hôtel de Ville**★ ⊘ in 1572; its bell-tower, **beffroi** ⊘, blends Flemish Gothic with Henri II-style ornamentation. It was destroyed in the First World War but rebuilt in 1919.

ARRAS

Maximilian Robespierre was born in Arras in 1758 to a well-to-do legal family. He too was called to the Bar before becoming a Deputy in 1789, a Republican in 1792, and a prominent member of the Committee of Public Safety in 1793. Frank, determined, indifferent to favours, "Robespierre the Incorruptible" embodied the spirit of the Revolution. Backed by Saint-Just and Couthon, he harried plotters and crushed deviationists, going so far as to take part in the condemnation of his allies the Girondins. Discredited in the end by the consequences of his extremist ideology, he fell victim to the guillotine on 27 July 1794.

Grand'Place, Arras

★★ Old Town (Les Places) – Dating from the 11C, the **Grand' Place, Place des Héros** and the **Rue de la Taillerie** linking them celebrate the city's status as an important regional market centre. Their present splendidly harmonious appearance is the fruit of the city fathers' purposeful civic design initiatives in the 17C and 18C. The existing Spanish Plateresque buildings of the 16C and 17C (Arras was effectively under Spanish rule from 1492 to 1640) were given Flemish Baroque façades from 1635 onward. The 155 brick and stone houses rest on 345 columns: their arcading sheltered traders and clients alike. With few projections, their regularly-proportioned façades give an impression of great unity, relieved by a rich variety of detail. This includes curvilinear gables, arcades with pilasters or corbelling, decorative tie-bars, and a number of sculpted merchants' signs (a whale, a harp, a bell...). To the north of the Grand' Place a brick building with a stone-built ground floor is topped by a stepped gable, the only one of its kind.

⊘ ►► Arras: Ancienne abbaye St-Vaast★★ (Musée des Beaux-Arts★).

EXCURSION

Vimy Ridge – *10 km* – *6 miles north*. The summit of this chalky rise was taken by the Canadian Expeditionary Force, part of the British Third Army, in April 1917. It is crowned by the **Canadian Memorial★**. There are extensive views over a farmed landscape dotted with the conical tips of coal mines. To the west are the cemetery and basilica of Notre-Dame-de-Lorette, and nearby, in the scrubby woodland, can be found some of the entrenchments and pitted landforms left by trench warfare.

Col d'AUBISQUE★★

Map p 8 – Map 85 fold 7 or 234 fold 43 – Green Guide Atlantic Coast

The main east-west axis of the Pyrenees is interrupted by a series of long narrow valleys running roughly north-south. Each of these valleys forms a distinct unit, with a characteristic landscape and way of life which often have more in common with the lowlands to the north or even with Spain than with the valleys on either side. A number of high passes permit east-west communication; the Tourmalet Pass at 2 114m – 6 936ft is the highest, but the Aubisque Pass (Col d'Aubisque) separating the Béarn from the Bigorre country is the most spectacular. From the southern summit of the pass *(TV relay station – 1/2 hour return on foot)* the immense **panorama★★★** extends over rocky slopes to the gentler, man-made landscape of the valleys far below, as well as taking in the magnificent rock formations of the Cirque de Gourette, marked from left to right by the Grand Gabizos, Pène Blanque and the Pic de Ger.

AUBUSSON

Population 5 097
Map p 9 – Michelin map 73 fold 1 or 239 fold 4
Green Guide Berry Limousin (in French)
Town plan in the current Michelin Red Guide France

With its old town huddled at the foot of a promontory on the right bank of the Creuse, Aubusson owes its fame to the art and craft of tapestry making. Its products were soon better known than those made at nearby Felletin *(11km – 7 miles south)* and went on to rival those made at the workshops in Gobelins and Beauvais.

Nowadays the industry's wares may be seen in the shops and boutiques lining the Grand'rue and Rue Vieille, in the **Musée départemental de la Tapisserie** ⊘ of the **Jean Lurçat Arts Centre★** and, in season, in the Town Hall, **Hôtel de Ville** ⊘.

Tapestry-making was probably brought to Aubusson in the early 14C by Flemish weavers. The workshops benefitted from the title of "Royal Manufactory" (Manufacture royale) conferred on them by Colbert in 1665, though 20 years later the forced emigration of much of its largely Protestant workforce (the result of the Revocation of the Edict of Nantes) almost closed them for good.

Aubusson's golden age was in the second half of the 18C. Its clientele consisted of the comfortably-off rather than the rich, who bought Aubusson's imitations of the products of other manufacturers, free interpretations of engravings or prints and reproductions of old designs, often on cartoons by Oudry or Boucher.

Political and economic crises, together with the competition of wallpaper and mechanised carpet production, resulted in long years of decline which were finally brought to an end by the efforts of the painter and designer, Jean Lurçat (1892-1966) *(qv)*.

His revival of tapestry-making was in part inspired by Cubism and is characterised by a limited range of colours, absence of perspective, flat backgrounds, coarse stitching and subjects of an illustrative rather than realistic nature.

Tapestries and carpets

The weaving of wool goes back very far in time, probably complementing the use of animal hides in caves and huts to create a modicum of comfort. It probably originated in Persia, and reached a high level of development in Greece, then in the Near East, before arriving in Europe by way of the Crusaders. As a process it is quite distinct from embroidery and needlework and has little in common with the machine-made products of the 19C and today.

Tapestry and carpet are distinguished primarily by their function rather than by their design or manufacture.

A **tapestry** is designed to be hung vertically on the wall for decoration. It is mainly made of wool, sometimes of silk, occasionally shot through with gold or silver threads. The design is usually representational, based on an artist's drawing (cartoon), and featuring stylised landscapes *(verdures)* or figures depicting allegorical subjects or legends.

A **carpet** differs in that it serves as a decorative floor covering; the pattern is designed to be viewed from all sides and the thickness of the pile is indicative of the degree of comfort.

Both tapestries and carpets are woven structures. **Weaving** involves stretching the longitudinal (warp) threads on a loom and interlacing the cross (weft) threads. The design is achieved by interlacing different-coloured wools in the warp following the shapes of the cartoon in order to create the design image. The result is a closely-woven structure with a smooth surface, the ends being tucked away on the reverse side. The designs are often geometrically complex. The most celebrated of all woven carpets are those of Kelim in Turkey and M'Zab in the Sahara.

To achieve a pile carpet, short strands of wool are knotted to the warp threads, creating a **knot stitch** *(point noué)*. The colour and arrangement of the wools determine the image or design of the carpet. Most carpets are made in this way, distinctions between them being dependent on the type of knot used, their density, the width and treatment of the border, and the choice and treatment of subject.

Beauvais carpets are very finely woven, those from the Savonnerie factory have a pile which is trimmed to give a velvety texture, while Aubusson is renowned for its smooth-faced tapestry-woven products.

The final result is the same whether tapestry or carpet is made on a vertical loom (high warp) – as at the Gobelins factory, or on a horizontal loom (low warp) – as at Beauvais and Aubusson.

AUCH★★

Population 23 136
Map p 8 – Michelin map 82 fold 5 or 234 fold 32
Green Guide Atlantic Coast
Town plan in the current Michelin Red Guide France

The origins of Auch go back to a fortified settlement of the Basques situated on the left bank of the Gers. For 2 000 years the city served as a staging-post on the old Toulouse-Bordeaux highway; its alignment avoided the treacherously-shifting course of the middle Garonne to the north.

The real d'Artagnan, Charles de Batz, was from this district. Another citizen remembered with pride is d'Etigny, who, as the city's Intendant, was responsible for its revival in the 18C. He was the first of a series of able administrators to reside in the former Bishops' Palace; its façade is distinguished by a rhythmic sequence of fluted pilasters.

★★ **Cathédrale Ste-Marie** – The cathedral's ambulatory contains a masterly series of Renaissance **stained glass windows**★★, completed in 1517 by the Gascon Arnaud de Moles. They are remarkable for their composition, their sophisticated use of colour (subtle nuances and gradations and half-tones, all in strong contrast to the pure colours, rigidly separated, of the Gothic), and for the way in which the central figure of each window is surrounded by vignettes elucidating its symbolism and prefiguration (a characteristic humanist device of the time). Adam and Eve, Jonah, and the Nativity are exceptionally fine.

The **choir-stalls**★★★ ⊘, an inspired work completed in 1554, are peopled by 1 500 different figures in an extraordinary wealth of detail. The backs are carved with representations of biblical and other personages; the faces crowding the dividers, elbow-rests, the panels and niches of the backs and the misericords provide an interest and stimulation which are inexhaustible. The opulence characteristic of the Flamboyant style survives in this work of the Renaissance.

AULNAY★★

Population 1 462
Map p 8 – Michelin map 72 fold 2 or 233 fold 17
Green Guide Atlantic Coast

Originally in the province of Poitiers, Aulnay was apportioned to Saintonge by virtue of the division of France into *départements* by the Constituent Assembly on 22 December 1789.

★★ **Église St-Pierre** – This fine Romanesque church stands among the cypresses of its ancient burial ground with its Gothic Hosanna Cross. It was built between 1140 and 1170 at a time when Eleanor of Aquitaine ruled southwestern France first as queen to Louis VII, then to Henry II of England. Its structure, notably its tribune-less triple nave, is essentially in the Romanesque style typical of the Poitou area while its sculpture is characteristic of Saintonge.

Although somewhat marred by massive 15C buttresses, the west front is remarkable for its sumptuously decorated arches and its large-scale figure sculptures. In the left portal is a poignant representation of St Peter hanging upside-down on his cross. Considering himself unworthy of the same treatment as his Master, he demanded this even crueller form of crucifixion for himself. This method of execution was not uncommon, even before the days of Nero; by lowering its centre of gravity, the cross could be made smaller, and thus less costly.

The doorway of the south transept has lofty corner columns and a great relieving arch; the second arch, supported by sitting atlantes and showing the Prophets and Apostles, is an achievement of the 13C Saintonge school of sculpture.

Within, the central window of the apse is famous for its unusually rich carving, characteristic of the level which decorative art had reached in the High Middle Ages. The capitals of the columns in the nave are also worthy of attention, as is the bell-tower with its 18C slate-clad spire; its lower levels are particularly attractive in spite of the insensitive addition of extra height in the 15C.

Crucifixion of St Peter, Aulnay

AUTUN**

Population 17 906

Map p 6 – Michelin map 69 fold 7 or 243 fold 25 – Green Guide Burgundy Jura
Town plan in the current Michelin Red Guide France

Autun was founded by the Emperor Augustus, half a century after Caesar's conquest of Gaul. The hilly site bestrode the Roman road linking Lyons with Sens and overlooked the wide Vale of Arroux. Rome was taken as the model for the new town; its 6km – 4 mile length of walls soon sheltered fine civic buildings (a theatre, an amphitheatre) and a thriving commercial life. From their stronghold at Bibracte on **Mount Beuvray** 29km – 18 miles away to the west, the Gallic Aedui tribe watched the city's growth with fascination and ended up moving there themselves.
In the Middle Ages the city consolidated itself on the upper part of its site.

★★ Cathédrale St-Lazare ⊘ – The great sandstone edifice was built between 1120 and 1146 and named after the friend of Christ whom He raised from the dead and whose relics had been brought here from Marseilles shortly before. Though its external appearance was altered by the addition of a tower and steeple in the 15C, it remains essentially a building of the Burgundian Romanesque; its barrel-vaulted nave has slightly pointed arches (an early example) and a blind triforium designed to enliven an otherwise bare wall. With a gallery identical to that of the city's Roman Arroux Gate (Porte d'Arroux), this triforium is striking evidence of the continuing influence of Antiquity well into the 12C.
The glory of the cathedral is its 12C Burgundian sculpture, most of it the achievement of Master Gislebertus, who came from Vézelay in 1125 and worked here for 20 years. The **tympanum**★★★ over the central doorway dates from about 1135 and has the Last Judgement as its subject. Less mystical in feeling than its equivalent at Moissac which predates it by some 30 years, it exhibits supreme mastery of technique and in the boldness of its design outshines all other contemporary work. What might pass for naive or grotesque elsewhere here becomes a powerful means for expressing a hierarchy of spiritual values. Look carefully for example at the joy of the saved, the agony of the damned and the use of scale in the treatment of the figure of Christ, the Apostles and other figures. The same mastery is evident in the **capitals**★★ in the nave *(lighting)* and in the chapter house, where more capitals (originally in the choir), are displayed at eye level.

⊘ ►► Musée Rolin★ – Gallo-Roman collections, paintings, sculpture; Porte St-André★ – Gallo-Roman gate.

AUXERRE**

Population 38 819

Map p 6 – Michelin map 65 fold 5 or 238 fold 10 – Green Guide Burgundy Jura
Town plan in the current Michelin Red Guide France

Capital of Lower Burgundy, Auxerre is a port on the navigable River Yonne. The countryside around consists of arable plateaux with much woodland, cut by valleys with slopes planted with vineyards and orchards. The city is sited on the west bank of the river and served as an important staging post on the great Roman highway which led from Lyons to Boulogne via Autun and Lutetia (Paris).

★ Abbaye St-Germain – The city's most venerable building, a focus of interest for historian and archaeologist. It is named after St Germanus (378-448), born in Auxerre and its first bishop, the successor to St Martin in the great work of converting Gaul to Christianity. A small basilica was probably erected over the saint's tomb early in the 6C by Clothilde, the wife of King Clovis. This building was extended in 841 to include an outer nave to the west and a crypt to the east; the relics were moved here on completion of the work 18 years later. The **abbey crypt**★ ⊘ therefore houses a raised cavity which was hollowed out in the 9C to hide the tomb from raiding Norsemen. In addition there is a false tomb designed to lead them astray, plus various other works carried out subsequently. In that part of the crypt dating from Merovingian times (6C) where the oratory was originally located, there are two oak beams carried on Gallo-Roman columns and also a 5C monogram of Christ. From the Carolingian period (8C-10C) there is a fresco showing the bishops of Auxerre, floor-tiling, and most moving of all, a capital based crudely on the Ionian Order, proof of the aesthetic poverty of the time.
The mid-12C bell-tower, a remarkable Romanesque structure, was isolated from the rest of the building by the destruction of several bays in the 19C. The eight sides of its squat spire have an almost imperceptible bulge.

⊘ ►► Cathédrale St-Étienne★★ – crypt★, treasury★, stained glass★.

AVEN ARMAND★★★

Map p 9 – Map 80 south of fold 5 or 240 fold 10 – Guide Pyrenees-Languedoc-Tarn Gorges

To the west of the Cévennes extends one of France's most remote landscapes, the Causses, arid limestone tablelands cut deeply by canyons. The monotonous tracts of the Causse Méjean leave a desolate impression; occasional groupings of drystone houses, patches of oats in the grudgingly fertile depressions known as *sotchs*, attempts at reafforestation with black pines on the slopes.

Deep within the limestone of the Causse Méjean the subterranean waters have created one of the wonders of the natural world, the **Aven Armand** ○ *(3/4 hour)*, a great chasm discovered in 1897 by Louis Armand, one of the collaborators of the pioneer speleologist Edouard-André Martel. Here the limestone has been eroded and dissolved to form a vast cavern, its floor littered with rock fallen from its roof. Four hundred stalagmites, the "Virgin Forest", make an extraordinary spectacle.

AVIGNON★★★

Conurbation 181 136
Map p 10 – Map 81 folds 11, 12 or 245 fold 16 or 246 fold 16
Green Guide Provence
Town plan in the current Michelin Red Guide France

Protected by its ramparts, the historic core of Avignon is a lively centre of art and culture. For 68 years it was the residence first of seven French Popes, then of three others once Pope Gregory XI had returned to Rome in 1377, then of the Papal Legates who remained here until the city was reunited with France in 1791.

At the beginning of the 14C the Popes had begun to feel the need to escape from the pressures of the turbulent political life of Rome. Avignon formed part of the Papal territories, albeit attached to Provence and under the protection of the Holy Roman Empire. In addition it occupied a central position in the Europe of the time. The case for moving there was made with some force by Philippe le Bel (the Fair), conceivably not without the ulterior motive of involving the Papacy in his own political manœuvrings. In 1309 Pope Clement V took the plunge, and Avignon thus became the capital of Christianity. The following year the Pope had to accept the dissolution of the Order of the Templars.

Between them, the Papal court and the administration of the Church built with enthusiasm, transforming the appearance of the city.

An influential centre for art and culture, Avignon owes much to Jean Vilar, who founded the **Drama Festival** in 1947. This prestigious annual event led to a blossoming of the arts which has served as a model to many other towns in Provence. As well as stage productions, Avignon hosts a variety of different cultural events: films, exhibitions, poetry readings, concerts, mime performances, ballets, etc. It is also keen on fostering international cooperation.

★★★ **Palais des Papes** (EY) ○ – The Old Palace (Palais Vieux) lies to the north, the New Palace (Palais Nouveau) to the south. The huge feudal structure, fortress as well as palace, conveys an overwhelming impression of defensive strength with its high, bare walls, its massive corbelled crenellations and stalwart buttresses.

Pont St-Bénézet and the Palais des Papes

AVIGNON

B	Hôtel des Monnaies	K	Hôtel de Fortia	N	Hôtel de Salvan Isoard
D	Hôtel de Rascas		de Montréal	P	Bureaux Préfectoraux
E	Palais du Roure	L	Hôtel Salvador	Q	Ecole des Beau-Arts
F	Hôtel de Sade	M¹	Musée Calvet	V	Cloître
H	Hôtel de Ville	M²	Musée Lapidaire	W	Hôtel Gasqui
K	Hôtel d'Honorati	M³	Musée Théodore-Aubanel		de la Bastide
K	Hôtel de Jonquerettes	M⁴	Musée Louis-Vouland	X	Hôtel de Fonseca
K	Hôtel Berton de Crillon	M⁵	Muséum Requiem	Y	Livrée Ceccano

The Popes at Avignon – The building of the Old Palace to accommodate the Church's archives and treasures was begun in 1334 by Benedict XII, a former Cistercian of austere ways. The Consistory, St John's Chapel, Banqueting Hall (Grand Tinel), St Martial's Chapel and three state rooms all date from this period. Clement VI *(qv)* followed him in 1342. A great patron of the arts, desirous of increasing the wealth and influence of the Church, he was responsible for the New Palace (Great Audience Chamber, Small Audience Chamber and Clementine Chapel) and succeeded in buying Avignon from Jeanne of Provence.

At the time France could stand comparison with Italy in architecture and sculpture, but not in painting. Clement called in Italian artists **(First School of Avignon)**; Simone Martini painted the fresco in the Consistory, Matteo Giovanetti decorated the Wardrobe Room (Chambre de la Garde-robe) using the foliage motifs popular at the time. The latter's mastery is evident too in his treatment of perspective in St Martial's Chapel and in his courtly Prophets in the Great Audience Chamber.

In response to the fears awakened by the Battle of Poitiers and the troubles of the Hundred Years War Innocent VI rebuilt the city's ramparts, using techniques of military engineering already obsolete (fewer machicolations, towers exposed on the side facing the town).

Sadly, little is left to remind us of the princely life of the Papal court; all the furniture has gone as has most of the decoration.

Second School of Avignon – Dissatisfied with the accession of Gregory XI, the cardinals at Rome elected another Pope in 1378, Clement VII, who returned to Avignon. A confusing period lasting 37 years followed in which two, sometimes three Popes (at Pisa as well as at Rome and Avignon) vied with and excommunicated each other. The Great Schism divided the West, threw Christianity into disarray, troubled men's minds and extinguished all artistic activity at the Papal court. This started up again at Avignon in 1418 with the establishment of the rule of the Papal Legates who created an island of calm in the midst of general European anarchy.

The Second School of Avignon (1440-1500) is marked by a compromise between the stylisation and the light effects of the Italians (15C works in the Museum of the Petit Palais) and the mystical realism of the Flemish masters. A "French" type of painting emerged, its main protagonist Enguerrand Quarton (his Pietà from Villeneuve-lès-Avignon is in the Louvre) together with Josse Lieferinxe and Nicolas Froment (whose triptych of the Burning Bush is in the cathedral at Aix-en-Provence).

★★ **Pont St-Bénézet** (EY) ⊙ – Begun in 1177, according to legend, by the shepherd-boy Bénézet himself, founder of the Bridge Brotherhood (Frères Pontifes). Until the Brotherhood built the St-Esprit bridge over a century later it was the only stone bridge over the Rhône. It helped the economic development of Avignon long before becoming a useful link with Villeneuve when the Cardinals built their villas there. 18 of its arches were carried away by the floodwaters of the river in the 17C.

⊙ ►► Avignon: Petit Palais★★ – Local and Italian paintings; Rocher des Doms★★ – views★★; Cathédrale – cupola★; Ramparts★; Musée Calvet★ M¹ – prehistory, metalwork, fine arts; Musée Louis-Vouland – faïence★; Hôtel des Monnaies – façade★; Musée Lapidaire★ Église St-Didier – frescoes★.

EXCURSIONS

★ **Villeneuve-lès-Avignon** – 2km – *just over a mile west, on the west bank of the river.* At the point where St Bénézet's bridge touched French territory Philip the Fair built a small fort. Half a century later, feeling hemmed in at Avignon, the Cardinals crossed the river and built themselves 15 fine houses *(livrées)* here. At the same time, John the Good erected the St-André fortress on the hill which was already crowned by an abbey. Protected by its walls and with a splendid twin-towered gatehouse, this vast building complex offers (from its Romanesque Chapel of Notre-Dame de Belzévet) one of the finest views over the Rhône valley. In the foreground is the St-André Gate, and beyond, on the far bank, the Palace of the Popes.

★ **Chartreuse du Val de Bénédiction** – In 1352 the General of the Carthusian Order had been elected Pope but humbly refused the throne. Pope Innocent VI, elected in his stead, founded this charterhouse to commemorate the gesture. It soon became the greatest in France. It has a monumental 17C gateway, small cloisters and graveyard cloisters, the latter fringed by the cells of the Fathers. The church contains the founder's tomb.

Strictly speaking, it was not St Bruno who founded the Order of Carthusians. But, by living the life of a hermit in the wild setting of the Chartreuse Massif (1084-90), it was he who was responsible for establishing the rigorous asceticism incorporated in the Order's constitution of 50 years later.

The Red Guides (hotels and restaurants)

Benelux – Deutschland – España Portugal – Europe – France – Great Britain and Ireland – Ireland – Italia – Portugal – Switzerland

The Green Guides (fine art, historical monuments, scenic routes)

Austria – Belgium and Luxembourg – Brussels – California – Canada – Chicago – England : the West Country – Europe – Florida – France – Germany – Great Britain – Greece – Ireland – Italy – London – Mexico – Netherlands – New England – New York – Paris – Portugal – Quebec – Rome – San Francisco – Scandinavia – Scotland – Spain – Switzerland – Tuscany – Wales – Washington – Venice

... and the collection of regional guides for France

Château d'AZAY-LE-RIDEAU★★★

Map p 5 – Michelin map 64 fold 14 or 232 fold 35
Green Guide Châteaux of the Loire

In a verdant setting where the waters of the Indre act as reflecting pools, **château d'Azay-le-Rideau** ⊘ *(3/4 hour)* was built for the financier Gilles Berthelot between 1518 and 1529.

In architectural terms it is French Gothic work of the 15C, with a corbelled sentry-walk, steep-pitched roof, great stumps of chimneys, mullioned windows and a heavily-ribbed door. But its defences (machicolated cornice, pepperpot towers and turrets) are purely decorative, the owner's status symbols.

By contrast, the decoration shows the influence of the Italianate style used in the François I wing at Blois: Florentine shells in the gable of the great dormer window, pilasters, moulded entablatures and above all the grand staircase with straight flights (at Blois it is still in the form of a spiral) and rectangular landings (still curved at Chenonceau). The interior is particularly notable for the French-style ceiling in the dining room and the chimney-piece in the François I Room.

EXCURSION

Marnay – *6 km – 3.5 miles Azay-le-Rideau via D57 west then into D20.* The **Musée Maurice-Dufresne★** ⊘ houses several machines linked to the history of locomotion.

BARCELONNETTE★

Population 2 976
Map p 10 – Michelin map 81 fold 8 or 245 folds 9, 10
Green Guide Alpes du Sud (in French)

The little capital of the Ubaye district was laid out as a bastide on a regular plan in 1231. It belonged to the House of Savoy until passing to France under the provisions of the Treaty of Utrecht in 1713. Many of its old houses are rendered and painted in warm colours and are protected from heavy snowfalls by massive projections. On the edge of town are the houses of the "Barcelonnettes" or "Mexicans", locals who made their fortunes in the textile trade in Mexico before returning home, the pioneers being the three Arnaud de Jausiers brothers who left the valley in 1821 to open their shop in the centre of Mexico City.

⊘ ►► Barcelonnette: Villa la Sapinière: Musée de la Vallée – local collection.

BAR-LE-DUC★

Population 17 545
Map p 7 – Map 62 fold 1 or 241 fold 31 – Green Guide Alsace Lorraine (in French)
Town plan in the current Michelin Red Guide France

This old capital of the Duchy of Bar is sited on the limestone plateau just back from the Côte des Bars, the escarpment marked by ancient strongholds like Bar-sur-Seine and Bar-sur-Aube. In appearance it suggests the proximity of Lorraine. The lower town laid out along the Ornain and the Rhine-Marne canal is industrial in character. The city became a possession of the Capetian kings in 1301 when Philippe le Bel (the Fair) persuaded the Count of Bar to accept him as sovereign. In 1484, it was absorbed by the Duchy of Lorraine and incorporated into France at the same time as that province, in 1766.

★ **Upper town** – Here, in the Place St-Pierre, are a number of houses dating from the 15C, 16C and 17C. The castle (now a museum) already dominated its surroundings in the 6C; its window-mouldings and carved imposts are characteristic of the Rhenish Renaissance. St Stephen's Church (Église St-Étienne) has a curious late 18C belfry-cum-porch in the medieval style; within are two works by the 16C master Ligier Richier, a relatively conventional figure of Christ *(behind the altar)* and a striking **Skeleton★★** which owes much to advances in dissection technique and is far removed from the serene recumbent figures of the Middle Ages.

EXCURSION

The "Voie Sacrée" **(Sacred Route)** – During the Battle of Verdun there were only two routes for supplies, reinforcements and removal of the wounded not to be cut by enemy gunfire. Both linked Verdun with Bar-le-Duc; one was a narrow-gauge railway with a capacity of up to 2 000 tons a day, the other a winding secondary road (today's N35), 56km – 35 miles long, and barely 6m – 20ft wide. It was this vital artery which became the "*Voie Sacrée*" of France's hard-pressed soldiers, the *poilus*. Its surface was quickly wrecked by the solid tyres of the 8 500 lorries – Berliets especially, but also Renaults and Peugeots – which used it every day, transporting 90 000 tons of material per week, but it was kept open by 10 000 Territorials constantly shovelling roadstone from quarries dug in the fields alongside.

★ **St-Mihiel** – *33km - 20 miles northeast* – Like many of the other towns along the Meuse, St-Mihiel's importance is due to its role as a river crossing in this zone where Gallic and Germanic claims to sovereignty have so often clashed. As early as September 1914, the invading German army established the St-Mihiel salient, thus cutting the direct valley route to Verdun and making the beleaguered city's reinforcement entirely dependent on the state of the *Voie Sacrée*.

St-Mihiel's ancient abbey was founded in the 8C and rebuilt in the 17C, but the town is best known for its elegant hall-church dedicated to St Stephen which houses the celebrated **Sepulchre**★★ by Ligier Richier, a native of the town. More theatrical in its effect than its equivalent at Chaumont, it was started in 1554 and never completed, since Richier, attracted by the ideas of the Reformation, left for Geneva in 1565. Nevertheless, the work reveals a strong sense of design and a dramatic intensity characteristic of the richness of provincial sculpture in Renaissance France.

La BAULE★★★

Population 14 688
Map p 4 – Michelin map 63 fold 14 or 230 fold 51, 52 – Green Guide Brittany
Town plan in the current Michelin Red Guide France

Perhaps the ultimate in modern seafront development in northwestern France, the resort of La Baule is an attraction on a European scale. Miles of beautiful and well frequented sandy beaches protected by the Points of **Penchâteau** and **Chémoulin** to the northwest and southeast respectively, numerous hotels and apartment complexes, some comfortable, others luxurious, the proximity of delightful resorts such as **Le Croisic**★, **Le Pouliguen**★ and **Pornichet**★, with their pleasure boat harbours, make La Baule, together with its neighbour **La Baule-les-Pins**★★, the ideal spot for discovering the splendour of the "**Côte d'Amour**" and the **Guérande Peninsula**.

Such has not always been the case. It was only in 1879 that construction of the town began, after 400ha - 1 000 acres of maritime pines had been planted to halt the steady encroachment of the sand dunes. The older houses retain much of their original charm and stand mostly hidden behind the more recent constructions, along the various shaded and well laid-out avenues.

Les BAUX-DE-PROVENCE★★★

Population 437
Map p 9 – Michelin map 83 fold 10 or 245 fold 29 or 246 fold 26 – Green Guide Provence

With its ruined castle and deserted houses capping an arid rocky spur plunging abruptly to steep ravines on either side, the old village of Baux has the most spectacular of **sites**★★★.

The 17C former Town Hall (Hôtel de ville) has rooms with ribbed vaulting. The original entrance into the town is guarded by the Eyguières Gate (Porte Eyguières). The **Place St-Vincent**★, pleasantly shaded by elms and lotus-trees, has a terrace giving views of the small Fontaine Valley and Val d'Enfer. The Church of St-Vincent (Église St-Vincent) dates from the 12C; dressed in their long capes, the shepherds from the Alpilles hills come here for their **Christmas festival**★★, celebrated at Midnight Mass. The **Rue du Trencat**★ was carved into the living rock which has subsequently been pitted and eroded by wind and rain.

Baux has given its name to bauxite, a mineral first discovered here in 1822 and which gave rise to the aluminium industry.

Château ⊘ – By the 11C the lords of Baux, "that race of eagles", were among the most powerful rulers in the south of France. Their turbulent ways, together with their support for the Reformation, were a great irritant to Louis XIII who in 1632 ordered the castle and ramparts to be dismantled; this was the town's death-blow.

From the remains of the 13C keep a fine **panorama**★★ unfolds over the Alpilles with the windmills of Fontvieille to the west. One of them is Daudet's Mill (Moulin de Daudet). It was here that **Alphonse Daudet**, the Nîmes-born author, is supposed to have written his delightful *Letters from My Mill*, creating the characters of the Woman of Arles (*L'Arlésienne*), Monsieur Seguin's goat, the Pope's grumpy mule and Dom Balaguère the gourmand.

⊘ ►► Cathédrale d'images★ – audio-visual show; Musée Yves Brayer★ – retrospective collection of the local artist.

BAYEUX★★

Population 14 704
Map p 5 – Michelin map 54 fold 15 or 231 fold 17 – Green Guide Normandy
Town plan in the current Michelin Red Guide France

The old capital of the lush pasturelands of the Bessin district, happily unscathed, was the first French town to be liberated, on D-Day + 1, 7 June 1944.

Bayeux was the home town of Alain Chartier (1385-1433), the chronicler who spared no effort in rousing all manner of Frenchmen to save their country in the Hundred Years War *(qv)*. Five centuries later, on D-Day + 7, General de Gaulle "on foot, going from street to street, visibly moved" made his first speech on French soil. Later, on 16 June, he was to set out his principles for the establishment of a new constitution.

★★ **Tapisserie de la Reine Mathilde** ⊘ – This extraordinary masterpiece of embroidery was probably made in England soon after the Conquest. It tells of the consequences of Harold's failure to keep the oath he swore at Bayeux recognising William's right to succeed Edward the Confessor.

Its 58 episodes with headings recount the epic of the Norman invasion with striking truthfulness; in addition it is an irreplacable source of information on the ships, weapons, clothes and way of life of the middle of the 11C.

The Norman Conquest

Edward the Confessor died without issue. His favourite, Harold, had sworn on sacred relics at Bayeux to honour the claim to the English throne of William the Bastard, Duke of Normandy (Edward's cousin). Whether through weakness or because of ambition, he reneged on his pledge. Secure in the support of the Pope and the neutrality of the King of France, encouraged by his barons and with the resources of the rich cities of Caen and Rouen at his disposal, William organised a punitive expedition in the space of seven months.

The main part of the Norman fleet was assembled at **Dives** *(48km – 30 miles east);* its 3 000 ships carried 50 000 soldiers and cavalry who were landed on the coast of Sussex on 28 September 1066. Within a few days battle had been joined just inland from Hastings and the Saxon army routed. Duke William had become the Conqueror.

Shortly after his great victory, at a coronation ceremony in Westminster Abbey on 25 December, he accepted the crown of England.

Though in accordance with feudal law, the situation was an ambiguous one; William was both King of England and Duke of Normandy; the latter title made him a vassal of the King of France. Difficulties soon arose, becoming even more serious in 1152 as a result of the divorce of Louis VII and Eleanor of Aquitaine, and were only to be resolved at the end of the Hundred Years War.

★★ **Cathédrale Notre-Dame** – Bayeux' much-venerated "mother-church" bears the marks of the many changes it has undergone over the centuries.

Of the Romanesque church (1049-97) there survive above all the groin-vaulted crypt and the lower part of the nave with its walls and cornerstones profusely decorated in the 12C with interlacing, knotwork and low-relief sculpture. In the second half of the 12C the nave pillars were encased in slim columns, its arches doubled and the aisles given rib-vaults.

In the 13C, the high water-mark of the Gothic, the Romanesque galleries were replaced and the new work supported by twin-spanned flying buttresses. Of the same period is the superb chancel with its radiating chapels, elegant triforium, Norman gallery and the four fluted pillars at its semi-circular eastern end.

Autorisation spéciale de la ville de Bayeux

The Normans set sail for England (detail of the Bayeux Tapestry)

The 13C also saw the covering-up of the Romanesque façade by new doorways and a gable, together with the construction of the transepts with their three-pointed arches and gallery with a fretwork design.

Later additions included the building of side-chapels along the aisles (14C), frescoes in the springs of the nave and in a niche in the crypt, an octagonal storey over the crossing (15C), and the embellishment of the cathedral with furnishings and works of art (16C, 17C and 18C). In the 19C the tower was in danger of collapsing; its foundations were rebuilt and the external lantern added.

⊙ ►► Musée mémorial de la Bataille de Normandie★ – Musée Baron Gérard – regional objects and 16 to 19C European paintings.

BEAULIEU-SUR-DORDOGNE★★

Population 1 265
Map p 9 – Michelin map 75 fold 19 or 239 fold 39
Green Guide Berry Limousin (in French)

Beaulieu's Benedictine abbey, which had fallen on difficult times, placed itself under the authority of Cluny in 1076. Its restoration began 25 years later.

★★ **Église St-Pierre** – This is the former abbey church. Situated on the borders of the Auvergne, Limousin and Quercy, it recalls Conques (tribunes and ambulatory), le Dorat and Solignac (Limoges-style arching, restrained decoration), and Cahors (treatment of the chancel).

Its fine **doorway★★**, dating from 1125, is the work of artists from Toulouse. It still has the stylisation of the Romanesque (highly compartmentalised composition, jambs and piers like those at Moissac, treatment of the folds of clothes as at Souillac and Cahors), but it also anticipates the more subtle presentation of personality characteristic of the Gothic (the expressive features of the Apostles). The theme is the opening stages of the Last Judgement, with the dead being summoned from their graves. The ecstasy of the Apostles, the magnificence of the Cross and of the instruments of the Passion, the display of Christ's wounds and the subjugation of Evil represented by monsters, all proclaim the imminence of judgement.

⊙ ►► Romanesque figure of Our Lady★ (in the Treasury).

BEAUNE★★

Population 21 289
Map p 7 – Michelin map 69 fold 9 or 243 fold 27 – Green Guide Burgundy Jura
Town plan in the current Michelin Red Guide France

The epicentre of one of the world's great wine regions, Beaune is also renowned for its artistic heritage. Fortified in 1368, it was the residence of the Dukes of Burgundy before they moved to Dijon.

La Côte – The vineyards stretch north and south from Beaune, as fine as they are prestigious. The vine was first planted here in Gallo-Roman times; the area devoted to it increased in the Middle Ages thanks to the clearing of waste and woodland by the monastic foundations. The reputation of the wines of Burgundy grew in the 15C along with the rise of its Ducal court. In the following century the great vineyards came into their own, as the monks mortgaged their lands and control passed into the hands of financial interests from the towns, eager to maximize returns from all their landholdings.

The "Côte" is formed by a long, straight escarpment rising above the alluvial plain of the Saône, fissured in places by deep combes. At its foot, depending on detailed conditions of soil, drainage, exposure and microclimate, grow the great vines, the most precious enclosed by walls. To the north is the **Côte de Nuits,** celebrated for its noble red wines made from the choice Pinot Noir grape (Nuits, Vosne, Vougeot, Chambolle, Morey, Gevrey...). To the south is the **Côte de Beaune** where the same grape makes other great red wines (Beaune, Pommard, Volnay, Chassagne-Montrachet, Santenay, Mercurey) and where the Chardonnay makes the finest of white wines (Meursault, Puligny-Montrachet...). On the third Sunday in November the auction takes place in Beaune of the wines of the Hospices.

The Hospices: a charitable foundation of the 15C – In 1443, **Nicolas Rolin** (1377-1461), Chancellor to Philip the Good *(qv),* founded the Hôtel-Dieu hospital in Beaune. Few rises have been as meteoric as his. Born of a modest Autun family, he became a lawyer, then a councillor to John the Fearless. In 1422 he was promoted to the high rank of Chancellor by Philip the Good. Whilst expertly promoting the prestige and interests of his master, he also acquired favour, fortune and power for himself to an unprecedented degree. It was he who succeeded in detaching Burgundy from its alliance with England and reconciling her with France by the Treaty of Arras in 1435.

Whether out of remorse for scruples forgotten while furthering his ambition, concern for his soul of a man aged 66, or genuine interest in the welfare of the needy, he founded a free hospital and guaranteed a perpetual income for it from a 1 300ha – 3 200 acre estate of woodland, arable land and vines between Aloxe-Corton and Meursault; today, 58ha – 143 acres of great vines suffice for the maintenance and restoration of this venerable institution.

In 1457 Rolin fell into disgrace; he died at Autun four years later.

★★ Hôtel-Dieu ⊘ – For 520 years, Rolin's foundation cared for the sick, from 1451 to 1971. It has come down to us intact. With its fine architecture, its elegant decoration (ironwork, gabled dormers, weathervanes), its multi-coloured glazed tiles and its old well, it seems more a palace of luxury than a place for the poor. Although the internal courtyard in Flemish-Burgundian style, the pharmacy, the nuns' quarters, the kitchens are fascinating it is the Great Hall (Grand'Salle) which most completely evokes the spiritual dimension of the hospitals of yesteryear. It remained in service up to 1959.

St Michael (detail from the Polyptych of the Last Judgement), Beaune

H. Champollion/OUEST-FRANCE

★★ Polyptych of the Last Judgement – Rolin himself commissioned this work from Rogier van der Weyden to go over the altar of the Great Hall. The master, with the help of assistants, completed it between 1443 and 1451. In its expression of emotion at this crucial moment and in its perfection of detail (which can be inspected with the aid of a giant magnifying glass), it is one of the greatest of Gothic paintings. At the time, its masterly evocation of the outcome to be expected from the living of a blameless life must have been reassuring too.

⊘ ►► Musée du vin de Bourgogne★ – relates the history of Burgundian vineyards; collégiale Notre-Dame★ – tapestries★★; Hôtel de la Rochepot★.

BEAUVAIS★★

Conurbation 57 704
Map p 6 – Michelin map 55 folds 9, 10 or 237 fold 5 – Green Guide Flanders, Picardy and the Paris Region — Town plan in the current Michelin Red Guide France

A fortified city rising from the surrounding marshlands, Beauvais became a town in its own right as early as 1099. It was here in 1357 that the peasants revolt known as the **Jacquerie** had its beginnings. The physicist Gilles Personne de Roberval was born here in 1602; in 1647, he proved the existence of atmospheric pressure (measured the following year by **Pascal** at the foot and summit of the Puy de Dôme), and in 1670, achieved fame through his invention of beam scales; he was also known as an opponent of Descartes' philosophy.

★★ Cathédrale St-Pierre – Only three western bays remain of the Carolingian cathedral. In 1225 the decision was taken by the Bishop of Beauvais to build the biggest and highest cathedral of the age in honour of St Peter. Its vaults were to top 48 metres – 157ft. Construction of the choir began in 1238 and by 1263 was completed. In 1272 the vault collapsed; it was rebuilt but fell again in 1284. Work had to start immediately on strengthening the abutments, building new buttresses, increasing the number of flying buttresses at the east end and using them like external struts at the very base of the roof, 40m – 131ft above ground, concealing the sheer daring of the original enterprise.

The interior was treated similarly. In the southern bays, additional pillars underpinned the structure above. The windows were given more lancets to subdivide and strengthen them, glazing was added to the elevation, lightening it considerably.

After the Hundred Years War *(qv)*, Martin Chambiges began the construction of the transepts and crossing. He designed the great gable and rose window of the south transept, then, instead of starting on the nave, he built the crossing tower. It was completed in 1539, a century later, but 11m – 36ft higher, than the tower of Strasbourg Cathedral. With no nave to buttress it, however, the great structure collapsed in 1573.

There is much decorative work to admire, from the Renaissance doors of the south portal, to the **stained glass windows★★** created by the Beauvais workshops founded by Ingrand Leprince. The south transept has beautiful hues of green in the triforium and a rose window by Nicolas Leprince, and the figures of the Sibyls in the north transept. Tapestries *(qv)* are exhibited regularly; their fame is linked to the work of Jean-Baptiste Oudry who was in charge of the Beauvais manufactory from 1734-53. Note the **astronomical clock★** ⊙.

★ **Église St-Étienne** – The aisles of the Romanesque nave have one of the earliest of ribbed vaults; the transverse arches have a slight horse-shoe shape and the ribbing is archaic in form. On the north side of the choir is a **Jesse Window★★★**. Jesse's descendants are depicted against a luminous blue background; the design of the window, its colours and transparency make it a rare masterpiece.

⊙ ►► Musée Départemental de l'Oise★ – regional ceramic, sculpture and archeological objects.

Abbaye du BEC-HELLOUIN★★

Map p 5 – Map 54 fold 19 or 231 fold 21 – Green Guide Normandy

The prestigious **Abbey** ⊙ rivalled that of Jumièges, its influence in matters of doctrine and oratory being without parallel.

In the year 1042, **Lanfranc** (1005-1089) appeared before the abbey gates. This great yet humble man, a fine teacher and master of jurisprudence, was in flight from the success his teaching had brought him at Avranches. Three years later, a sense of duty led him to start teaching again, making Le Bec one of the great intellectual centres of the West. After the Conquest, Lanfranc, who had become Duke William's Counsellor, was made Archbishop of Canterbury and Primate of all England. He took his church vigorously in hand, staffing its higher ranks with clerics from Le Bec. His successor at Le Bec was St Anselm (1033-1109), his former pupil, a philosopher and distinguished theologian whose thinking was of an almost experimental rigour in its drive for truth. His *Proslogion*, written here in 1078, is held to be one of the great sources of Western thought. In 1093 he too became Archbishop of Canterbury. In England Le Bec owned great estates which were lost at the Dissolution following Henry VIII's break with Rome (1534). But the Abbey's spiritual prestige remained intact, with both English Churches – Anglican and Roman Catholic – claiming St Anselm's succession and maintaining links with Le Bec which were only broken when the monks were expelled in 1792. They returned in 1948.

Destruction, Desecration, Restoration – The monks remaining at Le Bec were driven out at the time of the French Revolution. The Abbey's copper, lead, and the bronze from its bells were melted down, and its tapestries, archives, books and furniture dispersed. In 1809, following a decree which authorized the demolition of churches where there were two or more to a parish, the 13C abbey church and its chapter house were used as quarries.

From 1802 for nearly a century the abbey served as a remount depot and stud. In 1901 it was put in the charge of the Ministry of War.

Since 1948 considerable reconstruction has taken place, particularly of the St Nicholas Tower of 1467 and the Abbot's Lodging of 1735. But the great Abbey Church, whose 42m – 140ft choir was one of the wonders of the Christian world, has gone, though its spiritual power is undiminished.

BELFORT★

Conurbation 75 509

Map p 7 – Michelin map 66 fold 8 or 243 fold 10 – Green Guide Burgundy Jura
Town plan in the current Michelin Red Guide France

Belfort is divided by the Savoureuse into two distinct parts. On the river's west bank are extensive industrial and commercial areas and housing estates, on the east bank, at the foot of the rock on which the castle is sited, is the "impregnable" citadel built by Vauban. This 17C fortified town is the great military engineer's masterpiece. In the 19C, as pressure built up on the town to expand, its ramparts were demolished.

An invasion route – Lying between the Jura to the south and the Vosges to the north, the route through the Belfort Gap (or Burgundian Gate) has drawn successive waves of invaders, Celts, Germanic tribes, soldiers of the Holy Roman Empire... Belfort's history is a battered one.

In the course of the Franco-Prussian War of 1870 forty thousand German troops were held up for a month before Belfort by the Mobile Guards commanded by Colonel Denfert-Rochereau. Retiring in good order into the citadel, he and his men withstood a 103-day siege, only consenting to march out (with full battle honours) on the direct orders of the French government, 21 days after the armistice signed at Versailles. In the struggle between President Thiers and Bismarck, the German Chancellor, over the cession of French territory, this exemplary resistance made it possible for Belfort to escape the fate of Alsace and Lorraine; it became instead the centre of its own tiny territory.

In November 1944 the advance of the First French Army through the Belfort Gap towards the Rhine was held up by the retreating Wehrmacht. The night attack of 19 November on the Salbert Fort (northwest of the town) by Commandos of the Army of Africa led to Belfort's liberation on 22 November; the thrust in the direction of Mulhouse could now continue.

★★ **Le Lion** ⊙ – The great beast (22m – 72ft long and 11m – 36ft high) carved from red Vosges sandstone just below the castle symbolises the spirit and strength of Belfort's defenders in 1870 and marks the response of the French people to their heroism. It is the work of **Frédéric Bartholdi** (1834-1904) of Colmar, who here gave free rein to his patriotic fervour and ardent creativity. It was he who sculpted the *Trois Sièges (Three Seats)* monument in the town's Place de la République as well as *Liberty lighting the world* at the entrance to New York harbour.

⊙ ►► Belfort: Le Camp retranché★★ (the Citadel).

EXCURSION

Pays de Montbéliard – *19km – 12 miles south.* The principality of Montbéliard was converted early to Lutheranism, a result of its having been attached to the Duchy of Württemberg in 1397. Its annexation by France dates from 1793. Powerful families lived here, like the Moussons, the Montfaucons and the Châlons, whose name is recalled by Montbéliard's round-towered château. The great biologist **Jean Cuvier** *(qv)* was born here.

The industrial progress which marked the reign of Louis XVI produced interesting developments in the area. In 1773, **Georges-Frédéric Japy**, a farrier and grandson of a locksmith, started a clock-making works, which spawned other factories around Paris and in the North of France producing metalwork, electrical goods, typewriters, mechanical dolls...

Jean-Pierre Peugeot was descended from a long line of mill-owners (corn, dyes, tanning). In 1811, at his Sous-Cratet mill near Herimoncourt, he started working in metal, not without some set-backs. His sons, Armand and Eugène, went on to found an important industrial group, beginning with their bicycle factory in 1886 and the manufacture of a number of steam tricycles in 1889. At **Sochaux** is the **Musée Peugeot★** ⊙ which tells the story of this famous name. There are coffee-mills, bicycles, tools, and a vis-à-vis of 1892; among the other vehicles note especially a Double Phaeton of 1906, a Bébé Torpedo of 1913, a two-door Eclipse of 1936 and a 404 Diesel Records coupé of 1965.

BELLE-ÎLE★★

Population 4 489
Map p 4 – Michelin map 63 folds 11, 12 or 230 folds 48, 49
Green Guide Brittany

Belle-Île's interest lies as much in its history as in its wonderful coastline. In the Middle Ages the island belonged to the Counts of Cornouaille and was often raided by pirates (French as well as Dutch and English) because of its wealth in grain.

Le Palais – This is the island's capital, its natural harbour dominated by the citadel and the fortifications protecting the town. In 1548 an English attack had been repulsed, but the incident made Henri II aware of England's continuing interest in Aquitaine and France's Atlantic coast generally. His response was to build a fort along more solid lines than the previous monastic château.

In 1572, during the Wars of Religion Albert de Gondi was charged with the defence of the island; he was responsible for constructing the dungeons of the Le Palais gateway. The following year the island was taken by Gabriel de Lorgues. It was this gentleman, also known as Montgomery, who had fatally wounded Henri II at a joust in Paris, then, turned Huguenot, and fearful of Catherine de' Medici's revenge, had escaped from the St Barthomew's massacre (1572) to England. His sacking of the island came in between two inconclusive battles off La Rochelle, all serving to justify in retrospect the King's policy at the Treaty of Le Cateau-Cambrésis.

★ **Citadelle Vauban** ⊙ – The proximity of Belle-Île to the ports of the south coast of Brittany (e.g. Lorient) and the mouth of the Loire (Nantes), gave it great importance in the fight for the control of the high seas conducted by England and France, an aspect of that rivalry between them which was the dominating factor in international politics from the reign of Louis XIV to the fall of Napoleon. In the search for outlets for her growing manufactures, England came frequently into conflict with France, herself in pursuit of new overseas territories but with the additional burden of defending long land frontiers.

In 1658, the island came into the hands of Chancellor **Fouquet**. He consolidated the defences and installed 200 new batteries to defend against attack from the sea.

In 1674, at the time of the Dutch Wars, 70 ships of the United Provinces' fleet dropped anchor off Grands Sables beach. At this point Vauban was working at St Malo, Rochefort, Blaye and St-Martin-de-Ré, but from 1682, the great military engineer adapted the citadel to the needs arising from improvements in the technology of war, converting an old chapel (Henri II Tower) into a powder-magazine with a projecting roof to fend off broadsides, rebuilding the old arsenal as well as laying out an officers' walk (Promenade des Officiers) with a gallery giving fine sea views.

In 1696, during the War of the League of Augsburg *(1)*, the English succeeded in taking the nearby islands of Houat and Hoëdic and at one point landed on Belle-Île itself. From 1710 to 1713, during the War of the Spanish Succession, they based themselves at Grands Sables. This was the time at which Acadia and Newfoundland were taken from France. In 1723, the old Louis XIII bastion was altered and became the Sea Bastion (Bastion de la Mer). In 1746, during the War of the Austrian Succession, the English fleet sank the royal ship *L'Ardent* between le Palais and Quiberon. In 1761, during the Seven Years War, in which France lost Guadeloupe and Martinique in the Antilles as well as Pondicherry, Belle-Île's citadel fell after 38 days of siege. For two years, under the guns of a fleet of 130 vessels, the island became a virtual colony, governed by General Hogdson. By the Treaty of Paris, signed 10 February 1763, France recovered the Antilles but lost Canada; England gave back Belle-Île but made herself a Mediterranean base on Ibiza, convenient for her designs on Corsica.

In 1775 the Louis XVI Arsenal was the final major project carried out in the citadel. Three years later, the American War of Independence made it more necessary than ever to assert French sea power along the Breton coast and protect free access to its ports.

Anglo-French rivalry continued during both Revolution and Empire. In 1793 the Convention had to come to terms with the loss of Pondicherry, confront an Anglo-Spanish fleet off Toulon, in 1794 accept the loss of the Antilles and squash the Anglo-Corsican Kingdom, and in 1795 defeat the emigré forces at Quiberon. In 1802, while still First Consul, Napoleon had le Palais fortified; later, as Emperor, he had to face the loss of the Antilles again while dealing with the successive coalitions ranged against him.

★★★ **Côte Sauvage** – Belle-Île is a remnant of the ancient coastline of Brittany which once ran from the Penmarch peninsula to the Île d'Yeu. The rise in sea level following the retreat of the glaciers at the end of the last Ice Age some 8 000 years ago led to its separation from the mainland.

The Côte Sauvage, literally "wild coast", runs from the Pointe des Poulains to the Pointe de Talud. Battered by the Atlantic waves, the schists of which the island's plateau is composed have been formed into a series of spectacular coastal scenes.

Port-Donnant★★ has a splendid sandy beach between high cliffs but is known for its great rollers and perilous currents.

The **Aiguilles de Port-Coton**★★ are a series of pyramids hollowed out into caverns and grottoes. The different colours of the rock have been exposed by the action of the sea.

▶▶ Sauzon★; Pointe des Poulains★★; Port-Goulphar★.

---

(1) Four years earlier, during the same war, Louis XIV had tried to create a diversion by supporting James VII of Scotland (James II of England). But the operation failed, and the French fleet involved, commanded by Tourville, was destroyed by the Royal Navy off St-Vaast-la-Hougue between 2 and 5 June 1692.

Every year
the Michelin Red Guide France
revises the town plans :
– through routes, by-passes, new streets, one-way systems, car parks...
– the exact location of hotels, restaurants, public buildings...
Current information for easy driving in towns

BESANÇON**

Conurbation 122 623

Map p 7 – Michelin map 66 fold 15 or 243 fold 19 – Green Guide Burgundy Jura
Town plan in the current Michelin Red Guide France

Besançon is the capital of the Franche-Comté. The **site★★★** of the historic core of the city is unusual, framed as it is by a series of hills and enclosed by a meander of the River Doubs emerging from the Lomont Mountains by way of the Rivotte Valley. The strategic value of the site, already remarked on by Caesar, gave rise to a Gallo-Roman settlement; the Black Gate (Porte Noire), a 2C triumphal arch, survives. The axis formed by the Roman highway has become the modern Grande-Rue in the heart of **Old Besançon★** (Vieille ville). Already in Roman times, Besançon was an important stopping point on the commercial route to the Rhine, the Alps and Italy.

Every year, in early September, the city stages the **International Music Festival** of Besançon and France-Comté, during which a prize is awarded to the best young conductor.

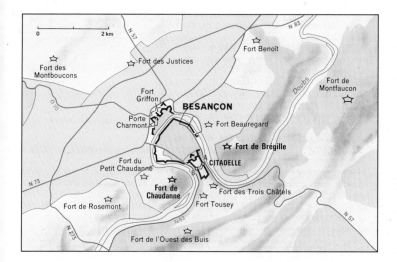

A city under Spanish rule, then French – In 1493, Emperor Maximilian of Austria granted the Franche-Comté to his son Philip the Fair who married Joan the Mad, heiress of Spain. Their son Charles V thus inherited Spain from his mother and Hapsburg lands, among them Flanders and the Franche-Comté, from his father. Having been Imperial, then Burgundian territory, the Franche-Comté, in the 16C, became Spanish.

The era marked a high point in the province's commercial life, illustrated by the rise of the Granvelle family. Starting from a humble peasant background in the Loue Valley, Perrenot, one of their number, became Chancellor to Charles V and built himself the **Palais Granvelle★**. This fine example of civil architecture of the 16C has a three-storey façade, divided by five horizontal bands of decoration, and a high mansard roof with crowstep gables. Its proportions and decorative details are those of the Early Renaissance (basket-handle arches, mouldings) while other features are quite new (Tuscan columns, and the superposition of Ionic and composite orders).

In 1674 Louis XIV conquered the Franche-Comté. He made Besançon, rather than Dole, the capital of the new French province, and, fully aware of the vulnerability of the new frontier, ordered Vauban to make the city impregnable. In carrying out his task the great engineer (qv) razed part of the Spanish fortifications of 1668 and from 1675 to 1711 constructed the **citadel★★ ⊙**; its great strength is best appreciated from the sentry-walk along the encircling ramparts. One prominent look-out is named for the King (**A**), another for the Queen (**B**) (Guérites du Roi, de la Reine).

Besançon's defences were later completed by the forts of Chaudanne, Beaure-gard and Brégille, as its military role superseded its commercial one.

The clock capital of France – Most of the great clock-making firms are represented at Besançon. Some of the most important advances in the art have been made here or in the Jura.

1660: **Mayet** created the first centre of clock-making in the province at Morbier.
1766: **Antide Janvier**, born at St-Claude, succeeded in making a planetarium. He subsequently manufactured astronomical clocks and opened a school of clock-making in Paris.

1771: **Georges-Frédéric Japy** *(qv)* set up the first workshop to produce watch-makers' callipers. In 1777 he founded a factory for machine engraving.

1790: **Laurent Mégévand** opened a clock manufactory.

1798: **Louis Perron** invented the double-pin escapement (a century later this invention was exploited in America when mass-production of alarm-clocks started); between 1817 and 1827 he made clocks and watches of highly original design.

1889: **Frederic L'Epée** exhibited musical boxes and manufactured escapement bearings.

1897: **Leroy** started to make the most complicated watch in the world, only completed in 1904 *(in the museum)*.

1920: **Maurice Favre-Bulle** produced the first electric clock.

1952: **CETEHOR** launched a clock powered by daylight. In the same year Lip made Europe's first electric watch.

1958: More innovations from Lip, firstly an electric wrist-watch, then in 1967, a quartz micro-oscillator for watches and, in 1971, the first French quartz wrist-watches.

Wall clock, Musée des Beaux Arts, Besançon

A room on the first floor of the **Musée des Beaux-Arts** ⊙ provides plenty of evidence of the long tradition of clock and watch-making in the Franche-Comté.

Hour-glasses, the earliest way of measuring the passage of time, a multiple-faced sundial anticipating the table-clocks of the 16C, alarm-watches and fob-watches of the 17C and 18C, hanging wall-clocks of the early Rococo style (*c*1710-30) and fine products of the 19C, the movements of striking clocks, bracket clocks, grandfather clocks, all proclaim the skill that has long gone into the making of timepieces and elevated the design of their cases into works of art.

⊙ ►► Besançon: Cathédrale St-Jean – Painting of the Virgin with Saints★, St-Jean Rose Window★; Astronomical Clock★ *(Horloge astronomique)*; Musée de la Citadelle★ – Natural History, Musée Agraire★★ – Traditional Agriculture, Folk Museum, Resistance and Deportation Museum; Musée des Beaux-Arts et d'Archéologie★★; Préfecture★; Bibliothèque municipale★ – manuscripts, incubula, drawings, etc.

Grottes de BÉTHARRAM★★

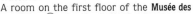

Map p 8 – Michelin map 85 north of fold 17 or 234 fold 39 – Green Guide Atlantic Coast

These **caves** ⊙, 12km – 7 miles from Lourdes, are one of the most visited natural wonders of the Pyrenees. There are galleries at five different levels corresponding to the successive beds of the underground river. A remarkable array of the various forms of subterranean erosion and deposition can be seen, from the great spongiform roof of the topmost level, the famous pillar which perfectly illustrates the process of stalactite and stalagmite formation, the 80m – 260ft deep swallow-hole, to the narrow fissure into which the river has disappeared.

BEYNAC-ET-CAZENAC★★

Map p 8 – Michelin map 75 fold 17 or 235 fold 5 – Green Guide Dordogne

One of the great castles of Périgord, **Château de Beynac**★★ ⊙ is famous for its history, its architecture and for its setting (**panorama**★★ from the nearby Calvary).

Defended on the north side by double walls, it looms over the river from a precipitous height of 150m – 500ft. Crouching beneath its cliff is a tiny village, once the home of the poet Paul Eluard as well as of the creator of Bibendum, O'Galop. A square keep existed here as early as 1115; it was strengthened at the time of the great rivalry between the Capetians and Plantagenets. During the Hundred Years War, the Dordogne frequently marked the border between French and English territory; stirring times for Beynac, face to face with its rival Castelnaud on the cliffs opposite. Once the English had finally departed, Périgord was organised into four baronies: Beynac, Biron, Bourdeilles, and Mareuil. The castle still has its great Hall of State.

BIARRITZ★★★

Population 28 742
Map p 8 – Michelin map 78 fold 18 or 234 fold 29 – Green Guide Atlantic Coast
Town plan in the current Michelin Red Guide France

With its splendid beaches of fine sand and modern facilities of all kinds (including its own airport, five golf courses and a conference centre), this Basque Coast resort enjoys an international reputation. Over a century ago, Biarritz was a place of no particular distinction, its beaches attracting people from nearby Bayonne. Fame came suddenly, with the visits of Empress Eugénie and Napoleon III, followed by many of the illustrious names of the period. Queen Victoria was here in 1889, and after 1906 Biarritz became one of the favourite resorts of Edward VII.

Now enhanced by modernisation, Biarritz continues to offer pleasures which never pall, its beaches, promenades and gardens to either side of the rocky promontory of the Plateau de l'Atalaye remaining as attractive as ever.

The shape of the seabed in this part of the Bay of Biscay and the orientation of the beaches produce fine Atlantic rollers, the delight of surf-riders.

Promenades – Pleasantly shaded and landscaped streets lead from the Grande Plage (Main beach) to the **Rocher de la Vierge★** (Virgin's Rock). To the south is the Perspective de la Côte des Basques offering an uninterrrupted **view★★** towards the mountain peaks of the Basque Country.

EXCURSIONS

★★ **Bayonne** – Biarritz, Anglet and Bayonne merge with one another to form a single urban area (conurbation 169 378) of which Bayonne, with its busy quaysides and old streets, is the commercial centre.

⊙ ►► Bayonne: Musée Bonnat★★ – painting collection ; Musée Basque★★ – one of the finest regional ethnographic museums in France; Cathédrale Ste-Marie★ (Cloisters★).

★ **Route Impériale des cimes (Napoleon I's Scenic Highway)** – *Bayonne to Hasparren 25km – 16 miles*. This section of the highway was part of an overall project to link Bayonne with St-Jean-Pied-de-Port for strategic reasons. It follows a highly sinuous alignment and affords fine **views★** of the Basque coast and countryside.

BITCHE

Population 5 517
Map p 7 – Michelin map 57 fold 18 or 242 fold 11
Green Guide Alsace et Lorraine (in French)

Among the forests of the "Little Vosges" between Alsace and Lorraine, the fortress-town of Bitche stands guard over the frontier.

★ **Citadelle** ⊙ – A castle stood here as early as the 12C. In 1683, on the orders of Louis XIV, Vauban drew up plans for a citadel. 15 years later, when the terms of the Treaty of Ryswick obliged France to abandon Lorraine, his work was razed to the ground. The citadel was rebuilt by Louis XV in 1741.

The Maginot Line

In the interval between the two World Wars, France decided to build a line of fortification in case of another conflict with Germany. The lessons of the Great War and the atrocities caused by gas, tanks and planes forced military authorities to rethink the defensive system of open trenches and isolated fortresses. The Maginot Line with its strongly fortified sectors, behind continuous fronts from 20 to 60 km (13 to 38 miles) long, and permanent underground fortifications, was better adapted to modern warfare.

By the end of the thirties, the Maginot Line – named after the War Minister André Maginot – was completed along the Franco-German border, stretching from Switzerland to the vicinity of the Belgian frontier near Montmédy. The north section was never completed due to financial and political problems. In 1940 the German army invaded France via Belgium.

The Line was composed of huge fortresses along with smaller defence posts or simple blockhouses. They were not all linked together but each fort was connected to its ammunition depot by long underground tracks, using small electric trains. The entire line formed a secret city were soldiers could live in a "peaceful" world surrounded by cooks, surgeons, hairdresser's and other guilds.

After the war, the line was part of the NATO defence organisation but in 1965. France ceased to maintain the line in working order and eventually sold the different substructures to towns, associations and even individuals. Several fortresses have now been restored and can be visited, taking the tourist back to the atmosphere of the pre-war years.

To appreciate the place's formidable strength (its massive red sandstone foundations, the complexity of its defensive system of moats, bastions, glacis...) it is necessary to walk round *(1/2 hour, taking the path before the second gateway)*.
The citadel lost its strategic value at the beginning of the 20C.

★ **Fort de Simserhof** ⊙ – *4km – just over 2 miles west*. This fort, one of the most important structures on the Maginot Line, was completed in 1935. It could house a combined arms garrison of 1200 men (infantry, artillery, engineers) with 3 months autonomy (food, petrol, ammunition). From the outside, only the east facing entrance block can be seen with its 7 tonne reinforced door, its side slit, its shooting and observation post.

BLOIS★★

Conurbation 65 132
Map p 5 – Michelin map 64 fold 7 or 238 fold 3
Green Guide Châteaux of the Loire
Town plan in the current Michelin Red Guide France

Blois looks northwards to the Beauce and south to the Sologne and is situated at that point on the Loire at which the limestone landscapes around Orléans give way almost imperceptibly to the chalk country of Touraine downstream. Originally defended by a medieval castle, the town was transformed from 1503 onwards when the kings moved there from Amboise, bringing in their train all the trades devoted to satisfying the royal taste for luxury.

★★★ **Château** ⊙ – The whole development of secular French architecture from feudalism to the classicism of Louis XIII's reign can be traced at Blois.
The medieval remains include the round towers, spiral stairways and steep-pitched roofs of the Foix Tower and the Chamber of the States General of 1205; with its panelled ceiling, this is where the States General held its Assemblies in 1576 and 1588.
The transition from the Gothic to the Renaissance is evident in the Charles of Orléans Gallery and particularly in the Louis XII Wing of 1498-1501. Louis had been born at Blois in 1462 and, together with Anne of Brittany, carried out a number of improvements including the construction of a new wing. This was right up to date with its triumphal arch doorways, Italianate arabesque decoration applied to the three Gothic pillars on the courtyard side, and the use of galleries to link rooms rather than having them run directly into one another.

Built only 15 years later, possibly by Claude de France, the François I wing exemplifies the preoccupation with ornamentation that swept in with the first phase of the French Renaissance. The work remained incomplete but the new taste for sumptuous decoration is very apparent, not only in the Façade des Loges (built 7m – 23ft in front of the old rampart) with its still irregular fenestration, but also in Pierre Trinquart's François I staircase; though somewhat over-restored in the view of some archaeologists, this is a richly decorated masterpiece with openings between its buttresses forming a series of balconies. The much-modified interior includes, on the first floor, Catherine de' Medici's study with its secret cupboards, and on the second floor, Henri III's apartments, scene of the murder of Henri de Guise *(qv)*.

François I staircase, Château de Blois

The style of Louis XIII appears in the Gaston of Orléans Wing (1632-37). The King's brother employed François Mansart, who, however, failed to deploy the full range of his talents, his work here being stiff rather than dignified. Building stopped when the birth of Louis XIV put paid to his uncle's hopes of succeeding to the throne.

⊙ ►► Église St-Nicolas★; Hôtel d'Alluye (galleries★).

Château de BONAGUIL★★

Map p 8 – Michelin map 79 fold 6 or 235 fold 9 – Green Guide Dordogne

This majestic **fortress** ⊘ on the border of Périgord Noir (Black Périgord, so-called because of its extensive woods) and Quercy, makes a stunning sight. It exemplifies the state of military architecture of the late 15C and of the 16C.

The castle *(1 1/2 hours)* was enlarged in 1445 around the existing 13C keep, and further extended between 1482 and 1520. It is unusual in that underneath its old-fashioned appearance of a traditional stronghold it is actually remarkably well adapted to the new firearms then coming into use, and thus has loopholes for both cannon and muskets. Furthermore, it was not conceived of as an offensive establishment to hold down territory or to threaten a rival, but as a place of refuge, able to withstand any attack, with its firearms used in a purely defensive role. In 1480-1520 this was something new, and anticipates the idea of the fort.

At a time when the châteaux along the Loire were being turned from castles into country houses, Bonaguil was, however, something of an anachronism.

BONIFACIO★★

Population 2 683
Map p 10 – Michelin map 90 fold 9 – Green Guide Corse (in French)

Greek and Roman remains have been found at Bonifacio and there is evidence that the site was occupied in prehistoric times, but the town's history really begins when Bonifacio, Marquis of Tuscany, gave it his name. The place's strategic value in terms of control of the Western Mediterranean was appreciated by the Genoese, who succeeded in taking it by trickery in 1187, and set up a colony here eight years later. Most of the rulers of Europe cast an envious eye on Bonifacio at one time or another; the town was besieged many times, most notably in 1420 by King Alphonse of Aragon. Legend has it that his soldiers cut the famous stairway of 187 steps into the cliff-face in the course of a single night.

★★★ **The site** – Bonifacio is magnificently sited on a long, narrow promontory protecting its "fjord" in the far south of Corsica and it is reached from the rest of the island across a vast, arid plain. The town is divided in two, the "**Marine**"★, the port quarter offering a safe anchorage for warships, fishing boats and pleasure craft, and the **Upper Town**★★ (Ville haute) overlooking the sea from 60m – 200ft high cliffs. Its old houses, many of them with four or five storeys, are joined together by what appear to be flying buttresses but are in fact rainwater channels feeding the town's cisterns.

The great loggia of the Church of Ste-Marie-Majeure is built over a cistern with a capacity of 650m³ – about 140 000 gallons; under Genoese rule this is where the affairs of the town were deliberated upon by four elders, who were elected for three months at a time. Twice a week the *podesta*, the mayor, who lived opposite, would mete out justice from here.

★ **Grotte du Sdragonato** – *3/4 hour by boat.* The dragon's cave is dimly lit by a shaft in the shape of Corsica in reverse. 12km – 7 miles away across the sometimes choppy waters of the Bonifacio Straits (Bouches de Bonifacio) is Sardinia. The trip gives good views of the high limestone cliffs of the promontory and of the King of Aragon's steps.

⊘ ►► Église St-Dominique★★.

BORDEAUX★★★

Conurbation 696 367
Map p 8 – Michelin map 71 fold 9 or 234 folds 3 and 7 – Green Guide Atlantic Coast
Town plan in the current Michelin Red Guide France

"Take Versailles, add Antwerp, and you have Bordeaux", was how the city was defined by Victor Hugo impressed by its 18C grandeur and its splendid tidal river. Bordeaux had, however, played an important role in the affairs of France long before Versailles had been thought of.

Eleanor's dowry – In 1137, Bordeaux' St Andrew's Cathedral was the setting for the wedding of the king's son (the future Louis VII) to Eleanor *(qv)*, the only daughter of Duke William of Aquitaine. The bride's dowry consisted of practically the whole of southwestern France. But, after 15 years of marital discord, the mismatch of a marriage broke up when the great statesman, Abbot Suger of St Denis, was no longer there to pacify the quarrelsome couple in the interests of his policy of expanding the kingdom. In 1152 the Council of Beaugency annulled the marriage. Eleanor had won back her freedom… and her dowry. Two months later she married Henry Plantagenet, Duke of Normandy, Count of Anjou, ruler of Touraine and Maine.

BORDEAUX

B	Tour St-Michel
D	Porte de la Grosse-Cloche
E	Tour Pey Berland
H	Hôtel de Ville
L	Maison de Jeanne de Lartigue
M¹	Musée des Douanes
M²	Musée des Arts décoratifs

M³	Musée des Beaux-Arts
M⁴	Musée d'Aquitaine
M⁵	Muséum d'Histoire naturelle
M⁷	Musée d'Art contemporain
M⁸	Centre Jean-Moulin
R	Monument aux Girondins

Another two months and her new husband inherited the English crown, becoming Henry II of England. It was a disaster for the House of Capet; the conflict it heralded between England and France would last three centuries.

From 1360, Bordeaux served as a base for the Black Prince in the expeditions against the French-held possessions in the southwest. Finally, in 1453, at Castillon-la-Bataille, Bordeaux and Guyenne (Old English for Aquitaine) were won back for France in the final battle of the Hundred Years War *(qv)*.

The Intendants – These high-ranking representatives of the French Crown in the provinces, first appointed by Richelieu, were made an effective instrument of government by Colbert. Their broad vision of a well-planned city to replace the tangle of medieval streets brought them into conflict with the local population, but in the course of the 18C they succeeded in transforming Bordeaux, giving it the classical face it wears today. The work of Claude Boucher, Tourny, Dupré and St-Maur can be seen in the grandiose set-pieces of urban design: the quaysides, the Place de la Bourse, the great avenues, the Town Hall (Hôtel de Ville), and the Grand Théâtre.

The Girondins – In the course of the French Revolution the Bordeaux *députés*, including Condorcet and Vergniaud, formed the grouping known as the Girondins. Essentially bourgeois in attitude, they enjoyed a majority in the Legislative Assembly and during the first few months of the Convention. But because of their federalist tendencies they were held responsible for the state of the country by the Montagnard faction, who accused them of conspiring against the Revolution. Twenty-two of them were tried in May 1793, condemned to death and executed.

Port – It was the English demand for wine under English rule that introduced Bordeaux to seafaring, and promoted the expansion of the area under vines. Even during the Hundred Years War *(qv)* claret continued to flow north to England, and right up to the 17C the trade took the form of an annual event, with Dutch as well as English ships participating. In the 18C goods from the Caribbean added to the traffic, stimulating the development of this great port lying 98km – 61 miles inland at the river's first bridging point. Nowadays, port activity has moved downstream to Verdon, Ambès and Bassens on the Gironde.

EIGHTEENTH CENTURY BORDEAUX

★★ **Grand Théâtre** (DX) ⊘ – Recently restored, this theatre is one of then finest in France. Its architect was Victor Louis (1731-1802), a proponent of the Louis XVI style; here he succeeded in creating a combined theatre and concert hall which recalls Antiquity not only in its sheer scale but also in its restrained use of decoration. A colonnade, one of his favourite devices, runs around the building; in front of the main façade it forms a peristyle surmounted by 12 huge statues of muses and goddesses. The interior too is a triumph, not only because of the great staircase (a concept taken up again by Garnier in his Paris Opera), but also in the auditorium with its pillars, ramps and cantilevered boxes. The design of the balconies, including the type of wood chosen, was carried out with the acoustic quality of this magnificent space in mind.

★ **Place du Parlement** (EX 109) – A good example of the urban planning carried out in the reign of Louis XV, the square has a number of houses with ground floor arcades, transom windows and decorative masks. The harmony and unity of the square is emphasized by the balcony running the whole length of the façades.

★ **Quartier des Chartrons** (DX) – This old neighbourhood, behind the quayside devoted to the wine trade and ships' chandlers, became fashionable in the 18C when the city's great families built their town houses here. Some of the streets (Rue Notre-Dame, Cours de la Martinique, **Cours Xavier Arnozan**) have many fine dwellings with classical façades, attics, **wrought-iron balconies**★ and transom windows with entablatures.

Monument des Girondins (R) – It consists of a column 50m – 164ft high topped by Liberty throwing off her chains and two bronze **fountains**★ symbolising the Triumph of the Republic (facing the Grand Théâtre) and the Triumph of Concord.

⊘ ►► Bordeaux: Musée des Beaux-Arts★★ **M³**; Cathédrale St-André★; Basilique St-Michel★; Place de la Bourse★★; Église Ste-Croix – façade★; Musée d'Aquitaine★★ **M⁴**; Musée d'Art Contemporain★ – Entrepôt Lainé★★ **M⁷**, Croiseur Colbert★ – a post WWII cruiser.

EXCURSIONS

★ **The Bordeaux Vineyards** – The Bordeaux wine region which extends over approximately 135 000 hectares – 333 585 acres in the Gironde département is the largest vineyard producing quality wines in the world.
The areas to the north produce red wines: Médoc on the west bank of the Gironde with Bourg on the east bank and St-Émilion and Pomerol north of the Dordogne. The remaining area is devoted to white wines: Entre-Deux-Mers between the Dordogne and the Garonne and Graves and Sauternes to the south.

Haut Médoc – It boasts the most prestigious "châteaux" which uphold a wine-making tradition dating back to the reign of Louis XIV. Some of the châteaux and the famous cellars are open to visitors, in particular Château Margaux, **Château Mouton-Rothschild**★ and Château Lafite.

★★ **St-Émilion** – The region is famous for its full-bodied and fragrant red wines produced under the strict control of the Jurade, a guild founded in the Middle Ages which was reconvened in 1948. *See St-Émilion.*

Sauternes – The vineyards on the slopes of the lower valley of the Ciron produce renowned white wines, in particular Château Yquem. The grapes are picked by hand at the "noble rot" stage when the flavour is highly concentrated.

Musée des Tumulus de BOUGON★★

Michelin map 68 fold 12 or 233 fold 7 – Northeast of La Mothe-St-Heray
Green Guide Atlantic Coast

This important Megalithic site (**Musée** ⊙), parts of which date back to *c*4500 BC, lies hidden in a wood near Bougon, a village known today for its goat's cheese. The complex comprises five tumuli or barrows (ancient burial mounds), either circular or rectangular in shape, which were built by Neolithic tribes living in the neighbourhood; of the tribes' dwellings, however, little or no trace remains.

A Megalithic Necropolis – The outer faces of the barrows are constructed of concentric, drystone walls. Inside, beneath the earth roofs, are **passage graves** comprising a passageway which leads to a funerary chamber, again circular or quadrangular; its walls are formed of large upright stone slabs, and its ceiling of a horizontal stone slab laid over the uprights.

The 300 or so skeletons found in these chambers were grouped together, in limited numbers, confirming that the barrows were designed as collective burial places, though reserved nevertheless for important members of the tribe.

In addition to their function as burial places, they seem also to have served as places of worship, which would make this group one of the oldest surviving sanctuaries in the world.

The site was abandoned *c*2000 BC.

BOULOGNE-SUR-MER★

Conurbation 95 930
Map p 5 – Michelin map 51 fold 1 or 236 fold 1
Green Guide Flanders, Picardy and the Paris Region
Town plan in the current Michelin Red Guide France

Boulogne's location along the chalk cliffs facing the English coast made it a cross-Channel port at an early date. It was from here that Emperor Claudius set sail to conquer Britain; he established regular boat services to Dover and built an enormous 12-storey landmark tower 200 Roman feet high which stood until the 16C.

Fishing has long been the town's mainstay, the activities of the ship-owners' guild being regulated as early as 1203. Today's fishing fleet ties up alongside the Quai Gambetta, its catch of fresh fish the largest in continental Europe. Boulogne's other deep-water docks and basins make it France's second passenger port and tenth largest commercial port.

The **Upper Town**★★ (Ville haute), Boulogne's historic core built on the site of the Roman fortress, is still surrounded by its 13C ramparts.

★ **Colonne de la Grande Armée** ⊙ – 3km – 2 miles north. This commemmorates the army assembled here by Napoleon in 1803 for the invasion of England. The project was abandoned when the entry of Russia and Austria into the war in August 1805 forced him to strike camp and redeploy his forces. A little to the west is the scene of the second great ceremony at which the award of the Légion d'Honneur was made (16 August 1804). A marker shows where the Emperor's throne was set up.

⊙ ►► Boulogne: Basilique Notre-Dame – dome★, crypt★ and treasury; Musée Château★; Nausicaa – national Sea Centre.

EXCURSION

★ **Côte d'Opale** – *See CALAIS: Excursions.*

Maps and town plans in Michelin Guides are oriented with north at the top

Bassin du BOURG-D'OISANS*

Map p 11 – Map 77 fold 6 or 244 fold 29
Green Guide Alpes du Nord (in French)

Le "**Bourg**" is the busy little capital of the Oisans area. The town is sited in a fertile **basin** which until the 13C was a glacial lake, now filled in by material brought down by the Romanche and its tributary, the Vénéon.

★★ The Oisans – Unlike Savoy, where the inhabitants live in scattered farmsteads, the population here is grouped in villages sited on terraces and reached by narrow roads with spectacular hairpin bends. Like most glacial valleys, that of the Romanche has a self-contained agricultural economy, pasture and arable land complementing each other. Further downstream, as it enters the sub-alpine depression south of Grenoble, the valley becomes one of the industrial corridors typical of the French Alps.

Écrins Massif – In character not unlike the other highlands making up the central part of the southern Alps, these bare mountains between the valleys of the Romanche, Drac and Durance look down on more than 100km² – some 40sq miles of glaciers. The Route des Grandes Alpes (p 225) gives fine views of the north and east faces of the massif (from the Col du Galibier, the Chazelet Oratory, and from La Grave), cut by isolated valleys with their typical way of life and served by long cul-de-sac roads; the best-known is the valley of the Vénéon leading to La Bérarde.

EXCURSION

★★ Vallée du Vénéon – 31km – 19 miles from Bourg-d'Oisans to La Bérarde. The road up to La Bérarde offers a spectacular lesson in glacial geomorphology made even more dramatic by the scale of the great U-shaped valley and the ruggedness of its high granite walls. It takes in the great rock bar at Bourg-d'Arud with its wilderness of tumbled boulders, the basin of Plan-du-Lac, the terraces of Le Clapier-de-St-Christophe (hairpin bends), Pré-Clot and Champhorent, the moraines planted with conifers and with birches (the pioneer tree of early post-glacial times), waterfalls cascading down from hanging valleys, and a number of compact little villages, before reaching La Bérarde, formerly a shepherds' hamlet and now a climbing centre.

►► Cascade de la Sarennes★; Gorges de la Lignarre★.

BOURG-EN-BRESSE★★

Population 40 972
Map p 10 – Michelin map 74 fold 3 or 243 fold 41 or 244 fold 4
Green Guide Burgundy Jura
Town plan in the current Michelin Red Guide France

Bourg is the capital of the Bresse area, a fertile plain much liable to flooding and famous for its delicately-fleshed poultry. To the south extend the Dombes; its many irregularly-shaped meres mark the furthest extent of the Alpine glaciers.

"Fortune infortune fort une" – The sadly appropriate motto of **Margaret of Austria** (1480-1530) can be translated as "Fate was very hard on one woman". As a child of two, Margaret lost her mother, Mary of Burgundy (qv). At three, she was chosen by Louis XI as the wife of the Dauphin Charles VIII because of her Burgundian inheritance; a form of wedding took place at Amboise. Then, at the age of 11, she was repudiated by the Crown in favour of Anne of Brittany (qv) and the marriage annulled. At the age of 21 she married John of Castile who left her a widow after less than a year. At 24 she re-married, this time to Philibert the Fair. He too was soon dead, of a cold caught while out hunting. For Margaret this was enough; from then on her life was devoted to prayer and to looking after the lands she had inherited. Adversity had strengthened her character; her rule over Burgundy, the Franche-Comté and Artois was marked by skilled diplomacy, financial rigour and great political wisdom. As a result, her father, the Emperor Maximilian, made her Regent of the Low Countries on the death of her brother Philip the Fair in 1506. Margaret, now 26 years old, moved to Brussels. It was at this point that she decided to transform the humble priory of Brou into a monastery, partly in fulfilment of a vow made 24 years earlier by her mother-in-law, Margaret of Bourbon, partly to assert her own high status and achievement and to symbolise her love for her husband.

★★ Église de Brou ⊙ – Work on building the monastery began straight away. The church itself took only 19 years to complete, from 1513-32; it is in late-Gothic style, harmonious but perhaps over-exuberant. The work was undertaken by a Flemish master-builder, Loys Van Boghem, and a team of artists and craftsmen, mostly from Flanders. Their decoration of the church is already much influenced by the Renaissance.

In the elegant nave built of pale stone from the Jura, a finely sculptured balustrade was substituted for the more usual triforium. The stone **rood-screen**★★ has three basket-handle arches and is profusely decorated with leaves, cable-moulding and scrolls.

The 74 **choir-stalls**★★ were built in the space of two years by local carpenters. An array of statuettes represents figures from the Old Testament (on the right) and from the New Testament (on the left). In the Margaret of Austria **chapel**★★★ is an altarpiece representing the Seven Joys of the Virgin, a masterwork of amazing craftsmanship. There are also superb **stained glass windows**★★ inspired by works by Dürer and Titian.

The three **tombs**★★★ give the church its truly regal character. On the right is that of Margaret of Bourbon. To conform to the taste of her time, it was housed in a Gothic niche with Flamboyant decoration. Philibert the Fair's tomb, in the middle, is completely Renaissance in character; up above, the prince, clad in decorative armour, lies recumbent, watched over by cherubs, while below his cadaver is guarded by delightful little statues representing his virtues. Margaret of Austria's tomb, on the left, forms part of the parclose screen; she is first shown lying in state on a black marble slab, then, underneath, in her shroud. With its richly carved canopy incorporating her motto, it is the most sumptuous of the three mausoleums.

Statuette on the tomb of Philibert the Fair, Bourg-en-Bresse

🕐 ►► Musée★ (in the monastery) – painting, sculpture, decorative arts.

BOURGES★★★

Conurbation 94 731
Map p 6 – Michelin map 69 fold 1 or 238 folds 30, 31
Green Guide Berry Limousin (in French)
Town plan in the current Michelin Red Guide France

Bourges was already a place of some importance at the time of the conquest of Gaul; in 52BC it was sacked by Julius Caesar, who is supposed to have massacred 40 000 of its inhabitants. In the 4C the city became the capital of the Roman province of Avaricum, part of Aquitaine. Its significance increased over the years, but it was only at the end of the 14C that it took on a national role, when **Jean de Berry**, the dynamic son of John the Good, made it his capital. A great patron, he made Bourges a centre of the arts to rival Dijon (Court of the Dukes of Burgundy) and Avignon (the Papal court), commissioning works like the *Très Riches Heures* from the Limbourg brothers, perhaps the most exquisite miniatures ever painted.

★★★ **Cathédrale St-Étienne** 🕐 – In the 12C, Bourges was the seat of an archbishopric linked by tradition to the royal territories to the north whereas the regions to the southwest came under the sphere of influence of the Angevin kingdom. The great new cathedrals of the Ile-de-France were taking shape, and the Archbishop, Henri de Sully, Primate of Aquitaine, dreamed of a similar great edifice for his city.

In drawing up his plans, the anonymous architect exploited all the new techniques of the Gothic in order to control and direct the thrusts exerted by and on his great structure. Other innovations of his included leaving out the transepts, retaining six sexpartite bays and incorporating the Romanesque portals of the old cathedral into the north and south doorways of the new building.

By 1200 the crypt was completed, by 1215, the choir. In 1220 the great nave with its splendid line of two-tiered flying buttresses was ready. Over-enthusiastic restoration at the start of the 19C included the remodelling of the external gables and the unfortunate addition of round windows, balustrades and pinnacles.

The huge **west front** has five doorways, anticipating the nave and four aisles adorned with the radiating motifs of the High Gothic (mid 13C-14C) style; they were begun in 1230. Ten years later the two right-hand portals were in place. By 1250, the central portal (Last Judgement) had been finished. But 60 years later, subsidence made it necessary to prop up the South Tower by means of a massive pillar-buttress and to strengthen the west front. This was to no avail; on 31 December 1506, the north tower fell in ruins. Guillaume Pellevoysin, the new architect, worked for 30 years on its replacement and on the construction of the two left-hand portals; he included many architectural and decorative features of the Early Renaissance.

The **east end** has the Gothic windows of the lower church inserted between the base of the chapels and the buttresses. Three-sided chapels radiate out from the outer ambulatory, while the inner ambulatory is spanned by the first tier of the double flying buttresses; the upper spans pierce the structure to hold the vault of the choir in place. The Lanceolate Gothic style here reaches a high point in its development.

Inside, the **nave** and four **aisles**, completed in 1270, make a striking impression by virtue of their great height and the light filtering through the stained glass. The outer aisles, lined by chapels, are already 9m – 30ft from floor to vault, the inner aisles, with a blind triforium, reach 21m – 70ft, while the nave rises to a full 37.15m – 122ft. With no gallery, and limited by the great size of its arches it is covered by a sexpartite vault; the alternating sequence of major and minor piers is cunningly disguised by the shafts wrapped around the columns. This rare arrangement was to be repeated soon afterwards in the choir at Le Mans. Beneath the choir a **crypt**★★ ⊘ of the same layout takes up a 6m – 20ft change in level of the ground. A fine example of a 13C crypt, it has an outer ambulatory with triangular vaulting and arcades mounted on twisted diagonal arches to allow the keystones to be set properly.

The **stained glass**★★★ – some of the finest in the whole of France – demonstrates the whole evolution of the art of glass-making between the 12C and 17C. The 13C windows in the choir recall the techniques of the master glass-makers of Chartres. The great nave is illuminated by light streaming in through all its windows, from the lowest (in the side-chapels), from the double windows in the inner aisles, and from the highest, which reach almost to the vaults of the central nave itself.

★★ **Palais Jacques-Cœur** ⊘ – The son of a Bourges fur-trader, Jacques Cœur (1395-1456) started out as a goldsmith, first at the court of Jean de Berry, then with Charles VII. He soon became aware of the economic recovery just beginning and of the opportunities opening up in the Mediterranean. Before long he had many commercial interests and he supplied the royal court with luxury goods and became the king's Minister of Finance. At the peak of his career at the age of 50 he decided to build himself a worthy residence.

Palais Jacques-Cœur

His palace, begun in 1445, was completed in the short space of 10 years. It shows how the will to build had revived after the stagnation due to war and also demonstrates the success of the Flamboyant Gothic style. It is a sumptuous building, incorporating certain pioneering comforts like a bath-house and an arcaded courtyard. Other innovations it contributed to the evolution of late medieval domestic architecture included the provision of a large number of rooms with independent access, sculptures indicating the purpose of the rooms served by the various staircases, and, in the chapel, two oratories reserved for the proprietor and his wife.

⊘ ►► Hôtel Cujas★ (Berry Provincial Museum); Hôtel Lallemant★; Hotel des Échevins (Musée Maurice-Estève★); Jardin des Prés-Fichaux★.

Lac du BOURGET★★

Map p 10 – Map 74 fold 15 or 244 folds 17, 18
Green Guide Alpes du Nord (in French)

This is France's largest (4 500ha – 11 000 acre) and most celebrated lake. It lies in a glaciated valley between the southern end of the Jura and the foothills of the Alps; its waters were once fed directly by the Rhône and stretched right to the foot of the Grand Colombier. Today it is linked to the river by the Savières Canal dug across the marshy Chantagne valley. Its steep western shore is dominated by the peaks of the Dent du Chat and the Mont de la Charvaz.

Lac du BOURGET

The lake and its banks form a rich and unusual habitat for wildlife. In its waters live pollans, migratory members of the salmon family, together with crayfish, originally imported a century ago from New England. Its varied birdlife includes 300 cormorants which winter on the west bank at La grande Cale.

It was on the shores of the lake that **Alphonse de Lamartine** (1790-1867) found his Muse. A young, distinguished consumptive, idling his time away between Burgundy, Italy and Paris, he met Mme Charles, Julie, here in October 1816. Though she was to die only 14 months later, it was through her that Lamartine achieved his maturity as a poet, while she, in turn, was immortalised as Elvire. In March 1820 his *Méditations poétiques* were published, a distillation of tender memories expressed in "a harmonious and half-blurred language which seems to flow below the level of consciousness" (Geoffrey Brereton). They brought him instant literary fame. In 1830 he turned to politics, establishing himself as an idealistic orator of considerable power. Though in opposition from 1833, his popularity was immense. In February 1848 it was he who proclaimed the Provisional Government and succeeded in saving the tricolour. But after Napoleon III's *coup d'état* of 2 December he was obliged to retire to his country estate. Plagued by debts, he sold his property and published many volumes on political history, and a potted *Course in Literature*. The last months of his life were eased by the proceeds of a national collection, patronised by Napoleon III.

►► Lakeside road★★.

★★ **Abbaye royale de Hautecombe** ⊙ – Restored in the 19C in a somewhat emphatic style, the church houses the tombs of 42 princely members of the House of Savoy. Over the centuries these rulers had looked westwards from their capital at Turin at the irritating chain of the Alps which split their domain in two. In 1857, in a determined effort to overcome this obstacle, Victor-Emmanuel II had a railway tunnel 13.7km – 8 1/2 miles long bored between Bardonecchia and Modane. This was the first tunnel to pierce the Alpine barrier; ironically, by the time of its completion in 1872, it lay entirely in French territory, since Savoy had opted for France in the plebiscite of 1860.

The abbey's little lakeside harbour has an unusual 12C building with covered moorings, allowing goods to be unloaded and stored under the same roof.

BRANTÔME★★

Population 2 080
Map p 8 – Michelin map 75 fold 5 or 233 fold 31 – Green Guide Dordogne

Few landscapes are as generously endowed as the smiling countryside of Perigord with its gently-sloping fields, walnut trees, solid stone farmhouses and meandering rivers hemmed in by limestone cliffs. At its heart lies Brantôme, its **setting★★** by the banks of the Dronne making it the most delightful of riverside villages. It has old dwellings with slate roofs built like little manor-houses, a crooked bridge seen across the tranquil surface of the water, great trees growing on the lawns of its lovely gardens. The 18C abbey has a fine west front and a Romanesque **bell-tower★★** ⊙.

Pierre de Bourdeilles (1540-1614) was commendatory abbot here. In 1589 he retired to the abbey after a fall from a horse, having also fallen from favour at court as the Bourbons replaced the Valois. Under the nom-de-plume of Brantôme, this former courtier and soldier of fortune amused himself with his memoirs, published posthumously as the *Lives (les Vies) of Illustrious Ladies, Illustrious Men, Great Leaders*, and of *Gallant Ladies*... These lively tales of licentious exploits have many piquant portraits penned by a chronicler whose own days of merry-making were sadly over.

Banks of the River Dronne, Brantôme

Château de la BRÈDE★

Map p 8 – Michelin map 71 fold 10 or 234 fold 7 – Green Guide Atlantic Coast

In the peaceful countryside of the Graves area the **Château de la Brède** ⊙, protected by its moat, still keeps its aristocratic 15C appearance. It was the birthplace of **Charles Montesquieu** (1689-1755), Baron de la Brède, a magistrate of Bordeaux, who took pleasure in the life of a country gentleman, devoting much time to the management of his vines, but also wrote extensively (*Persian Letters* – 1724) and travelled widely, notably to England, where he spent two decisive years (1729-31), returning with that somewhat idealised notion of English constitutionalism prevalent among French political thinkers of the 18C. Twenty years of philosophical reflection and hard writing led to the publication in 1748 of his *L'Esprit des lois* (The Nature of Laws), in which he expanded the theory of the separation of legislative, executive and judicial powers, sole guarantee of the citizen's liberty. Its 31 volumes are hardly read today but went through 22 editions in 18 months at the time. With them, political writings enter the mainstream of French literary history.

In the château, the bedroom and library help to evoke the life and work of this sympathetic figure.

BREST★

Conurbation 201 480
Map p 4 – Michelin maps 58 fold 4 or 230 fold 17 – Green Guide Brittany
Town plan in the current Michelin Red Guide France ·

Although used as a port by Gauls and Romans, Brest only really became important in the 13C. The town had to be completely rebuilt after the Second World War in which it suffered four years of air attack and a 43-day siege.

The Rue de Siam runs in a straight line between the arsenal and Place de la Liberté; it formed the main axis of the ancient town and its fame was spread world-wide by the sailors who frequented it.

In 1341, at the start of his struggle with Jeanne de Penthièvre for the Breton succession *(qv)*, Jean de Montfort allowed his ally, Edward III of England, to occupy Brest. Digging themselves well in, the English refused to budge, even when peace came and the Treaty of Guérande had been signed, three sieges notwithstanding. They were only persuaded to relinquish their prey in 1397, under the terms of the marriage contract between the new ruler of England, Richard II, and Isabella, the daughter of Charles VI. A French garrison moved in and has been there ever since.

At the beginning of the 17C, Richelieu's wish was to have French naval forces which could be permanently ready for action. Aware of the potential of Brest (as of Toulon), he founded the naval dockyard on the banks of the Penfeld river; its first warship was launched as early as 1634. His work was continued by Colbert, who created a college of marine guards as well as schools of gunnery, hydrography and naval architecture. The yard was further improved by Duquesne who also built the ramparts that Vauban improved in his turn in 1683. A number of sculptors were employed in the port, among them Coysevox who worked on figureheads and the decoration of poops. Breton sculpture of the late 17C was much influenced by the work of these naval craftsmen-artists.

In the 18C, the fortifications at Le Quélern out on the channel (le Goulet) linking the Brest roadstead to the sea are evidence of the need to safeguard French naval power at the time of the American War of Independence.

★ **Cours Dajot** – This fine promenade was laid out in 1769 on the old ramparts. It gives splendid **views**★★ of the activity of the port and of the great roadstead of 150km^2 – 58 square miles fed by the estuaries of the Elorn, Daoulas, Faou and Aulne and almost closed off by the Roscanvel peninsula. On the right the Brest Channel (Goulet de Brest) opens out; 55m – 180ft deep, 2km – 1 1/4 miles wide and 5km – 3 miles long, this channel is a spectacular example of a coastline drowned by the rise in sea level which accompanied the final melting of the glaciers. The same phenomenon produced the *abers,* the drowned valleys of Lower Brittany (aber Wrach, aber Benoît, aber Ildut...), the rivers of the south coast of Brittany (Auray, Pont-Aven, Etel...), as well as the rias of Galicia and their counterparts in Devon, Cornwall and South Wales and the coves *(calanques)* in the Provençal mountain range (Cassis).

★ **Musée des Beaux-Arts** ⊙ – The collections illustrate the advances made by the painters of the Pont-Aven School, for example *Yellow Sea (Mer jaune)* by Lacombe, as well as a curious study of the town of Ys *(see Quimper)*, Manet's *Parrots* and *Bouquet of Roses* by Suzanne Valadon.

Pont de Recouvrance – This is Europe's biggest lifting bridge, with an 87m – 285ft span. The *aber* of the Penfeld winds upstream between steep banks past the naval dockyard and base founded in the 17C.

Château – Together with the Tanguy Tower on the opposite bank of the Penfeld, this is a reminder of Brest's historic fortifications.

★★ **Oceanopolis** ☉ – *Moulin Blanc Marina.*

In this ultra-modern building, shaped like a giant crab, discover the marine life of Brittany's coastal waters in the saltwater aquariums (downstairs) and the many sea birds of the coast in their nesting places on the cliff face (entrance level).

EXCURSIONS

★★ **Calvaire de Plougastel Daoulas** – *11km – 7 miles east, south of the church.*
Built between 1602 and 1604 by the Priget brothers to mark an outbreak of plague four years earlier.

Its 180 figures are sculpted in the round; a certain stiffness of posture is set off by the size of the heads and the vigorous expressions. The 28 scenes illustrate the life of Christ (the Nativity, the Washing of Feet) and above all the Passion (Arrest and Scourging) and the Resurrection.

The monument itself is built from ochre Logonna sandstone in nice contrast to the episodes shown in **kerzanton**, a dark igneous coarse-textured rock of the diorite family containing much black mica. This used to be extracted at water-level from an inlet off the Brest roadstead; it is easy to work and hardens with exposure. It was this stone which helped establish the reputation of the sculpture made at Le Folgoët and for many years was the material used in Finistère for gravestones.

Christ washing the disciples' feet, the Calvary, Plougastel-Daoulas

★ **The Abers** – The term *aber* is of Celtic origin and is found in Scottish and Welsh place names such as Aberdeen, Aberdour, Aberystwyth, Abersoch... In Brittany *abers* are picturesque, fairly shallow estuaries on the low, rocky northwest coast of Finistère. Harbours are suitable only for yachts and other sailing craft.

The entrance to the **Aber-Wrac'h** is guarded by the small seaside resort of the same name near which there are fine views of the lighthouse on Vierge Island, the tallest in France (82.5m – 270ft). A **scenic road**★ runs along the rugged coastline through a number of charming resorts.

BRIANÇON★★

Population 11 041
Map p 10 – Michelin map 77 fold 18 or 244 folds 42, 43 or 189 fold 9
Green Guide Alpes du Sud (in French) – Town plan in the current Michelin Red Guide France

Briançon is best viewed from the terraces of the **citadelle** ☉ where stands the 9m – 30ft high statue of **France**★ sculpted by **Antoine Bourdelle**. This is the highest town in Europe (1 321m – 4 334ft), sited at the meeting-point of the valleys forming the upper part of the Durance basin. Since ancient times, two great routes into Italy have met here, one coming from the Romanche valley via the Col de Lautaret, the other following the Durance up from Embrun.

The strategic value of the site was appreciated by the Gauls. It seems likely that the survivors of the Germanic tribes routed by the Roman general Marius outside Aix-en-Provence found their way here, and Briançon may have provided a refuge too for some of the persecuted members of the Vaudois, a pre-Protestant sect in the 15C. The town played an important commercial and military role, the latter enhanced by the presence of great rock bars lending themselves naturally to fortification. The forts (Dauphin, Sallettes, les Trois-Têtes, Anjou, Randouillet) built by Vauban in the 17C proved their effectiveness in the year of Waterloo, when General Eberlé's triumphant resistance here held off the invading Austro-Sardinians for three months.

★★ **The Upper Town** – In January 1692, the War of the League of Augsburg had been raging for six years; mercenaries in the pay of Vittorio-Amadeo II, Duke of Savoy, invaded the Dauphiné and put Briançon to the torch – only two houses out of 258 escaped the conflagration. Vauban was working in Burgundy, but was immediately despatched by Louis XIV to Briançon (which he knew already) with a brief to rebuild the town and make it impregnable. A week sufficed for the great engineer to draw up his plans, but age and ill-health made it impossible for him to supervise their execution, and he was to deplore a number of modifications and compromises made to his project.

With its Pignerol Gate and its fortified church, Briançon-Vauban, in contrast to the lower town Briançon-Ste-Catherine, still has the look of a frontier town of Louis XIV's reign, while its narrow, steeply-sloping streets, especially the **Grande Gargouille**★ (also known as the Grande Rue), express the drama of its precipitous site.

➤➤ Pont d'Asfeld★.

BRIARE

Population 6 070
Map p 6 – Michelin map 65 fold 2 or 238 fold 8 – Green Guide Burgundy Jura

Briare is a busy town on the banks of the Loire, known for its ceramic floor mosaics and its stoneware.

★ **Pont-Canal** – The Loire was used by river traffic from the 14C to the 19C, but the navigation companies found it difficult to cope with the river's irregular flow on the one hand, and shallowness on the other. To rectify this, and as part of his policy of economic unification, Henri IV began building the Briare Canal in 1604; completed in 1642, it linked the basins of the Loire and the Seine via its junction with the River Loing at Montargis. It was the first connecting canal in Europe. The Loire Lateral Canal (1822-38) extends it south to Digoin. It crosses the Loire at Briare on an aqueduct built 1890-94 (58 years after those at Le Guétin and Digoin). The channel is the longest in the world (662.68m – 2 174ft 2in). It rests on 15 granite piers designed by G. Eiffel; their loading is constant, irrespective of the presence of barges or the weight of their cargo, a nice illustration of Archimedes' principle.

BRIOUDE★★

Population 7 295
Map p 9 – Map 76 fold 5 or 239 fold 32 – Green Guide Auvergne-Rhône Valley
Town plan in the current Michelin Red Guide France

Brioude is the market centre of the southern Limagne, an ancient lake-bed, now a fertile plain which contrasts with the ruggedness of the surrounding mountains.

★★ **Basilique St-Julien** – This was built at the spot where, according to tradition, Julian, a centurion of a Roman legion based at Vienne, was martyred in 304. For many years it attracted throngs of pilgrims on the road which, beyond Le Puy, passed through Langogne and Villefort, at the time the only route between the Auvergne and Languedoc. Work on the present building began with the narthex in 1060 and was completed in 1180 with the construction of the choir and east end. The nave was raised in height and given a rib-vault in 1259.

The **east end**★★ is one of the final examples of Romanesque architecture in the Auvergne. Its five slate-roofed radiating chapels have richly-decorated cornices and capitals, above which runs a band of mosaic masonry. The south **porch**★ has kept its typical Auvergne five-sided lintel, its wrought-iron strap-hinges and two fine bronze knockers. The warm colouring of the interior is due to the combination of sandstones and basalts of red, pink and brown hue. The nave is paved with cobblestones laid in the 16C and only recently exposed again. The presence locally of both sandstones and marble was a distinct advantage to the four, possibly even six masons' workshops responsible for the decoration of the church during the 12C and 13C. The **capitals**★★ are exceptional; note particularly *(in the south aisle near the entrance)* an armed knight, perhaps a participant involved in the First Crusade (which had been preached at Clermont-Ferrand), together with a usurer (the sculptor's social comment on this curse of the Middle Ages). Further up the south aisle are two 14C works, the Virgin Birth and Our Lord as a Leper. There are murals too, not, unfortunately, very well preserved, but covering an area of 140m – about 1 300 sq ft. There are two outstanding subjects, the figure of St Michael in the first bay of the nave, and the composition in the gallery of the narthex (south room): Christ in Glory, the Chosen and the Damned, the Virtues and the Vices and a hundred angels, and, on the timber wall, a stunning 13C Fall of Satan.

EXCURSION

★ **Lavaudieu** – *10km – 6 miles southeast.* The 11C Benedictine priory, attached to the great abbey at La Chaise-Dieu, has charming **cloisters**★ ⊙ with timber-built galleries and 14C **frescoes**★ in the chapel and refectory.

BROUAGE★

Population 498
Map p 8 – Michelin map 71 fold 14 or 233 fold 14 – Green Guide Atlantic Coast

A victim of the retreating coastline, the ancient port of Brouage – its ships once sailed to the Baltic – now lies among extensive grazing lands, which themselves were once washed by the sea. The great explorer of Canada and founder of Quebec City, Samuel Champlain, was born here in 1570. During the Wars of Religion the men of La Rochelle isolated Brouage by scuttling a number of ships weighed down with rocks in the channel linking it to the sea.

In the early 17C the English had attacked this coastline frequently, besieging the Ile de Ré and actively supporting the Protestant rebels of La Rochelle. Richelieu decided to make Brouage "the arsenal of the Atlantic", and built a new town protected by ramparts. But in spite of Vauban's efforts, the port and channel silted up and the marshes became disease-ridden; Brouage, once the rival of La Rochelle, was abandoned in favour of the new port of Rochefort.

★★ **Remparts** – Built between 1630-40, these ramparts are a fine example of defences of the pre-Vauban era, with gun-slits, fortified gateways and elegant corbelled turrets. Louis XIV came here after his wedding to Maria-Theresa at St-Jean-de-Luz, less to inspect the fortifications than to dream about his lost love, Marie Mancini, who had fled here in sorrow six months previously after her uncle, Cardinal Mazarin, had frowned on their passion.

CAEN★★★

Conurbation 189 000
Map p 5 – Map 54 fold 16 or 231 fold 30
Green Guide Normandy
Town plan in the current Michelin Red Guide France

Capital of Lower Normandy, Caen is an important river port, thanks to the canal linking it to the Orne. Its proximity to France's second largest iron-ore deposits has led to the development of works producing more than 1m tonnes of steel a year. The city was the birthplace of **François Malherbe** (1556), the poet and grammarian hailed by Boileau as a purifier of the French language.

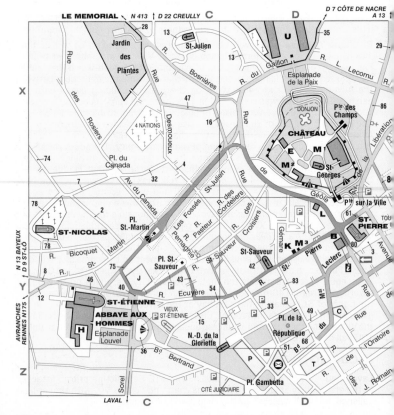

Caen stone – The Jurassic limestone quarried locally, often a light creamy colour, was used not only here but also in some of the great buildings undertaken by the Normans in England (Canterbury Cathedral, the white Tower at the Tower of London and Westminster Abbey).

"Caen the Crucible" – Chester Wilmot's pithy epithet (from *The Struggle for Europe*) evokes the sufferings undergone by the city during the summer of 1944 as well as the strategic role it played in the Battle of Normandy.

The first shells fell on Caen on D-Day itself; the city burned for 11 days. Liberated by the Canadians on 9 July, it was then continuously bombarded for another month by the Germans. The inhabitants huddled in the Abbey for Men, the Hospital of the Good Saviour and the quarries at Fleury; the final shell fell on 20 August. In the meantime a bitter battle was waged over the crossing of the Odon, an operation which cost the British more casualties than the crossing of the Rhine. But Montgomery's hammer-blows in the Caen sector helped lead to the break-out by the American armies further west, the pincer movement which crushed the Wehrmacht at Falaise Gap, and the subsequent liberation of most of France.

★★ **Le Mémorial, un musée pour la Paix** (CX) ⊘ – *Time: 2 hours minimum.* On the terrace overlooked by this austere building stand thirteen stone slabs, each representing one of the nations involved in the 1944 Battle of Normandy and each engraved with a message of peace. On 6 June 1944, the site was occupied by the command post of the German general Richter, whose troops put up fierce resistance to the invading Allies.

With the aid of the most advanced interpretative techniques, the Mémorial takes the visitor on a trip through the collective memory, from 1918 to the present, dealing successively with the failure of the peace treaty following the First World War, the Phoney War of 1939-40, the Occupation, the global spread of the conflict, D-Day (dramatically illustrated by means of simultaneous projection of Allied and German newsreels on to a giant screen), the Battle of Normandy and the liberation of France and of the rest of the Continent from the Nazi yoke. The sequence ends with "Hope", a multi-media depiction of the counterpoint of armed conflict and struggle for peace which has characterised the postwar period, inviting us to consider the close links between respect for human rights and the peaceful resolution of differences.

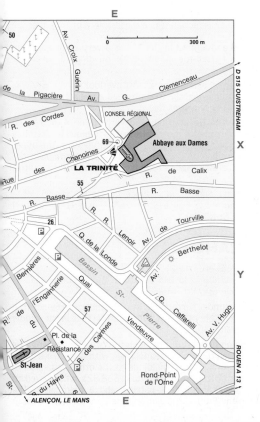

CAEN

B Hôtel d'Escoville
E Salle de l'Échiquier
K Maisons à pans de bois
L Maison des Quatrans
M¹ Musée des Beaux-Arts
M² Musée de Normandie
M³ Musée de la Poste et des Techniques de Communication
U Université

THE CITY OF THE NORMANS

Caen's architectural heritage is essentially the creation of the Norman school of the Romanesque and reveals the affection felt by William and Mathilda for the city.

After the invasions of the Norsemen in the 9C and 10C, and the establishment of the Dukedom of Normandy, the Benedictines set to work under the enthusiastic patronage of the Dukes. Their abbey churches were the first major religious buildings in Normandy. Externally, they are distinguished by the robust towers framing their west fronts, and by high lanterns over the crossing; internally by their generous dimensions and well-lit structure, and by the deliberate adoption of a timber roof rather than a stone barrel vault. Another Norman speciality is the inspection passage running just below the level of the upper windows.

Many of the city's medieval buildings are constructed of "Caen stone", a light creamy-yellow limestone also used extensively in England.

Proud Mathilda – Caen's importance grew in the 11C when it was chosen as their place of residence by William and his young bride Mathilda of Flanders. The Duke's wooing of his distant cousin had originally met with a rebuff, proud Mathilda having no time for the illegitimate offspring of Duke Robert the First's liaison with "La Belle Arlette" of Falaise. But, mad with love and anger, William returned to Lille and chastised his wife-to-be. Mathilda was won over, and accepted his proposal. They were married in about 1050, in the face of Papal opposition which arose because of their kinship. This led to their excommunication and the placing of Normandy under an interdict. In 1059 the great Lanfranc *(qv)* succeeded in having these sanctions lifted and the couple made amends, William by founding the Abbey for Men (Abbaye aux Hommes), Mathilda by founding the Abbey for Women (Abbaye aux Dames).

When William left to conquer England, faithful Mathilda became Regent and ruled the Duchy with a firm hand.

★★ **Église St-Étienne** (CY) – The church of the Abbey for Men was founded by the Conqueror; it was begun in 1066 and took 12 years to build. The west front with its soaring towers (the octagonal spires were added in the 13C) dates from this time. The nave is vast; it is a fine example of Romanesque construction with great square bays divided in two by minor piers and with high galleries over the aisles. The clerestory was altered in the 12C when the timber roof was replaced by sexpartite vaulting.

The great lantern-tower over the crossing is probably the work of Lanfranc and William themselves; in its simple perfection it is a masterpiece of Romanesque art.

The choir which was extended and altered in the 13C is a very early specimen of Norman Gothic which was to set the standard for buildings all over the province.

★ **Château** (DX) – This great fortress perched on a bluff overlooking the city was built by William in 1060, and subsequently strengthened and extended. From its ramparts there are extensive views over Caen.

★★ **Église de la Trinité** (EX) ⊙ – The Norman building with its nave of 9 bays, round-headed arches, and blind arcades in the triforium was founded by Mathilda in 1062 as the church of the Abbey for Women. As at St Stephen's, the upper storey was altered when the timber roof was replaced by sexpartite vaulting. The choir with its spacious 11C groined vaults has Mathilda's tomb at its centre. The crypt is well preserved.

⊙ ►► Caen: Musée des Beaux-Arts★★ **M**¹; Musée de Normandie★★ **M**² – archeology and ethnography; Église St-Pierre★ – east end★★; Hotel d'Escoville★ **B**; Église St-Nicolas★.

CAHORS★★

Population 19 735
Map p 9 – Michelin map 79 fold 8 or 235 fold 14 – Green Guide Dordogne
Town plan in the current Michelin Red Guide France

Sited on a limestone promontory almost surrounded by a meander of the Lot (the first river to be canalised in France), Cahors enjoyed fame and fortune in the Middle Ages as a commercial and university city.

Boulevard Gambetta – Running north-south through the city, this ancient axis is today a typically lively southern town promenade, lined with plane trees, with shops and cafés to one side, administrative buildings to the other. It bears the name of Cahors' most famous citizen, **Léon Gambetta** (1838-82), who moved to Paris aged 18, became a lawyer, an ardent patriot, and a member of the Legislative Assembly. During the Franco-Prussian War he took an active part in

R. G. Everts/RAPHO

Pont Valentré

the downfall of Napoleon III and in the proclamation of the Republic on 4 September 1870; he escaped the siege of Paris in a balloon a month later in order to organise the Army of the Loire.

★★ **Pont Valentré** ⊙ – The city's merchants were responsible for building this superb six-arched stone bridge; its construction lasted from 1308-78. Its fortifications are a reminder of the importance attached to the defence of Cahors by Philippe le Bel (the Fair), whose relationship with the city was based on an act of *pariage* (equality between a feudal lord and a town).

★ **Cathédrale St-Étienne** – In these much-troubled lands it was wise to fortify a place of worship as was done here. The cathedral is one of the first of the domed churches of Aquitaine; its twin domes (18m – 59ft in diameter, 32m – 105ft in height) are early examples of the systematic use of broken arches (lateral and transversal arches). They also have empirically designed pendentives, somewhat flattened and certainly far from the perfectly curved design.

The **north door**★★ depicts the Ascension. It was built in the 13C and shows the moment at which Christ is beginning to rise and the angels are stilling the fears of the disciples. The sculptors who created it had learned their skills at Moissac, and the compartmentalisation of the different scenes recalls the Languedoc School.

►► Barbacane and Tour St-Jean★.

CALAIS

Conurbation 101 768
Map p 6 – Michelin map 51 fold 2 or 236 fold 2
Green Guide Flanders, Picardy and the Paris Region
Town plan in the current Michelin Red Guide France

The proximity of the English coast a mere 38km – 24 miles away has determined the destiny of Calais, looking out over the straits to which, in French at least, it has given its name (Pas de Calais = Straits of Dover in English). The port handles more passengers than any other in France, being both the railhead for England and the point of departure for the great cities of the Continent.

In May 1347, eight months after his victory at Crécy over Philippe VI which marked the beginning of the Hundred Years War *(qv)*, Edward III succeeded in starving Calais into submission. The town was to remain English for more than two centuries until the Duke of Guise seized it in January 1558, just over a year before the Treaty of Le Cateau-Cambrésis *(qv)*. The loss of England's last possession in France provoked Mary Tudor's bitter comment "When I am dead and opened, you shall find 'Calais' lying in my heart".

In 1520 the famous meeting beween Henry VIII and François I took place at the Field of the Cloth of Gold, between Guînes and Ardres to the southwest of Calais. The proposed alliance in opposition to Charles V was not however concluded, no doubt in some measure due to the ostentatious display indulged in by both sovereigns.

★★ **Monument des Bourgeois de Calais** - *In front of the Town Hall (Hôtel de ville).* Rodin's group of bronze figures (1895) commemorates the self-sacrificing action of Eustache de Saint-Pierre and his five fellow-citizens; emaciated by the eight long months of siege, barefoot and clad in long robes, they came before Edward III offering themselves for execution provided the king spared their fellow-citizens. Ed-

Rodin's Burghers of Calais

ward accepted their plea and spared them too, doubtless with an eye to the governability of his new conquest. Rodin's huge talent comes over triumphantly in these vibrant figures, haughty in their humiliation *(photograph p. 313).*

Other examples of this sculpture may be seen in London (near the Houses of Parliament), in Los Angeles (at the Norton Simon Inc. Museum of Art) and in Washington (at the Hirshhorn Museum and Sculpture Garden).

⊙ ►► Calais: Views★★ from the lighthouse *(Phare);* Musée des Beaux Arts et de la Dentelle★ - history and artistic development of the town.

EXCURSION

★ **Côte d'Opale** - The road linking Calais and Boulogne takes the visitor along the most spectacular part of this coastline with its high chalk cliffs, heathlands and vast sandy beaches backed by grassy dunes.

Blériot-Plage - The little resort has a fine beach stretching as far as Cape Blanc-Nez. On a cliff-top knoll is the obelisk commemorating the **Dover Patrol,** mounted continuously between 1914-18 to protect the vital supply routes across the English Channel. At Les Baraques just to the west of the resort is a monument marking **Edouard Blériot's** flight across the Channel in 1909.

Between Blériot-Plage and **Sangatte** can be seen the French terminal for the Channel Tunnel.

The Channel Tunnel - Today the tunnel connecting Britain to the road and rail networks of continental Europe is a reality. The inauguration of the triple tunnel system in 1994 was the realisation of a series of dreams and schemes - many far-fetched. The passenger vehicle and freight shuttles (Le Shuttle) and the high-speed trains (Eurostar) make the crossing in about 35 minutes from Chariton Terminal near Folkestone to the French terminal near the village of Coquelles. Trains run round the clock with 2 to 4 departures per hour during the day and one an hour at night. The tunnel system consists of two single track rail tunnels and one service tunnel for safety and ventilation. The tunnels are 50.5 km - 31 miles long and run for most of the way 40m - 131ft under the sea bed.

★ **Cap Blanc-Nez** - From the top of the white cliffs the **view**★ extends from Calais to Cape Gris-Nez and right across the Channel to the English coast.

Wissant - With its superb beach of fine hard sand, one of France's main centres for land yachting, Wissant enjoys its privileged position in the middle of the National Conservation Area which includes both Cape Gris-Nez and Cape Blanc-Nez.

★★ **Cap Gris-Nez** - This splendid limestone headland marks the point where the English Channel joins the North Sea.

Ever since the end of the last Ice Age when the rise in sea level cut the land bridge which once linked Britain and France, Cape "Grey-nose" has protected the Flanders coastline to the north and influenced the way in which it has evolved. The chalk cliffs to the south have been eroded over the centuries to form promontories divided by deep combes, while to the north, longshore drift is continually adding to the sands of Wissant Bay.

Ambleteuse – This picturesque village lies at the mouth of the River Slack, at the half-way point between Boulogne and Cape Gris-Nez. The approach to the beach is commanded by **Fort Mahon**, a 17C structure built by Vauban to protect Ambleteuse in its days as a base for the French Navy. Part of the fleet assembled by Napoleon to invade England *(see Boulogne)* was stationed here.

Wimereux – This sizeable family resort is pleasantly situated between Alprech Cape (Cap d'Alprech) to the south and the cliffs running up to Cape Gris-Nez in the north. From the raised seafront promenade there are fine views over the Channel and along the coast from the Grand Arm Column to the port of Boulogne. Beyond the promenade, a footpath leads towards the headland **(Pointe aux Oies)** where the future Napoleon III landed in the course of his abortive attempt to raise the population of Boulogne against Louis-Philippe.

★ **Boulogne** – *See BOULOGNE.*

CANNES★★★

Population 68 676
Map p 11 – Michelin map 84 fold 9 or 195 folds 38, 39 or 245 fold 37
Green Guide French Riviera – Town plan in the current Michelin Red Guide France

Spread out between the Suquet Heights and La Croisette Point on the shore of La Napoule Bay, Cannes owes its popularity to the beauty of its **setting★★**, its mild climate and its magnificent festivals. In 1834, the former Lord Chancellor of Britain, Lord Brougham, was on his way to Italy when he was prevented from entering what was then Sardinian territory because of a cholera epidemic in Provence. Forced to retrace his steps, he made an overnight stop at Cannes, at the time no more than a fishing village. Enchanted by the place, he returned to it every winter, establishing a trend among the English aristocracy and stimulating Cannes' first period of growth.

Locals and visitors congregate along the elegant **Boulevard de la Croisette★★** with its succession of delightful gardens. To one side extends the resort's splendid sandy beach, while the landward side of the boulevard is lined with the dignified and impeccably maintained façades of luxury hotels, exclusive boutiques...
At the eastern end of La Croisette is a marina, busy with yachts and pleasure craft, and at its western end another, overlooked by the Festival and Conference Centre (Palais des Festivals et des Congrès). It is here that the Cannes Film Festival is held every May, the town's most spectacular and prestigious event.

Le Suquet – This is the old town of Cannes. From the Mount Chevalier Tower (Tour du Mont Chevalier) there is a fine **view★** over beach and bay, the Lérins Islands and the Esterel Heights.

EXCURSION

★★★ **Massif de l'Esterel** – The massif's jagged relief of volcanic rock (red porphyry) worn by erosion dips vertically into the deep blue sea between La Napoule and St-Raphael. The rugged coastline is fringed with rocks, islets and reefs. From its highest peak, **Mont Vinaigre★★★** (alt 618m – 2 027ft), a vast panorama unfolds over the surrounding area. The pine and cork oak forests clothing the wild and lonely massif have been ravaged by fire in recent years.

Église de la CANONICA★

Map p 10 – Michelin map 90 southeast of fold 3 – Green Guide Corse (in French)

The 12C **church-cathedral** of **La Canonica** ⊙ stands near the mouth of the Golo in the flat coastal plain stretching southwards from Bastia on the site of the veterans' colony founded by the Roman general Marius in 93BC.
The plan of the building is that of a basilica; it was begun around 1110, and consecrated in 1119. In its simplicity and sobriety, it is a fine example of the Pisan Romanesque style. It is built from calschist, a sort of marble which comes from the quarries at Cap Corse in a variety of colours ranging from greyish-yellow via blues and oranges to pale green. The polychrome effect is further enhanced by the blocks of stone being laid alternately with and against the grain.
A pattern of blind arcading and pilasters on the apse and the pediment above creates an attractive effect.

This guide, which is revised regularly,
incorporates tourist information provided at the time of going to press
Changes are however inevitable owing to improved facilities and fluctuations in the
cost of living

CARCASSONNE***

Population 43 470
Map p 9 – Michelin map 83 fold 11 or 86 fold 7 or 235 fold 39
Green Guide Pyrenees-Languedoc-Tarn Gorges
Town plan in the current Michelin Red Guide France

The centre of the wine-producing Aude department, Carcassonne is also a fortified town which by some wave of a magic wand seems to have been preserved untouched since the end of the Middle Ages.

This extraordinary vision of medieval military architecture crowns an escarpment commanding the great communication route which links Toulouse with the Mediterranean. The site was first fortified by the Gauls; their entrenched camp served Roman, Visigoth and Frank in turn. In the 9C, Carcassonne became the capital of a county, then of a viscounty subject to Toulouse. In common with the rest of the South of France it enjoyed a long period of prosperity which was brought to an end by the Crusade mounted to put down the Albigensian Heresy.

On 1 August 1209 the army of crusaders under the orders of Simon de Montfort arrived beneath the walls of Carcassonne and put the city to siege. Within a fortnight it was all over, the defenders broken by lack of water and the seizure of their chief negotiator Raymond-Roger Trencavel. In 1240 his son tried to recapture his inheritance with the aid of the townspeople, but the attempt failed; Louis IX razed the fortifications and sentenced the inhabitants to seven years of exile for their treachery. After serving their term they were allowed to settle here again, but only on the far bank of the River Aude, today's Lower Town (Ville basse). This was laid out in typical bastide fashion and the line of its ramparts is now marked by the ring of boulevards.

***THE FORTIFIED TOWN (LA CITÉ)

Louis IX restored and reinforced the Cité both to hold down France's new territorial acquisitions and to defend the kingdom against Spain. His son Philippe le Hardi (the Bold) strengthened the defences still further, making Carcassonne, "the Virgin of Languedoc", virtually impregnable. During the Hundred Years War the Black Prince, unwilling to risk a frontal assault, contented himself with burning the Lower Town to the ground.

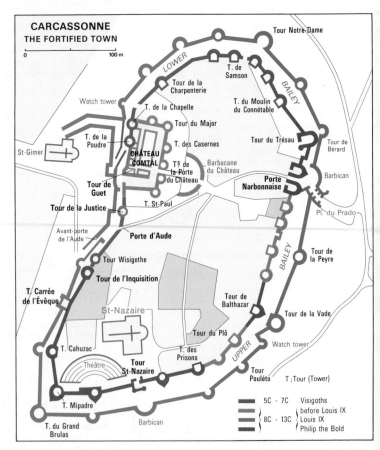

In 1659 Roussillon was incorporated into France, pushing the vulnerable frontier zone southward. This, together with the invention of modern artillery, meant that Carcassonne's strategic significance was now nil; abandonment and decay followed. Then, in the 19C, Romanticism brought the Middle Ages back into fashion; the writer **Prosper Mérimée**, with his taste for ruins, was made Government Inspector of Ancient Monuments; the architect **Viollet-le-Duc** surveyed the remains, wrote an enthusiastic report and in 1844 was put in charge of reconstructing the city. The restoration process lasted until 1910.

Fortifications – Carcassonne's defences enable us to imagine what medieval siege warfare was like; they are a veritable catalogue of the architectural ingenuity that went into resisting an attack. There are drawbridges and fixed bridges with portcullises, towers with projecting "beaks" or open on the inside, protected at the top by hoardings and at the base by flared footings, curtain walls with a sentry-walk behind the crenellations, watch-turrets, arrow-slits, machicolations... Even if the attackers succeeded in breaking in, they could be pinned down by covering fire.

Château Comtal ⊘ – Butting on to the Gallo-Roman ramparts, this was built in the 12C by the Viscounts, the Trencavels. A deep ditch and a barbican separate it from the interior.

Inner ramparts – These were first built in the 6C by the Visigoths, though altered and given extra height in the 13C. The original towers can be identified easily; they are slender, rounded on the outside and flat on the inside. The 13C additions include the remarkable "beaked" towers.

Outer ramparts – Begun by Louis IX and completed by Philippe le Hardi (the Bold). Most of the towers are open on the inside; if taken by the attackers they would be difficult to defend against a counter-attack from within.

There are also completely enclosed towers acting as redoubts from which the defence could harrass any attackers who had succeeded in gaining entry to the inner ward.

It is possible to date the fortifications by the way in which materials are used. The Gallo-Roman foundations are made up of large blocks fitted together without the use of mortar. The work of the Visigoths is characterised by the use of cube-shaped stones alternating with brick courses often laid in herring-bone fashion.

The Viscounts' buildings are constructed from yellowish sandstone laid rather crudely. The walls built by the kings of France are made up of rectangular stones laid in a regular fashion, smooth-faced under Louis IX, rusticated at the time of Philip the Bold in order to withstand impacts more easily. The curtain-walls and towers of the outer ramparts are unusual in that Roman or Visigothic work is visible at a higher level than the 13C walling. This is because additional work had to be carried out on the foundations when the ground level was lowered to form the outer ward.

►► Basilique St-Nazaire – stained glass★★, statues★★.

CARNAC★

Population 4 243

Map p 4 – Michelin map 63 fold 12 or 230 folds 35, 49 – Green Guide Brittany
Town plan in the current Michelin Red Guide France

In the bleak Breton countryside just north of the little town of Carnac are some of the world's most remarkable megalithic remains.

★★ **Megaliths** – The area containing the megaliths is somewhat divided up by roads and a number of stones have been lost, but altogether it comprises 2 792 menhirs, arranged in ten or eleven lines – *alignements* – including the **Ménec Lines**★★ with 1 169 menhirs, the **Kermario Lines**★ with 1 029 and the **Kerlescan Lines**★ with 594. As well as the lines there are also dolmens (burial places), cromlechs (semicircles) and tumuli.

Megalithic culture flourished during the Neolithic period, from about 4670 to 2000 BC. It was the creation of a settled population growing crops and with domestic animals (in contrast to the hunter-gatherers of Paleolithic times), who produced polished objects, pottery and basket-work and who traded in flints. The inhabitants of Carnac had commercial relations with people from Belgium and from Grand-Pressigny in the north of Poitou.

The markings on the megaliths represent an art of abstraction in contrast to the figurative cave-art of the Upper Paleolithic *(p 151)*, and the orientation of the lines in a west-northeasterly direction adds to their enigmatic character. Various theories have been advanced about their likely religious or astronomical significance.

Megaliths, Carnac

The tumuli and dolmens which appeared 40 centuries before the birth of Christ are collective burial-places and the mounds covering them, a thousand years older than the pyramids, may be "Mankind's most ancient built monuments".
4 000 centuries previously, the Carnac area was inhabited by prehistoric people, and, during the Lower Paleolithic, by nomads, contemporaries of the nomads of Tautavel, Terra Amata and the Ardèche Valley.
In the 5C BC, the Celts moved here. In Gallo-Roman times there was the great villa of the Bosseno. Later, the area was repopulated by immigrants from Britain and by monks from Ireland.

★ **Église St-Cornély** – In the centre of the old village of Carnac stands the church, one of the finet examples of Renaissance monuments to be found in the Morbihan; it was built in 1639 and dedicated to St Cornély, the patron saint of horned beasts; he is shown here on the west front standing between two oxen. The church's decoration dates from the 17C, 18C and 19C. The porch on the north side is surmounted by a baroque canopy in the form of a crown. Inside, the panelled vaulting has 17C paintings showing scenes from the life of Christ, of John the Baptist and of St Cornély himself. The 18C chancel grille and pulpit are of wrought iron.

⊙ ►► Musée de Préhistoire J.-Milun-Z.-Le-Rouzic★★; Tumulus St-Michel★.

CASSIS★

Population 7 967
Map p 10 – Michelin map 84 fold 13 or 246 fold M – Green Guide Provence
Town plan in the current Michelin Red Guide France

The little port of Cassis has a most attractive **setting**★ in a bay formed where the Provençal limestone ridges come down to the sea; to the east is **Cape Canaille★★★**, at 362m – 1 188ft the highest sea-cliff in France. At the beginning of the 20C, artists like Derain, Vlaminck, Matisse and Dufy were attracted here by the quality of the light.

★★ **Les Calanques** – *1 hour by boat.* To the west of Cassis the Puget Massif is cut into by inlets known as *calanques;* they occupy steep-sided valleys which were invaded by the sea when its level rose because of the melting of the glaciers at the end of the Ice Age. Sheltered by cliffs with a sparse cover of maritime pines, they make pleasant bathing-places. **En-Vau**, **Port-Pin** and **Port-Miou** are perhaps the most attractive.

CASTRES★

Population 44 812
Michelin map 83 fold 1 or 235 fold 31 – Green Guide Pyrenees-Languedoc-Tarn Gorges

Built on the banks of the **Agout** river, Castres is an ideal starting-point for trips to the **Sidobre**, the **Lacaune heights** and the **Montagne Noire**. Castres is a thriving city and the surrounding sector has been complemented by more recent industries such as chemistry, pharmacology and robotics.

★ **Musée Goya** ⊙ – Set up on the second floor of the former episcopal palace (presently the Town Hall), this museum specialises in Spanish painting and boasts an outstanding **collection**★★ of works by Goya, namely *Self-Portrait, The Disasters of War, Francisco del Mazo* and *The Junta of the Philippines led by Ferdinand VII.*

CAUDEBEC-EN-CAUX★

Population 2 265
Map p 5 – Map 52 fold 13 or 54 fold 9 or 231 fold 21 – Green Guide Normandy

A market-town since 1390 (market-day Saturday) on the north bank of the Seine, Caudebec possesses in **Église Notre-Dame**★ "the finest chapel in the kingdom" according to Henri IV; the monarch was struck by the harmonious relationship between this masterpiece of Flamboyant Gothic architecture and the sculpture which adorns it.

Among the architectural features note particularly the exquisitely carved spire, the parapet, the west front, and, within, the great nave and the pierced triforium which shows how the chalk of the region lent itself to being carved into intricate patterns. The wealth of sculpture includes, on the west front, a number of small figures with intriguing poses and expressions on the jambs as well as the canopies. Inside, the Chapel of the Holy Sepulchre (Chapelle du Sépulcre) has statues from Jumièges Abbey *(qv)* while the **keystone**★ of the Lady Chapel (Chapelle axiale) is an extraordinary seven-ton monolith with a 4.3m – 13ft pendentive. The font has panels with biblical scenes; each of the lower panels shows a scene from the New Testament while above it is the corresponding prophetic episode from the Old Testament.

Corniche des CÉVENNES★★★

Map p 9 – Michelin map 80 folds 6, 16, 17 or 240 folds 6, 10, 11, 15
Green Guide Pyrenees-Languedoc-Tarn Gorges

This highway was constructed at the beginning of the 18C in order to facilitate the movement of Louis XIV's troops engaged in putting down the Camisard rebellion.

From Florac to Anduze – *67km – 42 miles*. The scenic road follows a high ridge separating two rivers and leads past a number of splendid viewpoints offering stunning panoramas over the characteristic landscape of the Cévennes with its long straight ridges, deep valleys and limestone plateaux known as *causses*.
– The eastern escarpment of the Causse Méjean stands out as the road rises towards St-Laurent-de-Trèves;
– Dinosaur remains 190 million years old were discovered at St-Laurent; from here, there are fine **views**★ extending over the *causses* and as far as Mount Aigoual and Mount Lozère;
– Le Can de l'Hospitalet was one of the meeting-places of the Camisards;
– At the Col des Faïsses there is a fine general view over the Cévennes;
– At Le Pompidou, the limestone gives way to schists and chestnut trees begin to make their appearance. Further on is a network of long, narrow ridges.

La CHAISE-DIEU★★

Population 778
Map p 9 – Michelin map 76 fold 6 or 239 fold 33
Green Guide Auvergne-Rhône Valley

Over 1 000m – 3 300ft up on the high granite plateau of Livradois, La Chaise-Dieu Abbey was already famous in the 11C. In the 12C its importance was second only to that of Cluny and by the 13C its influence extended to Bordeaux, Spain, Sicily and Switzerland, with altogether 300 dependent congregations. Its finest hour came with the election at Avignon in 1342 of Pope Clement VI; as Pierre Roger, he had once been a novice and monk here before becoming prelate at Rouen, Bishop of Arras and Archbishop of Sens. The abbey's decline set in after 1518, when commendam was instituted; abbots were henceforth appointed by the king, with fiscal, rather than religious considerations taking first place. La Chaise-Dieu's commendatory abbots included Henri d'Angoulême, illegitimate son of Henri II, one of the assassins of the Huguenot leader Coligny; this pious churchman lost his life in a duel. Richelieu's reforms in the 17C failed to stop the slide into decadence which was only brought to an end by the abbey's dissolution at the time of the French Revolution.

★★ **Église abbatiale de St-Robert** ⊘ – The granite west front with its twin towers (the spires have disappeared) speaks strongly of the abbey's former grandeur and austerity. The impression of rigour is somewhat relieved by the arching of the doorway, albeit mutilated by the Huguenots, which is approached via a monumental stairway.

Within, the structure is of a noble simplicity, a single-storeyed elevation, aisles almost equal to the nave in height, the arches reaching up to the flattened vaults. The sobriety of the granite is offset by the soaring eight-sided chamfered piers.

★★ **Chœur des Moines** – This was built between 1344 and 1352 by Clement VI, who was also responsible for the New Palace at Avignon. A great patron of the arts, he had acquired a taste for the Gothic style of Northern France, and appointed the architect Hugues Morel to give his old monastery its abbey church. The result sets monastic values and the care of the needy above the ostentation prevailing at the Papal court, sacred geometry and its symbolism above decorative virtuosity. In 1348, Clement announced that he would be buried here.

The 14 Flemish **tapestries**★★★ (1500-18) of wool, linen and silk, came from Arras and Brussels. They illustrate scenes from the Life of Christ related to the corresponding prophetic episode of the Old Testament; the Temptation of Jesus, the Last Supper, and the empty Tomb are particularly fine. The tapestries are hung over the 15C **stalls**★★, 144 in number, fashioned from Limousin oak into floral or figurative patterns; those reserved for the Abbot and Dean, below the screen at the entrance to the choir, are decorated with more elaborate carvings. Clement's tomb was much restored after its mutilation by the Huguenots who seized the abbey in 1572. It still lacks its mourning figures, but the effigy of this French Pope lies on his tomb in serene state.

★ **Dance of Death** – 1470. An obsessive preoccupation with death and decay appeared towards the end of the 15C during the last convulsions of the Hundred Years War *(qv)*. Sermons spoke of the horrors of death, tombstones portrayed decomposing bodies (rather than the calm of final repose), artists painted Christ's wounds (rather than Last Judgements), and the Dance of Death became a favourite decorative subject (even forming the subject of a painting at the court of Dijon). At La Chaise-Dieu, figures of the mighty, of great ladies, or of clergymen are shown next to their likeness in death. The work provided Honegger with the inspiration for his 1938 composition entitled the *Dance of Death*.

West bays – Like the cloisters and Clement's Tower (Tour Clémentine), these were built by Gregory IX, the nephew of Clement VI, in order to provide for the increasing number of pilgrims. In the 16C they were closed off by the construction of the screen and its balcony which extends into one bay of the nave.

A great organ was installed at the west end in 1683 and enlarged in 1726; the **organ-case**★ is elaborately sculpted and contrasts with the spirit prevailing in the architecture of the choir.

►► Cloître★.

CHÂLONS-EN-CHAMPAGNE★★

Conurbation 62 452
Map p 6 – Michelin map 56 fold 17 or 241 fold 25
Green Guide Champagne (in French)
Town plan in the current Michelin Red Guide France

Châlons originated on an island site in the Marne. It lies at the centre of the chalklands of Champagne, an extensive plateau once notorious for its poverty, but now one of France's most prosperous agricultural regions, thanks to the artificial fertilisers which enable rich crops of cereals and sugar-beet to be grown.

The valley of the Aube to the southwest of the town was the setting in 451 for the series of battles known as the **Catalaunian Fields**. Having given up his intention of sacking Paris, then known as Lutetia, because of the intervention of St Genevieve, Attila the Hun was engaged here by the Roman army under Aetius; after fierce fighting, he quit the battlefield and fled eastwards.

Châlons was the birthplace in 1749 of Nicolas Appert, a pioneer of the food industry and the inventor of a system of preserving food by sterilisation.

★★ **Cathédrale St-Étienne** – The present building was begun around 1235 in the Lanceolate Gothic style invented 40 years previously at Chartres, though there is little evidence of stylistic development having taken place.

The cathedral is famous for its **stained glass**, Renaissance as well as medieval. The 13C glass includes the tall windows in the choir, the north transept (with the wonderful hues of green characteristic of the region), and the first bay on the north side (the Tanners' window – note the hanging skins). The finest windows however are those of Renaissance date, in the side-chapels of the south aisle, showing scenes from the Creation, the earthly Paradise, the Passion, the Life of Christ and the Lives of the Saints.

★ **Église Notre-Dame-en-Vaux** ⓥ – A typical early Gothic church with a characteristic four-tier elevation. Particularly noteworthy is the ambulatory, inspired by the one at St-Rémi in Rheims, together with the stained glass in the windows of the north aisle, again showing superb skill in the use of green.

To the left of the church, the **Musée du Cloître de Notre-Dame-en-Vaux**★★ ⓥ houses **sculptures**★★ from the old Romanesque cloisters.

CHALON-SUR-SAÔNE

Conurbation 62 452
Map p 10 – Michelin map 69 fold 9 or 243 fold 27 – Green Guide Burgundy Jura
Town plan in the current Michelin Red Guide France

Chalon is the urban centre for the fertile lowlands bordering the Saône as it makes its way between the Jura and the Massif Central.

The river is fed by a number of canals; at Corre it is joined by the Eastern Canal (Canal de l'Est – completed 1882), at Pontailler by the canal from the Marne (1907), at St-Jean-de-Losne by both the Rhine-Rhône Canal (1833) and the Burgundy Canal (1832). But it is only at Chalon, where it is joined by the Central Canal (completed 1790), that it becomes one of Europe's great commercial waterways, flowing south to join the Rhône at Lyons. Long before the present age, however, the Saône had been an important commercial route; a large number of amphora bases were found at Chalon, proof that wine was imported here from Naples before the introduction of the vine to Burgundy by the Romans.

Since the 18C the banks of the river have been a favoured site for industry, which includes the heavy engineering firm Schneider du Creusot as well as electrical works and nuclear power plants.

The origins of photography – Joseph Nicéphore Niepce (1765-1833) was a native of Chalon. His restlessly inventive disposition had already led him to design an internal combustion engine in 1807. He lacked talent as a draughtsman, but was fascinated by lithography. At the age of 48 he set himself the task of recording images through the spontaneous action of light.

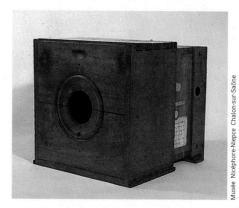

Nicéphore Niepce's camera in the museum,
Chalon-sur-Saône

Musée Nicéphore-Niepce Chalon-sur-Saône

He was already familiar with the optics of the *camera obscura* which had been studied by the Arab physicist El Hazen (11C), by Leonardo da Vinci and by various 18C men of science among them Jacques Charles, the husband of Lamartine's Elvire.

After three years' work he succeeded in making and fixing a positive image, and on 28 May 1816 he sent his brother a print made at his home in St-Loup-de-Varennes *(7km - 4 miles south)*; this was the very first photograph. **Daguerre** popularised Niepce's discovery and others developed it (eg Fox Talbot and Bayard).

Progressive refinement and invention have led from Niepce's simple apparatus to photography as an art form, to the Hasselblad used in lunar exploration and to the snaps in the family album...

The **Musée Nicéphore Niepce**★ ⓥ explains the fascinating history and techniques of photography and has much documentary material.

ⓥ ►► **Musée Denon**★ – paintings and archaeological collections.

The main through routes are clearly indicated on all town plans

CHAMBÉRY★★

Conurbation 102 548
Map p 11 – Michelin map 74 fold 15 or 244 fold 18
Green Guide Alpes du Nord (in French)
Town plan in the current Michelin Red Guide France

Chambéry lies in a valley dividing the Chartreuse and Bauges massifs. It was chosen as their capital by the Counts of Savoy in 1232; they made good use of its strategic position astride the ancient lines of communication with Italy and kept their liking for the place even after their seat was shifted to Turin.

The famous **Fontaine des Éléphants** is sited in the Rue de Boigne; its arcades make an urban composition reminiscent of the town planning of Northern Italy.

The **Sainte-Chapelle★**, part of the château, was built by Amadeus VIII to house the Holy Shroud, though this was removed to Turin when Savoy became part of France in 1860 (and is now known as the Turin shroud). Its charm lies in its Flamboyant architecture, Renaissance stained glass and *trompe-l'œil* painted vaults.

The country house known as **Les Charmettes** ⊙ was where Mme de Warens and Jean-Jacques Rousseau *(qv)* lived from 1736 to 1742.

⊙ ►► Vieille ville★; Château★; Musée Savoisien★ – prehistory, religious art, regional ethnography; Église St-Pierre de Lémenc – crypt.

Château de CHAMBORD★★★

Map p 6 – Michelin map 64 south of folds 7, 8 or 238 fold 3
Green Guide Châteaux of the Loire

The first of France's great classical palaces, **Chambord** ⊙ *(1/2 hour)* stands in a vast park enclosed by a 32km – 20 mile wall. Beyond stretches the forest of Sologne, teeming with the game which the rulers of France have long loved to hunt. At the age of 21, François I had just returned in triumph from his victory over the Swiss at Marignano which had given him possession of the Duchy of Milan. Dissatisfied with the old royal residence at Blois in spite of the improvements he had made, he had a vision of a dream castle to be built four leagues away on the forest edge. Leonardo da Vinci may have helped with the plans for this fabulous edifice; its feudal keep and corner towers belied its purpose as a palace of pleasure and status symbol for a Renaissance prince. The château was begun in 1519; later Philibert Delorme, Jean Bullant and the great Mansart all worked on it.

Hardly had Chambord started to rise from its foundations when the king suffered defeat and captivity at Pavia in 1525. On his return to France he judged it more suitable for a monarch to live close to his capital, at either Fontainebleau or St-Germain-en-Laye.

The château's double staircase is justly famous for its interlocking spirals opening on to internal loggias and for its vaults adorned with salamanders, François' crest. The extraordinary roof terrace was where the king and his entourage spent much of their time watching tournaments and festivals or the start and return of the hunt; its nooks and crannies lent themselves to the confidences, intrigues and assignations of courtly life, played out against this fantastic background of pepperpot turrets, chimney stacks, dormers peeping from the roofs, false windows embellished with shells, all decorated with inset slatework and dominated by the splendid lantern.

CHAMONIX-MONT-BLANC★★★

Population 9 700
Map p 11 – Michelin map 74 folds 8, 9 or 244 fold 21
Green Guide Alpes du Nord (in French)
Town plan in the current Michelin Red Guide France

Chamonix is France's mountaineering capital. It lies at the foot of the famous 3 000m – 10 000ft Chamonix Needles (Aiguilles de Chamonix) at a point where the glacial valley of the Arve widens out. All around are the high mountains of the Mont Blanc Massif; this is the most renowned of the massifs of the French Alps *(qv)*, because of its dramatic relief, crystalline rocks and glacial morphology. The dome of the great White Mountain is visible from the town.

The tongue of the 7km – 4 mile long Glacier des Bossons hangs 500m – 1 650ft above the valley on the approach to Chamonix.

The Geneva naturalist **Horace Benedict de Saussure** based himself here in the course of his scientific studies in Savoy. In 1760, he offered a reward for the first ascent of Mont Blanc. On 8 August 1786 Dr Michel Paccard and Jacques Balmat reached the summit, thereby inaugurating the age of mountaineering... as well as the development of the town as an Alpine resort.

EXCURSIONS

★★★ **Aiguille du Midi** ⊘ – *By two cableways. Allow 5 hours.* The **panorama**★★★, especially from the central peak (3 842m – 12 605ft), is staggering, taking in the snowy splendours of the high mountains, Mont Blanc, Mont-Maudit, the Grandes Jorasses, and the dome of the Goûter whose buttresses are buried in 30m – 100ft of ice. The domes and other rounded summits are of granite (Mont Blanc, Peuterey, Goûter), while the jagged shapes of the needles and spikes and the sharp ridges separating the snow-filled gullies are of schistitic rocks (Drus, Grandes Jorasses).

The **Vallée Blanche** ⊘, also known as the Giant's Glacier (Glacier du Géant), can be reached by taking the cablecar to Pointe Helbronner. From here can be seen the glacial cirques with their flanks worn down by the incessant attacks of the ice. The snow builds up in the cirques, hardens to form *névé* (a granular substance, half-snow, half-ice), then becomes a slowly-moving crystalline mass of ice, fissuring into crevasses, dividing into ice pinnacles *(séracs)* and scooping out the valley as it descends. It is in this way that the glaciers of the Géant and Mont-Blanc-de-Tacul form the upper part of the Mer de Glace.

Dru rock-pinnacles, Chamonix

A. Fournier/SCOPE

★★ **Mer de Glace** ⊘ – *2 1/2 hours by rack railway and cablecar.* The view from the upper station of the railway built in 1908 takes in the whole of this world-famous "sea of ice". The glacier is 14km – 9 miles long, in places 400m – 1 300ft thick, and moves 90m – 300ft a year. The rocky material it carries with it scores and scratches the mountain walls to either side as well as giving the glacier its characteristic rather grimy appearance (as the ice evaporates it is left on the surface). At the foot of the glacier this material is deposited, forming a terminal moraine.

Beyond, the eye is led from one soaring peak to another offering one of the most beautiful **panorama**★★★ in the region; the Grand-Charmoz, the Grépon, Blaitière, the Tacul, Pointe Helbronner, Dent du Géant, Grandes Jorasses, the Drus, the Aiguille Verte du Montenvers.

⊘ ►► Summit of the **Brévent**★★★; La Flégère viewpoint★★; Summit of the Aiguille des Grands-Montets★★★; Bellevue★★ (Les Houches) and the Nid d'Aigle★★ (glacier de Bionnassay – leave from St-Gervais-les-Bains).

Château de CHANTILLY★★★

Map p 6 – Michelin map 106 fold 8
Green Guide Flanders, Picardy and the Paris Region
Town plan in the current Michelin Red Guide France

A synonym for elegance, Chantilly evokes wonderful art collections, a great park and forest, and the cult of the horse as well as the château itself.

Château ⊘ – Anne de Montmorency, the great Constable of France who served six monarchs (from Louis XII to Charles IX), had a Renaissance castle built here in 1528. The foundations of an earlier building (1386) were reused by Pierre Chambiges. The finished building filled Charles V with admiration.

In 1560 the architect Jean Bullant designed a charming little château (Petit Château) to the south of the main building.

The Great Condé *(qv)* and his descendants later made the state rooms of the Petit Château into their living quarters; today, there is much to delight the eye, including Rococo woodwork, manuscripts, incunabula, silver caskets, icons, and, in the bedroom of Monsieur le Prince (the title given to the reigning prince of Condé), a chest of drawers by Riesener. The greatest treasure is in the Library (Cabinet des Livres); this is the **Limbourg** brothers' sumptuously illuminated *Book of Hours for the Duke of Berry (Les Très Riches Heures du Duc de Berry)* of about 1415, completed 60 years later by Jean Colombe (on display in reproduction).

Henri II of Bourbon-Condé acquired Chantilly through his marriage to Charlotte de Montmorency. Their son Louis II of Bourbon, known as the Great Condé, employed the men of talent of the time: Le Nôtre, who laid out the park and gardens (where the ornamental canals and their fountains so impressed Louis XIV that he determined to reproduce them on an even grander scale at Versailles), François Mansart, who redesigned the principal façade (thereby wiping out Chambiges' work) and the layout of the rooms, and Vatel, his major domo, who killed himself at a banquet, supposedly because the fish course had not been on time. At the time of the French Revolution, the château was dismantled to first floor level, the Petit Château was ruined and the park laid waste.

On his return from exile Louis-Joseph de Condé set about putting his house and grounds back into order. On his death, the estate passed into the hands of the Duke of Aumale (Henri of Orléans, the fifth son of Louis-Philippe), who rebuilt the great edifice between 1875-83 in a neo-Renaissance style, bequeathing to the Institut de France what was now a palace, mausoleum and museum.

The château houses a **museum**★★ (manuscripts, furniture, paintings, sculpture...) whose wealth would prove difficult to rival today.

★★ **Grandes Écuries** – These were built in 1721 by Jean Aubert for Louis-Henri of Bourbon, the Great Condé's great-grandson. Much admired in its time, it is the finest example of 18C building at Chantilly to have come down to us. The stables house the **Musée vivant du Cheval et du Poney**★ ⊙, which has stalls from the time of the Duke of Aumale, historic harnessing, costumes, and all kinds of objects associated with equitation. Riding displays take place in the central rotunda. More than 3 000 horses are stabled and trained in and around Chantilly; race-meetings and hunts both perpetuate the tradition begun on 15 May 1834 when France's first great official race-meeting was held, and maintain Chantilly's reputation as the country's thoroughbred capital.

⊙ ►► Park★★; Jardin anglais.

CHAOURCE★

Population 1 031
Map p 6 – Michelin map 61 fold 17 or 241 fold 10
Green Guide Champagne (in French)

Chaource lies at the centre of that part of the old province of Champagne known as "Champagne humide" (Champagne wetlands), to distinguish it from the drought-ridden chalklands of "Champagne crayeuse" to the west (p 19). The village has a particularly interesting Gothic **church**★ with a 12C chancel and a nave of the 15C and 16C.

Restored after war damage, the church is a veritable museum of regional sculpture, some of which has come here from churches no longer in use. Much of the work has a touching simplicity and truthfulness. Some of it is exceptional, like the 15C Man of Sorrows, the 16C (but still Gothic in feeling) St Martha (in the Lady Chapel – Chapelle de la Vierge), the **Entombment**★★, the Crib and the Pietà in the Paradise Chapel to the north (Chapelle du Paradis).

CHARLEVILLE-MÉZIÈRES

Conurbation 67 213
Map p 7 – Michelin map 53 fold 18 or 241 fold 10
Green Guide Champagne (in French)
Town plan in the current Red Guide France

Here are two towns in one. Mézières is the administrative and military town, evolving from the 10C onward at the foot of the château guarding the isthmus formed by the triple meander of the Meuse to the south; Charleville is the commercial centre, built in the 17C within the broader central meander.

Arthur Rimbaud was born here in 1854; in his revolt against society, this great symbolist poet penetrated the realm of the subconscious (Bateau ivre – The Drunken Boat), anticipating the surrealists' attempts at spontaneous writing.

★★ **Place Ducale** – Like the rest of the town, this square was built in 16 years from 1612. Its designer was Clément Métezeau, the younger brother of Louis Métezeau who completed the Place des Vosges in Paris in the same year. So there is a strong similarity of style between these two important examples of Renaissance town planning: careful geometry of the elevations, use of brick with stone dressings, unity achieved by the regular design of the arcades. Louis XIII pediments and bull's-eye windows have been reinstated in some of the buildings. On the west side of the square, the Law Courts (Palais de Justice) and the Town Hall (Hôtel de ville) are of later date and much less interesting in spite of their pilasters and projecting balconies.

In the centre of the square is the statue of Charles of Gonzaga who managed to get exemption from salt tax for the town he had just founded and which bears his name.

CHARTRES★★★

Population 39 595
Map p 6 – Michelin map 106 fold 37
Green Guide Flanders, Picardy and the Paris Region
Town plan in the current Michelin Red Guide France

Chartres' magnificent cathedral, the "Acropolis of France" (Rodin), still beckons to the pilgrim far off across the endless cornfields of the Beauce.

The area was occupied by the Carnutes and druids once worshipped here; there is also evidence of the pagan cult of a holy spring, and possibly also of a mother-goddess, whom the first missionaries may have christianised as a forerunner of the Virgin Mary.

Old Chartres★ lies at the point where the Eure cuts into the plain of the Beauce; its picturesque streets evoke the bustling activity of a medieval city of merchants and craftsmen. The banks of the Eure were once alive with the manifold trades of the riverside, millers, tanners, curriers, cobblers, fullers... Today, the old mill-races and laundry-houses have been restored, and a number of 17C houses have kept their embossed doorways topped by a bull's-eye. The most attractive townscape is to be found in the St-André quarter, by the riverbanks, and in Rue des Écuyers and Rue du Cygne. Loëns Granary (Grenier de Loëns) is a fine 12C building which once housed the tithes of grain and wine.

Chartres attracted pilgrims at an early date, first of all to Our Lady of the Underground Chapel (Notre-Dame-de-Sous-Terre), then to the cathedral which Bishop Fulbert built in the 11C but which was burnt down in 1194.

★★★ **Cathédrale Notre-Dame** ⊘ – Reconstruction began immediately and was completed in the short space of 25 years. The north and south porches were added only 20 years later and the building consequently has a unity of style possessed by few other Gothic churches. Pilgrims have now been coming here for almost eight centuries to fill the vast transept and the great chancel with its double ambulatory, and to admire the 175 representations of the Virgin Mary which adorn the cathedral. The most celebrated pilgrim was probably the writer Charles Péguy, who came here in the years before the First World War. Chartres inspired this socialist and unorthodox Catholic with an essentially medieval vision of a renewed France, whose lasting force is seen in the young peoples' pilgrimages which his writings initiated and which still take place today.

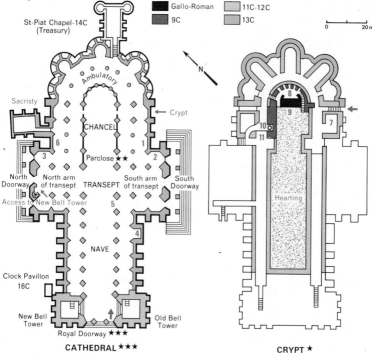

■ Gallo-Roman	▨ 11C-12C
■ 9C	▨ 13C

St-Piat Chapel-14C (Treasury)

Sacristy

Ambulatory

← Crypt

CHANCEL

Parclose ★★

North Doorway — North arm of transept — TRANSEPT — South arm of transept — South Doorway

Access to New Bell Tower

NAVE

Clock Pavillon 16C

New Bell Tower — Royal Doorway ★★★ — Old Bell Tower

CATHEDRAL ★★★

Hearting

Crypte St-Lubin (8)
Gallo-Roman wall (9)
Puits des Saints-Forts (10)
Chapelle Notre-Dame-de-Sous-Terre (11)
Chapelle St-Martin (7)

CRYPT ★

1 Notre-Dame-de-Belle-Verrière
2 St Fulbert's window
3 Window of Peace
4 Chapelle Vendôme
5 Organ
6 Vierge du Pilier

7 Chapelle St-Martin
8 Crypte St-Lubin
9 Gallo-Roman wall
10 Puits des Saints-Forts
11 Chapelle Notre-Dame-de-Sous-Terre

The new cathedral raised the Transitional Gothic style *(p 235)* to new levels of achievement. The bays of the nave, previously square in plan, are now oblong and have sexpartite vaults; the arches of arcades and windows are more pointed; a round opening is inserted in the space above the highest windows; the structural functions of galleries are taken over by flying buttresses and a narrow triforium (still windowless) forms an inspection gallery ⊙. All this signifies the emergence of the Lanceolate style.

Gothic verticality reigns outside too, but the architect wisely kept two Romanesque masterworks, the Old Bell Tower (Clocher vieux) of 1145, a marvel of audacity and lightness, and the Royal Doorway, **Portail Royal★★★**, of the west front, with its long-bodied but intensely expressive sculpted figures.

The cathedral's interior is subtly lit by its superb **stained glass★★★** which covers a total area of 2 700m² – 25 000sq ft and depicts 5 000 figures. 45 of the windows were donated by the city's guilds. Most of them date from the 12C and 13C and are the greatest achievement of this art form. "Chartres blue" is famous for its clarity and depth; its full range can best be seen in the wonderful Blue Madonna (Notre Dame de la Belle-Verrière) Window *(first window on the south side of the ambulatory)*. In 1964, the American Society of Architects gave a window *(in the south transept)* and in 1971 the German Friends of the Cathedral did likewise *(north transept)*.

⊙ ►► Musée des Beaux-Arts – enamels★; Église St-Pierre★ – stained glass★.

Massif de La CHARTREUSE★★

Map p 11 – Michelin map 74 fold 15 or 77 fold 5 or 244 folds 28, 29
Green Guide Alpes du Nord (in French)

The relatively low, fir-clad Chartreuse upland is bounded by the narrow transverse valleys in which Grenoble and Chambéry are sited and by the Graisivaudan lowland. In appearance it is not unlike the subalpine country to the north, with its rugged summits and deep valleys formed from much folded and faulted beds of Jurassic limestone.

It was in this isolated spot *(désert)* that St Bruno founded his monastery in 1084; it became the mother church of the celebrated Carthusian Order.

★★★ **Charmant-Som** – *1 1/2 hours Rtn on foot.* Panorama taking in the Chamechaude peak, the Guiers-Mort valley and the site of the monastery in its deep valley.

★★ **Pas du Frou** – A deep ravine hollowed out by the Guiers-Vif.

★★ **Col du Granier** – This great rock-wall has been formed by erosion at the base of a syncline.

★★ **Bec du Margain** – The summit of the Bec rises 820m – 2 700ft above the Graisivaudan, the best-known section of the Subalpine Trench which runs between the Central Alps and the Pre-Alps. First formed in ancient seas, then remodelled by the action of the glaciers and filled with the material brought down by the Isère, this busy valley is an important communication route. Its northwest flanks next to the Chartreuse are given over to farmland and vineyards, while the far side, under the shadow of the Belledonne, has a harsher, industrial character, with paper, chemical and engineering works and power stations. It was here, at Lancey, in 1891, that Aristide Berges converted the hydraulic installations of a paper-mill to the production of "white coal" – hydro-electric power. The **view** from here includes, from right to left, the Vercors, the Grandes Rousses, the Belledonne uplands, Mont-Blanc and the Bauges.

CHÂTILLON-SUR-SEINE★

Population 6 862
Map p 7 – Michelin map 65 fold 8 or 243 fold 2 – Green Guide Burgundy Jura

Close to the Celtic oppidum on Mount Lassois near Vix *(7km – 4 1/2 miles north)*, Châtillon occupied a strategic location on the ancient north-south trade route. It was here that the Seine ceased to be navigable; as a result, the place developed all the facilities that transhipment needed, and grew prosperous on the merchandise being exchanged between Cornwall and Etruria – amber, tin, coral, ceramics...

★★ **The Treasure of Vix** ⊙ – The first floor of the **museum** houses grave goods found in the tomb of a 30-year old queen who was buried at the very beginning of the 5C BC. They give some idea of the quality of material life of the elite of the time, who surrounded themselves with fine objects imported from Greece and Italy; the exhibits include a huge bronze vase, a masterpiece of Greek metalwork, Etruscan vases, gold jewellery (a diadem), and Gallic ironwork.

►► Source of the Douix★.

Château de CHAVANIAC-LAFAYETTE

Map p 9 – Michelin map 76 fold 6 or 239 fold 33
Green Guide Auvergne-Rhône Valley

Located on the lower slopes of the Livradois uplands overlooking the Allier valley, this **château** ⊘ *(3/4 hour)* is where Marie-Joseph-Gilbert, marquis de La Fayette was born on 6 September 1757. Here, the story of Franco-American friendship must take precedence over architectural considerations.

As a young lieutenant of 19, **La Fayette** was well aware of the conflict brewing up in Britain's American colonies, and engineered his release from service. A month later, the news of the Declaration of Independence reached Paris; Lafayette, filled with enthusiasm for the cause of the American rebels, set off on a self-financed expedition (he was immensely rich) to support their cause. On his arrival at Georgetown in 1777, he won Washington's friendship and fought at his side. In October, the victory at Saratoga rallied the French government to their cause; Louis XVI and **Benjamin Franklin** signed a treaty of alliance and French forces were dispatched across the Atlantic. On 17 October 1781, the Battle of Yorktown was fought; the victors were Washington, Lafayette and America itself, whose independence was recognised by the Treaty of Versailles signed on 3 September 1783. Lafayette was back in France again in time for the Revolution in which he played a leading role, at the same time as his friend Washington was elected President of the United States.

The château was acquired in 1916 by the Lafayette Memorial Inc. It houses rural furniture of the 17C and 18C, and above all many moving mementoes of the two great men.

Château de CHENONCEAU★★★

Map p 5 – Map 64 fold 16 or 238 fold 14 – Green Guide Châteaux of the Loire

Chenonceau *(1)* ⊘ *(2 hours)* is a jewel of Renaissance architecture built 1513-21 on the site of a fortified mill on the River Cher by Thomas Bohier, François I's treasurer. It is a rectangular building with corner-towers and bull's-eye dormer-windows decorated with cherubs. Over the years the place has been in the charge of six women, of whom three marked it strongly with their personality.

Catherine Briçonnet was the wife of Thomas Bohier. In his absence she supervised much of the building work. It is to her that we owe the central hall giving on to all the other rooms; its axial vault, broken by keystones, is a masterpiece. Another innovation is the introduction into the Loire Valley of an Italian staircase, that is, one that substitutes ramps for Gothic spirals, and is consequently much better adapted for receptions. However, here the returns are still curved and provided with steps.

In 1556 **Diane de Poitiers** commissioned Philibert Delorme, who had previously worked for her at Anet, to design the flower garden *(to the east)* as well as the bridge across the Cher.

Three years later, on the death of Henri II, **Catherine de' Medici** humiliated the former favourite by forcing her to exchange Chenonceau for Chaumont. Later, she added the extra two storeys to the bridge, laid out the gardens to the west and gave the windows their elaborate pediments.

There is much to see within the château; a fine fireplace by **Jean Goujon** (in the Diane de Poitiers room), the Library of 1521, the ceiling of the Green Cabinet, the portrait of Diane by Primaticcio, the tapestries and mantlepiece of the Louis XIV Salon, a fine Renaissance creation with its wealth of scrolls, baskets of fruit, cornucopias and fantastic beasts.

CHERBOURG

Conurbation 92 045
Map p 5 – Map 54 fold 2 or 231 fold 2 – Green Guide Normandy
Town plan in the current Michelin Red Guide France

At the very tip of the Cotentin peninsula, Cherbourg is a naval base and port for transatlantic ships and for ferries on the cross-Channel and Channel Islands routes. The military architect Vauban himself had appreciated the "bold location" of Cherbourg as early as the 17C, but without protection from the action of the waves the potential of the site could not be exploited. It was Captain de La Bretonnière, who first had the idea of constructing a great breakwater. Work began in 1776, and Louis XVI himself presided over the lowering into the sea of one of the giant timber cones filled with rubble and mortar, with which the dike was to be built. But the waves destroyed the work as fast as it was finished. The struggle lasted

---

(1) The village is spelt with an x, the castle without.

for three-quarters of a century before the breakwater was able to withstand the fury of the sea. In 1869 the first transatlantic liner dropped anchor in the roadstead. The military port, commissioned by Napoléon I, was officially inaugurated by Napoléon III in 1858.

Frogmen at work – The capture of Cherbourg on 26 and 27 June 1944 should have marked a decisive phase in the Battle of Normandy. But the 7th American Corps found that the harbour had been wrecked and sown with mines. With the help of Royal Navy frogmen, the port was cleared of every last wreck and mine and the remaining servicable installations immediately put into operation, thereby easing the load on the artificial Mulberry harbours at Arromanches to the east in the vital task of supplying the Allied armies.

It was at Cherbourg that PLUTO came ashore. The Pipe Line Under The Ocean ran from Dungeness in Kent and from 12 August 1944 brought essential fuel for the invasion armies.

From the Fort de Roule, where there is the **Musée de la Libération** ⊘, a fine **panorama★** unfolds over the varied activities of the port.

Château de CHEVERNY★★★

Map p 5 – Map 64 fold 17 or 238 fold 15 – Green Guide Châteaux of the Loire

Cheverny ⊘ *(3/4 hour)* was built between 1604-34 with that simplicity and distinction characteristic of the classical architecture of the reigns of Henri IV and Louis XIII.

The main façade is built in stone from **Bourré** *(28km – 17 miles southwest)* which whitens and grows harder with age. The elevation is strictly symmetrical, extending to either side of the well containing the staircase, and terminated by massive corner pavilions with square domes. The prominent slate roofs are in Louis XIII style, pierced with mansards and bull's-eye windows. The first-floor windows are crowned with scrolls; between them are medallions of Roman emperors (Julius Caesar in the central pediment). The elegant doorway is adorned with two concentric collars, outside, that of the Order of the Holy Ghost, inside, that of the Order of St Michael. The state rooms, served by a stately Louis XIII ramped staircase with massive balustrades and rich sculptural decoration, contain a fine collection of furniture from the 17C to the 19C.

Main façade of the Château de Cheverny

CHINON★★

Population 8 627
Map p 5 – Michelin map 67 fold 9 or 232 fold 34
Green Guide Châteaux of the Loire – Town plan in the current Michelin Red Guide France

Chinon occupies a sunny site on the Vienne surrounded by the fertile Veron countryside, and known for the mildness of its climate.

In 1494, **François Rabelais**, son of a Chinon lawyer, was born at **La Devinière** 8km – 5 miles to the southwest. He studied medicine at Montpellier and then practised at Lyons. Under the guise of ribaldry, he imparted to the awakening middle classes a healthy contempt for pedantry and false culture, and a respect for a social morality founded on the rectitude of free and upright men.

★★ **Old Chinon** - The town, Joan of Arc's Ville-Fort (fortified town) has kept its medieval and Renaissance appearance. The old gabled houses with corner turrets and the 16C and 17C mansions, most of them in white tufa, make up a most evocative townscape.

The main axis is formed by the Rue Voltaire, formerly Haute-St-Maurice. Along it are ranged: the Gothic dwelling where Richard Lionheart is supposed to have died in 1199 and where the States-General assembled in 1421 (now the museum), the Hôtel du Gouvernement with 17C arcades in its courtyard, the Palais du Bailliage, and the 16C Hôtel Poirier de Beauvais.

At the **Grand Carroi**★★ (Crossroads) the oldest houses of all press closely together. On her arrival from Vaucouleurs on Sunday 6

François Rabelais

Musée des Beaux-Arts, Orléans

March 1429, Joan of Arc is thought to have used the lip of the well-head here to dismount from her horse. The following day she picked out the Dauphin hiding amongst his courtiers, and declared, "You are the heir of France and true son of the king, Lieutenant of the King of Heaven who is King of France", a touching scene calculated to still the Dauphin's worries about his legitimacy. From here, Joan was sent to Poitiers. Back in Chinon again, she was equipped and given a troop of soldiers and sallied forth to meet her extraordinary and tragic destiny.

★★ **Château** ⊙ - The spur overlooking the town was the site of a Gallic oppidum, then of a fortress, long before Henry II of England (born at Le Mans in 1133) built the present castle to protect Anjou from Capetian designs. The castle was taken by Philippe Auguste in 1205 from John Lackland; it subsequently became a royal residence, was strengthened by Charles VII, but then abandoned by the court at the end of the 15C and gradually dismantled.

It was in the castle that the first meeting took place between Charles VII and Joan of Arc, here too that Agnes Sorel stayed and here that the leading Templars were imprisoned in 1308. On 10 December 1498 the Papal legate Ludovico Borgia came to the castle to hand Louis XII the Bull annulling his marriage to Joan of France, thereby allowing him to marry Anne of Brittany (qv).

The remains of the castle include, to the east, St George's Fort (Fort St-Georges), watching over the most vulnerable approach, the Middle Castle (Château du Milieu), which has a 14C clock tower, the royal apartments and gardens giving a fine view over the old town, and finally the Coudray Fort (Fort de Coudray) at the far end of the spur.

EXCURSIONS

★ **Champigny-sur-Veude** - *15km - 9 miles south.* Erected in the first half of the 16C by Louis of Bourbon and his son, the château of Champigny was demolished in 1635 on the orders of Richelieu, who felt that it might outshine his own pile, then a-building not far away. It was used by him as a source of materials, and today only some outbuildings and the chapel remain.

★ **Sainte-Chapelle** ⊙ - With its two side galleries the St Louis Chapel is a jewel of Renaissance architecture. Toussaint Chesneau's splendid porch of 1570 has antique scrolls, strapwork, and pilasters, as well as a terrace, the whole treated in a manner which anticipates classicism.

The chapel is lit by splendid Renaissance **stained glass**★★ of 1538-61, attributed to the brothers Pinaigrier, master-craftsmen of Tours, trained in the school of Jean Fouquet and Bourdichon. Some of the glass may be from a Bourbonnais workshop. The subjects represented include 34 portraits of the Bourbon-Montpensier family, episodes from the life of Louis IX, and scenes of the Passion. The lustre of the glass, above all of the Prussian blues with a hint of reddish-browns, has no equal.

★ **Richelieu** ⊙ - *25km - 15 1/2 miles south of Chinon.* The town built for Cardinal Richelieu by Lemercier (1631-42) is a rare example of classical town planning. Little remains of Richelieu's great château planned as the centrepiece of the vast park.

⊙ ►► Musée de l'hôtel de ville; steam railway (between Chinon and Richelieu).

CLERMONT-FERRAND★★

Conurbation 254 416
Map p 9 – Michelin map 73 fold 14 or 239 folds 19, 20
Green Guide Auvergne-Rhône Valley
Town plan in the current Michelin Red Guide France

The **site★★** of Clermont is unique; the old town, including the cathedral, is built on and from a volcano, whose black lava makes for an unusual townscape. To the north are the plateaux of Chanturgue and Les Côtes, once the site of a Gallic oppidum, and an example of the phenomenon known as relief inversion *(qv)* which has protected them from erosion and left them standing out from the surrounding country. To the west are the summits of the Puys *(qv)*, the mountain range which gives Clermont its incomparable setting, perhaps best viewed from the Place de la Poterne with its pretty **Amboise Fountain★** (Fontaine d'Amboise) of 1515.

Vercingétorix – By 58 BC, the security of the Roman Empire was no longer adequately secured simply by the possession of Gallia Narbonensis (corresponding roughly to modern Provence); all Gaul, with its agricultural produce and its trade routes for tin and amber, was to be the prize. Julius Caesar grasped at it, eager for glory, and, in the March of 52 BC marched his legions up to the gates of the great oppidum of the Arverni (the Celts who gave their name to the Auvergne). But within the space of a few days he met with a surprising defeat, which forced him to retreat through Berry, Burgundy and the Jura towards Italy. The victor of this encounter was the Gallic chieftain Vercingétorix (72-46 BC), whose spirited equestrian statue by Bartholdi stands at one end of Clermont's Place de Jaude. Before the summer was over, however, Caesar returned, this time winning a decisive battle, the site of which is still not certain. Vercingétorix had to wait six years in the Mamertine prison in Rome for execution of the sentence of death by strangulation meted out to him by Caesar.

The First Crusade – On 28 November 1095 Pope Urban II, a former Clunaic monk, closed the Synod which had been held here at Clermont because of the stable conditions prevailing in the province. In the presence of a great crowd of archbishops, bishops, abbots, barons, knights and common people, he called for the reconquest of the Holy Land. Over the century following the Frankish, Norman and Danish invasions, the population of the Auvergne had grown to such an extent

Portrait of Pascal (in the Musée du Ranquet)

J. D. Sudres/SCOPE

that the province could afford to see so many ardent crusaders depart with the ringing cry "It is God's will!" *(Dieu le veut!)*; countless of them were to perish before Godfrey of Bouillon succeeded in taking Jerusalem three years later.

Blaise Pascal – To the southwest of the cathedral a slab marks the birthplace of this writer and thinker of genius, a man whose temperament made him quite unable to accept received ideas. Though he was in poor health, his acute intelligence and interest in science showed itself at an early age; at 11 he was studying the laws of acoustics; at 12 he rediscovered, on his own, Euclid's 32nd proposition; at 16 he wrote his essay on conics which astounded Descartes among others, and at 19 he invented an adding machine (on display in the Ranquet Museum – Musée de Ranquet). Subsequently he developed the idea of a hydraulic press, formulated the principle of hydrostatics and anticipated the probability theory.

At 33, after a mystical experience two years previously, he put his literary talents to work in the service of Jansenism. At 34, he wrote his *Thoughts (Pensées)* which has been called the greatest literary work in French of the 17C. "The heart has its reasons that reason knows not" Blaise Pascal 1623-1662.

28 September 1665 – 30 January 1666 (Les Grands Jours d'Auvergne) – Far removed from the seat of government, the feudal lords of the Auvergne had become petty tyrants, putting down the periodic peasant revolts with great ferocity. To overcome this indiscipline, the king's commissioners arrived in Clermont on 28 September 1665 with full powers to deal with the situation and assert royal authority.

1 360 files were opened, but since the local nobility had fled as a man as soon as the first execution had taken place, most sentences were carried out in absentia, and effigies hanged in batches of 30. There was much rejoicing, restitution of confiscated property, and razing of castles which had escaped Richelieu's attention 40 years earlier. The power of the state and the force of the king's laws now prevailed throughout the land.

The capital of the motor tyre

Two men, Aristide Barbier and Édouard Daubrée came together around 1830 to make agricultural machinery as well as gunshot, and rubber belts and tubes. In 1889, their factory was taken over by the brothers **André** and **Édouard Michelin**, the grandsons of Barbier. Building on their tradition of applying scientific method to the work of industry, the company has subsequently flourished through study of the client's real needs, scrupulous observation of reality and the consolidation of previous experience. This process has led via the detachable bicycle tyre of 1891, the car tyre of 1895, the low pressure "Confort" tyre of 1923, the "Metalic" of 1937 (its steel-reinforced casing helped heavy road transport come of age), the radial tyre of 1946 (given the designation "X" in 1949), to today's achievements, with the introduction in the early 90's of the new Michelin Energy tyre. This new "green" tyre technology – based on reduced rolling resistance – will enable the driver to make considerable savings on fuel.

★★ **Basilique Notre-Dame du Port** (FV) – This is the finest of the larger Romanesque churches of the Lower Auvergne, unforgettable in its beautiful simplicity. It was built around 1150 over a crypt of the 11C. Its south doorway differs from those of Quercy and Burgundy in the clear differentiation of its subjects, in spite of their having suffered damage. To the left of the door stands the figure of Isiah, to the right that of John the Baptist. In the typically Auvergnat five-sided lintel is a highly-controlled, hierarchical composition, and above that, in the tympanum, a Christ in Majesty flanked by Seraphim. The south side of the building is also characteristic of the Romanesque style of the Auvergne, with its great buttressing arches, the three-bayed blind arcading and the polychrome stonework adorning the transept. The east end was much restored in the 19C.

Inside, both the structure itself and the materials from which it is built confirm the impression of robustness. The great arches at the crossing, though descended from the masterworks of Carolingian times, surpass them greatly in scale. Relieved by short arcades and patterned stonework, the high cross-walls

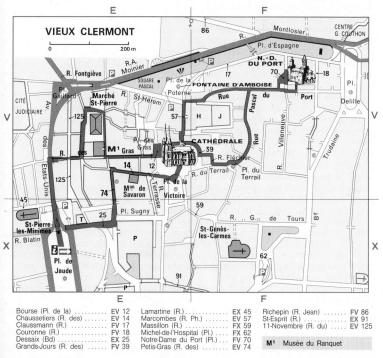

support the splendid dome on pendentives, best seen from the steps up to the ambulatory.

The small, raised **chancel**★★★, admirably proportioned, is divided from the ambulatory by eight slender columns; their **capitals**★★, together with those of the wall of the ambulatory, are among the finest in Auvergne because of their good state of preservation, their fascinating subjects, and their expressiveness. In the crypt is an ancient, possibly Celto-Gallic well, together with a Black Virgin, a copy of a Byzantine icon, which has been worshipped here since the 13C.

Rue Pascal (FV) – Lined with lava-built residences of somewhat severe aspect, this is one of the typical streets of **old Clermont**★★. No 22 has a façade in rusticated stone and a wrought-iron balcony, and a lava-patterned rose on the floor of the hall. No 4 (Hôtel de Chazerat) has an oval courtyard with Ionic pilasters. In the Place du Terrail is a pretty 17C fountain.

★★ **Cathédrale Notre-Dame-de-l'Assomption** (EFV) – The visitor coming here from Notre-Dame-du-Port is immediately struck by the revolutionary changes in architectural style which had occurred in the relatively short period of 100 years which separates the two buildings. The cathedral was begun in 1248 by Jean Deschamps, something along the lines of the new cathedrals of the north of France and recalling the High Gothic style. It symbolises the extension of Capetian power into the Auvergne. It has unusual terraces which hide the ambulatory and is built in sombre Volvic lava – its strength allowed the pillars to be more slender than usual. The west front, spires and first two bays of the nave are the work of **Viollet-le-Duc** in 1865.

The **stained glass**★★ medallions of the 12C-15C are copies of those in the Sainte-Chapelle in Paris. The warm tones of red and violet in the rose windows of the transepts are particularly striking.

St George's Chapel has a wall-painting showing a frieze of animals and the martyrdom of this patron saint of crusaders. In the axial chapel is a Romanesque Madonna, contemporary with those of Marsat (qv) and Orcival, and probably the descendant of the 10C Golden Madonna of Stephen II which was destroyed at the time of the French Revolution. **Treasure**★ ⊙.

⊙ ►► Old Montferrand★★; Église St-Léger★ (fortified church at Royat); Musée des Beaux-Arts.

CLUNY★

Population 4 430
Map p 9 – Michelin map 69 fold 19 or 243 fold 39 – Green Guide Burgundy Jura
Town plan in the current Michelin Red Guide France

The conditions for the future renown and prosperity of the great **Abbaye de Cluny**★★ ⊙ (1 hour) existed at the very moment of its foundation.

The abbey, founded in 910, lay deep in the forests of this frontier zone, far removed from the centres of power in either France or Germany; to the west the Carolingian king of France, Charles III, was absorbed by problems with Norse invaders, to the east, Ludwig IV was still an inexperienced adolescent, much weakened by rivalries between his barons and by troublesome Hungarians and Norsemen. The abbey's independence was absolute; it was subject to no authority other than that of the Pope himself; at the time when the great feudal estates were being broken up and seigneurial rights were crumbling, it answered – like its daughter houses and other dependencies – to no one but its elected abbot. In an unstable and entirely unscrupulous world, it represented in exemplary fashion the ascetic ideals of St Benedict. It thus became a powerful instrument for the Papacy in its own domains, in the struggle to maintain its authority in the face of the barons of Latium and in its ambitions for the reform of the Church.

Cluny's development was rapid, its prestige immense, and its influence pre-eminent at the very moment when Western culture was taking shape. In under a century, the abbey had amassed considerable political power as well as much property; already there were 1 184 daughter and dependent houses grouped in "provinces", but organised in a strictly hierarchical fashion. One hundred and fifty years later their numbers had risen to 3 000, scattered all over Europe. For two and a half centuries this capital of monasticism found leaders of exceptional calibre (St Mayeul, Saint Hugh, Peter the Venerable), some of whom ruled for a fruitful term of up to 60 years. The government of such an empire was not of course without problems of conformity to its Rule and to its ideal of poverty. The fight against temptation required qualities of intellect and will compared with which the struggle against external threats was but a minor affair. The decline of the order began in the 13C, but its prosperity lasted until the 18C.

Abbey Church – Started by St Hugh in 1088, it was completed in 1130 under Peter the Venerable. Its destruction was begun in 1798 and continued until 1823. All that remains of the narthex are the lower parts of two towers; of the nave and its aisles nothing at all; of the five bell-towers, the one known as "the **Holy Water**"★★ (Eau *bénite)* a superb octagon, and another known as the Clock Tower; of the great transept, the south arm with its two chapels and 32m – 105ft high octagonal vault; of the minor transept, the Bourbon chapel with sculpted heads of the Prophets.

Abbey buildings – Rebuilt in the 18C.

Flour store – Reduced in height in the 18C. It has a fine timber roof (13C) built like the hull of a boat and eight capitals from the abbey.

Ⓥ ►► Cluny: Musée Ochier★ – *sculpture.*

EXCURSION

★★ **Château de Cormatin** Ⓥ – *13km – 8 miles to the north.* The château *(4km – 2 1/2 miles north of Taizé),* probably built by Jacques II Androuet du Cerceau, is a good example of the Henri IV style (late 16C – early 17C): the monumental gates framed by antique orders, the basement built of stone and the windows decorated with mouldings. The mannerist style which evolved in the literary salons under Louis XIII (1610-43) reached its peak with the gilding and the lapis-lazuli decoration of the **St Cecilia Room**★★★.

COGNAC

Population 19 528

Map p 8 – Michelin map 72 fold 12 or 233 fold 28 – Green Guide Atlantic Coast
Town plan in the current Michelin Red Guide France

For many years Cognac was a river port on the calm waters of the Charente, exporting salt – the best in the world, so said the Scandinavians – and, from the 11C, wine. In 1570, it was one of the four strongholds conceded to the Protestants under the Treaty of St-Germain.

In the streets of the old part of the town on the west bank are a number of fascinating buildings. The Grande-Rue has a fine half-timbered example dating from the 15C, the Rue Saulnier a number of 16C houses with rusticated stonework and elaborate doorways and windows, while in the Rue de l'Île d'Or is the Hôtel de l'Échevinage (House of the Magistrates), distinguished by its corner niches.

The château was rebuilt by John the Good in 1450; its riverside façade has an austere air, enlivened somewhat by the King's Balcony"of 1515, a grand loggia resting on a bracket carved in the shape of a salamander, the emblem of François I.

Ⓥ ►► *Musée du cognac. Most prestigious Cognac houses offer guided tours of their chais.*

Cognac

The Ancients were fully aware of the properties of alcohol. It was studied in 1250 by Arnaud de Villeneuve who attributed quasi-miraculous powers to it. Of all the different kinds of spirit, it is cognac which has acquired a universal reputation. It was early in the 17C that the local vintners started to distil those of their wines that travelled badly, in order to help turnover, reduce excise dues and facilitate storage. The taste for the product spread first to Holland, Scandinavia and of course the British Isles, whose long association with brandy is reflected in some of the great names of Cognac, Hine, Martell, Hennessy...

A century later the accumulated stock became the subject of speculation. In addition, it was realised that ageing improved the quality of the spirit. Cognac was first divided into regions in 1887; today they comprise Grande Champagne, Petite Champagne, Borderies, Fins Bois, Bons Bois and Bois Ordinaires, reflecting, in that order, a decreasing proportion of chalk in the soil, an increasing earthiness of taste – *goût de terroir* – and ability to mature rapidly.

The production of cognac is the result of a two-stage distillation process, using the special still of the region. The 90 000ha – 220 000 acres of vineyards yield a white wine which is light, flowery and quite acid; it takes 9 litres of it to make one of brandy. It is then kept in barrels made of porous oak from the Limoges district for at least two and a half years, during which time the brandy absorbs tannin and resins from the wood, and oxygen from the atmosphere, to which it loses 2 1/2% of its volume per annum – the "angels' portion", equivalent to 2 million bottles a year!

The making of cognac has given rise to a very distinct way of life. People here have a fine sense of irony and a love of independence which has expressed itself in revolts against salt-tax, in peasant rebellions at the time of Louis XIV and in the disturbances of the Wars of Religion *(qv);* the chais where the cognac is stored, is the repository of the greater part of a family's savings.

COLMAR★★★

Conurbation 83 816
Map p 7 – Michelin map 62 fold 19 or 87 fold 17 or 242 fold 31
Green Guide Alsace et Lorraine (in French)
Town plan in the current Michelin Red Guide France

The capital of Upper Alsace is situated at the point where the Munster valley widens out into the broad plain of the Rhine. Since the 13C the town has prospered on the proceeds of the wine trade and boasts fine monuments. More recently, industries have spread along the Logelbach Canal.

In 1834 **Frédéric Bartholdi** was born here, the patriotic sculptor responsible not only for such striking achievements as the Lion of Belfort *(qv)* or the figure of General Rapp here in Colmar, but also for the Statue of Liberty.

Between 1871-1918, when Alsace and Lorraine formed part of the German Reich, the town distinguished itself by its obstinate Frenchness. A particular irritant to authority was the Colmar writer and caricaturist Jean-Jacques Waltz (1872-1951), known as "Hansi", who was imprisoned at the outbreak of war in 1914, but escaped to enlist in the French army.

★★★ **Isenheim Altarpiece** – In the chapel of the **Musée d'Unterlinden**★★★ Ⓥ. In 1512 **Matthias Grünewald** was called to Isenheim 22km – 14 miles south of Colmar to paint this altarpiece for the chapel of the Antonites' convent. This extraordinary work should be seen, not as a collection of separate masterpieces, but as an integrated whole, conceived and executed as a programme whose logic, while still puzzling to the specialist of today, probably lies in the convent superior's particular vision of the meaning of suffering. Everything contributes to the overall effect, not only the choice of themes and their relationship to one another, but also the pose and expression of the figures, the symbolic meaning of the various themes, animals and monsters and even the use of colour. Note for example the figure of Mary Magdalen at the foot of the cross; her pose conveys both the attraction exercised over her by the figure of Christ as well as the revulsion she feels in the face of His agony. Note too the way contrast is handled, with the generally gloomy tone of the paintings shot through with flashes of light.

Grünewald's stature as one of the truly great masters of Western religious painting is fully revealed in the central panel of the altarpiece, the harrowing Crucifixion.

★★ **Old Colmar** – The heart of the old town comprises the Place de l'Ancienne Douane (Customs House Square), Rue des Marchands (Merchant Street) and Rue Mercière (Haberdasher Street). There are many picturesque old houses, with corner turrets, oriel windows and half-timbering, and balconies gay with flowers. Particularly striking are the **Maison Pfister**★★, with frescoes and medallions and a pyramidal roof, and the Old Customs House, **Ancienne Douane**★ of 1480 with a timber gallery and canted staircase tower.

    Ⓥ ► Colmar: Église des Dominicains – stained glass★ and Virgin in the Rose Bower★★; Ancien Corps de Garde★ (Old Guard House); "Little Venice"★; Maison des Têtes★; Église St-Matthieu – Crucifixion window★.

Isenheim Altarpiece (central section), Colmar

COLOMBEY-LES-DEUX-ÉGLISES

Population 660
Map p 7 – Map 61 fold 19 or 241 fold 38
Green Guide Champagne (in French)

Situated in the far south of Champagne on the borders of Burgundy and Lorraine, Colombey owes its fame to **General de Gaulle**. This great Frenchman was born in Lille in 1890; in 1933 he bought the country-house here known as **La Boisserie** ⊙ (now a museum). Having withdrawn from affairs of state in 1969, he died here on 9 November 1970.

Both the Memorial, a great cross of Lorraine dominating the village, and the general's tomb have become places of pilgrimage.

COMPIÈGNE★★★

Conurbation 57 057
Map p 6 – Map 196 fold 10
Green Guide Flanders, Picardy and the Paris Region
Town plan in the current Michelin Red Guide France

The site of Compiègne had been appreciated by the Merovingians, long before Charles the Bald built a château here in the 9C. A fortified town grew up around this nucleus. In 1429, Philip the Good *(qv)*, Duke of Burgundy, had designs on Picardy, which he hoped to incorporate into his realm by means of a joint operation with the English. The French line of defence along the Oise was reinforced on the orders of Joan of Arc; disgusted with the inertia prevailing at Sully-sur-Loire where the French Court had established itself, she had come to Compiègne on her own initiative. But on the evening of 23 May 1430, she was seized by the Burgundians. Wary of possible consequences, Philip the Good sold her on to the English; one year later she was burnt at the stake in Rouen.

★★★ **Palace** ⊙ – Compiègne had been a royal residence since the time of the later Capetians, but Louis XV was dissatisfied with the ill-assorted and crumbling buildings inherited from his great-grandfather, and in 1738 he gave orders for the château to be reconstructed. The architect was **Ange-Jacques Gabriel**, who succeeded in building one of the great monuments of the Louis XV style. Begun in 1751, the great edifice made use of the foundations of the previous structure, partly for reasons of economy, partly because the site was pitted with old quarries. Gabriel chose to emphasise the horizontality of his buildings, stretching them out and providing them with flattened roofs with balustrades, themes he took up again in the Place de la Concorde and Ecole Militaire in Paris. The palace was 40 years a-building; after Gabriel's retirement the work was carried on by his draughtsman, and a general movement in the direction of greater simplicity is very evident, with features like entablatures, ornamental window-brackets and attic floors tending to disappear. This evolution can be traced in the left wing of the main courtyard (1755), the principal façade facing the park, which was designed in 1775 and completed 10 years later (Napoleon's staircase of 1801 spoils the effect wished for by Gabriel), and the peristyle of 1783.

While the place was still a building site, it formed the background to the first meeting (1770) between Louis XVI and Marie-Antoinette; then in 1810, it was where Napoleon met Marie-Louise, the latter's great-niece.

During the Second Empire, Napoleon III made Compiègne his favourite residence, where he took much pleasure in the house-parties to which like-minded celebrities would be invited, some 80 at a time.

Inside, the palace is decorated and furnished in 18C and Empire style (chests of drawers, applied ornament, wall-cupboards, tapestries).

★★ **Musée de la Voiture** ⊙ – In addition to 18C and 19C coaches, the vehicles exhibited include:

the **Mancelle** of 1898, a steam mail-coach designed by Amédée Bollée,

a No 2 **Panhard**,

a Type **A Renault** of 1899 with direct drive,

the **Jamais Contente** ("Never Satisfied") of 1899, an electric car with tyres by Michelin, the first to reach 100km/h-62.1mph,

a Type C **Renault** of 1900, one of the first cars to have enclosed bodywork (by Labourdette),

a **Citroën** half-track of 1924.

⊙ ►► Compiègne: Hôtel de ville★; Musée de la Figurine historique★ – Musée Vivenel - Greek vases★★, archaeology, fine arts.

EXCURSIONS

★★ **Clairière de l'Armistice** ⊙ – *8km – 5 miles east.* This is the place where, at 5.15am on 11 November 1918, the armistice was signed which put an end to the First World War at 11am on the same day. At the time the site was sheltered by forest trees. A restaurant-car identical to the **carriage** ⊙ used by Marshal Foch displays the original objects handled by the delegates in 1918. **Ferdinand Foch** (1851-1929) is generally held to have been the architect of Allied victory in the Great War *(qv)*. He was born in Tarbes in the Pyrénées in an 18C middle-class home (now a museum). He taught

Compiègne

strategy at the École de Guerre (Military Academy) then became its commandant. In 1914 he distinguished himself both in the Battle of the Frontiers in Lorraine and in the "Miracle of the Marne". After the German break-through in the Ludendorff offensive of early 1918, Foch was appointed supreme commander of the French and British armies. Promoted to marshal, it was he who launched the final Allied offensive on 8 August.

After the Battle of France in 1940, it was the turn of a French delegation to present itself here to the dignitaries of the Nazi regime in order to hear the victors' terms for an armistice.

★★ **Château de Pierrefonds** ⊙ – *14km – 9 miles southeast.* The stronghold seems to embody everything that a medieval castle should be as it looms over the village crouching at its feet. For the most part, however, it is a creation of the 19C. Pierrefonds was part of the Duchy of Valois, and its castle, whose origins go back as far as Carolingian times, was rebuilt in the middle of the Hundred Years War *(qv)* by Louis of Orléans, the brother of Charles VI, as part of a chain of defences between the rivers Oise and Ourcq. It was dismantled during the reign of Louis XIII. In 1857 Louis Napoleon commissioned **Viollet-le-Duc** (1814-1879) to restore the keep; four years later he was entrusted with a complete rebuilding of the castle for use as an Imperial residence and a picturesque place for receptions given to entertain the Emperor's guests at Compiègne.

Little of Louis of Orléans' building is left save the base of the walls and the towers visible from the track leading to the castle. Viollet-le-Duc's contributions, in the neo-Gothic style, are not without merit, but are notable more for originality than for strict historical accuracy, both in terms of architecture and decoration (arcading and gallery of the main façade in the courtyard, tribune in the chapel, roof of the Salle des Preuses...). Nevertheless, it gives an excellent idea of a castle's defensive system prior to the age of cannon (north rampart walk).

Château de Blérancourt – *31km – 19 miles northeast.* In the First World War, the château was taken over by Anne Morgan, who set up a temporary hospital here. Blérancourt subsequently became the headquarters for the organisation of relief for the civilian population.

When the war was over, Miss Morgan's efforts were directed towards the establishment of a museum of Franco-American history. In 1929, she presented the place to the French state, whereupon its name was changed to the **Musée National de la Coopération Franco-Américaine** ⊙. About a dozen rooms in the left wing (at present closed for reconstruction) are devoted to the American War of Independence.

The exhibits on show in the right wing (the Florence Gould Pavillion) illustrate aspects of the long and close relationship between the two countries; there are displays on the 1801 Treaty of Friendship, the Louisiana Purchase, emigration to the United States, the Gold Rush etc. Other rooms evoke the two world wars, notably by means of relics of the **La Fayette** Squadron and of the American Field Service.

CONCARNEAU★★

Population 18 630
Map p 4 – Michelin map 58 fold 15 or 230 folds 32, 33 – Green Guide Brittany
Town plan in the current Michelin Red Guide France

The growth of Concarneau *(2 hours)* is based on its importance as a fishing port. Trawlers and cargo-boats moor in the inner harbour up the estuary of the Moros, while the outer harbour is lively with pleasure craft. There are many vegetable and fish canneries and plenty of bustle as the catch is sold in the early morning at the *"criée"* (fish auction market).

★★ **Ville close (Walled town)** – On its islet in the bay, this was one of the strongholds of the ancient county of Cornouaille; as at Dinan and Guérande, its walls proclaim the determination of the citizens to maintain their independence, particularly in times of trouble (as during the War of the Breton Succession in 1341).

The English nevertheless seized the place in 1342, and were only thrown out by Du Guesclin in 1373.

The granite **ramparts** Ⓥ with their typically Breton corbelled machicolations, were started at the beginning of the 14C and completed at the end of the 15C. They were improved by Vauban at the end of the 17C at a time when England once more posed a threat to these coasts; he lowered the height of the towers and built gun emplacements into them.

The interior of the town gate is of the same period. It has impressive crenellations, regular stonework and gables. The **Musée de la Pêche**★ Ⓥ is nearby. At the heart of the walled town, Rue Vauban and Rue St-Guénolé are a demonstration of how medieval marketplaces arose more or less spontaneously through a simple widening of the street.

CONQUES★★★

Population 362
Map p 9 – Michelin map 80 north of folds 1, 2 or 235 fold 11
Green Guide Pyrenees-Languedoc-Tarn Gorges

This tiny medieval town has a splendid hillside **site**★★ best seen from the Bancarel rock *(3km - 2 miles south).*

★★ **Église St-Foy** – Completely rebuilt between 1045-60, this is one of the oldest Romanesque pilgrimage churches on the route to Santiago de Compostela. Its abbey had a chapel and hospice at Roncesvalles to serve the pilgrims as they made their way across the Pyrenees. Within, the spacious nave is flooded with light from the south tribune windows. The dimensions of the transept are exceptional and the ambulatory with its annular barrel vault is also remarkable.

The **tympanum**★★★ above the west door with its wealth of sculpture forms a striking contrast to the overall plainness of the west front. Traces of the original colouring can still be made out. It shows how sculpture had evolved away from the static solemnity characteristic of Burgundy and Languedoc, towards the greater freshness and spontaneity evident in the capitals of the churches of the Auvergne. It may be that the weighing of souls taking place below the figure of Christ is an expression of the idea – entirely new at the beginning of the 12C – of the personal nature of the Last Judgement.

It seems likely that the tympanum was moved forward by the length of a bay and integrated with the west front in the 15C in order to extend the nave; this move would have led to the displacement of the statues in the north transept.

★★★ **Treasury** Ⓥ – This is among the most important in Europe.

Its most precious object is the reliquary statue of St Faith (Ste-Foy). The saint's relics had been brought to Conques at the end of the 9C, when they were venerated by prisoners and by the blind. The statue was put together and added to over a long period; some of its features probably go back as far as the last years of the Roman Empire and consist of reused elements of Roman date (face-mask, intaglio work in precious stones, jewels); the gold and engraved crystal are of the Merovingian and Carolingian periods (7C-9C). At the close of the 10C the statue was renovated here at Conques and adorned with enamels, cabochons and other precious stones.

Four more of the treasures are of exceptional significance: the initial "A" given to the abbey, it is said, by Charlemagne (a fragment of the Holy Cross decorated in the 11C with intaglio work and with chased and gilded silver), two portable altars, one, St Faith's, in alabaster and chased silver, the other, Abbot Begon's, from the beginning of the 12C, in porphyry and silver inlaid with niello, and the reliquary of Pope Pascal with filigree work and diadems, also from the early 12C.

CORDES-SUR-CIEL★★

Population 932
Michelin map 79 fold 20 or 235 fold 23
Green Guide Pyrenees-Languedoc-Tarn Gorges

Nestling at the top of the puech de Mordagne, Cordes occupies a most attractive **site**★★ overlooking the Cérou valley.

The superb row of **Gothic houses**★★ dating from the 13 and 14C testify to the wealthy past of this quaint little town. Notice the **Maison du Grand Fauconnier**★ and the **Maison du Grand Veneur**★. For more than fifty years, artists and craftsmen have contributed to preserving and restoring local tradition.

CORTE★

Population 5 693
Map p 10 – Michelin map 90 fold 5 – Green Guide Corse (in French)

Corte owes its fame to its **site**★ among gorges and ravines, as well as to two great men, Gaffori and Paoli, who were instrumental in making it one of the strongholds of Corsican patriotism.

Jean-Pierre Gaffori (1704-53) was born here. He was a member of the Triumvirate elected as "Protectors of the Nation", who took up arms against Genoa. In 1746, supported by his indomitable wife Faustine, he succeeded in wresting the town from the Genoese. Four years later the latter returned, taking the citadel but failing to overcome the resolute defence of the old town; Gaffori's house still bears the marks made by the Genoese guns.

In June 1751, Gaffori was made "General of the Nation" and granted executive power. But two years later he was killed in an ambush, betrayed by his brother. After this assassination, an appeal was made for **Pascal Paoli** (1725-1807), then in exile in Italy, to return to his native land. He was proclaimed "General of the Nation" in his turn. By 1764, the island was united under his leadership, with only the Genoese coastal forts still able to hold out against him. For 14 years, watched closely by the European Powers, he made Corte his capital, drew up a constitution, founded a university, minted money, reformed the system of justice, encouraged industry and stimulated agricultural production.

Having failed to put down the Corsicans' long struggle for independence (1729-69) the Republic of Genoa requested the intervention of France. A mission of conciliation arrived, headed by the future French Governor, Marbeuf. Paoli, lacking somewhat in the skills of statesmanship, unwisely prevaricated, and was bypassed by events; on 15 May 1768, by the Treaty of Versailles, Genoa provisionally gave up its rights over the island to France. Paoli proclaimed a mass uprising, but was defeated at Ponte Nuovo on 8 May 1769.

Paoli went into exile, spent mostly in England, where he was lionized by the court of the young George III and was able to enjoy his friendship with James Boswell. Amnestied at the outbreak of the French Revolution, he met with a triumphal reception in Paris before returning to Corsica. Later, after his denunciation as a counterrevolutionary, he sought aid from the English. Nelson's victories over the French at St-Florent, Bastia and Calvi, did not however fulfil Paoli's hopes of independence under the English crown, but led to an Anglo-Corsican kingdom of limited durability (2 years) and renewed exile in London for Paoli himself. He died there in 1807.

★ **Upper town** – *2 hours.* Dominated by the **citadel** ⊙ perched high up on its rock, old Corte, with its cobbled and stepped streets and tall houses, still has the air of the island's capital it once was.

In the Place Paoli stands the statue of the great man, in bronze. Further up is the Place Gaffori, where, behind the monument to the General of the Nation, is his house, pitted with bullet holes from the siege of 1750. In the Rue de l'Ancien Collège is the old dwelling where Joseph Bonaparte was born. It was also the birthplace of Jean Thomas Arrighi de Casanova, one of the Empire's most brilliant generals.

A ramp opposite the National Palace (Palais National) leads to a **viewpoint**★ on a peak standing out from the main promontory on which the citadel is built. It offers a fine view of the town in its setting.

►► Chapelle Ste-Croix★.

COUTANCES★★

Population 9 715
Map p 5 – Map 54 fold 12 or 231 fold 26 – Green Guide Normandy
Town plan in the current Michelin Red Guide France

On its hilltop overlooking the woodlands and pastures *(bocage)* of the Cotentin peninsula, Coutances is famous as a cattle-breeding centre for Normandy dairy cows. The town is dominated by its cathedral, a wonderful synthesis of the local architectural traditions of Normandy and the Gothic style at the peak of its development.

★★★ **Cathédrale** – The present building (1220-75) made use of some of the remains of Geoffroy de Montbray's Norman cathedral, as well as drawing on the experience gained in the recently-completed abbey at Fécamp.

The west front is framed by two towers, whose soaring lines (a regional characteristic) are further emphasized by the tall and narrow corner turrets. The great octagonal lantern rises imposingly over the crossing; it too is flanked by turrets, and has strikingly delicate ribbing and slender openings. At the east end, the flying buttresses arch daringly over the double ambulatory to the point from which the ribs rise to support the choir vault.

Within, the Lanceolate phase of the Gothic is evident in the features of the nave, which has clustered piers and highly moulded arches, a triforium with double openings and tall windows behind the typically Norman balustraded inspection gallery.

The transept is in a more advanced style. Here, great piers reinforced by splendidly soaring shafts carry the pendentives on which the elegant octagon of the lantern rests. Built in 1274, it is a masterpiece of ingenious construction. The lower level of the drum is formed by a balustrade and twin arches; above it, the columns of a second gallery support the ribs of

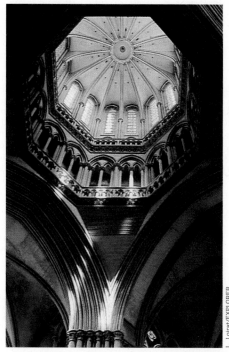

Lantern-tower of the cathedral, Coutances

the 16-part vault, while light floods in through 16 windows. The keystone is 40.85m – 134ft 4ins above the floor of the crossing.

The elevation of the choir and the inner ambulatory and the six coupled columns of the apse show the High Gothic style in all its perfection. Given the unusual height of the main arches, the search for an architecturally satisfying solution led to a lengthening of the clerestory windows and the omission of the triforium above the blind arcading (though the inspection gallery is retained), and justified the design of elaborate vaulting covering both the outer ambulatory and the radiating chapels.

►► Jardin des Plantes★.

La COUVERTOIRADE★

Population 148
Map p 9 – Michelin map 80 fold 15, or 240 folds 14, 18
Green Guide Pyrenees-Languedoc-Tarn Gorges

High up on the lonely Larzac *causse* (limestone plateau), La Couvertoirade is an old fortified settlement which once belonged to the Knights Templar. It has many robustly-built houses, typical of the region, with cisterns, outside stairways leading to the main floor, and a vaulted sheep-pen at ground level. Most date from the 17C.

The ramparts were erected around 1450, some 140 years after the Templars' Order had been disbanded, by the Knights of St John of Jerusalem; insecurity continued to prevail here in Upper Languedoc, even while the Hundred Years War was coming to an end in Guyenne.

The towers and the sentry-walk of the **ramparts** ⊘ are particularly interesting, and the visitor should also see the **fortified church** ⊘ (which has disc-shaped steles at the entrance to the chancel), the dismantled 12C-13C castle, the old houses in Rue Droite, and the de la Scipione and de Grailhe mansions.

The Michelin Green Guide France
makes tourism in France easier and more enjoyable
by highlighting the outstanding natural features and the works of man
Never visit France without a Michelin guide

DEAUVILLE★★★

Population 4 261
Map p 5 – Michelin map 54 fold 17 or 231 fold 19 – Green Guide Normandy
Town plan in the current Michelin Red Guide France

While the neighbouring little town of Trouville began to attract visitors as early as the 1830s, Deauville, on the opposite bank of the River Touques, was created virtually out of nothing from the 1860s onward by the efforts of one man, a Dr Oliffe, physician to the British Ambassador in Paris as well as to the renowned French financier Donon.

Deauville enjoys its world-wide reputation as a luxury resort to the sumptuousness of its facilities and the elegance of its social and sporting calendar which extends over the whole year but reaches a peak in summer; there are regattas, golf and tennis championships, galas, the American Film Festival, international yearling sales and horse-racing culminating in the Deauville Grand Prix.

Life in Deauville centres on the one hand around the Place de Morny and the yachting harbour, on the other around the sea front with its famous boardwalk, its casino and Port Deauville.

EXCURSIONS

★★ **Corniche Normande:** from Deauville-Trouville to Honfleur via the D513. – *21km – 13 miles.* This scenic route leads through typical Normandy countryside and affords fine views over the Seine Estuary.

★★ **Honfleur** – *See HONFLEUR.*

★★ **Côte Fleurie**: from Deauville-Trouville to Cabourg via the D513. – *19km – 12 miles.* The road passes through a number of attractive small resorts with excellent recreational facilities, among them **Villers-sur-Mer★★**, **Houlgate★★** and **Cabourg★★**.

Grotte des DEMOISELLES★★★

Map p 9 – Michelin map 80 folds 16, 17
Green Guide Pyrenees-Languedoc-Tarn Gorges

The **grotte des Demoiselles** ⊘ *(1 hour)* was first discovered in 1770. Before the massive upheavals of the Alpine-building period which raised the whole of the Massif Central far above its previous level, it was probably a sea-cave. Its roof fell in, enlarging it still further, as well as opening up an aven – a deep narrow trench – on the Thaurac plateau above.

Subsequent processes of evaporation and deposition of calcium carbonate have produced a scale and diversity of forms which are quite extraordinary, from stalactites and stalagmites and translucent draperies, to the great columns and huge organ case of this underground cathedral.

DIEPPE★★

Population 35 894
Map p 5 – Michelin map 52 fold 4 or 231 folds 10, 11
Green Guide Normandy
Town plan in the current Michelin Red Guide France

As well as being the nearest seaside resort to Paris, Dieppe is also the most venerable; its famous sea-front lawns were laid out in 1863 by Empress Eugénie and Napoleon III. The first docks were built in 1839 and today it is one of the main cross-Channel ports, with regular car-ferry services to Newhaven.

Its history as a port, however, goes back much further, to the days of the herring fisheries (beginning in the 11C), the English wool trade, and the import of spices from the Orient in Italian ships.

Dieppe Mariners – As early as the 14C sailors from Dieppe were landing on the coast of the Gulf of Guinea and Jean Cousin was exploring the South Atlantic. In 1402 Jean de Bethencourt founded the first European colony on the Canary Islands. Jean Ango (1480-1541), whose privateers once captured a fleet of 300 Portuguese vessels, was responsible for equipping many a voyage of discovery to remote shores. The Parmentier brothers made their way as far as Sumatra as well as drawing up charts of the globe. It was from Dieppe too that the Florentine Giovanni da Verrazano, in the service of France, set out on the journey that eventually took him through the Narrows named after him at the entrance to New York harbour (1524).

In the 16C the great explorer **Samuel de Champlain,** a Dieppe ship-owner, sailed out from Honfleur to found the French colony of Quebec. Later the port traded in sugar from the Antilles and ivory from Guinea.

The Canadian Raid – On 19 August 1942, Dieppe was the main target of Operation Jubilee, the first sortie on French soil after June 1940 by Allied troops under the command of Admiral Mountbatten. Seven thousand men, mostly Canadians, landed at dawn at eight different places on the coast. The tank crews gave their lives to protect the retreat under heavy artillery fire and with heavy losses including 3 500 Canadians.

★ **Dieppe ivories** – Dieppe ships had loaded elephant tusks from the West African coast ever since they had begun calling there on the return journey from Brazil in the early years of the 16C. The fragile ivory was filed and polished with great skill by artists encouraged to settle in Dieppe by Jean Ango. Whalebone and the teeth of sperm whales were worked as well. Production was interrupted when many of the craftsmen quit France after the revocation of the Edict of Nantes, but it started up again at the time of the rebuilding

Dieppe ivory

Musée de Dieppe, B. Régent/DIAF

of the town in the 18C. It was then that Jean Mauger and Michel Mollart, and later Pierre Baillou (1807-72) fashioned ravishing little objects very much in the spirit of the Rococo. In the castle is the **Museum**★ ⊙ where many of these meticulous masterpieces are displayed; they include ship-models, busts, medallions, snuff-boxes, as well as objects of religious or mythological significance.

⊙ ►► Dieppe: Cité de la Mer★; Église St Jacques★; Notre-Dame de Bon Secours Chapel – view★.

EXCURSION

★ **Alabaster Coast** ("Côte d'Albâtre")

From Dieppe to Etretat – *104km – 65 miles.* With its beaches and sheer white cliffs cut into by dry valleys *(valleuses),* this is a landscape reminiscent of the coastline of much of southern England. The chalk continues inland to form the Caux region, a vast plateau whose farmsteads shelter from the winds behind massive tree-topped hedgebanks.

Leave Dieppe by the D75 in the direction of Pourville.

A number of little resorts – **Pourville-sur-Mer, Ste-Marguerite-sur-Mer** and **Veules-les-Roses** – are sited at the seaward end of a succession of lush valleys, their half-timbered houses hidden among the hedgerows.

★ **Varengeville-sur-Mer** – The houses of this popular resort lie scattered in small groups along the roadside.
Overlooking the sea, the graveyard of the 11-15C church shelters the tomb of **Georges Braque;** among the achievements of the great Cubist are the stained-glass windows of **Chapelle St-Dominique** on the outskirts of Varengeville.

St-Valéry-en-Caux – In a gap in the cliffs halfway between Dieppe and Fécamp, St-Valéry (twin town, Inverness) is a fishing port as well as a popular resort. High up on the Amont cliff (Falaise d'Amont) are two monuments, one commemorating the last stand of the 51st Highland Division in June 1940, the other to the airmen Coste and Bellemont who completed the first east-west crossing of the Atlantic from Paris to New York in 1930.

★★ **Fécamp** – *See FÉCAMP.*

Yport – With its roofs of slate changing colour from blue to grey according to the weather, this little resort was once known for its *caiques,* flat-bottomed fishing boats which could be drawn up easily over the pebbly beach.

★★ **Étretat** – *See ÉTRETAT.*

DIJON★★★

Conurbation 226 025
Map p 7 – Michelin map 66 fold 12 or 243 fold 16 – Green Guide Burgundy Jura
Town plan in the current Michelin Red Guide France

Close to some of the world's finest vineyards, Dijon, former capital city of the Dukes of Burgundy, straddles important north-south and east-west communication routes and has a remarkable artistic heritage.

The great dukes of Burgundy – Dijon had been the capital of Burgundy ever since the rule of Robert the Pious at the beginning of the 11C. In 1361 Philip of Rouvres died without an heir, leaving the duchy without a ruler. In 1363, the French King Jean II le Bon (the Good) handed the duchy to his son Philip, the first of an illustrious line of Valois Dukes who made the Burgundian court at Dijon one of the most brilliant of Europe.

Philip became Duke in 1364, at the same time as his brother Charles V "the Wise" was acceding to the throne of France. Philip stood out as the most able of four royal brothers; cool, analytical on the one hand, well-named "the Bold" on the other. His marriage in 1369 to Margaret of Flanders made him the most powerful prince of Christian Europe. Anxious to provide a worthy burial place for himself and his successors, he founded the Champmol Charterhouse in Dijon in 1383, and set out to attract to the city the best sculptors, painters, goldsmiths and illuminators from his possessions in Flanders. They included Jean de Marville (who designed his tomb), Jean de Beaumetz from Artois (who worked for five years on the altar of the Charterhouse), Claus Sluter and Melchior Broederlam (who succeeded Marville as Court painter), and Malouel from Gelderland who gave Burgundian-Flemish style its distinct identity (his great circular Pietà can be seen in the Louvre).

In an attempt to redress the cultural balance in France's favour, Jean de Berry, virtual ruler of the kingdom as a consequence of Charles VI's growing madness, encouraged other artists to settle and work in Bourges, Poitiers and Riom.

John the Fearless, Charles VI's cousin, became Duke in 1404 at the age of 33. While continuing to employ the artists chosen by his father, John nourished political ambitions, spurred on by the insanity of the king and the Dauphin's unease about his legitimacy. But John's attempt to make himself master of France came to an end in 1419, when he was assassinated on the bridge at Montereau on his way to negotiate with the Dauphin.

The odious crime of Montereau led to **Philip the Good** inheriting the title at the age of 23. Burgundy's alliance with England helped Henry V acquire the Crown of France by the Treaty of Troyes in 1420. From this time on, Burgundy slowly saw its cultural importance waning in favour of the Netherlands and Flanders, where Renaissance ideas were blossoming. Nevertheless, artistic production continued throughout his long reign of 48 years. Among the talents working at Dijon were Claus de Werve, Henri Bellechose from Brabant (whose St Denis altarpiece is in the Louvre), Rogier van der Weyden, and, it seems probable, Robert Campin, the likely **Master of Flémalle.** Working at Bruges in the service of the Duke was Van Eyck, the founder of the Flemish School, who was responsible for perfecting the techniques of painting in oils.

At the same time, Nicolas Rolin, the Duke's Chancellor, was establishing the Hôtel-Dieu at Beaune.

The boundaries of the Burgundian state had never been more extensive nor the life of its court more exuberant; on his wedding day in 1429, Philip founded the Order of the Golden Fleece; never had the French king and his court, lurking in relative obscurity at Bourges, been more pitiful.

But the alliance with England had now become embarrassing, even unpopular; it was beginning to threaten the dominance of Burgundy at the very moment when Joan of Arc was awakening national sentiment. Subtle policies were required; the Duke found it convenient to allow Charles VII to cross Burgundian territory in order to have himself crowned at Rheims. Then, aged 33, Philip, who hitherto had always conducted himself like any other non-French monarch, submitted himself to the feudal authority of the French king, thus marking the beginning of the end of the interminable Hundred Years War (qv).

Charles the Bold succeeded in 1467; he was the last and perhaps the most renowned of all the Valois Dukes of Burgundy. Consumed by ambition, he squandered his resources in the search for glory. But now, after a century, the balance of power had been reversed; the Duke found himself faced with the wily Louis XI, devoting himself stubbornly and with great effect to the interests of the French kingdom. Charles' death at the siege of Nancy in 1477 marked the end of the great days of the Burgundian dynasty, but not the end of the problems besetting the French throne. It was in the same year that Mary of Burgundy, Charles' daughter, married the Hapsburg Maximilian, Holy Roman Emperor, in spite of her godfather Louis XI's fierce opposition. She was to be the mother of Philip the Fair who in turn fathered the future Emperor Charles V. The recovery of Burgundy and the other lands making up her dowry cost France more than two and a half centuries of struggle.

THE DUCAL CITY *3 hours*

★ Palais des ducs et des États de Bourgogne – The ducal palace had been neglected since the death of Charles the Bold. In the 17C, it was restored and adapted and given a setting of dignified classical buildings. At the time the city was concerned to emphasise its parliamentary role and needed a suitable building in which the States-General of Burgundy could meet in session. Plans were drawn up by Mansart. The exterior of the Great Hall of the States-General (Salle des États) recalls the Marble Court at Versailles. By contrast, the east wing with its peristyle anticipates the architectural style of the 18C.

Mansart was also responsible for the semi-circular Place de la Libération (formerly Place Royale). With its arcades crowned by an elegant stone balustrade, it is designed to show off the main courtyard of the palace.

Painting and sculpture at the time of the Dukes – As a great European centre of artistic activity, Dijon tended towards a certain ostentation. But though the works of some of its artists may have been lacking in refinement, they more than made up for it by their sumptuousness, vigour and power.

★★★ Salle des Gardes – *On the first floor of the Musée des Beaux-Arts* ⓥ. This is the Ducal Palace's most important interior. Its centrepiece is formed by two tombs which before the French Revolution were in the chapel of the Champmol Charterhouse. The tomb of Philip the Bold was designed by Jean de Marville; its decoration was in the hands of Claus Sluter followed by his nephew Claus de Werve who succeeded in softening somewhat the severity of Marville's conception. Flamboyant Gothic inventiveness and exuberance are expressed in the procession of hooded mourners making its way around the cloisters formed by the four sides of the monument.

The adjacent tomb of John the Fearless and Margaret of Bavaria repeats this pattern. There are also two altarpieces dazzling in the richness of their decoration: one, sculpted by Jacques de Baerze and painted and gilded by Broederlam, shows saints and martyrs; the other, depicting the Crucifixion, has famous paintings by Broederlam on the reverse side of its panels. A portrait of Philip the Good by Rogier van der Weyden (born in Tournai, a pupil of Van Eyck and perhaps of Campin too, then teacher to Memling) is remarkable for its psychological insight.

In an adjoining room is a fine Nativity of 1425 by the Master of Flémalle.

★ Ancienne Chartreuse de Champmol ⓥ – *Entrance No 1 Boulevard Chanoine-Kir (now a hospital)*. All that is left of the Charterhouse is **Moses' Well★★** and the **Chapel Doorway★**, both the work of Claus Sluter, the foremost among the sculptors of the Dijon School. Born in Holland, he learnt his skills in Brabant.

Moses' Well was originally the pedestal of a Calvary. The head of the figure of Christ is now in the Archaeological Museum. Six great statues of Moses and the Prophets face outwards from the hexagonal base; their treatment shows a striking realism and sense of movement, notably in the folds of the clothing. The statues of Philip the Bold and Margaret of Flanders in the chapel doorway are thought to be actual portraits.

ⓥ ►► Musée des Beaux-Arts★★; Rue des Forges★; Église Notre-Dame★; Crypte of the Cathédrale St-Bénigne; Musée Archéologique; Église St-Michel.

DINAN★★

Population 11 591

Map p 4 – Michelin map 59 folds 15, 16 or 230 fold 25 – Green Guide Brittany
Town plan in the current Michelin Red Guide France

Dinan is situated at the head of the Rance estuary on which its little port is built, but the wall-girt town itself rises from the plateau 30m – 100ft above the river.

Bertrand du Guesclin (c1315-80) – In the town is a statue of this redoubtable warrior. John the Good had been taken prisoner by the English at the Battle of Poitiers in 1356. During the four years of captivity he spent in England he became aware of the extent to which feudal rights imposed limitations on royal power and conceived the idea of a body of knights attached to the monarch. In pursuit of this aim, he took Du Guesclin into his service shortly after his release and return to France. This middle-aged knight had until then experienced little but rebuffs and difficulties due to his modest ancestry, lack of means and exceptionally ugly appearance. John's successor, Charles V, kept him on, doubtless in view of his great popularity and reckless bravery and his implacable hatred of the English (which at one point in his youth had led him to support Charles of Blois. In 1366, after ridding France of the "Free Companies" (marauding bands of mercenaries), he was made High Constable of France. He freed Périgord from English rule in 1370 and Normandy in 1378. In 1379 he handed his sword to the king rather than use it against his rebellious Breton compatriots. In 1380 he died beneath the walls of Châteauneuf-de-Randon in the south.

★★ **Old Dinan** - *1 1/2 hours*. The houses of the old town cluster together behind the 2.5km - 1 1/2 miles long circuit of walls built by the Dukes of Brittany in the 14C in order to protect the place's commercial activity and to defend their domain against the Normans, the English, and, after the accession of Louis XI, the French.

★ **Château** ⊘ - Begun by Duke John IV about the middle of the 14C. Its 15C towers project outwards in order to facilitate enfilading fire. The exceptionally fine machicolations of Duchess Anne's Keep (Donjon de la Duchesse Anne) are of interest.

Basilique St-Sauveur - The west front is much influenced by the Poitiers version of the Romanesque. In the north aisle is the Evangelists' Window, a fine example of late 15C Breton glass, famous for its yellows. In the north transept is the cenotaph containing the heart of Du Guesclin.

Town houses - Duke John was happy to let Dinan run its own affairs, and the town's consequent prosperity is reflected in the rebuilding of many old timber houses in stone. A most picturesque townscape results from the many buildings with overhanging upper stories, angle-posts, half-timbering on stone footings, arcades carried on timber beams, and granite side-walls.
The most interesting houses are on Rue de l'Apport (the 15C Mère Pourcel House), **Place des Merciers**★ (triangular gables and porches), **Rue du Jerzual**★ which links the main part of the town with the port (15C and 16C shops where craftsmen have worked for six centuries) and on Place Du Guesclin (17C and 18C town houses).

DINARD★★★

Population 9 918
Map p 4 - Michelin map 59 fold 5 or 230 fold 11 - Green Guide Brittany
Town plan in the current Michelin Red Guide France

On the magnificent estuary of the River Rance, Dinard is an elegant resort with sheltered sandy beaches and luxuriant Mediterranean vegetation flourishing in the mild climate.
It was little more than a small fishing harbour, an offshoot of nearby St-Enogat, when in 1850 a rich American by the name of Coppinger decided to build himself a château here. He was followed two years later by a British family, who in turn attracted many of their fellow-countrymen; Dinard's period of fame had begun. Its success as a resort owed much to the fashion for sea-bathing which developed at the time of Napoleon III. It was formally inaugurated by Empress Eugénie in 1868, and by the end of the 19C its reputation rivalled that of Brighton; sumptuous villas and luxurious hotels abounded, frequented by an international smart set, their evenings spent in sophisticated revelry.
Nowadays many of Dinard's grand hotels are no more than a memory, but plenty of well-tended villas remain to tell of past glories.

Dinard's beaches and coastline - Seaside promenades lead from the **Plage de l'Écluse**★ (or **Grande Plage**) to the Plage du Prieuré, giving fine views over the coast and the Rance estuary. From the **Pointe du Moulinet**★★, the view extends as far as Cap Fréhel to the west and to the ramparts of St-Malo to the east. In summer, the **Promenade du Clair de Lune**★ with its pretty parterres and Mediterranean plants forms an attractive setting for evening concerts.

DISNEYLAND PARIS★★★

Michelin map 106 fold 22 - Green Guide Disneyland Paris

Nestling in the Brie Plain, twenty miles away from Paris, a leisure centre unique in Europe has been set up at Marne-la-Vallée. This huge complex, scheduled to expand until the year 2017, already includes a Disneyland Paris theme park, as well as numerous recreational activities and facilities for accommodation. These consist of six hotels, each focusing on one particular region in the United States, a camping and caravanning site, **Davy Crockett Ranch**, an twenty-seven hole golf course (Golf Disneyland Paris), and an entertainment centre **(Festival Disney)** portraying the American way of life. The resort also features restaurants, shops, a discotheque and a mounted show **(Buffalo Bill's Wild West Show**★★**)** reproducing the adventurous lifestyle of the Far West.

★★★ **Disneyland Paris Theme Parc** ⊘ - Like its counterparts in the United States and Japan, this resort is the perfect illustration of Walt Disney's dream: "a small, magic garden where both children and grown-ups could have fun together".

© Disney

Disneyland Paris occupies a total area of 55 hectares – 135 acres and includes five lands devoted to a particular theme (**Main Street USA**, **Frontierland**, **Adventureland**, **Fantasyland** and **Discoveryland**). Each land stages spectacular shows featuring amazing automatons that move in sumptuous, elaborate settings. It also has its own boutiques and restaurants (table-service and self-service).

DOMME★★

Population 1 030
Map p 8 – Michelin map 75 fold 17 or 235 fold 6
Green Guide Dordogne

One of the many medieval fortified towns *(bastides)* founded in southwest France by both French and English, Domme was laid out by Philippe le Hardi (the Bold) in 1281. The normal rectangular plan of such settlements was here distorted in order to fit it to the rocky crag overlooking the Dordogne 145m – 475ft below.

★★ **Panorama** – There are splendid views over the alluvial valley of the Dordogne from the Barre belvedere or, better still, from the cliff-top walk (Promenade des Falaises – *no parapet*) just below the public gardens.

Although the river meanders here are not so well-formed as those upstream at Trémolat nor as perfect as the one at Luzech on the Lot, their sinuous pattern is enhanced in a most satisfactory way by the curving cliffs, lines of poplars and the layout of field boundaries and the crops growing within them.

The regularity of the river channel, the equilibrium reached between the forces of erosion and deposition, and the present stable state of the meanders mean that the Dordogne here is a regulated river. All around is the opulent landscape so characteristic of Périgord, castles perched on the heights, well-wooded slopes dotted with stone-built villages, and the rich alluvial lands with their lush meadows, walnut trees, and crops of tobacco and corn.

*The current edition of the annual **Michelin Red Guide France** offers a selection of pleasant and quiet hotels in convenient locations*
Each entry includes the facilities available (swimming pools, tennis courts, private beaches and gardens...) and dates of annual closure
The selection also includes establishments which are known for the quality of their cuisine : carefully prepared meals at reasonable prices ; Michelin stars for good cooking

DOMRÉMY-LA-PUCELLE★

Population 182
Map p 7 – Michelin map 62 fold 3 or 242 fold 25
Green Guide Alsace et Lorraine (in French)

Joan of Arc was born in this village in the Meuse valley on 6 January 1412. It was at Bois-Chenu 1.5km – 1 mile south that she heard the voices of St Catherine, St Margaret and St Michael calling upon her to deliver France from the misery inflicted on her by the English and their Burgundian allies. Having with some difficulty convinced the local lord, Robert de Baudricourt, of the divine nature of her mission, she left Vaucouleurs on 23 February 1429 at the age of 17. In the next 15 months there followed the journey to Chinon, the testing time at Poitiers, the relief of Orléans, the coronation at Rheims, the campaigns of Paris, the Loire and the Oise, and finally the funeral pyre at Rouen, during the course of which there emerged for the first time the stirring of a truly French national feeling in opposition to the horrors of the Hundred Years War, the sufferings of the occupied territories and the insubordination of the Burgundians.

★ **Maison natale de Jeanne d'Arc** ⊘ – Joan was born into a family of prosperous peasants. The modest home with its stout walls is moving in its simplicity (small museum).

Le DORAT★

Population 2 203
Map p 5 – Michelin map 72 fold 7 or 233 fold 22
Green Guide Berry Limousin (in French)

Le Dorat lies in the gently rolling countryside of the old province of Marche, whose patchwork of pastureland feeds the yellowish-fawn Limousin cattle bought and sold in the great market at **St-Yrieix-la-Perche** 41km – 25 miles south of Limoges. The little town has a collegiate church of impressive size and harmonious proportions.

★★ **Collégiale St-Pierre** – The great edifice was rebuilt in Romanesque style over a period of fifty years beginning in 1112. It is firmly rooted in its region by virtue of its siting, the coarse granite from which it is built, and by a number of characteristic Limousin features. These include the massive square west tower flanked by bell-turrets, the portal with its scalloped archivolts, the openwork lantern (inspired by the one built 50 years earlier at St-Junien 45km – 28 miles south but vastly more original), and the mouldings used in the arches and arcades throughout the building.
The late 11C **crypt** ⊘ dedicated to St Anne has crudely hewn columns and simple capitals, only one of which is sculpted, openwork barrel vaulting in granite in the ambulatory and groined vaults in the chapels. Compared with the crypt in the church at Uzerche it shows the architectural progress achieved within a period of fifty years.

DOUAI★

Population 42 175
Map p 6 – Michelin map 53 fold 3 or 236 fold 16
Green Guide Flanders, Picardy and the Paris Region
Town plan in the currrent Michelin Red Guide France

In the 11C and 12C, like Valenciennes, Douai provided winter quarters for merchants and merchandise using the great trading routes of Northern Europe. The town was laid out on both sides of the River Scarpe; on the west bank the depots and workshops and a charterhouse (now a museum) on what was then an isolated site; on the east bank the town centre, with its burghers' houses and monuments such as the bell-tower, town hall, Notre-Dame church and latterly some fine 18C residences. Douai was a free town from the late 12C and from 1713-89 was the seat of the Parliament of Flanders, whose successor is the present Court of Appeal. The painter **Jean Bellegambe** (1470-1534) was born here. He probably learnt his skills in Marmion's studio in Valenciennes before returning to work in his native town and its surroundings. His paintings, mostly of religious subjects, are medieval still in their treatment of familiar details, Renaissance in their decoration (colonnades, shells) and specifically Flemish in their realism. His **Polyptych of the Trinity**★ (in the former charterhouse) is justly famous.
Around 1605, a number of Benedictine monks from England and Wales came to Douai and established the monastery of St Gregory the Great. It was here that the "Douai Bible", an English version of the Old Testament, was published in 1609. The monastery buildings were destroyed at the time of the French Revolution, and the community recrossed the Channel, eventually settling at Stratton-on-the-Fosse in Somerset, where they founded **Downside Abbey.**

★ **Beffroi** ⊙ – The is one of the best of its kind in the North of France. Both Victor Hugo and Corot were much taken by the Gothic tower of 1390 with its elaborate crown. The Flemish Renaissance courtyard front was rebuilt in 1860.

Northern Coalfield – The Louis XV Aoust building (Hôtel d'Aoust) with its Rococo doorway and allegorical sculptures was the management headquarters for what used to be an important mining district. Douai lies on the edge of the great coalfield which extends from the Ruhr through southern Belgium into France. Between the Belgian border and Artois it runs for some 120km – 75 miles; the six pits used to supply coking plants and power stations.
Coal was mined here from the 18C to 1990. The history of the area has been marked by such tragedies as the disaster at Courrières in 1906 when 1 200 miners lost their lives in a fire-damp explosion.

⊙ ►► Douai: Charterhouse★ (Ancienne Chartreuse) – painting; Museum★.

DOUARNENEZ★

Population 16 457
Michelin map 58 fold 14 or 230 fold 17 – Green Guide Brittany

Douarnenez, Ploaré, Pouldavid and Tréboul were amalgamated to form the *commune* of Douarnenez, a great fishing and canning centre. Tréboul is joined to the rest of the community by a big steel bridge across the Port-Rhu, estuary and is a much frequented seaside resort.
The site of the town, deep in a great bay with gracefully curving shores, the lively and colourful picture of its quays, and the streets of the old district, zigzagging down to the sea, are Douarnenez's chief attractions.

★★ **Port-Musée** ⊙ – This museum is both a centre of conservation of boats and a permanent workshop where expertise in this field is passed on. It offers a good opportunity to rediscover the recent maritime past. The various elements of the Port Museum, established on the wonderful site of Port-Rhu, once the commercial harbour of Douarnenez, contain displays on all aspects of maritime and harbour life, from ships afloat, to construction sites and an onshore museum containing 200 boats.

Saut du DOUBS★★★

Map p 7 – Michelin map 66 south of fold 18 or 243 folds 21, 22
Green Guide Burgundy Jura

The gorges of the River Doubs downstream from Villers-le-Lac mark the frontier between France and Switzerland. The river has cut down deeply into the highly folded Jurassic limestone, but here its course has been blocked by eroded material to form Lake Chaillexon (Lac de Chaillexon). Its waters escape from the lake over the 28m – 92ft high Doubs Falls (Saut de Doubs).
Follow a footpath through the woods to reach the main viewpoint *(3/4 hour Rtn)*: beyond, a very steep path descends to the lake itself, from where there is another most impressive view of the falls crashing down into the narrow defile.

DUNKERQUE

Dunkirk
Population 70 331
Map p 6 – Michelin map 51 folds 3, 4 or 236 fold 4
Green Guide Flanders, Picardy and the Paris Region
Town plan in the current Michelin Red Guide France

Dunkirk (Church of the Dunes in Flemish) was originally a fishing village, whose transformation into the principal port of Flanders began as early as the 14C. Handling timber form Scandinavia, wool from England and wine from Bordeaux, by the 17C it had become a pawn in the political manœuvres of the European powers. It was taken by Turenne after his victory in the Battle of the Dunes in 1658, but was given to England immediately afterwards in recognition of her help in the struggle against Spain. The town was repurchased by France in 1662, the crowning achievement of the shrewd diplomatic campaign waged on Louis XIV's behalf by the diplomat Lionne. It was now that Dunkirk became the abode of smugglers and of pirates pressed into the service of the king. In the course of Louis XIV's wars, a total of 3 000 foreign ships were captured or destroyed and the trade of the Netherlands completely wrecked. The most intrepid of these privateers was **Jean Bart** (1651-1702); his statue of 1848 by David d'Angers stands in the square named after him.

DUNKERQUE

Demolition of the fortifications in 1713 (one of the conditions of the Treaty of Utrecht) brought about a decline in Dunkirk's fortunes, notwithstanding the efforts made by the Intendant Calonne in the mid-18C to improve the port facilities. Later, in Napoleon's scheme of things, Dunkirk played second fiddle to Antwerp.

The German breakthrough at Sedan in mid-May 1940 and subsequent dash to the coast near Abbeville had led to the Allied forces in the north being trapped with their backs to the sea.

Defeat was turned into partial victory by the "Miracle of Dunkirk", the name given to the successful evacuation between 27 May and 2 June of more than a third of a million troops from the beaches of Dunkirk itself and its outlying resorts of Malo, Zuydcoote and Bray-Dunes, an operation carried out in the face of intense bombardment on land and from the air.

★★ **Port** - Dunkirk is the third port in France with a total of over 40 million tonnes of traffic in 1993. A vast industrial zone has emerged, based on shipbuilding, steelworks, refineries, petrochemicals...

⊘ ►► Musée d'Art Contemporain★★; Musée des Beaux-Arts★ - Malo-les-Bains★.

Basilique Notre-Dame de L'ÉPINE★★

Map p 6 - Map 56 fold 18 or 241 fold 26
Green Guide Champagne (in French)

The village nestles at the foot of its great pilgrimage church. Its houses, with a courtyard separating them from the road, eschew the crumbling local chalk in favour of half-timbering as their preferred building material.

The Notre-Dame Basilica (Basilique Notre-Dame) was started in 1410, beginning with the crossing and the lower walls of the nave continuing with the west front in about 1450 and finishing with the east end in 1510. Its fine Flamboyant Gothic features include the slender gable over the main portal, the delicate openwork structure of the south spire (the north spire was rebuilt in the 19C) and the grotesque **gargoyles**★ which took the fancy of both Huysmans and Victor Hugo.

Within, the round piers with their engaged columns are a throw-back to the Lanceolate Gothic style, while the false triforium seems to have been inspired by the one in Rheims cathedral which is over two hundred years older. The elegant rood-screen and its monumental rood-beam are 15C work. The south side of the choir screen is Gothic, the north Renaissance in date. The splendid Jesse Window *(in the easternmost bay of the south aisle)* is a masterpiece of local work in Renaissance style, carefully composed, with finely-modelled faces and an impressive range of green hues.

The Red Guides (hotels and restaurants)

Benelux - Deutschland - España Portugal - Europe - France -
Great Britain and Ireland - Ireland - Italia - Portugal - Switzerland

The Green Guides (fine art, historical monuments, scenic routes)

Austria - Belgium and Luxembourg - Brussels - California - Canada -
Chicago - England : the West Country - Europe - Florida - France -
Germany - Great Britain - Greece - Ireland - Italy - London - Mexico -
Netherlands - New England - New York - Paris - Portugal - Quebec -
Rome - San Francisco - Scandinavia - Scotland - Spain - Switzerland -
Tuscany - Wales - Washington - Venice

... and the collection of regional guides for France

ÉTRETAT★★

Population 1 565
Map p 5 Map 52 fold 11 or 54 folds 7, 8 or 231 fold 8
Green Guide Normandy – Town plan in the current Michelin Red Guide France

Sited where a dry valley in the chalk country of the Caux region meets the sea, Étretat was a humble fishing village well into the 19C. It was then favoured by writers such as Maupassant and painters like Courbet and Eugène Isabey.

Two excursions on foot allow the visitor to appreciate the distinctive character of the "Alabaster Coast" with its chalk cliffs seamed by bands of dark flints and yellowish marls.

★★★ **Falaise d'Aval** - *1 hour Rtn on foot from the end of the promenade. Take the steps and then the path to the cliff-top known as Porte d'Aval.*

There are fine views of the magnificent Manneport Arch, the solitary 70m – 200ft Needle (Aiguille), the long shingle beach and the Amont Cliff on the far side of the bay. The play of colours changes constantly with the time of day and conditions of sky and sea.

★★ **Falaise d'Amont** - *3/4 hour from the Nungesser and Coli Memorial.*

Situated at the end of the promenade, the memorial was put up to mark the spot from which the two aviators were last glimpsed as they set out in their *"White Bird" (Oiseau Blanc)* on their attempt to make a non-stop westward crossing of the Atlantic (8 May 1927). It is not known whether these brave men perished under the ocean's waves or in the forests of New England. A footpath with steps cut into the cliff leads to the sea.

Cliffs at Étretat

ÉVREUX★★

Conurbation 57 968
Map p 5 – Michelin map 55 folds 16, 17 or 231 fold 35 – Green Guide Normandy
Town plan in the current Michelin Red Guide France

The history of Évreux could read like a series of unmitigated disasters, from the burnings and sackings perpetrated by Vandals, Vikings and Plantagenets to the more recent devastation wreaked from the air by Luftwaffe (in 1940) and Allied air forces (in 1944). But after each disaster the townspeople have recreated prosperity from ruin. Evidence of this spirit can be seen in the promenade laid out on the old Roman rampart on the banks of the River Iton and in the treatment of the Clock Tower (Tour de l'Horloge) which was built by Henry V in 1417, two years after his victory over the French at Agincourt.

★ **Cathédrale Notre-Dame** - The cathedral, begun in the 12C under Henry II of England and continued under the Norman and Plantagenet dynasties (the choir was completed in about 1260), is essentially a harmonious Gothic building of the 13C.

It did not escape the troubles which beset the town, much restoration having to take place for example after John the Good's siege in 1356 and during the reign of Louis XI (1461-83). In the 16C the aisles of the nave were rebuilt in Flamboyant style and after the Second World War much of the upper part of the cathedral was replaced.

The **stained glass**★ gives an excellent insight into the evolution of this art form. Late 13C: the windows of the south aisle have a wonderful intensity of colour. 14C: in the fourth chapel on the right of the ambulatory it is noticeable how the glass has acquired a greater degree of elegance. The windows of the choir were installed in about 1330. Their clarity, the delicacy of their golden tones and the transparency of their colours are admirable and illustrate the gradual change from translucent decoration to elaborate scenes which occurred from 1330 to the end of the century.

15C: the second window in the clerestory on the north side of the nave has very subtle grisaille effects which include a pearly white. The windows of the axial chapel are a fascinating source of information on the reign of Louis XI.

16C: there is a fine Last Judgement in the rose window of the north transept.

17C: glass in the third chapel of the north part of the ambulatory.

⊘ ►► Musée Municipal★★ – archaeology, medieval religious art; Église St Taurin – Choir★★.

Les EYZIES-DE-TAYAC★★

Population 853

Map p 8 – Michelin map 75 fold 16 or 235 fold 1 – Green Guide Dordogne

The discovery here of cave-paintings and of shelters cut into the base of the cliffs contibuted to the beginnings more than a century ago of the scientific investigation of prehistory.

Largely French in their origins, prehistoric studies got under way early in the 19C, following the work carried out by Boucher de Perthes in the Somme region, at Acheul and Abbeville *(qv)*. He was succeeded by other investigators, who concentrated their attention on the wealth of evidence here in the Vézère valley; among the eminent pioneers who laid the foundations on which modern archaeology is based – Lartet, Mortillet, the abbots A. and J. Bouyssonie and Lemozi, Dr Capitan, D. Peyrony, Rivière, Cartailhac, Lantier and Abbot Breuil – was an English banker, Henry Christy.

ABC of Prehistory – The Quaternary Age, the most recent and shortest of the periods into which geological history is divided, began some 2 000 millennia ago. During this time the great glaciers spread outwards from the high mountains, a result of the general cooling of the global atmosphere, but the period is marked above all by the movement into Asia and Europe of early people who had first made their appearance in Africa 1 000 millennia previously.

Towards the end of Tertiary times, about 3 000 000 years ago *(1)*, it seems that the first glimmerings of reflective – not simply instinctive – thought occured in the minds of the pre-hominids, thus distinguishing mankind's oldest

QUATERNARY ERA	Years BC
Birth of Christ	
Foundation of Rome	753
IRON	900
BRONZE	2 500
AGE OF METALS	
The Pyramids	2 800
NEOLITHIC	7 500
MESOLITHIC	10 000
PALEOLITHIC — UPPER	35 000
MIDDLE	150 000
STONE AGE — LOWER	2 000 000
Appearance of Man	

ancestors from other species. For most purposes, the Quaternary Age as defined by geologists corresponds to "prehistoric times" as defined by anthropologists, and the Paleolithic, marked by the manufacture and use of knapped flint tools, takes up most of the period.

Lower Paleolithic – 2 000 000 to 150 000 years BC. The first tools are made and various human species succeed one another, evolving all the time; Australopithecus from southern Africa, Pithecanthropus from Java, Sinothropus from northern China, Atlanthropus from North Africa. Traces have been found of the encampments made by auroch hunters as they pursued their quarry across the steppes, notably in the Pyrenees (the skull found at the Caune d'Arago cavern near Tautavel, the jaw at Montmaurin). At Nice studies have been made of the print made by a human foot and also of the Terra Amata site used by hunters in the Paillon and Var valleys, a beach now some 26m – 85ft above the present level of the Mediterranean. To the same period belong the deposits found in the Lower Ardèche and around Carnac as well as the bifaces and other flint tools discovered at Gouzeaucourt *(17km – 11 miles south of Cambrai)*.

---

(1) Estimated dates and periods are given in millenia as regards geological data and in years for prehistory.

The fragments of skull belonging to Fontechevade Man *(southeast of La Rochefoucauld)* have been linked to the Tayacian culture marking the transition from the Lower to the Middle Paleolithic.

Middle Paleolithic – 150 000 to 35 000 years BC. A human skeleton of the Neanderthal type was found at Chapelle-aux-Saints near Brive-la-Gaillarde in 1908; Neanderthal Man first appeared about 150 000 years ago, possibly as a descendant of Atlanthropus, but died out some 35 000 years ago. The first tombs date from this period.

Upper Paleolithic – 35 000 to 10 000 years BC. Skeletons dating from the early part of this period were found at Cro-Magnon in the Dordogne in 1868. Cro-Magnon people were tall, with nimble hands and possessed of great inventiveness, the first examples of modern man, Homo sapiens. Another branch of the same species, characterised likewise by large brains, sophisticated language and self-awareness, is formed by the people known as the Chancelade race, remains of whom were discovered at Chancelade near Périgueux in 1888.

The Aurignacian and Perigordian cultures, though contemporary, do not seem to have been in contact with each other and differ in a number of respects, although both are characterised by a continuous improvement in tool-making and the development of hunting techniques which allowed time to be set aside for the creation of works of art (line-drawings and paintings). Aurignacian industry (Aurignac map 82 fold 16) brought forth very finely knapped flints, gravers and scrapers and perforated batons made from reindeer horn. The culture reached its peak about 25 000 years ago; its achievements can be seen in the famous drawings in the Pair-non-Pair caves at Marcamps (map 71 fold 8), in the cave at La Grèze and in the **Poisson shelter** ⊘, all of which mark the beginnings of human activity in the lower Vézère valley.

Solutrian culture, named after the rock near Mâcon at the foot of which important discoveries were made, is very well represented in the Dordogne. It is characterised by the manufacture of very fine flint blades and weapons with serrated points and by the appearance of needles with eyes.

THE UPPER PALEOLITHIC

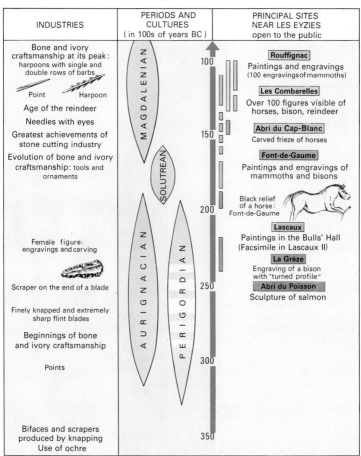

The warming-up of the climate at the end of the Magdalenian period encouraged people to live more in the open as at Pincevent and Étiolles in the Île-de-France. Later, in the Azilian period (named after the Mas d'Azil cave – *qv* – in the Pyrenean foothills), people once again lived in caves, both in the Pyrenees and the Dordogne. The Paleolithic was followed by the Mesolithic (10 000 to 7 500 years ago) which was marked by a decline in artistic output, although increasingly sophisticated implements were made like the miniaturised tools and new types of harpoon found at Mas d'Azil. There followed the Neolithic, the period in which the first settled agricultural societies appear and which leads us out of prehistoric times into the era of writing and recorded history.

The slow pace of human progress stuns the imagination; it took people about 30 000 centuries to learn to polish stone; in contrast, the 50 centuries which followed saw the rise of the brilliant civilisations of the Near East and Egypt and the discovery and use of metal (bronze).

CAPITAL OF PREHISTORY

There are almost 200 prehistoric sites in the Dordogne, more than half of them in the vicinity of Les Eyzies. The area has easily-accessible natural **caves** ⊙ and shelters as well as rock projections forming a natural habitat. Prehistoric people have left many traces of their activities. Two hundred centuries before civilisations arose along the Tigris and the Nile, the valley of the Vézère was inhabited by accomplished artists who carved in ivory and reindeer horn and painted on the walls of caves. Les Eyzies was one of humanity's capitals long before Nineveh; the deposits at **Laugerie-Haute** ⊙ are all of six metres – 20ft thick; they reveal to us 7 000 years of civilisation (Solutrean and Magdalenian cultures).

⊙ ►► Grotte du Grand-Roc★★; Musée National de la Préhistoire★★; Grotte de Font-de-Gaume.

Le FAOUËT

Population 2 869
Map p 4 – Michelin map 58 fold 17 or 230 fold 20 – Green Guide Brittany

Pleasantly sited in well-wooded countryside, this large village attests to the period of great prosperity which followed the troubled times brought about by the War of the Breton Succession. In the 15C, nine fairs a year were held here, leading to the construction of the great market hall.

Halle – Built at the beginning of the 16C, it is divided into three naves, each of 15 bays; its massive timber roof is covered with slates and supported on granite columns.

★ **Chapelle St-Fiacre** – *2.5km – 1 1/2 miles south.* – The Breton countryside is dotted with many such isolated rural chapels. The Bouteville family were anxious to emulate their rivals, the great de Rohans, who were building the church and hospital at Kernascleden; begun in 1450, the chapel here took 30 years to complete and was probably endowed with a hospice for pilgrims and the sick.

Flanked by two bell-turrets, the west front is dominated by a central belfry with a tall spire and projecting balcony like that of the Kreisker Chapel (*p 291*).

The Flamboyant **rood-screen**★★ of 1480 is a superb example of Breton painted wood sculpture.

The 16C windows, divided horizontally, mark that moment in the art of stained glass when it evolves from a series of medallions to a planned composition. Particularly fine are the scenes of the Passion in the main window of the chancel, the Life of John the Baptist in the south transept, and a Jesse Tree and the Life of St Fiacre in the north transept.

Rood-screen in the Chapelle St-Fiacre, Le Faouët

FÉCAMP★★

Population 20 808
Map p 5 – Michelin map 52 fold 12 or 54 fold 8 or 231 fold 8
Green Guide Normandy

Fécamp's main activity is still its port, a long-standing "capital" for cod fishing in French Newfoundland; today it caters for both industry (timber, bulk goods) and fishing (herring and mackerel). Several smoking and deep-freezing factories have been set up nearby.

As early as the 11C Fécamp had seen considerable monastic activity as a result of the efforts of Guglielmo da Volpiano. This energetic cleric had been Abbot of St-Bénigne at Dijon where he had implemented the important reform which had originated from Cluny and which involved the worship of the Precious Blood and of the Holy Trinity. That master of the short story, **Guy de Maupassant** (1850-93), lived in the town and used it as the setting for much of his literary output.

★★ **Église de la Trinité** – As big as any cathedral, the ancient abbey church marks an important stage in the evolution of Gothic architecture in Normandy. Built for the most part between 1168 and 1219, it was much influenced by the developments taking place in the Île de France (use of tribunes as in the churches derived from St Denis outside Paris, the combination of flying buttresses and triforium pioneered at Chartres which made the tribunes redundant and which here is seen in the south wall of the chancel).

Norman regionalism reasserts itself however in a number of ways: in the slender lantern tower high above the crossing and in the inspection gallery at the base of the triforium windows.

In the south transept chapel is a beautiful **Dormition of the Virgin**★.

⊘ ►► Palais Bénédictine★★ – objets d'art, history and production of Benedictine; Musée des Terre Neuvas et de la Grande Pêche★; Musée Centre des Arts★ – ceramics, ivory, archaeology, regional furniture.

FENIOUX★

Population 133
Map p 8 – Michelin map 71 fold 4 or 233 fold 16 – Green Guide Atlantic Coast

The 11C country **church**★ at Fenioux is pleasing in its simplicity. On the south side of the building are the ruined cloisters of an earlier Carolingian edifice retained by the architects who reconstructed the rest of the church between 1000 and 1050.

The west front has perhaps the finest example of the didactic sculpture of the Saintonge School; the signs of the Zodiac emphasise the passage of time, the cycle of the months, the Wise and Foolish Virgins, and the Vices and Virtues (the triumph of Good over Evil).

The little north doorway is charmingly decorated with leaves and with the flowers of the clematis which adorns so many houses in the Saintonge area. The belfry is a masterpiece of delicate construction in spite of a certain stiffness resulting from its restoration by followers of Viollet-le-Duc in the 19C.

★ **Lanterne des Morts** – These unusual constructions were common in the region in the 11C and 12C. They consist of a sepulchre, steps leading up to an altar, a hollow column, the top of which housed an eternal flame, the whole surmounted by a little roof and a splendid cross. This is a particularly fine example.

FERNEY-VOLTAIRE

Population 6 408
Map p 11 – Michelin map 70 south of fold 16 or 243 fold 44
Green Guide Burgundy Jura

Located right on France's frontier with Switzerland, Ferney was the home of one of the sharpest minds of 18C Europe.

François-Marie Arouet (1694-1778), who took the name of **Voltaire,** acquired the Ferney estate in 1758. Its proximity to the border enabled him to dodge the difficulties his provocative plays caused when performed before the good citizens of Geneva, as well as allowing him to slip across the frontier whenever he needed a refuge away from France.

In 1758, this "genial jack of all trades" (E. Faguet) settled down in the château at Ferney. By this time he had already spent two years in England, whose political life he tended to view through rose-coloured spectacles, and three years at the court of Frederick the Great as a kind of cultural ambassador. He had written in all the main literary genres; epic, in the *Henriade* of 1723, tragedy with *Mérope* in 1743, history in 1751 with *The Century of Louis XIV* and the *Essay on Manners (Essai sur les mœurs).* Now his philosophical period was about to begin. A tireless enemy of privilege and fanaticism, he also fought for the rehabilitation of priests and Protestants. At the age of 70, more than half his output of correspondence and pamphlets remained to be written. Because of their often perverse destructiveness the latter were nicknamed "Voltaire's rockets". Ferney became a place of pilgrimage for all sorts of admirers, people of power as well as men of letters. The little town benefited from the attentions of its progressive lord of the manor, acquiring a hospital, a school, clock-making enterprises and solid stone houses.

At the age of 83 he received a triumphal welcome in Paris where he had gone to see a production of his *Irène* at the Tuileries Palace. This liveliest of men, the spokesman of his age, was

Houdon's bust of Voltaire
(Musée du Louvre, Paris)

lionized. But the excitement proved too much; Voltaire, who was widely acclaimed as the champion of the oppressed and whose *Candide* is known "wherever French is read" (G. Brereton), passed away in Paris, filled with regret that his work had not been completed.

Visiting conditions at the château are somewhat restrictive and homage to the great man is best paid at the commemorative statue to him in the town centre.

FIGEAC★★

Population 9 549
Michelin map 79 fold 10 or 235 fold 11 – Green Guide Dordogne
Town plan in the current Michelin Red Guide France

Sprawled along the north bank of the Célé, Figeac's development began at the point where the Auvergne meets Upper Quercy. A commercial town, it had a prestigious past as is shown in the architecture of its tall sandstone town houses.

The small city's main industrial concern is Ratier, a company which specialises in aeronautical construction.

Jean-François Champollion - Champollion, the outstanding Orientalist, whose brilliance enabled Egyptology to make such great strides, was born at Figeac in December 1790. At the beginning of the 19C, Ancien Egyptian civilization was still a mystery, since the meaning of hieroglyphics (the word means "sacred carving") had not yet been deciphered.

By the time Champollion was 14, he had a command of Greek, Latin, Hebrew, Arabic, Chaldean and Syrian. After his studies in Paris, he lectured in history, at the youthful age of 19, at Grenoble University.

He set himself the task of deciphering a polished basalt tablet, showing three different inscriptions (Egyptian hieroglyphics, demotic – simplified Egyptian script which appeared around 650 BC – and Greek), which had been discovered in 1799 by members of Napoleon's expedition to Egypt near Rosetta in the northwest Nile delta, from which it derives its name – the Rosetta Stone.

In 1826, he founded the Egyptology Museum at the Louvre Palace, Paris, and became its first curator. In 1831, he was appointed Professor of Archaeology at the Collège de France, however he gave only three lecture courses before dying a year later, worn out by all his hard work.

★OLD FIGEAC

The old quarter, surrounded by boulevards which trace the line of the former moats, has kept its medieval town plan with its narrow and tortuous alleys. The buildings, built in elegant beige sandstone, exemplify the architecture of the 13, 14 and 15C. Generally the ground floor was opened by large pointed arches and the first floor had a gallery of arcaded bays. Underneath the flat tiled roof was the *soleilho*, an open attic, which was used to dry laundry, store wood, grow plants etc. Its openings were separated by columns or pillars in wood or stone, sometimes even brick, which held up the roof. Other noticeable period architectural features to be discovered during your tour of the old quarter are: corbelled towers, doorways, spiral staircases and some of the top storeys, which are half-timbered and of brick.

⊙ ➤ Hôtel de la Monnaie★; Musée Champollion.★

FILITOSA★★

Map p 10 – Michelin map 90 fold 18 – Green Guide Corse (in French)

This fascinating site was discovered in 1946; the beginnings of Corsican history are all visible here, from the Neolithic (6000-2000 BC), to the Megalithic (3000-1000 BC) and the Torreen (1500-800 BC), and finally to the Roman.

The **Megalithic people** interred their dead in caves or beneath dolmens. Peaceful in their ways, they made granite sculptures using tools fashioned from imported obsidian. About 1800 BC they raised menhirs to their chiefs, prototypical statues in which the head is already distinct from the body. Around 1500 BC, the representation of anatomy becomes more precise, with the spine and shoulder-blades shown. Finally, in the hope of acquiring their powers, they depicted their enemies as armed men killed in combat; these are the Torreens.

The **Torreens** were a sea-faring, warlike people, technically advanced, with clothes made of leather, breast-plates and weapons of bronze and iron. They had already harassed the empires around the edge of the Mediterranean and caused concern to the Egypt of Rameses III. But they were essentially a race of builders, and in time began to lead a more settled existence, involving trading and other links with the peoples of Italy and Sardinia. Over a period of some 500 years they gradually pushed the Megalithic people into the northern part of Corsica before they themselves abandoned the island around 800 BC, probably making for Sardinia.

★★ **Station préhistorique** ⊙ – By the path leading to the site stands the superb menhir known as Filitosa V bearing, in front a long sword and an oblique dagger, and behind, anatomical or clothinq details.

A stone wall built by the Megalithic people encloses the site. Within it, four striking groups of monuments testify to the domination exercised by the Torreens: the **East Monument** (Monument est) which they filled in; the remains of **huts** which they reused, the circular **Central Monument**, and the fragments of menhir-statues. The latter had been made by the Megalithic people; the Torreens cut them up and re-used them, face downwards, in the construction of the Central Monument, doubtless to signal their supremacy. Some of them, however, have been stood upright again, and Filitosa IX and XIII frame the way into the Central Monument. The **West Monument** (Monument ouest) is Torreen, and is built on Megalithic foundations.

The five menhir-statues near an age-old olive-tree on the far slope of the valley mark the end of the Megalithic period in this area.

FOIX★

Population 9 660
Map p 9 – Michelin map 86 folds 4, 5 or 235 fold 42
Green Guide Pyrenees-Languedoc-Tarn Gorges
Town plan in the current Michelin Red Guide France

Foix is both the name of a region – pays de Foix – and of its capital on the Ariège between the high hills of the Plantaurel and the Pyrenees proper. In the Middle Ages the town enjoyed some importance as the capital of the colourful Counts of Foix. At the conclusion of the Albigensian Crusade (qv), the Counts, who had favoured the heresy, were obliged to submit to the King of France. At the end of the 13C they inherited that other Pyrenean statelet, the Béarn, which still enjoyed its independence, and decided to reside there. Their fondness for Foix, their ancestral home, was undimmed, although they failed to maintain it properly, and in the end had to dismantle much of its massive fortifications. But the three great towers remained intact, symbols of their pride, property and power.

The greatest of the Counts was Gaston Febus (1331-91), a brilliant figure whose wide culture did not however stop him killing both his brother and his only son. Henri IV was a member of the family; his accession to the French throne in 1589 meant the formal union of the Pays de Foix with France.

★ **Panorama** – From the **Château** ⊙ rock high above the river there are extensive views over the surrounding region. To the southwest are the green Plantaurel hills, characterized by their remarkably regular relief. To the south are the Pyrenees themselves; among the many summits can be picked out the Trois Seigneurs (2 199m – 7 215ft) and St-Barthélemy (2 368m – 7 769ft). Eastward lies the high and windy Sault plateau from which rise a number of pointed peaks resembling the one on which the Cathar fortress of Montségur (qv) is built.

EXCURSION

★★ **Grotte de Niaux** ⊙ – Michelin map 86 southeast of fold 4 or 235 fold 46 Located in the Vicdessos valley, this cave is famed for its remarkably well preserved prehistoric wall drawings, in particular those depicting animals in the "Black Hall" (Salon noir); the pure, sober lines and high craftsmanship mark the summit of Magdalenian art.

FONTAINEBLEAU★★★

Population 15 714
Map p 6 – Michelin map 106 folds 45, 46
Green Guide Flanders, Picardy and the Paris Region
Town plan in the current Michelin Red Guide France

As early as the 12C, the Capetian kings had built a hunting lodge here, drawn by
the abundant game which thrived in the vast forest.
The woodland covers 25 000ha – 62 000 acres, much of it high forest of sessile
oaks, Norway pines and beeches. It grows on the low east-west sandstone ridges,
among the crags and boulders of stony wastelands, and in the sandy depressions
between the ridges. The Forest is traversed by a network of well-signposted
footpaths. Since the days of Colbert's Forestry Ordinance of 1669, "a masterpiece
of forestry administration" (J.L. Reed), it has been carefully managed to ensure
its long-term survival.
In spite of the forest's fame and popularity, it is the palace begun by François I
which has made the reputation of Fontainebleau.
A taste for natural surroundings together with its role as a military base (notably
for cavalry) led to the growth of the town of Fontainebleau in the 19C. Between
1947-67 it was home to the headquarters of NATO.

★★★ **Palace** ⊙ – From the days of the Capetian kings to the time of Napoleon III,
the Palace of Fontainebleau has been lived in, added to and altered by the
sovereigns of France. Napoleon Bonaparte liked it; here, in contrast to at
Versailles, he was free of the overwhelming presence of Louis XIV, a formidable
predecessor in the quest for glory. He called Fontainebleau "the house of
Eternity", furnished it in Empire style and set about altering it for himself, for
Josephine, and for Pope Pius VII.
In 1528, François I commissioned Gilles Le Breton to replace the existing
medieval buildings by two structures linked by a gallery. Like his predecessor
Charles VIII, while campaigning in Italy, François had acquired a taste for
agreeable surroundings adorned with works of art. He brought in gifted and
prolific artists who are known as the **First School of Fontainebleau**. They included
Rosso (of Florence), Primaticcio (from Perugia), Niccolo dell'Abbate (from
Parma), as well as architects, thinkers, cabinet-makers, goldsmiths, decorators... He also acquired works of art including Leonardo's *Mona Lisa* and
paintings by Raphael. France was thus permeated by Renaissance taste, by
Renaissance mathematics and by an appreciation of the rules of proportion
derived from the architecture of Greece and Rome. The pleasures of life were
savoured anew, and painters and sculptors abandoned religious subjects in favour
of older divinities.

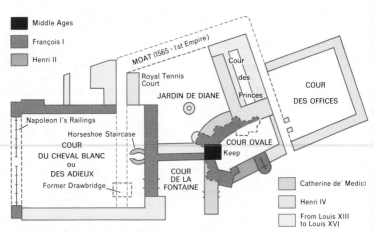

This era endowed the palace with many of its most splendid features: on the
outside, the left wing and façade of the **Court of the White Horse** or **Farewell Court★★**
(Cour du Cheval Blanc or des Adieux), the concave section of the **Oval Court★** (Cour
Ovale), the **Golden Gate★** (Porte dorée) with its loggia painted by Primaticcio, and
on the inside, the **François I Gallery★★★** (Galerie François I) by Rosso, the first
important French interior to mix frescoes and stucco work, and the **Ballroom★★★**
(Salle de bal) painted by Primaticcio and dell'Abbate and completed by Philibert
Delorme in the reign of Henri II.
Henri II, Catherine de' Medici and Charles IX carried on the work initiated during
this most creative and productive period.

Henri IV enlarged the palace further by building the real tennis court (Jeu de Paume), and the Diana Gallery (Galerie de Diane). He also completed the enclosure of the Oval Court. There was a change of style; the Second School of Fontainebleau looked to Flanders for its inspiration and found its artists in the Ile de France; oil was now the preferred medium for painting.

Louis XIII completed the Farewell Court. It was here, from the famous horseshoe staircase built by Du Cerceau, that Napoleon bade his men farewell on 20 April 1814 following his abdication.

◉ ►► First floor State Rooms★★★ (Ensemble des Grands Appartements); Ground floor State Rooms★ (Petits Appartements); Musée Napoléon★; Gardens★ (Jardins).

La FONTAINE-DE-VAUCLUSE★★★

Map p 10 – Michelin map 81 fold 13 or 245 fold 17 or 246 fold 11
Green Guide Provence

An excursion *(1 hour Rtn on foot)* from the village of the same name, takes in this resurgent spring which was famous enough to figure in Strabo's Geography more than 2 000 years ago; the word Vauclusian is used world-wide to define springs of this type. Gushing forth at the foot of one of the cliffs marking the limits of the Vaucluse upland, it is one of the most spectacular phenomena of its kind in the world.

It is fed by rain falling high up on the Vaucluse, the Ventoux Massif and Mount Lure; water penetrates these highly fissured limestone uplands with their 400-plus chasms *(avens)* and collects in a vast, still unexplored cavern from which it is forced out under pressure to the surface by way of a fault-line.

For more than a century attempts have been made to explore the depths. In 1983 Hasenmayer went down 200m - 656ft below the surface; a remote-controlled video-equipped device reached a depth of 315m - 1 033ft in 1985 without however touching bottom.

Towards the end of the winter, the flow from the underground source can amount to 100m³ - 3 631 cubic feet per second. At such times the waters of the River Sorgue foam and spray against the rocks, a magnificent natural spectacle. In the dry season screens of trees mark out the strata of the plateau which is pitted by pot holes.

Abbaye de FONTENAY★★★

Map p 6 – Michelin map 65 southwest of fold 8 or 243 fold 2
Green Guide Burgundy Jura

Tucked away in its lonely valley near the River Brenne, Fontenay is very evocative of the self-sufficient life of a Cistercian abbey of the 12C.

Saint Bernard (1091-1153) – By the end of the 11C there had arisen a longing for a greater degree of asceticism, spirituality and a renunciation of self in religious life, which could not be satisfied by the wealth and power represented by Cluny. One response was the founding of the Cistercian Order in 1198 by Robert, Abbot of Molesme, at Cîteaux, 23km - 14 miles south of Dijon. Bernard, a young nobleman born at the Château of Fontaine near Dijon, came to Cîteaux in 1112 and before long had restored the fortunes of the abbey which had fallen on hard times. He was made responsible for establishing the abbey at Clairvaux on the River Aube, then, in 1118, at the age of 27, he founded Fontenay, his "second daughter".

Saint Bernard was one of the great spiritual leaders of the Middle Ages, a writer, preacher, theologian, philosopher and statesman. Though diminished physically by fasting and self-mortification, he was quite tireless. He could be gentle and humble, but above all possessed an extraordinary will which he put entirely in the service of the Church. By the time of his death, at Clairvaux, he had witnessed the founding of 167 Cistercian monasteries. At the end of the 13C their number had risen to 700 and the Order enriched by donations was no longer in a position to admonish Cluny. ·

Ancienne abbaye ◉ – Fontenay is the architectural expression of the ideas of St Bernard; its buildings form the perfect setting for monastic life led according to the Rule of St Benedict. The harmonious apportionment of time between prayer, work (manual as well as intellectual, unlike Cluny), and sleep found its physical equivalent in the functional arrangement of external and internal spaces: church, cloisters, chapter house, scriptorium (where manuscripts were copied), dormitory, forge...

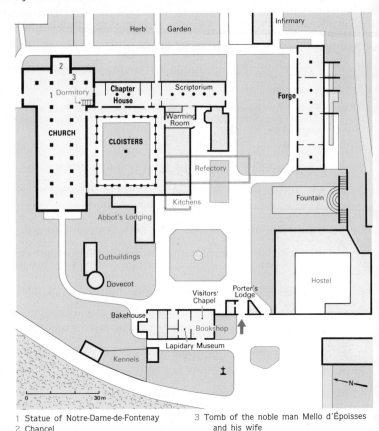

Abbaye de FONTENAY

1 Statue of Notre-Dame-de-Fontenay
2 Chancel

3 Tomb of the noble man Mello d'Époisses
   and his wife

The ravages of time have left the abbey in a sad state. It was sacked by the English and plundered by marauding bands of mercenaries in the Hundred Years War *(qv)*; it suffered during the Wars of Religion *(qv)* and under the regime of Commendam (when abbots were nominated by royal favour and were only interested in the revenues). It was sold during the French Revolution and became a paper mill. Since 1906 its owners have been endeavouring to restore it to its original condition.

The **abbey church** was built between 1139 and 1147. It is the first example of the "monastic simplicity" characteristic of the architecture promoted by St Bernard, and is laid out in the most straightforward way, with a square chancel and chapels of square plan. The nave has a broken barrel-vault, solidly supported by cross-vaulted aisles. The lesson of Cluny, whose ambitious vault had collapsed in 1125, had clearly been learnt.

FONTEVRAUD L'ABBAYE★★

Map p 5
Michelin map 64 southwest of fold 13 or 232 fold 33
Green Guide Châteaux of the Loire

The Order of Fontevraud was founded in 1099 as a result of the failure in France of Pope Gregory's reform which had been designed to enhance both the competence and the respectability of the clergy.

In many ways the Plantagenets considered themselves to be more Angevin than English, and chose the abbey as their last resting place. When Eleanor of Aquitaine died at Fontevraud in 1204, her husband Henry II and her son Richard Lionheart were already buried here.

The Order was aristocratic in nature and accommodated both sexes. It was presided over by an abbess (this at a time when the cult of the Virgin Mary was growing and influencing the status of womanhood). The abbey formed the largest monastic grouping in France and comprised five distinct elements: St Mary (nuns), St-Jean-de-l'Habit (monks), St Benedict (hospice), St Lazarus (lepers) and St Mary Magdalen (fallen women).

Having suffered in their time from the assaults of Huguenots and Revolutionaries and from use as a penitentiary, the abbey buildings are now the subject of thoroughgoing restoration.

★★ **Église abbatiale** ⊙ – *Time: 1 hour*. Built between 1104 and 1150, this abbey church is closer in style to the architecture of southwestern France than to that of the Île-de-France, with which Anjou had no political ties at the time.

Characteristically southwestern is the sequence of four domes forming the roof of the nave, while the delicately carved capitals with their foliated scrolls and palm leaves recall the workmanship of the Saintonge and Angoulême areas and the pyramidal dome over the crossing is very much in the manner of the Church of St-Ours at Loches.

The chancel is graceful in its clarity and simplicity.

In the transept crossing are a number of **Plantagenet tombs**★, good examples of Gothic funerary sculpture. The figures of Henry Plantagenet (died 1189), of Richard Lionheart (died 1199) and of Eleanor of Aquitaine (died 1204) are in painted tufa, while the figure of Isabel of Angoulême, John Lackland's wife (died 1218), is of polychrome wood.

★★ **Kitchen (cuisine)** – This highly individual structure, 27m – 89ft high, dates from around 1160 and was restored in 1902. It is a rare example of a Romanesque kitchen, with a tiled roof characteristic of the Poitiers area. It is built up in alternately square and octagonal stages. Its main function was as a smoke-house (meat and fish, especially salmon). Its fireplaces, arranged in pairs, could be lit according to the direction of the wind.

► ► Église St-Michel★.

Château de FOUGÈRES★★

Map p 5 – Michelin map 59 fold 18 or 230 fold 28 – Green Guide Brittany
Town plan in the current Michelin Red Guide France

In the 19C Fougères was the most industrialised town in Brittany, having abandoned cloth-making in favour of shoe-production. The area formed part of the frontier region taken from the Franks in 850 AD by **Nominoé** *(qv)*.

Château ⊙ – It is set on a rocky promontory protected by an easily-flooded meander which formed an effective defence right up to the invention of artillery. The first fortifications date from the 10C, built in response to the entry of the Vikings into Normandy under the terms of the Treaty of St-Clair-sur-Epte of 911.

Baron Raoul II began to rebuild in stone in 1173. In the 13C the castle's mighty towers served to protect Brittany from Capetian France; round or square, with their machicolations and stonework of schist strengthened with granite, they mark the progress of military architecture. After its important role in the War of the Breton Succession *(qv)* in the 14C, the castle was partly demolished by Richelieu in pursuit of his centralising policy designed to limit the power of the great feudal lords.

► ► Église St-Sulpice★; Public Gardens★.

Cap FRÉHEL★★★

Map p 5 – Michelin map 59 fold 5 or 230 fold 10 – Green Guide Brittany

Located near the lighthouse *(1/2 hour Rtn on foot)*, this is one of the most magnificent **sights** ⊙ the Breton coast has to offer. The action of the waves has worn away the softer rocks around, and the great cliff of red sandstone rises 70m – 230ft above the reefs at its foot.

Despite the abundant rainfall, the porosity of the rock and the exposure to wind mean that only plants which are well adapted to dry conditions can flourish here (heather and rushes).

The **panorama**★★★ from the cliff-top is superb, taking in the Channel Islands and the Cotentin Peninsula.

For a quiet place to stay
Consult the annual **Michelin Red Guide France** *(hotels and restaurants)*
and the **Michelin Guide Camping Caravaning France**
which offer a choice of pleasant hotels and quiet campsites
in convenient locations

Le FUTUROSCOPE★★

Michelin map 68 folds 13, 14 and 232 fold 46 (southeast)
Green Guide Atlantic Coast

This vast 70ha – 173 acre development on the northern outskirts of Poitiers was created to introduce the public to the realities of modern technology and to give it an insight into future developments in a world dominated by screen images.

The complex, the **European Park of the Moving Image** or more simply **Le Futuroscope** ⊙, presents a modernistic architectural universe of steel and glass which was conceived by the French architect Denis Laming; it is dominated by a symbolic sphere above the Communication Pavilion. Numerous attractions, both educational and purely entertaining, are on offer.

Advances in the field of communications are on display in several buildings and halls. Among the most astonishing shows, the **Lac enchanté** and its **Théâtre Alphanumérique** which present performances and productions incorporating the technology of the future. **Kinémax, Omnimax** and **Solido** will enable the visitor to view films from a different angle (3D films, hemispherical cinema etc.).

Cirque de GAVARNIE★★★

Map p 8 – Michelin map 85 fold 18 or 243 folds 47, 48
Green Guide Atlantic Coast

The village of Gavarnie lies near the upper end of a blind valley high in the Central Pyrenees; its fame is due to its cirque, a natural amphitheatre forming one of Europe's most magnificent mountain landscapes.

The Cirque de Gavarnie *(3 1/2 hours Rtn on foot from the village horses or donkeys can be hired)* rises in a series of huge steps (formed by more resistant strata and marked by permanent deposits of snow and ice) to the crest-line from which a number of peaks stand out at more than 3 000m – 10 000ft. The base of the cirque is 3 1/2km – 2 miles across while the crest-line extends over 14km – 9 miles.

Innumerable falls cascade down the rock walls, the greatest of them (the Grande Cascade), 422m – 1 385ft high, fed by meltwater from the Marboré snowfields and from the frozen lake of Mont-Perdu.

Downstream from the cirque, below the restaurant, the waters of the torrent have carved a gorge through the rock bar and a pine forest has colonised the stony wastes of the moraine. Further downstream other typically glacial features like hanging valleys and secondary moraines make their appearance; together with the extensive grasslands, they compose a landscape of great serenity and charm. Some distance further northwards, as the torrent approaches the little town of Luz-St-Sauveur it has carved a deep and narrow gorge through the marble outcrop. The splendours of Gavarnie excited people's imagination well before **Victor Hugo** sang its praises; the great cleft in the rock wall visible from as far away as Gèdre has long been known as Roland's Breach (La Brèche de Roland). The dying Christian knight is supposed to have tried in vain to smash his sword Durandal against the rock here in order to stop it falling into the hands of the pursuing infidels. In fact, the rear-guard of Charlemagne's army was ambushed by the Basques 115km – some 70 miles to the west at the Pass of Roncesvalles in 778. The **Song of Roland** was the first French verse-chronicle *(chanson de geste)*. Probably 11C in date, it is outstanding in epic literature in that it depicts the psychological state of its hero as defeat and death loom rather than simply concentrating on his glorious feats of arms or celebrating the courage of Charlemagne's twelve peers as they tried vainly to fight off their attackers.

GORDES★

Population 2 031
Map p 10 – Michelin map 81 fold 13 or 245 fold 17 or 246 fold 11
Green Guide Provence

The **site**★ of Gordes is a spectacular one; the village's buildings rise in sun-soaked tiers up the rocky slopes on the edge of the Vaucluse plateau. The Vaucluse forms one of the distinct landscapes of the southernmost Alps; its succession of limestone outcrops carry an impoverished *garrigue* vegetation, though some of its lower-lying areas support vines and fruit-trees in spite of the difficulties of irrigation.

Château ⊙ – Rebuilt at the time of the Renaissance it has a splendid **chimneypiece**★ of 1541. It houses the Victor Vasarely Foundation and the **Musée Didactique Vasarely**★, gathering together paintings and decorative panels by this artist from Pécs in Southern Hungary. As early as 1930, Vasarely was making studies of the ways in which line and colour could be manipulated to create optical effects. His pioneering work led him from the *Graphisms* of 1929 via his Denfert and Black and White periods to the *Permutations* and *Expanding Structures* of 1964-76

EXCURSIONS

★★ **Abbaye de Sénanque** ⊙ – *4km – 2 1/2 miles north.* Founded in 1148, this is a characteristically Cistercian abbey, in a remote **site**★ conducive to the contemplative life and the renunciation of self. The buildings grouped together to form the monastic community are almost complete; the abbey church is notable for its purity of line and lack of distracting ornamentation and for the table tracing the links between the daughter houses of the Cistercian Order *(qv)* in the 12C.

★ **Village des Bories** ⊙ – *3.5km – 2 miles southwest.* Corbelled drystone structures of this kind are to be found from Iceland to the Middle East as well as in many other parts of France. In Provence they have existed for almost 4 000 years and seem to have been built in great numbers on the Vaucluse between the 14C and the 19C. Their purposes appear to have been manifold, some serving as field shelters, others as dwellings. They are marvels of craftsmanslike handling of the simplest of materials.
The village consists of a number of dwellings as well as structures for threshing, baking, oil pressing and housing animals.

GRAND COLOMBIER★★

Map p 11 – Michelin map 74 fold 5 or 244 fold 17 – Green Guide Burgundy Jura

At 1 571m – 5 154ft the Grand Colombier forms the highest point in the Bugey area. The viewpoint at the summit is one of the finest in the whole of the Jura and the only one accessible by car. In geological terms, the structure here consists of limestone beds forming a dome which has been subsequently eroded, exposing the older rocks making up its core.

From Virieu-le-Petit to Culoz

– *29km – 18 miles.* The road rises steeply (maximum gradient 19%) passing first through splendid fir-woods. At the summit with its cross and triangulation-point there is the widest of panoramas, taking in the Jura, the Dombes plateau, the valley of the Rhône, the Massif Central and the Alps. The features of the landscape read almost like a geological section, with the domes of anticlines and troughs of synclines clearly distinguishable. In the distance the Grand Fene-strez (**Observatory**★★) rears up from the Culoz plain which can be reached by car via a boldly-designed hairpin road.

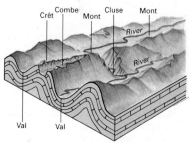

Diagram showing the typical structure of the folded Jura.

The synclines form valleys *(vals)* running parallel to each other, separated by anticlinal ridges *(monts).*
Transversal valleys *(cluses)* cut across anticlines to link two main valleys.
A high-level depression *(combe)* occupies a hollowed-out ridge: it has steep inward-facing scarps *(crêts).*

Écomusée de la GRANDE LANDE★

Map p 8 – Michelin map 78 folds 1 to 5 or 79 folds 1 to 11
or 233 folds 6 to 11 or 234 fold 18
Green Guide Atlantic Coast

The Grande Lande Open-air Museum comprises three seperate sites in the heart of the Parc naturel régional des Landes de Gascogne. Between them they evoke the daily life and traditional activities of the region in the 18 and 19C.
The clearing was once inhabited by three families; its thirty or so buildings have been restored or replaced on their original site. As well as the master's dwelling *(marquèze)*, there is an array of other structures serving a variety of purposes, none of them with foundations and relying for their stability on the soundness of their timber construction. A flock of sheep, hives of tiny black bees and an orchard complete the picture of life as led in this locality.

Marquèze ⊙ – *Access only by train (2 1/2 hours) from Sabres:* built in 1824 of stout beams and cob walls and with a three-pitched roof.
Les Brassiers: the more modest servants' quarters.
Moulin de Bas: the corn-mill.
Les charbonnières: the production of charcoal by means of slow combustion.
The traditional industry based on resin products is interpreted at Luxey *(22km – 14 miles northeast).*

The **Landes** were once a marine depression, subsequently filled with fine sands deposited by the Pyrenean glaciers of Quaternary times. These sands are quite distinct from those on the coast. The vast tract is poorly drained, and below the surface is a hard impermeable pan, further reducing its fertility.

Man's conquest over Nature

Since Roman times, the pine forest growing on the better-drained soils has tended to fluctuate in extent, reflecting the changing demands made on it by the local population as well as changes in climatic and other conditions. In the late 18C, Brémontier followed his success in stabilising the coastal dunes when he fixed some 4 000ha – 10 000 acres of inland sands by planting pines, broom and gorse in a matrix of faggots.

The problem of drainage remained to be tackled. It was solved in 1857 by Chambrelent who enabled the area to be put into productive use by means of a system of ditches and filtering wells. Napoleon III set a good example by purchasing the 8 000ha – 20 000 acre Solferino estate. By 1890, the area under maritime pines was 840km² – 325sq miles; today the area under woodland continues to grow at the expense of arable and pasture land. The pines of the Landes would be capable of supplying the whole of France's needs for resin products, though because of competition from Asia the present proportion is a mere 6%. But the wood serves any number of useful purposes, sawn timber, veneers, paper pulp, wood charcoal, wood alcohol...

GRENOBLE★★

Conurbation 400 141
Map p 10 – Michelin map 77 fold 5 or 244 fold 28
Green Guide Alpes du Nord (in French)
Town plan in the current Michelin Red Guide France

Undisputed capital of the French Alps, modern Grenoble is a flourishing city of broad boulevards. It was held back in the past by the precarious nature of its communication links; though well-sited on the roads leading from the Rhône valley to Turin and Cannes, frequent floods and challenging gradients made travelling an uncertain business.

Fort de la Bastille ⓥ – *Access by cablecar.*
The fort was built in the 16C and strengthened in the 19C. Its function was to protect the approaches to the city.

It has the best **view★★★** over the town set magnificently between the Vercors plateau to the southwest, the long narrow Taillefer ridge to the southeast and the Chartreuse Massif (Massif de la Chartreuse) to the north. Far below is the Isère, flowing in stately fashion from the Grésivaudan; it is joined here by the vigorous waters of the Drac which has forced the bigger stream to the north. Between them, the two rivers bring down some 20 000 tons of material a day. Their mingled waters have carved out the valley separating the Chartreuse and Vercors massifs which forms an important communications axis.

Église St-Laurent ⓥ – The 11C-12C Romanesque church is built over its predecessor which dates back to Merovingian times. The latter constitutes the **crypt★**. It has four apses, a colonnade whose shafts are of Roman date, and capitals carved with primitive Christian motifs.

★ **Old Grenoble** – The vast quantities of material brought down by the restless River Drac ("that most brutal, most violent of Alpine tributaries" R. Blanchard) formed an alluvial fan on which a fortified Roman town was sited, close to the present-day Place Granette (celebrated by Stendhal) and on either side of the Grande-Rue, itself a Roman road. By the 13C the town had spread northeastwards as far as the Isère where today a number of courtyards and porches dating from the 16C can be found (No 8 Rue Brocherie, nos 8 and 10 Rue Chenoise). In the reign of Henri IV the city was captured by Lesdiguières, commander of the armies of Piedmont and Savoy, who fortified it further, thereby accommodating the urban growth due to the beginnings of industrial activity. His son-in-law, Marshal Créqui, extended this work to the west. Later fortifications, the Enceinte Haxo, doubled the area of the city to the south and catered for the expansion which took place at the end of the 19C.

The inventor Vaucanson (1709-82) was born in the old town. He designed a water-pump, a slide-lathe and various devices to regulate silk-throwing. But he was led astray by his success, and is best known for his wonderful automata.

Cathédrale – On the right of the chancel is an unusual Flamboyant **ciborium★** of the 14C in polychrome stone.

★ **Palais de Justice** – To the left is a wing in Flamboyant style; the right wing is of Renaissance date, still with a certain irregularity in the arrangement of the windows from one floor to the other. Between the wings is the apse of the chapel, also in Flamboyant style.

★★ **Musée de Grenoble** ⊘ – Built on the bank of the river Isère in the heart of the old town, this museum, inaugurated in 1994, is an example of architectural sobriety. In the main hall, the collection is concentrated on the first floor. On each side of a white gallery, alcoves house 16-19C works. Further on, the rounded end of the building is the setting for a collection of modern and contemporary art where the natural lighting is modulated according to each work of art.

Huge windows enable the visitor to observe the numerous and massive sculptures which "animate" the parvis and the Parc Michallon, outside the north building. This is one of France's most important provincial museums. The collections include fine modern works like Matisse's *Interior with Aubergines* and Picasso's *Woman Reading* as well as Old Masters like de Champaigne's *John the Baptist*, Rubens' *Pope Gregory surrounded by Saints* or de La Tour's *St Jerome*. Most art movements after 1945 are represented: Art Informel, New Realism, "Supports-surfaces", Pop Art and Minimalism.

⊘ ►► Musée Dauphinois★ – popular art and traditions.

GRIGNAN★

Map p 10 – Michelin map 81 fold 2 or 245 fold 3 or 246 folds 8, 22
Green Guide Provence

The old town of Grignan is dominated by its château which was the home of Count François de Grignan, Louis XIV's Lieutenant General of Provence. In 1669, at the age of 40, with two marriages already behind him, he married Françoise-Marguerite, the daughter of Mme de Sévigné, who became a frequent visitor. The letters written by mother to daughter over a period of 27 years were to create a new literary genre; full of keen observation, wit and spontaneity, they are an inexhaustible source of information to historians of the age of Louis XIV.

Built in 1556, the Renaissance south front of the **château**★★ ⊘ was restored early in the 20C following a fire. With its superimposed columns, moulded pilasters, mullioned windows and shell-decorated niches, it marks the arrival of Renaissance architecture in Provence.

The original courtyard is flanked by a Gothic pavilion and opens out onto the terrace constructed over the Church of St-Sauveur. From here there is a **view**★ over the Tricastin area, Mount Ventoux and the plain of the old Comtat Venaissin. Inside the château are evocative **furnishings**★ of many periods, Louis XIII, Régence and Louis XV.

GUÉRANDE★

Population 11 665
Map p 4 – Michelin map 63 fold 3 or 230 fold 51 – Green Guide Brittany

Secure behind its well-preserved ramparts, Guérande has kept the look of a proud little medieval town which once sent its delegates to the States of Brittany. It is set between the marshlands of the Grande Brière (now a Regional Nature Park) and the extensive salt-marshes of the former gulf. Until the 15C it was a port of some importance which shipped quantities of salt to the Baltic, but then lost out to the more dynamic port towns of Nantes on the Loire and Le Croisic at the entrance to the gulf.

★ **Ramparts** – Begun in 1343, they were only completed in 1476 in the reign of Duke Francis II (Governor's Residence – Logis du Gouverneur). They are a reminder of difficult and insecure times when towns were forced to protect themselves with such elaborate defences.

★ **Collégiale St-Aubin** – Built between the 12C and the 16C, the church has a striking west front in granite. Embedded in a buttress on the right is an outdoor pulpit. On the south side, a 16C portal in the form of a porch is distinguished by Renaissance motifs.

The nave with its high Gothic arches was re-roofed in brick in the 19C. The capitals are decorated with grotesque figures and foliage. The chancel is lit by a magnificent stained glass window showing the Assumption of the Virgin Mary (much restored in the 19C); to the north is another window depicting the Life of St Peter. There is a Louis XIV pulpit, and, to the south, a "crypt" with 6C sarcophagi.

Abbaye d'HAMBYE★★

Map p 5 – Michelin map 59 north of fold 8 or 231 fold 27
Green Guide Normandy

The 12C abbey of Hambye is charmingly sited in the green valley of the Sienne. Its ruins evoke the serenity of Benedictine life and seem to gain from having the heavens as their vault.

The group of buildings is dominated by the **abbey church**★★ ⊘ with slender columns and sharply pointed arches around the choir (1180-1200). The high bell-tower whose upper stage is pierced by round-headed arches was once crowned by a lantern.

The chapter house stands somewhat apart. It is a masterpiece of Norman Gothic, divided into two by six central pillars, the final one of which gathers together the arches of the apse in a masterly way.

Château de HAUTEFORT★★

Map p 8 – Michelin map 75 fold 7 or 233 fold 44 – Green Guide Dordogne

More like a Loire château than a Périgord fortress, the **Château d'Hautefort** ⊘ (1 hour) rises up proudly on its hilltop site, overlooking its extensive and well-kept grounds. Although substantial traces of the former medieval castle are still to be seen, the building is essentially the work of the architect Nicolas Rambourg. A native from Alsace, he rebuilt it between 1625-70 in accordance with the rules of classical architecture then very much in vogue, albeit keeping domes based on the 16C circular plan like those at Valençay château on the Loire river.

Château de Hautefort

In the 11C, the castle passed into the hands of the de Born family whose most famous offspring was the troubadour Bertrand de Born, born here in about 1140.

The virtuous and beautiful Marie de Hautefort (1616-91) added to the place's fame. Lady-in-waiting to Anne of Austria, she inspired Louis XIII's Platonic love. Thereafter, she presided over the salons of the so-called *Précieuses*, ladies dedicated, not without a certain pretension, to refinement in spoken and written expression.

The château was badly damaged by a fire in 1968 but has since undergone a meticulous programme of restoration.

The interior has fine Flemish tapestries saved from the flames, a 17C Felletin landscape, some good pieces of furniture and above all some unusual paved floors. The tower has magnificent **timberwork**★★.

Château du HAUT-KŒNIGSBOURG★★

Map p 7 – Michelin map 62 fold 19 or 87 fold 16 or 242 fold 27
Green Guide Alsace et Lorraine (in French)

This vast mock-medieval edifice ⊘ in pink sandstone overlooks the Alsace plain from its lofty rock rising through the treetops of the Vosges forest **(panorama**★★**)**. Little remains either of the 12C castle nor of the rebuilding carried out by the Counts of Thierstein at the end of the 15C, since the place was besieged, plundered and then dismantled in 1633 by Swedish troops in the course of the Thirty Years War.

The present building is the outcome of an almost complete reconstruction which was carried out on the orders of Emperor William II between 1900-08 during the period when Alsace and Lorraine had been reincorporated into Germany. In the neo-feudal style popular at the time, it provoked bitter controversy, offending archaeologists and architectural purists as well as infuriating French patriots who saw in it a particularly flagrant symbol of the German presence on the west bank of the Rhine.

Le HAVRE★★

Conurbation 250 000
Map p 5 – Michelin map 52 fold 11 or 54 fold 7 or 231 fold 19
Green Guide Normandy
Town plan in the current Michelin Red Guide France

The **port**★★ of Le Havre is where the great urbanised axis stretching from Paris down the Seine finally meets the sea. It is France's second, and Europe's third most important harbour and has car-ferry links to both Britain and Ireland.

A judicious choice – By 1517 the harbour at Harfleur had silted up. To remedy the situation, François I ordered the building of a new port which was to be called "Havre-de-Grâce" (Harbour of Grace). The marshy site selected by Admiral Bonnivet seemed unpromising, but his choice was a genial one since the tide remained at the flood two hours longer here than elsewhere. The port area has subsequently spread some 20km – 12 miles upstream with a parallel development, mostly on the north bank, of chemical, engineering and motor industries, shipyards and refineries.

Le Havre's great men – These include Bernardin de Saint-Pierre (1737-1814), author of the novel *Paul et Virginie* (1787); its mingling of exotic and pastoral elements won him a prominent place in French literature. Claude Monet made the name of Ste-Adresse famous through his *Terrace at Ste-Adresse* (in the Metropolitan Museum in New York), painted in 1867. This is a key work of Impressionism, with fleeting effects of light and a wonderful clarity of subject. The old town and resort of **Ste-Adresse**★★ is still a pleasant place; from the cliff-top at La Hève there are fine views out over the estuary and the English Channel.
André Siegfried (1875-1959) is noted for his sociological and economic studies of Britain and America and for his work on French politics, while Arthur Honegger (1892-1955) was responsible for breathing fresh life into the composition and staging of choral works (*King David*, 1924).

★ **Modern Town** – The bombing which preceded Le Havre's liberation on 13 September 1944 was a total disaster for the town. The old centre was obliterated and more than 4 000 people killed; the besieged Germans completed the destruction by a thorough dynamiting of the port facilities.
The architect **Auguste Perret** (1874-1954), a pioneer of modern architecture already famous for his innovating work with reinforced concrete and promotion of standardised components, was given the task of rebuilding the devastated town from scratch. His initial concept involved a vast deck covering all the new city's services (energy, pipelines, gas, traffic...). The very boldness of his scheme led to its rejection.
Perret consequently abandoned his advanced ideas and laid out the town using the principal elements of the old street pattern. But the design of his buildings remained in an uncompromisingly modern idiom.

★ **Place de l'Hôtel de Ville** – One of the largest squares in Europe, it is notable for the contrast of verticals (the town hall with its tower, 10-storey blocks) and horizontals (the 3-storey buildings lining the square's irregular sides).

★ **Avenue Foch** – The vista leading down to the Ocean Gate (Porte Océane) and the sea is emphasised by the balconies of the buildings lining the avenue and by the regular lines of trees.

★ **Église St-Joseph** – The tall bell-tower soars to a height of 109m – 325ft. Inside, the church's walls are a lattice of stained glass through which the light pours.

Rue de Paris. – Gives lateral views of the Commercial Dock (Bassin de Commerce) and leads to the South Promenade (Front de Mer Sud).

★ **Musée des Beaux-Arts André Malraux** ⊙ – Built entirely of glass and metal it houses the **Eugène Boudin Collections**★. This painter was a citizen of Le Havre by adoption; he was responsible for freshening up the palette of the painters of the Barbizon School *(qv)* and was much admired by Baudelaire who called him "King of the Skies" *(Yellow Boats at Étretat, Breton Church Interior)*. There is also a good selection of pictures by Raoul Dufy, a native of Le Havre *(Amphitrite, Sea Goddess)*.

EXCURSION

★★ **Pont de Normandie** – This cable-stayed bridge was inaugurated in January 1995. It crosses the Seine estuary from the outskirts of Le Havre to Honfleur. The bridge has a record-breaking main span of 856m (2 808ft) between its 214m (705ft) high towers and a clearance of 50m (164ft) at high tide.

Cascade du HÉRISSON★★★

Map p 10 – Michelin map 70 fold 15 or 243 fold 31 – Green Guide Burgundy Jura

High up at the foot of the cirque of Chaux-de-Dombief is little Lake Bonlieu, drained by the River Hérisson (hedgehog). The river crosses the narrow Frasnois plateau, then, in the space of 3km – 2 miles drops via a series of rapids and falls through its famous wooded gorge to the Champagnole plain 200m – 650ft below.

> Follow the footpath which starts 8km – 5 miles east of Doucier as far as the Ilay crossroads – *3 hours Rtn.* The path climbs over a series of limestone outcrops rising above areas of alluvial deposits where lakes have formed and where a rich vegetation flourishes. The limestones were laid down over a period of 35 million years during Jurassic times; it is they which form the succession of splendid falls, the **Éventail**★★★ (Fan Falls), the **Grand Saut**★★ (Great Leap), Château Garnier the **Saut de la Forge**★ and Saut Girard.

HONFLEUR★★

Population 8 272
Map p 5 – Michelin map 54 fold 8 or 231 fold 20 – Green Guide Normandy
Town plan in the current Michelin Red Guide France

Honfleur lies at the foot of the **Côte de Grâce hill**★★ overlooking the wide waters of the Seine estuary. Bathed in the soft light of the northern sea, it is the most picturesque of ports, appealing greatly to 19C painters like the English water-colourist Bonington as well as many French artists such as the Normandy-born Eugène Boudin *(above)* and later the Impressionists. Erik Satie composed some of his music in Honfleur and writers lived and worked here too, like the historian Albert Sorel, the humourist Alphonse Allais and the poets Henri de Régnier and Lucie Delarue-Mardrus.

Many maritime ventures began on the quayside at Honfleur. Paulmier de Gouneville sailed from here to Brazil in 1503 and in 1506 Jean Denis explored the mouth of the St Lawrence River. In 1608 Samuel de Champlain set out to found Quebec City and in 1681 La Salle started the voyage which was to make him the first European to descend the Mississipi all the way to the sea, thereby opening up those vast territories to which he gave the name Louisiana in honour of his king, Louis XIV.

★★ **Old Honfleur** – The streets and quaysides of the ancient port are full of character. The **Old Harbour**★★ (Vieux bassin) shelters a fishing fleet as well as yachts and pleasure craft. A richly varied townscape, the delight of painters and photographers, is formed by the fine stone residences along the St-Etienne Quay, the narrow, slate-faced houses on the St-Catherine Quay, the St-Etienne Church, the Governor's House (Lieutenance), all seen against the foreground of masts and rigging.

Nearby is the **Église Ste-Catherine**★ with its detached **bell-tower**★ ⊘. The church was rebuilt after the Hundred Years War by the carpenters from the adjacent shipyards. All around are houses built in like fashion, making up a fine group of timber buildings, an unusual phenomenon in Western Europe.

The Rue Haute, a former pathway outside the fortifications, has kept many fine houses of brick, stone and timber once lived in by shipbuilders.

⊘ ►► Musée Eugène Boudin – paintings in the Honfleur tradition; Pont de Normandie★★ (see LE HAVRE).

Old Harbour, Honfleur

HUNSPACH★★

Population 615
Map p 7 – Michelin map 57 folds 19, 20 or 242 fold 16
Green Guide Alsace et Lorraine (in French)

Carefully preserved and free from incongruous modern additions, Hunspach is one of Alsace's most charming villages. Flowers fill the streets of timber-framed houses with their projecting roofs and bull's-eye windows (a Baroque feature). Many of the buildings are in fact old farm-houses, with yards opening off the street; orchards, vines and long-handled pumps complete the picturesque scene.

ISSOIRE★★

Population 13 559
Map p 9 – Michelin map 73 folds 14, 15 or 239 fold 20
Green Guide Auvergne-Rhône Valley
Town plan in the current Michelin Red Guide France

This old Auvergne town is situated at the point where the Pavin valley meets the flatter fertile country of the southern Limagne. In 1540 the town became a notable centre of Protestantism.
More recently it has acquired an industrial character, with important engineering works (heavy pressing machinery and aluminium alloys).

★★ **Ancienne abbatiale St-Austremoine** – Built around 1135, this is the largest Romanesque church in the Auvergne. It was extensively restored in the 19C (west front, roof, bell-tower, many of the capitals, the polychrome interior decoration).
The **east end**★★ is a fine example of Auvergne Romanesque, generously and harmoniously proportioned and rich in detail (cornices, ornamental brackets, mosaic stonework and sculpture).
Inside, an impression of strength and solidity, characteristic of these Auvergne churches, is given by the four great arches at the crossing and by the ambulatory with its ribbed vault. The influence of the Mozac School of sculpture *(qv)* is clearly seen in the **capitals**★ (*c* 1140) carved from the local volcanic rock; particularly fine are those showing the Last Supper and Christ washing the feet of the disciples.
In the narthex is a 15C mural of the **Last Judgement**★ ⊙, a favourite subject of the time, here treated with great verve and a degree of satire.

Château de JOSSELIN★★

Map p 4 – Michelin map 63 fold 4 or 230 fold 37
Green Guide Brittany

This stronghold has stood guard over the crossing of the Oust for nine hundred years. The **War of the Breton Succession**, which started in 1341, set rival heirs to the Duchy against each other, Jeanne de Penthièvre, grand-daughter of John II of Brittany, and John de Montfort, John III's half-brother. The struggle, long and confused, overlapped with the early stages of the Hundred Years War. Jeanne was married to Charles of Blois and her claim, supported by the Valois rulers of France, was based on established Breton custom. The ousted de Montfort allied himself to the Plantagenets who had won the great naval battle of Sluys the previous year. He was able to persuade them to set a terrible example by laying waste the area around Tréguier; this action took place during the period which also saw the triumph of English arms at Crécy and Calais.
The garrison at Josselin faced the defenders of Ploërmel Castle, 12km – 8 miles to the east; between them they ravaged the countryside without any decisive outcome. A solution to the impasse was sought by arranging a contest between 30 knights from each camp. The **Battle of the Thirty** took place in 1351, half-way between the two towns. Ploërmel's champions consisted of four Bretons, six Germans and twenty Englishmen. Josselin emerged victorious, but even this dramatic settling of accounts did not prove decisive.
The war was finally brought to an end in 1364 by the death of Charles of Blois at the Battle of Auray. In 1365 de Montfort was acknowledged as ruler of the Duchy, albeit subject to the Capetian kings of France.

After the war the **château** ⊙ *(3/4 hour)* was rebuilt by Olivier de Clisson. His work can still be seen in the massive walls overlooking the river; their medieval robustness contrasts with the refinement of the upper parts belonging to the reconstruction of the 15C-16C. The marriage of Anne of Brittany to Charles VIII of France in 1491 had led to a lessening of tension between the Duchy and the French kingdom, and John of Laval was able to rebuild the old castle in accordance with the new ideas of Renaissance architecture.

What had been a fortress now became a palace. The transformation is particularly evident in the courtyard, where the roof **balustrade**★★ has a splendid variety of motifs: pinnacles, tracery and mouldings.

Inside there is an innovative staircase with straight ramps.

In the 17C the keep and five of the towers were demolished on the orders of Richelieu. A park was laid out in 1760 and in 1882 the castle was restored.

► ► Basilique Notre-Dame-du-Roncier★; mausoleum★ of Olivier de Clisson.

Forêt de la JOUX★★

Map p 10 – Michelin map 70 fold 5 or 243 fold 31 – Green Guide Burgundy Jura

This is one of France's finest coniferous forests; adjoining it are other forests, the Forêt de Levier, the Forêt de Chapois and the Forêt de la Fresse, making up a vast wooded tract of some 670km² – 174 square miles.

★★ **Route des Sapins** – *45km – 28 miles from Levier to Champagnole.* The drive is marked by a number of remarkable individual trees including the splendid Président de la Joux, a fir tree more than 200 years old and 45m – 148ft tall. Life in the Jura has always been intimately bound up with the forest and its manifold uses; these ranged from timber, to firewood and furniture. The modern forest feeds industry and is managed in such a way that the removal of timber in any one year does not exceed the annual increment of new growth.

Abbaye de JUMIÈGES★★★

Map p 5 – Map 54 fold 10 or 231 fold 22 – Green Guide Normandy

The great **abbey** ⊘ in its splendid setting on the Lower Seine forms one of the most evocative groups of ruins in France.

It was founded in the 7C by Saint Philibert and within 50 years housed a community of 700 monks and 1 500 lay-brothers. Its great wealth was based on the generosity of the Merovingian rulers and on the tithes drawn from a vast area.

Destroyed by the Vikings, the abbey was raised again in the early 11C by a new generation of builder abbots. It suffered in the Wars of Religion and was subject to the abuses of commendam rule. The few remaining monks were scattered at the outbreak of the French Revolution. In 1793 it was put up for auction and one of its later owners saw fit to use it as a source of building stone, blowing up the chancel and lantern tower in the process. In 1852 a new owner saved it from complete destruction but by then the great edifice was already a ruin.

The most striking feature of the abbey is the west front of the **Église Notre-Dame** with its two magnificent towers, 43m – 141ft high, the oldest and grandest of any Norman abbey.

The power of the building to move the beholder is enhanced by the absence of vaults which permits the eye to soar freely skywards. The ruins seem to express deeply spiritual qualities too, from the stately double bays of the nave (1052-67) and the single remaining wall of the lantern tower with its great high arch to the bases of the walls of the chancel, the ambulatory and the axial chapel.

To the south of the abbey is the **Église St-Pierre**; the porch and first few bays of the nave with their intersecting arcades are typical of the architecture of Carolingian times in Normandy.

KAYSERSBERG★★

Population 2 755
Map p 7 – Michelin map 62 fold 18 or 87 fold 17 or 242 fold 31
Green Guide Alsace et Lorraine (in French)

Located where the Weiss valley meets the Alsace lowlands, Kaysersberg commands what was in Roman times an important route between Gaul and the Rhineland. In the Middle Ages it was one of the confederation of ten free cities known as the Decapolis, set up to resist feudal demands on their burgeoning urban culture. Its flower-bedecked streets have many old houses, some of them dating from the 16C, and behind the pretty little town rise the serried ranks of vines.

It was here that **Albert Schweitzer** (1875-1965) was born, at **no 124** Rue du Général de Gaulle (next to the Musée Albert-Schweitzer) ⊘. In his early years he was a gifted organist, specialising in the works of Bach; he became a philosopher, with a doctoral thesis on Kant, and a theologian. At the age of 30 he began to study medecine, with the aim of succouring the sick of Gabon, where he built his first hospital near Lambaréné "on the edge of the primaeval forest" in 1913.

During the First World War he was interned for a time as a German national. In 1924 he returned to Africa. He was able to found two further hospitals thanks to the proceeds of the recitals he gave in Europe and in Colorado in 1949 and to the resources which he was able to command after winning the Nobel Peace Prize.

Albert Schweitzer was in the forefront of the struggle to relieve the sufferings of the Third World and was also a powerful advocate of Franco-German reconciliation.

ROGER VIOLET

Albert Schweitzer

His writings are considered as classics, particularly in Japan and the United States.

►► Church★ and altarpiece★★ Hôtel de ville★; Old houses★; Fortified bridge★; Maison Brief★.

KERNASCLÉDEN★★

Population 434
Map p 4 – Michelin map 58 fold 18 or 230 north of fold 35 – Green Guide Brittany

The group formed by pilgrimage church and hospital grew up in the 15C under the protection of the powerful Rohan family.

★★ **Church (Église)** – Built in granite between 1430 and 1455, the church typifies the Breton version of Flamboyant Gothic. It has a characteristic belfry with a balcony, a spire with foliated decoration, buttresses with pinnacles, a roof balustrade and two **porches** on the south side (one of them with statues of the Apostles★). Inside there is a fine window at the east end and an untypically low and heavy granite vault.

The **frescoes★★** (1470-85) which have made the church famous are probably the work of a local workshop whose painters were familar with the work of the miniaturists of the Loire Valley.

The choir vault depicts 24 scenes from the Life of the Virgin, notably the Resurrection (over the triumphal arch), the Burial of the Virgin (south side) and above all the Annunciation and the Marriage of the Virgin (north side). The artists have used much ingenuity to overcome the difficulties presented by the ribs and concave surfaces of the vaulting.

In the north transept the elegance of the celestial choir (note particularly the folds of their clothes) recalls the refinement of the court surrounding the Rohans. On the wall of the south transept is the Passion, and a Dance of Death *(qv)* with the dead dragging the living to their doom against a background of sulphureous yellow symbolic of the Beyond. Below, the damned are depicted undergoing an extraordinary variety of torments.

Château de LANGEAIS★★

Map p 5 – Michelin map 64 fold 14 or 232 folds 34, 35
Green Guide Châteaux of the Loire

As early as the 10C the great Angevin ruler Foulques Nerra built a sturdy keep to command the Loire Valley. Completed in 994, now in ruins in the park of the château, it is considered to be the oldest such building in the whole of France. Fearful of the Breton threat to the Loire Valley, Louis XI began the present **château** ⊘ *(1 hour)* in 1465. It was completed in the unusually short time of four years, but events a mere 22 years later made it redundant.

Seen from outside, the château still looks like Louis' medieval fortress, with its drawbridge, towers, battlemented sentry-walk and almost windowless walls. But the façade facing the courtyard has the features of a Renaissance country house, including pointed dormers, turrets, sculptures and mullioned windows.

The **apartments★★★** have kept their medieval layout, one room commanding the next through narrow doors and laid out along diagonal lines. The last owner, Jacques Siegfried (a mill and ship-owner and banker from Le Havre), refurnished the interior in a much more thoroughgoing way than is the case with most such châteaux, with the result that Langeais now gives a good impression of aristocratic life as lived in the reign of Louis XI and in the early Renaissance period.

The rooms contain fine Flanders tapestries together with some *mille-fleurs* tapestries, examples of the girdle of the Franciscan Tertiaries and the interlaced monograms K and A (Charles VIII and Anne of Brittany).

On the first floor are an early four-poster bed, a credence table and a Gothic chest. In the Charles VIII Room is a 17C clock with a single hand.

Anne of Brittany's marriages – Louis XI felt threatened by both Burgundy to the southeast and Brittany to the west. Since the death of Charles the Bold he had been hoping to reclaim the Duchy of Burgundy, a prize that had escaped his grasp following the marriage of Mary of Burgundy to the Hapsburg Maximilian. Mary died in 1482, leaving two children, Philip the Fair and the two-year old Margaret of Austria *(qv)*. Louis seized his chance and organised the marriage of the infant to the Dauphin Charles VIII who had been born in 1470. Margaret came to Paris in 1483 and went on to Amboise where a form of wedding was held.

By 1488 Louis XI had been dead for five years. The eight-year old Margaret was growing up and being educated at the French court. At this point, Duke François II of Brittany, an implacable adversary of the French Crown, died too. He left a daughter, Anne, aged 11, whose marriage prospects were subject to royal assent, an arrangement which had already been invoked in order to get rid of Alain d'Albret as a suitor. As sole heir to the Duchy, Anne was an attractive match. To begin with, she followed her father's preference for Maximilian of Hapsburg; the couple were married by proxy, but the "penniless emperor" could never afford to come to Nantes.

For his part, Charles VIII, now 21 years old, came down in favour of an immediate union with Brittany rather than a hypothetical future one with Burgundy; he broke with Margaret and pressed Anne to do the same with Maximilian. Advised by her tutors, Anne was well aware of what the English occupation of the previous century and the ravages of the War of the Breton Succession had done to her duchy; faced with the subordination of Brittany to the interests of Tudors or Hapsburgs, she chose to integrate her inheritance with a France still suffused with the prestige of Saint Louis. The wedding took place at Langeais on Tuesday 16 December 1491. Anne was still only 14.

Maximilian was doubly offended, firstly as Anne's putative husband, secondly as Margaret's father. Relations between France and the Holy Roman Empire sank to a new low.

Charles VIII was killed accidentally in 1498. While he was away campaigning in Italy, Anne showed herself to be a wise ruler of both duchy and kingdom. At the age of 22, still the sole heir to Brittany since she had no living descendant, and possessed of a certain attractiveness despite somewhat mean features and the handicap of a limp, she married Louis XII, Charles' cousin, whose marriage to Joan of France had been annulled by the Church. She presented him with two children, one of them Claude, subsequently the wife of François I to whom she brought Brittany as her dowry (1514).

LAON★★

Population 26 490
Map p 6 – Michelin map 56 fold 5 or 236 fold 38
Green Guide Flanders, Picardy and the Paris Region
Town plan in the current Michelin Red Guide France

This ancient town dominates the surrounding countryside from its magnificent hilltop site★★, a 100m – 330ft high limestone outlier rising abruptly from the plain. Its defensive potential was noted by the Carolingian kings who made it their capital for 150 years, from the reign of Charles le Chauve (the Bald) (840) to Louis V (987). It was only in the reign of Hugh Capet that the capital was moved to the Île-de-France. At the time of the communal movement directed against episcopal rule the city was the scene of bloody and destructive riots (1111 and 1114).

The city was the birthplace of the three **Le Nain** brothers, adept painters of rural life. The works of Louis Le Nain (1599-1648) were particularly successful. They show a prosperous peasantry already enjoying the high standard of living which Colbert was to promote some 30 years later.

★★ **Cathédrale Notre-Dame** – The present cathedral was begun in 1160 and completed towards 1230. It is in the early Gothic style, still caught up in the Romanesque idiom (as in its Norman-style lantern-tower). The west front is a masterpiece, with its deep porches and stepped towers flanked by openwork turrets.

The immensely long **nave★★★** shows the persistence of Carolingian traditions, but "nowhere else did the development of 12C Gothic achieve such breadth and unity" (Henri Focillon). The elevation is four-storeyed, with great arches carried on circular columns, a gallery with bold double arches, a blind triforium and a clerestorey. In the nave, transept and chancel the bays are marked – still in a less emphatic way than at either Sens (1140) or Senlis (1153) – by a pattern of major and minor clustered columns, the former with five, the latter with three engaged columns.

⊘ ►► Cathedral quarter★★; Southern ramparts★ *(Rempart du Midi)* – views★; Musée★ – painting and archaeology; Chapelle des Templiers★; Église St-Martin★; Porte de Soissons★.

Château de LAPALISSE★★

Map p 9 – Michelin map 73 fold 6 or 239 fold 9 – Green Guide Auvergne-Rhône Valley

The little crossroads town has grown up at the foot of the **Château** ⊘ which has commanded the crossing of the Besbre since the 11C. Its most famous owner was Jacques II de Chabannes (1470-1525), a Marshal of France who distinguished himself in the conquest of Milan but who was killed by a blast from an arquebus received during the Battle of Pavia.

Little remains of the medieval castle. The present building, started at the beginning of the 16C, is very much in the style of the early Renaissance, the work of Florentine craftsmen brought from Italy by Jacques. The courtyard façade is enlivened by heraldic motifs and polychrome brickwork, by sandstone courses on the towers and around the windows, by bracketed lintels and mullioned windows, by medallions in the portal of the central tower, by foliated scrolls, pilasters and Corinthian capitals.
Inside, there is interesting Louis XIII furniture in the main reception room. The **Salon doré** has a coffered ceiling and 15C Flemish tapestries. The chapel, built in granite, is in Flamboyant style, and there is a fine timber ceiling in the **service range.**

Grotte de LASCAUX

Map p 8 – Michelin map 75 fold 7 or 233 fold 44 – Green Guide Dordogne

The world-famous cave paintings of Lascaux were discovered by accident on 12 September 1940 by a young man looking for his dog which had disappeared down a hole. Most of the paintings appear to date from the end of the Aurignacian period, others from the Magdalenian. They cover the walls and roofs of the cave with a bestiary of bulls, cows, horses, deer and bison, depicted with such skill as to justify Abbot Breuil's epithet "the Sistine Chapel of prehistoric times".

The cave itself is not open to the public, but one may visit a full-size **replica, Lascaux II★★** ⊘, which has reproductions of many of the paintings.

N. Anjou/ay/Département d'art pariétal CNP, Périgueux

Wall-painting, Lascaux

The chapter on art and architecture in this guide gives an outline of artistic achievement in the country providing the context of the buildings and works of art described in the Sights section
This chapter may also provide ideas for touring It is advisable to read it at leisure

Les Îles de LÉRINS**

Map p 11 – Michelin map 195 fold 39
Green Guide French Riviera

The **islands** ⓥ *(boat service from Cannes)* are clad in a rich vegetation of pines, cypresses and eucalyptus and have a fascinating historic and archaeological heritage. The fine view back to the coast of the mainland stretches from Cap Roux to Cap d'Antibes.

** **Ile Ste-Marguerite** – A Celto-Ligurian population once lived here and the place formed a safe anchorage off the marshy coast of La Napoule Bay. There are fine **forest walks**★★ to the Bataigner, Dragon and Convention headlands, as well as through the botanical collection and along the Eucalyptus Avenue. Pines of many species soar above an undergrowth of arbutus, tree heathers, cistus, thyme and rosemary.
Fort Royal was built for coastal defence by Richelieu. During the Thirty Years War it was occupied by the Spanish for two years (1635-37); reconstructed by Vauban in 1712, it was restored under the Convention. It served as a prison for Huguenot pastors, for the Man in the Iron Mask (from 1687-98) and for Marshal Bazaine *(qv)*, condemned in 1873 as a traitor for his role in the Franco-Prussian War. From the terrace there is an extensive **view**★ of the coast.

** **Ile St-Honorat** – Saint Honoratus founded one of the first monasteries of Roman Gaul here in the early years of the 5C. It became one of the most famous and powerful of the period, not least because Provence was not yet affected by the barbarian invasions.
In 1073, the monks built a **keep**★ on a headland on the south side of the island. It was here that they took refuge from the raids of pirates from the Barbary Coast. It has two-storeyed cloisters, fine stonework and a remarkable **view**★★ from its battlements.
The monastery itself was rebuilt in the 19C in a neo-Romanesque style.

LESSAY★

Population 1 719
Map p 5 – Michelin map 54 fold 12 or 231 fold 14 – Green Guide Normandy

Lessay lies on the edge of moorland country whose harsh beauty was sung by Barbey d'Aurevilly (1808-89), who helped establish a distinct Norman literature. The town comes to life every September at the time of the Holy Cross Fair.

** **Eglise abbatiale** – Founded in 1056, this is not only one of the most perfect examples of Romanesque architecture in Normandy, but also a tribute to the extraordinary skill and devotion of the chief architect of the Historic Monuments Institute, Yves Froidevaux, who rebuilt the church after it had been blown up by the Wehrmacht in 1944.

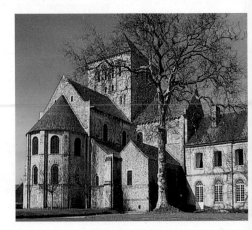

Abbey Church, Lessay

From the east there is a fine view of the rounded apse backed by a flat gable and dominated by the massive tower.
Inside there are the typically Norman features of great nave arches, triforium and inspection gallery running underneath the clerestory windows.
But Lessay also marks the architectural transition from groined vaults (as used in the 11C aisles) to quadripartite vaults, used somewhat crudely in the choir (end of the 11C), then with greater confidence, in the nave (beginning of the 12C). This revolutionary development led directly to the great achievements of Gothic architecture, with its high-flung vaults and walls of glass.

Centre historique minier de LEWARDE★★

Michelin map 53 fold 3 or 236 fold 16 (8km – 5 miles southeast of Douai)
Green Guide Flanders, Picardy and the Paris Region

The Lewarde Mining Heritage Centre (Centre Historique Minier de Lewarde) ⊘ is housed in the converted building of the Delloye Collery which closed in 1971. The museum's design has adapted the original structure to provide exhibition rooms, a restaurant, a lecture room etc.

The tour partly guided by ex-miners, follows the miners different activities up to the descent in the cage; from cloakroom shower room – or "hanging room" (salle de pendus) because of the hooks on which the clothes, boots and heimets were hung – lamp room, infirmary... A small train leads to Pit no 2. where the descent to the seams is by lift. A 450m – over

Centre historique Minier, Lewarde

Tour of the mine-Lewarde

3/4 mile long circuit traces the evolution of mining work since the 1930s. A tour of the processing building (extraction machines, coal-screening room) and the pit stables completes the visit. A vast collection of fossils is also on display, shown in the context of the formation of the mining basin 300 million years ago.

LILLE★★

Conurbation 950 265
Map p 6 – Michelin map 51 fold 6 or 236 fold 16 or 111
Green Guide Flanders, Picardy and the Paris Region
Region plan in the current Michelin Red Guide France

Lille is the centre of a sprawling conurbation which includes the industrial cities of Roubaix and Tourcoing and which has a total population of nearly a million. The early development of the city was slowed down by the disadvantages of its poorly drained site; nevertheless, its position at the head of the navigable river Deule made it the point of exchange between industrial Flanders to the north and agricultural Artois to the south. This medieval commercial role later changed to an industrial one, with cloth predominating in the 14C and wool in the 16C; by the middle of the 19C, Lille had become the epitome of the overcrowded, polluted, northern industrial city.

Bouvines – *12km – 8 miles southeast.* The fall of Gaillard Castle *(qv)* in 1204 marked the beginning of King Philippe Auguste's campaign to win back his kingdom from the Plantagenets. As a counter-measure, John Lackland allied himself with the German Emperor Otto IV who had his own reasons for wishing to weaken the French king. Their stragegy was to defeat Philippe by means of a pincer movement. John landed at La Rochelle, but was defeated at Roche-aux-Moines near Angers on 2 July 1214 by Philippe's son. Setting out from Aachen, Otto and his mercenaries took the invasion route through Flanders only to be soundly beaten by the king here on the plain of Bouvines. This first great victory of the House of Capet strengthened the monarchy and won popular support. It also marked the end of 60 years of conflict between the House of Anjou and the kings of France. The outbreak of the Hundred Years War lay far in the future.

From Burgundian to Spanish rule – In the 15C Lille belonged to Burgundy; in 1454 Philip the Good *(qv)* was responsible for the fine brick-built Rihour Palace. But the marriage of Mary of Burgundy to Charles V brought first Austrian, then Spanish rule.

During this period the **Comtesse Hospice**★ ⊘ (1650) was rebuilt; it is a fine example of local building, with its monumental gateway, its walls of brick and sandstone, and the superb **timber roof**★★ of its Great Hall (Salle des malades).

The **Old Exchange**★★ (vieille bourse) of virtually the same date (1652) is altogether different, an example of the persistence of the Louis XIII style adapted to Flemish tastes (doors with broken pediments, caryatids supporting the entablatures, columns, pilasters and window-surrounds in sandstone, fruit and floral decoration and a little bell-tower). The whole building proclaims the importance of textile manufacturing in the life of the city as well as paying tribute to great men and their contributions to progress by the statues lining the arcades.

Lille becomes French – After only nine days of siege, Lille fell to the armies of Louis XIV, subsequently becoming the capital of France's northern provinces. This stimulated activity of all kinds and the city's growth was rapid.

★ **Citadelle** ⊙ – Within four months of the end of the siege, **Vauban** began to reconstruct the citadel. The great complex is set in a marshy site of some 1 700ha – 4 200 acres which could be flooded when necessary. With its masterly handling of brick and sandstone, its economical design, its logical plan and its response to the geometry of artillery, it was the great engineer's masterpiece, the "queen of citadels".

Within the Royal Gate (Porte Royale), the citadel consisted of 12 barrack blocks, the arsenal and several magazines, all laid out around the vast Parade Ground (Place d'Armes – 1). Its defensive strength was such that it took Marlborough and his Dutch allies 62 days to break into the city and a further 48 to reduce the citadel itself. The high quality of construction is evident in the allegorical pediments of the Royal Gate, in the lively treatment of the tympanum of the arsenal and in the vaulting of the Ste-Barbe postern-gate. The Jesuit-style Chapel (3) has unfortunately lost its classical decoration.

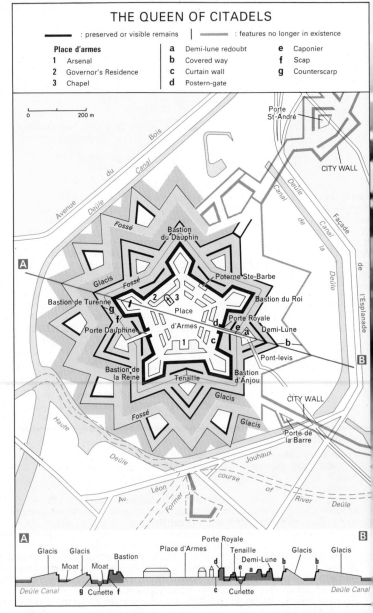

THE QUEEN OF CITADELS

▬▬▬ : preserved or visible remains   │ ▬▬▬ : features no longer in existence

Place d'armes
1 Arsenal
2 Governor's Residence
3 Chapel

a Demi-lune redoubt
b Covered way
c Curtain wall
d Postern-gate

e Caponier
f Scap
g Counterscarp

Sébastien Le Prestre (1633-1707) was born at St-Léger *(25km – 16 miles southeast of Avallon in the Morvan)*. Better known as the Marquis de **Vauban**, he was one of the truly great figures of the age of Louis XIV, a soldier who personally conducted 53 sieges , an engineer who created the French army's corps of engineers and who studied the science of gunnery, and not least an architect and town planner who redesigned ports, dug canals, spanned the Eure at Maintenon with a fine aqueduct, and built from scratch 33 new fortresses as well as improving no less than 300 others (many have of course disappeared). Appointed Commissioner of Fortifications in 1678, he took his inspiration first of all from his predecessors, bringing their work to a new peak of perfection; in the case of Belfort he added a second external line of defences as well as strengthening the existing bastions by means of demilunes and a deep moat, while at Neuf-Brisach his innovations included supplementing the internal walls with bastions and placing demilunes in front of the redoubts. But above all he was able to assimilate new inventions and changes in tactics, and to adapt his designs to the particular characteristics of the site.

His main concern was to defend France's new, expanded frontiers. His work thus took him to Flanders, the Ardennes and Alsace, to the Franche-Comté, to the Pyrenees, the Alps and to many places along the country's coastline. Some of his fortresses proved their worth to the retreating French and British forces in 1940.

Many patriotic French people met their end in the Turenne Bastion, which served as a place of execution during both world wars.

★★ **Musée des Beaux-Arts** ⊙ – The collection includes many masterpieces of French painting, among them the *Mystical Fountain* by Jean Bellegambe (16C) with its symbolic treatment of renewal and redemption, a serenely classical *Nativity* by Philippe de Champaigne (1674), a beautifully modelled portrait of *Madame Pélerin* by Quentin de la Tour and another portrait, *J. Forest* (1746), by Nicolas de Largillière.

➤➤ Old Lille★★; Demeure de Gilles de la Boé★; Rue de la Monnaie★, Église St-Maurice★; Porte de Paris★.

LIMOGES★

Conurbation 170 065
Map p 8 – Michelin map 72 fold 17 or 239 fold 13
Green Guide Berry Limousin (in French)
Town plan in the current Michelin Red Guide France

Limoges originated as a ford over the River Vienne at the meeting-point of the great Roman highways from Lyons to Saintes and Bourges to Bordeaux. Nevertheless, it was only in the early 19C that it became a commercial centre of considerable importance, requiring a fleet of 5 000 waggons and 20 000 horses to handle its road traffic. Then came the manufacture of porcelain, which moved here from St-Yrieix *(40km – 25 miles south)* where there were kaolin deposits but no workforce. Later, shoe-making became established, based on the already-existing tanneries.

The town has been the birthplace of a large number of great men, including:

Léonard Limosin (1505-76), an enameller and painter who worked with Primaticcio at Fontainebleau and who was the leading figure in the 16C Limoges School of enamel-workers;

Pierre Vergniaud (1753-93), a prominent Girondin in the Legislative Assembly and later in the Convention;

Jean-Baptiste Jourdan (1762-1833), the victor of the Battle of Fleurus in 1794 which opened up Belgium to the French armies;

Thomas Bugeaud (1784-1849), promoted corporal at the Battle of Austerlitz, who later pacified Algeria and oversaw its colonisation;

Sadi Carnot (1837-94), who became President of France in 1887;

Auguste Renoir (1841-1919), one of the initiators of Impressionism.

★ **Musée Municipal** ⊙ – In the former Bishops' Palace, it houses a stunning collection of some 300 *champlevé* or *cloisonné* enamels by Limoges masters.

Porcelain – All vessels made from baked clay come under the generic term **pottery**, but porcelain has certain important characteristics of its own, notably its whiteness, its hardness and its translucence; when baked, it becomes vitrified. **Soft-paste porcelain** was first made in Europe in the 17C and 18C in an attempt to recapture the perfection of Chinese porcelain. A white clay was used, given a first firing and then ground and mixed to yield the paste. The paste, which was not particularly easy to work, was then formed into the shape of the vessel or object required, to which glazes and enamels were applied before firing at a temperature of some 1 400 °C. From the 18C new enamels unable to withstand such high temperatures were used, and consequently a third and even a fourth firing took place with progressively lower temperatures, allowing a great variety of colour as well as the use of gold.

It was soft-paste porcelain that made Sèvres' reputation from the 1760s on.

Hard-paste or true **porcelain** was first produced in Europe in Meissen early in the 18C and came to France around 1770. It is based on

Limoges porcelain from the Comte d'Artois manufactory, Musée Adrien-Dubouché

kaolin (a very pure kind of clay) and feldspar. It is particularly translucent, resists scratching with steel and gives off a pure tone when rung. The vessel is formed directly from the paste and fired at a temperature of around 500°C. A first coat of enamel is then applied and a second firing at a high temperature takes place, followed sometimes by other firings at lower temperatures to take account of more vulnerable enamels.

Biscuit-bake is the term used to describe firing at a high temperature when no coloured enamel has been applied.

Faïence or **tin-glazed ware** is an imitation of porcelain, made from a soft and porous paste, to which an opaque white glaze of tin oxide is applied which can then be decorated. The oldest and most difficult decorative process is one in which the decoration is applied and given a single firing at a high temperature, therby limiting the choice of colours and excluding any subsequent retouching.

Most porcelain factories use broadly the same operational processes, the differences in the product depending on the skill of the workforce, the size and form of the objects produced, the way in which they are decorated and in the relative proportion of certain ingredients.

Virtually all the porcelain produced at Limoges is of the hard-paste type. Production began in 1771, some 30 years later than at Strasbourg or Niderviller in Lorraine, stimulated by the discovery of a particularly pure deposit of kaolin at St-Yrieix by a local surgeon, one Darnet.

★★ **Musée Adrien-Dubouché** ⊙ - The masterpieces assembled here of this most decorative of the arts illustrate the evolution in time and space of all branches of ceramics. Limoges ware is dealt with in showcases 61 and 62 (when its beginnings were closely linked with production at Sèvres, qv), in the salon d'honneur (19C work), and in the left wing of the ground floor (contemporary work).

Town - Early on in its evolution, Limoges developed two rival centres, known as City (Cité) and Castle (Château).

City - Overlooking the Vienne, this is the historic core of Limoges. It spreads out around the **Cathédrale St-Étienne★** which has a fine **portal★** (portail St-Jean) and which has kept its **rood-screen★** of 1533, now located at the west end of the nave. In the chancel are a number of **tombs★**.

Limoges Enamel

Enamel has been known since the days of Antiquity. In the 12C Limoges became an important centre of production, partly thanks to the variety of minerals to be found in the surrounding area; its exquisite wares were exported all over Europe. The technique consists of crushing leadglass, coloured with metal oxides, applying it to a metal surface, gold, silver or copper, then heating it to a temperature of up to 800 °C. resulting in a crystalline effect. In the 12C Limoges specialised in *champlevé* enamels, in which the enamel is poured into grooves let into a copper surface, then polished level with the metal. In the 14C painted enamels made their appearance.

In the reign of François I, Léonard Limosin was made Director of the Manufactory, which produced enamels of great brilliance and colour.

Castle Quarter – This is the modern centre of Limoges, with busy shopping streets. **St-Michel-des-Lions**★ is an old hall-church which has retained its original rectangular plan.

It was in this part of the town that the great St-Martial Abbey was sited. Originally founded on the grave of a third century missionary, by the 11C it had become one of the important Romanesque churches on the pilgrimage route to Santiago de Compostela, just as important as St-Rémi at Reims or St-Sernin at Toulouse. It stretched southwestwards from today's Place de la République but was demolished at the time of the French Revolution *(its plan is traced out on the paving)*.

► ► Cour du Temple★.

LISIEUX★★

Population 23 703
Map p 5 – Michelin map 54 fold 18 or 231 fold 32
Green Guide Normandy
Town plan in the current Michelin Red Guide France

Lisieux is the market centre of the Auge region. With its closely-packed hedgerows, thatched cottages and old manors, this is a pastoral countryside of great charm, the quintessence of the Normandy sung by the poetess Lucie Delarue-Madrus.

St Teresa of Lisieux – Thérèse Martin (1873-97) was born at Alençon into a deeply religious family. Her father was a watchmaker, her mother a lace-maker. On the death of her mother the family moved to Lisieux, to the house known as Les Buissonnets. At the age of 15, Thérèse left the family home for good, having been given the Pope's permission to enter the Carmelite Order.

In the convent, "Little Teresa", as she wished to be known, scaled the steep stairway towards perfection. "A soul such as she needs no dispensations" said her Prioress. Teresa's short life ended in the Carmelite hospital only a few days after she had finished the manuscript of her *History of a Soul*. She was canonised on 17 May 1925.

The Pilgrimage – Teresa's house, **Les Buissonnets** ⊘, can be visited. Her effigy can be seen in the **Carmelite Chapel** ⊘ and there is a **Reliquary Chamber** (Salle des Reliques) where relics are displayed.

Mass pilgrimages take place to the vast basilica on its site to the southeast of the town.

Manor Houses of the Auge Region – The farmhouses and manors of this tranquil landscape are set within an enclosure planted with apple trees and defined by a hedge. All the buildings are timber-framed, from the house itself, to the cider-press, apple-store, stables and dairy grouped around it. Among the finest are the moated site at **Coupesarte** ⊘ *(16km – 10 miles southwest)* and **Château Crèvecœur**★ *(18km – 11 miles west)* with its **Musée Schlumberger** ⊘ devoted to the story of petroleum research.

► ► Cathédrale St-Pierre★.

LOCHES★★

Population 7 133
Map p 6 – Michelin map 68 fold 6 or 238 fold 14
Green Guide Châteaux of the Loire
Town plan in the current Michelin Red Guide France

Modern Loches lies mostly on the left bank of the Indre, at the foot of the fortified bluff which dominates the valley and which set natural limits to the growth of the medieval town.

★★ **Medieval Loches** – *2 hours.* The old town is contained within a continuous wall some 1 000m - about 1 100 yards long in which there are only two gates. To the south, the great square **keep**★★ ⊘ was built by the Counts of Anjou in the 11C on even earlier foundations. In the 13C, it was strengthened by wide ditches hewn into the solid rock, by buttress towers and the Martelet Tower with its impressive dungeons, then given additional accommodation including service buildings.

In the centre of the old town is the **St-Ours Church**★, with its Angevin porch built around a Romanesque portal and pyramid vaults in its nave.

To the north is the **Château**★★ ⊘, begun at the end of the 14C as an extension of the 13C watchtower known as Agnes Sorel's Tower. Part of the royal apartments are medieval (Vieux logis), part Renaissance (Nouveau logis). It was in the great hall of the Vieux Logis on 3 and 5 June 1429 that Joan of Arc persuaded the Dauphin to undertake his coronation journey to Rheims.

There is a tiny Flamboyant oratory dedicated to Anne of Brittany decorated with the ermine of Brittany and the girdle of St Francis, and, in the Charles VIII Room, the **recumbent figure of Agnes Sorel★**, Charles VII's "Lady of Beauty".

► ► Royal Gate★ (Porte Royale) – Ramparts★.

Recumbent figure of Agnes Sorel, Château de Loches

LOCRONAN★★

Population 796
Map p 4 – Michelin map 58 folds 14, 15 or 230 fold 18
Green Guide Brittany

Locronan is sited at the foot of its granite hill at the meeting point of the roads from Quimper to Châteaulin and from Crozon to Douarnenez.

The little town once flourished on the proceeds of flax-growing and on the manufacture of sailcloth which was exported from the port of Douarnenez.

The traditional crafts of the area are evoked in the museum and in a number of workshops; they include the making of baskets, glass and clogs, stone-masonry, and above all the weaving of flax, wool, cotton and silk.

★★ **Place de l'Église** – This little square with its well is like many others in Brittany, having grown up over the centuries in a haphazard way without any overall plan, but with a unity due to the consistent use of granite. Because of the strength of the westerly winds, the walls on that side of the weavers' houses are windowless. In the 17C many of the houses were given an additional storey in stone. The lofts are lit by means of dormer windows let into the roof.

★★ **Église St-Ronan et Chapelle du Penity** – This is a 15C pilgrimage church with stone vaults. Its architect endowed it with the plain east end current in Brittany at the time, thereby letting more light into what would otherwise be a somewhat dark interior. Behind the altar, the main window has fine 15C stained glass depicting scenes from the Passion. The **pulpit★** of 1707 has panels illustrating the life of St Ronan.

The Penity Chapel in the south aisle has a 16C altarpiece with a **low-relief★** of the Last Supper, a St Michael in armour *(on the pillar)* weighing souls, and an early 15C effigy of St Ronan, carved from the dark kerzanton stone.

⊘ ► ► Conservatoire de l'Affiche en Bretagne; collection of posters.

LONS-LE-SAUNIER★

Population 19 144
Map p 10 – Michelin map 70 folds 4, 14 or 243 fold 30
Green Guide Burgundy Jura
Town plan in the current Michelin Red Guide France

Lons owes the second part of its name (saunier = salt-merchant) to the salt-works which, like those at **Salins** *(52km – 32 miles northeast)*, are based on deposits laid down in Secondary times and subsequently uncovered by erosion. The town is also a spa, applying its salty waters to the treatment of rheumatism and problems associated with growth.

The town's most famous son was **Claude Rouget de l'Isle** (1760-1836) who wrote the music, and possibly the words too, of the Marseillaise. His statue stands at the western end of the Promenade de la Chevalerie and the theatre clock picks out a couple of bars of the national anthem before striking the hour. He was a Captain of Engineers, but more of an artist than a soldier. His "Marching Song of the Army of the Rhine", one amongst many of his compositions, owes its definitive title to the men of Marseilles who sang it in Paris during the insurrection of August 1792; it became an official national song in July 1795, was forbidden at the time of the Restoration, but was proclaimed the national anthem on 14 February 1879.

★ **Rue du Commerce** – The town was ravaged by fire between 25 June and 4 July 1636 when it was attacked by Condé on Richelieu's orders. Seven years later, the population was amnestied by Mazarin and allowed to return. The Rue du Commerce was rebuilt in accordance with a detailed plan in the second half of the 17C; it is elegantly laid out on a slight curve and is famous for its great variety of shops with their attractive displays.

What might have been a monotonous piece of planning reflects instead a local love of independence and appreciation of good design. Note particularly the high roofs with their mansards and tall chimneys, the 146 stone arcades (some of them of Romanesque date) of many different shapes and sizes, the trapdoors leading to the cellars, sculpted heads, and balconies and window decoration in wrought iron. No 24 is the birthplace of Rouget de l'Isle.

EXCURSION

★★★ **Cirque de Baume** – *19km – 7 miles east.* This is one of the most spectacular of the blind valleys characteristic of the western rim of the Jura. The action of water has been particularly significant here in undermining the upper beds of limestone, which have caved in, thus forming the impressive gorge we see today. The viewpoint at Roches de Baume *(near the D 471)* gives splendid prospects over this great natural amphitheatre with its 200m – 650ft walls marking the boundary between the high plateau of the western Jura and the Bresse plain.

Source de la LOUE★★★

Map p 7 – Map 70 fold 6 or 243 south of fold 20 – Green Guide Burgundy Jura

The River Loue rises in one of the blind valleys which penetrate deeply into the high plateau of the Jura. In its setting of high cliffs and luxuriant vegetation, it is one of the region's finest natural sites.

The fully-formed river appears from a cave at the foot of a 100m – 300ft high cliff. The cave should be entered for the power of the waters surging up from the underground world to be fully appreciated. The source is fed by rain falling on the plateau and by water loss from the Doubs and Drugeon rivers into the porous and highly fissured limestone near Pontarlier.

The Loue rejoins the Doubs downstream from Dole.

LOURDES★★★

Population 16,300
Map p 8 – Michelin map 85 north of fold 18 or 234 fold 39
Green Guide Atlantic Coast
Town plan in the current Michelin Red Guide France

This little market town, sited at the meeting point of mountain and plain, became a pilgrimage place of world renown in the 19C.

The town's setting – The summit of the **Béout** mountain *(reached by cable-car then 3/4 hour Rtn on foot)* is littered with great erratic blocks which give some idea of the power of the Quaternary glaciers. The **view**★ is an object lesson in physical geography; it extends northwards from the exits of the Lavedan valleys over the morainic terraces through which the Pau torrent winds its sinuous course, to the glacial rock-bar on which the castle is sited and finally to the great terminal moraine which forces the stream to make an abrupt turn to the west.

The pilgrims' town – On the 11 February 1858, **Bernadette Soubirous** (1844-79) had the first of the 18 visions which led to Lourdes' becoming a world-famous centre of the cult of Mary, with the grotto and its surroundings attracting pilgrims from all five continents, with a special place reserved for the lame and the sick (70 000 out of 55 million visitors in 1993).

1858: the first visions.
1862: Bernadette becomes a novice at the Sisters of Charity convent of St-Gildard at Nevers.
1866: the building of the first sanctuary is begun.
1871: construction of the upper basilica.
1886: opening of the crypt.
1889: Basilica of the Rosary built in Romano-Byzantine style.
1925: beatification of Bernadette (followed by canonization in 1933).
1959: St Pius X Underground Basilica built.

Grotto area – *Appropriate dress essential.* In the summer months the great local, national and international pilgrimages are held here. The degree of spirituality is evident in the scale of the ceremonial and the devotion of the participants.

Esplanade: 500m – 550 yards long, the site of daily processions.

Basilica of the Rosary: in neo-Byzantine style. The two curving approach ramps have fixed the image of the great building in the popular mind.

Crypt: a realm of devotion, contemplation and silence.

Upper Basilica: dedicated to the Immaculate Conception and with a vast nave of five bays.

St Pius X Underground Basilica: ellipse-shaped, one of the world's largest sanctuaries.

Grotto of the Miracles: the site of the visions, where the most moving manifestations of faith take place.

Fountains: Lourdes water collected by pilgrims.

Pools: immersion of the sick.

Stations of the Cross: overlooking the basilicas and the Pau torrent.

⊙ ►► Château★ (Musée du Folklore Pyrénéen★); Musée Grévin de Lourdes (*Wax museum*).

EXCURSION

★★★ **Pic du Pibestre** – This peak (*2 hour 20 min climb from Ouzous on D 202*) provides one of the best viewpoints in the central Pyrénées.

LUNÉVILLE★

Population 20 711
Map p 7 – Michelin map 62 fold 6 or 242 fold 22
Green Guide Alsace et Lorraine (in French)
Town plan in the current Michelin Red Guide France

The development of Lunéville parallels that of Lorraine itself, owing much to the enterprise of the ruling Dukes and beginning with an upsurge of intellectual and artistic activity in the 17C. In 1620, **Georges de la Tour** (1593-1652), born at Vic-sur-Seille (*26km – 16 miles north*) became the town's official painter. He seems to have been a ruthless opportunist, but his work, with its mastery of nocturnal effects, has a serene, almost mystical quality. In the 18C, under Duke Leopold, Lunéville was for several years the seat of the ducal court, a concession by Leopold to his Duchess, Charlotte, who enjoyed life here, whereas the Duke himself much preferred Nancy. The wide streets of the town, the great park and the **château★** ⊙ of 1719 were all designed by Boffand, who took Versailles as his model. The prestige of the House of Lorraine is expressed in the château's great colonnaded portico and in the wealth of statuary and trophies, while the roofs are concealed behind a high balustrade.

Later in the 18C, Duke Stanislas, "The Magnificent", held court here several times, and continued Leopold's work on the splendid edifice.

On 9 February 1801, the Treaty of Lunéville was signed, thereby giving Hapsburg recognition to France's eastern frontier which the conquests of the Revolution had pushed to the Rhine. One of its unforeseen consequences was to promote German unity by consenting to a reduction in number of the multitude of German states and principalities.

►► Lunéville: Parc des Bosquets★; Panelling★ in the Église St-Jacques.

LYON★★★

Conurbation 1 262 223
Map p 9 – Michelin map 246 folds B, C, F, G and plan 30 (single sheet)
or plan 31 (with street index)
Green Guide Auvergne-Rhône Valley – Town plan in the current Michelin Red Guide France

Two millenia of history, a site at the meeting point of the Rhône and Saône corridors and an exceptionally enterprising population have combined to make Lyon France's second city. Its past periods of greatness, in Roman and Renaissance times, are matched by its present industrial, commercial and cultural dynamism.

FOURVIÈRE HILL Plan 31 J 8, J 9

A Celtic, then Gallic settlement, Lyon was chosen as a base camp by Julius Caesar for his conquest of Gaul. Under Augustus it became the capital of the Roman Empire's "Three Gauls" (Aquitaine, Belgium and the province around Lyon) complementing the older province centred on Narbonne. Agrippa was responsible for choosing Lyon as the hub of the road system, constructed originally in pursuit of political ends. It was here that the great route coming north from Arles met the other highways from Saintes, Orléans and Rouen, from Geneva and Aosta, and from Chalon with its links to Amiens, Trier and Basle.

The manufacture of pottery became established here as early as the first century AD, only to move later to La Graufesenque on the Tarn *(qv)*. The Amphitheatre of the Three Gauls on the Croix-Rousse hill was joined by the Temple of Rome and of Augustus and by the Federal Sanctuary where the noisy annual assembly of the 60 tribes of Gaul was held under Roman supervision.

Christianity reached Lyon via Vienne by the middle of the 2C, brought by soldiers, traders and Greek missionaries. In 177, there were riots on the occasion of the annual assembly, and Saints Pothinus and Blandina, along with 48 others, became the city's first Christian martyrs. 20 years later, Saint Irenaeus, head of the Church in Lyon, was to meet the same fate. According to St Gregory of Tours, the Gospel was reintroduced to Lyon around 250 by Roman missionaries, and, under Constantine, Christianity is supposed to have flourished here as in the other cities of the Empire.

Fourvière (ET) – The name of the hill is derived from the old forum *(Forum vetus)* which was still here in the reign of King Louis I in the 9C. Its site is now occupied by the pilgrimage chapel (with its Black Virgin) next to the basilica of 1870. Roman Lyon had numerous public buildings, including the imperial palace (the capitol) giving on to the forum, a theatre and an odeon (both rebuilt) on the slope of the hill, baths, a circus building and several temples, as well as the amphitheatre on the east bank of the river.

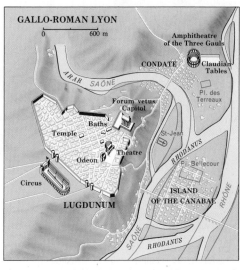

The terrace to the north of the basilica forms a splendid **viewpoint** overlooking the confluence of the Rhône and Saône and encompassing the hills and Dauphiné plain over which the great city has spread.

★★ **Musée de la Civilisation Gallo-Romaine** (ET M³) ⊘ – J 8. The most striking exhibit is perhaps formed by the **Claudian Tables** of bronze, discovered in 1528. They record the speech made by Claudius in 48AD which gave the citizens of Gaul the right to become senators. It is possible to compare this ponderous "official" version with the more witty and revealing transcription made by Tacitus.

★★ **OLD LYON** Plan 31 H 9, J 9, K 9

The medieval and Renaissance quarter of Lyon, the precursor of today's city, extends along the west bank of the Saône at the foot of the Fourvière hill.

★ **Primatiale St-Jean** (ET) ⊘ – J 9. Begun in 1192, today's church was preceded by a number of sanctuaries, including an early Christian baptistery, remains of which are on the north side of the building. The cathedral was enlarged in the reigns of Philippe Auguste and St Louis, beginning with the Romanesque east end. The 280 medallions adorning the west front were begun in 1310; in their wealth of detail and great variety they are comparable with those of Rouen cathedral or the chapel of Papal Palace at Avignon, though the juxtaposition of the sacred, profane and grotesque is sometimes disconcerting.

Inside, the apse, with its fluted pilasters below a blind arcade and a frieze of palm-leaves, is typical of the architecture of the Rhône valley. It is lit by a 13C stained glass axial window with a fine medallion depicting the Redemption. There is a 14C astronomical clock with original ironwork.

★★ **Quartier St-Jean** (ET) – J 9. Lyon was incorporated into the French kingdom at the beginning of the 14C. In the Middle Ages it was a border town facing the Dauphiné, Savoy, and the Holy Roman Empire. Charles VII made it a trading centre of European importance when he founded the twice-yearly fair in 1419. Louis XI introduced the weaving of raw silk imported from the Levant and from Italy, but local opposition led the only silk-mill to transfer its operations to Tours. 44 years later, Louis doubled the number of fairs; long-distance trade was encouraged and patterns of commercial activity developed which were far in advance of the time; accommodation at inns and hostels was improved, and clearing houses were set up, forerunners of the great bank founded in the 16C. Trade flourished, and with it came a period of great prosperity for the city, its merchants, bankers and high officials. Lyon seethed with activity and ideas; its streets were lined with elegant Flamboyant Gothic façades with asymmetrical window patterns; behind them, down narrow alleys, lay courtyards like the ones at Nos 11 and 58 in Rue St-Jean. More numerous are houses of Renaissance date, decorated with Italianate motifs (polygonal turrets, superimposed galleries, basket-handle arches and corner signs like the figure of the ox at the junction of Rue du Bœuf (Hôtel Paterin, 4 Rue de la Juiverie), sculpted in the 16C by John of Bologna.

Ch. Delpal/EXPLORER

Guignol and his friends

The **Hôtel Gadagne**★ (**ET M¹**) houses the **Musée historique**★ and the **Musée de la Marionnette**★, the latter created by Laurent Mourget (1769-1844), whose Guignol is the very embodiment of the spirit of the Lyon populace. With the development of the characteristic forms of the French Renaissance come superimposed orders as in the Hôtel Bullioud (8, Rue de la Juiverie) with its gallery and corner pavilions.

Printing had been invented in Korea in 1403, then again at Mainz in 1447. It made its first appearance on the banks of the Saône in 1485. The world of the transcriber or of the illuminator would never be the same again. The spread of books transformed Europe with its diffusion of learning, in literature, science and technology and accounts of voyages. The Reformation, born from widespread reading of the Bible, came about some 50 years after the invention of the printing press.

This was also the age of Louise Labe, known as la "Belle Cordière" (Rope-maker's wife), whose salon became a centre for literature and the arts; among those writing was the Lyon poet Maurice Scève.

By 1548 there were almost 400 printers working in the city, including Sébastien Gryphe, Guillaume Rouille and Étienne Dolet, the publisher of Marot and of Rabelais *(qv)*; the latter served as a doctor at the Pont-du-Rhône hospital for three years, carrying on a correspondence with Erasmus and Du Bellay. It was Du Bellay who published **Rabelais'** *Pantagruel* in 1532 and *Gargantua* in 1534 to coincide with the Lyon fairs.

It was here that the Florentine Angelo Benedetto produced white porcelain. Other manufacturers were active too, including Julio Gambiu, who moved away to Nevers around 1565.

★★ **Musée de l'Imprimerie et de la Banque (FT M⁵)** ☉ – H 10, J 10. The museum traces the evolution of printing from its very beginnings in Lyon, from the first wood engravings to the discovery of typography and to photocomposition, as well as evoking the great age of banking (Guérin, Crédit Lyonnais) post-1863 with its support for silk-making, trade generally, and the great Paris-Lyon-Mediterranean Railway.

LYON'S PENINSULA

Plan 31 H 10, J 10, K 9, K 10, L 9

The modern centre of the city is sited on a long tongue of alluvial material brought down by the Rhône. The formation of the "Peninsula" has shifted the junction of the two rivers 4km – 2 1/2 miles southwards since Roman times.

The area was first of all a military encampment, then its proximity to the two rivers made it a favourable place for trading and warehousing. Finally it became the very core of the city; its development along classical lines begun under Henri IV and Louis XIII was continued in the 18C and 19C until the urban area spread outwards to the modern suburbs and beyond. The great city's character comes across not only in the busy Rue de la République with its fine 19C façades and elegant shops but also in the pleasantly shaded Place de la République (**FT**) with its trees and fountains.

LA PRESQU'ÎLE

H   Hôtel de Ville
M¹   Hôtel de Gadagne
M³   Musée de la Civilisation
       gallo-romaine
M⁴   Musée des Hospices civils
M⁵   Musée de l'Imprimerie et de
       la Banque

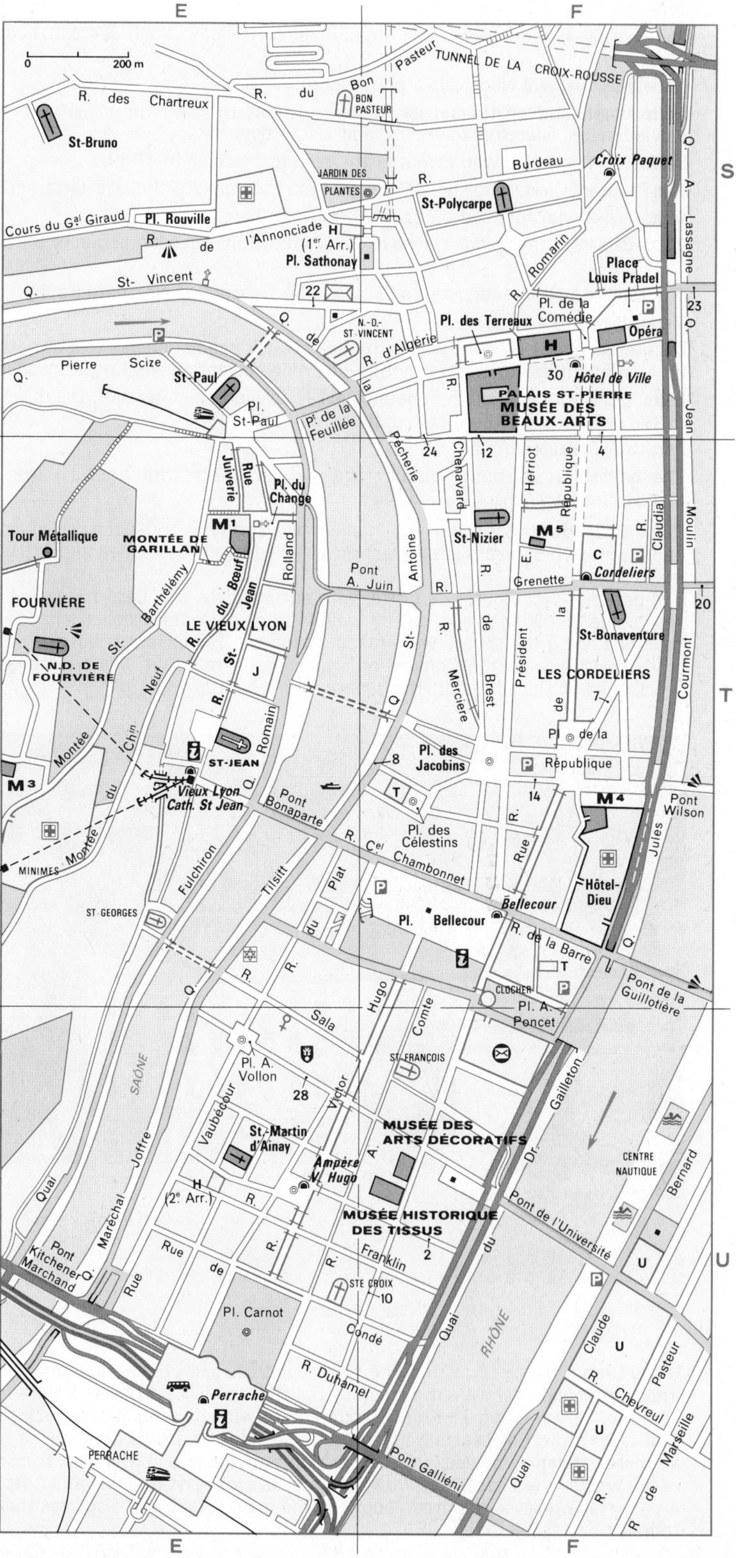

183

The era of invention – Lyon played a leading role in science and technology at this time. Among its eminent men should be noted the following:

The **brothers Jussieu** (Antoine, Bernard and Joseph), 18C botanists.

Claude Bourgelat, a passionate devotee of horse-racing, who founded Europe's first veterinary school.

Jouffroy d'Albans who sailed up the Rhône in his pyroscaphe, the first steam paddle-boat.

Marie-Joseph Jaquard who built a power-loom in 1804.

André Ampère, a deep thinker as well as a mathematician, the inventor of the galvanometer, electromagnetism, and electrodynamics.

Barthélemy Thimonnier, who invented the sewing machine in 1829.

Jean-Baptiste Guimet, who, in 1834, succeeded in making the dye ultramarine.

Émile Guimet who founded an oriental museum here in 1879.

Claude Bernard, a physiologist, who established the glycogenic function of the liver in 1853.

The **Lumière brothers** (Auguste and Louis), the creators of cinematography.

Marius Berliet *(qv)*.

Louis Lépine, a civil servant, who introduced traffic regulations as well as setting up a competition for the promotion of French inventions and other products.

Hector Guimard, one of the founders of Art Nouveau in architecture, the designer of the entrances to the metro stations of Paris.

Antoine de St-Exupéry *(qv)*.

The **brothers Voisin**, both aviators and car designers with a sharp eye for aerodynamic forms.

Place Bellecour (FT) – K 9, K 10. Planned by Henri IV in 1609, the project could only be started 50 years later when the city had finally succeeded in purchasing the land.

The designer was Robert de Cotte, who arranged the avenues of trees on the south side of the square in such a way as to disguise its irregular shape. The buildings lining the square were razed during the Terror in retribution for the city's resistance to the Convention. "Lyon is no more" it was triumphantly proclaimed at the time, but the square was rebuilt in the 19C.

Place Bellecour, Lyon

Hôtel-Dieu (FT) – J 10, K 10. The plans for this, one of the kingdom's most important buildings, were drawn up by Soufflot in 1740. It marks a significant stage in the evolution of French architecture with its long façade facing the Rhône, its projecting central section with Ionic columns and its dome rising from a square base and crowned with a square lantern. The way in which the transoms of the windows are decorated with linen motifs evokes its function as a hospital. A balustrade relieves the great length of the main façade and disguises the low roofs.

Place des Terreaux (FS) – H 10. This is sited where the Saône flowed into the Rhône in Roman times. The older inhabitants of the city are particularly fond of the square with its **fountain**★ by Bartholdi, which has four eager horses representing rivers bounding oceanwards. The town hall dates from the reign of Louis XIII, although its façade was rebuilt by Robert de Cotte after a fire and is typically 18C, with a dome and a rounded tympanum supported by atlantes.

★★ **Musée des Beaux-Arts** ⊘ – Housed in the St-Pierre Palace (FS). Among the representative selection of French painting should be mentioned Géricault's *Madwoman (Folle)*, Delacroix' *Woman with Parrot (Femme au perroquet)*, a drawing by Daumier entitled *After the Audience (Après l'audience)* and two portraits by Puvis de Chavannes, one of his wife and one of Suzanne Valadon (his niece).

★★★ **Musée historique des Tissus** (FU) ⊘ – K 10. Apart from its exhibits devoted to very early examples of the weaver's art, the collection consists mostly of Lyons silk from the 17C onward, by masters such as Philippe de Lasalle. There are Louis XV lampas and embroidered satins, embroidery, and cut velvets of the Empire and Restauration periods. The museum also houses the **Centre International d'études des textiles anciens**.

Silk

From the 1740s onward, Lyon supplied France and the whole of Europe with silk goods of all kinds, its silk painted with decorative motifs being particularly favoured. In 1744 there was a long and bitter strike of the silkworkers, caused by the rise in the cost of living. The movement revived in 1875, the workers attributing their penury this time to the introduction of mechanical looms.

On the slopes of the Croix-Rousse hill is a network of covered passageways called Traboules (FS), once used to protect the precious sheets of silk from the weather. They proved their worth during the French Revolution too and were much used by the Resistance in the Second World War.

⊘ ►► Lyon: Musée lyonnais des arts décoratifs★★ FU; Musée Guimet★★ – Oriental art and natural history; Musée des Hospices civils – pharmacy★ FT M⁴; Basilique St-Martin d'Ainay – capitals; Église St-Nizier – Virgin with the Infant Jésus★; Église St-Paul – Lantern-tower★; Garillan Hill★ ET; Parc de la Tête d'Or★; Place Rouville – view★ ES.

EXCURSIONS

★★ **Musée Henri-Malartre** ⊘ – *At Rochetaillée, 10km – 6 miles north of the Clemenceau Bridge.* The château and its ancilliary buildings house a collection the greater part of which was brought together by Henri Malartre. He found his true vocation in 1931 when he discovered, amongst a lot of old iron, a Rochet-Schneider of 1898 complete with engine still in working order.

The earliest automobiles in France were Cugnot's trolley of 1769, Beau de Rochas' four-stroke Otto of 1862, Bollée's *"Obéissante" (p 153)* of 1873 and the steam-driven Jacquot of 1878.

At the beginning of this century there were some 150 manufacturers of motor vehicles in the area. One of them was **Marius Berliet** (1866-1849). He built his first streamliner in 1896, but then based his reputation on the robustness of his chassis, on his monobloc motors (1913) and on the reliability of his CBA lorries (for their role on the Voie Sacrée *p 74*). He brought out diesels in 1931, then heavy trucks of 20 and 30 tons in 1932.

The museum makes it possible to appreciate some of the important French contributions to motoring technology, notably:

Scotte (1892): Steam omnibus with fire-tube boiler.

Rochet-Schneider (1895): a vis-à-vis.

Noël-Benet (1900): a two-seater phaeton with front-wheel drive, fitted with Michelin 810x90 tyres.

Mildé (1900): with two electric motors (one on each rear wheel) and moveable front-wheel drive.

Corre (1904): a tonneau fitted with Beaujeu elastic wheels.

Berliet (1908): a four-cylinder double phaeton.

Citroën (1922): an all-steel open tourer with side-valves.

Lorraine-Dietrich (1925): a Le Mans winner fitted with twin ignition.

Voisin: a 1932 streamliner with twin carburettor and aluminium body.

Renault (1933): Vivastella, once owned by the Lumière brothers.

Citroën (1938): the TPV (toute petite voiture = ultra-small car) was the ancestor of the renowned 2CV.

Le MAINE-GIRAUD

Map p 8 – Michelin map 72 fold 13 or 233 fold 29 – Green Guide Atlantic Coast

The modest **manor house** ⊙ of Le Maine-Giraud stands in lonely countryside 4km – 2 1/2 miles north of Blanzac. Since the 17C it has produced a celebrated *eau-de-vie*.

In 1838, **Alfred de Vigny** (1797-1863) shut himself away from the world here on his family estate. An aristocrat of modest means and a semi-detached member of the Romantic Movement, his life was marked by a degree of suffering and estrangement from society. His marriage to his English wife was a disappointment, his liaison with the second-rate actress Marie Dorval (celebrated in his play *Chatterton*) a less than satisfactory affair. It was at Le Maine-Giraud that Vigny wrote some of the masterpieces included in the posthumous collection of his poems entitled *Les Destinées* (1864), like *La Mort du Loup (Death of the Wolf)*, advocating acceptance of the burdens of duty, and *La Maison du Berger (The Shepherd's House)*, a description of the inward journey to solitude.

More interested in ideas than in artistic creation, Vigny's virile Romanticism resulted in a kind of noble, somewhat impersonal poetry. His three tales of army life, *Servitude et grandeur militaire* (1835), are "full of a stoic virtue" (Geoffrey Brereton). But here, on his estate, the poet was also a vine-grower, concerned to make the most of his resources and to distil the "purest cognac possible".

Le MANS★★

Conurbation 189 107
Map p 5 – Michelin map 60 fold 13 and 64 fold 3 or 232 fold 10
Green Guide Châteaux of the Loire
Town plan in the current Michelin Red Guide France

The county of Maine was seized in 1063 by William the Conqueror, and for two centuries Le Mans and its beautiful surrounding countryside shared the history of the Norman state to the west.

The **historic centre**★★ of Le Mans (Vieux Mans) stands on the site of a Celtic settlement, overlooking the lowlands on either side of the Sarthe. This part of the city is still enclosed within its 4C Gallo-Roman ramparts, some of the few still extant in western France **(Queen Berengaria's House**★ ⊙ – Maison de la Reine Bérengère and Red Pillar House – Maison du Pilier Rouge).

★★ **Cathédrale St-Julien** – The transition from nave to choir is one of the clearest demonstrations anywhere – even for the architecturally uninitiated – of the great technical and stylistic changes which took place over a period of some 160 years.

Romanesque nave – 1060-1120. The west front is in a very archaic style; behind it extends the Romanesque nave, strengthened and stone-vaulted in 1158, its simplicity relieved by a series of arcades. The Ascension Window *(the second in the south aisle)* dates from 1140 and has remarkable stained glass.

Outside, the arches of the south porch are pleasingly decorated with dog-tooth moulding, and the **doorway**★★ has splendid statue-columns. The flying buttresses were added in 1419.

East end of the cathedral, Le Mans

Gothic choir and transept – 1217-1448. The choir which lacks a triforium was completed in 1254; with its two-stage elevation, it is of a graceful simplicity. Below the clerestory windows runs that characteristically Norman feature, an inspection gallery. There is a double ambulatory whose inside gallery rises to a height of 22m – 72ft at triforium level. The whole is lit by 13C **stained glass windows★★** on three levels; in the chapels opening out on to the outer ambulatory, in the inner ambulatory and in the clerestory.

Note how in the south transept (1385-92) the junction has been effected between the Gothic choir and the older, Romanesque transept.

The north transept was built between 1425 and 1448 in identical style. In the baptismal chapel are two remarkable Renaissance **tombs★★**; the one on the left in Italianate style was made for Charles V of Anjou, brother of King Réné *(qv)*, and exhibits a taste for Antiquity; the other tomb is that of Guillaume du Bellay (a cousin of the poet Joachim du Bellay), who is shown recumbent on a sarcophagus ravishingly decorated with nautical divinities.

Outside, the **chevet★★★** is a spectacular demonstration of the boldness and ambition of its architect, and of his consummate understanding of the interplay of forces in such a complex undertaking. It should be viewed from the foot of the steps leading to Place des Jacobins. The famous Y-shaped flying buttresses "seem not so much to prop the structure as to hoist it skywards with their vertical impetus" (Henri Focillon – the Art of the West).

★★ Musée de l'Automobile ○ – *5km – 3 miles south, in the Le Mans circuit.*

By the middle of the 19C, Le Mans had become an industrial city. In 1873, **Amédée Bollée** (1844-1917), a bell-founder, built his first automobile, 104 years after Cugnot's trolley. He named it *L'Obéissante* (Obedient) – it is now in the Technical Museum in Paris – and followed it with *La Mancelle* (Lady of Le Mans), helped by his sons, Amadée and Léon.

On 26 June 1906, the first Grand Prix took place, on the 103.180km – 64.11 mile long Sarthe Circuit.

The victor was Szisz, driving a Renault fitted with Michelin detachable rims. In 1923 the 24 hour Le Mans race was initiated.

The museum has something of the air of a sanctuary, laid out as it is in the heart of the 24 Hour Circuit. It enables the visitor to appreciate some of France's contributions to the evolution of the automobile. Particularly notable are:

De Dion Bouton (1885), a steam vehicle with two engines.

Henry Vallée (1897) with a tubular chassis and suspension by triangulated struts.

Krieger (1908) electric car with twin motors and front-wheel drive.

Zèbre (1909) the prototype of all cars aimed at the liberal professions.

Saiga (1912), an innovatory machine with streamlining.

De Dion (1912) with a V8 engine.

Citroën Type A (1919), the first mass-produced car in Europe.

Sara (1926) with air-cooling.

Voisin aerodyne (1935) with six valveless cylinders.

CGE Tudor Electrique (1940).

Grégoire Socema (1952) gas turbine vehicle.

Citroën DS with streamlining added in 1962, giving a rocket-like effect.

Citroën M35 (1970) with a rotary engine.

Racing vehicles include:

DB Panhard (1960) a top performer at Le Mans.

Porsche 904 GTS (1964) used as a test vehicle by Michelin, with variable suspension and adjustable wheel rake and play.

Matra-Simca (1974) high-tech vehicle using titanium alloys.

Renault (1978) turbine-powered, subjected to endurance testing at Le Mans.

Peugeot WM P88 (1981).

Rondeau (1983) with a top speed of 335kmh – 208mph. Took part in the 1983 "24 Hours".

Covgar (1990) Porsche engine.

○ ►► Musée de Tessé★ – paintings; Église de la Couture★; Église Ste-Jeanne d'Arc★; Notre-Dame de L'Épau★ *4km – 2 miles east.*

The annual Michelin Red Guide France
offers an up-to-date selection
of hotels and restaurants
serving carefully prepared meals at reasonable prices

MARAIS POITEVIN★

Map p 8 – Michelin map 71 folds 1, 2, 11, 12 or 233 folds 3, 4, 5
Green Guide Atlantic Coast

The vast Poitou marshlands occupy what was once a wide bay, the Golfe du Poitou. Up until the beginnings of historic times, the tides washed the foot of the old cliffline, and the barely perceptible rises which form the sites of today's villages ③ were once islands. The marsh rests on a bed of hardened marine silts; it is drained by an extensive network of channels and protected from floods and high water by dikes and sluices.

The lack of a stable foundation forced the builders of the railway between Luçon and La Rochelle to make a long detour and to align the track on the firmer ground of the old shoreline and the "islands".

The marsh has a total area of some 80 000 ha – 97 680 acres. The larger part, nearer the sea, consists of "dry" marshland, with dark soils requiring the application of fertiliser. Here can be seen the punt-like craft of the mussel breeders. Inland lies the "wet" marshland, known as "green Venice" because of the abundant duckweed in its watery labyrinth. Well-treed with poplars, alders and willows, it is grazed by cattle as well as producing good market-garden crops. The work of reclamation, involving the digging of drainage channels, the building of sluices and the parcelling out of the new-won lands, was begun by the monks from the abbeys as early as the 11C, and continued, once the Wars of Religion were over, by Henri IV.

The marsh is linked to the ocean by **Aiguillon Bay** (anse d'Aiguillon). It is protected from the waves by **Arçay Point** (Pointe d'Arçay) ② and its sandbanks and by the Aiguillon dike built by Dutch engineers.

The bay is in the process of silting up and evolving into a marsh. It has already shifted southwards and westwards. The effect of currents ① is added to by that of the tides which transport material eroded by the waves or brought down by the river Sèvre. The deposition of this material is tending to even out the irregularities in the line of the coast and to provide good conditions for oyster and mussel breeding. The bay makes a grand sight at high water, but it is only when the tide is out that its full interest is revealed.

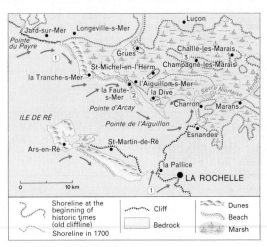

MARSEILLE★★★

Conurbation 1 087 370
Map p 10 – Michelin map 84 fold 13 or 245 fold 44 or 246 folds K, L, M
Green Guide Provence – Town plan in the current Michelin Red Guide France

The 19C Romano-Byzantine Basilica of Notre-Dame-de-la-Garde stands in a commanding position overlooking this great Mediterranean seaport. The **view**★★★ from the church is immense, taking in the islands standing guard in the bay, the harbour, and the background of limestone hills as well as the sprawling city itself. Marseille owes everything to the sea. It began life as a trading post set up by Greeks from Asia Minor around 600BC. Its inhabitants soon established other commercial bases both in the interior and on the coast, at Nice, Antibes, the Lérins Islands, Agde, Glanum (St-Rémy), and Arles. By the 3C-2C BC the city they called Massilia covered an area of some 50ha - 125 acres to the north of the Old Port, and the knolls rising above the busy streets were crowned with temples. A cultural as well as a commercial centre, the city aroused the interest and envy of the Celto-Ligurians of Entremont, and in 123BC Massilia found it prudent to conclude an alliance with Rome. The Senate took the opportunity thus offered to put its communications with its possessions in Spain on a sounder footing, and began its programme of expansion into Provence and subsequently Gaul.

70 years later, when Caesar and Pompey were engaged in civil war, Marseille was obliged to take sides and had the ill fortune to choose the loser. The victorious Caesar besieged the city and sacked it in 49BC. Narbonne, Arles and Fréjus grew prosperous on the spoils, and Marseille went into decline.

In the 19C, the city's fortunes revived with the expansion of French (and European) colonial activity in the Orient as well as in Africa.

★ **Basilique St-Victor** – A Christian quarter grew up opposite the old Graeco-Roman city. It was here that St Victor is supposed to have met a martyr's death at the very beginning of the 4C, and here too that a fortified abbey is said to have been built in his memory around 420AD.

The basilica was rebuilt in 1040 and its crypt and nave altered at the beginning of the Gothic period. In the **crypt★★** ⊘ are a number of 4C sarcophagi, examples of the individualism which distinguishes Christian art from that of the Classical world. The sarcophagi showing the Council of the Apostles and the Companions of St Maurice are justly famous.

The Vieux-Port

★★ **Old Port (Vieux-Port) and surrounding area** – On the south side of the Old Port is the bust of Vincent Scotto (1876-1952), the composer of much-loved popular melodies, surveying what is almost always a highly animated scene. To the east is the Canebière, the city's busy main artery, whose fame has been spread around the world by the mariners of Marseille.

Even after its sack by Caesar, Marseille remained a free city, and its life as a port carried on, with many ups and downs, based on the "Horn" (corne), the original basin sited to the northeast of today's Old Port, which itself came more and more into use as an outer harbour. Nevertheless, the decline of the city as a whole made it difficult to maintain the installations **Musée des Docks romains★** (**M³**) ⊘ and the original harbour gradually silted up, finally becoming completely blocked in the 11C.

The Crusades, together with the growth of the rivalry between Pisa and Genoa led to a revival of the city's fortunes in the 12C. Further expansion followed, with the incorporation of Provence into the French kingdom in 1481 and even more with the construction of new quays under Louis XIII (a blow to its old rival Arles).

The archaeological site, part of the **Musée d'Histoire de Marseille★** (**M¹**) known as the **Garden of Ruins** (Jardin des Vestiges) (**K**) gives some fascinating insights into the city's long history. The "horn" formed by the first harbour is dramatically visible, and inside there is a 3C boat recently excavated from the mud.

MARSEILLE

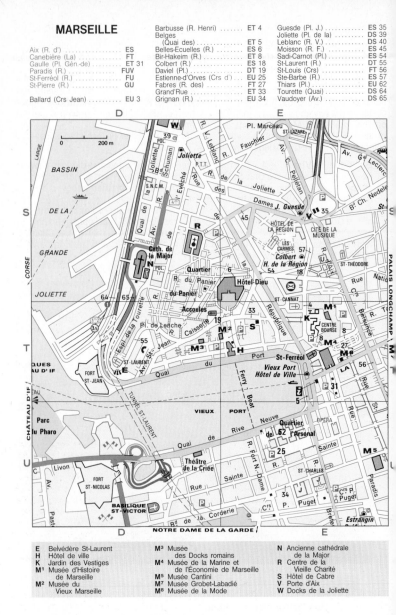

E	Belvédère St-Laurent	M³	Musée	N	Ancienne cathédrale
H	Hôtel de ville		des Docks romains		de la Major
K	Jardin des Vestiges	M⁴	Musée de la Marine et	R	Centre de la
M¹	Musée d'Histoire		de l'Économie de Marseille		Vieille Charité
	de Marseille	M⁵	Musée Cantini	S	Hôtel de Cabre
M²	Musée du	M⁷	Musée Grobet-Labadié	V	Porte d'Aix
	Vieux Marseille	M⁸	Musée de la Mode	W	Docks de la Joliette

★★ **Centre de la Vieille Charité** (DS R) ⊙ – The old workhouse and hospice has been carefully restored. The **chapel**★ is a masterpiece by Pierre Puget, a Marseille man; it has a little ambulatory and recessed steps allowing the different categories of inmates to make their separate ways to the chapels and galleries, and a central, oval-shaped cupola resting on a drum and supported by Ionic columns and pilasters.

⊙ ►► Musée du Vieux-Marseille★ M²; Ancienne cathédrale de la Major★ N; Musée Cantini★ M⁵ – Contemporary art, faïence; Corniche President J.-F.-Kennedy★★; Musée d'Archéologie méditerranéenne★; Musée Grobet Labadié★★ – decorative arts, painting M⁷; Palais Longchamp - fine arts; Port★★; Château d'If★★.

The chapter on art and architecture in this guide gives
an outline of artistic achievement in the country
providing the context of the buildings and works of art
described in the Sights section

This chapter may also provide ideas for touring
It is advisable to read it at leisure

Grotte du MAS-D'AZIL★★

Map p 9 – Michelin map 86 fold 4 or 235 fold 42
Green Guide Pyrenees-Languedoc-Tarn Gorges

This **cave** Ⓥ is one of the outstanding natural phenomena of southwestern France as well as a prehistoric site of the first importance.

The River Arize has hollowed out a 420m – 1 380ft tunnel through the Plantaurel heights which once barred its way; a meandering dry valley to the east testifies to its former course. The entrance to the tunnel is formed by a magnificent 65m – 213ft arch, the exit by a much lower opening made in a sheer rock rising to a height of 140m – 460ft.

The site was first excavated by **Edouard Piette** (1827-1906), who communicated his passion for prehistory to the young seminary student who later became Abbot Breuil. In 1887, Piette discovered a human habitat intermediate between the Magdalenian and the Neolithic *(qv)*, the Azilian. It was at this site that Azilian industry was studied and defined. Practised between 11000 and 9500 BC, it is characterised by miniaturised tools, by flat harpoons made from stags' antlers (the reindeer having moved northwards following the change to warmer conditions after the Wurm glaciation), and by the making of flattened pebbles. The latter carry enigmatic markings done in a red paint made from calcinated ferric oxide; they have been interpreted to be lunar or menstrual calendars, or possibly the beginnings of abstract numbering. The dark-skinned, round-headed people who made these objects probably had their origin in the great Asiatic population reservoir; drawn here by the mildness of the climate, they brought about considerable changes in the way men lived, and contibuted greatly to the peopling of Europe.

Nevertheless, they were not the first to use this cavern; as is the case all along the fringes of the Pyrenees, human occupation goes back much further, to Magdalenian times (15000 BC).

MEAUX★

Conurbation 63 006
Map p 7 – Michelin map 106 folds 22, 23
Green Guide Flanders, Picardy and the Paris Region
Town plan in the current Michelin Red Guide France

In the early years of the 16C, the bishop of Meaux, Guillaume de Briçonnet, was an advocate of ecclesiastical reform, and the town sheltered numerous adherents of Calvinism. In 1682, the bishopric passed into the hands of **Jacques-Bénigne Bossuet** (1627-1704), a meagre recompense for the frustrating years spent as tutor to the Dauphin. But Bossuet gave himself wholeheartedly to the task of running his diocese and to the fight against quietism and against Gallicanism, that specifically French movement favouring a reduction of Papal power. In an age when the influence of the pulpit orator equalled that of today's media commentator, the "Eagle of Meaux" was one of the greatest orators of his time, noted particularly for the eloquence of the funeral speeches made on the deaths of the Grand Condé *(qv)* and Maria-Theresa, Louis XIV's wife. With his solid Burgundian temperament, he was also one of France's great classical writers, his careful phrasing vibrating with an astonishing lyricism.

★ **Cathédrale St-Étienne** – 12C-16C. All the major phases of French Gothic architecture are represented here. There are interesting, albeit headless, sculptures on the outside of the south transept, while the central portal of the Flamboyant west front is adorned with a vast composition depicting the Last Judgement carried out in the 15C but in the style of the 13C. The clarity of the interior is striking, its apparent height enhanced by the removal of the tribunes in the 13C (though their arches have been preserved in the first three bays on the south side of the choir).

Ⓥ ►► Episcopal Palace★; Musée Bossuet – mementoes of Bossuet, archaeology, fine arts.

Château de MEILLANT★★

Map p 9 – Map 69 fold 1 or 238 fold 31 – Green Guide Berry Limousin (in French)

This **château** Ⓥ *(3/4 hour)* is a fine example of how stylistic change was allied to the growing desire for domestic comfort towards the end of the 15C to transform what had been a typical medieval castle into an agreeable country residence. Like the Jacques-Cœur Palace in Bourges and the châteaux at Chaumont and Chenonceaux, it demonstrates the spread of early, Italianate Renaissance motifs in the southern part of the Loire valley.

Among the great families to which the château belonged and who left their mark on it were the Amboises, the Béthune-Charost and the Mortemarts.

Château de MEILLANT

The medieval south front is particularly fine, while the Renaissance north front has the air of having been applied like a veneer to the older structure behind it. It suffered excessive restoration in 1842. The interior, notably the principal living room, is furnished with period pieces, fireplaces, tapestries, carpets...

EXCURSION

Bruère-Allichamps – *6km – 4 miles west*. A Roman milestone was found here in 1757. It stands at the centre of the village and is popularly thought to mark the geographical centre of France.

MENTON★★

Population 29 141
Map p 11 – Michelin map 84 fold 10, 20 or 195 fold 28
Green Guide French Riviera – Town plan in the current Michelin Red Guide France

Between mountain and Mediterranean, Menton stretches out agreeably on its sunny **site★★** on the lower slopes of the natural amphitheatre dominated by Mount Agel and the Gorbio and St Agnes Heights. The picturesque qualities of the landscape belie the poverty of its soils and the severe erosion to which it is prone and which is the cause of frequent landslides. On the cliffs around are the remains of fortifications, castellars, evidence of human settlement going back to Neolithic times. The town was bought by the **Grimaldi** family of Monaco in the 14C, then incorporated into the French kingdom when the county of Nice was annexed.
Menton's gardens are many; together with the abundant olive, orange and lemon trees, they give the town a most pleasant park-like character. The **Tropical Garden★★** (jardin botanique exotique) is outstanding.

Hôtel de ville ⊙ – The town hall is a pretty building in Italianate style, with pilasters and Corinthian capitals and a cream-coloured cornice contrasting with the rosy rendering of the walls. The **Registry Office★** (Salle des mariages) was decorated by Cocteau in 1958.

★★ **Old Menton** – The old town nestles underneath the hill just above Rue Longue and Rue St-Michel, whose alignment marks the course of the Roman Via Giulia Augusta.

★★ **Parvis St-Michel** – This is a charming square in the Italian style, laid out on two levels by the Grimaldis, whose monogram can be seen in the pebble mosaic forming the paving. It is bordered by a number of houses in the local style, by the pink-walled Chapel of the Conception and by the **Église St-Michel★** ⊙, a fine Baroque building dating from the middle of the 17C, extensively restored after the earthquake of 1887.

Rampe St-Michel – Monumental stairway with pebble paving and twin ramps.

EXCURSION

★★ **Roquebrune-Cap Martin** – *Immediately southwest of Menton*. Roquebrune is a most picturesque **hill-top village★★**, where the tourist can stroll through the small streets towards the **keep★** ⊙. From the top, wonderful **panorama★★** on the sea, Cap Martin, the Principality of Monaco and the Mont Agel.

⊙ ►► Menton: Promenade du Soleil★★; Musée du palais Carnolès★ – paintings.

METZ★★

Conurbation 193 117
Map p 7 – Michelin map 57 folds 13, 14 or 242 fold 9
Green Guide Alsace et Lorraine (in French)
Town plan in the current Michelin Red Guide France

From the limestone escarpment of the Côtes de Moselle high above Metz, the Lorraine plateau can be seen stretching away eastwards towards the German frontier. The city itself lies at the meeting point of the Moselle with the Seille, a strategic site whose importance was appreciated by the Romans; it was here that their great highways leading from the Channel coast to the Rhine and from Trier to Italy were linked, their course marked today by Metz' busy shopping street, Rue Serpenoise.
In the 4C, as a response to the threat posed by the Germanic tribes to the east, fortifications were built, together with a basilica which later became the church of a monastery, the original Church of St Peter of the Novitiates (St-Pierre-aux-Nonnains). In the early part of the Middle Ages, the city was the residence of the

Merovingian rulers of Eastern Gaul (Austrasia); it then became the capital of the kingdom of Lotharingia (Lorraine), before being attached to the Holy Roman Empire. In the 12C Metz declared itself the capital of a republican city-state, with an elected High Magistrate as ruler. But in 1552, together with Verdun and Toul, it was annexed by a French kingdom seeking to push its frontier eastwards, and its role henceforth was that of a fortress-town standing guard over the border.

1871-1918-1944 – On the 6 August 1870, the Prussian armies invaded Lorraine, defeating the incompetent Marshal Bazaine *(qv)* in a series of battles and locking up his forces in Metz. On 27 October Bazaine surrendered the city which seven months later became part of the newly-declared German Empire.

The city lost a quarter of its population, people who chose to resettle in France; artists left and so did many businessmen, at the very moment when industry was expanding rapidly. Metz' loss was Nancy's gain.

The townscape began to take on a Germanic character. In 1898 the cathedral was given a neo-Gothic portal, complete with a statue of the Prophet Daniel looking uncommonly like Kaiser Wilhelm II (though his moustache was subsequently clipped). With its surrounding forts, Metz became the centre of the greatest fortified camp in the world. From 1902-08 the area around the station was rebuilt; the station itself was constructed in a style which mixed Rhenish neo-Romanesque and Second Reich symbolism (the Emperor himself designed the bell-tower); an imposing central post office rose nearby, together with hotels providing accomodation for the officers of the garrison and their guests. Metz was in fact the lynch-pin of the Schlieffen Plan, the strategy to be followed in the event of a future war with France; this envisaged the adoption of a defensive posture to the south of the city coupled with a vast turning movement to the northwest which would sweep through Belgium and then descend on Paris. In 1914 the plan all but succeeded; the German armies marched steadily forward for six weeks, coming within 50km – 30 miles of Paris, only to be thrown back by Joffre at the Miracle of the Marne.

In the inter-war period, the ring of forts around Metz was incorporated into the Maginot Line. Their defensive strength was such that the Allied armies took two and a half months to eject their German occupants in the autumn of 1944.

★★★ **Cathédrale St-Étienne** ⊘ – The cathedral grew out of the joining together around 1240 of two churches which up to then had been separated by an alley-way and had faced in different directions.

The 13C and 14C interior recalls the Gothic style of Champagne; its relative narrowness combines with the modest height of the aisles to exaggerate the loftiness of the nave, which does in fact reach 41.77m – 137ft. The late Gothic chancel, crossing and transepts were completed at the beginning of the 16C. The **stained glass windows**★★★ have led to the cathedral being known as "God's Lantern" – lanterne du Bon Dieu. They have a total area of 6 500m^2 – about 60 000sq ft. The rose window of the west front is 14C work, the lower part of the north transept window 15C, and the upper part of this window together with the glass of the south transept and the chancel, 16C. Contemporary glass can be seen beneath the towers (abstract designs by Bissière) and above all in the north ambulatory and on the southwest side of the north transept (the *Earthly Paradise* by Chagall).

⊘ ►► Musée La cour d'or★★ (archeological department★★★ – Grenier de Chèvremont★) – Porte des Allemands★ – Place St-Louis★ – Église St-Maximin – St Pierre-aux-Nonnains Church.

Massif du MÉZENC

Map p 9 – Michelin map 76 fold 18 or 239 fold 47
Green Guide Auvergne-Rhône Valley

These volcanic uplands in the southern part of the Velay region form the watershed between Atlantic and Mediterranean. They lie at the centre of a belt of igneous rocks cutting across the axis of the Cévennes. The first burst of volcanic activity occurred in Tertiary times, when molten rock was released by the faulting and uplift of the ancient central plateau during the formation of the Alps. A second phase of activity resulted in a series of basalt table-lands, the *planèzes,* like the Devès uplands, and a third volcanic period, towards the end of Tertiary times, was responsible for today's rock pinnacles, the *sucs*. A final set of eruptions released massive flows of lava into the valleys.

Mont Mézenc – *2 hours Rtn on foot from the Croix de Boutières pass.*
Two great lava flows extend downwards from the twin summits of the mountain, from which a vast **panorama**★★★ extends over the Velay. The southern of the two peaks overlooks the luxuriant landscape marked by the *sucs* and the central part of the huge eroded crater of the volcano, while the north peak with its cross dominates a landscape of huge fields running down to the deep ravines of Les Boutières in the east. Quite close at hand can be seen the village of Les Estables.

Gerbier de Jonc

★★ **Gerbier de Jonc** – *1 1/2 hours Rtn on foot.* This lava pinnacle, a typical *suc*, was of too thick a consistency to flow. Its screes of bright phonolite clatter under the feet of the many who clamber to its summit, from which there is a fine *view*★. At the foot of the pinnacle, in a stable, is a fountain which is held to be the source of the Loire, though some geographers consider the streams threading the damp pasturelands near Estables to be the river's true origin.

★★ **Cascade du Ray-Pic** – *11km – 7 miles south of the Gerbier de Jonc – 1 1/2 hours Rtn on foot.* In a harsh setting formed by a succession of lava flows, the Bourges torrent drops in a series of falls, the main one strikingly framed by prisms of basalt. In the bed of the stream, the boulders and pebbles of the dark basalt contrast with those of the much lighter granite.

★ **Lac d'Issarlès** – *20km – 12 miles east of the Gerbier de Jonc.* This pretty, rounded lake with its blue waters occupies the crater of an extinct volcano, 138m – 450ft deep. It forms part of the Montpezat hydro-electric scheme straddling the Atlantic-Mediterranean watershed and incorporating a 13km – 8 mile tunnel with a drop of 650m – 2 100ft.

Pic du MIDI DE BIGORRE★★★

Map p 8 – Michelin map 85 fold 18 or 234 fold 44 – Green Guide Atlantic Coast

A vertiginous mountain road winds over the Tourmalet Pass (Col du Tourmalet), whose name "the bad way round" reflects the difficulties heaped upon intrepid travellers by the severity of the elements. From the top of the pass (2 114m

View, of the Néouvielle Massif from the Pic de Bigorre

- 6 936ft) a **toll road** ⊙, one of the highest in Europe, leads to the place known as Les Laquets; from here a cable-car or a rough path *(two hours Rtn)* give access to the summit of the Pic du Midi de Bigorre, now reduced in level to the 2 865m - 9 400ft contour in order to accommodate the television transmitter.

★★★ **Panorama** - The primary rocks of which the Pic du Midi is made form an isolated mass projecting northwards into the Bigorre lowlands, making a spectacular viewpoint which takes in the Pyrenees from La Rhune to Andorra. To the south rise the summits of the Néouvielle Massif, that extraordinary museum of glacial relief.

Observatory and Institute of World Physics ⊙ - The factors favouring the siting here of an observatory include the great height, the purity of the atmosphere and the all-round viewing possibilities. The observatory, founded by General Nansouty, was originally intended for botanical and meteorological studies, but the astronomical function was soon added. It was here in 1706 that the first observations were made of the solar corona during a total eclipse of the sun. In the 19C, Vaussenat set up a 20cm equatorial telescope here, and at the beginning of the 20C, Jules Baillaud and his son built the great observatory dome and installed reflecting telescopes.

Today, the observatory and the institute attached to it form one of the most important scientific stations of its kind in the world, carrying out research into the solar corona, lunar mapping, cosmic radiation and nocturnal luminescence.

MILLAU★

Population 21 788
Map p 9 - Michelin map 80 fold 14 or 240 northwest of fold 14
Green Guide Pyrenees-Languedoc-Tarn Gorges
Town plan in the current Michelin Red Guide France

Millau huddles between two high limestone plateaux, the Causse du Larzac and the Causse Noir, at the meeting-point of the Tarn and the Dourbie. The site of a ford in ancient times, it acquired a bridge in the Middle Ages and became a trading centre of some importance.

As early as the 2C AD, ewes' milk was used to make Roquefort cheese, a process involving the sacrifice of their lambs. This was turned to advantage by finding uses for lambskin and eventually developing the manufacture of fine gloves.

In its sheltered valley Millau enjoys a much milder climate than that of the harsh plateau high above; with its streets lined with plane trees, its fountains and its bustling air, it has a very southern character. The varied orientation of the edge of the plateau, the depth of the valleys and the rising air currents have made it an important centre for hang gliding.

La Graufesenque ⊙ - This 10ha - 24 acre archaeological site on the south bank of the Dourbie was an important centre for the manufacture of pottery in ancient times. It flourished for over two centuries, between the reigns of Augustus and Hadrian, activity peaking during Nero's rule.

During the first hundred years of its existence, some 400 potters toiled to produce more than 800 000 numbered pieces in 100 kilns heated to 950°C for a period of two weeks. In spite of transport problems, their wares found customers in Britain, central Europe and around the Mediterranean Sea. Vases, cups, bowls and plates were moulded or turned with great care to patterns which probably originated in Arezzo in Tuscany; they were of high quality, decorated with seals and featuring a vitrified reddish surface.

Around 170AD, the seam of clay began to run out, leading to the decline and then abandonment of the site. Manufacture, on an even bigger scale, then began at Lezoux, near Clermont-Ferrand.

There is an **archaeological museum** ⊙ with a fine **pottery collection**★.

EXCURSION

★★★ **Chaos de Montpellier-le-Vieux** ⊙ - *18km - 11 miles northeast - 2 hours Rtn on foot.* This extraordinary ruined city of rocks extending over some 120ha - 300 acres was formed by the erosive effects of water on the limestones of the Causse Noir. For long inaccessible, it was held by the people of the locality to be the abode of the devil, but the surrounding dense woodland was eventually cleared, and in 1883 the site was explored by J. and L. de Malafosse.

The bewildering variety of rock formations (the Sphinx, the Elephant, the Gates of Mycaenae...) is due to the different ways in which the constituents of dolomite react to weathering; the magnesium carbonate has a much greater resistance than calcium carbonate, which decomposes rapidly into sand. The contrasting properties of the rock are further expressed in the pattern of vegetation, with species favouring lime soils and dry conditions (lavander and box) growing in close proximity to plants (thyme, juniper) which prefer siliceous sands.

MOISSAC★★

Population 11 971
Map p 8 – Michelin map 79 folds 16, 17 or 235 fold 21
Green Guide Pyrenees-Languedoc-Tarn Gorges
Town plan in the current Michelin Red Guide France

Moissac is sited on a low rise overlooking the fertile flood plain near the meeting point of the Tarn with the Garonne. The place is famous for the white Chasselas dessert grape which grows here in abundance.

★ **Église St-Pierre** – The Benedictines founded an abbey here in the 7C. Its church was consecrated in 1063 and the **cloisters**★ completed 35 years later; its capitals depict a great variety of themes and served as a model for similar work all over 12C Europe. The church originally had dome vaults like those of Périgord, but was transformed in the 15C into a typical southern French building with a single nave. The work of this period is easily recognisable, having been carried out in brick. The church's **south doorway**★★★ is one of the great triumphs of Romanesque sculpture; in its perfect synthesis of the sculptor's art with the 11C Abbot Roger's profound understanding of the meaning of the Scriptures, it passes beyond beauty into the realm of mysticism.

The subject of the tympanum is the Apocalypse such as it is described by St John. To read Chapter 4 of the Book of Revelation while standing in front of this masterpiece is indeed a moving experience; everything is there, from the "throne set in Heaven", to the "four and twenty Elders with crowns of gold" and the "four beasts (the Evangelists) full of eyes".

MONACO★★★

Population 27 876
Map p 10 – Michelin map 84 folds 19, 20 or 245 fold 38 or 195 folds 27, 28
Green Guide French Riviera – Town plan in the current Michelin Red Guide France

The Principality of Monaco is a sovereign state covering an area of 192ha – less than a square mile. Inhabited since prehistoric times and later a Greek settlement (5C BC) and a Roman port (1C AD), its history really began when the **Grimaldi** family bought it from the Republic of Genoa in 1308.

★★ **The Rock (Le Rocher)** – This is the historic core of the principality, and its capital, the miniature city of Monaco. It is built on a rocky peninsula 60m – 200ft above the sea.

MONACO

Albert-Ier (Bd)	BXY
Grimaldi (R.)	BXY
Princesse-Caroline (R.)	BY 48

Armes (Pl. d')	BY 2
Basse (R.)	BY 3
Bellando-de 6 Castro	
(R. du Colonel)	BY 7
Comte-Félix-Gastaldi (R.) ...	BY 10
Major (Rampe)	BY 27

Palais (Pl. du)	BY 35
Pêcheurs (Chemin des)	CY 37
Princesse Marie-	
de-Lorraine (R.)	BCY 54
Ste-Barbe (Promenade)	BY 60
Suffren-Reymond (R.)	BY 64

E	Centre d'acclimatation zoologique
D	Chapelle de la Miséricorde
M²	Collection des voitures anciennes
M³	Historial des Princes de Monaco
M⁴	Musée Naval

196

The **Musée Océanographique**★★ (CY) ⊙ has a splendid aquarium with tropical and Mediterranean species of marine life as well as skeletons of sea nammals. It is also a scientific research centre, and there are exhibits of marine laboratories, the technology of underwater exploration and applied oceanography.

In the **cathedral (BY)** are a number of **early paintings of the Nice School**★, including a St Nicholas altarpiece by Louis Bréa.

The **Palais du Prince**★ ⊙ overlooks the **Place du Palais**★, a square ornamented with cannon presented by Louis XIV. With its medieval battlements and walls strengthened by Vauban, the palace makes a most picturesque composition. An imposing gateway leads into the Court of Honour with its arcades; inside the Palace is the Throne Room and state apartments decorated with fine furniture and hung with signed portraits by Old Masters.

★★ **Jardin Exotique** (AY) ⊙ – The gardens cascade down a steep rock face which has its own microclimate supporting a luxuriant variety of vegetation; there are many semi-desert species together with plants from the southern hemisphere.

★★★ **Monte-Carlo** (BY) – Europe's gambling capital was launched by François Blanc, director of the casino in Bad Homburg in Germany. The place's success has led to building at a very high density indeed, but Monte-Carlo retains its attractiveness with its luxurious casino, its sumptuous villas, its de luxe shops and its pretty gardens.

⊙ ►► Grotte de l'Observatoire★; Musée d'Anthropologie préhistorique★; Jardins St-Martin★; Musée Napoléonien★; Musée des Poupées et Automates★.

Château de MONTAIGNE

Map p 8 – Michelin map 75 fold 13 or 234 fold 4 – Green Guide Atlantic Coast

The **Château** ⊙ was rebuilt after a fire in 1885, and little remains of the original construction apart from some outbuildings and the late 13C tower frequented by the great writer and moralist during the last twenty years of his life.

The Essays (1580) – At the age of 47, **Michel de Montaigne** (1533-92), published his *Essays,* a work which enhanced the reputation of the French language abroad, but above all expressed the inquiring spirit of its author, who made the question "What do I know?" *(Que sais-je?)* into his motto. Montaigne was a man of varied experience, much travelled, familiar with the company of the mighty, and himself a magistrate and mayor of Bordeaux. As a humanist, he was appalled by the atrocities of the Wars of Religion, and distrusted change: "to make a choice or a change is to presume to judge".

Even more evocative of Montaigne's engaging personality than his bedroom is his library, arranged much as he left it, with its 1 000 books and its beams painted with Greek and Latin sentences...

Musée Condé Chantilly/GIRAUDON-LAUROS

Michel de Montaigne

MONTAUBAN★

Population 51 224
Map 79 folds 17 and 18 or 235 fold 22
Green Guide Pyrenees-Languedoc-Tarn Gorges

On the boundary between the hillsides of Bas Quercy and the rich alluvial plains of the Garonne and the Tarn, the old *bastide* of Montauban, built with a geometric street layout, is an important crossroads and a good point of departure for excursions into the Aveyron gorges. It is an active market-town, selling fruit and vegetables from market gardens from all over the region.

The almost exclusive use of pink brick lends the buildings here a distinctive character, which is also found in most of the towns and villages in Bas Quercy and the Toulouse area.

★★ **Musée Ingres** ⊙ – The museum is housed in what used to be the bishop's palace. The first floor features some of the artist's best examples of paintings: *Ruggiero freeing Angelica, Ossian's Dream, Jesus among the Doctors*, completed with a selection of his 4 000 **drawings**, displayed in rotation.

MONTHERMÉ★

Population 2 866

Map p 7 – Map 53 fold 18 or 241 fold 6 – Green Guide Champagne (in French)

Monthermé has a spectacular **site**★ just downstream from the meeting-point of the Semoy with the Meuse, which here has hollowed out a meander in the schists of the Rocroi Massif. The setting of the little town can be enjoyed from three viewpoints in particular:

Longue Roche★★ *(1 hour Rtn on foot)*, a high spur on the outer side of the meander;

Roche aux 7 Villages★★ *(1/4 hour Rtn on foot)*, giving wide **views**★★ over the high plateau of the Ardennes and of the industrial town of Château-Regnault on its river bend dominated by the Quatre Fils Aymon rock;

Roc de la Tour★★ *(1/4 hour Rtn on foot)*, formed from quartzite intruded into the schists.

EXCURSION

★★ **The Meuse Gorge: through the Ardennes from Charleville-Mézières to Givet** – *72km – 45 miles.* One of Europe's great rivers, 950 km – 590 miles in length, the Meuse rises on the Langres uplands. It flows between the escarpment of the Côte des Bars and the dip-slope of the Côte de la Meuse, before penetrating the schists of the high plateau of the Ardennes in a deep gorge. Its meanders here mark the course it traced out in Tertiary times; since then the plateau has been uplifted, but the river has succeeded in entrenching itself in the schists, a process known as superimposition. From Charleville-Mézières to Givet there is a succession of single meanders (Monthermé, Fumay, Chooz), double (Revin) and even triple ones (Charleville). The valley has long formed a corridor of human activity, with its water, rail and road communications, and with a skilled workforce producing engineering products and domestic appliances. At the beginning of the century, Monthermé was a centre of trade union activity, with considerable conflict between workers and employers.

Downstream from Monthermé the most interesting sites are: the **Laifour Rocks**★ (Roches de Laifour) and the **Ladies of the Meuse**★ (Dames de Meuse) opposite one another; Revin, where the old town and the industrial area each occupy their own peninsula; Fumay, with its old quarter, once famous for its quarries producing violet slate; Chooz, with its nuclear power stations; Givet, sited at the exit from a side valley originally fortified by Charles V and strengthened by Vauban. The composer Mehul (1763-1817) was born here, best known for his *Chant du Départ*, a patriotic song of the French Revolution.

MONT-LOUIS★

Population 200

Map p 9 – Michelin map 86 fold 16 or 235 folds 55

Green Guide Pyrenees-Languedoc-Tarn Gorges

Mont-Louis occupies a strategic site at the meeting point of three valleys. To the north is the valley of the Aude; its broad upper course is known as the **Capcir**. To the southwest is the Sègre, a tributary of the Ebro, which here flows through the **Cerdagne**, an upland basin; its elevated position (1 200m – 4 000ft) diminishes the apparent height of the surrounding peaks, and its high sunshine level led to the construction here in 1949 of the first "**solar oven**" ⊘ using parabolic mirrors. Finally, to the west, is the valley of the Têt, which flows out of the Lac des Bouillouses to form the **Conflent**, the major routeway linking the Cerdagne with Perpignan.

The site's importance was confirmed following the **Treaty of the Pyrenees** in 1659, which, by restoring Roussillon to the French crown, made the Pyrenees the legal as well as the natural boundary of France. Louis XIV set about giving his newly acquired lands some more solid protection than that afforded by a signature; the great Vauban carried out his survey of Roussillon and the Cerdagne in 1679, and, from 1681 onwards, directed the construction of Mont-Louis.

Thus came into being this austere little fortified town, completely contained by its massive **ramparts**★ and protected by its citadel.

The chapter on art and architecture in this guide gives
an outline of artistic achievement in the country
providing the context of the buildings and works of art
described in the Sights section
This chapter may also provide ideas for touring
It is advisable to read it at leisure

MONTPELLIER★★

Population 207 936
Map p 9 – Michelin map 83 fold 7 or 240 fold 23
Green Guide Pyrenees-Languedoc-Tarn Gorges
Town plan in the current Michelin Red Guide France

By the 11C, Montpellier was already an inland port served by the Maguelone lagoon and by the Camargue canal. At the time of the first Crusades, trade with the eastern Mediterranean encouraged spice merchants to find out more about the medicinal and other plants they were dealing in; one way of doing this was to read the works of Hippocrates, and directly and indirectly this led to the founding here in 1137 of Europe's first medical school. In the space of a hundred years it equalled Salerno in reputation and achieved the status of a university in 1289.

The town had passed by marriage into the hands of the king of Aragon, but was bought back by Philippe VI of Valois in 1349. Louis XIV made it the capital of Lower Languedoc, opening a period of high architectural achievement.

★★ **Promenade du Peyrou** – This was laid out in 1688 in the upper part of the town by Charles d'Aviler (1653-1700). In the 18C, the construction of the St-Clément aqueduct to supply the town's fountains led to the redevelopment of the site by Jean-Antoine Giral, who cut into the hill, built terraces and camouflaged the reservoir with a charming little octagonal temple. From here there is a fine **view**★ over the Garrigue and the Cévennes.

★★ **Old Montpellier** – In the course of the 17C and 18C the townscape of old Languedoc houses was embellished by the addition of fine town residences (*hôtels*).

The **Hôtel des Trésoriers de la bourse**★ has kept its fine staircase carried on four central pillars, a Louis XIII feature.

The **Hôtel de Varennes**★ integrates Romanesque and Gothic elements in a harmonious way.

The **Hôtel des Trésoriers de France** has a dignified courtyard with twin columns, superimposed orders and a staircase with a fine wrought-iron grille and straight flights with angle pendentives.

There are many other *hôtels*, with names like Manse, Beaulac, Baudon de Maury, Richer de Belleval, Cambacérès-Murles, Montcalm, St-Côme, each with its own character but all conforming to common rules of taste.

⊘ ►► Musée Fabre★★ – paintings; Musée Atger★ – drawings.

EXCURSION

★ **La Grande Motte** – This resort on the Languedoc coast is famous for its original architecture: imposing pyramids, small residential complexes (villas, low houses) and rounded, shell-shaped buildings. The resort is built on poor agricultural land, mostly dunes, between the Or and Ponant marshes.

It is a holiday-maker's paradise: beaches, fishing, water-sports, seafront promenades, pedestrian precincts and shopping-mall.

Le MONT-ST-MICHEL★★★

Population 72
Map p 5 – Michelin map 59 fold 7 or 231 fold 38 – Green Guide Normandy

Mont-St-Michel has been called "the Wonder of the Western World"; its extraordinary site, its rich and influential history and its glorious architecture combine to make it the most splendid of all the abbeys of France.

The rock of the archangel – At the beginning of the 8C St Michael appeared to Aubert, the bishop of Avranches. Aubert founded an oratory on an island then known as Mount Tombe. This was soon replaced by an abbey, which adopted the Benedictine Rule in the 10C, thereby assuring its importance. Two centuries later the Romanesque abbey reached its peak of development. In the 13C, following a fire, a great rebuilding in Gothic style took place, known as *la Merveille* – the Marvel. It was then, however, that the Hundred Years War intervened, one of the most critical periods in French history. The greater part of the kingdom, the West, the North and the East passed into other hands. The population suffered decades of misery. The framework of the state weakened to the point at which Henry V of England managed to get himself crowned, in Paris, as King of France. Charles VII himself, son of a madman, was no sovereign, merely a pale incarnation of the idea of royalty.

This sombre century was nevertheless the period when Mont-St-Michel enjoyed its greatest influence. Even though the English blockaded it and besieged it twice (for a time they occupied the adjacent Tombelaine rock), the Mount was the only place in the whole of northern and western France to avoid falling into the hands of the

Le MONT-ST-MICHEL

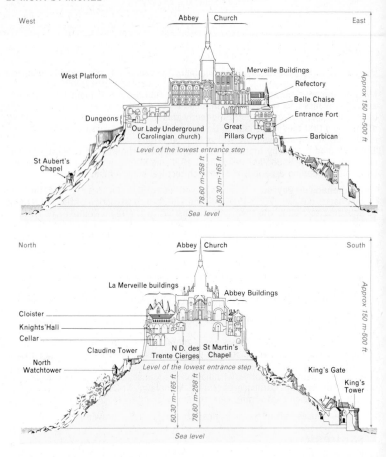

invader, and at no point did it cease being a destination for pilgrimages. The archangel who "watches over God's chosen people" (Book of Daniel) evidently did his work well. Joan of Arc *(qv)* was well aware of all this; her rallying cry was *"St-Michel-Montjoie!"*. St Michael fitted into the plans of Louis XI for strengthening the prestige of his aristocracy when, in 1469, the King founded the Order of St Michael to rival the Order of the Garter created in 1348 by Edward III and the Order of the Golden Fleece instituted in 1429 by Philip the Good of Burgundy.

It is thus hardly surprising that many sanctuaries have been dedicated to the archangel, nor that there are no less than 76 localities named after him in France.

★★★ **Abbey** ⊙ – The original architectural style of the Abbey was determined by the constraints imposed by the rock on which it was erected. The various elements of the complex (barbican, fort, crypt, chapel, cellars, great hall) all had to to be built over one another rather in the manner of a skyscraper. Crowned as it is by the Abbey church and the buildings of the *Merveille* (c1225), the result bears little resemblance to the conventionally-planned Benedictine monastery.

Plate-forme de l'Ouest – From this terrace, there are extensive views over the bay, including the Tombelaine rock, and on 8 November, the autumn Feast of St Michael, the sun sets directly behind Mount Dol, where the Saint once wrestled with the Devil.

★★ **Church** – From this terrace, There is a striking contrast between the stern character of the Romanesque nave and the light-filled Flamboyant choir. The axis of the sanctuary is aligned on the rising sun on the 8 May, the spring Feast of St Michael according to the eastern calendar.

★★★ **La Merveille** – This is the name given to the group of buildings on the north side of the Mount.

The **Guests' Hall★** is a masterpiece of High Gothic.

Suspended between sea and sky, the **Cloisters★★★**, with their slim columns in pink granite arranged in a quincunx pattern, make a magic garden conducive to serenity and inner joy.

The **Refectory**★ (Réfectoire) is filled with light from its recessed windows. It hangs 45m – 148ft high, a bold achievement on the part of its architect who was unable to use buttresses on the sheer rock face.

The vast **Knights' Hall**★ (Salle des Chevaliers) is divided into four parts. It may be so named after the chivalric Order established here.

★ **Abbey Gardens** – From here there is a view of the North face of the Mount, the "most beautiful wall in all the world" according to Victor Hugo.

►► The village★ (Grande-Rue)★ – Ramparts★.

Château de MONTSÉGUR★

Map p 9 – Michelin map 86 fold 5 or 235 fold 46
Green Guide Pyrenees-Languedoc-Tarn Gorges

It was on this fearsome peak that the last episode of the Albigensian Crusade took place, when its Cathar defenders were massacred and Languedoc eclipsed by the central power of the French kingdom.

At the beginning of the 13C the **Cathars** built a castle here to replace an old, since demolished fortress. 40 years later, the stronghold was occupied by some 400 soldiers and adherents to the faith, from whose ranks was drawn the fierce band which marched on Avignonet *(70km – 44 miles north)* to put to the sword the members of the Inquisition meeting there. This action sealed the fate of Montségur; in the absence of Louis IX who was dealing with disturbances in Saintonge, Blanche de Castille ordered the Crusaders to put the castle to siege. On 2 March 1244 the resistance of the defenders was overcome, but 200 of the faithful refused to retract their beliefs, even after being granted a fortnight in which to consider the matter. On 16 March, they were brought down from the mountain to be burnt on a huge pyre at a place known from then on as the "Field of the Burnt Ones" (Camp des Crémats).

Catharism – the name is derived from a Greek word meaning "pure" – was based on the principle of the total separation of Good and Evil, of the spiritual from the material. Its adherents comprised ordinary believers and the *"Perfecti"*, the latter living lives of exemplary purity in the light of God. Their austerity contrasted awkwardly with the laxity of the clergy. Their bitter enemy was St Dominic, who died 23 years before the events of Montségur.

The rebuilding of the **château** ⊘ was begun in the year following the siege, on the same **site**★. It was the third stronghold to be built here, and its ruins crown the summit today. Not long after its reconstruction, it became part of the line of French defences facing the kingdom of Aragon. Its great keep and its fine staircase, concealed from the outside, bear witness to the skill of its builders.

⊘ ►► Musée archéologique.

MOULINS★

Population 22 799
Map p 9 – Michelin map 69 fold 14 or 238 fold 46
Green Guide Auvergne-Rhône Valley
Town plan in the current Michelin Red Guide France

Moulins is the capital of the Bourbonnais region. The city was founded by the Bourbon lords at the end of the 11C in the course of their efforts to extend their territory in the direction of Autun, and to control the crossing of the Allier. Over time, the Bourbons' clever manipulation of military, political and marital alliances (Beatrice de Bourbon married Robert, the son of Louis IX) helped them rise first to the rank of counts, then, in 1327, dukes. In the 15C, their court boasted musicians like Jean Ockeghem, sculptors like Jacques Morel, Michel Colombe and his followers, and above all the painter known as the **Master of Moulins.**

Once Burgundy and Brittany had been incorporated into the French kingdom, the continued independent existence of the Bourbonnais, albeit as a vassal dukedom, became an irritant to the king. François I took advantage of the supposed treason of Charles III, the Ninth Duke, to confiscate his estates. Charles sought the aid of both the Emperor Charles V and England's Henry VIII, and confronted the armies of his sovereign in a series of battles at Pavia, Milan, and finally at Rome, where he was killed (1527). The Bourbonnais was attached to the French Crown in 1531.

★★ **Triptych of the Master of Moulins** ⊘ – This is the cathedral's most important work of art, a triumph of late Gothic painting. It dates from about 1498. The Master has never been conclusively identified; Jean Bourdichon, Jean Perréal and

Jean Prévost have all been suggested, while contemporary expert opinion favours Jean Hey. The poses of the figures depicted suggest the Flemish School, while their faces recall the work of Florentine masters. The figures of the donors are painted in a very realistic manner, in contrast to the idealised treatment of the central panel. The painting appears to be rich in symbolism, the use of the numbers 7 and 12, in particular, representing the Gothic idea of perfection.

⊙ ►► Cathédrale★ – stained glass★★; Jaquemart Belltower★; Mausolée du Duc de Montmorency★; Musée d'art et d'archéologie.

MULHOUSE★★

Population 223 856
Map p 7 – Michelin map 66 folds 9, 10 or 242 fold 39
Green Guide Alsace Lorraine (in French)
Town plan in the current Michelin Red Guide France

Mulhouse (= Mill-house) became a free Imperial city as early as the end of the 13C, and in the 16C formed part of the *Decapolis*, the league of ten towns of Alsace. Between 1466 and 1586, the city's independent spirit led it into an association with the cantons of Switzerland. It joined France voluntarily in 1798.

Mulhouse was already established as a textile centre, when, in 1746, three of its citizens, J.-J. Schmaltzer, the painter J.-H. Dollfus and the merchant S. Koechlin together founded the first mill producing calico cotton fabrics. Their capital investment, use of machinery, division of labour and sales organisation all foreshadowed the techniques of modern large-scale industry. Production advanced by leaps and bounds. In 1812 the Dollfus and Mieg mill was the first to install steam power.

Since 1558, the **City Hall**★ (Hôtel de Ville) has symbolised Mulhouse's civic and political liberties. It is a fine building of the Rhineland Renaissance, much restored, painted in the same colour as the red sandstone of the area with *trompe-l'œil* effects.

Bugatti "Royale"

★★★ **Musée de l'Automobile – Schlumpf collection** ⊙ – Nearly all the vehicles here are from the collection lovingly built up over the years by the mill-owning Schlumpf brothers. Industrial troubles and over-enthusiastic buying of expensive items for the collection led to bankruptcy, the acquistion of the museum by an association and its opening to the public in 1982.

What a magnificent obsession on the part of the brothers to have brought together this extraordinary range of motor vehicles! Some of them are real works of art, with elegant bodywork and flowing lines, their wheels, hub-caps, controls and a myriad of other details beautifully finished in a variety of materials, and with radiator grilles and manufacturers' nameplates designed to proclaim their identity with pride.

The Bugattis form a collection within the collection. There are 123 versions of the marque, racing cars, sports cars, luxury cars. Ettore Bugatti (1881-1947) founded his works in Molsheim in 1909. 340 patents attest to the quality and finish of his vehicles which dominated the circuits and won 3 000 first prizes; the famous "35" alone had no less than 1 851 victories in 1925, 1926 and 1927. The collection gives many insights into changing tastes and preoccupations, from, for example, the total refinement of the luxury car to today's hi-tech research. There is much evidence too of success (and occasional failure) in the solving of technical problems posed by type of fuel, carburation, transmission, suspension, steering, roadholding, safety...

Panhard et Levassor (1893) with a two-cylinder V-type engine (under licence from Daimler). This car formed part of a range which was the first to be marketed, with a catalogue setting out the available models and their variants together with their price;

Clément Bayard "Light" (1895);

Renault (1900) with a direct drive single cylinder vertically-mounted engine;

Peugeot (1903) tonneau with front-mounted engine;

Sizaire et Naudin (1908) racing car with independent front suspension;

Delahaye (1912) landaulet with wood and metal bodywork;

Peugeot (1913) *Bébé* derived from a Bugatti prototype;

Citroën (1922) *"Trèfle"*;

Bugatti 35 (1924) Landaulet Type NM with de luxe interior and bodywork by Kellner;

Panhard et Levassor (1926) with 7.9 litre valveless engine;

Amilcar (1926) with six-cylinder compressor engine, capable of more than 200km/h-125mph;

Peugeot "Coach 174" top-of-the-range model (1927) with powerful valveless engine;

Hispano-Suiza (1928) prestige coupé with its exceptionally responsive and silent motor and robust transmission;

Bugatti "Royale" (1929) "Founder's Own" Napoleon Coupé with bodywork by his son, Jean Bugatti, and with an 8-cylinder, 12.76 litre engine;

Voisin (1933) limousine with valveless 3.3 litre motor;

Citroën (1934) front wheel drive with hydraulic braking and torsion bar;

Panhard (1948) Dynavia experimental model with streamlining;

Bugatti single-seater racer (1955) Type 251;

Apart from these products of the French motor industry there are also fine vehicles from abroad, such as a Swiss **Dufaux** racing car, a **Mercedes** W 154 12-cylinder single-seat racer, a **Porsche** 917K (fastest time ever at Le Mans), a **Ferrari** 275 twelve-cylinder two-seater, several **Rolls-Royces**...

★★ **Musée français du Chemin de fer** ⊙ – This well-presented collection relates the evolution of the railways from their origins to the present day. In addition to the different engines, the collection also shows a wide variety of equipment: signals, tracks, switches, coupler heads, swing bridge, etc. In the main hall, visitors will discover the fascinating world of railways: video films, animated presentations, possibility of going under trains, into the driver's cab or coaches... Highlights include the 1844 Saint-Pierre engine, made out of teak, which ran between Paris and Rouen; the 1852 **Crampton** high speed train (120 kph – 75 mph); the 232 UI (1949), the last steam engine built. Electric trains are also present with the 1900 first electric version also known as the *"boîte à sel"* (salt box), which was built to tow trains between the Parisian stations of Orsay and Austerlitz. Visitors should not miss the BB 9004, the fastest train in 1955, the Bugatti "Presidentiel" or the **Micheline** tyre-equiped XM 5005 railcars.

⊙ ►► Musée de l'Impression sur Étoffes★★; Musée Historique★★; Temple St-Étienne – stained glass windows★; Park and Botanical Gardens★★; Musée du Papier-peint★ at Rixheim (6 km – 4 miles east of Mulhouse); Écomusée d'Alsace★★ (at Ungershein – 12 km – 8 miles north of Mulhouse).

EXCURSIONS

★★ **Murbach Church** – *21km – 12 miles northwest*. Built around 1145, this is one of the finest Romanesque churches in Alsace. It lost its nave in the course of rebuilding in 1738, but its east end and transepts still stand in the attractive setting of the wooded Guebwiller valley.

Dominated by the transept towers, the flat apse is a masterpiece of harmonious design. Supported by a number of shallowly-projecting buttresses, it is covered in lively patterns of arcading. The influence of the great basilicas of the Rhineland is apparent, as is a decorative sense derived from the master-builders of Pisa and Lucca some 80 years previously, and exemplified here in the contrasting play of light and dark arches.

Ottmarsheim – *7.5km – 5 miles east*. Although much-restored, the **church**★ here goes back to around 1040. Its layout recalls Charlemagne's chapel at Aachen, a type of plan rarely found elsewhere, and known as Carolingian or Ottonian. On two levels around a central eight-sided cupola, it consists of two concentric octagons, the second serving as a kind of ambulatory to the central part of the building. In the east chapels of both levels are 15C frescoes.

The **hydro-electric power station**★ ⊙ with its impressive feeder-channel and 185m – 600ft locks is one of the key features of the Grand Canal of Alsace, itself part of a wider scheme for the management of the Rhine for navigation and power generation.

NANCY★★★

Conurbation 310 628
Map p 7 – Michelin map 62 fold 5 or 242 folds 17, 18
Green Guide Alsace et Lorraine (in French)
Town plan in the current Michelin Red Guide France

Capital of the industrial area of Lorraine, Nancy is sited on the low-lying land between the River Meurthe and the Moselle Heights *(Côtes de Moselle)*. The city was founded in the 11C but its history really begins with the death of Charles the Bold, Duke of Burgundy, on 5 January 1477. Charles had spent a fortune on undertakings to enhance his prestige and in an attempt to counter the financial pressures exerted by the Florentine bankers who supported Louis XI, he planned to consolidate his Flemish and Burgundian possessions. In 1476, Charles had ruthlessly incorporated Lorraine into his dukedom, but the standard of revolt was raised in Nancy following his defeat by the Swiss at Murten. Furious, he hastened back to put down the rebellion, but was killed in the course of operations. His body, half devoured by wolves, was found in the freezing mud of an icy pond.

Forty-five years later, the Dukes of Lorraine added Renaissance ornament to their Flamboyant Gothic palace and provided it with a new gallery. To the north of the Triumphal Arch – Arc de Triomphe – the district now known as the old quarter of Nancy (Vieux Nancy) began to take shape.

17C Nancy – Charles III encouraged the laying-out of a new district to the south of Rue Ste-Catherine and Rue Stanislas. The "New Town" was planned on a regular pattern; it was depicted by the artist **Claude Gellée**, known as **Claude Lorrain** (1600-82), whose luminous landscapes were sought out assiduously by English milords as souvenirs of the Grand Tour. His *Paysage pastoral* is in Nancy's Fine Arts Museum.

In 1699, Duke Leopold presented himself to Louis XIV at Versailles, following completion of a mission to Vienna. He was accompanied by his wife, Charlotte, Louis' niece. Their tour of the palace,

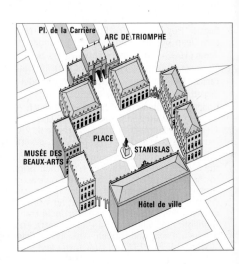

guided by the the King's architect Mansart, brought home to them the decrepitude of their own palace at Nancy. It seems that it was Louis' gratitude for the services rendered by Leopold at Vienna, rather than affection for his niece, that moved him to lend the couple his architect, who subsequently designed the **Government Palace★**. Though not finally completed until 1753, its balustrade, **Ionic colonnade★** and horizontal entablature are typical of Mansart's work.

EIGHTEENTH CENTURY NANCY

Ever since the Treaty of Munster in 1648, the Duchy of Lorraine had been in a precarious situation; an enclave in French territory, it still formed part of the Holy Roman Empire. Though French in language and culture, its people were proud of their independence and much attached to their princes.

In 1738, following the War of the Polish Succession, Duke Francis I, son of Leopold and husband of Maria-Theresa of Austria, found himself having to cede Lorraine in exchange for Tuscany. In his place, Louis XV appointed, as ruler for life, his own father-in-law Stanislas Leszczynski, and by 1766 the Duchy had been painlessly incorporated into the French kingdom, a notable success for Cardinal Fleury's foreign policy. Four years later an event took place which can be considered either as an irony of history or as evidence of the cunning match-making of the Viennese court. Marie-Antoinette, daughter of Francis I and Maria Theresa, had lost her putative claim to Lorraine 17 years before her birth. In 1770, she married Louis XVI and began her reign at Versailles. Known as "the Austrian" because of her mother, Marie-Antoinette was, through her father, just as much a Lorrainer and a Frenchwoman. Stanislas was a man of peace, fond of his daughter the Queen of France, a lover of good living and the opposite sex, and a passionate builder. He set out to join together the old quarter of Nancy with the "New Town" by means of a set-piece of civic design in honour of his son-in-law. The great project was completed in the short space of three years, between 1752-55.

★★ Place Stanislas – In charge of the work were the architect Emmanuel Héré (1705-63) and Jean Lamour, a metal-worker of genius.

Héré designed the City Hall (Hôtel de ville) and the flanking buildings with their fine façades.

At ground level, the City Hall has a central projecting section with arcades and colossal pilasters separating the windows; on the upper level are balconies and wrought iron window-ledges.

The four flanking buildings are of similar design, though without the centre section; to the north the square is defined by two further buildings, again similar in general treatment, though with only one storey and with an attic and balustrade separated by a later mansard roof. The whole forms a space of exceptional elegance and clarity of structure, ornamented with urns and trophies and balustrades to conceal the roofs.

Further enclosure is achieved by Jean Lamour's brilliant ironwork. Perfectly integrated into the architectural concept, his gilded railings *(photograph p 53)* with their crests and floral decoration are of inimitable gracefulness. He was also responsible for the window ledges, the balcony and the double curve of the internal staircase of the City Hall.

⊘ ►► Palais Ducal**★★** and Musée Historique Lorrain**★★★**; Musée des Beaux-Arts**★★**; Arc de Triomphe**★**; Place de la Carrière**★**; Église**★** and Couvent des Cordeliers – Couvent Chapel**★**; Porte de la Craffe**★**; Musée de l'École de Nancy**★★**; Église de Notre-Dame-de-Bon-Secours**★**.

NANTES**★★★**

Conurbation 492 255
Map p 5 – Michelin map 67 fold 3 or 232 fold 28 – Green Guide Brittany
Town plan in the current Michelin Red Guide France

Nantes is Brittany's largest city, sited at the point at which the mighty Loire becomes tidal. The presence of islets (inhabited from the 17C on) in the river had long facilitated the building of bridges, making Nantes the focus of trade and movement between Lower Brittany and Poitou.

In the 9C, the city was disputed between Nominoé, the first Duke of Brittany, and the Franks to the east. In 939, it was chosen as his capital by King Alain Barbe-Torte (Crookbeard). By the 14C, Nantes had become a trading port, with a fleet of 1 300 ships, but it was only in the 15C, under Duke François II, that the city reached its full importance.

In the early 18C Nantes grew rich on sugar; cane was imported from the West Indies to be distributed in France or re-exported to England and Scandinavia. This formed part of the profitable "ebony trade", the discreet name given to the triangle of commerce involving the export of fancy goods to Africa, the shipping of slaves to the Indies, and the import of cane. Nantes became France's premier port. But the loss of French territories abroad under Louis XV, the abolition of slavery, the substitution of sugar-beet for cane sugar (a result of the British blockade in the Napoleonic wars) and the increasing size of ships led to the port's decline.

In the 19C and 20C the construction of downstream harbour facilities has contributed towards Nantes' continuing prosperity.

Un bon vin blanc – This expression, well known for being part of a phonetics exercise for Anglo-Saxon learners of French – literally "a fine white wine" – adequately describes the local *Muscadet*, dry but not too sharp, perfect with seafood. The vineyards are located to the south and east of Nantes, alongside or near the Sèvre and towards Ancenis on the banks of the Loire.

★★ Château des Ducs de Bretagne (HY) ⊘ – "God's teeth! No small beer, these dukes of Brittany!" exclaimed Henri IV on seeing this massive stronghold for the first time. The castle was much rebuilt and strengthened from 1466 on by Duke François II who saw in it the guarantee of his independence from Louis XI. His daughter Anne of Brittany continued the work.

The great edifice is defended by deep ditches of considerable width, which could be flooded when necessary, and by six stout towers with characteristically Breton pyramidal machicolations.

The interior reflects the castle's role as a palace of government and residence, known for its high life of feasts and jousting. Many of its features are of great interest, like the **Golden Crown Tower★★** (Tour de la Couronne d'or), the Main Building (Grand-Logis) with its massive dormer windows, the Governor's Major Palace (Grand Gouvernement) rebuilt at the end of the 17C, and the **well★★** with its wrought-iron well-head incorporating ducal crown motifs.

There are two museums in the castle; the **Musée des Salorges★**, a maritime museum and the **Musée d'Art populaire★** featuring Breton coiffes, dress and furniture.

Cathédrale St-Pierre et St-Paul (HY) ⊘ –
Although the building of the cathedral
extended over a period of 450 years, it has
a great unity of style. The use of a white
calcareous tufa in the **interior**★★ enhances
the impression of boldness and purity of
line resulting from the mouldings of the
pillars which soar without a break in their
flight up into the keystones of the vaults.
Duke John V wished to make it the greatest
of all the churches in Brittany to provide
a worthy setting for the tomb of his father.
It was here, on 13 April 1598, that Henri IV
signed the **Edict of Nantes**, thereby establishing equality between Catholics and Protestants, and explicitly granting the latter
privileges regarding political organisation
and the right to maintain fortified strongholds. The Edict had 92 articles, some of
them secret; it succeeded others of a
similar nature issued by Catherine de'
Medici, the first in Europe concerning
religious tolerance. This time, however,
their efficacy was backed by a ruler in a
position to neutralise any lingering opposition to them. In the reign of Louis XIV,
some Protestants were persuaded to convert to Catholicism, but the king, misled
about the number of conversions, revoked
the Edict in 1685 "since it no longer served
any useful purpose", thereby provoking the
Huguenot exodus of around 200 000 people to England, Holland and Germany and
depriving France of some of its most
valuable human resources.

In the south transept of the cathedral is the
tomb of François II★★ (1502), commissioned
by Duchess Anne for her father and her
mother Marguerite of Foix. It is the work
of Michel Colombe and probably also of
Jean Perreal; while its recumbent figures and their cortège are still medieval in
feeling, the Renaissance is announced by the use of black and white Italian
marble, by the arabesques and by the figures of the Virtues.

⊘ ►► Musée des Beaux-Arts★★ **M¹**; Musée d'Histoire Naturelle★★ **M²**; the 19C
Town★; Palais Dobrée★ – decorative art; Musée Jules-Verne★; Musée
archéologique★ **M³**, Jardin des Plantes★; Ancienne Île Feydeau.

NANTES

B Maison de "la duchesse de Berry"
D La Psalette

EXCURSION

St-Nazaire – *60km – 38 miles west on the N165 and N171.* A great shipbuilding
centre and port, St-Nazaire became an important German submarine base during
the Second World War. On 27 March 1942 it was the scene of the heroic deeds
of a Canadian-British commando whose aim was to neutralise the installations.
The destroyer *Campbeltown* broke through the entrance lock and subsequently
blew itself up. The operation was a success, albeit with heavy losses.

NARBONNE★

Population 45 849
Map p 9 – Michelin map 83 fold 14 or 235 fold 40 or 240 folds 29, 30
Green Guide Pyrenees-Languedoc-Tarn Gorges
Town plan in the current Michelin Red Guide France

The history of this ancient Mediterranean city is a long one; it may well have served
as the harbour for a 7C BC Gallic settlement on the Montaurès hill to the north.
After the defeat of Hannibal, the conquest of Catalonia, La Mancha and Andalusia,
the Roman Empire felt the need to secure its land communications with Spain.
Narbonne was chosen to be a Senatorial (rather than governmental) colony;
the city became the commercial centre of the Celtic province, with an artificial port
created by diverting an arm of the river Aude. Finally it was made the capital of
Gallia Narbonensis - Provence - and flourished right up to the end of the Empire
and the arrival of the Visigoths, who made it the capital of their kingdom.

Some trading activity continued, and Muslim raiders from Spain found the city still
worth looting in 793. Medieval shipping made use of the extensive lagoons lining
the coast behind the rampart of sand bars. But in the 14C a storm brought the

NARBONNE

Aude back into its old bed, and Narbonne declined as its bay silted up. The construction of the Canal du Midi at the end of the 17C and the building of the railway in the 19C helped to reverse the process of decline.

★★ **Cathédrale St-Just** – The present building was begun in 1272, but construction was halted 82 years later in order to preserve the ramparts which would otherwise have been breached to accommodate the nave. The choir remains, its vaulting reaching the dizzy height of 41m – 135ft. It is in the High Gothic style, with a fine triforium – its columns extend upwards into the lancets of the clerestorey windows. The great arches of the apse are crowned with battlements and loopholes. The lofty cloisters (1349-1417) are built in crumbling limestone on the site of a Carolingian church.

The cathedral **treasury** ⊙ has a wonderful late 15C Flemish **Tapestry**★★ featuring the **Creation** woven in silk and gold thread, a 10C ivory missal plaque and a rare marriage casket in rock crystal with intaglio decoration.

Palais des archevêques ⊙ – Many building styles are represented here, from the 12C Old Palace (Palais Vieux), the 13C Madeleine Tower (donjon de la Madeleine) and **Gilles Aycelin Tower**★ (donjon Gilles Aycelin) ⊙, the 14C St Martial Tower (tour St-Martial) and New Palace (Palais Neuf), the 17C Archbishops' Residence (Residence des archevêques) with its Louis XIII staircase to the City Hall (Hôtel de ville), with its 19C façade.

⊙ ►► Musée Archéologique★; Musée d'Art et d'Histoire★; Basilique St-Paul-St-Serge; Musée Lapidaire★.

EXCURSION

★★ **Abbaye de Fontfroide** ⊙ – *15 km – 9 miles to the southwest.*
This former Cistercian abbey nestles in a quiet, restful corner of the countryside, planted with cypress trees and reminiscent of the gentle landscape of Tuscany. The fine flame-coloured shades of yellow ochre and pink in the Corbières sandstone used to build the abbey enhance the serenity of the sight, particularly at sunset. Most of the buildings date from the 12C and 13C.

Seuil de NAUROUZE

Map p 9 – Michelin map 82 fold 19 or 235 fold 34
Green Guide Pyrenees-Languedoc-Tarn Gorges

This pass (alt 194m – 636ft) forms the watershed between Atlantic and Mediterranean; the notion of a canal enabling shipping to avoid the long route via Gibraltar had preoccupied not only the Romans but also François I, Henri IV and Richelieu. The natural obstacles seemed however insurmountable.

In 1662, **Pierre-Paul Riquet** (1604-1680) succeeded in interesting Colbert in his project; with the latter's support he gained the necessary authorisations four years later. But the canal was to prove his ruin; all the work had to be carried out at his own expense and he died six months before the opening. In 1825 Riquier's successors, finally freed of the burden of debt, built an obelisk here to commemorate the great man and his work. The canal passed into state ownership in 1897. The completed Canal du Midi is 240km – 149 miles long and has 103 locks.

Cirque de NAVACELLES★★★

Map p 9 – Michelin map 80 fold 16 or 240 north of fold 18
Green Guide Pyrenees-Languedoc-Tarn Gorges

This 300m – 1 000ft deep natural amphitheatre, separating the Causses – high plateaux – of Larzac and Blandas, marks the former course of the River Vis before it cut through the base of the meander.

On the outer sweep of the meander great screes have been formed; the upper parts of the cliffs are made up of exceptionally thick beds, thinning out at the lower levels where traces remain of old buildings and terraces on the marl and clay deposits. On the valley floor a pretty single-arched bridge leads to the village of Navacelles (which once had a priory). The little settlement clings to a rocky outcrop in order to conserve as much as possible of the belt of cultivable land in the former bed of the river.

In contrast to the harsh conditions prevailing on the arid, windswept causses, the valley floor has a mild microclimate which allows figs to be grown.

Massif de NÉOUVIELLE★★

Map p 8 – Michelin map 85 fold 19 or 234 fold 44 – Green Guide Atlantic Coast

In 1976 the Bielsa road tunnel was opened linking France with Lerida in Spain, and making the little mountain resort of **St-Lary-Soulan**★ an important trans-Pyrenean staging-post.

St-Lary is the starting-point for the spectacular scenic route rising up to 1 362m – 4 435ft and leading, via dark fir-woods and many hairpin bends, to the **Cap de Long dam**★, **Lake d'Oredon**★ and **Lake d'Aumar**★ (46km – 29 miles Rtn).

The Néouvielle Massif, forming part of the high central spine of the Pyrenees, is made up of granite; it is a veritable museum of glacial topography, with virtually all the features characterising such landscapes, from high, ice-smoothed cliffs and cirques separated by narrow ridges to hanging valleys, rock-steps and a multitude of lakes and erratic boulders.

The Cap de Long dam forms a key part of the Pragnères hydro-electric scheme with its many miles of tunnels channelling the waters from a number of different valleys to feed the turbines.

NEVERS★

Conurbation 58 915
Map p 6 – Michelin map 69 folds 3, 4 or 238 fold 33 – Green Guide Burgundy Jura
Town plan in the current Michelin Red Guide France

From the red sandstone bridge spanning the Loire there is a fine view of the old town of Nevers set in terraces on its limestone hill, its tall town houses with their roofs of slate and tile dominated by the high square tower of the great cathedral and the graceful silhouette of the ducal palace.

As was usual all along the Loire, it was height above the river which was the most important determinant of the town's location. At the meeting-point of the Loire with the Nièvre, Nevers flourished as a port until the 19C when the Loire ceased to be navigable. The abundant and reliable flow of the Nièvre encouraged the development of potteries and iron working along its banks as early as the 16C. The area around Nevers was known for its everyday pottery in the Middle Ages. Artistic pottery seems to have been brought here in the 1560s by Italian craftsmen from Lyons like Giulio Gambini; at the time the secrets of enamelling were jealously guarded, and the techniques discovered 45 years previously at Rouen by Abaquesne had not spread. Progress at Nevers was encouraged by the humanist Lodovico di Gonzaga, who became Duke of Nevers in 1565, and whose wide interests included the advancement of the arts and technology. In the time of Louis XIII and Louis XIV the town was one of the great centres of faience production, with 12 manufactories employing 1 800 workers and producing some of the finest Blue Persian work ever made. There is a good **collection**★ of Nevers pottery in the **Municipal Museum** ⊙.

Nevers pottery (late 17C – early 18C)
Musée municipal, Nevers

J. Guillot/C.D.A. EDIMEDIA

Following her visionary experiences at Lourdes, Bernadette Soubirous came to Nevers in 1866 to enter the **St-Gildard convent**★ ⊙ here. Her body, exhumed three times, was unaffected by decay; the object of pilgrimages and the veneration of the faithful, it is displayed in a reliquary in the convent chapel.

★ **Palais ducal** – The former residence of the Dukes of Nevers is a fine example of the secular architecture of the French Renaissance. The centrepiece of the main façade is formed by an elegant five-sided projecting staircase topped by a small belfry.

★ **Église St-Étienne** – This splendid Romanesque church has a magnificently tiered east end and a beautiful overall pattern of windows in the style of the great abbey church of Cluny. It has a false triforium modelled on Burgundian precedents but above all it is the height of the interior which is impressive, particularly for a building of its date (1063-97); this feat of construction was necessitated by the introduction of a row of windows immediately below the barrel-vaulting.

►► Cathédrale St-Cyr-et-Ste-Julitte★★ ⊙; Porte du Croux★.

NICE★★★

Conurbation 475 507
Map p 11 – Michelin map 84 folds 9, 10, 19 or 115 fold 26 or 245 fold 38
Green Guide French Riviera
Town plan in the current Michelin Red Guide France

Some 400 000 years ago, bands of elephant hunters made their encampments on the fossil beach at Terra Amata, 26m – 85ft above the present level of the sea. In the 6C BC, Celto-Ligurians settled on the castle hill; a little later it was the turn of merchants and sailors from Marseilles; they established themselves around the harbour, followed by the Romans, who favoured the Cimiez district. In 1388, aided and abetted by the **Grimaldi** family, Count Amadeus VII of Savoy incorporated Provence into his domain and made a triumphal entry into Nice.

As a result of the alliance of 1859 between France and Sardinia, Napoleon III undertook to help drive out the Austrians from Lombardy and the Veneto; in return, France was to receive from the House of Savoy the lands to the west of the Alps and around Nice which had once been hers. A plebiscite produced an overwhelming vote in favour of a return to France (25 743 for, 260 against) and the ceremony of annexation took place on 14 June 1860.

★ **Old Nice** – The core of the city, huddling at the foot of the castle hill, has a lively, utterly Mediterranean character.

Château (LR) – The landscaped slopes of the castle hill with their umbrella pines shading pleasant walks reach a height of 92m – 300ft. The summit provided a place of refuge for the denizens of Cimiez at the time of the fall of the Roman Empire. In the 12C, the Counts of Provence built a castle here which was subsequently strengthened by the Angevin princes and the Dukes of Savoy but was demolished by Louis XIV in 1706. From the top there is a fine **view**★★ over the city, the Pre-Alps and the bay (Baie des Anges).

NICE

B Ancien Palais du Gouvernement	**M⁵** Galerie de malacologie
E Monument de Catherine Ségurane	**M⁹** Musée d'Art moderne
F Chapelle du Saint Sépulcre	et d'Art contemporain
K Palais Lascaris	**R** Chapelle de l'Annonciation
S Chapelle de la Miséricorde	
X Galerie-Musée Alexis et	
Gustave-Adolf Mossa	
Y Galerie-Musée Raoul Dufy	

Place Garibaldi (LQ) – The square is named after the great fighter for Italian unity who was born in Nice. The ochre walls and arcading of the buildings along its sides recall the urbane elegance characteristic of Piedmontese town planning in the 18C.

Cathédrale Ste-Reparata (KR) – This is a fine example of the Baroque style as it developed in Nice. The west front, a gay mixture of greens and yellows, is decorated with niches and medallions, topped by an imposing entablature and supported by buttress-pillars with composite capitals. The **interior★** is enlivened by an elaborate cornice and in the choir is a frieze lined out in white and gold and decorated with little figures of angels.

★ **Église St-Jacques (LR)** – The west front recalls the Gesù church in Rome. Behind it lies a nave whose severity is relieved by an abundance of sculpture. The barrel vault opens into side chapels containing loggias where the local nobility once worshipped.

Place Masséna (KR) – The linear park laid out on what was once the bed of the river Paillon is interrupted by this square begun in 1815. Its buildings with their façades rendered in reddish ochre and their arcades recall the planned urban spaces of Turin.

★★ **Cimiez** – This part of the city originated in the Roman settlement whose growth soon eclipsed that of the older town laid out around the harbour.
The **Gallo-Roman archaeological site★** ⊘ consists mostly of medium amphitheatres and the area around the baths.
There is a **monastery★** whose church possesses a Pietà of 1475 *(to the right of the entrance);* though an early work of Louis Bréa, and executed in Gothic style, it is one of his finest achievements, notably in its portrayal of the grieving Mary. To the left of the choir is a later Renaissance work by the same artist, a Crucifixion.
The **Musée Matisse★** ⊘ is housed in the Villa des Arènes; it traces the artist's evolution, from his *Still Life with Books* (1890) to the *Rococo Armchair* (1947) and the *Blue Nude* (1952).

The **Musée Marc-Chagall**★★ ⓥ was designed to display the 17 great paintings making up the artist's Biblical Message (painted between 1954-67).

ⓥ ►► Sea Front★★; Musée des Beaux-Arts★★; Musée Masséna★ – painting, decorative arts, local history; Musée International d'Art Naïf★; Palais des Arts★ – contemporary art; Chapelle de la Miséricorde★ **S**; Église St-Martin-St-Augustin – interior★.

EXCURSION

★★ **The Riviera Corniche roads** – *Circular tour of 41km – 26 miles – allow 3 hours.*
The Lower Corniche road skirts the foot of Mount Boron, giving fine views over Villefranche-sur-Mer and its bay. The highly indented coastline is the result of the recent folding and subsequent drowning of the limestone Pre-Alps.
Both **Cap Ferrat**★★ and nearby St-Hospice Point offer splendid views of the Riviera with its corniche roads; the village of Èze-Bord-de-Mer, the fashionable resort of Beaulieu, Cap d'Ail can all be identified and rising out of the sea in the distance is Cap Martin. Clinging to its inaccessible high rock, **Èze**★★ seems the very archetype of a hill village. It was inhabited by the Ligurians and by the Phoenicians, then fortified against raiders from the sea. In 1706 both the village and its castle were demolished on the orders of Louis XIV, but it was rebuilt after 1760.

NÎMES★★★

Conurbation 138 527
Map p 9 – Michelin map 80 fold 19 or 83 fold 3 or 240 fold 20
or 245 fold 27 or 246 folds 25, 26
Green Guide Provence – Town plan in the current Michelin Red Guide France

Nîmes lies between the limestone hills of the Garrigue to the north and the alluvial plain of the Costière du Gard to the south. Its elegant and bustling boulevards are shaded by lotus-trees. The quality of its Roman remains is outstanding.

★★ **Arènes** ⓥ – This superb structure was built in the reign of Augustus, possibly some 80 years before the amphitheatre at Arles. Its barrel-vaulted galleries are characteristically Roman.
To gain a full appreciation of the huge task the Roman architects set themselves and the boldness with which they carried it out, it is necessary to climb to the covered gallery of the top level (from which there are good views over the town), as well as inspecting the first floor gallery (note particularly the size of the lintels supporting the vaulting) and part of the barrel-vaulted double gallery on the ground floor. The scale of the great structure is extraordinarily impressive, as is the builders' achievement in cutting, transporting and placing stonework of such dimensions with such precision.

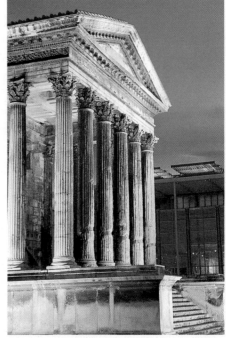

★★ **Maison Carrée** ⓥ – Known as the Square House, this is the purest, as well as the best preserved, of all Roman temples.

★★ **Jardin de la Fontaine** – In Roman times this site was occupied by a spring, a theatre, a temple and baths. Today's shady gardens exemplify the subtle use of water in the landscapes of Languedoc. They were laid out in the characteristic manner of the 18C, with pools leading into a canal, balustraded walks, porticoes...

ⓥ ►► Musée d'Archéologie★; Musée des Beaux-Arts★; Musée du Vieux-Nîmes★; Carré d'art★.

J. P. Lescourret/EXPLORER

Maison Carrée

NOHANT

Map p 9 – Michelin map 68 fold 19 or 238 fold 41
6km – 4 miles north of La Châtre
Green Guide Berry Limousin (in French)

The hamlet of Nohant with its little square shaded by great elms owes its fame to the novelist **George Sand** (1804-76). This controversial figure, an early fighter for women's right to emotional freedom, was a descendant of Frederick of Saxony, King of Poland, and Aurore, the illegitimate daughter of the Marshal de Saxe who had acquired the Nohant estate in 1793 when it was much more extensive than it is today.

Château ⊙ – The house, built in the 18C, was extended in the 19C. The literary output generated here – 80 novels and some 12 000 letters – together with the authoress's notoriety, made the place famous throughout Europe. In her pastoral novels George Sand depicted the countryside of the Black Vale – Vallée noire – and the Boischaut, a landscape of small hedged fields with farmsteads half-hidden in the generous greenery. It was here that she received many of the celebrities of the age, Chopin, Liszt, Delacroix... George Sand's life is touchingly evoked in the theatre designed by Chopin, by the limewood marionettes made by her son Maurice for which she sewed the costumes, and in the Blue Room where she died.

Portrait of George Sand by C. Blaize

Église de Vic – *2km – 1 1/2 miles northwest.* – St Martin's Church houses an unusual series of **frescoes**★ dating from the early 12C and depicting the Redemption. They are pleasing both as a group and also in the conventional way in which the individual figures are disposed and related to one another. They are related to the art of Aquitaine and even of Catalonia both in technique and in the way in which movement is evoked. Together with Prosper Mérimée, George Sand helped bring them to the attention of the public.

Some hotels have their own tennis court, swimming pool,
private beach or garden
Consult the current edition of the annual **Michelin Red Guide France**

Abbaye de NOIRLAC★★

Map p 9 – Michelin map 69 south of fold 1 or 238 fold 31
Green Guide Berry Limousin (in French)

Noirlac is a Cistercian foundation of 1136 whose plan exemplifies the kind of layout envisaged by St Bernard for an abbey of this type. It is the most complete of the 12 surviving Benedictine abbeys in France (out of an original 345), though by no means without its share of upheavals; the Hundred Years War, the Wars of Religion, the commendatory regime, 18C additions, conversion into a porcelain factory in 1822, use as a centre for refugees in the First World War and the Spanish Civil War, and a final role as an old people's home before its restoration in 1975.

The **abbey church** ⊙ dates from 1150-60. With its plain east end, its great transepts and its vast aisles it follows (like Fontenay Abbey in Burgundy) the plan of the great abbey at Clairvaux. Dating from the end of the Romanesque (in the design of the pillars) and the beginning of the Gothic (vaults still without ribs), it shows clearly how advanced this region was in the development of architectural style. The building of the final two bays of the nave at the beginning of the 13C marked the completion of the great edifice. The modern grisaille glass is the work of Jean-Pierre Raynaud, aided by craftsmen from Chartres and Bourges; it adds a certain subtlety of lighting to the perfect simplicity of the architecture.

Among the conventual buildings, the chapter house was built in the 12C and the refectory and the Gothic cloisters in the 13C.

OBERNAI★★

Population 9 610
Map p 7 – Michelin map 62 fold 9 or 242 fold 23 or 87 folds 4,5
Green Guide Alsace et Lorraine (in French)

Sited where the lower, vine-covered slopes of Mount Ste-Odile meet the plain, its ruined walls eloquent of its ancient independence and its narrow, winding streets lined with high-gabled houses, the little town of Obernai seems to represent the very essence of Alsace. In the 14C it was one of the cities of the urban league known as the Decapolis. A period of great prosperity followed in the 16C, then, in 1679, it was annexed by Louis XIV.

★★ **Place du Marché** – With its cheerfully-coloured timber-framed buildings, the picturesque market place is the centrepiece of Obernai, graced by a fountain of 1904 with a statue of St Odile. It has a **Town Hall★** (Hôtel de ville) of the 15C-16C with a fine oriel window and sculpted balcony, a 16C **Corn Hall★** (Ancienne halle aux blés) much restored but with a stork's nest above its doorway, and the **Chapel Tower★** (Tour de la Chapelle), a 13C bell-tower topped by a spire 60m – nearly 200ft above the ground.

  ►► Obernai: Old houses★.

EXCURSION

★★ **Mont Ste-Odile** – 12km – 7 miles southwest. Its associations with St Odile, the province's patron saint, help make this the most popular summit in the whole of Alsace. The high sandstone crag rises 764m – 2 500ft above the plain, offering a spectacular **panorama★★**.

Such a site was bound to attract attention; the Celts were the first to fortify it; their so-called **Pagan Wall** (Mur païen), running for more than 10km – 6 miles is the best known and the most important of their defensive works, with stonework on a truly Cyclopean scale. The wall was remodelled by the Romans.

At the centre of a magnificent firwood is the **convent** built in honour of St Odile. Often added to and restored over time, it is an important place of pilgrimage.

OMAHA BEACH

Map p 5 – Michelin map 54 folds 4, 14 or 231 fold 16
Green Guide Normandy Historical maps Battle of Normandy 102 and 105

Until 6 June 1944 this name only existed as an Allied code word designating one of the sections of Normandy coastline to be assaulted in the early hours of that fateful day. Including the beaches of St-Laurent, Colleville-sur-Mer and Vierville-sur-Mer, it was here that the U.S. First Division made its first contact with French soil and it was here that the bloodiest engagement of D-Day was fought. The St-Laurent military cemetery stands as a moving testimony to the thousands of young men who came from far shores to liberate an oppressed continent and who were cut down here and on the other invasion beaches by a tenacious defence.

The Allied landings – Sword Beach (Colleville-Montgomery, Lion-sur-Mer, St-Aubin), where British and Free French troops landed, marks the easternmost point of the invasion perimeter; to the west came the Canadians at Juno Beach (Bernières and Courseulles), the British again at Gold Beach (Ver-sur-Mer and Asnelles), then the Americans at Omaha Beach and **Utah Beach** (la Madeleine and the Varreville dunes at the base of the Cotentin peninsula).

The assault on the beaches had been preceded by airborne landings at Pegasus Bridge and Ste-Mère-Église which were intended to neutralise the enemy on either flank of the attack.

The **Pointe du Hoc**, between Omaha and Utah Beaches, offered the enemy command of the entire invasion front, and was stormed by the Second Rangers Battalion early on D-Day. The first Mulberry (artificial harbour) was in place at Arromanches by the end of D-Day.

The Normandy invasion, and its significance in European and world history, is marked all along this coastline and its hinterland by military cemeteries, monuments, viewing points and museums.

  ⊙ ►► Utah Beach: Musée du débarquement.

Many campsites have shops, bars, restaurants and laundries
they may also have games rooms, tennis courts, miniature golf courses,
playgrounds, swimming pools...
Consult the current edition of the **Michelin Camping Caravaning France**

ORADOUR-SUR-GLANE

Population 1 998
Map p 8 – Michelin map 72 folds 6, 7 or 233 fold 22
Green Guide Berry Limousin (in French)

The stark walls of the burnt-out village of Oradour-sur-Glane have been kept as an eloquent reminder of the horrors of war. On 10 June 1944, a few days after the Normandy landings, an SS Division was being moved from southwestern France to reinforce the front. Harrassed by the Resistance, the troops made a characteristically brutal example of this entirely innocent place, massacring its inhabitants (men, women, and children), and laying waste the village ⊘ itself. The 642 victims are buried in the village cemetery; a memorial commemorates the terrible deed.

ORANGE★★

Population 26 964
Map p 9 – Michelin map 81 folds 11, 12 or 245 fold 16 or 246 fold 24
Green Guide Provence – Town plan in the current Michelin Red Guide France

Orange flourished in the days of the Pax Romana as an important staging-post on the great highway between Arles and Lyons. In the 16C, it came into the possession of William the Silent, ruler of the German principality of Nassau, then *Stadtholder* of the United Provinces. He took the title of Prince of Orange and founded the Orange-Nassau line. Orange is still proud of its association with the royal house of the Netherlands, whose preferred title is Prince (or Princess) of Orange.

★★★ **Théâtre antique** ⊘ – Dating from the reign of Augustus, this theatre is the best preserved structure of its type in the whole of the Roman world.
The stage wall measures 103x36m – 340x120ft; Louis XIV called it "the finest wall in all the kingdom". Built of granite and African breccia, its outer face is of striking simplicity, interrupted only by the mounts for the poles supporting the awnings shading the audience from the sun.
On the auditorium side, the wall has lost its marble facing and mosaic decoration, its columns and its statues. The great statue of Augustus has been replaced in its central niche; together with some remaining hammer-finished granite blocks, it gives some idea of the how the theatre must have appeared originally.

★★ **Arc de Triomphe** – This was built between the years 21 and 26 AD. On its north and east sides are reliefs depicting the exploits of the Second Legion in Gaul (weapons both of the Gauls and of Amazons), the triumph of Rome (captured Gauls in chains) and Roman domination of the seas following the naval battle of Actium (anchors, oars, warships).

ORCIVAL★★

Population 381
Map p 9 – Michelin maps 73
fold 13 or 239 fold 18
Green Guide Auvergne
– Rhône Valley

MICHELIN

Basilique Notre-Dame, Orcival

Many houses in this tiny Auvergne hill-town still have their original roof coverings of tiles cut from the phonolithic lavas of the nearby Tuilière Rock, the core of an ancient volcano.

★★ **Basilique Notre-Dame** – Set hard against the hillside and completed around 1130, this basilica is a typical structure of the Auvergne Romanesque, with a many-tiered apse and side-walls strengthened by powerful buttresses and massive arches. The south doorway, dedicated to St John, topped by rows of arches, has elaborate original strapwork and hinges in wrought iron.

Inside, the majestic crossing is lit by 14 windows and supported by sturdy transverse arches, while both chancel and crypt, the latter with a spacious ambulatory, are masterpieces of their kind.

Among the capitals is a 12C one of the Miser or the Money-Lender, illustrating vice, no longer by means of an individual personification, but by its consequences. In the chancel is a **Virgin Enthroned**★ still with its original gilt ornamentation; one side of the face (left) is that of an Auvergne peasant woman, the other (right) of a society lady, an affirmation of the universality of the "throne of wisdom".

Aven d'ORGNAC★★

Map p 9 – Michelin map 80 fold 9 or 246 fold 23 – Green Guide Provence

This extraordinary chasm, **Aven d'Orgnac**, lies among the woods covering the Ardèche plateau. It was first explored by **Robert de Joly** (1887-1968) on 19 August 1935. Joly was an electrical engineer, fascinated by cars and planes but above all by speleology; it was due to his efforts that the mysteries of France's underground world were revealed, he himself being responsible for numerous "firsts".

Of the four caverns at Orgnac, only **Orgnac I** ⊘ *(1 hour)* has so far been opened up to the public. The caverns owe their origin to an underground stream which infiltrated a fault-line in Tertiary times and linked up the Cèze and Ardèche rivers. Over the millenia the slow and silent processes of erosion and corrosion have resulted in the build-up of the extraordinary concretions visible here. Towards the end of the Tertiary era, earthquakes associated with the uplifting of the Alps shattered stalactites and threw down stalagmites, while the Quaternary age, with its alternation of hot and cold periods, brought other changes. A mass of rubble separates the two upper chambers from the lower one, whose stalagmites have developed a variety of forms: bayonet-like spikes marking a resurgence of activity following the removal of an obstruction to the supply of water, "stacks of plates" where the height of the vault has inhibited the formation of pillars, and "pine-cones" where the build-up of material was irregular.

Orgnac III was inhabited 300 000 years ago; the **museum** ⊘ has displays on the cultures which flourished between the Rhône and the Cévennes from Paleolithic times to the Bronze Age.

ORLÉANS★

Conurbation 243 153
Map p 6 – Michelin map 64 fold 9 or 237 fold 40 or 238 fold 5
Green Guide Châteaux of the Loire

Orléans grew up on the great bend in the Loire between the rich cornfield of the Beauce to the north and the heaths and forests of the Sologne to the south. For a time the city was the capital of France, its cathedral the setting for the coronation in 996 of Hugh Capet's son, Robert the Pious. Place du Martroi, with its statue of Joan of Arc, is the centre of the historic town.

The Siege of 1428-29 – This memorable siege was one of the great episodes in the history of France, marking the country's rebirth after a period of despair. It began on 12 October 1428, as the Earl of Salisbury attempted to take the bridge

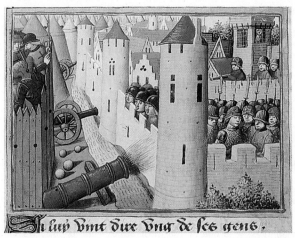

The Siege of Orléans

over the Loire and thus link up with the other English forces in central and southern France. Lasting almost seven months, the siege was the scene of one of the first ever (albeit inconclusive) artillery duels. On 29 April 1429, **Joan of Arc** arrived from Chinon *(qv)*; she skirted Orléans to the south and entered the city by the Burgundy Gate (Porte de Bourgogne), several days in advance of the army advancing along the north bank of the river. By 7 May, victory seemed assured, and on the 8th the English capitulated. In Orléans, Joan enjoyed the hospitality of Jacques Boucher, whose fine half-timbered dwelling with its museum is now known as **Joan of Arc House★**.

★★ **Musée des Beaux-Arts** (EY M¹) ⓥ – This museum houses some of the richest collections in France. The painting section constitutes most of the collection, especially the French school from the 16C to the 20C. Among the most famous: Le Nain, Ph. de Champagne, Courbet, Boudin, Gauguin, Vigée-Lebrun, Rouault, Gromaire, Soutine, Zao Wou-ki and even Max Jacob (better known as a writer).

★ **Cathédrale Ste-Croix** – Construction of the cathedral lasted from the 13C to the 16C. The nave was torn down by the Huguenots in 1568, but rebuilt in composite Gothic style by **Henri IV** mindful of the city's loyalty to him.
The **choirstalls★★** of 1706 have splendidly carved medallions and panels adorning the high backs.
In the **crypte** ⓥ are traces of the three buildings which preceded the present cathedral, and two sarcophagi, one of which belonged to bishop Robert de Courtenay (13C) who collected the most precious items in the **Treasury** ⓥ.

ⓥ ►► Musée historique★; Musée des Sciences naturelles★; Parc Floral de la Source★★ (at Olivet).

Ile d'OUESSANT★★

Population 1 062
Map p 4 – Michelin map 58 fold 2 or 230 fold 1 – Green Guide Brittany

The **Île d'Ouessant** ⓥ is a detached fragment of the Léon plateau on the mainland, 25 km – 16 miles away. Two outcrops of granite running northeast-southwest enclose a sunken area of mica-schist much eroded by the sea to form Lampaul Bay (Baie de Lampaul) to the southwest and Stiff Bay (Baie du Stiff) to the northeast. Many of the male onhabitants are French Navy men or work for the merchant navy; the few fishermen trap lobsters. The population lives in scattered hamlets or in the little capital of Lampaul, with its tiny harbour and the mausoleum where the Proella crosses representing those lost at sea are assembled.
Where there is shelter from the wind, camelias, aloes and agaves can grow, but the characteristic vegetation of the island is heather and dwarf gorse. The meagre grasses nourish a small flock of sheep. The cliffs of Ushant and its neighbouring islands house numbers of migrating and nesting birds.

★★★ **Côte Sauvage** – *4 hours return on foot starting at Lampaul.* The headlands and inlets of Ushant's rocky northwestern coastline have a rugged and dramatic beauty. In winter the wind is master, hurling the breakers against reefs and cliffs with utmost fury. The most spectacular locations include Keller Island (Île de Keller), Penn-ar-Ru-Meur and the Cardoran islet.
The 300 or so vessels which pass each day are guided by five great lighthouses. The one at Creac'h, which houses the **Centre d'Interpretation des phares et Balises** ⓥ, an historial museum on lighthouses and beacons, is the most powerful in the world; together wth its counterpart at Land's End in Cornwall it marks the western limit of the English Channel. The light at Stiff ⓥ with its towers built by Vauban in 1695 gives a splendid **view★★★** over the spreading sea. The lighthouses play a vital role; Ushant is notorious for its fogs, treacherous reefs and currents. Over the last hundred years 54 wrecks have been recorded.

Gouffre de PADIRAC★★★

Map p 8 – Michelin map 75 fold 19 or 235 fold 6 or 239 fold 39
Green Guide Dordogne

Padirac Chasm (Gouffre de Padirac) ⓥ, hollowed out of the limestone mass of the Gramat plateau (Causse de Gramat), is one of the most extraordinary natural phenomena of the Massif Central.
The chasm *(1 1/2 hours)* itself is a gigantic well *(aven)* of striking width (99m – 325ft around its rim) and depth (75m – 246ft to the rubble cone formed by the collapse of the original roof). With its walls covered in vegetation and the overflow from stalagmites, it is one of the most atmospheric of France's underground domains.

Guy de Lavaur (1903-86), a follower of Robert de Joly *(see under Aven d'Orgnac)*, originally devoted himself to the exploration of dry caves, but later turned to the development of techniques for investigating underground watercourses. In 1938 he came to Padirac and succeeded in finding a way through the siphons which had proved inaccessible to his predecessor Édouard-Alfred Martel. As a result of his efforts, the total length of the subterranean network at Padirac rose from 2km – 1 1/2 miles to 15km – 9 miles.

The underground river flows 103m – 340ft beneath the surface of the plateau to reappear on the surface near the natural amphitheatre at Montvalent 11km – 7 miles away on the Dordogne. Some 5km – 3 miles of its main channel and tributaries have been explored.

The Grand Pilier, Grande Pendeloque of the Lac de la Pluie and the Salle du Grand Dôme are among the most striking of all natural monuments of the underground world.

Films about Paris

Hôtel du Nord (1938) directed bay Marcel Carné – This film contains the famous line spoken by Arletty. "Atmosphere, atmosphere, do I look like I've got atmosphere ?" The Hôtel du Nord still exists, near the Canal St-Martin whose bridges and locks are inseparably linked to the film, although it was, in fact, shot on a studio set.

Les Enfants du Paradis (Children of Paradise, 1943-1945) directed by Marcel Carné – Arletty/Garance, Jean-Louis Barrault/Baptiste, Frédéric Lemaître/Pierre Brasseur, Maria Casarès, dialogue by Prévert... thes film is one of cinema's all-time classics.

Gigi (1948) directed by Claude Dolbert – This period movie is full of local colour. The story of a young girl, brought up by her aunt, is married off to a rake. Not to be confused with the musical version.

Zazie dans le métro (Zazie on the Underground, 1959) directed by Louis Malle – A burlesque comedy which is a screen adaptation of an idea by Raymond Queneau.

A bout de souffle (Breathless, 1959) – A light touch on the camera and natural settings. Jean-Luc Godard's film laid down the basic principles of the New Wave.

Les 400 coups (The 400 blows, 1959) directed by François Truffaut – A lively spontaneous Parisian lad, Antoine Doinel, ends up in a borstal-type institution. The unforgettable shots of the streets of Paris are reminiscent of the photographic art of Doisneau.

Charade (1962) directed by Stanley Donen – Audrey Hepburn is chased through Paris by a gang of ruffians and helped by Cary Grant. Is he or is he not interested in the missing 250 000 dollars ?

Last Tango in Paris (12972) – Bernardo Bertolucci directs this fatefus story of obsessive love in Paris. Stars include Marlon Brando and Maria Schneider.

Le locataire (The Tenant, 1976) directed by Roman Polanski – A lonely young man falls victim to a conspiracy in an apartment block full of hostile neighbours.

Le dernier Métro (The Last Metro, 1980) directed by François Truffaut – The oppressive atmosphere of Paris during the German Occupation.

La passante de Sans-Souci (1981) directed by Jacques Rouffio – A moving performance by Romy Schneider in her last film. Having fled to Paris (Hôtel George V then Pigalle) to escape Nazi killers, she is finally caught.

Diva (1981) directed by Beneix – Paris serves as a refined context for two very different themes. A beautiful black opera singer gets indirectly entangled with the harsh and violent underworld.

Subway (1985) directed by Luc Besson – This was filmed like a video clip, with musical backing by Eric Serra. The leading actors (Isabelle Adjani and Christophe Lambert) express their love in the labyrinthine world of the Paris Metro.

Les amants du Pont-Neuf (1991) directed by Léo Carax – The décors are artificial and heighten the unreal atmosphere of the life led by two young homeless lovers in the middle of the Pont-Neuf while work is being carried out on the bridge.

La Tour Eiffel

PARIS***

Population 2 152 333
Map p 7 – Michelin map 101 and plan 10 (single sheet)
or 11 (atlas with street index) – Green Guide Paris

The dominance of Paris in France's intellectual, artistic, scientific and political life can be traced back to the 12C when the Capetian kings made it their capital.

A STROLL THROUGH THE CITY'S HISTORY

Middle Ages (476-1492)

At the time of the fall of the Roman Empire towards the end of the 5C, Paris was a modest township founded seven centuries previously by Gallic fishermen. Following its occupation by the Roman legions of Labienus, the settlement had been extended south of the river to where the remains of the Cluny Baths and a 2C amphitheatre now stand. In the 3C St Denis, Paris' first bishop, had met his martyrdom and the Barbarians had razed the place to the ground. This destruction, together with the threat posed by Attila's hordes (but averted by the intervention of St Genevieve), had caused the inhabitants to withdraw to the security of the Île de la Cité.

Clovis, King of the Franks, settled in Paris in 508. Two years later, he founded an abbey south of the Seine in honour of St Genevieve, just as 35 years previously a basilica had been erected over the tomb of St Denis. In 885, for the fifth time in 40 years, the Norsemen sailed up the river and put Paris to siege; Eudes, son of Robert the Strong, bravely led the local resistance, and was elected king of "France" in 888; from then on, the town became the royal seat, albeit with some interruptions.

The Capetian dynasty (987-1328)

The original abbey of St-Germain-des-Prés was wrecked by the Norsemen; around the turn of the millenium, it was rebuilt in Romanesque style and has been much altered subsequently.

Peter Abelard, master of logic and theology and lover of Heloise, taught in Paris at the beginning of the 11C; in 1136, Abbot Suger rebuilt the abbey church of St-Denis in the revolutionary Gothic style, an example soon followed by Maurice de Sully at Notre-Dame. Between 1180 and 1210, Philippe Auguste surrounded the growing city with a continuous ring of fortifications anchored on the Louvre fortress. In 1215 France's first university was founded on the Ste-Geneviève hill.

D'après photo PIX

In 1246, the Sainte-Chapelle was built by St Louis (Louis IX), that sturdy defender of the rights of kings and commoners. A marvel of the Gothic style, it was intended to house the relics of the Passion. The king also founded the Quinze-Vingts (15 × 20 = 300) Hospital to house 300 blind persons, and (together with Robert of Sorbon), the college which was to develop into the mighty Sorbonne.

Seal of the Watermen's Guild.
(1210)

In the early years of the 14C, Philippe le Bel (the Fair) built the Conciergerie; on 30 October 1307, he ordered the arrest of all the Templars in France, then, after persuading the Pope to dissolve their Order (1314), he had their Grand Master Jacques de Molay and 54 of his associates burnt alive.

The House of Valois (1328-1589)

Philippe Auguste had built a manor house at Vincennes, Louis IX a chapel. Philippe VI added a castle, its keep designed according to the most advanced principles of military architecture. The work was carried on by his son John until his imprisonment in England.

On 22 February 1358, Étienne Marcel, the merchants' provost, succeeded in rousing the townsfolk to break into the Law Courts (Palais de Justice); entering the Dauphin's apartments, he slew two of the future Charles V's counsellors before his very eyes. On becoming king, Charles quit this place of ill memory to set up court, first in the huge Hôtel St-Paul (now destroyed), then at Vincennes. He was also responsible for making the Louvre habitable and providing it with a library, then, in 1370, he built himself a stronghold in the eastern part of the city, the Bastille, which became the centrepiece of a new ring of fortifications.

From the reign of Charles VII onward the monarchs spent much of their time in the châteaux of the Loire Valley, transporting kitchenware and furniture with them. In 1407, the king's brother, Louis of Orléans, was assassinated by followers of John the Fearless, thereby unleashing civil war between the Armagnacs and Burgundians. Paris was delivered up to the English in 1418 and Joan of Arc was wounded in front of the St-Honoré Gate trying to retake the city in 1429. Paris was only won back for France eight years later by Charles VII.

The Flamboyant variant of the Gothic style was used in the ambulatory of St-Séverin's Church, in the transept of St-Étienne-du-Mont and in the porch of St-Germain-l'Auxerrois which became the royal parish church when the rulers from the House of Valois took up residence in the Louvre. It was at this time that François Villon, thief and reprobate, made his reputation as the poet of the down-and-outs, with a talent far in advance of his time but expressed in a language which was already out-of-date. Louis XI provided printers from Mainz in the Rhineland with facilities at the Sorbonne. In 1475 the Hôtel de Sens was built; together with the Hôtel de Cluny, it is one of Paris' few surviving late medieval residences; the influence of the court's Italian artists is apparent in the mouldings of the windows, the brackets and the dormers.

The modern era (1492-1789)

In 1492, the discovery of America marked the start of the modern age. The Neapolitan artists brought back by Charles VIII from his campaigns in Italy were introducing new trends in taste and thought; the influence of the Renaissance became apparent in many ways, in the semicircular arches of St Eustache's Church, in the decoration of the choir-screen of St-Étienne-du-Mont and even in the entreaties of Guillaume Budé which persuaded François I to found the Collège de France.

In the middle of the 16C the Hôtel Carnavalet was built, followed by the Pierre Lescot wing of the Louvre which now forms one side of the impressive courtyard of the old palace, the Cour Carrée; Lescot commissioned Jean Goujon to carry out the sculptural decoration. In 1549, Joachim du Bellay published his *"Defence and Illustration of the French Language"* which became the manifesto of the literary movement known as the *Pléiade*.

In 1559, the court went into mourning for Henri II, fatally wounded in the Rue St-Antoine in the course of a tournament celebrating the wedding of his daughter. His widow, Catherine de' Medici, put Philibert Delorme in charge of the construction of the Tuileries Palace. A few years later Germain Pilon was to sculpt the *Three Graces* in the idealised style of the previous century for the tomb of Henri II. The brothers Androuet Du Cerceau drew up the plans for the Flore Pavilion abutting the Louvre to the west, then set about the construction of the Pont Neuf (New Bridge), which today is the city's oldest surviving bridge. At the same time, Ambroise Paré, a surgeon at the Hôtel-Dieu Hospital was making great advances in orthopaedics.

On 24 August 1572, the bells rang out from the tower of St-Germain-l'Auxerrois to signal the start of the St Bartholomew's Day Massacre; Henry of Navarre, the future Henri IV, just married to Marguerite of Valois, barely escaped with his life. In 1588, in reaction to the monarchy's centralising policy which had left the country at the mercy of growing Spanish hegemony, the Catholic League turned against Henri III; after the so-called Day of the Barricades (12 May 1588), the king was obliged to flee the city. But with the help of Henry of Navarre, he returned to the attack, only to be assassinated at Saint-Cloud in 1589 by the monk Jacques Clément. This violent act marked the end of the Valois line.

The Bourbons (1589-1789)

In 1594 Paris opened its gates to Henri IV, the new king who had renounced his Protestant faith and succeeded in pacifying the country. The Arsenal was built to the plans of Philibert Delorme while Louis Métezeau laid out the elegantly symmetrical Place Royale, since renamed Place des Vosges. But on 14 May 1610 in the Rue de la Ferronerie, this monarch too fell victim to an assassin.

The reign of Louis XIII – 1610-43. Under Louis XIII, Métezeau designed an imposing classical west front for St-Gervais Church, the first of its kind in Paris; Salomon de Brosse built the Luxembourg Palace for Marie de' Medici; Jean Androuet Du Cerceau laid out the courtyards and gardens of the Hôtel de Béthune-Sully; as well as erecting a church for the Sorbonne with classical columns on its courtyard side, Lemercier built the Palais Royal for Richelieu. In 1636, Pierre Corneille, a Rouen laywer, put on his play *Le Cid* at the theatre in the Hôtel de Bourgogne in the Marais district. Six years later, Lemercier constructed the Clock Pavilion (Pavillon de l'Horloge) forming the centrepiece of the west side of the Louvre's Cour Carrée. In the following year, Cardinal de la Rochefoucauld founded the Hospital for Incurable Diseases; the Laënnec building retains two sides of the original courtyard. On the king's death in 1643, Anne of Austria became Regent, acting in concert with Mazarin and continuing the policies of Richelieu. It was during this period that

Guillaume Coustou sculpted the famous *Horses of Marly*. While François Mansart was building the Hôtel Guénégaud and Le Vau was busy with the construction of the Pavilions of the King and Queen at Vincennes, Paris fell prey to the series of disturbances caused by unrest among the nobility and known as the Fronde; the young king came to the conclusion that it might be advantageous to separate Court from city.

The century of Louis XIV – The 23-year-old king began his long and highly personal reign in 1661. The classical style which had been maturing during the Regency now came into its own. Even more than the splendour of court life, it was the extraordinary advancement of the arts and literature at this time that gave France such prestige in Europe. Under the protection of a king keen to encourage artistic endeavour and promote creative confidence, writers, painters, sculptors and landscapers flourished as never before. In the space of 20 years, the great Le Nôtre redesigned the parterres of the Tuileries; Claude Perrault provided the Louvre with its fine colonnade and built the Observatory; Le Vau completed the greater part of both the Louvre and the Institute of France, the "College of Four Nations" endowed by Mazarin. After building the chapel of the Salpêtrière Hospital, Libéral Bruant drew up his grandiose plans for the Invalides, the barracks founded by the king for his old soldiers.

With the aim of improving the quality of goods and thereby contributing to the country's prosperity, Colbert founded the Gobelins manufactory. Jean-Baptiste Lully created the classical form of opera and collaborated with Molière on his ballet-plays; his recitatives accompanied on the clavicord are masterpieces of measured expressiveness. Lully also founded the Royal Academy of Music.

Bossuet delivered his funeral orations in honour of great figures of the period, while La Fontaine wrote the scabrous anecdotes known as the *Contes et Nouvelles*, followed by his *Fables*, a wonderful combination of literary enchantment and psychological analysis. At the age of 28 Jean Racine produced his *Andromaque*, the first of the great line of tragedies which include *Britannicus, Bérénice, Phèdre* and *Athalie*. His verses of "incantatory power but magical simplicity" (G. Bréreton) expressed such unbridled passions that he eventually returned in penitence to the Jansenist fold he had once deserted. Molière came back to Paris after a long apprenticeship, notably in the South; out of this came the *École des Femmes (School for Wives* – 1662*), followed by Don Juan*, the *Misanthrope, Amphytrion, L'Avare (the Miser), Le Tartuffe (the Hypocrite), Les Femmes Savantes (the Wise Women)*, comedies shot through with *"that masculine gaiety of such sadness and depth to make us mingle tears with our mirth"* (Alfred de Musset). The great playwright died on 17 February 1673 in 40 Rue de Richelieu after being taken ill on stage while playing the role of the *Malade Imaginaire (the Hypocondriac)*.

During this decade, a scandal about the use of poison to secure inheritance and involving the aristocracy touched the throne itself, casting a shadow on a court still avidly in pursuit of youthful pleasures and leading to the disgrace of the king's mistress, Mme de Montespan.

This was the time during which André Boulle gave his name to furniture with elaborate marquetry of tortoiseshell and brass and when François Couperin became known for his mastery of the harpsicord and his exquisitely elegant suites. La Bruyère, whose masterly prose and trenchant comment aroused conflicting passions with his *Characters*, while Charles Perrault, brother of Claude *(p 231)* fascinated his public with his marvellous tales of *Cinderella* and *Sleeping Beauty*. Coysevox sculpted his group of winged horses to grace the Tuileries, and 10 years later, Colbert's tomb in the St-Eustache Church. Hardouin-Mansart planned the Place Vendôme and Delamair designed the Soubise Palace and the Hôtel de Rohan in the Marais district. France's "Century of Greatness" came to an end with Louis XIV's death in 1715.

The Age of Enlightenment – On Louis XIV's death, the country found itself, for the second time in its history, under the rule of a five-year-old. The running of the country was therefore put into the hands of a regent, Philippe d'Orléans; the first action of the court was to pack its bags and quit the boredom of Versailles for the gaiety of the capital. A long period of peace accompanied the years of corruption; for 77 years France experi-

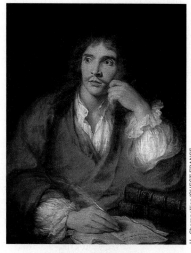

H. Champollion/OUEST-FRANCE

Molière, by Charles Coypel

enced no foreign incursions. Chancellor Auguesseau continued the work begun by Colbert with his administrative reforms, but the period was also marked by the dramatic bankruptcy of the Scots financier John Law, when the speculation he had fuelled with promissory notes issued from his bank in the Rue Quincampoix finally crashed in 1720.

Literary salons flourished, notably those of the Marquise de Lambert, Mme Du Deffand and Mme Geoffrin, all helping the spread of new ideas. The Palais Bourbon (1722-28), which now houses the National Assembly, was erected at this time. The Esplanade des Invalides was laid out by Robert de Cotte. The work of the furniture-maker Charles Cressent was characterised by opulent forms and elaborate bronze mounts; in many ways it heralds an age when the fashionable world was enthused by fine furniture, and the craftsmen and shopkeepers of the Rue St-Eustache and the Faubourg St-Antoine were kept busy. Jean-Philippe Rameau expressed his theories in his *Treatise on Harmony* and introduced innovative compositional ideas into his operas and opera-ballets *(Les Indes Galantes);* in 1723 he composed a number of suites for harpsicord which broke new ground in melodic invention. In 1730 Marivaux wrote the best-known of his delicately amorous comedies, *Le Jeu de l'amour et du hasard (The Game of Love and Chance).* In 1739, the naturalist Georges Buffon laid out the Jardin des Plantes (Botanical Gardens) and in the following year, the sculptor Bouchardon completed his beautiful *Fountain of the Four Seasons (Fontaine des Quatre Saisons)* in the St-Germain district.

The reign of Louis XV – The personal rule exercised by Louis XV was discredited by his favourites, but was nevertheless marked by a number of personalities such as Charles de la Condamine, a surveyor and naturalist responsible for the discovery of rubber (1751); Jussieu, incumbent of the Chair in Botany at the Botanical Gardens, responsible for a systematic classification of plants (1759) and for many advances in pharmacology; Diderot, author, together with d'Alambert, of the great *Encyclopaedia,* a splendid summary of the technology of the age; Chardin, who had lodgings in the Louvre, devoted himself to working in pastel; Robert Pothier, who wrote the *Treatise of Obligations;* Ange-Jacques Gabriel, the last and most famous of a line of architects linked to Mansart and Robert de Cotte, who between them gave France a hundred years of architectural unity; it was he who designed the magnificent façades fronting the Place de la Concorde, the west front of St-Roch Church and the École Militaire (Military Academy). Finally there was Soufflot, creator of the dome which crowns the Panthéon.

Distinguished furniture-makers were at work too: Lardin with his cabinets and commodes with rosewood inlay, and Boudin with his virtuoso marquetry and secret compartments; they anticipate the masters who were to emerge in the following reign.

The reign of Louis XVI (1774-92) – After making tables and writing-desks, Lacroix showed his skill in the perfect curves of his commodes and cabinets. From his workshops near the St-Martin Gate, Georges Jacob presided over the whole field of furniture-making, making the definitive chairs of the age as well as his famous armchairs *"à la reine".* But it was above all Jean Riesener with his workshop in the Rue St-Honoré who helped create the Louis XVI style; his commodes and his mahogany desks with bronze decoration are triumphs of sobriety and distinction. Chalgrin designed the organ-case for the imposing St-Sulpice Church; Gluck wrote *Orpheus* and exerted his influence over Mehul; Antoine built the Hôtel des Monnaies; Baudelocque pioneered the study of obstetrics; Pilâtre du Rosier rose above the rooftops of the St-Antoine quarter in his "Montgolfière" and sailed across the city; after his *Barber of Seville,* Beaumarchais presented the *Marriage of Figaro* at the Théâtre Français on 27 April 1784, thereby gaining the reputation of a "defender of the oppressed"; 9 years after his visionary plans for Arc-et-Senans, Ledoux built 57 toll-houses for the wall enclosing the city; the court painter Élisabeth Vigée-Lebrun portrayed Queen Marie-Antoinette and her children with a seductive grace and tenderness.

Revolution and Empire (1789-1814)

The contemporary period (from 1789)

In 1788, the King decided to convene the States-General. The delegates assembled at Versailles on 5 May 1789.

The Constituent Assembly – On 17 June, the States-General transformed itself into a National Assembly which styled itself the Constituent Assembly on 9 July; the monarchy would eventually become a constitutional one.

On 14 July, in the space of less than an hour, the people of Paris took over the Bastille in the hope of finding arms there; the outline of the demolished fortress can still be traced in the paving on the west side of the Place de la Bastille (14 July became a day of national celebration in 1879). On 17 July, in the City Hall, Louis XVI kissed the recently adopted tricolour cockade. The feudal system was abolished on 4 August, and the Declaration of the Rights of Man adopted on 26 August; on 5 October, the Assembly moved into the riding-school of the Tuileries, and the royal family was brought from Versailles and installed in the Tuileries Palace.

On 22 December, the Assembly divided up the country into 83 *départements*, thereby carrying out a proposal first suggested by d'Argenson in 1764.

On 12 July 1790 the Church became subject to the Civil Constitution for the Clergy. Two days later, a great crowd gathered on the Champ-de-Mars to celebrate the anniversary of the fall of the Bastille; Talleyrand, Bishop of Autun as well as statesman and diplomat, celebrated mass on the altar of the nation and the king reaffirmed his oath of loyalty to the country.

After his attempt to join Bouillé's army at Metz had been foiled, Louis was brought back to Paris on 25 June 1791; on 30 September, he was forced to accept the constitution adopted by the Assembly which then dissolved itself.

The Legislative Assembly – The new deputies met the following day in the Tuileries Riding School. On 20 June 1792, encouraged by the moderate revolutionary faction known as the Girondins, rioters invaded the Tuileries and made Louis put on the red bonnet of liberty. On 11 July, the Assembly declared France to be in danger and during the night of 9 August, the mob *(sans-culottes)* instituted a "revolutionary commune" with the status of an organ of government; the next day the Tuileries were sacked and 600 of the Swiss Guards massacred. The Assembly responded by depriving the king of his few remaining responsibilities and confining him with his family in the tower of the Templar Prison. Soon after, the "September Massacres" began; 1 200 prisoners, some "politicals", but most of them common offenders, were hauled from the city's jails and arbitrarily executed on the Buci cross-roads in a frenzy of fear and panic precipitated by fear of invasion. This grisly event marked the beginning of the Terror. On 21 September, the day after Valmy *(qv)*, the Legislative Assembly gave way to the Convention.

Louis XVI wearing a
"liberty bonnet"

Collection Soalhat/SIPA-PRESS

The Convention – At its very first meeting, the new assembly, now in the hands of the Girondins, formally abolished the monarchy and proclaimed the Republic. This day, 21 September 1792, became Day 1 of Year One in the new revolutionary calendar, which remained in force until 31 December 1805. On 11 December, the trial of Louis Capet opened at the Riding School. The monarch was guillotined on 21 January 1793 in the Place de la Concorde. At the end of May, beset by difficulties at home and abroad and bereft of popular support, the Girondins fell, to be replaced by the "Mountain" (the extreme Jacobin faction, so-called because they occupied the upper tiers of seating in the Assembly).

One of the acts of the Mountain-dominated Convention was to open the Louvre as a Museum of the Republic, on 10 August 1793. On 17 September, the Law of Suspects was passed, legalising the Terror. The first to be executed by the revolutionary tribunals were the Girondins, in October 1793. On 8 June 1794, Robespierre the "Incorruptible" presided over the Festival of the Supreme Being. The event was orchestrated by the painter David, beginning in the Tuileries Gardens and proceeding to the Champ-de-Mars.

On 10 June (9 Prairial), the Great Terror began. Over a period of two months, the "national razor", as the guillotine was known, was to slice off 2 561 heads. Among those executed was Lavoisier, former Farmer-General and eminent chemist, responsible for the formulation of the theory of the conservation of mass on which much of modern chemistry rests, and André Chénier, the lyric poet who had condemned the excesses of the regime in his verse. The end of the Terror came with the fall and execution of Robespierre himself, on 27 July (9 Thermidor).

The Thermidorian Convention now attempted to put the sickening spectacle of the scaffold behind it with a policy calculated to promote stability in the nation. Among its most important achievements were measures designed to advance science and learning, including the founding of the École Polytechnique (School of Engineering) by Monge (1794), known for his work on descriptive geometry and electromagnetism; the creation of the Conservatoire des Arts et Métiers (National Technical Institution) on the initiative of Abbot Grégoire, and the setting up of the École Normale (the prestigious pedagogical college). In 1795, the metric system was adopted and the Office of Longitudes founded. Just before the Assembly's dissolution on 25 October, public education was instituted and the Institut de France founded, embracing the nation's learned academies (including the Académie Française).

The Directory and the Consulate – The period of the Directory was marked, in 1798, by the very first Universal Exhibition, but was brought to an end with the *coup d'état* of 9 November (18 Brumaire) 1799, when the Council of Elders persuaded the legislature to move to St-Cloud as a precautionary measure against

Jacobin plots. On the following day, Napoleon Bonaparte entered the chamber to address the delegates, but was booed; he was saved by the presence of mind of his brother Lucien, who used the guard to disperse the members. By the same evening, power was in the hands of three consuls; it was the end of the Revolution.

In less than five years, the Consulate allowed Napoleon to centralise power, opening the way to the realisation of his Imperial ambitions. A period of consolidation began; the Legion of Honour was created and Catholic opinion propitiated by a Concordat with the Vatican. Bonaparte's religious policy dovetailed (conveniently for its author) with the views on religion expressed in Chateaubriand's work The *Genius of Christianity.*

Long before the onset of the Industrial Revolution, Babeuf put forward his "system of socialism" and the mathematician Lagrange was studying the functions and equations of dynamics; Lebon's "thermolamp" inaugurated the era of lighting by gas, and the great anatomist and physiologist Bichat defined the nature of body tissue. In 1803 the Pont des Arts was built, the first iron bridge in France, reserved for the exclusive use of pedestrians. In order to deter the plots being organised against him by royalist *émigrés* and the English, Napoleon ordered the Duke d'Enghien to be executed; the sentence was carried out in the small hours of 21 March 1804 in the moat at Vincennes, sending shock waves throughout the whole of Europe.

The Empire – Proclaimed Emperor of the French by the Senate on 18 May 1804, Napoleon I was anointed on 2 December by Pope Pius VII at Notre-Dame, though it was he himself who actually put the crown on his head in a ceremony immortalised by David. His reign was marked by the promulgation in 1804 of the Civil Code, which he had helped draft himself when he was still First Consul, and which, as the *Code Napoléon,* has since formed the legal basis of many societies. In order to make Paris into a truly imperial capital, Napoleon ordered the erection of a great column in the Place Vendôme; cast from the melted-down metal of guns taken at the Battle of Austerlitz (Slavkov), it commemorated the victories of his *Grande Armée.* Vignon was commissioned to design a temple which nearly became a railway station before ending up as the Madeleine Church; Chalgrin was put to work drawing up plans for a great triumphal arch (Arc de Triomphe); Brongniart built the Stock Exchange (Bourse); Percier and Fontaine, the promotors of the Empire style, constructed the north wing of the Louvre and the Carrousel Arch (Arc du Carrousel); Gros painted the battles and Géricault the cavalry of the *Grande Armée.*

On 31 March 1814, despite the strong resistance offered by Daumesnil at Vincennes, the Allies occupied Paris. On 11 April, the Emperor, "the sole obstacle to peace in Europe", put his signature to the document of abdication at Fontainebleau.

Coronation of Napoleon by David

The Restoration (May 1814-February 1848)

The reign of Louis XVIII – 1814-24. The period of rule of Louis XVI's brother was interrupted by the Hundred Days of Napoleon's attempt to reestablish himself between his sojourn on Elba and his final exile to St Helena. During the years of Louis XVIII's reign, Laënnec invented the stethoscope, wrote his *Treatise on Mediate Auscultation* and founded the anatomo-clinical school together with Bayle and Dupuytren; Pinel studied mental illness at the Salpêtrière Hospital; Cuvier put biology on a sounder footing, formulated the principles of subordination of organs to their function and established a zoological classification; Bertholet studied the composition of acids, Sadi Carnot thermodynamics and temperature equilibrium, and Arago electromagnetism and the polarisation of light; Daguerre laid the foundations of his fame with his dioramas and Lamartine conquered literary society with his *Méditations Poétiques* – its elegaic rhythms soothed Talleyrand's sleepless nights.

The reign of Charles X – 1824-30. Painting flourished with the brilliant sweep of Delacroix' great canvases and Corot's landscapes. At the same time, Laplace was establishing the fundamental laws of mathematical analysis and providing a firm basis for astronomical mechanics, and Berlioz was composing his *Fantastic Symphony*, the key work of the Romantic Movement in music.
On 21 February 1830, Victor Hugo's drama *Hernani* provoked a literary battle between "moderns" and "classicals" in which the latter were temporarily routed. In the summer, Charles' press ordinances provoked a crisis which led to his abdication; he was succeeded by Louis Philippe, a member of the cadet branch of the Bourbons.

The reign of Louis-Philippe – 1830-48. During the 1830s, the mathematician Evariste Galois put forward the theory of sets; his concepts were developed by Cauchy; Victor Hugo wrote *Notre-Dame de Paris* and Alfred de Musset *Caprices*. Chopin, the darling of Parisian society, composed scherzos, waltzes and his celebrated *Polonaises*. In 1838, while on holiday in Paris, Stendhal wrote *The Charterhouse of Parma*, a masterpiece of psychological observation which can be read on a number of levels. The first news agency was founded by Charles Havas. In 1839, a railway line was opened between Paris and St-Germain. The 1840s saw the publication of the *Mysteries of Paris* by Eugène Sue, the *Count of Monte Cristo* and the *Three Musketeers* by Dumas and many of the works of Balzac's prodigious *Human Comedy* as well as the *Treatise on Parasitology* by Raspail; the abuses of the July monarchy were brilliantly satirised in the drawings of Daumier.
At the age of 79, Chateaubriand brought his finely chiselled *Memories from beyond the Tomb* to a triumphant conclusion. On 23 February in 1848, the barricades went up on the Boulevard des Capucines and the monarchy fell; the next day, at the City Hall, amid scenes of wild enthusiasm, Lamartine saluted the tricolour "the flag which has spread the name of France, freedom and glory around the wide world".

Second Republic and Second Empire (1848-70)

Second Republic – The abolition of the National Workshops in June 1848 brought about rioting in the St-Antoine district, in which the archbishop of Paris was killed. In 1849, Léon Foucault proved the rotation and spherical nature of the earth by means of a pendulum (the experiment was repeated in 1855 from the dome of the Pantheon). On the 2 December 1851 the short life of the Second Republic was ended by a *coup d'état*.

Second Empire – 1852-70. Two great exhibitions (in 1855 and 1867) proclaimed the prosperity France enjoyed under the rule of Bonaparte's nephew, Napoleon III. Baron Haussmann, Prefect of the *Département* of the Seine, was responsible for an ambitious programme of public works which transformed the capital, giving it many of the features which now seem quintessentially Parisian. Among them were the laying out of the Bois de Boulogne and the Bois de Vincennes, and the building of railway stations and the North Wing of the Louvre. But the Baron is remembered above all for the ruthless surgery he performed on the capital's ancient urban tissue, opening up new focal points (Place de l'Opéra) and linking them with great axial roadways (Grands Boulevards), splendid exercises in traffic engineering and riot control.
In 1852, Alexandre Dumas wrote *The Lady of the Camelias* at the same time as Rudé was working on the memorial to Marshal Ney which was to be placed on the very spot near the Observatory where the great soldier had been executed in 1815; in Rodin's opinion, it was Paris' finest statue. The following year, Claude Bernard, Professor of Physiology at the Collège de France, analysed the glycogenic function of the liver and wrote his *Introduction to the Study of Experimental Medecine*. In 1857 Baudelaire, the first poet of the teeming modern metropolis, published *Les Fleurs du Mal (the Flowers of Evil)*. In 1858, the resident organist at the Madeleine Church, Saint-Saëns, composed Oratorios and Cantatas, and the following year Gounod presented *Faust* at the Opéra Lyrique. In 1860, Étienne Lenoir registered his first patent for the internal combustion engine which was to be perfected 28 years later by Fernand Forest.

PARIS

The year 1863 was marked by the scandals caused by Manet's *Déjeuner sur l'herbe* and *Olympia;* Baltard masked the masterly iron structure of the St-Augustin Church with the stone cladding still obligatory in a religious building; iron was used again by Labrouste, in his case to lend lightness to the supports in the reading room of the National Library (Bibliothèque Nationale); the buildings surrounding the Étoile were given their neo-classical façades by Hittorf. In 1896, Pierre de Coubertin created the International Olympic Committee.

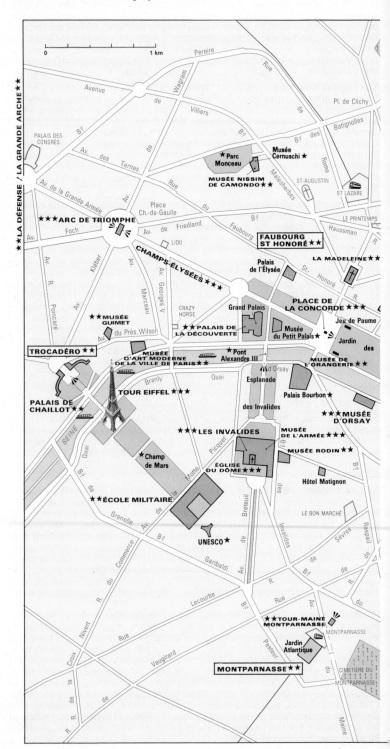

Republican Continuity (1870 to the present day)

On 4 September 1870, the mob which had invaded the National Assembly was led by Gambetta to the City Hall where the Republic was proclaimed. The new government busied itself in preparing to defend Paris against the advancing Prussians; the St-Cloud château was set on fire and a fierce battle took place at Le Bourget.

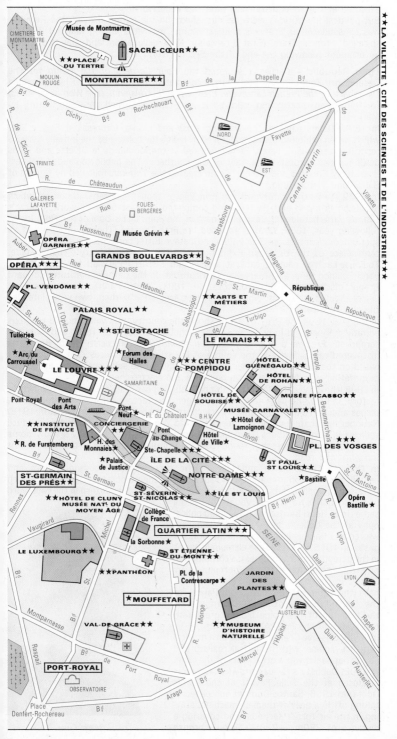

The ensuing siege subjected the population of Paris to terrible hardships; food ran out and the winter was exceptionally severe. The city surrendered on 28 January 1871. The revolutionary **Commune** was ruthlessly suppressed by military force, not before the Communards had burnt down the City Hall, the Tuileries and the Audit Office (Cours des Comptes – on the site of what is now the Orsay Museum), pulled down the column in the Place Vendôme and shot their prisoners at the Hostages' Wall in the Rue Haxo. They made their last stand in the Père-Lachaise Cemetery, where those of their number who had survived the bitter fighting were summarily executed at the Federalists' Wall (Mur des Fédérés).

But political institutions were reestablished and the nation revived; the Republic was consolidated as France's political regime, notwithstanding Marshal Pétain's so-called French State (État Français), Nazi occupation and the provisional government following the end of the Second World War.

Third Republic – Carpeaux sculpted the *Four Corners of the World* for the Observatory Fountain and Émile Littré completed the publication of his renowned *Dictionary of the French Language*. Bizet wrote *L'Arlésienne (the Woman of Arles)* for the Odéon theatre and followed it with *Carmen*, based on a short story by Mérimée.

In 1874, Degas painted *The Dancing Class* and Monet *Impression: Rising Sun*, which, when exhibited by his dealer Nadar, led to the coining of the initially derisive term Impressionism. Later, Renoir worked at the Moulin de la Galette and Puvis de Chavannes decorated the walls of the Panthéon. The public applauded Delibes' innovatory *Coppelia* and *Lakme*. Rodin created the *Thinker*, followed by figures of Balzac and Victor Hugo.

In 1879, Seulecq put forward the principle of sequential transmission on which television is based and Pasteur *(qv)* completed his vast body of work. Seurat's *Grande Jatte* heralded the establishment of the Pointillist school of painting. In the following year, 1887, Antoine founded the Free Theatre (Théâtre libre) based on spontaneous expression. The engineer Gustave Eiffel completed his great tower, centrepiece of the Universal Exhibition of 1889. In the century's final decade, Toulouse-Lautrec painted cabaret scenes and Pissarro Parisian townscapes and Forain gained fame as a marvellous caricaturist. In the Catholic Institute, Édouard Branly discovered radio-conductors. In 1891, René Panhard built the first petrol-engined motor-car, which drove right across Paris, then, two years later, all the way to Nice.

In the year 1894 the Dreyfus affair shook the country, re-awakening old religious enmities; Vincent d'Indy founded the Schola cantorum in 1896 and Debussy composed *Prélude à l'après-midi d'un faune.* The physicist Henri Becquerel discovered radioactivity in the course of his studies on fluorescence, themselves based on the work of his father who had analysed the solar spectrum, and of his grandfather who had worked on batteries and electro-chemistry.

In 1898, the 21-year-old Louis Renault built his first car, then founded his Billancourt factory; in 1902 he patented a turbocharger. The factory turned out cars, lorries, planes and, in 1917, light tanks which contributed to the German defeat in 1918. Nationalised at the end of the Second World War, the firm continued to produce vehicles in large numbers (Renaults are on display at the company's showrooms on the Champs Élysées; they range from the Voiturette of 1898 to the most recent model on the road.

In October 1898 Pierre and Marie Curie succeeded in isolating radium and established the atomic character of radioactivity; their laboratory was a shed which has since disappeared, but its outline is shown in the paving pattern in the courtyard of the school at No 10 Rue Vauquelin. At the same time, Henri Bergson was teaching philosophy at the Collège de France and Langevin was conducting his investigations into ionised gases (in 1915, he was to use ultrasonic waves in the detection of submarines); a combination of steel, stone and glass was employed by Girault in the construction of the exhibition halls (the Grand Palais and the Petit Palais) for the 1900 Exhibition; this occasion also saw the bridging of the Seine by the great flattened arch of the Pont Alexandre III.

In 1900, Gustave Charpentier put on a musical romance *Louise;* with its lyrical realism and popular appeal it was a great "hit" of the time. In 1902, Debussy's *Pelléas and Mélisande* was produced at the Salle Favart of the Comic Opera. In 1906, Santos-Dumont succeeded in taking off in a heavier-than-air machine, staying in the air for 21 seconds, and covering a distance of 220m – 720ft. Dalou's bronze

Marie Curie

group entitled *The Triumph of the Republic* graced the Place de la Nation, while at Montparnasse the re-erected Wine Pavilion from the 1900 Exhibition provided lodgings and studios for Soutine, Zadkine, Chagall, Modigliani and Léger; other innovative artists included the sculptor Maillol and the painter Utrillo, while Brancusi's work was evolving away from cubism towards abstraction *(The Sleeping Muse);* the Perret brothers built the Théâtre des Champs-Élysees in reinforced concrete; its façade was adorned with eight relief panels by Bourdelle. The theatre was opened in 1913 with a performance of Stravinsky's *Rite of Spring;* its music and choreography outraged an unprepared audience.

In 1914 the construction of the Sacré-Cœur Church (begun in 1878 by the architect Abadie) on the Montmartre heights was completed. On the evening of 31 July, the eve of general mobilisation, Jean Jaurès was assassinated.

The Great War of 1914-18 put civilians as well as soldiers to the severest of tests; after three years of conflict, Clemenceau was made head of government, and, by restoring the country's confidence, earned the title of "Father of Victory".

In 1920, the interment of an unknown soldier at the Arc de Triomphe marked France's recognition of the sacrifices made by her ordinary soldiers, the unshaven *"poilus"* of the trenches.

In the course of the 20s, Le Corbusier built the La Roche Villa, and Bourdelle sculpted *"France"* at the Palais de Tokyo; Georges Rouault, with his predilection for religious themes, completed his *Miserere,* and Landowsky carved the figure of St Genevieve for the Tournelle Bridge; in the course of a fortnight, Maurice Ravel composed *Bolero* for the dancer Ida Rubinstein; with its subtle instrumentation and rhythmic precision it popularised the name of this aristocratic composer; Poulbot created the archetypal Montmartre urchin; Cocteau wrote *Les Enfants Terribles;* the dynamism of the theatrical scene was marked by many fine actors and producers, notably the Cartel of Four (Cartel des Quatre) consisting of Charles Dullin (at the Sarah Bernhardt Theatre), Gaston Baty (at the Montparnasse), Louis Jouvet (at the Champs-Élysées then the Athénée) and Georges Pitoëff (at the Mathurins).

At the end of the 19C, Émile Roux had studied the causes of and cure for diptheria; he was now in charge of the Pasteur Institute, and brought to Paris the scientists Calmette and Guérin who had worked on vaccination against tuberculosis.

In 1934, André Citroën brought out the Traction Avant (Front-Wheel Drive) car; 15 years previously, his Type A had been Europe's first mass-produced car; 21 years later, he was to unveil the innovative DS 19.

In 1940, Paris was bombed, then occupied by the German army. Between 16 and 17 July 1942, many victims of the Nazi racial myth were rounded up at the Vélodrome d'Hiver prior to their deportation eastwards; 4 500 members of the Resistance met their deaths in the clearing on Mount Valérien where the National Memorial of Fighting France now stands. Finally, on 19 August 1944, Paris was liberated.

Fourth and Fifth Republics – In 1950, Alfred Kastler, working in the laboratories of the École Normale Supérieure, succeeded in verifying the principle of "optical pumping", which has subsequently become the basis of one of the methods of producing a laser beam. The *Symphony for a Single Man* by Maurice Béjart, presented at the Étoile Theatre on 3 August 1955, was danced to *musique concrète* composed by Pierre Henry and Pierre Schaeffer, and led to many innovations in ballet throughout Europe. The beginning of the transformation of the Défense district was marked in 1959 by the construction of the CNIT building with its upturned concrete shell, an extraordinary achievement, and by the Y-shaped Unesco building with its Calder mobile. Jean-Michel Jarre, son of Maurice Jarre, used a synthesizer to produce the unprecedented sounds of *"Oxygène"*.

Placed in the very heart of an old neighbourhood in central Paris, the Pompidou Centre unabashedly displays its entire structural framework and brightly coloured service ducts on the outside. In summer 1989, 8.4km – 5 miles from the Louvre's Cour Carrée, La Grande Arche de la Défense was completed, 110m – 360ft high, faced in marble and glass, a dramatic new landmark for the city's western horizon.

In 1994, the **Conservatoire National Superieur de Musique et de Danse de Paris** was moved to the **Cité de la Musique** at La Villette. The architect Christian de Portzamparc has imagined a multi-purpose **concert hall** (1 200 seats) and a **Musée de la Musique** which was inaugurated in 1995.

PARIS THE CAPITAL

THE CITY'S MONUMENTS

Civil architecture

★★★ **Palais du Louvre** – 11 page 31 – H13. Neither the Merovingians nor the Carolingians, nor even the Capet kings lived in the Louvre which then lay beyond the city limits; instead, they preferred the Law Courts (Palais de Justice), their *hôtels* in the Marais, the manor at Vincennes, their own châteaux or those of their liegemen in the Loire Valley.

The monarchs and their contribution

Philippe Auguste – Lived in the Law Courts. He built the Louvre fortress on the right bank of the river in order to house his archives. The original defensive ditches can still be seen *(access via the museum)*. The fortress was sited in the southwestern quadrant of the present Cour Carrée.

Saint Louis (Louis IX) – Lived in the Law Courts, but added a great hall and a chapel to the fortress his grandfather had built.

Philip the Fair – Lived in the Law Courts, using the Louvre as arsenal and treasury.

Charles V – Lived in the *hôtels* in the Marais. For this king, the Louvre was a place for relaxation; it was here that he kept his library of 973 books (where the Clock Pavilion – Pavillon de l'Horloge – now stands), and protected it with a defensive wall. His "lovely

The Louvre at the time of Charles V

Louvre" is shown in one of the paintings in the Book of Hours known as the *Très Riches Heures du Duc de Berry*.

Charles VI resided in the Hôtel St-Paul. Charles VII, Louis XI, Charles VIII and Louis XII lived in the Loire châteaux, or, when in Paris, in the Hôtel des Tournelles.

François I – Lived mostly on the Loire and in the Marais. He had the old Louvre pulled down, and, in 1546, commissioned Pierre Lescot to build the palace which was to become the residence of the kings of France. Lescot's work 1 is regarded as the most prestigious part of the Louvre; it was he who brought the Italian Renaissance style, already flowering on the Loire, to the banks of the Seine; the façade he built is a delight of proportion, balance and decoration, to which the sculptor Jean Goujon (designer of the nymphs of the Fountain of the Innocents) added his brilliant contribution.

Henri II – Lived in the Louvre. Lescot showed his appreciation of his patron's support by marking the façade with emblazoned monograms interlacing C, H and D (Catherine de' Medici, Henri, Diane de Poitiers).

Charles IX – On the death of his brother François II, the new monarch was only ten years old; the Florentine **Catherine de' Medici** was made Regent. With Auvergnat blood on her mother's side, this niece of two Popes had been married in France at the age of 14; her qualities of political tolerance were much in evidence in the negotiations with the Huguenots which led up to the Treaty of St-Germain. She lived in the Louvre on the floor since known as the Queens' Lodging (Logis des Reines) 2, but the idea of residing in the middle of Lescot's building site did not appeal, and she ordered Philibert Delorme (succeeded by Jean Bullant) to build the Tuileries. The site of this new palace was some 500m – 550 yards away, just beyond the fortifications built by Charles V, and, to link it with the Louvre, Catherine planned a covered way following the line of the Seine, with a smaller gallery at right angles.

Charles IX completed the southwestern part of the Cour Carrée, the courtyard which is the most impressive part of the Old Louvre to remain, embellishing it with his monogram (K = Carolus).

Henri III – Lived in the Louvre. He was responsible for the southeastern part of the Cour Carrée (which bears the monogram H).

Henri IV – Lived in the Louvre. From 1595, he had the work on the Great Gallery (Grande Galerie) continued by Louis Métezeau (the letters H and G standing for Henri and Gabrielle d'Estrées were all removed, save for a single pair, by Marie de' Medici). He also had the Flora Pavilion (Pavillon de Flore) built by Jacques II Androuet Du Cerceau, completed the Small Gallery (Petite Galerie) (its first floor was occupied by Marie de' Medici and Anne of Austria hence the monogram AA), and erected the upper part of the Henri III wing in the Cour Carrée, marked by his monogram.

Louis XIII – Lived in the Louvre. Encouraged by Richelieu, he continued with the construction of the Cour Carrée. At the same time as he was building the Sorbonne and the Palais-Royal, the architect Lemercier erected the Clock Pavilion (Pavillon de l'Horloge) together with the northwest corner of the courtyard, a classical response to Lescot's work (the monogram LA = Louis and Anne). Anne of Austria lived in the Queens' Lodging; the bathroom designed for her by Lemercier now houses the *Venus de Milo*. In 1638, Charles V's rampart was razed and the moat filled in.

EVOLUTION OF THE LOUVRE PALACE

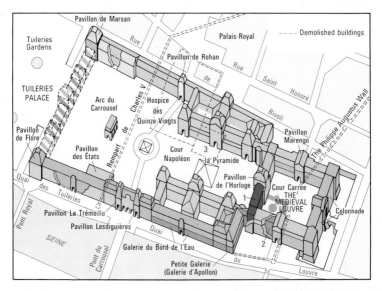

Pavillon de Marsan
Palais-Royal
Tuileries Gardens
Rue
- - - - Demolished buildings
Pavillon de Rohan
Rue
de
Saint
TUILERIES PALACE
Arc du Carrousel
Hospice des Quinze-Vingts
Honoré
Rivoli
The Philippe Augustus Wall
Pavillon de Flore
Rempart de Charles V
Cour Napoléon
3
la Pyramide
Pavillon Marengo
Pavillon des États
Pavillon de l'Horloge
1
Cour Carrée THE MEDIEVAL LOUVRE
Colonnade
Quai des Tuileries
Pont Royal
Pavillon La Trémoille
Pavillon Lesdiguières
Quai
du
Louvre
SEINE
Pont du Carrousel
Galerie du Bord de l'Eau
Petite Galerie (Galerie d'Apollon)
2

Louis XIV – On the death of Louis XIII, Anne became Regent and moved to the Palais-Royal with the young Louis. Nine years later, however, having been made aware of the palace's vulnerability by the uprising of the nobility (the Fronde), she took up residence in the Louvre again. In 1662, the young king, who had married Maria-Theresa the year before, organised a grand celebration to mark the birth of the Dauphin; the centrepiece was an equestrian fete (a *carrousel*) which led to the place being named the Place du Carrousel. The king moved into the Tuileries in 1664 for a period of three years. The architect Le Vau was now working at the Tuileries and on the Louvre, his personal style evident in the Small Gallery, started again after a fire in 1661, and in the Apollo Gallery; he continued the enclosure of the Cour Carrée by adding a storey on to the western part of the north wing (monogram LMT = Louis, Maria-Theresa) and by building the Marengo Pavilion (Pavillon Marengo) (with the monogram LB = Louis XIV de Bourbon). All this while he was already busy on the Great Apartment and the Queen's Suite at Versailles.

But the palace still needed a monumental façade facing the city; Colbert had just refused permission for a number of projects designed with this in mind. An appeal was made to the master-architect of the Italian Baroque, Bernini, already 67 years old. But his proposals were turned down too, since they would have either destroyed or clashed with Lescot's façade. In the end it fell to Claude Perrault, aided by Le Brun and Le Vau, to design an imposing colonnaded façade. Begun in 1667, but only completed in 1811, it masks Le Vau's work on the east side of the courtyard as well as necessitating a solemn extension on the outside of the south wing which made Le Vau's wall into a partition wall.

In 1682, the king left Paris for Versailles. The Louvre now housed the Academy as well as a less desirable population. In 1715, the Court returned to Paris for a period of 7 years; the young King Louis XV lived in the Tuileries and the Regent in the Palais-Royal. Coustou continued the work on the colonnade.

Louis XVI resided at Versailles until brought back to Paris on 6 October 1789; he lived in the Tuileries before being incarcerated in the Templar Prison.

The Revolution – The Convention used the Louvre theatre for its deliberations. The Committee of Public Safety convened in the state rooms of the Tuileries which were subsequently appropriated for his own use by Napoleon.

Napoleon I – Lived in the Tuileries. Percier and Fontaine completed the Cour Carrée by adding a second floor to the north and south wings. They also provided a wing linking the Rohan and Marsan Pavilions and gave it a façade identical to Du Cerceau's Grande Galerie, as well as enlarging the Place du Caroussel to enable Napoleon to review his legions and embellished it with a triumphal arch commemorating the Emperor's victories, its design based on the Arch of Septimus Severus.

Louis XVIII – Lived in the Tuileries. Percier and Fontaine constructed the Rohan Pavilion.

Charles X – Lived in the Tuileries, which was pillaged following the 1830 Revolution.

Louis-Philippe – Lived in the Tuileries, which in 1848 was sacked once more.

Napoleon III – Lived in the Tuileries. He decided to enclose the large courtyard on the north, confiding the task to Visconti, then to Lefuel, whose design was intended to conceal the disparity between the two wings; the architects razed the Hôtel de Rambouillet 3 which had housed the literary *Salon des Précieuses* under Louis XIII, replacing it with the present pavilions. They also restored the Rohan Pavilion (the monogram LN = Louis Napoléon). Lefuel restored the Flora Pavilion together with the wing extending it eastwards; his design is a not altogether successful copy of Métezeau's work; the gallery bears the monogram NE (= Napoleon, Eugénie).

The Republic – Since 1873, the official residence of the presidents of the Republic has been the Élysée Palace. During the night of 23 May 1871, the Communards burnt down the Tuileries and half of Napoleon I's North Wing, as well as the Richelieu and Turgot Pavilions and the East Wing attached to the Flora Pavilion. In 1875, under the presidency of Mac-Mahon, Lefuel continued the work of Visconti with some modifications; he restored and extended the North Wing as well as refurbishing the Marsan Pavilion and providing it with the monogram RF (République Française); in addition, he rebuilt the Riverside Gallery (Galerie du Bord de l'Eau) and the La Trémoille and Flora Pavilions.

In 1883, under the presidency of Jules Grévy, the Tuileries Palace was demolished; the place where Rameau had once composed his masterpieces was no more, and the city was deprived of one of the key buildings of its architectural history. In 1984, President Mitterrand voted the "Great Louvre and Pyramid" project. He commissioned the architect Ieoth Ming Pei to expand the services and reception area of the world famous museum. Beneath the Cour Napoléon, a vast hall offering information and documentation services is lit up by the glass **Pyramid★** which marks the main entrance to the museum.

★★★ **Hôtel des Invalides** – 11 page 29 – J10. The plans for the vast edifice were drawn up by Libéral Bruant between 1671 and 1676; their implementation was placed under the direction of Louvois. The main façade, nearly 200m – 650ft long, is majestic without being monotonous; it is dominated by an attic storey decorated with masks and dormer windows in the form of trophies. Napoleon used to parade his troops in the main courtyard (Cour d'honneur); here the South (Midi) Pavilion forms the façade of the St-Louis Church, the resting-place of some of France's great soldiers; the interior is hung with flags taken from the enemy. It was here, in 1837, that Berlioz' *Requiem* was performed for the first time.

★★★ **Église du Dôme** ⊙ this church, designed by the master of proportion, **Jules-Hardouin Mansart**, was begun in 1677. It is one of the great works of the Louis XIV style, bringing to a peak of perfection the classicism already introduced in the churches of the Sorbonne and the Val-de-Grâce, an ecclesiatical equivalent of the secular architecture of Versailles.

The façade facing Place Vauban is Doric at ground level and Corinthian above, finished off by a pediment carved by Coysevox. The soaring dome itself is carried on a great drum; the columns support the balconies and the consoles; it

1) Tomb of Joseph Bonaparte, elder brother of Napoleon, King of Spain.

2) Monument to Vauban by Etex. The Emperor himself commanded that the military architect's heart be brought to the Invalides.

3) Marshal Foch's tomb by Landowsky.

4) Ornate high altar surrounded by twisted columns and covered by a baldachin by Visconti. Vaulting decoration by Coypel.

5) General Duroc's tomb.

6) General Bertrand's tomb.

7) At the back – the heart of La Tour d'Auvergne, first grenadier of the Republic; in the centre, the tomb of Marshal Lyautey.

8) Marshal Turenne's tomb by Tuby.

9) St Jerome's Chapel (carvings by Nicolas Coustou). The tomb at the foot of the wall is Jerome Bonaparte's, Napoleon's younger brother and King of Westphalia.

10) The Emperor's tomb.

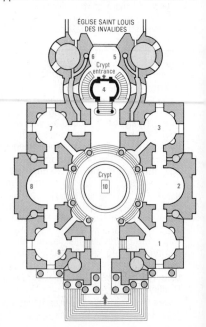

ÉGLISE SAINT LOUIS DES INVALIDES

terminates in an elegant lantern 107m – 352ft above ground level. In 1735, Robert de Cotte completed the building by replacing the planned south colonnade and portico by the splendid vista offered by the Avenue de Breteuil. On the far side he laid out the Esplanade and set up the guns captured at Vienna in 1805 by Napoleon to defend the gardens and fire ceremonial salvoes on great national occasions.

The **church** took on its role as military necropolis when Napoleon had Marshal Turenne (d 1675) buried here. Note also the memorial to Vauban, the great military architect, and the tomb of Marshal Foch. In Visconti's crypt of green granite from the Vosges stands the "cloak of glory", the unmarked red porphyry mausoleum, **Napoleon's Tomb**★★★, completed in 1861 to receive the Emperor's mortal remains. In 1940, the body of Napoleon's son, King of Rome and Duke of Reichstadt, was brought here too.

★★★ **Arc de Triomphe** ⊘ – 11 page 16 – F8. Together with the **Place Charles de Gaulle**★★★ and its 12 radiating avenues, the great triumphal arch makes up one of Paris' principal focal points, known as the Étoile (Star). The arch was designed by Chalgrin in 1806 to serve as one of the landmarks of Napoleon's imperial capital. But the architect died (in 1811) before the monument had risen very far above the ground, and this, combined with military failures, meant that the work was only completed in the reign of Louis Philippe, in 1836.

The façades of the buildings around the Étoile were designed in a harmonious style by Hittorff as part of Haussmann's plans for the metropolis.

The Arc de Triomphe was the scene on 14 July 1919 of the great victory parade and, on 11 November 1920, of the burial of the Unknown Soldier. Three years later the flame of remembrance was kindled for the first time. The arch is ornamented with much sculpture; the names of 128 battles and 558 generals cover the flat surfaces; caryatids, sculptures in high relief, the great frieze adorning the upper cornice... all pale into insignificance before Rude's masterpiece of 1836; known as the *Marseillaise*, and touched by the breath of genius, it shows the departure of volunteers to fight the invading Prussians (1792).

Place de la Concorde

★★★ **Place de la Concorde** – 11 page 30 – G11. A perfect expression of the Louis XV style, it was designed by Ange-Jacques Gabriel in 1755 and completed over a period of 20 years. On 21 January 1793, near where the statue of Brest now stands, the guillotine was set up for the execution of Louis XVI and other victims of the Terror.

The square owes its monumental character to the colonnaded buildings defining it to the north, its octagonal plan, and to the massive pedestals intended for allegorical statues of French cities. Two great urban **axes**★★★ intersect here; one runs from the Madeleine Church to the Palais-Bourbon, the other from Coysevox's *Winged Horses* which mark the entrance to the Tuileries to the magnificent marble sculptures (copies) by Nicolas and Guillaume Coustou which flank the Champs Élysées. The pink granite Luxor Obelisk, 3 300 years old, covered with hieroglyphics, was brought here from Egypt in 1836. The square's fountains are particularly fine.

★★★ **Tour Eiffel** ⓥ - 11 page 28 - J7. This is Paris' most famous symbol.
The first proposal for a tower was made in 1884; construction was completed in 26 months and the tower opened in March 1889 for the Universal Exhibition of that year. The structure is evidence of Eiffel's imagination and daring; in spite of its weight of 7 000 tonnes and a height of 320.75m - 1 051ft and the use of 2 1/2 million rivets, it is a masterpiece of lightness. It is difficult to believe that the tower actually weighs less than the volume of air surrounding it and that the pressure it exerts on the ground is that of a man sitting on a chair.

★★★ **Palais de Justice** - 11 page 31 - J14. Known as the Palace (Palais), this is the principal seat of civil and judicial authority. Before becoming the royal palace of the rulers of medieval France, it had been the residence of Roman governors, Merovingian kings and the children of Clovis, the mint of Dagobert and Duke Eudes' fortress. The Capetian kings gave it a chapel and a keep. Saint Louis lived in what is now the Civil Chamber (Chambre Civile). Philip the Fair entrusted Enguerrand de Marigny with the building of the Conciergerie as well as with the extension and embellishment of the palace; its Gothic halls of 1313 were widely admired. Later, Charles V built the Clock Tower (Tour de l'Horloge), the city's first public clock; he also installed Parliament here, the country's supreme court. Charles VII abandoned the place to its new occupants, preferring to live elsewhere. Survivals from this period include the Great Hall (Salle des gens d'Armes) with its fine capitals, the Guard Room (Salle des Gardes) with its magnificent pillars, and the kitchens with their monumental corner fire-places. The great hall on the first floor was restored by Salomon de Brosse after the fire of 1618; it was refurbished again in 1840 and once more after the fire of 1871.
The First Civil Court is in the former Parliamentary Grand Chamber, the place where the kings dispensed justice, where the 16-year-old Louis XIV dictated his orders to Parliament, where that body in its turn demanded the convocation of the States-General in 1788, and where the Revolutionary Tribunal was set up under Fouquier-Tinville.
The entrance to the royal palace was once guarded by the twin towers gracing the north front of the great complex; this is the oldest part of the building, albeit now hiding behind a 19C neo-Gothic façade.
The **Conciergerie**★★ ⓥ served as antechamber to the guillotine during the Terror, housing up to 1 200 detainees at any one time. The Prisoners' Gallery, Marie-Antoinette's cell and the Girondins' Chapel are particularly moving.

★★ **Palais-Royal** - 11 page 31 - H13. In 1632, Richelieu ordered Lemercier to build the huge edifice which came to be known as the Cardinal's Palace when it was extended in 1639. It is remarkable for its impressive central façade, surmounted by allegorical statues and a curved pediment. On his deathbed, Richelieu bequeathed it to Louis XIII, whereupon its name was changed to the Palais-Royal. The king did not outlive his minister for long, and after his death Anne of Austria moved here with the young Louis XIV in preference to the now somewhat old-fashioned Louvre with its never-ending rebuilding and extension.
The first meetings of the Académie Française (founded by Richelieu) were held here in 1635. In 1783, Victor Louis laid out the charming formal gardens and the arcades which enclose them and which house a number of specialist shops and boutiques. In 1787, the same architect built the adjoining Théâtre-Français and in so doing altered the appearance of Lemercier's building which heralded the classical style.
In 1986, Daniel Buren designed the quincunx of columns, 260 in number and all of different height, which occupy the outer courtyard.

★★ **École Militaire** - 11 page 29 - K9. Though the original design could not be fully implemented because of lack of financial resources, the Military Academy by Jacques-Ange Gabriel is one of the outstanding examples of French 18C architecture. It was begun in 1752, financed in part by Mme de Pompadour, and completed in 1773. Under the Second Empire, cavalry and artillery buildings of nondescript design were added, together with the low-lying wings which frame the main building. True to its original function, it now houses the French Army's Staff College.
The main façade consists of a projecting central section with great Corinthian columns rising a full two stories, crowned with a quadrangular dome and ornamented with allegorical figures and military trophies.
The superb **main courtyard**★★, lined on either side by beautiful porticoes with paired columns, is approached via an exercise yard; the imposing central section and the projecting wings form a harmonious composition.

★★ **Panthéon** ⓥ - 11 page 43 - L14. In 1744, Louis XV had made a vow at Metz to replace the half-ruined church of St Genevieve's Abbey. 14 years later Soufflot began the construction of the new building on the highest point of the Left Bank. The scale of the building was such that its collapse was confidently predicted and the pretensions of its architect ridiculed. The present building has been much changed since Soufflot's day; its towers have gone, its pediments have been remodelled, its windows blocked up. In 1791, the Constituent Assembly closed the church to worshippers in order to convert it into the last resting place of the "great men of the epoch of French liberty". Successively a church, a necropolis, headquarters of the Commune, a lay temple, the Pantheon is representative of the time in which churches lost their dominant position in the urban landscape. Still crowned by Soufflot's dome, the great edifice is built in the shape of a Greek Cross. It has a fine portico with Corinthian columns and a pediment carved by David d'Angers in 1831. In the crypt are the tombs of the famous.

★★ **Opéra Garnier** ⊙ – 11 page 18 – F12. This is the National Academy of Music, and was until 1990 France's premier home of opera. It opened in 1875 and it is the work of Charles Garnier, who had dreamed of creating an authentic Second Empire style. But the huge edifice, "more operatic than any opera" (Ian Nairn), magnificent though it was, lacked sufficient originality to inspire a new school of architecture. The interior, with its Great Staircase, foyer and auditorium, is of the utmost sumptuousness. Garnier used marble from all the quarries of France, and there is a ceiling by Chagall.

★★ **Palais de Chaillot** – 11 page 26 – H7. This remarkable example of interwar architecture was built for the 1937 Exhibition. Its twin pavilions are linked by a portico and extended by wings which curve to frame the wide terrace with its statues in gilded bronze. From here there is a wonderful **view**★★★ in Paris; in the foreground are the Trocadero Gardens with their spectacular fountains, and beyond the curving river the Eiffel Tower, the Champ-de-Mars, and the École Militaire.

The Palais houses the Théâtre de Chaillot, the **Musée de l'Homme**★★, **Musée de la Marine**★★, **Musée des Monuments Français**★★ and **Musée du Cinéma Henri-Langlois**★.

Ecclesiastical architecture

★★★ **Cathédrale Notre-Dame** – 11 page 32 – K15. The metropolitan church of Paris is one of the triumphs of French architecture. People have worshipped here for 2 000 years and the present building has witnessed the great events of French history; in many ways Notre-Dame is the cathedral of the nation.

Work on the cathedral was begun by Maurice de Sully in 1163. He was already familiar both with the early Gothic of Suger's St-Denis Cathedral and with the Transitional style in evidence at Sens, Noyon, Senlis, Laon and in the recently-consecrated choir at St-Germain-des-Prés a short distance away. Notre-Dame is the last great galleried church building and one of the first with flying buttresses. Its successive architects have for the most part kept to the original plan, while at the same time not being afraid to innovate, sometimes in ways which set subsequent standards.

The chancel was built under Louis VII and consecrated in 1182 in the reign of Philippe Auguste. It is still enclosed with sturdy cylindrical columns as near to the Romanesque as to Early Gothic, but the double ambulatory and the tracery reinforcing the wide windows set new trends. Furthermore, there is still a gallery, but, for extra support, there are flying buttresses as used a few years previously at St-Germer-de-Fly. Here, for the first time, they are extended by a spout in order to throw rainwater clear of the foundations, thereby forming the first gargoyles.

By 1210, the first bays of the nave had been built, together with the seatings for the west front; within 10 years the nave was completed, the 28 statues of the Kings' Gallery were in place, and by 1225 the west front rose as high as the great rose window. In 1245 the bulk of the work was complete and St Louis held a ceremony for the knighting of his son and also placed the Crown of Thorns in the cathedral until the Sainte-Chapelle was ready to receive it. In 1250 the twin towers were finished and the nave provided with side-chapels to consolidate the whole structure.

In 1430, the cathedral was the setting for the coronation of the young Henry VI of England as King of France; in 1455, a ceremony was conducted to rehabilitate Joan of Arc; in 1558, Mary Stuart was crowned here on becoming Queen of France by her marriage to François II and, in 1572, the Huguenot Henri IV waited at the door as his bride, Marguerite of Valois stood alone in the chancel; in 1594 the king converted to the Catholic faith.

The great building was not spared mutilations of various kinds; in 1699 the choir-screen was demolished, and later some of the original stained glass was removed to let in more light and the central portal demolished (18C) to allow processions to move more freely. During the Revolution statues were destroyed and the cathedral declared a Temple of Reason. It was in a much-dilapidated building that Napoleon Bonaparte crowned himself Emperor and the King of Rome was baptized. In 1831, public opinion was alerted by Hugo's novel *Notre-Dame de Paris* to the state of the building, and in 1841 Louis-Philippe charged Viollet-le-Duc with its restoration. In the space of 24 years, the great architect-archeologist had completed his work in accordance with his own, idealised vision of the Gothic style; though open to criticism, it needs to be seen in the context of the wholesale demolition of the medieval Île-de-la-Cité and its replacement with administrative buildings.

Exterior – The cathedral square is the point from which the distances along the great highways – *routes nationales* – radiating from Paris are measured. It was the scene, in 1452, of a performance of one of the long mystery plays of the time, *The True Mystery of the Passion*, by Arnoul Greban; its 34 000 lines took three days to recite.

In the belfry of the south tower hangs Emmanuel, the famous bell weighing 13 tonnes. Its pure tone is said to be due to the gold and silver jewellery thrown by the ladies of Paris into the molten bronze on the occasion of the bell's re-

West front of Notre-Dame

casting in the 17C. Above the Kings' Gallery is the great rose window, still with its medieval glass. An enterprise of considerable daring – it was the largest such window of its time – its design is so accomplished that it shows no sign of distortion after 700 years and has often been imitated.

The South Portal, dedicated to St-Anne, has the cathedral's oldest statues and, at the apex of the tympanum, a somewhat stiff Virgin in Majesty, still very much in the Romanesque tradition. The strapwork of the doors is particularly fine.

The Portal of the Last Judgement, in the centre, depicts Christ in Majesty and, in the archivolts, the Heavenly Kingdom.

To the north is the Portal to the Virgin, based on the one at Senlis and divided into horizontal registers; it was a model to sculptors throughout the Middle Ages. The magnificent Cloister Portal (north transept) is 30 years later than the west front portals; with its richly carved gables and smiling figure of the Virgin – the only one of the original large sculptures to have survived – it demonstrates clearly how far the art of sculpture had advanced over the period.

Further east is the Red Door, showing the Coronation of the Virgin.

At the beginning of the 14C, the bold array of flying buttresses was sent soaring over ambulatory and galleries to hold in place the high vaults of the east end. The South Portal was begun in 1258 by Jean de Chelles; it depicts the Martyrdom of St Stephen; few sculpted scenes had ever been so full of feeling.

Interior – The boldness of its layout and the noble uplift of its lines testify to the pre-eminence of the French school of architecture in the early 13C. The addition of side-chapels in the 13C and 14C by guilds and corporations widened the building and made it necessary to extend the transepts. Jean de Chelles took advantage of the opportunity and of the experience gained at the Sainte-Chapelle to construct rose-windows of daring dimensions but with exceptionally delicate tracery above a pierced triforium. The rose-window in the north transept has particularly fine stained glass of a deep blueish-mauve. Finally, at the entrance to the chancel, on the right, is a Virgin and Child of the 14C, depicted with even greater nobility and idealism than the equivalent in the Cloister Portal, exemplifying the degree to which sculpture had evolved over the course of a hundred years.

★★★ **Sainte-Chapelle** ⊙ – 11 page 31 – J14. Only 80 years separate this definitive masterpiece of the High Gothic from the Transitional Gothic of Notre-Dame, but the difference is striking; in the lightness and clarity of its structure, the Sainte-Chapelle exceeds in ambition even the achievements of the Lanceolate style of Chartres and Amiens, pushing Gothic logic to its limits. The relatively modest dimensions of the building allowed its architect, Pierre de Montreuil, to support it by means of conventional buttresses capped by pinnacles.

The chapel was built on the orders of St Louis to house the recently acquired relics of the Passion within the precincts of the royal palace; it was completed in the record time of thirty-three months. Like other palatine chapels (Laon, Meaux), it is built on two storeys, the upper for the monarch, the lower for the staff of the palace.

Stained glass – The upper chapel resembles a shrine with walls made almost entirely of stained glass covering a total area of 618m² – 6 672sq ft; 1 134 differ-

Stained glass medallion in the Sainte-Chapelle

ent scenes are depicted, of which 720 are made of original glass. The windows rise to a height of 15m – nearly 50ft. By 1240, the stained glass at Chartres had been completed, and the king was thus able to call on the master-craftsmen who had worked on them to come to Paris; this explains the similarity between the glass of cathedral and chapel in terms of the scenes shown and the luminous colour which eclipses the simplicity of the design.

The theme is Christ's Passion, including its foretelling by the Prophets and by John the Baptist, together with the episodes which lead up to it. The original rose window is shown in a scene from the *Très Riches Heures du Duc de Berry*; the present rose window is a product of the Flamboyant Gothic, ordered by Charles VII, and showing the Apocalypse of St John. It is characteristic of its age in the design of its tracery and in the subtle variations of colour which had replaced the earlier method of juxtaposing a great number of small coloured panes. The glass of the Sainte-Chapelle has been much imitated, even in architecturally inappropriate situations.

★★ **Église de St-Germain-des-Prés** – 11 page 31 – J13. This most venerable of the city's churches reveals more than visual delights to those who know something of the history of its ancient stones. With the exception of Clovis, the Merovingian kings were buried here. The church was subsequently destroyed by the Normans, but restored in the course of the 10C and 11C. Understandably, the tower rising above the west front has a fortress-like character. Around 1160, the nave was enlarged and the chancel rebuilt in the new Gothic style. "Improvements" followed in the 17C (triforium and chancel windows) and in 1822 a somewhat over-zealous restoration took place.

But the church's years of glory were between 1631 and 1789, when the austere Congregation of St Maur made it a centre of learning and spirituality; the monks studied ancient inscriptions (epigraphy) and writing (paleography), the Church Fathers (Patristics), archaeology, cartography... Their library was confiscated at the time of the French Revolution.

★★ **Église St-Séverin-St-Nicolas** – 11 page 43 – K14. This much-loved Latin Quarter Church has features from a number of architectural styles. The lower part of the portal and the first three bays of the nave are High Gothic, while much of the rest of the building was remodelled in Flamboyant style (upper part of the tower, the remainder of the nave, the secondary aisle, the highly-compartmental-ised vaulting of the chancel and the famous spiral pillar in the ambulatory). In the 18C, the pillars in the chancel were clad in wood and marble.

★★ **Église St-Eustache** – 11 page 31 – H14. This was once the richest church in Paris, centre of the parish which included the areas around the Palais-Royal and the Halles market; its layout was modelled on that of Notre-Dame when building began in 1532. But St-Eustache took over a hundred years to complete; tastes changed, and the Gothic skeleton of the great building is fleshed out with Renaissance finishes and detail.

The Flamboyant style is evident in the three-storeyed interior elevation, in the vaulting of the choir, crossing and nave, in the lofty side aisles and in the flying buttresses. The Renaissance is exemplified in the Corinthian columns and in the return to the use of semicircular arches, and classicism in P. de Champaigne's choir windows and in Colbert's tomb, designed by Le Brun in collaboration with Coysevox and Tuby. In the St-Joseph Chapel is the English sculptor Raymond Mason's colourful commemoration of the fruit and vegetable market's move out of Paris in 1969.

★★ **Église Notre-Dame-du-Val-de-Grâce** – 11 page 43 – M14. After many childless years, Anne of Austria commissioned François Mansart to design a magnificent church in thanksgiving for the birth of Louis XIV in 1638. The work was completed by Lemercier and Le Muet. The church recalls the Renaissance architecture of Rome; the dome, rising above the two-tier west front with its double triangular pediment, is particularly ornate and obviously inspired by St Peter's. Inside, the spirit of the Baroque prevails; there is polychrome paving, highly-sculptured vaulting over the nave, massive crossing pillars and a monumental baldachin with six wreathed columns. The **cupola**★★ was decorated by Mignard with a fresco featuring 200 figures.

Urban Design

Since the sweeping away of much of medieval Paris in the 19C, three central districts have come to typify particular stages in the city's evolution.

★★★ **The Marais** – 11 pages 32 – H16, J16 and 33 – H17, J17. Renaissance, Louis XIII and Louis XIV. Charles V's move to the Hôtel St-Paul in the Marais district in the 14C signalled the incorporation of a suburban area into Paris. The area soon became fashionable, and Rue St-Antoine the city's finest street. It was here that that characteristic French town house, the *hôtel*, took on its definitive form with the collaboration of the finest architects and artists; it became the setting for that other distinctive feature of Parisian life, the literary or philosophical salon.

Place des Vosges

The **Hôtel Lamoignon**★★ of 1584 is a typical example of a mansion in the Henri III style. For the first time in Paris, its architect, Jean-Baptiste Androuet Du Cerceau, used the Giant Order with its flattened pilasters, Corinthian capitals and sculpted string-course.

The Henri IV style makes its appearance in the **Place des Vosges**★★★ designed by Louis Métezeau and completed in 1612. The 36 houses retain their original symmetrical appearance with arcades, two storeys with alternate brick and stone facings and steeply-pitched slate roofs pierced with dormer windows. The King's Pavilion (Pavillon du Roi) is sited at the southern end of the square, balanced by the Queen's Pavilion (Pavillon de la Reine) at the sunnier northern end.

Louis XIII's reign heralds the classical style. In 1624, Jean Androuet Du Cerceau built the **Hôtel de Béthune-Sully**★ with a gateway framed between massive pavilions and a main courtyard with triangular and curved pediments complemented by the scrolled dormer windows; beyond is an exquisite inner courtyard. The early Louis XIV style is seen in Mansart's **Hôtel Guénégaud**★★ of 1648, with its plain harmonious lines, majestic staircase, and small formal garden one of the finest houses of the Marais, in Le Pautre's **Hôtel de Beauvais**★ with its curved balcony on brackets and its ingenious internal layout, in the **Hôtel Carnavalet**★, a Renaissance house rebuilt by Mansart in 1655, and in Cottard's **Hôtel Amelot-de-Bisseuil**★ of somewhat theatrical design with its cornice and curved pediment decorated with allegorical figures.

The later Louis XIV style features in two adjoining *hôtels* built by Delamair; the **Hôtel de Rohan**★★ with its wonderful sculpture of the *Horses of Apollo* by Robert Le Lorrain, and the **Hôtel de Soubise**★★ with its horseshoe-shaped courtyard and double colonnade. They are characterised by their raised ground floors, massive windows, roof balustrades and by the sculpture of their projecting central sections.

★★★ **From the Tuileries to the Arc de Triomphe** (La Voie Triomphale) – 11 pages 31, 30, 29, 17 – H13, H12, G10, G11, F9, F8. A great axis leading from the courtyard of the Louvre to St Germain had been planned by Colbert, but today's "Triumphal Way" was laid out under Louis XVI, Napoleon III and during the years of the Third Republic.

★★ **Arc de Triomphe du Carrousel** – This delightful pastiche of a Roman arch is decorated with statues of Napoleonic military men in full uniform. An observer standing in the Place du Carrousel commands an extraordinary perspective which runs from the Louvre, through the arch, to the obelisk in the Place de la Concorde, then onward and upward to the Grande Arche at the Défense.

★ **Jardin des Tuileries** – The gardens were first laid out in the 1560s by Catherine de' Medici in the Italian style. A century later, they were remodelled by Le Nôtre, who here created the archetypal French garden, a formal setting for the elegant pleasures of outdoor life. The Riverside Terrace became the playground of royal princes and of the sons of the two Napoleons, then of all the children of Paris.

★★ **Place de la Concorde** – *Page 233*.

★★★ **Champs-Élysées** – In 1667, Le Nôtre extended the axis from the Tuileries to a new focal point, the Rond-Point, which he laid out himself. The avenue was then a service road for the houses facing the Rue du Faubourg-St-Honoré, but very soon refreshment stalls were set up and crowds flocked to the area. In 1724, the Duke of Antin planted rows of elms to extend the "Elysian Fields" up to the Étoile. In 1729, street lanterns lit the evening scene. 48 years on, and the avenue had descended the gentle slope beyond the Étoile to reach the Seine at the Neuilly Bridge. The buildings lining it included taverns and wine-shops, the later haunt of Robespierre and his friends. Finally, in 1836, the **Arc de Triomphe**★★★ *(p 233)* was completed by Louis-Philippe.

The Champs-Élysées became fashionable during the reign of Louis-Napoléon, when high society flocked to the restaurants (like Ledoyen's), to the theatres (like the Folies Marigny and the Bouffes d'Été where Offenbach's operettas were performed), or to receptions in the grand houses (like no 25, today occupied by the Travellers' Club, with its doors of bronze and onyx staircase).

The avenue has undergone much change since 1914. Its character nowadays is determined by its luxury shops, expensive cafes, and motor showrooms; but it nevertheless remains the capital's rallying point at times of high national emotion (the Liberation, 30 May 1968, the funeral of De Gaulle in 1970 and annually on July 14).

★★ **La Défense** – 11 pages 65, 66. An outstanding architectural achievement, La Défense has nothing in common with the traditional business districts found in most city centres. A 1 200 m – 4 000 ft terraced podium, pleasantly punctuated with gardens, fountains, sculptures and shaded spots, runs from the Seine up to La Grande Arche. It is lined with an impressive ensemble of huge towers (Fiat Tower: 178 m – 583 ft) that compose a dazzling tableau of radiant light.

★★ **La Grande Arche** ⊙ – The Danish architect Johan Otto von Spreckelsen designed this vast hollow cube which stands at the end of the esplanade and houses private firms as well as several ministries. Each side of the cube is 110 m – 360 ft long. Towering 100 m – 328 ft above the esplanade, the 1 ha (2.4 acres) terrace-roof is partly taken up by temporary exhibition rooms. From the belvedere visitors will also be able to admire Paris ans its suburbs. At the foot of the arch lies the Palais de la Défence (**CNIT**): it was the first to be built (1958) and has recently been "rejuvenated". Now it is an important business centre focusing on three main areas of activity: technology, world trade and corporate communication.

Exterior decoration – La Défense is also noted for its many public sculptures, which turn the district into an informal, open-air museum: *Two Figures* by Miro, Calder's *Red Stabile*, his very last work, Julio Silva's *Lady Moon*, Agam's *Fountain*, Moretti's *Monster*, Attila's *Cloud Sculptor*, Leygues' *Corollas of the Day*, Philoloas' *Mechanical Bird*, Derbré's *Earth*, etc. The statue representing the Defense of Paris, belonging to a different tradition altogether, has been reinstated on its original site.

PARIS THE POLITICAL CAPITAL

Palais de l'Élysée – 11 page 17 – F10. The palace has been the Paris residence of the President of France since 1873. It was built in 1718 by Henri de La Tour d'Auvergne and was once the property of the Marquise de Pompadour. During the Revolution it housed a public dance-hall, a gaming saloon, and a picture gallery. In Napoleon's time, Marie-Louise had a boudoir here in a pavilion overlooking the Rue de l'Élysée, and the young King of Rome a set of rooms. It was here, on 22 June 1815, that the Emperor signed his second act of abdication.

The architectural treatment of the palace is a reminder of the taste for comfort which accompanied the revival of court and society life during the period of the Régence.

Hôtel Matignon – 11 page 30 – J11. Like the Élysée, this attractive town house of 1721 exemplifies the early 18C's quest for architectural refinement; it has been the residence of the French Prime Minister since 1958. Between 1808 and 1811 it belonged to the statesman Talleyrand, whose lavish receptions here enjoyed great renown. Its carriage-door (*porte-cochère*) is flanked by Ionic columns and the balconies of its projecting central section are adorned with trophies.

★ **Palais Bourbon** – 11 page 30 – H11. The palace has been the seat of the Lower House of France's parliament, the Assemblée Nationale, for more than 150 years. The role of the Assembly, which consists of directly-elected deputies, is to examine and where necessary, amend, all draft legislation. The vote must be carried on a text after its wording has been approved by both Assembly and Senate.

The palace was built in 1722; during the Revolution, it was the seat of the Council of Five Hundred. The decorative treatment of the façade (1804) which faces the Place de la Concorde was decided upon by Napoleon. The Antique-style south façade giving on to the courtyard has balconies, a roof balustrade and a portico decorated with an allegorical pediment by Cortot.

Palais du Luxembourg

★★ **Palais du Luxembourg** – 11 page 43 – K13. This is the seat of the Senate, the French Upper House, which is composed of 283 members chosen by an electoral college consisting of deputies, departmental and municipal councillors. They are elected for a period of 9 years, but a staggered system ensures that a third of them are changed every three years. The president of the Senate exercises the functions of Head of State if the Presidency falls vacant.

In 1615, the Tuileries Palace, begun by Catherine de' Medici, had been a-building for half a century. The Regent, Marie de' Medici, had come to dislike the Louvre since the death of her husband the king; she now wished to emulate her cousin Catherine and have a palace of her own which would remind her of the Pitti Palace in Florence. The work was given to Salomon de Brosse. The exterior has ringed columns and rusticated stonework of very Florentine character. The splendid courtyard displays the architect's command of the classical repertory with a Doric ground floor with semi-circular window-openings, columns and curved pediments in the central section, portals with columns, an upper storey emphasized with balconies and roof balustrades on the wings. The south façade has a fine central section with a quadrangular dome, a massive pediment, and garden terraces.

In 1625, Marie de' Medici decorated her gallery with huge paintings (now in the Louvre) ordered three years previously from Rubens. They were intended to glorify her person and her reign; the sense of fleeting colour and movement was a new experience in France.

★ **Hôtel de Ville** – 11 page 32 – J15. It is from here that central Paris is governed. Municipal government was introduced in the 13C, under the direction of leading members of the powerful watermen's guild appointed by Louis IX. The council was headed by a merchant provost, one of whom was Étienne Marcel, "champion of French unity", who openly challenged royal power *(p 219)*.

The place has long been the epicentre of uprising and revolt. Throughout the French Revolution it was in the hands of the Commune and in 1848, it was the seat of the Provisional Government. The Republic was proclaimed from here in 1870, and, on 24 March 1871, the Communards burnt it down. It was rebuilt from 1874; the central section of the main façade is a reproduction of Il Boccadoro's design for François I; the grand staircase is based on a project of Philibert Delorme's, and the decoration gives a good idea of official taste under the Third Republic.

PARIS THE INTELLECTUAL AND ARTISTIC CAPITAL

Intellectual life

The city as a whole functions as the capital of the country's intellectual life; there is nevertheless a particular concentration on the Left Bank, in the Fifth and Sixth arrondissements. On the slopes of Mount Ste-Geneviève and the surrounding area are concentrated many of the capital's most venerable institutions, around them the ebb and flow of a perpetually youthful tide, the students and other young people who make up the population of the "Latin" Quarter (so-called because Latin was the language of instruction right up to the French Revolution). Here, in the University and other great institutions of learning, the dogmas of Church and State have been continuously challenged for seven centuries, in lecture-hall and library, and sometimes on the street.

The area abounds in publishing houses, many of them highly specialised (fine art, science, languages, philosophy..), in bookshops, purveyors of scientific equipment, and of course in terrace cafés, places in which to refashion the world as well as to have a drink; they include the Flore, the Deux-Magots and Procope, and, in Montparnasse, the Dôme, La Coupole, La Closerie des Lilas...

★★ **Institut de France** – 11 page 31 – J13. The Institute originated as the College of Four Nations founded by Mazarin for scholars from the provinces incorporated into France during his ministry (Piedmont, Alsace, Artois and Roussillon). Dating from 1662, its building was designed by Le Vau and stands on the far side of the river from the Louvre, on the site of the Nesle Tower which had formed part of Philippe Auguste's ring of fortifications. It is famous for its cupola, its semi-circular flanking buildings and the tomb of Mazarin in the vestibule.

The Institute is made up of five academies:

The **Académie Française**, the most prestigious of all. Founded in 1635 by Richelieu, its membership is limited to 40. Its meetings are held beneath the oval cupola of the former chapel. Its members, the "Immortals", devote themselves to upholding the quality of the French language and enshrining it in the great *Dictionnaire de la langue française*, the country's standard dictionary.

The **Académie des Beaux-Arts** dates from 1816. It has 50 members, divided into sections representing painting, sculpture, architecture, engraving and music.

The **Académie des Inscriptions et Belles Lettres** was founded by Colbert in 1663. It deals with literary history and maintains an archive for original documents.

The **Académie des Sciences**, also founded by Colbert, in 1666, has 66 members involved in astronomy, mathematics, medecine, natural science and research.

The **Académie des Sciences morales et politiques** was founded by the Convention in 1795. It has 40 members and is concerned with philosophy, ethics, law, geography and history.

Collège de France – 11 page 43 – K14. Its origins can be traced to six "King's Readers", and it was founded in 1529 by François I at Guillaume Budé's request under the name of the College of Three Languages (Latin, Greek, Hebrew) in order to combat the narrow scholasticism of the Sorbonne. The present buildings date from the time of Louis XIII when the subjects taught were increasing in number; the king renamed it the Royal College of France (Collège Royal de France). Chalgrin supervised a major reconstruction in 1778. Among the great figures of the era of individual research who were active here were Gassendi, Picard and Roberval, and Claude Bernard, who worked in the laboratories for 30 years. It was here, in 1948, that Frédéric Joliot-Curie formulated the laws controlling the process of nuclear fission and built a cyclotron to test his theories. The college is not subject to administrative constraints dictated by set courses of study and does not award any qualifications. No charge is made for its courses, which are given by leading authorities and often attended by other experts in the particular field.

Sorbonne – 11 page 43 – K14. This is the most illustrious of all the country's universities. It is the successor to the theological college founded in 1253 by Robert de Sorbon for 16 poor scholars. The first printing press in France was installed here by Louis XI in 1469. For many years, the university's tribunal constituted the highest ecclesiastical authority after that of the Pope. During his period as Rector, Cardinal Richelieu, faced with crumbling university buildings, was responsible for much reconstruction, including that of the church. Rebuilt and extended at the end of the 19C, the Sorbonne is the seat of the Paris-III and Paris-IV Universities.

The **Sorbonne Church**★, built by Lemercier from 1635 on, is a fine example of Jesuit architecture; the façade overlooking the courtyard is remarkable for its Corinthian columns and its dome. Inside is **Richelieu's tomb**★ (1694) by Girardon.

Higher education and research – The prestige of French universities (17 Nobel Prizes between 1901-39) is largely due to the state's encouragement of innovation. Paris alone has 13 universities (five of them, plus the five Technical Universities, in the suburbs) as well as a number of teaching hospitals of equivalent status.

Other institutes of higher education include the Grandes Écoles; these either prepare a student for an advanced course or deliver it themselves. They include the École Normale Supérieure (teacher training), the École Polytechnique (engineering), Ecole des Ponts et Chaussées (civil engineering), Ecole des Mines (mining engineering)... Places are limited, and subject to fierce competition. Many of these institutions have recently been resited in the outskirts of Paris or in the provinces.

The National Centre for Scientific Research (Centre National de Recherche Scientifique), set up in 1941, promotes scientific progress by supporting research of all kinds.

Libraries – Paris has several hundred institutional libraries and 62 municipal ones. Apart from the National Library, the Mazarin Library and the Ste-Geneviève Library, the most popular are those in the Arsenal, the Pompidou Centre (BPI), the Museum of Decorative Arts (Musée des Arts Décoratifs) and the National Technical Museum (Conservatoire National des Arts et Métiers).

The capital of entertainment and culture

This chapter gives an outline of the city's wide range of entertainment and cultural attractions. Full information about what is on at any one time is contained in a number of specialised publications like *L'Officiel des Spectacles*, *Une Semaine à Paris* and *Pariscope*, or in the daily press.

The monthly booklet "**Paris Selection**", edited by the Paris Tourist Office, lists the different exhibitions, shows and other events in the capital.

Entertainment – Paris may be said to be one huge "living stage" as it boasts a total of 100 **theatres** and other venues devoted to the performing arts, representing altogether a seating capacity of 56 000. Most of these are located near the Opéra and the Madeleine but from Montmartre to Montparnasse, from the Bastille to the Latin Quarter and from Boulevard Haussmann to the Porte Maillot, state-funded theatres (Opéra Garnier, Opéra Bastille, Comédie Française, Odéon, Chaillot, La Colline) are to be found side by side with local and private theatres, singing cabarets and *cafés-théâtres*. Not to mention television studios and the large auditoriums where radio and TV programmes are regularly recorded in public.

Cinemas, more than 400 in number, are to be found in every part of the city, with particular concentrations in the same areas as the theatres and on the Champs-Élysées.

Music-hall, variety shows and **reviews** can be enjoyed at such places as the Alcazar de Paris, the Crazy Horse, the Lido, the Paradis Latin, the Casino de Paris, the Folies Bergère and the Moulin Rouge.

As well as the Opéra Garnier, the Opéra-Bastille and the Comic Opera (Opéra-Comique), there are a number of **concert halls** with resident orchestras like the Orchestre de Paris at the Salle Pleyel, the Ensemble Orchestral de Paris at the Salle Gaveau and the orchestras of the French Radio at the Maison de Radio-France. In addition there are many other halls in which full-scale performances are put on (Théâtre des Champs-Élysées, Châtelet, Salle Cortot, Espace Wagram, Maison de la Chimie, Palais des Sports, Palais Omnisports de Bercy, Palais des Congrès, Théâtre de la Ville, Zénith...).

Besides this there are nightclubs, cabarets, dens where *chansonniers* can be heard, *café-theatres*, television shows open to the public, concerts and recitals in churches, circuses...

Exhibitions – The city has a total of 87 museums and over one hundred art galleries. In addition, there are around 30 places where temporary exhibitions are held and a whole array of studios (particularly around the Rue St-Honoré, Avenue Matignon and the Rue de la Seine), as well as libraries and other institutions. Between them, they offer the visitor a continuously changing view of past and present artistic achievement and aspiration. The most famous include the Grand Palais, the Palais de Tokyo, the Pavillon des Arts, the Petit Palais, the Pompidou Centre and the Grande Halle de la Villette.

Tourist Paris – Certain parts of the city have come to be identified in the visitor's mind with the very idea of Paris itself.

The Sacré-Cœur by S Valadon

★★ **Montmartre** – The "Martyrs' Mound" was a real village before becoming the haunt of artists and Bohemians in the late 19C, and it still has something of the picturesque quality of a village in its steep and narrow lanes and precipitous stairways. The "Butte", or mound, rises abruptly from the city's sea of roofs; at its centre is the **Place du Tertre★★** with the former town hall at no 3, still enjoying some semblance of local life, at least in the morning; by the afternoon, tourism has taken over, and the "art market" is in full swing.

Not far away from all this activity rises the exotic outline of the **Sacré-Cœur Basilica★★**, a place of perpetual pilgrimage. From here, particularly from the gallery of the dome, there is an incomparable **panorama★★★** over the whole metropolitan area.

★★ **Champs-Élysées** – *Page 239.*

★★ **Tour Eiffel** – *Page 234.*

★★ **Musée du Louvre** – One of the world's great museums.

★★ **Cathédral Notre-Dame** – *Page 235.*

★★ **The Marais** – *Page 238.*

★★ **St-Germain-des-Prés area** – Antique dealers, literary cafés, the night life of side streets... all combine to make the reputation of this former centre of international Bohemian life.

★★ **Centre Georges-Pompidou** – The Centre seeks to demonstrate that there is a close correlation between art and daily activities. For both the specialists and the general public, this multi-purpose cultural centre offers an astonishing variety of activities and modern communication techniques encouraging curiosity and participation. The Centre includes four departments; the **Bibliothèque Publique d'Information** (BPI), offering a wide variety of French and foreign books, slides, films, periodicals, reference catalogues..., the **Centre de Création Industrielle** (CCI), demonstrating the relationship between individuals and spaces, objects and signs through architecture, urbanism, industrial design and visual communication; the **Institut de Recherche et Coordination Acoustique/Musique** (IRCAM), bringing together musicians, composers and scientists for the purpose of sound experimentation; and the **Musée National d'Art Modern** (MNAM), presenting collections of paintings, sculptures and drawings from 1905 to the present time.

★★ **Latin Quarter** – With its core on Mount Ste-Geneviève, this home of students and the young of all nationalities extends north to the St-Séverin and Maubert areas, south to the Rue Mouffetard and eastwards to the Jardin des Plantes.

★★ **La Défense area** – *Page 239.*

★★ **Palais de Chaillot** – *Page 235.*

La Géode at La Villette

★★ **La Villette** – The **Parc**★★ de la Villette is the largest architectural ensemble to be found within the city boundaries. The 55ha – 135 acre site houses an impressive urban complex featuring the City of Science and Industry and its cinema La Géode, the Zenith concert hall, the Paris-Villette Theatre, La Grande Halle and the Cité de la Musique.

★★★ **Cité des Sciences et de l'Industrie** – Built in response to the growing need of both children and adults to understand the scientific and industrial world, this living museum encourages visitors to investigate, learn and have fun through a wide range of edifying scenarios.

★★★ **La Géode** ⊘ – This spherical cinema and its circular screen (diameter: 36m – 118ft), which rests on a sheet of water, is a remarkable technical achievement, whose bold conception and perfect execution is the work of the engineer Chamayou.

THE MUSEUMS OF PARIS:
A SELECTION FROM THEIR TREASURES

★★★ Musée du Louvre ⊘

When the Grand Louvre was opened to the public in 1994, the different collections were divided into three large departments, **Sully**, **Denon** and **Richelieu** which are located in the two wings and around the Cour Carrée.

SULLY:

History of the Louvre *Entresol*
Medieval Louvre *Entresol*
Oriental Antiquities (Levantine Art) *Ground floor*
Greek Antiquities (Salle des Caryatides, Hellenistic Period) *Ground floor*
Egyptian Antiquities *Ground and 1st floor*
Greek Antiquities (Bronzes) *1st floor*
Objets d'art (Restoration and 18C) *1st floor*
French-Painting (17C and 19C) 2nd floor
Beistegui Collection *2nd floor*

DENON:

Italian Sculpture *Entresol and ground floor*
Northern Schools; Sculpture *Entresol and ground floor*
Etruscan Antiquites *Ground floor*
Roman and Palaeo-Christian Antiquities *Ground floor*
Greek antiquities *Ground and 1st floors*
Objets d'art (Galerie d'Apollon, Crown Jewels) *1st floor*
Large Format 18C French Painting *1st floor*
Italian Painting *1st floor*
Spanish Painting *1st floor*

RICHELIEU:

Oriental Antiquities

Statues of Gudea and Ur-Ningirsu - Mesopotamia: *c*2150BC
Code of Hammurabi - Babylon: *c*1750BC
Frieze of the Archers from Darius' palace: Susa 6C BC
Low-reliefs from Nineveh and Khorsabad - Assyria: 7C BC
Vase from Amathus - Cyprus: early 5C BC

Egyptian Antiquities

Funerary chapel of Akhout-Hetep - Fifth Dynasty
Gebel-el-Arak knife - Egypt: end of prehistoric times
Sphinx of the Crypt - Egypt: end of the Old Kingdom
Seated Scribe from Sakkara - Egypt: Fifth Dynasty
Fragments from the Coptic monastery of Bawit - 5C
Jewellery of Rameses II - middle of second millenium

Classical Antiquities

Hera of Samos - Greece: archaic period
Apollo of Piombino - Greece: archaic period
Parthenon fragments - Greece: Classical period
Venus de Milo - Greece: Hellenistic period
Etruscan terracotta sarcophagus from Cerveteri, Italy: 6C BC
Winged Victory of Samothrace - Greece; Hellenistic period

Sculpture

Limewood Madonna from the Church of the Antonites, Isenheim - late 15C
Diana the Huntress (fountain) from Anet Château - French Renaissance
The Three Graces (funerary monument for Henri II) by Germain Pilon
The Four Evangelists by Jean Goujon
Madonna and Child (terracotta) by Donatello - Florence *c*1450
Marble bust of Voltaire by Houdon: 1778
The Slaves by Michaelangelo - Florence: early 16C

Painting

Malouel's circular Pietà - Dijon: early 15C
St Denis Altarpiece by Henri Bellechose - Dijon 15C
Avignon Pietà by Enguerrand Quarton - *c*1440
Portrait of François I by Jean Clouet - Loire Valley School
St Thomas by La Tour - 17C
The Magistrates of Paris by Philippe de Champaigne: 17C
Gilles by Watteau - 18C
Portrait of Mme Récamier and The Coronation of Napoleon by David
The Turkish Bath and Grande Odalisque by Ingres
Scenes of the Massacres of Chios by Delacroix - 1824
Raft of the Medusa by Géricault - 1819
Virgin with Angels by Cimabue - Florence: 13C
Coronation of the Virgin by Fra Angelico - Florence: 15C
The Gioconda (Mona Lisa) by Leonardo da Vinci - Florence; early 16C
The Wedding at Cana by Veronese - Venice: 16C
Death of the Virgin by Caravaggio - Naples; early 17C
Madonna with Chancellor Rolin by Van Eyck - Dijon; 15C
Charles I of England by Van Dyck - England 17C
Allegorical paintings of the Life of Marie de' Medici by Rubens
Pilgrims at Emmaus by Rembrandt

Objets d'art

The Regent Diamond and Crown Jewels of France
Ivory figure of the Virgin Mary from the Sainte-Chapelle, Paris: middle of the 13C
The Hunts of Maximilian tapestries - Brussels: 1537
The study of the Elector of Bavaria by Boulle - early 18C
Clock in ebony case inlaid with tortoiseshell by Boulle - early 18C
Monkey commode (gilded bronze) by Charles Cressent - 1740
The Loves of the Gods tapestries - Gobelins; middle 18C
Writing-desk, table and commode in the Oeben room - middle 18C
Medici vase (Sèvres porcelain, bronzes by Thomire)

★★★ Musée d'Orsay ⊙

The Spring by Ingres
Burial at Ornans by Courbet – 1849
Gleaners and Angelus by Jean-François Millet
Déjeuner sur l'herbe and Olympia by Manet
The Dance by Jean-Baptiste Carpeaux – 1869
L'Estaque from Marseilles Bay by Cézanne – 1878
Blue Dancers by Degas
The church at Auvers-sur-Oise and Self-Portrait by Van Gogh
The Circus by Seurat
Arearea Pranks (Women of Tahiti) by Gauguin – 1892
Jane Avril Dancing by Toulouse-Lautrec
Balzac by Rodin – 1897
The Mediterranean by Maillol – 1902
Pendant and chain by René Lalique
Hercules the Archer in bronze by Antoine Bourdelle – 1909
Women Bathing by Renoir – 1918

★★★ Musée national d'art moderne (Centre Georges-Pompidou) ⊙

The Street Bedecked with Bunting by Dufy – Fauvism: early 20C
Table by Braque – Cubism: 1911
Nudes by Matisse – beginnings of abstraction: 1916
Harlequin by Picasso – mature Cubism: 1923
Spectral Cow by Dali – beginnings of hyper-realism: 1928
Seal by Brancusi – Surrealism in sculpture: 1935

★★ Hôtel de Cluny (Musée du Moyen-Âge) ⊙

Ivory casket – Constantinople: early 11C
Gilt altar-front made for Henri II – Basle cathedral: 11C
29 medallions from the stained glass of the Sainte-Chapelle – Paris: 13C
Limoges reliquaries in *champlevé* enamel – 13C
Golden rose given by Pope Clement V to the Prince-Bishop of Basle: early 14C
Eagle of St John (brass lectern) – Tournai cathedral: 1383
Life of St Stephen tapestry – Arras: middle 15C
Altarpiece from Limburg in painted and gilded wood – late 15C
Lady with the Unicorn tapestries – Brussels: late 15C
Mary Magdalen (probable likeness of Mary of Burgundy) – Flanders

★★ Musée de l'Orangerie ⊙

Portrait of Mme Cézanne by Cézanne
Woman Bathing and The Letter-Writer by Renoir
Nude on red background by Picasso – 1906
Pere Junier's Cart by Douanier Rousseau – 1908
Berlioz' House and Clignancourt Church by Utrillo
Antonia by Modigliani
The Three Sisters by Matisse
The Little Pastry-cook and Garçon d'étage by Soutine – 1922
Harlequin with Guitar and Blond Model by Derain

★★★ Musée de l'Armée (Hôtel des Invalides) ⊙

Seussenhofer's suit of armour for François I – 1539
The cannon-ball which killed Marshal Turenne in 1675
Model of the city of Perpignan (one of a series ordered by Vauban in 1696)
Napoleon's flag of farewell flown at Fontainebleau on 20 April 1814
The room where Napoleon died on St Helena (reconstruction)
Renault tank
The Armistice Bugle (which sounded the cease-fire at 9pm on 7 November 1918)

★★★ Cité des Sciences et de l'Industrie (la Villette) ⊙

La Nautile (exploded model of research submarine)
Superphénix (fast-breeder reactor)
Ariane rocket (upper stage)

★★ Palais de la Découverte ⊙

Lunakhod (Soviet moon buggy) – 12 November 1970
Fragment of moon-rock – Apollo Mission XVII: 1972
The number Pi and the 703 prime numbers of the 16 000 000 decimals calculated
Model of the Saturn V rocket
Astronomical camera for use in space

★★ Conservatoire national des Arts et Métiers (Musée des Techniques) ⊙

Microscope belonging to the Duke of Chaulnes – middle 18C
Cugnot's steam-carriage of 1771
Marie-Antoinette's automaton "Dulcimer-Player" – 1784

Jaquard loom
Thimonnier's sewing-machine – 1825
L'Obéissante automobile by Amédée Bollée Snr – Le Mans: 1873
The Lumière brothers' cinematographic apparatus – 1895
Transmitting station from the Eiffel Tower
Blériot's No 9 aeroplane (in which he made the first cross-Channel flight)

THE COMMERCIAL CAPITAL

Greater Paris is the industrial and commercial capital of France, the country's undisputed centre of economic activity. The distribution and consumption of energy, food, and of products of all kinds take place on a vast scale, and are accompanied by geographical specialisation; shopping particularly is marked by a high degree of concentration in certain areas, particularly where luxury goods are concerned. The range of goods offered by the great department stores is unparalleled, while the city plays host to numerous trade fairs of national and international significance.

Shopping districts – Most boutiques are concentrated in a few districts whose name alone is suggestive of Parisien opulence.

Champs-Elysées: all along this celebrated avenue and in the surrounding streets (avenue Montaigne), visitors can admire dazzling window-displays and covered shopping malls (Galerie Elysée Rond-Point, Galerie Point-Show, Arcades du Lido) devoted to fashion, cosmetics and luxury cars.

Rue du Faubourg-Saint-Honoré: here haute couture and ready-to-wear clothing are displayed alongside perfume, fine leather goods and furs.

Place Vendôme: some of the most prestigious jewellery shops (Cartier, Van Cleef & Arpels, Boucheron, Chaumet) stand facing the Ritz Hotel and the Ministry of Justice.

Place de la Madeleine and rue Tronchet: an impressive showcase for shoes, ready-to-wear clothing, luggage, leather goods and fine tableware.

Department stores – For tourists who are pressed for time, this is probably the ideal solution as most leading names are represented. Department stores are usually open from 9.30am to 7pm Monday to Saturday. **Bazar de l'Hôtel de Ville** (4th) – **Galeries Lafayette** (9th) – **Magasins du Printemps** (9th) – **Samaritaine** (1st) – **Au Bon Marché** (7th) – See Michelin plan of Paris No 11.

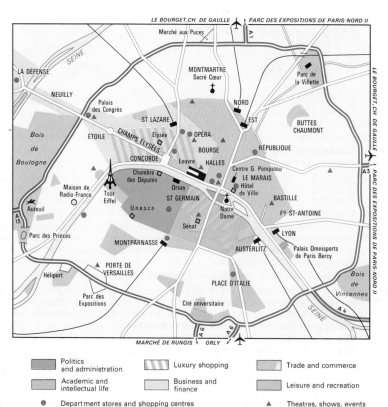

| Politics and administration | Luxury shopping | Trade and commerce |
| Academic and intellectual life | Business and finance | Leisure and recreation |

● Department stores and shopping centres   ▲ Theatres, shows, events

Antique shops and dealers – Le Louvre des Antiquaires (1st), Le Village Suisse (15th), the Richelieu-Drouot auction room and the rues Bonaparte and La Boétie are specialised in antique objects and furniture. Good bargains can also be found browsing through the flea market at the Porte de Montreuil and Porte de Saint-Ouen (Saturdays, Sundays and Mondays).

Fairs – Paris hosts a great number of world fairs and exhibitions all year round. The following events are among the most important.

Parc des Expositions de Paris (Porte de Versailles): International Agricultural Show and World Fair of Tourism and Travel in March; Foire Internationale de Paris in April; International Fair of Photography, Video and Sound in late September; International Motor Show in early October (even years); International Boat Show in mid-December.

Parc International d'Expositions (Paris-Nord Villepinte): International Fair of Farming Machinery (SIMA) in March; World Exhibition of Computer Science, Office Equipment and Technology (SICOB) in October.

Parc des Expositions (Le Bourget aerodrome): International Fair of Space and Aeronautics (odd years).

Grand Palais: International Fair of Museums and Exhibitions (SIME) in early January; International Book Fair in late March; International Fair of Classical Music (MUSICORA) in mid-April.

THE SPORTS CAPITAL

Among the most popular sporting events held in and around Paris are the International Roland Garros Tennis Championships, the Paris Marathon, the legendary Tour de France with its triumphant arrival along the Champs-Elysées and several prestigious horse races (Prix du Président de la République in Auteuil, Prix d'Amérique in Vincennes, Prix de l'Arc de Triomphe in Longchamp). The Parc des Princes stadium is host to the great football and rugby finals, attended by an enthusiastic crowd, and the Palais Omnisport de Paris-Bercy (POPB) organises the most unexpected indoor competitions: indoor surfing, North American rodeos, figure ice-skating, tennis championships (Open de Paris) motocross races and martial arts.

PLACES TO VISIT AROUND PARIS

Green Guide Flanders, Picardy and the Paris Region

★★ **Barbizon** – 196 fold 45. The landscapes of the Forest of Fontainebleau and the Bière plateau inspired a group of landscape painters who worked directly from nature (1830-60) and came to be known as the Barbizon School. Together with their leader, Théodore Rousseau (1812-67), these forerunners of Impressionism favoured dark tones, soft light and stormy skies. The **Père Ganne's Old Inn** ⊘ where they used to stay is now a **museum** ⊘.

★★ **Château de Champs** – 101 south of fold 19. *Time: 1 1/2 hours.* An 18C mansion and landscape. The **park★★** was designed in typically French style, while the internal layout of the **château** ⊘ broke new ground in its time: the rooms are no longer directly connected with one another and each is provided with a closet and dressing-room; a separate dining-room makes its appearance. There is fine Rococo **wainscoting★** and a **Chinese Room★★**.

★★★ **Château de Chantilly** – *See Château de CHANTILLY.*

Coupvray – 196 fold 22 – *11km – 6 miles southwest of Meaux.* In the canalside village is the birthplace of the great benefactor of humanity **Louis Braille** (1809-52), inventor of the alphabet for the blind which bears his name. **Museum** ⊘.

★★ **Château d'Écouen** ⊘ – 101 fold 6. *Time: 1 hour.* The château is a good example of the progress made in architecture between the Early and High Renaissance. It houses a **Musée de la Renaissance★★** which has furniture, tapestries and embroidery, ceramics, enamels...

★ **Enghien** – *See Main Resorts in Introduction.*

★ **Château de Gros-Bois** ⊘ – 101 fold 28. *Time: 1 hour.* The early 17C château houses a fascinating **furniture collection★★** of the classical and Empire periods; there is a mahogany bed with gilded bronze decoration, porphyry candelabra and bronzes by Thomire, and furniture by Jacob.

★ **Château de Maisons-Laffitte** ⊘ – 101 fold 13. Built 1642-51 by Mansart in early Louis XIV style, the château subordinates considerations of domestic well-being to the creation of grandiose effects (dominance of its site, majestic scale, use of columns and pilasters, lofty pediments).

★ **Meaux** – *See MEAUX.*

★ **Port-Royal-des-Champs** – *See PORT-ROYAL-DES-CHAMPS.*

* **Rambouillet** - 196 fold 28. The small town attracts many visitors because of its **château** ⊙ **(Rococo woodwork★)**, its **park★** with formal parterres, water gardens, **Royal Dairy★** (Laiterie de la Reine), **Shell Cottage★** (Chaumière des Coquillages) ⊙ and the splendid walks offered by its vast forest. The château is the summer residence of the President of France.

** **Abbaye de Royaumont** ⊙ - 196 fold 7. Founded by Louis IX in 1228. The extent of the original abbey church is indicated by the still-extant bases of its columns, while the splendid Gothic refectory and the 14C Madonna of Royaumont evoke the spirit of the Middle Ages.

** **Rueil-Malmaison** ⊙ - 101 fold 13. Malmaison is a place of pilgrimage for all those fascinated by the figure of Napoleon. In 1799, three years after her marriage to Bonaparte, Josephine bought the château and its park from the actor Talma. The First Consul spent much of his free time here with her; it was the happiest period of their life together and it was to Malmaison that Josephine returned after their divorce (1809). In June 1815, at the end of the Hundred Days (Josephine had been dead for more than a year), Napoleon fled here, staying with her daughter Hortense until his final departure from France.
Lemercier worked on the château around 1625; the building is interesting for its decoration by Percier and Fontaine and for its **collections★★**, which include busts of the Imperial family, Jacob furniture and many other ornamental objects. The **Château de Bois-Préau★** has many moving mementoes of Bonaparte's exile and of the eventual return of his remains to France.

** **Cathédrale St-Denis** - See Cathédrale ST-DENIS.

** **St-Germain-en-Laye** - See ST-GERMAIN-EN-LAYE.

** **Senlis** - See SENLIS.

** **Sèvres** - 101 fold 24. Sèvres owes its fame to the porcelain made here. In 1756, on the orders of Louis XV, the original factory at Vincennes was moved to Sèvres, half-way between Paris and Versailles; the government saw the move as an opportunity to assuage the concerns that had arisen as a result of the beginnings of the development of industry. Not unnaturally, Sèvres products are featured in the **Musée de Céramique★★** ⊙ which also has examples of the work from the world's other great porcelain makers. On the ground floor is an "Etruscan vase" (19C), while the first floor has plates, cups, dinner services and a range of objects illustrating the differences between hard and soft-paste porcelain from 1770 onwards.

** **Château de Vaux-le-Vicomte** - See Château de VAUX-LE-VICOMTE.

** **Versailles** - See VERSAILLES.

** **Château de Vincennes** ⊙ - 101 south of fold 17 (Green Guide Paris). *It is presently being restored and is closed intil 1999.* This "Versailles of the Middle Ages" originated in the manor-house built by Philippe Auguste. Louis IX was wont to dispense justice here in the shade of an oak-tree; he also built a chapel. The fortress begun by Philippe VI was completed by Charles V whose place of birth it was.
In the 17C, Mazarin ordered Le Vau to build the King and Queen Pavilions together with the portico linking them. The **château** ⊙ subsequently became a state prison.
Built in 1337, the **keep★★** is a masterpiece of 14C military architecture. Henri II completed the **chapel★**; the choir has fine **stained-glass★** made in 1556 in a Paris workshop.

PAU★★

Pop 85 766
Map p 8 - Michelin map 85 folds 6, 7 or 234 fold 35
Green Guide Atlantic Coast - Town plan in the current Michelin Red Guide France

Overlooking the busy waters of the torrent (Gave de Pau), the town has guarded the route to Spain via the Somport pass since Roman times. Since 1450 it has been the capital of the Béarn country, in touch with both the lowlands and the high mountains of this ancient southwestern province of France.

The Béarn and its people - The province has a diversified and attractive agricultural landscape with some arable cultivation, vines (yielding Jurançon, Madiran and rosé wine), and orchards on the spurs separating the river valleys; grazing the mountain pastures are sheep, some of whose milk goes into the making of Roquefort cheese.
The inhabitants live in large houses with steep-pitched slate roofs. Since the 11C they have practised a virtually autonomous form of pastoral democracy *(fors)*. They identify strongly with a number of historical figures. **Gaston IV Fébus** (1331-91) was not only a notable huntsman but also an authoritarian ruler who surrounded himself with men of letters; he was the first to fortify Pau. **Jean II d'Albret** acquired the Foix

country by his marraige to Catherine de Foix in 1484, but was obliged to abandon southern Navarre to the King of Spain. In 1527, his son Henri II married Marguerite d'Angoulême, the sister of François I: it was she who brought the art of the Renaissance to the castle, and, fired with Reformation zeal, made the place one of the foremost intellectual centres of Europe. Their daughter, **Jeanne d'Albret**, married Antoine de Bourbon, a descendant of Louis IX; this enabled her own son Henry of Navarre (the future Henri IV) to garner the inheritance of the House of Valois on the extinction of the line *(qv)*, thereby "incorporating France into Gascony by way of the Béarn" *(Henri IV)*.

★★ **Boulevard des Pyrénées** – From this splendid panoramic road there is a view★★★ over the valley to the Pyrenean foothills, and, in clear weather, far beyond, to the Pic du Midi de Bigorre and the Pic d'Anie.

◷ ►► Château★★ – tapestry collection★★★; Musée des Beaux-Arts★.

Grotte du PECH-MERLE★★

Map p 9 – Michelin map 79 fold 235 fold 14 – Green Guide Dordogne

Sited high above the River Célé just before it flows into the Lot, the **Pech-Merle cave** ◷ *(time: 1 3/4 hours)* is of the greatest interest in terms of both prehistory and speleology. On the lower level of the cave are paintings of a fish, two horses covered in coloured dots, and of "negative hands" (made by stencilling around hands placed flat against the rock). Something like a three-dimensional effect is produced by the way in which the Late Perigordian artists *(qv)* integrated their work with the irregularities of the rock surface. There are also representations of bisons and mammoths, as well as petrified human footprints from the Early Magdalenian. The upper level has strange, disc-like concretions, "cave pearls", and eccentrics with protruberances defying the laws of gravity.

Pointe de PENHIR★★★

Map p 4 – Michelin map 58 fold 3 or 230 fold 16 – Green Guide Brittany

Penhir Point is the most impressive of the four headlands of the Crozon Peninsula which lies between the Brest roadstead to the north and Douarnenez Bay to the south. The peninsula's high cliffs and deep inlets are the result of the faulting and fracturing of this part of the Armorican plateau. The processes of coastal erosion have worn away the sandstone matrix from which the cliffs were formed, exposing the seams of quartzite. In rough weather, the violence of the waves crashing against the differently-coloured rocks makes a magnificent spectacle. Offshore, the line of isolated rocks known as the Tas de Pois marks where the ancient coastline used to be; there is an unusual view of them from the grassy strip called the Chambre Verte.

★★★ **Other sites on the Crozon Peninsula** – The peninsula has some of the finest coastal landscapes in the whole of Brittany.

★★ **Pointe des Espagnols** – From here there is a panorama of the port of Brest and its approaches.

★★ **Pointe de Dinan** – Fine coastal views. "Le Château de Dinan" (Dinan Castle) is a great rocky mass linked to the mainland by a natural bridge; one day the action of the waves will make it an island. To the north stretch the vast sandy beaches of the Dinan inlet.

★ **Grottes de Morgat** ◷ – The caves tunnel into the cliffs at either end of Morgat's sandy bay. Their walls and roofs are attractively coloured, and a covering of seaweed helps protect them from erosion. The Grotte de l'**Autel** (80m – 25ft deep 15m – 5ft high) is probably the most beautiful of all.

★ **Cap de la Chèvre** – The panorama takes in the headlands of Finistère, Raz and Penhir with the Tas de Pois, while Sein Island can be glimpsed in the far distance.

Les Tas de Pois Rocks, Pointe de Penhir

PÉRIGUEUX★★

Conurbation 51 450
Map p 8 – Michelin map 75 fold 5 or 233 fold 42 – Green Guide Dordogne
Town plan in the current Michelin Red Guide France

Five distinct historical periods have contributed to the formation of this ancient town. First of all there was the Gaulish settlement which prospered in Roman times under the name of Vesunna; its site, the "Cité" is marked by the amphitheatre gardens and St Stephen's Church (St-Étienne). In the Middle Ages, the quarter known as "Puy St-Front" became established on a rise to the north; the cathedral was built here and the area became the heart of Périgueux, eventually, in 1251, absorbing the older Cité. In the 18C, the provincial governors, the Intendants, were responsible for a planned northward extension of the city, which linked the two districts by means of broad streets lined by public buildings. At the end of the 19C, the station area was developed, and more recently vast modern suburbs have grown up on the outskirts.

★ **Domed churches** – The city has two important examples of the domed churches characteristic of Périgord.

★ **St-Étienne-de-la-Cité** ⊘ – Two of the domes of the original sanctuary have survived. The earlier is thought to have been built in 1117 and may well have been the inspiration for the domed churches of Aquitaine; it is built directly on two massive transverse arches and on two lateral arches; it is dimly lit by a number of small windows opening on to the top of the dome. The second dome, erected half a century later, is altogether lighter; it rests on pointed arches supported by square pillars made less heavy in appearance by twinned columns and has a lofty open passage resting on an elegant blind arcade.

★ **Cathédrale St-Front** ⊘ – Of the original early Romanesque church there only remain two small domes at the eastern end of the nave. They are octagonal in shape and rest on high drums.

The church was an important stopping-place for pilgrims on their way to Santiago de Compostela since it was here that the remains of St Front, the apostle of Périgord, could be seen. His tomb dates from 1077.

The cathedral was virtually rebuilt from 1852 onwards by Abadie, the architect who designed the Sacré-Cœur in Paris, very much in the spirit of the Second Empire; it nevertheless remains impressive on account of its sheer size and the remarkable simplicity of its lines.

⊘ ►► Puy-St-Front quarter★; Rue Limogeanne★; Périgord Museum★ *(Musée du Périgord)* – prehistory, archaeology, ethnography and painting.

PÉROUGES★★

Population 851
Map p 10 – Michelin map 74 folds 2, 3 or 88 folds 8, 9
or 244 fold 15 or 246 fold A – Green Guide Auvergne-Rhône Valley

On its hilltop site dominating the Ain valley, this fortified village was originally founded by settlers who came from Perugia in central Italy long before Caesar's invasion of Gaul.

One of its lords was **Claude Vaugelas** (1585-1650), who was born at Meximieux a short distance to the east. This influential grammarian of the French language founded his precepts on logic, good taste, clarity of expression and on the language as actually used.

★★ **Fortified village** – Tightly contained within the ramparts, the tortuous streets and ancient houses of Pérouges have formed the perfect setting for many a period film.

The place was virtually rebuilt in its entirety after the war of 1468 with Savoy. The older buildings are timber-framed with projecting upper storeys. The modest artisans' houses contrast with those of the richer townsfolk and gentry which have mullioned windows and basket-handle arches, characteristic of the local response to Renaissance influences.

The **Upper Gate**★ (Porte d'en Haut) is the principal entrance to the village; the main square, the **Place de la Halle**★★★, has a splendid hostelry and the **Musée du Vieux-Pérouges** ⊘, as well as a Liberty Lime planted in 1792.

►► Outer rampart walk (Promenade des Terreaux)★; Rue.

PERPIGNAN★★

Conurbation 138 735
Map p 9 – Michelin map 86 fold 19 or 235 fold 52 or 240 fold 41
Green Guide Pyrenees-Languedoc-Tarn Gorges
Town plan in the current Michelin Red Guide France

Thoroughly French, Perpignan is nevertheless second only to Barcelona in the league of Catalan cities. It is a lively and attractive place, full of memories of great people who have left their mark on the city and its surroundings.

In the square which bears his name is a statue to **Hyacinthe Rigaud** (1653-1743). This local man, deeply attached to his home town and to his family, became a celebrated master of portraiture, painting Louis XIV and his courtiers with a rare degree of cool insight into the character of his sitters. A number of his canvases, including his *Self-portrait in a Turban* and his *Portrait of Cardinal Fleury*, are in the Perpignan museum.

Another square, the Place François-Arago, shady with palm-trees and magnolias, is named after the scientist **François Arago** (1786-1853), born at nearby Estagel, who worked on the sun's chromospere, the polarisation of light, and magnetisation.

In the Place de la Loge is the Loge de Mer, the fine 14C and 16C building which long served as stock exchange and maritime tribunal. The square has been the scene of Holy Week processions, political upsets, Louis XIV's celebrations to mark his reconquest of Roussillon as well as of the *sardanes* which are still danced here in summer.

The sculptor **Aristide Maillol** (1861-1944) was born at Banyuls, the last town on the coast road before the frontier with Spain; the square is graced by his *Venus*, while the nearby Town Hall has his *Méditerranée*; both statues embody that lively southern sensuality characteristic of the artist's female nudes.

Perpignan station found an artistic admirer in the person of the Surrealist painter and master exhibitionist, **Salvador Dali** (1904-89), another Catalan, albeit from just over the border.

CATALAN PERPIGNAN

★ **Palais des rois de Majorque** ⊙ – The origin of the palace lay in the desire of James I of Aragon to make his younger son ruler of the "Kingdom of Majorca" with its mainland seat in Perpignan. The ephemeral dynasty lasted long enough (68 years) for this characteristically Majorcan stronghold to be built on an eminence overlooking the modest township on the banks of the Rivers Basse and Têt. The plain central courtyard has a Romanesque ground floor and high Gothic arches above; flints and pebbles are used to make decorative patterns in the brickwork.

Among the other characteristic features of this school of architecture are the great hall known as the Salle de Majorque, the lower Queen's Chapel with traces of medieval frescoes on the squinches, the upper chapel with its fine Catalan figure of Christ, and the royal apartments.

★ **Civic buildings** – These make a fine architectural group along Rue de la Loge. The **Loge de Mer★** (**E**) once housed the tribunal regulating Perpignan's sea-trade. Its walls are of the finest stonework with tall Gothic arches at ground level. The windows let into the upper floor are of much later date (1540), as is the roof balustrade.

The **Town Hall★** (**H**) has been rebuilt a number of times. The upper floor is made of bands of pebbles held in place by brick coursing. The three projecting bronze arms are supposed to symbolize the three Estates representing the city's inhabitants, but in fact were designed to hold flares. The Renaissance courtyard has arcades and 18C wrought-iron grilles.

The **Députation★** (**B**) was once the seat of the Catalan "Corts"; it has a high arched doorway and window-openings with delicate columns made of marble from the Montjuich quarry far away to the south in Catalonia proper.

★ **Castillet** ⊙ – This pink brick citadel is all that survived from the 1904 demolition of Vauban's ramparts. It dates from the reign of Peter IV of Aragon, while the adjacent Notre-Dame Gate was built during the occupation of the city by Louis XI. The Casa Pairal is a Catalan folk museum.

★ **Cathédrale St-Jean** – Work on the cathedral was begun by Sancho of Aragon in 1324 but the building was only completed in 1509. The bell-tower is topped by an 18C wrought-iron cage housing a great 15C bell. Inside, the stately single nave is characteristic of the architecture of Languedoc; the altar-pieces of the high altar and the north chapels are fine work of the 15C and 16C, and in the Romanesque Chapel of Notre-Dame-del-Correchs is a collection of reliquaries. In an outside chapel, on the south side of the cathedral is a touching carved wood **Crucifixion★**, known as the Devout Christ. Such realistic depictions of Christ's suffering became widespread in Europe following Louis IX's acquisition of the relics of the Passion which included the Crown of Thorns.

EXCURSION

★★ **La Côte Vermeille** – South of Perpignan, between Argelès Beach and the Spanish border, small towns and ports huddle in the bays along the indented coastline created as the last foothills of the Albères Mountains drop sheer into the sea.

★★ **Collioure** – Hemmed in between the royal castle and the Church of Our Lady of the Angels (N.-Dame-des-Anges) with its domed belltower, this picturesque town attracted artists of the Fauve School in the early 20C and is still very popular with painters.

Banyuls-sur-Mer – This resort is also famous for its vineyard which produces a wine served as aperitif and as dessert wine.

The D 86 wich runs through the hinterland leads to the **Madeloc Tower** (alt 652m – 2139ft): wide **panorama★★** of the Albères, the Côte Vermeille and the Roussillon.

Château de PEYREPERTUSE★★★

Map p 9 – Michelin map 86 fold 8 or 235 fold 48 or 240 fold 37
Green Guide Pyrenees-Languedoc-Tarn Gorges

Visitors should have a good head for heights and take great care while exploring the castle.

The dramatic barrier of the Corbières was defended by a number of strongholds of which the ruins of the **Château de Peyrepertuse** ⊙ *(2 hours)*, separated into two distinct castles on their rocky promontory are the most imposing.

The Lower Castle (Château Bas) to the east came under Aragonese rule in 1162, enabling it to remain aloof to some extent from the troubles of the Cathar period, at least in their early stages. In 1240, it surrendered almost without resistance to the Seneschal of Carcassonne acting in the name of the king. Louis IX subsequently ordered a stairway to be built giving improved access to the castle. Under the terms of the Treaty of Corbeil in 1258, it became part of the fortified French border facing Spanish Roussillon.

The spectacular northern curtain wall running to a dramatic point, together with the ruins of the main building, the keep and chapel, give an idea of the successive stages of improvement and modernisation of the defences which took place over the centuries.

On the far side of the open area separating the two castles, a monumental stairway has been hewn into the living rock. *Use the chains which serve as a handrail.*

The royal castle raised on this western height is known as St George's Castle. It was built in the course of a single campaign, probably by Philip the Bold. There are remains of a cistern and a chapel. From its western extremity the view extends over the fortifications capping the neighbouring crests.

In 1659, the incorporation of Roussillon into France by the Treaty of the Pyrenees stripped Peyrepertuse of its strategic importance, but improvements in artillery had already made it obsolete.

Admission times and charges for the sights described are listed at the end of this guide
The clockface symbol ⊙ printed in blue in the Sights section of this guide indicates those sights for which the Admission Times and Charges are given

Haras du PIN★

Map p 5 – Michelin map 60 fold 3 or 231 fold 43 – Green Guide Normandy

The opening of Deauville's racecourse in 1864 helped spread the English fashion of owning a stable as a status symbol. 800 years previously it had been different; the Saxons had been so taken by the fine figure cut by the Norman horsemen that they had come here to study the breeding of their mounts.

Thoroughbreds have been raised here since the beginning of the 18C, flourishing on the rich pastures of the Argentan countryside.

In its setting of elegantly laid-out parkland, the **Le Pin Stud** ⊙ *(3/4 hour)* is one of France's premier centres of horse-breeding. The estate was bought by Louis XIV in 1660 and shortly afterwards Colbert instituted a public stud-farm and Mansart built a château. Dignified buildings, trim hedges and the fresh white paint of estate fences make Le Pin the most attractive of such establishments.

POITIERS★★

Conurbation 105 268
Map p 8 – Michelin map 68 folds 13, 14 or 233 fold 8
Green Guide Atlantic Coast – Town plan in the current Michelin Red Guide France

Poitiers was first established in Gallo-Roman times on a promontory overlooking a bend in the River Clain. Fertile land lay around in plenty, but the town's founders chose instead this site which had the advantage of commanding the "Gate of Poitou", the almost imperceptible rise in the land some 30km – 20 miles south which divides the Paris Basin from Aquitaine.

Key events in France's history have occurred in and around Poitiers, and have left their mark in an array of buildings of exceptional interest.

A CITY CHARGED WITH HISTORY

Antiquity – Poitiers has one of France's most venerable Christian buildings, **Baptistère St-Jean**★ ⊙. The narthex and baptistry proper have the characteristic architecture of 4C Gaul. The narthex was restored in the 10C and is polygonal in form; there are panels of Roman brickwork under its windows and beneath the gables are strange pilasters with capitals carved in low relief.

The baptistry interior has marble columns and arcades with richly-decorated capitals. Right up until the 17C, the octagonal pool was the city's sole place of baptism, originally by total immersion.

The building, which now houses an interesting lapidary museum, goes back to the time when St Hilary was elected Bishop of Poitiers, 27 years after the Edict of Constantine. Hilary played a leading role in the conversion of Gaul and was an ardent defender of the consubstantial indivisibility of the Trinity at the Council of Milan in the year 355. In 361, he received St Martin at nearby **Ligugé**, becoming his spiritual leader and encouraging him in his promotion of monastic life throughout Gaul.

The early spread of Christianity in the area around Poitiers seems to be proved by the presence of the famous **Merovingian necropolis**★ at Civaux, where more than 500 sarcophagi and coffins have been found.

The Dark Ages – A memorial in the old village of **Vouillé** recalls King Clovis' victory in 507 over Alaric II in a battle which not only marked the end of the rule of the Visigoths in Aquitaine but also the decline of a culture which had straddled the Pyrenees, stretching from Toledo to the the foothills of the Massif Central.

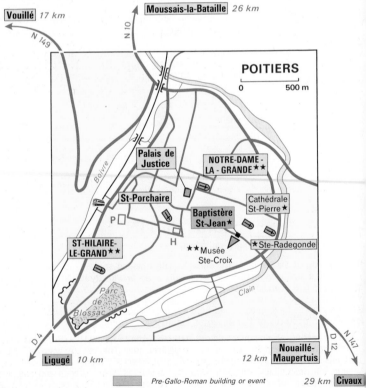

52 years later, in 559, St Radegund, Queen of France and wife of the Merovingian King Clotaire I, founded the Ste-Croix monastery (where the museum of the same name now stands) near St John's Baptistery and retired thence.

It was on an October Saturday in 732 that Charles Martel (688-741) won his famous victory at **Moussais-la-Bataille** on the banks of the Clain over the invading Arab forces. After a week spent in careful observation, Martel succeeded in drawing the Saracen cavalry on to the lances of his soldiers, cutting them to pieces and thereby saving Christian Europe from Islamic domination.

Romanesque era – This is the period to which Poitiers owes its most important monuments.

Église St-Porchaire – It has a fine 11C belfry-cum-porch.

★★ **Église St-Hilaire-le-Grand** – This great Romanesque edifice was built in 1049; it was an important staging-post on the pilgrimage route to Santiago de Compostela and in architectural terms is Poitiers' most interesting church. In 1100, it was given stone vaults to replace the original wooden roof which had been destroyed by fire. The distance it was possible to span in stone was naturally less than in timber, and the designer consequently had to reduce the width of the nave and increase the number of aisles; in doing this, he set up a double row of columns linked in ingenious fashion with the original walls and carrying a whole series of domes. The final arrangement is the unusual one of a nave flanked by three aisles on either side.

The choir, built over the tomb of St Hilary, is at a higher level than the nave where the crowds of pilgrims would assemble; it has a hemicycle of eight columns with iron grilles dating from the 12C.

★★ **Église Notre-Dame-La-Grande** – The church is a good example of the local version of the Romanesque style as it had developed around 1140. Its harmonious appearance is due to the great height of its rib-vaulted aisles. It has a splendid 12C **west front★★★**, richly decorated with sculpture based on the theme of the Incarnation, including figures of Adam and Eve, the Prophets, the Annunciation, St Joseph and the Infant Jesus being bathed.

Six round columns hold up the choir vault, which was painted in the 12C with a fresco depicting the Virgin in Majesty and Christ in Glory.

Église Notre-Dame-la-Grande, Poitiers

J.-D. Sudres/SCOPE

Gothic period – For a long time, Poitiers was English, part of Eleanor of Aquitaine's dowry *(qv)*. From the 13C to the 16C, the city was an occasional residence of the French kings, and, during the Hundred Years War, found itself allied with Aquitaine in confronting the forces of the Black Prince *(qv)*.

On 19 September 1356, a famous episode in this interminable Anglo-French conflict took place at **Nouaillé-Maupertuis** on the steep banks of the River Miosson. Jean II le Bon (the Good) was encumbered by the eye-pieces of his helmet, but fought bravely on, harking to his son's cries of "Watch out to your right, father! Watch out to your left!" In the event the French were defeated, largely because of the redoubtable English archers, able to reload their longbows three times as fast as their crossbow-equipped opponents. The Black Prince accepted the exhausted John's surrender, and the King of France passed into comfortable exile in London.

The disaster created a revolutionary situation in France; a wave of popular indignation swept the country at this further manifestation of the aristocracy's neglect of its responsibilities. The eventual result was the signing four years later of the Treaty of Brétigny which gave Poitiers to the English.

In 1372, Du Guesclin retook the town, presenting it to the king's representative, Duke Jean de Berry, brother of Charles V. In 1418, the fleeing Charles VII set up his court and parliament here; four years later he was proclaimed king. In March 1429, in the Gothic **Great Hall★** of Poitiers' recently rebuilt Law Courts, **Palais de Justice** ⊙, Joan of Arc was subjected to a humiliating investigation by an ecclesiastical commission, only to emerge three weeks later with an enhanced sense of her sacred mission.

The vast hall, scene of solemn audiences, great trials and the sessions of the Provincial Estates, was built under the Plantagenets and restored by Jean de Berry. It has a great gable wall with monumental chimneys, a balcony and Flamboyant windows.

The Renaissance – In the 16C the frontiers of France had been greatly extended, and border problems no longer affected Poitiers. Now the country's third-largest city, it played host to Rabelais, then Calvin and the writers of the Pléiade. In 1569, the place was besieged for seven weeks by a Protestant army under Coligny. In the 18C, under the rule of the centrally-appointed governors known as Intendants, Poitiers became a tranquil provincial capital.

⊙ ►► Cathédrale St-Pierre★; Musée Ste-Croix★★ – archaeology, ethnology, fine arts; Église Ste-Radegonde★.

The Practical Information section at the end of the guide lists :
– information about travel, motoring, accommodation, recreation
– local or national organisations providing additional information
– calendar of events
– admission times and charges for the sights described in the guide

PONTARLIER

Population 18 104
Map p 10 – Michelin map 70 fold 6 or 243 fold 32 – Green Guide Burgundy Jura
Town plan in the current Michelin Red Guide France

Between the 13C and 17C this proud upland town, which still commands the internationally important Besançon-Lausanne highway, was the capital of the area known as the Baroichage. This statelet, consisting of Pontarlier and the 18 surrounding villages, enjoyed an independent regime of republican character which was only extinguished by Louis XIV's conquest of the Franche-Comté.

Today, Pontarlier is a busy resort and commercial centre, advantageously sited on the approaches to the Jura mountains.

EXCURSIONS

★★ **Cluse de Pontarlier** – *5km – 3 miles south.* The Jura has many such *cluses,* lateral clefts through the high ridges separating two valleys which enable them to communicate with each other more easily. This example, with the road and railway tightly squeezed together in the narrow defile, is strategically located on the route to Switzerland and overlooked by the Larmont and Joux forts high above.

★ **Lac de St-Point** – *8km – 5 miles south.* Nearly 7km – 4 miles long and covering an area of 398ha – 983 acres, it is the largest lake in the Jura, fed by the waters of the River Doubs and attractively sited among mountain pastures and firwoods.

Le PONT DU GARD★★★

Map p 9 – Michelin map 80 fold 19 or 240 fold 16 or 245 fold 15
or 246 fold 45 – Green Guide Provence

One of the wonders of Antiquity, this superb aqueduct ⊙ was built between 40 and 60 AD. It formed part of a water supply system with a total length of 49km – 30 miles, stretching from its source near Uzès via a whole series of cuttings, trenches, bridges and tunnels to supply the growing Roman city of Nîmes with up to 20 000 cubic metres – nearly 3/4 million cubic feet of fresh water every day.

The three great lines of arches of the aqueduct rise 49m – 160ft above the valley of the Gardon.
One can imagine the effect such a structure must have had on the imagination of the local Gauls, impressing with the power and prestige of Roman achievement, as indeed it still does today. A slight curve in the upstream direction increases its ability to withstand seasonal high waters, while the independent construction of the arches lends a certain flexibility to the whole. Careful calculation of the dimensions of the huge blocks of stone (some of them weighing more than six tonnes) meant that they could be put in place without the use of mortar. The channel on the topmost level was faced with stone in order to maintain water quality and alongside it ran the carriageway of a Roman road. The Pont du Gard fulfilled its function until the 9C, when lack of maintenance and blocking by deposits of lime finally put it out of use.

Abbaye de PORT-ROYAL-DES-CHAMPS★

Map p 7 – Michelin map 101 fold 21
Green Guide Flanders, Picardy and the Paris Region

Much of the 17C in France was marked by religious conflict, not only between Catholic and Protestant, but between Jesuits and Jansenists. One focus of the latter struggle was the abbey of Port-Royal in its valley setting.

The abbey dates from 1204. In 1602, its nuns, who had departed somewhat from the strict rules of their calling, were given a new Mother Superior, Angélique Arnauld, only 11 years old at the time. In the space of seven years, this young woman succeeded, mostly by her own example, in restoring the self-respect and prestige of the abbey.

Jansenism and the "Solitaires" – By 1625, the abbey had become cramped for space, and it was decided to move to new quarters in Paris. In 1633 the Abbot of Saint-Cyran was appointed as spiritual director, and Jansenism, closely related to Calvinism, began to make its influence felt. Jansenius, a former bishop of Ypres in Flanders, had written a book, the *Augustinus*, in which he refuted the view put forward by a Spanish Jesuit that Man could improve himself by his own will, reaffirming instead St Augustine's doctrines on the need for grace and the power of predestination.

By 1648, the Paris buildings had become over-crowded in their turn, and part of the community returned to the original abbey in the Chevreuse valley where Mother Angélique was still in residence. It was now that the convent entered its period of greatest fame and influence. Some of the best minds of the time (Arnauld, the Master of Sacy, Jean Hamon...) settled here, eventually to be known as the *Solitaires*. In the outbuildings referred to as Les Granges (Barns) they founded the most progressive school of the age, called the "Petites Écoles". Racine was one of their pupils. The institution enjoyed a modest degree of success, but it was enough to call down on their heads the disapproval of Richelieu and of the Jesuits, who found their ideas too close to those of Jansenius. The *Solitaires* had to face polemics and persecution; the *Augustinus* was denounced at the Sorbonne in 1641, the *Five Propositions* summarising the work were condemned by Rome in 1653, and in 1656, on suspicion of subversion, the Petites Écoles were shut down. The importance of the issue and the deeply-held convictions on both sides made compromise impossible. In its turn, Port-Royal studied the *Five Propositions* and denounced them too, but pointed out that they were not to be found in the book. The whole country was affected by the quarrel. The cause of Port-Royal was taken up by Pascal *(qv)*, who carried the offensive into the enemy camp with the publication in 1656-7 of the 18 letters he entitled *Provinciales*, satirizing the pettifogging ecclesiastical habit of microscopic textual analysis in order to make an argument out of nothing. His grasp of the truth of the situation was altogether convincing. In 1668, Pope Clement IX, moved by the evident integrity of the *Solitaires*, accepted a formulation to which all parties could subscribe.

With passions calmed, Port-Royal now experienced an Indian summer, albeit still regarded somewhat askance by the Crown as a potential centre of resistance to absolutism. Arnauld was obliged to go into exile in Flanders, and from 1679 the nuns were no longer allowed to take in novices. Thirty years later, the convent was closed and its buildings razed.

Jansenism may have lost the argument about dogma, but the moral stature of its adherents influenced most of the contemporary intellectual elite, La Fontaine, Boileau, Perrault, Saint-Simon, Mme de Sévigné... and the 17C is beholden to it for much of its cultural achievement. It survived until the French Revolution in the policy of Gallicanism and in the collective hysteria of the convulsionaries of St-Médard.

> **Musée national des Granges de Port-Royal** ⊙ – The spirit of Jansenism is captured in a magnificent painting by Philippe de Champaigne, *Ecce Homo*, whose power lies in its restraint and profound acceptance of suffering to come. The museum also has a copy of the *Augustinius*.

PROVINS★★

Pop 11 608
Map p 6 – Michelin map 61 fold 4 or 237 fold 33 – Green Guide Champagne (in French)
Town plan in the current Michelin Red Guide France

The ancient fortified city of Provins sits atop a ridge overlooking the Seine valley and the Champagne chalklands, roughly equidistant from both Paris and Troyes. The town has a famous outline (once painted by Turner), dominated by Caesar's Tower and the dome of St-Quiriace Church.

Provins' role as an important centre of commerce was confirmed in the 12C when it became one of the two capitals of the County of Champagne. Its annual fairs were renowned, part of a round of such events which also took place at Lagny, Bar-sur-Aube and Troyes.

PROVINS

For a number of years in the 13C, Edmund of Lancaster was lord of Provins, at a time when the place was known for its roses, in those days a rare flower. He incorporated a red rose into his emblem; a century and a half later it was this flower which triumphed over the white rose of York in the Wars of the Roses.

★★ **Ville Haute** – Still protected to north and west by its 12C and 13C **walls**★★, its most splendid feature is the **Tour de César**★★ ⊙, a massive 12C keep with an additional rampart built by the English in the Hundred Years War as an artillery emplacement. There is also a roughly-built 13C **Grange aux Dîmes,** which belonged to the canons of St-Quiriace.

▶▶ Provins: Église St-Ayoul – group of statues★★.

EXCURSION

★ **Église de St-Loup-de-Naud** – *11km – 6 miles southwest.* The church belonged to a Benedictine priory of the Archbishopric of Sens, and was one of the first in the area to be vaulted in stone.

Erected in the 11C and 12C, it demonstrates the gradual evolution of the Romanesque into Early Gothic (in 1874, the vaulting was subjected to major restoration). The choir dates from the 11C as does the early Romanesque cradle-vault next to it. The dome over the crossing, the barely-projecting transepts and the first two bays of the nave were built at the beginning of the 12C. Finally, around 1160, the last two bays of the nave were completed; they are square in plan and have alternating pillars and twin columns on the model of Sens cathedral. The well preserved **doorway**★★, under the main porch, shows similarities with the Royal Doorway of Chartres Cathedral; Christ in Majesty surrounded by symbols of the Evangelists on the tympanum, apostles in arched niches on the lintel, statue-columns in the splays, figures in between the arch mouldings. The sculptures of St-Loup mark the beginning of a transition which gave birth to Gothic Realism.

PUY DE DÔME★★★

Map p 9 – Map 73 folds 13, 14 or 237 fold 19 – Green Guide Auvergne-Rhône Valley

With its summit rising to 1 465m – 4 806ft, this is the highest as well as the oldest of all the peaks making up the extraordinary volcanic landscape known as the Puys. Long before the Romans built a temple to Mercury here, the Gauls had erected a sanctuary to their god Lug. In 1648, Pascal was responsible for the experiment which proved Torricelli's theory about atmospheric weight; he arranged for his brother-in-law Florin Périer to take simultaneous readings of the height of a column of mercury on the top of the Puy de Dôme and down in Clermont-Ferrand; the difference was a decisive 8.4cm.

The Puys

On 7 March 1911, only three years after Henri Farman had successfully flown the first kilometre in a closed circuit, the aviator Eugène Renaux and his passenger landed on the summit of the Puy de Dôme five hours and eleven minutes after leaving Paris, thereby winning the Michelin Grand Prix of 100 000 francs.

★★★ **Panorama** – From the summit there is a vast panorama over the city of Clermont-Ferrand, the Grande Limagne basin, the complex volcanic structure of the Monts Dore and the Puys themselves. The Puys, or the Monts Dômes as they are sometimes known, extend over an area 30km – 19 miles long and 5km – 3 miles wide; in it, there is a total of 112 extinct volcanoes, all more than 50 000 years old, all distinct from one another and aligned along the fault line which borders the Limagne to the west. Between them they exhibit virtually all the forms of volcanic relief; some, to the north, are of "Peleean-dome" type, with craterless extrusive domes; they include the Puy de Dôme itself, built up by slowly extruded domite, the Clerziou, Puy Chopine and the Grand Sarcoui, all formed from trachytic lava.

Others are of Strombolian type, with craters and cones of ejected material around their vents; some have a single crater (Gravenoire, La Nugère, Les Goules); some have had the sides of their craters ripped out by explosions and have given birth to great lava-flows (La Vache, Lassolas, Louchadière), while the Puy de Côme has a double crater with a cone on the outer rim.

Other kinds of volcanic material have been injected into sedimentary rocks which have subsequently been eroded, leaving pinnacles, as at Puy de Monton and Montrognon, or sills, as at Montadoux.

Elsewhere (Gergovie, Mount Serre and the Chanturgue upland), lava flows have created the phenomenon known as relief inversion.

PUY DE SANCY★★★

Map p 9 – Map 73 fold 13 or 239 fold 18 – Green Guide Auvergne-Rhône Valley

The Puy de Sancy rises from the Mont Dore massif to 1 885m – 6 184ft, the highest point in Central France.

★★★ **Panorama** – *1 1/2 hours Rtn to the summit on foot by rough path from the top station of the cable railway.* With the heights of the Mont Dore massif in the foreground, the immense views extend northeastwards over the Puys and to the Cantal massif in the south.

The Puy de Sancy, the Banne d'Ordanche and the Puy de l'Aiguiller form the centre of the Mont Dore volcanic massif, an area three times greater than that of Vesuvius. Towards the end of the Tertiary era, more than 100 openings spewed forth lava from the great volcano, the successive flows building up to thicknesses of more than 1 000m – 3 300ft. In Quaternary times, radiating valleys were gouged out of the sides of the volcano by glacial action. The Puy de Sancy itself is a trachyte plug whose outer covering has been worn away by erosion. The hedged fields of the valley bottoms give way, between 1 100 and 1 400m (3 600 – 4 600ft), to forest of beech, spruce and fir, while the landscape as a whole is enhanced by the presence of volcanic lakes.

★ **Besse-en-Chandesse** – *On the eastern slopes of the massif.* This is a mountain village, made of lava, with picturesque **streets** and houses, a barbican and a severe little **church**★ with sturdy columns, rough capitals, and a choir screen and stalls decorated with Italian-style grotesques of the 16C.

Around the village are a number of volcanic lakes, each with its own character. The **Lac Pavin**★★ occupies a crater which was formed by the explosion of a pocketof gas on the slopes of the **Puy de Montchal**★★; Lake Chauvet has filled the void left by the effects of an implosion, while Lakes Montcineyre and the **Lac Chambon**★★ were formed when the volcano Tartaret erupted into the Vallée de la Couze's floor and blocked the outflow of water.

Le PUY DU FOU★

Michelin Map 67 fold 15 or 232 fold 42 – Green Guide Atlantic Coast

On summer evenings the château sparkles under the lights of its famous *Son et Lumière* show in which a cast of hundreds stages an open-air historical pageant; by day the museum here evokes the past of the Vendée region, while various attractions lure visitors into the 12ha – 30 acres of grounds.

The name Puy du Fou is derived from the Latin: Puy (from *podium*) means an eminence, a knoll; Fou (from *fagus*) designates a beech tree. Thus "A hill where a beech tree grows" or, less lyrically "Beechmount".

Château – It is likely that the original castle, built in the 15C and 16C, was never completed; it was in any case partly destroyed by fire during the Wars of the Vendée *(qv)*. There remains nevertheless a fine late Renaissance pavilion at the far end of the courtyard, preceded by a peristyle with engaged Ionic columns. This now serves as the entrance to the open-air museum, **Écomusée de la Vendée★★** ⊙. The left wing of the château is built over a long gallery.

★★★ **Cinéscénie** ⊙ – The terrace below the rear façade of the château, together with the ornamental lake below it, makes an agreeable background for the spectacular "*Cinéscénie*" in which "Jacques Maupillier, peasant of the Vendée" directs a company of 700 actors and 50 horsemen in a dazzling show. The history of the Vendée is re-lived with the help of an impressive array of special effects, fountains, fireworks laser and other lighting displays...

Le PUY-EN-VELAY★★★

Pop 21 743

Map p 9 – Michelin map 76 fold 7 or 239 fold 34 – Green Guide Auvergne-Rhône Valley
Town plan in the current Michelin Red Guide France

The town occupies the centre of a basin owed to the collapse of the Vellave plateau. Sediments stripped from the surrounding hills then partly filled the basin in which a gorge was cut by the river Loire. At the end of the Tertiary era, a series of volcanic eruptions convulsed the region leaving huge and resistant cones of basalt flows. Le Puy, capital of the Velay district, is famous for its spectacular site and splendid monuments, its pilgrimages and its fine lace.

LE PUY-EN-VELAY

Aiguières (R. Porte-)	AZ 2
Chaussade (R.)	BZ
Fayolle (Bd Mar.)	BZ
Foch (Av. Mar.)	BZ
Pannessac (R.)	AY
Raphaël (R.)	AY 39
St-Gilles (R.)	AZ
St-Louis (Bd)	AZ
Becdelièvre (R.)	AY 3

Bouillon (R. du)	BY 5
Card.-de-Polignac (R.)	BY 8
Chamarlenc (R. du)	AY 10
Chênebouterie (R.)	AY 13
Collège (R. du)	BZ 17
Consulat (R. du)	AY 19
Courrerie (R.)	AZ 20
Crozatier (R.)	BZ 23
Dr-Chantemesse (Bd)	AY 24
For (Pl. du)	BY 27
Gambetta (Bd)	AY 30
Gouteyron (R.)	AY 31
Grangevieille (R.)	AY 32
Martouret (Pl. du)	ABZ 34
Monteil (R. A. de)	AY 35

Philibert (R.)	AY 36
Pierret (R.)	BZ 37
Plot (Pl. du)	AZ 38
République (Bd. de la)	BY 40
Roche-Taillade (R.)	AY 42
St-François-Régis (R.)	BY 43
St-Georges (R.)	BY 45
St-Jean (R. du Fg)	BY 46
St-Maurice (Pl.)	AY 47
Séguret (R.)	AY 48
Tables (Pl. des)	AY 49
Tables (R. des)	AY 52
Vallès (R. J.)	AY 54
Vaneau (R.)	AY 55
Verdun (R.)	BY 58

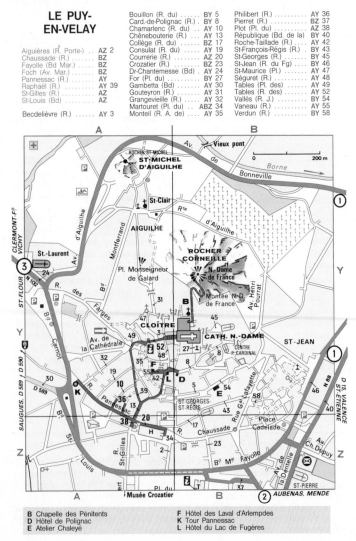

B	Chapelle des Pénitents	**F**	Hôtel des Laval d'Arlempdes
D	Hôtel de Polignac	**K**	Tour Pannessac
E	Atelier Chaleyé	**L**	Hôtel du Lac de Fugères

Lace

Lace-making was widespread in the area around Le Puy as early as the 17C, though its high point was reached in the 19C, in part due to the efforts of Théodore Falcon (1804-56), who encouraged high standards in both design and quality. Before the First World War, bobbin lace and needlepoint lace were equally popular, but after 1919, the former (also known as pillow lace) became dominant, with threads of linen, silk and wool used to form patterns of great variety and delicacy.

On the first floor of the **Musée Crozatier (AZ)** ⊘ is a **lace collection★** of great richness; it includes a magnificent square of 500 bobbins with the pins in place, a complex piece of work begun with gold thread and still awaiting completion. Also on display are the first sample-books (18C), giving hints on salesmanship and identification of the different types of stitch.

Detail of lace, Le Puy

Rocher Corneille (BY) ⊘ – This is an outlier of the volcano of which the St-Michel Rock was the vent. It is topped by a 16m – 52ft statue of Notre-Dame of France made in 1860 from melted-down cannons captured at the Siege of Sebastopol. The terrace at the foot of the statue offers the best viewpoint over the extraordinary **site★★★** of Le Puy.

★★ **Cathedral quarter** – The city's growth dates from the 11C, when it took over the urban functions of nearby St-Paulien and when it formed an important destination on the pilgrimage road to Santiago de Compostela. The cathedral's fortifications are evidence of the bishops' quarrels with the local lords (the Polignacs, Montlaurs, Mercœurs...) over sovereignty and over the taxes raised from the pilgrims...

The area around the cathedral has a sombre air, with its buildings of granite and lava, arcaded entranceways, mullioned windows, heavy iron grilles and paving stones.

★★★ **Cathédrale Notre-Dame (BY)** ⊘ – The first building to occupy the site was a Roman temple. This was followed around 430 by a sanctuary dedicated to the Virgin Mary, built at the same time as Santa Maria Maggiore at Rome. Rebuilding and extension took place from the 10C on, and in the 19C major restoration was carried out.

The lofty west front rises from its monumental steps to dominate the Rue des Taules. The windows in the third storey mark the extension to the nave which took place at the end of the 12C and which is supported on massive arcading. The overall impression is a highly ornamental one, due to the pierced or blind Romanesque arches, the use of polychrome granite and basalt stonework, the mosaics in the gables and the columns with carved lava capitals.

The steps continue to rise, giving a good view of the carved doors (which were once painted) of the Golden Doorway (Porte Dorée) with, on the left, a depiction of the Nativity, and on the right, Christ's Passion. In the 10C and 11C, the apse was rebuilt and the transepts and first two bays of the nave erected. At the beginning of the 12C the two adjacent bays were built and vaulted with splendid domes; here there is a carved 14C figure of Christ and a 17C pulpit. The two last bays were added at the end of the 12C.

★★ **Cloisters** ⊘ – Dating from the 11C and 12C, the cathedral cloisters have polychrome mosaics, an allegorical Romanesque frieze at the base of the roof, a fine 12C wroughtiron **grille★** and, in the Reliquary Chapel, a celebrated Renaissance fresco depicting the Liberal Arts.

★★ **Chapelle St-Michel-d'Aiguilhe (AY)** ⊘ – 268 steps lead to the chapel perched on its 82m – 270ft lava pinnacle. Arabesques and polychrome mosaics of Byzantine inspiration decorate the chapel doorway. Inside, the complex vaulting gives some indication of the difficulties the 11C architect had to overcome in transforming the original Carolingian sanctuary; one of his contributions was the addition of a gallery to the narthex. Note two capitals re-used in the smaller gallery, the 10C murals in the apse depicting the heavenly kingdom, and a Romanesque Christ-reliquary carved in wood.

► ► Le Puy: Cathedral Treasury★★ (Trésor); Religious Art Collection★★ (in the cloisters).

EXCURSIONS

Château de Polignac ⊙ – *5km – 3 miles northwest.* – There is a striking view of this medieval fortress from the N102 main road. Its defences were so strong that its lords were known as the "Kings of the Mountain". From the 17C to the 19C, their descendants held prominent positions in political and diplomatic life. The ruined walls and keep rise from a basalt platform, a fragment of one of the lava flows from the Mont-Denise volcano which poured along the floor of an ancient valley and then solidified. The strata beneath it were thus protected from erosion, while the material all around was being carried away by the waters of the Loire, the Borne and their tributaries. The resulting tableland stands nearly 100m – some 300ft above the surrounding land, a good example of relief inversion.

★ **Lac du Bouchet** – *21km – 13 miles southwest.* The clear waters of the lake, surrounded by coniferous woodland, occupy the almost perfectly circular crater of an ancient volcano. Around it stretch the extensive Devès uplands, formed by a series of fissure-eruptions and overlying the even older granite foundation of the landscape.

PUY MARY★★★

Map p 9 – Michelin map 76 southwest of fold 3 or 239 south of fold 30
Green Guide Auvergne-Rhône Valley

At 1 787m – 5 863ft, Puy Mary is one of the main peaks of the immense Cantal volcano, which when active was a true rival to Etna, with a circumference of 60km – 37 miles and a cone rising to 3 000m – nearly 10 000ft.

★★★ **Panorama** – *The summit is reached by a steep path from Pas-de-Peyrol – 1 1/2 hours Rtn on foot.* Glacial action has decapitated the volcano and worn it down. The view from the top takes in a landscape punctuated by the remains of volcanic vents (Griou, Violent, Élancère, Chavaroche) and lava flows which seem to have only just cooled. The **Pas-de-Peyrol**★★ too affords nice views.

The way in which this spectacular geological heritage has been fashioned by man for his various purposes is unusually fascinating. Sharp ridges divide the country up into a series of amphitheatres, in each of which the same set of activities is carefully staged. Meadows and cropland fill the valley bottoms, where the villages are also sited, though in areas less exposed to the sun, there are birchwoods, grown for fuel. On the middle slopes are beeches, used for a whole range of purposes, and recently planted conifers. Higher still come the upland pastures, dotted with stone-built huts used until lately as summer-dwellings by shepherds or for cheese-making. Known as *burons*, they are planted round with ash-trees, a useful source of fodder in times of drought.

The basaltic lava (unlike the trachytes of Mont Dore) yields rich herbage which is grazed by the reddish Salers cattle, who in their turn yield the milk for which Cantal cheese is famous.

QUIMPER★★

Conurbation 59 437
Map p 4 – Michelin map 58 fold 15 or 230 fold 18 – Green Guide Brittany
Town plan in the current Michelin Red Guide France

Quimper was first of all a Gaulish foundation, sited on the north bank of the Odet estuary 16km – 10 miles inland at the tidal limit. Towards the end of the 5C BC, Celts sailed over from Britain (hence the area's name of Cornouaille = Cornwall) and put the original inhabitants to flight. This was the era of the legendary King Gradlon and of the fabulous city of Ys which is supposed to have sunk beneath the waves of Douarnenez Bay. Tales such as these are considered by some authorities to represent the folk-memory of the most recent episodes of marine transgression (the post-glacial rise in sea level), which would have been witnessed by prehistoric people.

★★ **Cathédrale St-Corentin** – The extent to which the choir is out of alignment with the nave is striking, a consequence of the re-use of the foundations of earlier buildings on the site. The choir itself (currently undergoing extensive restoration) is remarkable for its deeply-moulded pillars, its imposing triforium and the design of the vault spanning both ambulatory and radiating chapels.

★ **Old Quimper** – The medieval town lies between the cathedral and the Odet and its tributary, the Steyr. There are fine old houses with granite ground floors and timber-framed projecting upper storeys, notably in the **Rue Kereon★**.

⊙ ►► Musée des Beaux-Arts★★; Musée Départemental breton★ – local history; Musée de la faïence Jules-Verlingue★.

EXCURSIONS

★★ **La Cornouaille** – Although the area today is limited to the coast and immediate hinterland west of its capital Quimper, Cornouaille was once the Duchy of medieval Brittany, stretching as far north as Morlaix. Brittany's "Cornwall" juts out into the Atlantic just like its counterpart across the Channel. The spectacular coastline with its two peninsulas **Penmarch★** and **Cape Sizun★★** culminates in the breathtaking **Pointe du Raz★★★** *(see below)*.

Pointe du RAZ★★★

Map p 4 – Michelin map 58 fold 13 or 230 fold 16 – Green Guide Brittany

Formed from a particularly hard-wearing granulite, Raz Point is one of France's most spectacular coastal landscapes. Its jagged cliffs, battered by the waves and seamed with caves, rise to over 70m – 220ft. The **Point★★** overlooks the fearsome Raz de Sein or tide race with its multitude of reefs and rocky islands (on the outermost of which is sited the Vieille Lighthouse); this was once dry land, but was drowned by the rise in sea level following the melting of the Quaternary glaciers. The outline of Sein Island can be seen on the horizon. To the north lies **Van Point**, perhaps less impressive, but having the distinct advantage of being off the tourists' beaten track.

A coastal path *(difficult in places, 1 1/2 hours Rtn on foot – to be avoided in bad weather or high winds)* leads round the Point; the sheer walls of the Plogoff Inferno (Enfer de Plogoff) dropping down to the boiling ocean are particularly impressive *(safety rope)*. To the north of the Point, **baie des Trépassés** cuts into the schists; it was from here that the bodies of druids are supposed to have been taken over to Sein Island for burial.

REIMS★★★

Population 206 362
Map p 6 – Michelin map 56 folds 6, 16 or 241 fold 17
Green Guide Champagne (in French)
Town plan in the current Michelin Red Guide France

Along with Troyes, Reims is one of the capitals of the province of Champagne. The city has always looked towards the Ardennes to the northeast and was the metropolis of Roman Belgica, the forerunner of modern Belgium.

It was at Reims, in 496, that **Clovis** was baptised by St Remigius (St-Rémi). This was a political event of some significance, since it made the ambitious 35-year-old warrior the only Christian ruler in the chaotic times consequent upon the collapse of the Roman Empire.

Strengthened by the support of the Church, Clovis became a symbol of order in a confused world. Within the space of a few years he had drawn his scattered subjects together; it was he who halted the advance of the Visigoths at Poitiers, subsquently pushing them back, firstly to Toulouse, then all the way into Spain. With him, the source of political authority in Gaul passed from Provence to the Seine Valley.

At the time of the Carolingians, a feeling for beauty became evident at Reims; ancient texts were carefully copied, manuscripts illuminated, ivory carved and masterpieces of the goldsmith's art created. The period produced Charlemagne's Talisman (now in the Bishops' Palace) as well as the Épernay Gospel. In 816, Louis I the Pious had himself crowned here, as Charlemagne had done at Rome 16 years before. It was from this point that the dynasty acquired a sort of religious character, though it was not until the crowning of Louis VIII, four hundred years later, that the city became the recognised place for coronations, with a ceremonial ever more elaborate and charged with symbolism. By the time of Charles X, 25 kings had been crowned here. The most moving coronation was that of Charles VII on 17 July 1429, which took place in the middle of the Hundred Years War in the presence of Joan of Arc; the Maid of Orléans had given Frenchmen the first inklings of national identity, and had persuaded the king to make his way to Reims, even though this involved him in crossing the hostile Burgundian territory of Philip the Good.

On 7 May 1945, in a modern technical college near the station, the document was signed which marked the surrender of Germany. Confirmed the day after in Berlin, this brought to an end the Second World War in Europe.

Champagne

Though covering only 2% of the total area planted with vines in France, this northernmost of the country's wine-growing regions is perhaps its most prestigious. The product was known in Roman times, when it was a still wine. It was Dom Pérignon (1638-1715), cellar-master of Hautvillers Abbey, who had the idea of making it sparkle by means of double fermentation, a process carried out today by the use of cane sugar and yeasts.

The vines are spread over an area totalling 30 000ha – nearly 74 000 acres, on the lower slopes of the chalk escarpment of the Côte de l'Île-de-France for preference. The most renowned vineyards are the Montagne de Reims (robust, full-bodied wines), the valley of the Marne (fruity wines with plenty of bouquet) and the Côte des Blancs (fresh and elegant wines). Champagne is a blended, branded wine, the prestige of the great labels dependent on the expertise of the master-blenders.

Some 215 million bottles are produced in an average year, with over 75 million of them for export.

★★★ **Cathédrale Notre-Dame** – The present building was begun in 1211. It is one of the great cathedrals of France, built in the Lanceolate Gothic style pioneered at Chartres, but with more sophisticated ornamentation, its window tracery above all. Four architects were involved in its construction; Jean d'Orbay (choir and transepts) up to 1228, Jean Le Loup (who designed a west front to rival Amiens) up to 1244, Gaucher de Reims (nave side of the west front) up to 1252, and Bernard de Soissons up to 1287. The west front has wonderfully soaring

P. Viard/PIX

lines and superb 13C sculpture, the output of four workshops, whose masterpiece is the world-famous *Smiling Angel* (in a splay of the north portal). Inside is one of the greatest achievements of the Gothic, the west end of the nave, best seen towards the end of the afternoon when the sun lights up the two rose windows.

The martyrdom of the cathedral – Reims was occupied by the German army between 3-12 September 1914, and for four years remained in the battle zone. By the end of the war, out of a total of 14 130 houses, only 60 remained habitable. The cathedral, one of the country's most precious buildings in terms of both artistic and historic value, was in ruins. The artillery bombardments of 19 September 1914 and April 1917 had been particularly destructive. The skilful restoration has largely been financed by the Rockefeller Foundation.

★★ **Palais du Tau** ⓥ – Dating from 1690, the former palace of the bishops of Reims was built by Mansart and Robert de Cotte. In it is housed some of the cathedral's original statuary, including the Coronation of the Virgin from the gable of the central doorway, and monumental figures of St Paul and of Goliath. There are also tapestries, among them two huge 15C examples from the Arras manufactory depicting scenes from the life of Clovis.

The treasury has many objects of outstanding interest, such as the 9C Talisman of Charlemagne, the 11C cut-glass Holy Thorn reliquary, the 12C coronation chalice, the St Ursula reliquary with its cornelian casket, the Holy Ampula reliquary, and a collar of the Order of the Holy Ghost.

★★ **Basilique St-Rémi** – Dating from 1007, this is the city's most venerable church, though successive restorations have left little that is Romanesque and even less that is Carolingian.

The west front was rebuilt in the course of the major restoration of 1170; it is remarkable for its Romanesque south tower. The façade of the south transept with its statue of St Michael was reconstructed in the 14C and 15C.

The sombre **interior**★★★ is remarkable for its extraordinary length (122m – 400ft) in proportion to its width (26m – 85ft). The oldest part of the church consists of the 11C transepts. In the 12C, the choir was rebuilt in the Early Gothic manner, with a blind triforium which is really no more than a roof to the galleries. All around the choir a series of double columns separates the chapel vaults from those of the ambulatory, an elegant solution which found favour throughout the province.

At the same time, the two westernmost bays of the nave were rebuilt and the whole nave given Gothic vaulting, while an imposing gallery was provided above the original aisles which were themselves given rib-vaults.

In the choir is the tomb of St Remigius (rebuilt in 1847) with statues of the twelve peers of France, clergy to the right, lay peers to the left, none of whom ever missed a coronation.

ⓥ ►► Musée St-Rémi★★ – local art and architecture, arms and armour; Champagne Cellars★; Musée des Beaux-Arts – paintings; Musée St-Denis★★; Place Royale★; Porte de Mars★; Musée-Hôtel le Vergeur★ – paintings and sculpture, Dürer engravings; Hôtel de la Salle★; Chapelle Foujita★; Centre historique de l'automobile française★.

RENNES★★

Conurbation 245 065
Map p 5 – Michelin map 59 fold 17 or 230 fold 26 – Green Guide Brittany
Town plan in the current Michelin Red Guide France

Originally founded by the Gauls, Rennes grew up around the meeting point of the great highways linking St-Malo to Nantes and Le Mans to Brest.

When Brittany won its independence in the 12C, Rennes became the capital of the Duchy's eastern march.

Its role as the capital of the whole of Brittany dates from the province's incorporation into France in the 16C.

★★ **Palais de Justice** (BY) ⓥ – *Closed for repair work following fire damage in early 1994.* This is the former seat of the Breton Parliament. The splendid south front of the building with its two corner pavilions was designed in 1618 by Salomon de Brosse; it is an early and characteristically severe example of the classical style of architecture, with a rusticated ground floor in granite supporting an upper storey rhythmically divided up by flattened pilasters. The façade is completed by an elaborately sculpted cornice and a balustrade, above which rises an unusually steeply pitched roof. The building was originally graced by a terrace with a double stairway, but this disappeared in 1726, when the square was replanned on monumental lines by Jacques-Jules Gabriel.

The interior is currently under restoration.

RENNES

B Portes Mordelaises
D Palais St-Georges
E Palais du Commerce
H Hôtel de Ville
M Musées de Bretagne et des Beaux-Arts
T Théâtre

★ **Old Rennes** (AY) – The city was devastated in 1720 by a great fire which raged for 8 days and engulfed almost 1 000 houses. Enough buildings were spared however to make a walk through the old part of Rennes an architecturally rewarding experience. The medieval houses crowd picturesquely together in the narrow streets, identifiable, like the Early Renaissance (pre-1580) houses among them, by their timber construction, their projecting upper floors and their sculptured decoration. No 3 Rue St-Guillaume is called the **Du Guesclin House★**, although it actually dates from a later period than that of the Breton hero. It has a deeply-carved door flanked by figures of St Sebastian and one of his tormentors with his bow.

Even in the 17C, after the completion of the Law Courts, the people of Rennes continued to build in timber; though oversailing upper floors were abandoned and ground floor walls sometimes built in granite, exuberant timber patterning still found favour. The city's notables had houses built at this time in which the granite ground floor supports one or two upper floors with walls of tufa or Charentes limestone. One such house, the **Hôtel de Brie★** (8 Rue du Chapitre), with a fine doorway and upper stories nicely defined by an entablature, is of such refinement that it has been attributed to Mansart.

In the meantime, some of the more distinguished houses were given a central staircase with no newel, a feature particularly characteristic of Rennes. These might have straight or curved flights, be hung from brackets or squinches or built with a timber frame (good examples are shown below by means of a letter E against the house number).

In the 18C, after the great fire, Rennes was rebuilt according to a plan drawn up by Jacques-Jules Gabriel. The streets were realigned and widened and lined with fine new buildings with granite ground floors, frequently in the form of arcades, and upper floors of stone. In the 19C, urban planning emphasised the unity of the French state; the banks of the River Vilaine were laid out as a grand axis and the city provided with pompous public buildings (high school, city hall, churches...). The following are Rennes' finest houses:

Rue St-Georges: nos 2 (E) – 3 – 6 – 7 – 8 – 10 – 12 – 18 – 22 (E) – 30 – 32;
Rue du Chapitre: nos 3 – 6-8 (Hôtel de Blossac) – 11 – 18 – 22 (E); **Rue de la Psalette:** nos 4 – 6 – 12; **Rue du Champ-Jaquet:** nos 5 – 11 – 13 – 15 (E) – 19; **Rue St-Guillaume:** no 3 (**Du Guesclin House★**); **Rue St-Sauveur:** 18C houses, nos 6 – 7 – 9.

★★ **Musée des Beaux-Arts** (M) ⊘ – This important gallery has a fine picture collection. It includes *The Newborn* (c 1630) by Georges de la Tour, a masterpiece of glowing colour, subtle lighting and deep tranquillity.

⊘ ►► Musée de Bretagne★★; Cathédrale St-Pierre – interior★; altarpiece★★; Ecomusée du pays de Rennes★; Jardin du Thabor★.

RIOM★★

Population 18 793
Map p 9 – Map 73 fold 4 or 239 fold 19 – Green Guide Auvergne-Rhône Valley
Town plan in the current Michelin Red Guide France

Riom lies at the foot of the scarp slope marking the eastern edge of the range of ancient volcanoes known as the Puys. It is the market centre of the Limagne district, a down-faulted Tertiary basin whose rich soils support a prosperous farming industry. Beginning in the 14C, the town was rebuilt in the black granite quarried either at Volvic, the "lava city", from the lava flow which once poured from the Puy-de-la-Nugère, or from the volcano itself. This hard stone is highly resistant to the sculptor's chisel, but is much appreciated by the architect for its strength and durability.

Old Riom – The medieval town is entirely contained within the ring of boulevards laid out on the line of its now-demolished walls. In the Middle Ages it was the capital of the Duchy of Auvergne, then the seat of important courts of law in the 16C and an administrative centre in the 17C, and it is to its former population of lawyers and magistrats that it owes its heritage of fine 16C-18C town houses.

★ **Église Notre-Dame-du-Marthuret** – Dating from 1583, it houses the splendid late 14C **Virgin with a bird★★★**. This famous sculpture, with its finely modelled face, is a masterpiece of harmonious proportion; it is a product of the school of sculpture patronised by Duke Jean de Berry, the reputation of which rivalled that of the sculptors of Dijon.

Rue du Commerce – The modern sculptures made of lava contrast with the traditional decoration of the houses using the same material (No 36 has 17C caryatids).

Rue de l'Hôtel-de-ville – The 16C **Maison des Consuls★**, No 5 has a corner-turret set on corbels and Italian-style busts on either side of its doorway. The Hôtel de ville has retained its 16C Renaissance arcades and statuettes of Hercules and Cupid mounted on small engaged columns.

Rue de l'Horloge – The Renaissance Clock Tower (Tour de l'Horloge) replaced a medieval bell-tower; it is crowned by a delightful little 18C domed temple. The 16C **Hôtel Guimoneau★** has a famous corner-tower staircase, Italian medallions enlivening its façade and balustrade, and statues of the Annunciation and of Venus which recall the work of the Loire School and which have been attributed to Michel Colombe.

Ⓥ ►► Riom: Ste-Chapelle★; Musée régional d'Auvergne★ – folk art and local customs; Musée Mandet★ – painting and decorative arts.

EXCURSIONS

★ **Église de Mozac** Ⓥ – *2km – 1 mile west.* This ancient abbey was founded towards the end of the 7C by St Calminus, becoming subordinated to Cluny in 1095.

Until its collapse in 1460, the abbey church was one of the finest in Auvergne. Of the building of 1095, all that remains are arches and pillars and the north aisle, together with the 47 **capitals★★** which are the oldest and perhaps the most beautiful in the whole of the province. They are products of a workshop which was active from the end of the 11C until the middle of the 12C and which enjoyed considerable influence. Those depicting Jonah (1st bay of the nave), the Apocalypse (on the ground in the choir), and the Centaur (3rd pillar on the left), Qare justly famous, but it is the capital showing the Resurrection which is truly outstanding (on the ground at the end of the nave); it is a faithful account of St Mark's text, but in its sober depiction of pose, gesture and expression, goes beyond the telling of a story to convey inner truths.

The **Shrine of St Calminus★★** in *champlevé* enamel is an exquisite example of Limoges work with chased and gilded inlay figures.

Église de Marsat – *3km – 2 miles southwest.* The church here has

The Resurrection Capital, Mozac

J.D Sudres/SCOPE

267

one of Auvergne's great works of medieval art, a 12C **Black Virgin**★★ *(in the choir of the north chapel)*. Few will be untouched by this depiction of Mary as a simple countrywoman, holding out the Child in a maternal gesture of great dignity.

★★ **Château de Tournoël** ⊘ – *8km – 5 miles west*. This is one of the province's most celebrated castles. It dominates the town of **Volvic**, famous not only for its lava quarry, but also for its spring water, whose exceptional purity is due to the filtering effect of one of the lava flows from the Puy-de-la-Nugère. Picturesquely perched on a crag, the castle has two keeps, one round, one square, joined together by ancillary buildings now in ruins. Mullioned windows of Renaissance date look down on to the courtyard, some of them blocked up to avoid the payment of window tax.

★ **Gour de Tazenat** – *22km – 14 miles northeast*. This lovely upland lake (32ha – 79 acres, 60m – 200ft deep) in its wooded setting marks the northern limit of the Auvergne volcanoes, one of whose craters it now fills.

RIQUEWIHR★★★

Population 1 075
Map p 7 – Michelin map 62 folds 18, 19 or 87 fold 17 or 242 fold 31
Green Guide Alsace et Lorraine (in French)

Unlike other French wines, those of Alsace are named according to the grape from which they are made rather than the locality. Protected by the Vosges from cold and wet westerly winds, the region's vineyards benefit from their southeasterly orientation, while the subtle bouquet of their wines is enhanced by the late ripening of the grapes in the soft September sun.

The tiny town of Riquewihr prides itself on its fine Riesling; the vintners' houses in its picturesque streets were designed with the production of wine more in mind than the comfort of the residents. A variety of building materials enlivens the scene, brick, red sandstone, timber, rendered and painted façades... while every balcony is adorned with flowers. Some of the dwellings (like the De Hugel house of 1494) go back to the end of the 15C, others to Renaissance times (like the Cour de Strasbourg house of 1597); most of them, however, are of 17C date, but they are all ornamented in the Rhineland Renaissance style which persisted longer in Alsace than elsewhere.

⊘ ►► Dolder Gate★ (1291) – local history museum; Liebrich (1535), Kiener (1574), Dissler (1610) and Preiss-Zimmer (1686) houses★.

ROCAMADOUR★★★

Population 627
Map p 9 – Michelin map 75 folds 18, 19 or 235 fold 6 or 239 fold 38
Green Guide Dordogne

Clinging dramatically to the cliffs of the gorge cut by the little River Alzou, the tiny medieval town of Rocamadour is one of the most visited places in the Dordogne.
All around stretches the **Causse de Gramat**★, a vast limestone plateau, known as good sheep country and for its pâté de foie gras.

★★★ **Site** – Rocamadour should be viewed from the Hospitalet belevedere *(2km – 1 1/2 miles northeast)*, as well as from the Couzou road. The castle, rising 125m – 420ft above the valley floor, dominates the scene; below it is a picturesque confusion of old houses, stepped streets, towers, gateways, churches and chapels.

A place of pilgrimage – Long ago, Rocamadour was chosen by a hermit, Saint Amadour, as his place

Rocamadour

of retreat. Legend identifies him with the figure of Zaccheus, husband of St Veronica, both of whom fled here from the Holy Land. From the 12C onwards, and above all during the 13C, Rocamadour was one of the most popular places of pilgrimage in the whole of Christendom. Just as they do today, souvenir stalls tempted the throngs of tourists, amongst them Henry III of England, who experienced a miraculous cure here.

A stairway with 216 steps leads to the Place St-Amadour (or **Parvis des églises**) around which are grouped seven sanctuaires, including the Chapel of Notre-Dame or Miraculous Chapel.

The stream of pilgrims eventually dried up, unsurprisingly, in view of the destruction which was caused by the great rock-fall of 1476 and completed by the Huguenots a century later. In the 19C, the place was restored by the Bishops of Cahors in an attempt to revive the pilgrimages.

Ⓥ ►► Hôtel de ville – tapestries★; Musée trésor Francis-Poulenc★ – sacred art.

ROCHEFORT★

Population 25 561
Map p 8 – Michelin map 71 fold 13 or 233 folds 14, 15
Green Guide Atlantic Coast – Town plan in the current Michelin Red Guide France

In 1664, the French Secretary for the Navy, Colbert, became aware of the vulnerability of France's Atlantic coast to attack by the English. Between Lorient in Brittany and the Spanish frontier there were hardly any defences worthy of the name; the bay at La Rochelle was very exposed and the ancient port of Brouage was silting up. In 1665, he chose a site 22km – 14 miles up the River Charente and charged Vauban with extending the defences of the fort already built there. Though the place had few natural advantages as a port, the presence of easily fortifiable islands and promontories facilitated the great engineer's task.

Seven years later, the work, which included a harbour for the navy, was complete, and by 1690 Rochefort rivalled the naval bases of Toulon and Brest. The increasing draught of modern vessels led to the harbour's obsolescence, however, and on 31 December 1926, the base was closed down.

Rochefort's fascinating history has left many traces: houses richly ornamented with entablatures, window brackets, balustrades and balconies, the stately St-Louis Church of classical design, the former **ropewalk**★★, 374m – 1 200ft long, the great timber hall built by naval carpenters (now a covered market and conference centre), and the Sun Gateway (Porte du Soleil) which formed the entrance to Colbert's arsenal.

Pierre Loti (1850-1923) – Born Julian Viaud, this native of Rochefort and lover of the exotic was intimately familiar as a young man with the life of the port and its links with the wider world. As a naval officer, he sailed the seven seas, evoking the sights and sounds of distant places in a series of novels under the nom de plume Pierre Loti. His house, **Maison de Pierre Loti**★ Ⓥ, now a museum, is equally evocative of his travels.

Ⓥ ►► Musée Naval★; Musée d'Art et d'histoire de la ville★.

EXCURSION

Moëze – 11km – 6 miles southwest. In the cemetery is a **Hosanna Cross**★, also known as the "Temple du Moëze", one of the finest in southwestern France. It crowns a small early 16C Corinthian temple, whose square plan and porticoes are evidence of growing Renaissance interest in the architecture of the ancient world. The region's Hosanna crosses are so named because they formed the setting for Palm Sunday celebrations, the "palm" branches strewn on the ground being referred to as "hosannas".

Château de La ROCHEFOUCAULD★

Map p 8 – Michelin map 72 fold 14 or 233 fold 30 – Green Guide Atlantic Coast

The **château** Ⓥ is the seat of a noble family which gave the name François to all its first-born sons and which produced many a soldier, statesman, artist and churchman. In 1494, François I de la Rochefoucauld became godfather to King François I; encouraged by his wife Anne de Polignac, he transformed the stronghold he had inherited into a sophisticated residence, albeit retaining the medieval towers which contrast with the fine Renaissance façade.

François XII (1747-1827) was a characteristic figure of the late 18C, an "Improver" in the English mould, a founder of technical colleges and savings banks, who also set up a model farm to apply the progressive agricultural techniques he had studied in England. In the previous century, **François VI** (1613-1680) had established his reputation as the greatest of France's maxim-writers. In his younger days, this Duke de la Rochefoucauld had been a brave soldier but a somewhat inept plotter; he had been imprisoned by Richelieu, ignored by Mazarin and fought on the wrong side in the Fronde; almost blinded by a blast from an arquebus, he retired to his country seat. Here, in the West Tower of the castle, a perception of the world sharpened by an understandable pessimism and filtered through a somewhat Jansenist temperament led him to produce the *Maxims* for which he is famous. Expressed in short, incisive phrases, they convey his assumption that it is self-respect *(amour-propre)* which underlies all human activity. Many of his *Maxims* have passed into languages other than French:

"Hypocrisy is the tribute vice pays to virtue."

"We are all brave enough to bear other people's misfortunes."

La ROCHELLE★★

Population 100 264

Map p 8 – Michelin map 71 fold 12 or 233 fold 14 – Green Guide Atlantic Coast
Town plan in the current Michelin Red Guide France

The port of La Rochelle is also the capital of the ancient province of Aunis. It is a lively place, much frequented by artists, but still retains that slightly secretive air characteristic of those French towns laid out on classical lines. It owes its origin to the fort built in the 11C to guard the entrance to the Aiguillon inlet; during the centuries of almost continuous English rule it was an important trading centre, exporting salt and wine, while Genoese ships landed Mediterranean produce on its quaysides.

A Protestant stronghold – La Rochelle was one of the first places in France where the Reformation took hold, becoming known as the "French Geneva". In 1570, at the end of the Third War of Religion, the town was one of the four fortified places permitted the Protestants as a guarantee of their liberty of conscience and worship. After the St Bartholemew's Day Massacre, La Rochelle became one of the main centres of Protestant resistance. Besieged by the Duke of Anjou, the town was granted an honourable surrender in 1573 after an English fleet commanded by Gabriel de Montgomery had failed to relieve it but had occupied Belle-Île.

The religious freedoms secured by the Edict of Nantes in 1598 brought several years of peace to La Rochelle. By 1627, however, the town's continued adherence to Protestantism had become intolerable to Richelieu, not least because of its English connection; the Duke of Buckingham had set up camp on the Île de Ré, and English forces had even landed on the mainland.

Richelieu directed the siege of La Rochelle in person. A fortified perimeter, 12km – 7 miles long was created and extended seawards by means of a dyke (designed by the architect Métezeau) which blocked the entrance to the harbour. It took 15 months to starve the town into submission. Richelieu made his entrance into La Rochelle on 30 October 1628, followed two days later by Louis XIII. 23 000 citizens had perished in the course of the siege; the 5 000 who had survived were spared, though a number of their leaders, including the mayor, Jean Guiton, who had embodied the spirit of resistance, were forced to leave the place for a period of several months.

★★ **Old Port – the New World** – The old port was originally laid out by Eleanor of Aquitaine; its entrance is guarded by two towers, probably built by the English in the 14C and once forming part of the town's ring of fortifications. The **Tour St Nicholas**★ (z) ⊘ to the east has rested on its foundation of oak piles for six centuries; 42m – 138ft high and with immensely thick walls, it is a fortress in its own right.

La Rochelle has contributed more than its share to the opening up of the world beyond Europe; in the 15C, it was from here that the first colonists embarked for Canada and Jean de Béthencourt sailed off to discover the Canary Islands; in the 16C, the La Rochelle fishing fleet operated in the rich fishing grounds off Newfoundland. Other explorers to set out from here were de la Salle, who sailed down the Mississipi to the Gulf of Mexico in 1681-2, and René Caillié, the first European to get back from Timbuctoo alive. La Rochelle's shipowners profited mightily from trade with Canada, Louisiana and above all with the West Indies, where they owned vast estates producing spices, sugar, cocoa, coffee and vanilla; they drew their wealth too from the triangular trade involving the sale of cloth and purchase of slaves in West Africa, transport and disposal of the slaves in America and a lucrative trip home with a full load of colonial produce.

In 1890 a new deep-water port was created at La Pallice, capable of taking shipping at all states of the tide.

LA ROCHELLE

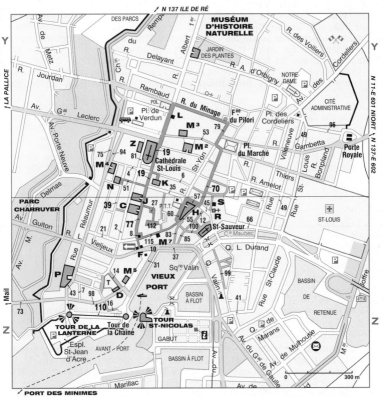

C Hôtel de la Bourse	**L** Café de la Paix	**M⁷** Musée du Flacon à parfum
D Ancienne chapelle des Carmes	**M²** Musée du Nouveau Monde	**N** Maison Venette
F Porte de la Grosse Horloge	**M³** Musée des Beaux-Arts	**P** Préfecture
H Hôtel de Ville	**M⁴** Musée d'Orbigny-Bernon	**R** Temple protestant
J Palais de Justice	**M⁵** Musée Grévin	**S** Cloître des Dames Blanches
K Maison Henri II	**M⁶** Musée rochelais de la Dernière Guerre	**Z** Ancien hôtel de l'Intendance

★★ **The 17C and 18C town** – The 18C **Porte de la Grosse-Horloge**★ (**Z F**) leads to the Old Town. Here, as well as timber-framed medieval houses with hung slates to keep out the damp and fine residences of Renaissance date, there are substantial 18C stone town houses adorned with some astonishing gargoyles. Arcades of pleasingly varied design enliven the urban scene, which reaches a climax in the splendid **Hôtel de ville**★ (**H**). Built in Tuscan style in the reign of Henri IV, this has a courtyard **façade**★ of 1606, with an arcaded gallery. Probably built by the great architect Du Cerceau (himself a Huguenot), it is evidence not only of the growing taste for things Italian but also of the economic recovery following the Wars of Religion.

⊙ ►► La Rochelle: Old Town streets★; Museum d'Histoire Naturelle★★; Musée du Nouveau-Monde **M²**; Musée des Beaux-Arts★ **M³**; Musée d'Orbigny **M⁴** – local history, ceramics; Tour de la Lanterne★; Parc Charruyer★.

EXCURSION

★ **Île de Ré** – The island, which is also known as White Island and has been linked to the mainland by a viaduct since 1988, is a popular resort. Part of the salt-marshes to the north has been set aside as a bird sanctuary.

ROCROI

Population 2 555
Map p 6 – Michelin map 53 fold 18 or 241 fold 6
Green Guide Champagne (in French)

First laid out in the 16C in a clearing in the Ardennes forest, Rocroi is a typical Renaissance fortified town.

After the principality of Sedan had been incorporated into France in 1642, the death of Richelieu and the ill-health of Louis XIII made a long period of uncertain rule by a regent seem likely. The prospect whetted the expansionist appetites of Philip IV of Spain, for whom the capture of Rocroi would open the way to Paris via the valleys of the Aisne and the Marne.

On 19 May 1643, three days after the death of Louis XIII, a bold manœuvre by the Duke d'Enghien – the future Grand Condé – routed the redoubtable Spanish infantry which never succeeded in regrouping. This, the first French victory over the Spaniards for more than a century, reverberated around Europe (it is commemmorated by a monument in the leafy countryside 3km – 2 miles to the south). Fortune now began to smile on France, and Mazarin was able to implement Richelieu's foreign policy, using the generation of officers trained by the farsighted Cardinal.

Later, after his involvement in the disturbances known as the Fronde, Condé went over to the Spaniards, and, in 1658, was responsible for capturing Rocroi for them. But in the following year, the Treaty of the Pyrenees gave the fortress town back to France and Condé to his king.

The **ramparts** of Rocroi were improved by **Vauban**. With their glacis, bastions, demilunes and deep defensive ditches they are a fine example of the great engineer's mastery of his art.

RODEZ★

Population 24 701
Map p 9 – Michelin map 80 fold 2 or 235 fold 16
Green Guide Pyrenees-Languedoc-Tarn Gorges
Town plan in the current Michelin Red Guide France

The origins of Rodez go back to a stronghold built by the Gauls on the rocky spur high above one of the meanders of the river Aveyron.

The layout of the town reflects the ancient rivalry of secular and ecclesiastical power; the areas around both cathedral and castle (the latter marked by today's Place du Bourg) were each provided with their own ring of fortifications.

★★ **Cathédrale Notre-Dame** – The red sandstone edifice was probably begun in 1277 by Jean Deschamps, the architect who had set himself the task of propagating the new Gothic style of the Île de France throughout Central and Southern France in parallel with the spread of Capetian power.

The impressive fortress-like west front was originally a bastion protruding from the city wall. Its Flamboyant Gothic portals were completed in 1475; 35 years later, the construction of the magnificent **bell-tower**★★★ was begun, incorporating an existing tower of 14C date. The top three storeys are richly decorated, the third with large arches with very pronounced mouldings, the fourth with statues of the Apostles in niches and the fifth with Flamboyant turrets and pinnacles. Among all this luxuriance, the Renaissance belfry rising above the balustrade looks a little delicate.

The interior was completed in the 16C but still in the style of the 13C. Four works in particular are worthy of attention; a rare example of a Romanesque altar-table with scalloped decoration (in the axial chapel); the former **rood-screen**★ of 15C date (in the south transept); a famous 16C **Holy Sepulchre**★ (in one of the chapels on the south side of the nave) and the superb 17C carved wooden **organ case**★.

⊘ ►► Musée Fenaille – prehistoric and medieval collections, archaeology.

MICHELIN GREEN GUIDES

Art and Architecture
Ancient monuments
Scenic routes
Landscape
Geography
History
Touring programmes
Plans of towns and buildings

A selection of guides for holidays at home and abroad

Chapelle de RONCHAMP★★

Map p 7 – Michelin map 66 fold 7 or 242 fold 38 or 243 fold 9
Green Guide Burgundy Jura

Built by **Le Corbusier** (Charles-Édouard Jeanneret 1887-1965), the **Chapelle Notre-Dame-du-Haut** ⊙ high up on its hilltop site is one of the few great works of religious architecture produced by the Modern Movement of the early to mid-20C.

The characteristically Corbusian use of fluid, interpenetrating space, first deployed in his La Roche Villa at Paris – today the Le Corbusier Foundation – appears here again to great effect.

> The apparent simplicity of the building's curving lines and asymmetrical surfaces can be deceptive, as can the architect's subtle use of light falling from the "periscopes" in the side-chapels, filtering in from the base of the convex vault or streaming through the irregular wall-openings which constitute the building's main decoration. Only slowly does one come to appreciate the fusion of feeling and technology which is the measure of the greatness of this unique work of art.

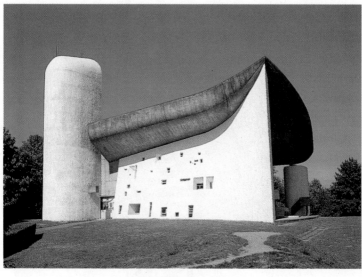

F. Jalain/EXPLORER

Chapelle Notre-Dame-du-Haut

ROUEN★★★

Conurbation 380 161
Map p 5 – Michelin map 55 fold 6 or 231 folds 22, 23 – Green Guide Normandy
Town plan in the current Michelin Red Guide France

With its skyline of towers and spires, Rouen is the capital of Lower Normandy, its importance from Roman times onwards being due to its role as the lowest bridging-point on the Seine; the alignment of its two main streets (Rue du Gros-Horloge and Rue des Carmes) still reflects the layout of the early city.

Normandy is as renowned for its architecture as much as for its orchards and rich pastures, and Rouen, with its heritage of fine building and its many museums, offers its visitors a wealth of artistic delights.

Literature and art – Although the birthplace of a number of scientists, it is men of letters and artists who have contributed most to Rouen's fame.

Pierre Corneille was born here in 1606. Trained as a lawyer, he subsequently became the first of France's great tragedians. A quartet of plays *(The Cid, Horace, Cinna* and *Polyeucte)* celebrate love, courage, clemency and faith; written between 1636-41, their heroes come from a classical mould, noble beings, able to subordinate both emotion and action to the exercise of will.

Gustave Flaubert (1821-80) was the son of Rouen's chief surgeon. Living for reasons of health at the village of Croisset *(west of the city),* he seems divided between the wish to portray the human soul in all its detail and a taste for vivid expression. His major works include the celebrated *Madame Bovary* (1857), in which the village of Ry *(20km – 12 miles east)* is described under the name of Yonville, *Salammbô,* and *L'Éducation Sentimentale.*

Théodore Géricault (1791-1824) was the Romantic painter par excellence; his feeling for movement and love of the theatrical are displayed to great effect in works such as the *Raft of the Medusa* (in the Louvre, Paris).

ROUEN

Map of Rouen

D   Archevêché
E   Hôtel d'Étancourt
K   Église Ste-Jeanne-d'Arc
M²   Musée
        de la Céramique
M³   Musée Le Secq
        des Tournelles
M⁴   Musée Jeanne-d'Arc
M⁵   Musée Corneille
M⁷   Musée des Antiquités
        de la Seine-Maritime
M⁸   Muséum d'Histoire
        naturelle, d'Ethnographie
        et de Préhistoire
M⁹   Musée de l'Éducation
N   Le Gros-Horloge
R   Hôtel de Bourgtheroulde
S   Tour
        Jeanne-d'Arc
X   Fontaine Ste-Marie
Z   Fierte St-Romain

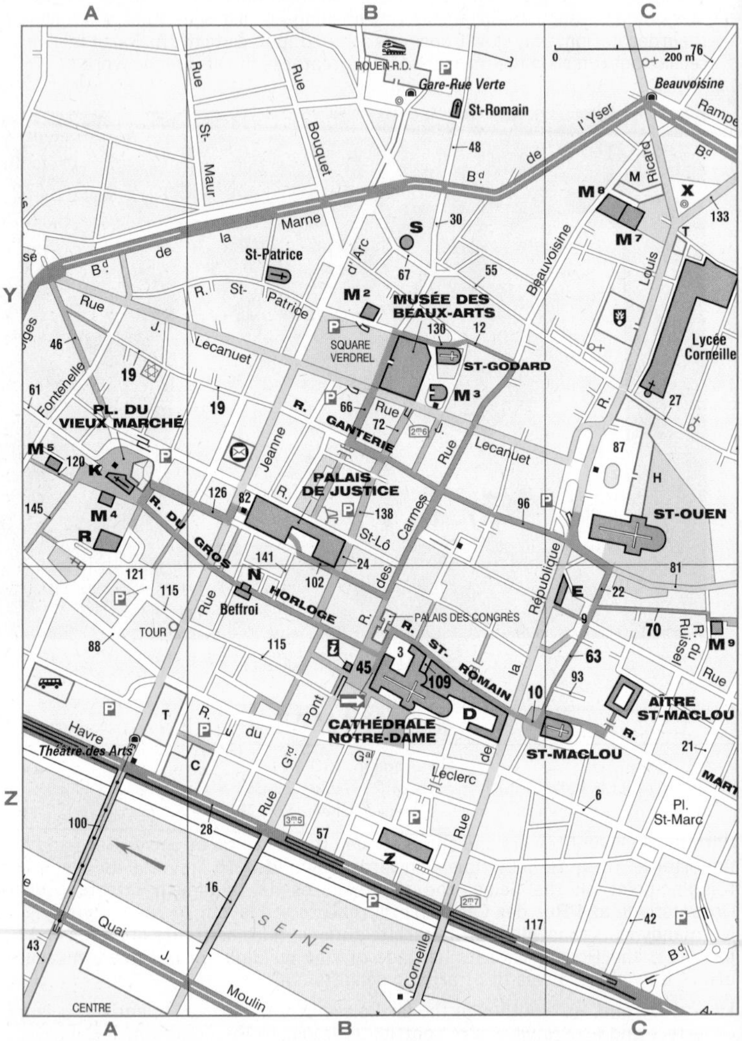

★★★ **Cathédrale Notre-Dame** (BZ) ⊙ – This is one of the finest achievements of the French Gothic. Like the great buildings which preceded it towards the end of the 12C, it is in the Lanceolate style, in spite of having been rebuilt after a terrible fire in 1200. Thanks to the generosity of John Lackland, Duke of Normandy as well as King of England, reconstruction was swift and bold in scope; the transepts were extended and the choir enlarged in accordance with the latest techniques. It had originally been intended to place galleries above the arcades, but by the 13C, the development of flying buttresses at Chartres had made them superfluous.

The spaciousness of the interior is striking. The nave has eleven bays and a sexpartite vault, while the lantern-tower, rising 51m - 167ft from the floor of the crossing, achieves a kind of sublime perfection. The choir, with its 14 soaring pillars and delicate triforium, is a masterpiece of harmonious proportion.

The great edifice seems to have been under repair for most of its existence for varied reasons: a consequence of the fire of 1200, the Hundred Years War, another fire in 1514, the misdeeds of the Calvinists, the hurricane of 1683, the French Revolution, the burning-down of the spire in 1822 and the aerial bombardment of the night of 19 April 1944. This most recent disaster threatened the whole structure, and restoration work still goes on today.

★★★ **Old Rouen** - The old town's narrow streets, many of them pedestrianised, are lined with more than 800 timber-framed houses, large and small, elegant or picturesquely askew, all characteristic examples of medieval building techniques. They consist of a skeleton of vertical posts and horizontal beams, reinforced by studwork and diagonals. Infilling is with plaster or rubble. Up until 1520, the upper floors were jetted out for reasons of economy and greater floor-space.

★★ **Rue St-Romain (BZ)** - One of the old town's most fascinating streets, with many timber-framed houses dating from the 15C to the 18C. No 74 is a Gothic building still with its 15C windows.

★★ **Église St-Maclou (CZ)** - When compared to the cathedral, the church provides striking evidence of the evolution of the Gothic style. It was begun in 1437 and is a fine example of the Flamboyant style at its purest. Nevertheless its decoration is of the Renaissance (doors, stairs, gallery and organ-case). At the north corner of the west front is a fountain with two mannekins performing the same act as their counterpart at Brussels, albeit with somewhat less finesse.

★★ **Aître St-Maclou (CZ)** - This is a rare example of a medieval plague cemetery. It is enclosed by half-timbered buildings decorated with macabre carvings showing the Dance of Death, skulls and crossbones, grave-diggers' tools...

★★ **Église St-Ouen (CY)** ⊙ - Built in the 14C, this former abbey church marks the peak of achievement of the High Gothic style. Its architect was complete master of the forces acting on his building, leading them at will via ogee arches on to flying-buttresses weighted by pinnacles, thence to foundations beyond the walls. The structural problem solved, he was then able to concentrate on designing the shell of the building. With no structural role, walls could become windows, flooding the interior with light and thereby encouraging an increasingly literate congregation to follow the service with the missals now coming into use.

A few years on, and the Gothic had fulfilled its architectural potential; its final phase, the Flamboyant, is a virtuoso style, delighting in ornamental excess rather than structural innovation.

★★ **Rue du Gros-Horloge** - This bustling street, lined with old houses and given over to pedestrians, is one of the city centre's main attractions for visitors. The Gros-Horloge clock (**BZ N**) on its arch has only one hand; next to it is the Belfry from the top of which there is a fine view over the city and its surroundings.

★ **Place du Vieux-Marché (AY)** - This modern complex occupies the site where Joan of Arc, aged only 19, was burned at the stake following her trial as a heretic; 25 years later she was rehabilitated (qv). In the centre of the square is the great Cross of Rehabilitation, marking the place where Joan of Arc was burnt. There is also a covered market and a church incorporating **stained glass windows**★★ of 16C date.

★★ **Musée des Beaux-Arts (BY)** ⊙ - The museum was renovated in 1992 but until all the work is completed, collections are limited to the 16 and 17C. Among the pictures on display, visitors should see Gérard David's *Virgin and Saints*, an oil painting on wood, on of the masterpieces of Flemish Primitive art, as well as several choice pieces from the French School: *Diana Bathing* by François Clouet, *The Concert of Angels* by Philippe de Champaigne, and *Venus Arming Aeneas* by Nicolas Poussin. Other outstanding works from European countries are *The Adoration of the Shepherds* by Rubens, *Saint Barnabé Healing the Sick* by Veronese and especially *Democritus* by Velasquez.

★★ **Musée de la Céramique (BY M²)** ⊙ - In 1530, a citizen of Rouen, Masséot Abaquesne, succeeded in making faience, hitherto a secret process which had originated in Faenza in Italy in the 14C. Rouen's moment of glory in the production of this most aristocratic of ceramics came in the more settled times which followed the troubled start to the 17C. It was at this time that the Poterat workshop flourished. The liking for Chinoiserie and lambrequin ornament, together with royalty's desire to replace outmoded metal plates and dishes with ceramics (p 144), helped assure Rouen's success with ewers, fountains, spice pots... The fine bust of Apollo of c1740 from the Fouquay workshop exemplifies both taste and technique.

⊙ ► Palais de Justice★★; Musée Le Secq des Tournelles – wrought ironwork **M³**; Musée des Antiquités de la Seine Maritime **M⁷**; Église St-Godard; Panorama from Côte-Ste-Catherine★★★; Jardin des Plantes.

ROUTE DES CRÊTES★★★

Map p 7 – Michelin map 62 fold 18, 66 fold 9 or 87 folds 17, 18, 19 or 242 folds 31, 35
Green Guide Alsace et Lorraine (in French)

In the First World War, the French and German armies confronted each other along the old frontier between the two countries formed by the crest-line of the Vosges. Hugging the ridge is the strategic north-south road planned by French military engineers to serve the front; today it forms a fine scenic route, the Vosges Scenic Road, running for 63km – 39 miles from the Bonhomme Pass (Col du Bonhomme) in the north to Thann in the south. It offers the visitor a splendid introduction to the varied landscapes of these uplands, which include the sweeping pasturelands of the summits, an array of lakes, and the broad valleys of the Fisch and the Thur.

Col du Bonhomme – 949m – 3 114ft high, this is the pass linking the provinces of Alsace and Lorraine.

Col de la Schlucht – 1 139m – 3 737ft. This is the steepest, but also one of the busiest of the routes through the Vosges. The eastern slopes are subject to intense erosion because of the gradient of the torrential rivers; at a distance of only 9km – 5 miles from the pass, the town of **Munster**★ lies 877m – 2 877ft below, while Colmar, 26km – 16 miles away is 1 065m – 3 494ft lower.

★★★ **Hohneck** – 1 362m – 4 469ft. Rising near the central point of the range, this is one of the most visited of the Vosges summits. From the top there are superb **views**★★★; to the east, the **Munster Valley**★★ plunges steeply down towards the broad expanses of the Alsace plain, while to the west is the Lorraine plateau, cut into by the valley of the Vologne.

★★★ **Grand Ballon** – 1 424m – 4 672ft. The Grand Ballon forms the highest point of the Vosges. From the top *(1/2 hour on foot return)* the magnificent **panorama**★★★ extends over the southern part of the range, whose physionomy can be fully appreciated. The eastern and western slopes are quite unlike each other; the drop to the Alsace plain is abrupt, while to the west the land falls away gently to the Lorraine plateau. Glacial action in the Quaternary era is responsible for many features like the massive rounded humps of the summits *(ballons)*, and the morainic lakes in the blocked valleys. Above the tree-line, the forest clothing the hillsides gives way to the short grass of the wide upland grazing grounds known as the Hautes-Chaumes.

★★ **Vieil-Armand** – The war memorial ⊙ marks one of the most bitterly-contested battlefields of the First World War.

ROUTE DES GRANDES ALPES★★★

Map p 10 – Michelin map 70, 74, 77, 81, 89, 115 or 244, 245 – Local map p 226
Green Guides Alpes du Nord (in French), Alpes du Sud (in French) and French Riviera

Among the many routes which invite the visitor to explore the French Alps, this high altitude road is the most famous. Rarely far from the frontier, the Great Alpine Road links Lake Geneva with the Riviera, crossing 25 passes in all as it leaps from valley to valley. It is only open from end to end during the summer months.

The great arc of the Alps running from Vienna to Nice was formed in Tertiary times by earth-movements which brought the plateau-continent of Africa and the Hercynian foreland of Europe closer together, subjecting the deep sedimentary beds laid down in the geosyncline between them to intense pressure, uplifting, folding and transporting them. The High Alps in France comprise two main divisions. In a central position rise ancient crystalline massifs, remains of the ancient Hercynian system which were eroded, then covered by sedimentary rocks in Secondary times. The shocks of the Tertiary age uplifted them violently; subsequent denudation has left a varied pattern of rounded summits and dramatic pinnacled peaks. The sparsely populated landscapes of this part of the Alps with their forests of larch are lit by intense sunshine from the clearest of skies. To the east of the crystalline massifs lies the Sedimentary Zone, whose uplifted rocks, often metamorphosed under extreme pressure and heat, have formed broad sunlit valleys which enjoy a mild climate.

During Quaternary times, the landscape was refashioned by the erosive powers of great rivers and by four successive glaciations.

At the foot of the northern High Alps is the Sub-Alpine Furrow; running roughly north-south, this broad valley some 177km – 110 miles long is fed by the mountain streams draining into the Isère and the Drac; it forms one of the most important communications routes in the French Alps. The Durance valley plays a similar role in the southern Alps.

The High Alps are approached via a more or less continuous zone of rugged calcareous mountains, the Pre-Alps, which reach their widest extent in the south.

Two-day programme.

By driving hard it is indeed possible to get from Thonon to Menton in two days, but to do so would be to deprive oneself of a number of sights which in themselves would make the trip worthwhile; they include Chamonix with the Aiguille du Midi and the Vallée Blanche, La Grave and the splendid viewpoint at Le Chazelet, St-Véran...

Six-day programme.

- Thonon-Beaufort: *144km – 90 miles – allow 5 1/2hours including sightseeing.*
- Beaufort-Val d'Isère: *71km – 44 miles – allow 3 hours including sightseeing.*
- Val d'Isère-Briançon: *180km – 112 miles – allow 7 1/2hours including sightseeing*
- Briançon-Barcelonnette: *133km – 83 miles – allow 6 1/2hours including sightseeing*
- Barcelonnette-Menton: *206km – 128 miles – allow 6 hours including sightseeing.*

FROM THONON TO MENTON *734km – 458 miles*

★★ **Thonon** – *See Main Resorts in Introduction.* From the Place du Château the view extends over the great sweep of **Lake Geneva**★★★. On the Swiss shore to the north rise the terraces of the great Lavaux vineyard and beyond are the mountains of the Vaudois Alps (to the east) and the Jura. Saint Francis of Sales once preached in St Hippolytus' Church (Église St-Hippolyte); its **vault**★ has retained its original stucco and 18 painted medallions together with the stucco decoration of its false pillars (visible from the adjoining basilica), all done by the Italian craftsmen who restored the interior in Rococo style in the 18C.

The road rises in a series of steps through the damp beech woodland of the gorges cut by the River Dranse de Morzine. This marks the transition between the gently rolling hill country fringing the great lake and the **Chablais**★★ massif, a complex of high ridges and peaks, with rich pastures grazed by Abondance cattle. The most spectacular part of the route is known as the **Devil's Bridge Gorge**★★ (Gorges du Pont du Diable), marked by a number of rock-falls, one of which has formed the bridge attributed to the Evil One.

★★ **Morzine** – *See Main Resorts in Introduction.* The valleys around the resort are dotted with hamlets; the chalets have patterned balconies. All around grow sombre forests of spruce.

After the pass at Les Gets, the small industrial town of Tanninges marks the beginning of the **Faucigny**★★ country. Drained by the Giffre, this is a landscape of pastures and sprucewoods, fashioned by the action of glacial moraines on calcareous rocks deposited here far from their point of origin.

Cluses – The town commands the most important lateral valley *(cluse)* in the French Alps. The River Arve has cut down directly through the folded rocks of the Aravis range to make its gorge. Clocks and watches and precision metal products are made here.

Above Cluses, the broad glacial valley of the Arve separates the Chablais and the **Giffre** (to the northeast) from the Aranis (to the southwest) also known as the Genevois. The upland Sallanches basin is bounded to the north by the dramatic peaks of a number of ranges, but dominating all is the great mass of Mont Blanc itself, the "Giant of the Alps".

★★ **La Clusaz** – The most important ski resort in the **Massif des Aravis** owes its name to the deep gorge or *cluse*, downstream of it, through which the Nom torrent gushes. The village, situated in the middle of pine forests and mountain pasture, is tightly huddled around the big church characterised by its onion dome tower. The jagged outlines of the Aravis mountains can be seen stretching away into the distance.

In the summer, La Clusaz offers an excellent setting for walking and in winter, this well-equipped resort provides plenty of thrills for ski enthusiats.

At the top of the climb out of the Arly Valley, the Notre-Dame de Bellecombe road gives good views first of all of the Aravis massif, then of the wooded gorges cut by the Arly.

Col des Saisies – It is at this point that the route leaves the Sub-Alpine Furrow; from here as far as St-Martin-d'Entraunes to the south of the Cayolle Pass (Col de Cayolle), its course lies entirely within the High Alps.

The broad depression of the Saisies Pass, 1 633m – 5 358ft high, is one of the most characteristic alpine grazing grounds to be seen along the route; it is browsed by sturdy little reddish-brown cattle as well as by the dark brown Tarines breed and the white-spotted Abondances. The landscape is studded with innumerable chalets.

Beaufort – This little crossroads town (its church has fine woodcarvings and interesting sculptures) has given its name to the **Beaufortain**★★ country, an area of folded limestone beds on a base of ancient crystalline rocks. Virtually continuous forest cover forms a background to sweeping alpine pastures. Above

High Alps	Ancient crystalline massifs			Boundary between the Northern and Southern Alps
	Sedimentary zone			
Pre-Alps				District boundary
Sub-Alpine Furrow				Route des Grandes Alpes
Principal massifs				Route Napoléon

the 1 450m – 4 750ft contour, the pastoral economy is marked by the seasonal movement of the herds up and down the slopes. The village of **Boudin**★ *(7km – 4 miles south)* is particularly picturesque.

★ **Cormet de Roselend** - This long valley, 1 900m – 6 200ft high, links the Roselend and Chapieux valleys. It is a vast, treeless, lonely place, dotted with rocks and a few shepherds' huts.

A rushing mountain stream descends the steep **Chapieux valley**★ in a series of abrupt steps towards **Bourg-St-Maurice.** This strategically-sited town commands the routes coming down from the Beaufortin country and the Little St Bernard and Iseran Passes. Around it is the **Tarentaise**★★ country of the upper Isère valley where transhumance is still practised. By the time the route reaches Ste-Foy in the upper Tarentaise, the landscape has become decidedly more mountainous in character. The Tignes valley (Val de Tignes) is characterized by a striking series of gorges and glacial bars; the avalanche protection works are impressive, as is the **Tignes Dam**★★, a major engineering feat of the 1950s.

★★ **Val d'Isère** – *See Main Resorts in Introduction.* In its high valley 1 000m – 3 300ft above Bourg-St-Maurice, this is the most important place in the upper Tarentaise. With an excellent sunshine record, the resort is surrounded by splendid mountain landscapes; to the south and west are the glaciers and peaks (several of them rising to more than 3 500m – 11 500ft) of the Vanoise National Park, an important habitat for alpine flora and fauna, much favoured by walkers.

★ **Col d'Iseran** – 2 770m – 9 088ft. The road across this high pass was built as recently as 1936; it is the only link between the Tarentaise and the **Maurienne** country to the south. The latter region centres on the long valley of the River Arc; industry is more important there than agriculture, with metal-working and electro-chemical plants at places like Bonneval, Lansevillard, Modane, St-Michel-de-Maurienne and St-Jean-de-Maurienne. The location of settlements has been determined by the sharp breaks in slope marked by glacial bars.

Modane – This is a border town, sited at the French end of rail and road tunnels leading to Italy. The 13 657m – 8 1/2 mile rail link (completed in 1872) was begun on the initiative of the Sardinian monarchy which wished to unite those parts of its domain lying to either side of the Alpine barrier. The road tunnel which came into service in 1980 is shorter - 12 870m – 8 miles.

At Valloire, the route once more enters the ancient Hercynian mountains and begins to climb towards the Galibier Pass.

★★ **Col du Galibier** – 2 642m – 8 668ft. From the viewing table there is a superb panorama which takes in the Maurienne country (to the north), and the Pelvoux region (to the south), which is separated from the Briançonnais country by the high ridge of the Écrins massif. The pass marks the dividing line between the northern and southern part of the French Alps.

At the **Col du Lautaret**★★ with its fine views of the Meije mountains, turn right in the direction of La Grave in the **Romanche valley**, then turn left at the entrance to the second tunnel.

★★ **Oratoire du Chazelet** – From the viewing table, the view extends over the high peaks of the Écrins National Park from the Col des Ruillans on the right to the broken ridges of the Meije (including le Doigt de Dieu – The Finger of God – at 3 974m – 13 025ft). The upper course of the glacier, fed by frequent snowfall, is of a staggering whiteness. This part of the Alps provides good conditions for high-altitude skiing.

★ **La Grave** – The village has a particularly fine **site**★★ in the Romanche valley at the foot of the Meije. A two-stage cable-car ride takes the visitor to a height of 3 200m – 10 500ft at the col on the western flank of Mount Rateau from where there are unforgettable views over the Meije and the Écrins glaciers.

View of La Meije from the Oratoire du Chazelet

D. Hée/MICHELIN

Back at the Lauteret Pass, the route now enters the southern part of the French Alps. At Monêtier in the Guisanne valley, it re-enters the sedimentary zone of the High Alps; oak, beech and ash reappear, the valleys open out and the whole landscape takes on a lighter air.

★★ **Briançon** – *See BRIANÇON.*

★★ **Col d'Izoard** – 2 361m – 7 746ft. The pass is in a desolate setting fringed by dramatic peaks. From the viewing tables magnificent views extend over the Briançonnais to the north and the Queyras country to the south.

The road descends in a series of hairpin bends through a strange landscape of screes and jagged rocks known as the **Casse Déserte★★**. At this high altitude, the processes of erosion are greatly accelerated by the extremes of temperature to which the rocks are exposed.

The high **Queyras★★** country is centred on the valley of the River Guil. Closed off downstream from the outside world by a series of narrow gorges, and cut off from main communication routes, it has fine examples of alpine houses. Above Château-Queyras, the valley sides are sharply differentiated; the gentler south-facing slopes are covered with well-watered meadows, while the north-facing slopes grow only larches and Arolla pines.

★★ **St-Véran** – Lying between the 1 990m – 6 530ft contour and the 2 040m – 6 690ft contour, this is the highest community in Europe. Its chalets, timber-built on a basement of schist, are a unique example of adaptation to the rigours of a high altitude mountain life which combines arable cultivation and grazing, forestry, and the exercise of craft skills during the long winters. The south-facing dwellings are sited in groups, most of them with hay-barns and the balconies on which cereals are ripened. The village has a strange sculpture showing Christ's Agony.

The little town of **Guillestre**, with its church characterised by a beautiful **porch★** is situated at the end of the **Combe du Queyras★★**, a canyon carved out by the clear and abundant waters of the River Guil.

★ **Embrun** – *24km – 15 miles southwest of Guillestre.* High up on its terrace overlooking the River Durance as it emerges from the mountains, the little town was once a cathedral city, the seat of an archbishop. From the Place de l'Archevêché there are fine views over the valley slopes with their well-cultivated terraced fields. The torrents entering the main valley have spread their debris over its floor in alluvial fans, forcing some of the local roads to follow a tortuous alignment. The upper slopes have been gouged by deep ravines, while dominating the scene are the bare and sombre crests of the high mountains.

The former **Notre-Dame Cathedral** ⊙, the finest church in the whole of the Dauphiné Alps, dates from the close of the 12C; it has fine black and white marble stonework and the **north porch★** « Le Réal », in North Italian style, is supported on pretty pink columns.

Col de Vars – 2 111m – 6 893ft. This pass forms the gateway to the Ubaye valley. The landscape is made up of highly laminated schists; the valley floor, littered with boulders and studded with gloomy ponds, is grazed by herds of sheep.

Beyond the pass, the south-facing slopes with their scattered hamlets are given over entirely to stock-farming. In its upper reaches, the River Ubaye has cut deeply into the dark schists; its course is frequently impeded by the alluvial fans of the side-torrents which feed it. Near La Condamine, the 19C Fort Tournoux seems part of the high rock on which it is built. After Jausiers, the route enters the Barcelonnette basin; the valley pastures are interspersed with woodland and the scene becomes more cheerful altogether.

★ **Barcelonnette** – *See BARCELONNETTE.*

At this point, those visitors who are already familiar with the Cayolle Pass (Col de la Cayolle) can get to the central Var valley via the Restefond Pass (Col de Restefond), the Bonnette Peak (Cime de la Bonnette) (involving an extra climb of 535m – 1 755ft), and the Tinée valley, or alternatively via the Allos Pass (Col d'Allos) and the upper Verdon (36km – 22 miles further). See details below.

The road climbs around the flank of Mount Pelat, the highest (3 035m – 10 164ft) peak in the Provence Alps.

★★ **Col de la Cayolle** – 2 327m – 7 635ft. This pass links the Ubaye country and the Upper Verdon to the upper reaches of the Var. From the top there are views over the deep valley of the Var towards the Grasse Pre-Alps in the far distance.

★★ **The Upper valley of the River Var** – The source of the **Var** is on the left as the road drops away from the pass to follow the river as it threads its way through the sombre mountains. At St-Martin-d'Entraunes, the route passes from the High Alps into the sedimentary zone again, this time into the Pre-Alps of Provence. Downstream from Villeneuve, the clear water coursing through the drainage channels draws the visitor's attention to the changes that take place in the landscape of the countryside around Guillaume.

★★ **Gorges de Daluis** – These deep gorges have been cut by the river into thick beds of red porphyry and Urgonian limestone, giving striking colour effects.
The road from **Guillaume** to **Beuil** leads to the **Gorges du Cians** situated in the upper stretch of the river Var.
The road climbs steadily to the **Col de Valberg** offering varied views of the different sides of the valley : woody to the north, compared to the southern one covered with vineyards and fruit trees. The descent towards **Roubion** from the **Col de Couilloie** (1 678 m – 5 503 ft) reveals the valleys of **La Vionèse** and **La Tinée**.
After the impressive **site**★★ of Roubion (the village is perched 1 300 m – 4 264 ft up on a ridge), the road travels through a red schistose landscape, enlivened by several waterfalls.

★ **Roure** – This village is characterised by its architectural unity: houses with red schist walls and limestone tile roofs *(lauze)*.
The route then follows the river Vionèse until it flows into the river Tinée at **St-Sauveur-sur-Tinée**. Outside the village, on the left, a small road leads to the extraordinary **site**★ of **Ramplas**, a village built on a ridge.

La Bolline – This pleasant summer resort is situated in the middle of a chestnut grove.

La Colmiane – The chalets and hotels of this winter sports resort are amidst a wonderful larch forest.
From the **Col de St-Martin**, there is a possibility of taking a chairlift up to the **Pic de Colmiane**★★ (beautiful **panorama**★★ from the top).

★ **St-Martin-Vésubie** – From this famous mountaineering centre, visitors can go rambling in the **Vallon du Boréon**★★ or the **Vallon de la Madone de Fenestre**★.

Roquebillière – This large village has been rebuilt six times since the 6C.

La Bollène-Vésubie – The concentric streets of this peaceful village, in the middle of a beautiful chestnut grove, converge on the church, which crowns the hill.
The **Forest of Turini**★★, which spreads across the valleys of the Vésubie and of the Bévéra, demarcates the southern border of the **Parc national du Mercantour**.

★★ **Le Massif de l'Authion** – North of the **Col de Turini**, this massif constitutes a wonderful natural fortress which seems to stand guard over the roads between the Vésubie and Roya valleys. This strategic value has caused it to be, throughout the centuries, the stage for several conflicts. In April 1945, it was the last sector of France to be liberated. A stele commemorates the fierceness of the combats. After crossing the forest of Turini, the river Bévéra winds its way towards the **Gorges du Piaon**★★ where the corniche road overlooks the river. The road then goes through **Moulinet**, a charming village set in a verdant valley before passing the **Chapelle de Notre-Dame-La-Menour** with its Renaissance facade.

★ **Sospel** – This Alpine resort was once a bishopric, during the Great Schism. On the Nice road, 1 km-0.6 miles from the centre of the village, stands the **Fort St-Roch** (1) one of the last evidence of the "Alpine Maginot line" built in the 1930s. The road follows the old railway line which used to link Sospel to Menton, along the course of the Merlanson, a tributary of the Bévéra. On the opposite side of the valley, the road to Nice via the **Col de Braus**, winds its way, amidst olive groves, towards the capital of the French Riviera.

★★ **Menton** – *See MENTON*.

ROUTE NAPOLÉON★

Map p 11 – Michelin map 84, 81, 77 or 245, 244 – Local Map p 226
Green Guides Alpes du Sud, Alpes du Nord (in French) and French Riviera

This scenic highway (Napoleon's Highway – N 85) runs from the Mediterranean shore at Golfe-Juan to Grenoble, following the route taken by Napoleon on his return from Elba in 1815. Inaugurated in 1932, it leads from the Riviera northwestwards through the southern Pre-Alps and is marked throughout its length by the flying eagle symbol inspired by Napoleon's remark "The eagle will fly from steeple to steeple until he reaches the towers of Notre-Dame".

Napoleon's return – The Emperor escaped from Elba on 26 February 1815, landing on the beach at Golfe-Juan on 1 March.

An imperial eagle, Laffray

FOC, Grenoble, Meylan

2 March. After a brief overnight stop at Cannes, Napoleon and his little troop halted just outside Grasse and then took to the mule tracks of the countryside. The next night was spent at Seranon.

3 March. Midday halt at Castellane and overnight in Barrème.

4 March. The party found its way back on to the main highway at Digne, then passed the night at the Château de Malijai.

5 March. The Emperor lunched at Sisteron, then left the town in an atmosphere of growing enthusiasm. Overnight at Gap.

6 March. At Les Barraques, Napoleon declined the offer of the local peasants to join his force. Overnight at Corps.

7 March. Near Laffrey, the way forward was barred by troops. Ordered to fire, they first hesitated, then broke ranks to shouts of "Vive l'Empereur!" Escorted by the men of the 7th Regiment, Napoleon made his triumphal entry into Grenoble at 7 o'clock in the evening.

FROM GOLFE-JUAN TO GRENOBLE

336km - 209 miles - allow a whole day

Leading across the southern Pre-Alps to the long valley known as the Sub-Alpine Furrow, the route can be followed throughout the year.

Golfe-Juan - *Leave Golfe-Juan by the N7.*

★★ **Antibes** - The first settlement here was a trading post founded by Greek merchants from Marseilles in the 4C BC. Reconstructed in the 16C, the **Grimaldi Castle** dates from the 12C, when it was built on the site of a Roman encampment to protect the coast from the incursions of Barbary pirates. Inside, the **Picasso Museum★** (Musée Picasso) ⊙ has a good selection of the master's works, including drawings, prints and tapestries *(The Lobster, Two Nudes and a Mirror)*, as well as paintings *(Still Life with Watermelon)*... The town was purchased from the Grimaldi family by Henri IV because of its strategic position in relation to the Kingdom of Savoy. It was fortified first by François I, then by Vauban. To the west of the **Cap d'Antibes★★** *(p 51)* stretches the fine sandy beach of Golfe-Juan.

★★ **Grasse** - Prettily located on the slopes of the Grasse Pre-Alps, the **Old Town★** has picturesque streets lined with tall Provencal houses. Grasse's most famous son was Jean-Honoré Fragonard (1732-1806), the painter best known for his witty depictions of the frivolities of 18C court life. The **Fragonard Room★** in the **Villa-Museum Fragonard** ⊙ has two of the artist's self-portraits as well as his *Three Graces*.

For the past three centuries, Grasse has been an important centre of the perfume industry. The products which emerge from the secrecy of the town's laboratories owe much to the sensitivity of certain highly developed "noses". It takes one tonne of jasmin blossom to manufacture just three grammes of the mixture of perfume and wax known as "concrète". An International Perfume Museum, **Musée international de la Parfumerie** ⊙ recently opened its doors in Grasse.

To the north of the **Pas de la Faye** with its **view★★** over mountains and Mediterranean, the road enters Upper Provence (Haute Provence) through the Seranon valley.

★ **Castellane** - The sheep-grazed valley in which the town is situated is overlooked by the "Roc", a limestone cliff 184m - 604ft high.

The Castellane Pre-Alps extend over a wide area; they consist of a series of bare ridges through which the River Asse has cut its deep valley. To the north of the former cathedral city of Senez lie the Digne Pre-Alps, the most desolate of all the Southern Alps, a harsh landscape with a meagre mantle of garrigue vegetation, deeply scored by the beds of torrents. A complex geological history has produced a series of folded ridges through which the rivers have cut their gorges, as well as long crests of pale rock to the east and broad fertile valleys to the north.

★ **Digne-les-Bains** - Digne spreads out along its valley **site★** at the foot of the rise on which its old town is situated. There are dramatic **views★** of the whole area from the hill-top village of **Courbons★**, 6km - 4 miles to the north. In the Place General-de-Gaulle is a memorial to Pierre Gassendi (1592-1655), born at nearby Champtercier. This natural philosopher was provost of the cathedral here; much of his scientific work was devoted to studying the properties of sound.

At **Malijai**, the route enters the **Durance basin**, an alluvial plain 6km - 4 miles wide in places, lying between the Valensole plateau to the east and the Vaucluse to the west. The Durance is the great river of the southern Alps, tracing its meanders through the gravel terraces on which a prosperous agricultural pattern has developed, favoured by the mildness of the climate. The best crops are grown on those sites which have been effectively drained; the wetter areas are occupied by woodland.

★★ Sisteron – *See SISTERON.*

★ Gap – Gap is pleasantly sited in the valley carved out by the glacier which was the ancestor of the Durance. The town's prosperity was built on the rich soils of its agricultural hinterland, one of the most fertile areas of the southern Alps. Founded by the Gauls, Gap became a staging-post along the Roman road from Turin to Valence, then a fortified cathedral town.

The **Col Bayard** (1 246m – 4 088ft) links the southern and northern Alps. From the viewing table at Chauvet on the south side of the pass the view extends over the valley around Gap. To the north is the beginning of the Sub-Alpine Furrow which the road enters by way of the Drac valley, hollowed out in the beds of schist by the action of the Quaternary glaciers. This is an ancient highway, once travelled by merchants on their way to the fairs at St-Bonnet. Terraced villages line the route, their roofs tiled in brown stone. To the left are the precipitous slopes and savage peaks of the Dévoluy Massif, to the right the Valgaudemar valley threading its way deep into the Écrins National Park.

Corps – A small bustling town in the Sub-Alpine Furrow. The road passes through areas of well-cultivated farmland interrupted by glacial bars, one of which has been used in the siting of the **Sautet Dam★★** *(5km – 3 miles west)*, with its deep lake hemmed in by high canyon-like walls; far below its surface is the hidden confluence of the Drac with the Souloise.
Around La Mure, the Trièves country is overlooked by the broad summit of Mount Aiguille (2 086m – 6 880ft), also known as the "unclimbable mountain" though it was actually conquered as long ago as 1492.

★ Laffrey – Just south of the village is the spot known as the "**Prairie de la Rencontre★**" where the vain attempt was made to bar Napoleon's progress northwards *(see p 229)*.

The road now descends towards **Vizille★** and Grenoble.

★★ Grenoble – *See GRENOBLE.*

Abbaye de ST-BENOÎT-SUR-LOIRE★★

Map p 6 – Michelin map 64 fold 10 or 238 fold 6 – Green Guide Châteaux of the Loire

In 675 AD, the original abbey founded here on a river terrace well above flood level was presented with the remains of St Benedict and of his sister, St Scholastica, brought all the way from Monte Cassino in Italy. Hitherto known simply as Fleury Abbey, the monastery now rededicated itself to the founder of Western monasticism (St Benedict = St-Benoît in French). The abbey's influence waxed at the beginning of the 9C with the appointment of Theodulf by the Emperor Charlemagne; this great abbot served his master by introducing the study of the Scriptures and of Roman law, and by promoting the conservation of ancient texts.

★★ Basilica ⓥ – Built between 1067-1108, the Romanesque edifice has a fine **crypt★** with a double ambulatory and a central pillar containing the relics of St Benedict. The **choir★★** is remarkable for its paving (a Roman mosaic brought here from Italy) and for the elegant arcading setting off the plain walls of its elevation, while the crossing carries the cupola of the central bell-tower on superimposed squinches.
Outside, the belfry **porch★★** is one of the finest examples of Romanesque art in France. Originally free-standing, it was joined to the basilica when the nave was extended in the middle of the 12C.

Plain-chant score, St-Benoît-sur-Loire

Bibliothèque municipale, Orléans/MICHELIN

It evokes in stone the vision of Paradise as described in the Apocalypse of St John, with three gateways facing each point of the compass (north, south, east and west), ever-open to receive the souls of the elect. A total of 16 sturdy pillars with engaged columns have beautifully carved capitals (*c*1120) depicting the same theme.

EXCURSION

★ **Germigny-des-Prés** – *5.5km – 3 miles northwest.* The much restored church is the **oratory** ⊘ which Abbot Theodulf built for himself. It is a typical example of Carolingian architecture of the 9C, with an unusual plan, alabaster window-panes filtering the light and above all a remarkable **mosaic**★★ in the dome of the east apse; this conforms to the iconography of the time, which rejected all forms of personal representation of the divinity. Its design centres on the Ark of the Covenant which symbolises the figure of Christ and which is surmounted by two cherubim flanked by two archangels.

ST-BERTRAND-DE-COMMINGES★

Population 217
Map p 8 – Michelin map 85 fold 20 or 234 fold 44
Green Guide Atlantic Coast

King Herod is supposed to have spent his years of exile in the substantial town which had been founded here in 72 BC by Pompey. In AD 585 the Burgundians descended on the place and laid it waste. For centuries the site lay abandoned, until in 1073 St Bernard saw its potential for the building of a cathedral and monastery. Here the rules of the religious reforms of Pope Gregory VII were applied, making the little city the spiritual centre of Comminges, endowing the awkwardly-shaped county (sandwiched as it was between the territories belonging to the House of Foix-Béarn and dotted with enclaves) with a religious significance far outweighing its political importance.

The sanctuaries of this area, with their wealth of highly-prized relics, were often adorned with sculpture, which here reaches a high point in its development. The Romanesque portal of the cathedral is made up of several independently sculpted panels showing the Adoration of the Magi and a figure of St Bertrand without a halo (i.e. before his canonisation in 1218), recalling the work of the School of Toulouse at St Sernin. The **cloisters**★★ are built over the 12-15C ramparts; the south side is open, giving fine views over the Upper Garonne countryside, and there is a famous pillar in primitive style with statues of the four Evangelists.

In the **cathedral**★ ⊘ are splendid **choir-stalls**★★ of 1535 in Italian Renaissance style; features to note particularly include the bishop's throne, a Jesse Tree and a Madonna and Child.

★ **Basilique St-Just** – *At Valcabrère, 2km – 1 mile northwest.* Standing in isolation among the cypresses of a country cemetery, the church was built in the 11C-12C with materials from an older building. Four fine statuecolumns grace its north portal, but its most unusual feature is its apse, where a number of triangular niches frame a central opening with a window giving on to a funerary recess.

ST-CLAUDE★★

Population 12 704
Map p 10 – Michelin map 70 fold 15 or 243 fold 43
Green Guide Burgundy Jura – Town plan in the current Michelin Red Guide France

The historic core of St-Claude sits high up on a **site**★★ overlooking the meeting-point of the Tacon with the Bienne.

Lying as it does in the heart of the Jura forests, the town has long produced wooden articles of all kinds, notably the briar pipes which have been made here for over 200 years (exhibition).

Chapeau de Gendarme – *8km – 5 miles southeast.* This geological oddity owes its name to the shape made by the folded beds of limestone. These were originally laid down in Secondary times, but during the Tertiary era they were compressed and uplifted at the same time as the Alps were being formed; they were folded without however being split, and forced upward into dome-like shapes with symmetrical sides, a text-book example of the formation of an anticline.

▶► Cathédrale St-Pierre★ – choir-stalls★★ – altarpiece★; Place Louis-XI – view★.

In this guide
town plans show the main streets and the way to the sights
local maps show not only the main roads but also the roads recommended in a round tour

Cathédrale ST-DENIS***

Map p 6 – Michelin map 101 fold 16 – Green Guide Flanders, Picardy and the Paris Region

St-Denis is an important manufacturing centre immediately to the north of Paris. It owes its name to the great missionary who became the first bishop of Paris when it was still Roman Lutetia. St Denis was beheaded at Montmartre around 250 AD; legend has it that he walked all the way here with his head in his hands before finally expiring.

The cathedral is of central importance in the evolution of the Early Gothic style in architecture. Although work had begun on the cathedral at Sens eight years earlier, St-Denis precedes Noyon, Senlis and Laon by several years and Notre-Dame at Paris by a good quarter-century. The building is the achievement of two great masters, Abbot Suger in the 12C and Pierre de Montreuil in the 13C. Suger was responsible for the first two bays of the nave, begun in 1136 and completed four years later, where the Romanesque tribunes and semicircular arches sit together with the pointed arches heralding the Gothic. Similar juxtapositions are evident in the chancel and ambulatory (only the lower part of which survives) completed in 1143, giving "an effect of lightness, of air circulating freely, of supple
curves and energetic concentration" (Nikolaus Pevsner). A century later, Pierre de Montreuil rebuilt the upper parts of the chancel and transept, which he treated as a pre-chancel, giving it sufficient width to accommodate the royal tombs. He also built the nave, a masterpiece of High Gothic.

The many **royal tombs*** in chancel and pre-chancel make the cathedral a veritable museum of funerary art from the Middle Ages to the Renaissance; there is a total of 79 recumbent figures. Note the splendid **crypt**★★.

Since the French Revolution the tombs have been empty, but it is nevertheless possible to trace the evolution of this particular form of sculpture as it developed in France.

To begin with, the recumbent figure, like the one depicting Clovis, was simply placed on a slab. In 1260, Louis IX ordered symbolic effigies to be carved of all the rulers who had gone before him since the 7C. The first attempt at producing a likeness appears in 1285 with the statue of Philip the Bold. By the middle of the 14C, authentic portraits (e.g. that of Charles V – 1350) were the result of the work being commissioned while the subject was still alive.

In Renaissance times, fashion replaced effigies by mausoleums, often of the most elaborate character, with representations of the deceased in highly studied poses. The tomb of Henri II and Catherine de' Medici was designed by Primaticcio in the form of a little temple, with bronze sculptures by Germain Pilon depicting the Virtues and other praying figures.

ST-ÉMILION**

Population 2 799
Map p 8 – Michelin map 75 fold 12 – Green Guide Atlantic Coast

St-Émilion, like many towns in wine-producing regions, offers simple and sophisticated attractions to art lovers and gourmets alike. The town, which is named after the Breton hermit who retired here around 750, is divided into two hill sites with the Royal Castle and Deanery (Doyenné) symbolising the age-old rivalry between the civil and religious authorities. Its sunbaked, pantile-roofed stone houses nestle in an **amphitheatre**★★ on the slope of a limestone plateau.

St-Émilion has an unusual underground **church**★ hollowed out of a single rock in the limestone strata between the 8C and the 12C. The nave and two aisles are 38m – 125ft long, 20m – 65ft wide and 11m – 33ft high.

ST-FLOUR**

Population 7 417
Map p 9 – Michelin map 76 folds 4, 14 or 239 south of fold 31
Green Guide Auvergne-Rhône Valley – Town plan in the current Michelin Red Guide France

This ancient town was once the capital of Upper Auvergne (Haute Auvergne); it occupies a spectacular **site**★★ high above the Lander valley at the eastern tip of one of the lava flows from the vast Cantal volcano.

During the Hundred Years War, its virtually impregnable fortifications helped guard French Auvergne from English Guyenne.

At the eastern end of the upper town with its old lava-built houses stands the **cathedral**★, erected in the 15C in Southern French style. From the Terrasse des Roches nearby there are extensive views over the rich grasslands of the Planèze de St-Flour; this is an inclined plateau, the result of the piling up on one another of successive lava flows whose mineralogical composition is very diverse.

EXCURSIONS

★★ **Viaduc du Garabit** ⓥ – *12km – 7 miles south.* This daring steel structure carries the Clermont-Ferrand-Millau railway across the Truyère valley with its many hydroelectric works. Its central arch is 116m – 381ft across. It was built between 1882-84 by Gustave Eiffel using plans drawn up by Boyer.

The river changes its course abruptly just here; long ago, it flowed northward towards the Allier, but the effects of the fold-movements of Tertiary times, together with the blocking of its valley by a lava-flow, meant that its waters were diverted southwestward to feed the Lot. Boat trips ⓥ are possible on the Grandval.

★★ **Château d'Alleuze** – *26km – 16 miles west from Garabit via the Mallet viewpoint and the Grandval Dam.* The square keep and round towers of this most romantic of **ruins**★★ loom menacingly over the lake held back by the Grandval Dam. During the course of the Hundred Years War *(qv)*, an adventurer in the pay of the English, one Bernard de Garlan, got hold of the place by trickery. For seven years he terrorised the neighbourhood, until a band of soldiers from St-Flour sent him packing. They also dismantled the castle in order to prevent any recurrence of the trouble in 1405.

*Consult the key on the inside front cover to interpret
all the information provided on town plans*

ST-GERMAIN-EN-LAYE★★

Population 39 926
Map p 6 – Michelin map 101 fold 12
Green Guide Flanders, Picardy and the Paris Region
Town plan in the current Michelin Red Guide France

Now a pleasant residential town just to the west of Paris, St-Germain's significance in the course of French history goes back hundreds, if not thousands of years.

Proximity to the capital and a strategic site 60m – 200ft above a bend in the Seine persuaded Louis VI the Fat to build a stronghold here . Later, when the Hundred Years War was at its height, the castle was restored by Charles V.

Some of the French kings were born at St-Germain (Charles IX, Henri II, Louis XIV), as were any number of princes, writers, historians, composers... Louis XIII died here. It was here that the negotiations took place between the Huguenot leader Gaspar de Coligny and the representatives of Catherine de' Medici which put an end to the Third War of Religion by the Treaty of St-Germain, signed on 8 August 1570, and it was here that in 1641 Richelieu promulgated the edict limiting the rights of the French parliament.

On 28 February 1837, the first passenger-carrying railway line in France was inaugurated; following the alignment of today's RER (Paris Express Network), it linked a ferry landing-stage in Paris with the one at Le Pecq, on the far side of the river from St-Germain.

On 10 September 1919, the Treaty of St-Germain laid down the new frontiers of a defeated Austria and limited the size of her armed forces.

★ **Château** – Its appearance is still much as it was when François I had it rebuilt by Pierre de Chambiges; over the foundations of the medieval castle the architect raised an edifice more to the taste of the 16C, though his upper brick courses and roof terrace with its ornamental balustrade caused a sensation at the time. The Court spent much of its time here between the reigns of Henri IV and Louis XIV; the latter brought in Mansart, who replaced the corner turrets by pavilions, and Le Nôtre, who designed the park, laid out the enormously long terrace, and replanted the forest.

The château houses the **Musée des Antiquités nationales**★★ ⓥ; its priceless collection of archeological exhibits traces French history through space and time from the Paleolithic to the Middle Ages.

Most of the objects displayed are original; they illustrate the slow progress of humanity from the days of the Pebble Culture (some 4 000 000 years ago) to the industries and arts of Paleolithic times (the tiny head of the Dame de Brassempouy, the first known representation of a human face), via the Mesolithic and Neolithic cultures (the Bronze Age, followed by the Iron Age with the Halstatt and La Tène periods), to Gallo-Roman and Merovingian times, when skills decisive for the course of human evolution were developed (weapons, tools, utensils...).

ⓥ ►► Terrace★★; Ste-Chapelle★ (in the château); Musée du Prieuré★ – paintings of the Pont-Aven School and of the Nabis' movement.

ST-GUILHEM-LE-DÉSERT★

Population 190
Map p 9 – Michelin map 83 fold 6 or 240 fold 18
Green Guide Pyrenees-Languedoc-Tarn Gorges

In its remote **site★** where the Val de l'Infernet runs into the valley of the Hérault, this 9C **village★** grew up around an abbey founded by William of Aquitaine, one of Charlemagne's most valiant lieutenants.

★ **Église abbatiale** – This is a Romanesque structure of striking simplicity, famed for its possession of a fragment of the True Cross *(in the south transept)*. It has a doorway with dog-tooth moulding and an apse with massive buttresses and an elegant little arcade. Inside, the width of apse and transept is the result of a rebuilding undertaken in the 11C.

Of the 11C-12C cloisters, nothing remains apart from the ground floor of the north walk and part of the west walk. The vigorously-sculpted 13C capitals which once graced the galleries are now among the treasures of the Cloisters Museum, high above the Hudson in New York.

★★ **Grotte de Clamouse** ⊙ – *3km-2 miles south.* The caves run beneath the Larzac plateau. They are a product of the violent earth movements of the Tertiary era when fissures were opened up which subsequently became part of a network of underground streams. There are remarkable stalactites and stalagmites, but above all it is the splen-

R. Delon/Castelet, Boulogne-Billancourt

Aragonite bush, Grotte de Clamouse

did crystallisations which impress the visitor (calcite flowers, aragonite bushes, frosted bunches of grapes...).

ST-JEAN-DE-LUZ★★

Population 13 031
Map p 8 – Michelin map 85 fold 2 or 234 fold 29 – Green Guide Atlantic Coast
Town plan in the current Michelin Red Guide France

A harbour town at the mouth of the river Nivelle, St-Jean-de-Luz is one of the principal centres of the French Basque country.

The port and the Barre Quarter – As early as the 11C, sailors from St-Jean were hunting whales off Labrador. By the 15C, their quarry had changed to the abundant cod of the great fishing grounds off Newfoundland. When the Treaty of Utrecht forbade this activity, they turned to piracy, creating a fearsome reputation for their home port. Eventually they returned to more law-abiding ways, fishing for sardines off the coasts of Portugal and Morocco and for tuna off Senegal and Mauretania. The part of the town known as La Barre was where the ship-owners lived; its growth was intimately linked to the fortunes of its fleet. The 16C and 17C brought good times, though the place was burned down by the Spaniards in 1558, then ravaged by high tides in 1749 and 1785. Among the fine old houses, the most venerable is the one which survived the 1558 fire, once the property of Carquiou Kailu.

The marriage of Louis XIV – The marriage of Louis XIV to the infant Maria-Theresa was held up, first by one of the clauses in the Treaty of the Pyrenees, then by the king's passion for Marie Mancini, but in the end was solemnized here, on 9 June 1660. The king had been staying since 8 May in an imposing dwelling belonging to the ship-owner Lohobiague, which ever since has been known as the **Maison Louis XIV★** ⊙; the interior is particularly interesting, with a sturdy staircase built by ships' carpenters, 18C furniture in the drawing-room and fine panelling in the dining room.

Maria-Theresa was lodged in an elegant brick and stone **house** (Maison de l'infante) nearby. For a while, St-Jean-de-Luz became the capital of France. Court and government moved here, and days and nights were spent in feasting and revelry.

★★ **Église St-Jean Baptiste** – Work on enlarging the church had began in 1649 and had still not been completed when the royal wedding took place within its walls. It is the finest church in the French Basque country, with a resplendent 17C gilded **altarpiece**★ attributed to Martin de Bidache, a painted wooden ceiling and oak-built galleries on several levels. The main altar is raised above the sacristy, a feature of churches in the ancient Basque provinces of Labourd (in France) and Guipuzcoa (in Spain).

★ **Falaise de Socoa** - *14km - 9 miles south, then extending southward to Hendaye.* This unusual example of coastal relief is best seen at low tide. Following the drowning of the former coastline by the waters released by the melting of the Quaternary glaciers, the beds of highly laminated schists were attacked by wave action; the strata dip sharply seaward, projecting sharp saw-tooth ridges of the more resistant rock from the wave-cut platform at the foot of the cliffs.

EXCURSION

★★ **La Rhune** - *14km - 9 miles southeast, then as far as Sare.* Towards the end of the 6C, the Basques were probably pushed northwards by the Visigoths. Those of their number who settled in the plains of Aquitaine intermarried with the other local people eventually to become the Gascons. But those that remained in the mountains kept their independence and their enigmatic language, thus guaranteeing their very distinct identity.

The mountain called La Rhune ("good grazing" in Basque) is one of the symbols of the Basque country; its summit *(accessible by rack-and-pinion railway)* rises to a height of 900m - *c*3 000ft, offering a wonderful **panorama**★★★ ⊘ of the Bay of Biscay, the Landes and the ancient provinces of Labourd, Navarre and Guipuzcoa.

At the foot of the mountain lie the villages of **Ascain**★ and **Sare**★, both with many characteristically Basque features. The houses are timber-framed; the white rendering of the walls makes a pleasant contrast to the reddish-brown colour usually applied to the timber, while the cemeteries adjoining the churches have the typical discoidal tombstones arranged in a circle.

If visitors are lucky, they may see the local people dancing the chaste but passionate fandango or taking part in pigeon-hunts.

ST-JEAN-PIED-DE-PORT★

Population 1 432
Map p 8 - Michelin map 85 fold 3 or 234 fold 37 - Green Guide Atlantic Coast
Town plan in the current Michelin Red Guide France

The little town owes its name to its position at the foot of the important Roncesvalles pass *(port)* through the Pyrenees. In the days when numberless pilgrims trod the dusty road to Santiago de Compostella, St-Jean was the last staging-post in France before the steep ascent towards the Spanish frontier. The pilgrims would normally have taken the Ports de Cize road, now no longer a highway but an official long distance footpath (GR 65); today's tourist traffic on the Rue d'Espagne still evokes something of the bustle of medieval times.

The northern side of the town was fortified in the 15C by the Navarrese. In 1512, the place became capital of Lower Navarre, the rump left to the Albret family by Ferdinand the Catholic after he had dispossessed them of their lands in Spain. In the Rue de la Citadelle are a number of red sandstone houses built at this time or in the 16C and 17C, distinguished by their rounded doorways and sculpted lintels. The fortifications on the far bank of the river protecting the road to Spain, together with the citadel itself, are part of a system of defences designed by Vauban.

ST-MALO★★★

Population 48 057
Map p 4 - Michelin map 59 fold 6 or 230 fold 11 - Green Guide Brittany
Town plan in the current Michelin Red Guide France

The **site**★★★ of the walled town of St Malo on the east bank of the Rance is unique in France, making the ancient port one of the country's great tourist attractions. The town's real prosperity began in the 16C. In 1534, **Jacques Cartier** had set out from here on the voyage which led to the discovery and naming of Canada; very soon a thriving commerce had begun, based on the abundant furs brought back from the deep interior of the new country by trappers and traders. Cod fishing developed too, as the Breton sailors exploited the teeming grounds off Newfoundland (though this did lead to a reduction in the dried fish export trade). St Malo waxed rich.

From the end of the 16C, the local ship-owners began to build themselves fine manor-houses in the surrounding countryside, as well as tall timber-built residences in the town itself. By the sixties of the following century, their boats were trading around the coasts of the Pacific, and their ever-increasing wealth enabled them to build in granite. But from this time onwards, Parisian architectural fashions and the centralising tendencies of the monarchy began to prevail over local traditions. Anticipating the coming naval rivalry between England and France, Colbert became aware of the vulnerability of his country's western coasts; in 1689, Vauban was commissioned to strengthen the defences of St-Malo, particularly on the landward side of the town to the north and the east. The two countries contested command of the seas and of the lands beyond throughout the 18C; a prominent part in the struggle was played by men from St-Malo like the privateers Dugay-Trouin and Surcouf, while the Falkland Islands were given their French name (Isles Malouines) by colonists who came from here.

In the 19C, the invention of floating docks ended the advantage which the great tidal range of the port had long given its ship-builders and repairers.

ST-MALO

E Quic-en-Groigne
M¹ Musée de
    la Poupée
    et du Jouet ancien
M² Musée
    d'Histoire de la ville
    et d'Ethnographie
    du pays malouin

★★ Ramparts – It is possible to walk right around the town on top of the walls (allow an hour). There are fine views up the valley of the Rance and towards Dinard on the far side of the estuary. Nearer at hand is Grand Bé Island, which low tide leaves stranded; the simple tomb of **Chateaubriand** (born in St-Malo in 1768) (p 183) is here, facing seaward. Within the walls is the old town, almost entirely rebuilt after near-total destruction in 1944, but in such a way as to recapture the spirit of the place; solid walls of granite, relieved only by horizontal bands between each storey, steep mansard roofs and formidable chimney stacks (essential on this windy western coast), all combine to give an effect of harsh dignity and strong identity. The houses along the Rue de Dinan and those facing the walls are particularly fine.

★★ Château – This still has the façades of the 17C and 18C barracks.

Cathédrale St-Vincent – The nave vault of 1160 is one of the oldest in Brittany, albeit rebuilt after the last war. It is of Angevin type; at the time Brittany was a Plantagenet fiefdom. However, the effect of lightness achieved elsewhere is absent here, owing to the use of granite and its solidity of appearance (an original vault survives in the north aisle). Note the **stained-glass windows★** by Jean Le Moal.

  ⊙ ►► Musée d'histoire de la ville et d'Ethnolographie du Pays Malovin★ (**M¹**) – history of the town and its famous men; Quic-en-Groigne Tower★ **E** – wax museum; Fort National★.

EXCURSION

★★ Côte d'Émeraude – The name has been given to the picturesque northern coast of Brittany stretching from Cancale to Le Val André in the west. The Emerald Coast scenic road runs through the major resorts (Dinard, St Malo) and offers detours to the tips of the numerous headlands, including the renowned **Cap Fréhel★★★**, from which the **views** of the jagged coastline are in places quite spectacular.

ST-NECTAIRE★★

Population 664
Map p 9 – Map 73 fold 14 or 239 fold 19
Green Guide Auvergne-Rhône Valley

The upper part of the village of St-Nectaire (St-Nectaire-le-Haut) is sited on Mount Cornadore, a place inhabited since Celtic times.

★★ **Church** (Église) ⊘ – This little Romanesque church enjoys a spectacular location on the eastern slopes of the Dore mountains (Monts Dore). Built around 1160 as a dependency of the great Chaise-Dieu monastery, it suffered much damage during the French Revolution, and underwent major restoration (towers, west front) in 1875.

The interior has a number of notable features in addition to the dome on squinches; they include the unusual arrangement of nave vaults supported on columns rather than on pillars, a massive narthex and the characteristically Auvergnat mitred arches of the transepts.

The church's 103 **capitals**★★ (most are 12C) are justly famous. Carved from igneous rock (trachyte and andesite), they depict animals, foliage and Bible scenes. The finest of them, in the chancel, seem to owe much to the work of the sculptors of Mozac (qv); 87 figures illustrate scenes from the Life of Christ (the kiss of Judas, the road to Calvary) and the Resurrection (Doubting Thomas).

The **Treasury**★★ (north transept) houses a statue of Notre-Dame-du-Mont-Cornadore (a Virgin in Majesty of the 12C see p 218), a **reliquary bust of St Baudime**★★, a 12C Limoges masterpiece with a penetrating gaze and beautifully-rendered hands, as well as a reliquary arm of St Nectaire in repoussé silver and a pair of Limoges book plates of about 1170.

EXCURSION

★★ **Château de Murol** ⊘ – 6km – 4 miles east. The ruined castle rises from a basalt platform formed by a lava flow from the Tartaret volcano. The site with its polygonal keep was fortified as early as the 12C because of its strategic position between Auvergne and Cantal. At the end of the 14C, it became one of the main seigneurial residences of the province; Guillaume de Murol was responsible for those features which still distinguish the stronghold today (internal courtyard, main tower and north and east walls) and which serve to remind us both of the medieval obsession with security and of the fiercely guarded independence of the Auvergnat nobility.

A century later, the castle underwent alterations to bring it more into line with Renaissance tastes, including a tilting-ground with grandstand, a tympanum decorated with heraldic devices, and ornamental mantlepieces. But the troubled times associated with the **Catholic League** and the Wars of Religion led to the place being modernized in a military sense, with the building of bastions, watch-towers, as well as an outer wall rising directly from the cliff, all reinforcing the site's natural defensive ability to withstand bombardment or sapping. Now impregnable, the fortress was spared by Richelieu's demolition programme, but fell into ruin in the 18C.

ST-NICOLAS-DE-PORT★★

Population 7 702
Map p 7 – Michelin map 62 fold 5 or 242 fold 22
Green Guide Alsace et Lorraine (in French)

Located on the River Meurthe and the Marne-Rhine canal, St-Nicolas is an industrial town. It is the home of the Solvay Company's soda works, France's oldest, based on a 70m – 230ft thick deposit of rock salt which has been extracted since 1872 by solution and brine pumping. The splendid 15C-16C Church of St Nicolas rises somewhat incongruously from these workaday surroundings.

★★ **Basilique** ⊘ – The building is perhaps the finest example of the Flamboyant Gothic style in Lorraine. It was built between 1481 and 1560, at a time when the style had passed its peak and was indulging in all kinds of extravagant embellishment. A number of the church's features are of this kind, not only the west front with its heavy decoration and sculpture and the delicate arcading which in places relieves otherwise bare walls, but also the false transept; here a pair of bold 28m – 92ft columns (the tallest in France) help hold up the vaulting with its elaborate play of liernes and tiercerons. The transept is lit by windows with unusually complex tracery.

The influence of the neighbouring province of Champagne can be seen in the inspection gallery running below the transept windows. The side chapels were built in Renaissance style after the completion of the main part of the building.

ST-OMER★★

Population 14 434
Map p 6 – Michelin map 51 fold 3 or 236 fold 4
Green Guide Flanders, Picardy and the Paris Region
Town plan in the current Michelin Red Guide France

A market centre of some importance, St-Omer has kept many fine town houses dating from the classical period. The town lies at the junction of Inland Flanders, with its watery landscapes of poplars, elms and willows, and Coastal Flanders, won from the sea in medieval times and now dominated by industry and arable farming.

38km – 24 miles to the south lies the site of the Battle of **Agincourt** (Azincourt), where, on 25 October 1415, France suffered its gravest defeat of the Hundred Years War at the hands of Henry V of England. The French cavalry, lacking any sort of unified command, moved in extended order against a less numerous but highly mobile foe; their horses, weighed down by their riders' armour and stumbling in the heavy ground, made good targets for English bowmanship. Once unhorsed, the knights in their armour were no match for the agile English infantrymen. The captured Duke of Orleans became the prisoner poet of the Tower of London.

The disaster bled the French nobility white; ten thousand of their number had been cut down, while English casualties were negligible.

"O God, thine arm was here", cried Shakespeare's Henry V,
"When, without stratagem,
But in plain shock and even play of battle,
Was ever known so great and little loss
On one part or the other?"

Now Normandy lay open to invasion, Paris was defenceless against John the Fearless of Burgundy and nothing stood between Henry V and the crown of France he coveted.

The battle is commemorated by a cross and an inscription on a standing stone.

A border town, St-Omer was in turn part of the Holy Roman Empire, Flanders, Burgundy and then Spain, finally passing into French hands in 1677.

The town's industry, predominantly metal-working, chemicals and glass-making, is concentrated in the Arques district.

★★ **Cathédrale Notre-Dame** – Completed at the end of the Hundred Years War, the building shows signs of the influence of the English Perpendicular style; the tower is treated with an overall pattern of lancet arches and, inside, the triforium of transept and chancel has very tall, slender colonnettes.

Works of art★★ are numerous and of high quality; there is 18C woodwork (pulpit base with scenes from the life of St Dominic, choir-stalls panelling, organ-case), and very rare 13C floor tiles in the ambulatory and chancel. Others survive in the two radiating chapels and in the first bay of the south transept, with subjects such as the Shrouding of the Virgin, the liberal arts, signs of the Zodiac... They are probably the work of 13C sculptors who originally came from Italy.

⊙ ►► Hôtel Sandelin★★: decorative arts; Ancienne Chapelle des Jésuites★; Public Gardens★.

ST-POL-DE-LÉON★

Population 7 261
Map p 4 – Michelin map 58 fold 6 or 230 fold 5 – Green Guide Brittany

St-Pol is one of the main market-gardening centres of the rich band of fertile soils running all round the Breton coast from St-Malo to St-Nazaire. Where the wind can be kept out, the otherwise mild climate allows excellent crops of vegetables to be grown, artichokes, onions, early potatoes, cauliflowers, salad vegetables... eagerly bought in the markets of Paris and on the far side of the English Channel. Mechanisation means that much of the characteristic pattern of tiny fields bounded by stone walls is doomed to disappear.

★ **Chapelle du Kreisker** ⊙ – The chapel was rebuilt around 1375; in the 15C, when the coastal towns were prospering from their seaborne trade, it housed the meetings of the town council. In about 1430, Duke John V of Brittany, who had spent his boyhood at the Burgundian court, then married Joan of France, felt it opportune to introduce the Gothic style into Brittany in order to boost his prestige. But the response of the Breton architects was to adapt Flamboyant Gothic to local ways; they shunned highly designed and decorated façades which were difficult to reconcile with the dour qualities of the granites of the region, and favoured a flattened apse (a reflection of the influence of both English architecture and that of the mendicant orders). They thereby eliminated the problems caused by vaults with a circular or polygonal plan, as well as enabling the interior to be lit by a single large window. In addition, the use of a coffered ceiling and a lightweight slate roof allowed them to dispense with flying buttresses.

The chapel was subsequently enlarged, and, between 1436-39, given its **belfry★★**, the finest in the province. Interest in it has increased due to the loss of the tower of Notre-Dame-du-Mur at Morlaix on which it is supposed to have been modelled. In its vertical emphasis, it is reminiscent of the churches of Normandy; it has a pointed steeple and pinnacles so delicate they had to be tied in to the main structure by braces to enable them to resist the force of the wind. The tall openings below reinforce this impression. The English Perpendicular style is recalled by the mullions of the windows, by the overhanging balustrade and by the entablatures expressing the different levels.

★ **Ancienne cathédrale** – Erected on 12C foundations in the 13C and 14C, this fine building with its characteristically Breton balustraded belfry was restored by the Dukes of Brittany from 1431 onwards. Seven bays of the nave still

Belfry of the Chapelle du Kreisker, St-Pol-de-Léon

have their original vaults; the nave itself, unlike most of the rest of the cathedral where local granite was used, was built in Caen stone, a clear indication of Norman influence. Norman too is the inspection gallery which runs below the triforium.

In the north side of the chancel, below the funerary niches, are a number of wooden reliquaries with skulls dug up in a nearby cemetery, while in the sanctuary a palm tree carved in wood contains a ciborium for the Host (1770).

EXCURSION

★ **Roscoff** – *5km – 3 miles north.* The harbour town with its fishing fleet and important export trade (vegetables) to Britain also has ferry services linking Brittany to Plymouth and Cork. It is a flourishing resort and a medical centre using sea water treatment.

Not far from the harbour in the town centre is the **church of Notre-Dame-de-Kroaz-Batz★** with its remarkable **lantern turret belfry★** of Renaissance date. Inside, four **alabaster statues★** grace the altarpiece of one of the altars in the south aisle.

ST-QUENTIN

Conurbation 69 188
Map p 6 – Michelin map 53 fold 14 or 236 fold 27
Green Guide Flanders, Picardy and the Paris Region
Town plan in the current Michelin Red Guide France

On its hill overlooking the Somme, the industrial town of St-Quentin was granted the charter guaranteeing its civic privileges as early as 1080.

The Battle of St Quentin and its aftermath – In August 1557, the Constable of France, Montmorency, had been taken prisoner by the Spaniards besieging St Quentin and his forces scattered. His king, Henri II, was plagued by worries, not only about the consequences of this grave defeat, but also about the course the Reformation was taking; to the grumblings of the peasants was added the malignant effect of German-influenced Protestant preachers on the morale of the army. The successes of the Duke of Guise at Calais (recovered by France after 211 years of English occupation) and Thionville were not enough to reassure him. The **Treaty of Le Cateau-Cambrésis** was signed on 2 April 1559 with England and with Spain the following day, but the final negotiations leading up to it had unsettled the king even more, making him acutely aware of his country's vulnerability.

Historians still argue about the significance of this treaty. It certainly restored Calais to France, gave implicit recognition of her rights over Metz, Toul and Verdun, and put an end to the conflicts in Italy. Some see in it a failure on France's part to make its provisions work in her favour, and consider Henri II to have been duped by Philip II of Spain into relinquishing no less than 189 strongholds, together with Nice, Bresse, Savoy, Corsica, the Italian territories dependent on Florence and Siena... According to others, more subtle considerations were at work. Faced with heresy at home and abroad, it suited the king to effect a reconciliation with the Catholic powers at whatever cost, even if this meant putting off the acquistion of secure frontiers to some uncertain point in the future. It is conceivable that the continued pursuit of such a policy could have spared France the disasters of the Wars of Religion. But it was not to be; three months after the signing of the treaty, Henri II succumbed to the effects of a wound received in the course of a joust. He was succeeded by François II, a sickly 15-year-old; in the period which followed, the lack of any strong authority meant that the political crisis grew worse.

Musée Antoine-Lécuyer ⊙ – The artist Maurice Quentin de La Tour (1704-88), known above all for his works in pastel, was born and died in St-Quentin. The museum houses a total of 78 of his **portraits★★**, masterpieces all in their anatomy of personality, whether it be impulsive, malicious, ironic, mocking, kindly, cynical... His introspective self-portrait also has this penetrating quality.

★ **Basilique** – This is a building in Lanceolate style, with the elevation characteristic of this version of the Gothic. In addition, it has a double transept and an ambulatory of the type prevalent in the neighbouring province of Champagne; on its south side is an arrangement of twin columns supporting the chapels in the manner of the church of St-Remi at Reims. Traced out on the floor of the nave is a rare example of a labyrinth.

EXCURSION

★ **Château fort des ducs de Guise** ⊙ – *28 km – 18 miles northeast by N29-E44.* Built in a combination of limestone, brick and Ardennes sandstone, this 11C fortress was one of the first fortified strongholds erected in France. It belonged to the celebrated Guise family, the elder branch of the House of Lorraine. The whole ensemble covers an area of 17 hectares – 42 acres. Since 1952, a group of volunteers have worked towards restoring the castle, badly hit during the First World War.

The Michelin Green Guide France

makes tourism in France easier and more enjoyable
by highlighting the outstanding natural features and the works of man
Never visit France without a Michelin guide

ST-RÉMY-DE-PROVENCE★

Population 9 340
Map p 10 – Michelin map 84 fold 1 or 245 fold 29 or 246 fold 26
Green Guide Provence
Town plan in the current Michelin Red Guide France

Just to the north of the jagged peaks of the Alpilles, St-Rémy encapsulates the character of inland Provence; plane trees shade its boulevards from the intense light and there are charming old alleyways. The Place de la République is Renaissance in style.

★★ **Les Antiques** – *Just to the south of the town.* These fascinating remains mark the site of the prosperous Roman city of Glanum.
The **Mausolée★★** of the 1C BC is the best preserved of its kind in the Roman world; it was erected in memory of the Emperor Augustus' grandsons Gaius and Lucius, whose early death deprived them of their Imperial inheritance.
The **Arc municipal★**, which is much damaged, dates from the beginning of Augustus' reign and is one of the oldest such structures in the south of the country. Its decorative sculpture (garlands of flowers, groups of prisoners and symbols of victory) demonstrates the continued existence of Greek art in Provence.
The **ruines de Glanum★** ⊙ have revealed the city's history. The original settlement here was founded by the Celts because of the existence of a spring. Later, in the 6C BC, it was extended by Greek merchants, and fine houses in Hellenic style were erected in the following centuries. The place was destroyed by the Teutons, probably not long before their defeat by Marius near Aix in 125BC; it was restored by Caesar, only to be laid waste again by Germanic tribes in the 3C AD.
From this time on the city was more or less abandoned, and its streets and canals slowly filled up with material washed down from the Alpilles.

ST-RIQUIER★

Population 1 166
Map p 6 – Michelin map 52 fold 7 or 236 folds 22, 23
Green Guide Flanders, Picardy and the Paris Region

The Benedictine abbey of St-Riquier was already famous when Charlemagne's son-in-law, Angilbert became Abbot and rebuilt the church towards the year 800. But the wealth of the place excited the envy of the Normans, and in 1131, the abbey, with its buildings in both Carolingian and Romanesque style, was burnt down. Restoration eventually took place in the 13C.

Like the rest of Picardy, St-Riquier suffered during the Hundred Years War (in 1356, the Battle of Crécy was fought not far to the northwest), then again in the course of the disputes between Louis XI and Charles the Bold and between Louis XII and Philip II of Spain.

★ **Abbey Church** ⊙ – Work on the abbey began again in 1511, at a time when the Flamboyant Gothic style was beginning to be subject to Renaissance influences; the lower parts of the chancel and transepts were kept, but rivalry with nearby Abbeville led to the rebuilding of the west front, dominated by a high square tower in the English manner with particularly ornate sculptural decoration.

The **interior**★★ has a dignity and simplicity which is striking, bathed as it is in the soft light diffused by the pale Somme limestone. The 2-storey nave elevation is emphasized by a 16C frieze and a 17C balustrade. The final two bays of the south aisle have complex vaults with liernes and tiercerons which seem to prefigure the coffered ceilings of the Renaissance. The choir is beautifully furnished in the style of the 17C; the wrought-iron **grille**★ of 1685 is particularly fine.

⊙ ►► Trésorerie; Musée départemental – handicrafts.

ST-SAVIN★★

Population 1 089
Map p 8 – Michelin map 68 fold 15 or 233 fold 10
Green Guide Atlantic Coast

St-Savin lies among the pasturelands of the eastern border of the old province of Poitou, an area of sandy clay soils known as Les Brandes. Its former **Abbey Church**★★ ⊙ *(1 hour)* still draws many visitors in spite of the depredations of the centuries. It is now difficult to imagine how the place must have looked in its days of glory before the Hundred Years War, when the whole interior glowed with Romanesque wall-paintings, when none of the furnishings had been removed, and when the impact of insensitive restoration had not been felt.

The church was mostly built in the space of 50 years, between 1040-90. The base of the tower dates from the 11C; above it rise two storeys added in the 12C and a slender 14C steeple (rebuilt in the middle of the 19C). Inside, tall columns divide the nave from the transepts, and in the six chapels which open off the choir and transepts are Romanesque altar tables still with their original carved inscriptions.

The fame of St-Savin rests on its stunning series of Romanesque **murals**★★★, the finest in the whole of France. They seem to have been painted around 1100 by a single team of artists over a period of only three to four years. The colours consist only of black and white, green, and reddish or yellowish ochre; they were applied flat, without gradations. Some of the paintings have withstood the ravages of time (and men) better

Abraham in the presence of God, fresco in the nave vault, St-Savin

than others; they include a monumental treatment of the Apocalypse (in the narthex), the Creation (nave), the Book of Abraham (in the vaulting of the first three bays of the nave), then the stories of Moses, Abel, Noah and Joseph (in the remaining six bays), Christ in Majesty, the Evangelists and the Saints (in the crypts).

Enclos paroissial de ST-THÉGONNEC★★

Map p 4 – Michelin map 58 fold 6 or 230 fold 5
Green Guide Brittany

The parish close *(enclos paroissial)* is one of the most characteristic features of the Breton landscape, particularly in the Elorn valley, on the slopes of the Arrée Hills and in the Léon district. The one at St-Thégonnec is among the most famous of these monumental groupings of church, cemetery, calvary and charnel house.

Parish closes began to develop in this form during the second half of the 16C at the time of the Counter-Reformation. They formed a powerful instrument in the hands of the Roman Catholic Church, helping it to consolidate its dogmas and to promote the veneration of apostles and saints in opposition to spontaneous local cults. Their effectiveness was increased by the presentation of their subject matter somewhat in the manner of a strip cartoon, with exaggerated features and dramatic gestures.

Much of the religious life of the community (masses, sermons, processions) took place in the close, emphasising the indivisibilty of the living and the dead.

Ph. Beuzen/SCOPE

The Scourging, figures on the Calvary, St-Thégonnec

This parish close is approached through a Renaissance **triumphal arch**★ (1587) lavishly decorated with cannon balls, shells, pilasters and little lanterns.

The **calvary**★★ dates from 1610. It is the work of Rolland Doré, and the last of its type to be carved from the mica-rich igneous rock known as **kerzanton**. On the lower arm of the cross are figures of angels collecting Christ's blood, while the base shows scenes of the Passion and Resurrection. Note particularly the depiction of Christ's tormentors and also the symbolic use of clothing, with Our Lord and His followers dressed according to Christian tradition, while the representatives of worldly power wear the fashions of the time of Henri IV.

The **funerary chapel**★ ⊙ of 1676 illustrates the survival of traditional decorative motifs in the province (altarpiece with spiral columns and a Holy Sepulchre in painted oak).

The 15C **church**★ was rebuilt and refurnished several times in the 17C and early 18C in an entirely harmonious way. The **pulpit**★★ has a remarkable polygonal base (1683) carved by master carpenters from the naval yards at Brest, as well as a fine medallion at the back and a Louis XV sounding-board.

By the end of the 17C, Anglo-French naval rivalry *(p 79)* had brought to an end the Léon district's maritime prosperity; local patrons of the arts now had little to spare and the artists themselves suffered a diminution of their imaginative powers.

St-Thégonnec was to be the last of the great parish closes of Brittany.

EXCURSION

★★ **Enclos paroissial de Guimiliau** – *8km – 5 miles southwest.* This example of a parish close predates the one at St-Thégonnec by some thirty years.

The **calvary**★★ (1581) has an attractively naive quality; its 200 figures are full of a sense of vigorous movement and are carved in a robust way which recalls the sculpture of the Romanesque period, notably in the episodes from the life of Christ and the scenes from the Passion depicted in the frieze. Also of interest is the terrifying sculpture showing the Gates of Hell, with the struggling figure of Catel Gollet (Lost Kate in Breton), the flirtatious serving girl who failed to reveal all at Confession. The funerary chapel of 1642 has an outdoor pulpit of earlier (15C) date.

The **church**★ ⊙ has a Renaissance **porch**★★ dating from 1606 with an unusual wealth and variety of ornament; the arching depicts scenes from both the Old and the New Testament. Panelled vaulting is a feature of the interior, which has a fine Baroque **baptistry**★★ with a baldachin and spiral columns decorated with pampres and foliage. The pulpit, with its sculpted panels of about 1675, is also in the Baroque style.

ST-TROPEZ★★

Population 5 754
Map p 11 – Michelin map 84 fold 17 or 114 fold 37 or 245 fold 49
Green Guide French Riviera

The foothills of the Maures Massif rise behind the narrow streets of the village of St-Tropez.

The harbour where luxury yachts are moored teems with life. The old fishing village which was discovered by the painter **Paul Signac** and attracted the major figures of the Post-Impressionist School – paintings in the **Musée de L'Annonciade**★★ ⊘ – has become a fashionable resort frequented by writers and artists and more recently by celebrities from the entertainment world.

EXCURSION

★★★ **Massif des Maures** – The long, low parallel ranges of the massif unfold from Fréjus to Hyères. Its fine forests of pine, cork oak and chestnut trees have been devastated by fire. Chapels, monasteries and small villages are dotted in the hinterland while the coast is fringed by coves and bays.

SAINTES★★

Population 25 874
Map p 8 – Michelin map 71 fold 4 or 233 fold 27 – Green Guide Atlantic Coast
Town plan in the current Michelin Red Guide France

Saintes was already a regional capital in Roman times, with a bridge over the Charente aligned on today's Rue Victor-Hugo. In the Middle Ages, the town was an important staging-post on the pilgrims' route to Santiago de Compostela. Two great religious establishments developed on its outskirts, St-Eutrope on the west bank of the river, the Abbey for Women (Abbaye aux Dames) on the east bank. **Bernard Palissy** (1510-90) came from Périgord. He was known for his works on technology and philosophy; his greatest fame nevertheless came from the glassware and pottery made here in a studio close to one of the towers of Saintes' ramparts. His total commitment to this work (he is even supposed to have chopped up his furniture to fire his kiln) enabled him to discover for himself the technique of making enamel, a secret jealously guarded by Masséot Abaquesne at Rouen for more than 20 years.
The historic core of the town, built on the site of the Gallo-Roman city, has been restored and pedestrianised.

Roman Saintes – The **Arch of Germanicus**★ was built in 19 AD at a point on the east bank of the Charente where the roads from Poitiers and Limoges converged on the Roman bridge. An archaeological museum houses objects saved when the ruins of the Roman city were demolished.
To the west, on the slopes of the west bank of the river, is an **amphitheatre**★ (arènes), one of the oldest (1C AD) in the Roman world.

Romanesque Saintes – On the left bank, the **crypt**★★ of the Église St-Eutrope once served as a **parish church, inferior in status**★★ to the pilgrimage church above. This upper part of the building was monastic in origin; it has retained two very fine capitals from the pillars of the former transept (visible from the gallery).
On the east bank is the **church**★ of the Abbaye aux Dames ⊘. It is a notable achievement of Romanesque local style, with fine carving in the excellent local stone showing the influence of the sculpture gracing St Peter's Church at Aulnay. The design of the **west front** is typical; it has rich carving in the arching, particularly around the central portal, featuring angels, symbols of the Evangelists, martyrs and the Elders of the Apocalypse. The harmoniously proportioned tower, with its rotunda divided up into twin bays and its mosaic arcading, is topped by a conical roof covered in fish-scale tiles.

⊘ ►► Saintes: Musée des Beaux-Arts★.

EXCURSION

Église de Rioux – 15km – 9 miles south. Among the many fine Romanesque churches of the Saintonge countryside, this one is well-known for its west front and particularly for its **apse**★. This is divided into sections by columnar buttresses and has an extraordinary wealth of geometric motifs emphasising windows, arcades and even the bonding of the stonework. With this display of decorative perfection, the Saintonge Romanesque can be said to have reached the end of its evolution, any further development being attributable to the virtuosity of individual sculptors.

SALERS★★

Population 439
Map p 9 – Michelin map 76 fold 2 or 239 fold 29 – Green Guide Auvergne-Rhône Valley

High up among the vast grazing grounds of the volcanic Cantal uplands, Salers has long been a market centre and staging-post for travellers. The tiny town seems to have been laid out to confuse possible attackers, with a maze of tortuous streets leading to the **Grande-Place★★**.

This square is something of a stage-set, overlooked by the corner-towers and turrets of the grand lava-built houses of the local notables; the effect is completed by a fountain. External staircases, arched doorways and dormer windows peering out from the schist-tiled roofs are among the features characterising the 15C and 16C houses. The Renaissance building known as the Ancien Bailliage has typically Auvergnat window-mouldings and angle-towers, while the canted Flojeac House (Maison de Flojeac) protects its windows behind massive iron grilles; the Hôtel de la Ronade

Grande-Place, Salers

is distinguished by a Gothic turret rising five-storeys high.

The **church★** has a 12C porch with a very simple doorway as well as a tower (restored in the 19C) with mitred arches very much in the local Auvergne style. Inside there is a fine polychrome sculpture of the **Entombment★** dating from 1495.

Fort de SALSES★★

Map p 9 – Michelin map 86 fold 9 or 235 fold 48 or 240 fold 37
Green Guide Pyrenees-Languedoc-Tarn Gorges

Ever since Roman times Salses has guarded the main road linking France and Spain at the pinch point where the Corbières range approaches the Mediterranean shore. The site's strategic importance was not lost on Ferdinand of Aragon, who erected a fort here in 1497 to protect the northern frontier of a Spain which, since 1493, had once more included Catalan-speaking Roussillon (the place still marks the language frontier between Languedoc and Catalan today).

Designed for Ferdinand by Francisco Ramirez, the **fort** ⊙ *(1 hour)* is an unusual example in France of such a structure of Spanish type, albeit subsequently much modified by Vauban in the 17C.

Salses changed hands more than once during the long years of Franco-Spanish conflict, but finally, in September 1642 – Perpignan had just been retaken by Louis XIII – its Spanish garrison marched forth from its gates and headed southwards for the last time.

17 years later, the Treaty of the Pyrenees ended the border problem by incorporating Roussillon into France. Nevertheless, Vauban's considered opinion was that the fort was obsolete; in 1691 he reduced the height of the keep and protected the walls and bastions with convex additions designed to make shells ricochet off them.

Église SAN MICHELE DE MURATO★★

Map p 10 – Michelin map 90 fold 3 – Green Guide Corse (in French)

On its lonely hilltop site just to the north of the village of Murato, this little **church** ⊙ is a good example of the archaeological and tourist attractions in Corsica.

Built around 1280, it belongs to the end of the second period of the Pisan Romanesque; as it developed in the island, this style was often characterised by polychrome stonework and a degree of sculptural decoration. The green serpentine and white limestone have been expertly cut into blocks of different sizes to avoid any impression of monotony.

The sculpture has a strangely naive quality; crudely fashioned figures of animals and people decorate the west front, while the side windows are surrounded with foliated scrolls and strapwork and the apse has ornamental brackets and modillions.

SAORGE★★

Population 362
Map p 11 – Michelin map 84 fold 20 or 115 fold 18 or 245 fold 26
Green Guide French Riviera

The **Upper Roya valley**★★ has been carved out between the schists of the Mercantour massif and the limestone rocks of the southern Pre-Alps. Its **gorges**★★ form a spectacular **setting**★★ for the village of Saorge clinging to the steep south-facing slopes which rise abruptly from the river far below.

The place is dominated by the belfries of its churches and monasteries, which overlook terraces and balconies, tall old houses with open-fronted drying lofts *(p 228)* and roofs tiled with heavy stone slabs. A maze of stepped and tunnelled streets completes this highly picturesque townscape.

EXCURSION

★★ **Notre-Dame-des-Fontaines** ⊘ – *17km –*
11 miles northeast via St-Dalmas-de-Tende.
The key to the chapel is kept at La Brigue.
A pagan temple dedicated to water gods once stood in this lonely valley at the foot of Mont Noir (Black Mountain). The chancel of the present building dates from the 12C; the nave added in the 15C was raised in height in the 18C and given a new ceiling. Most of the chapel's well-preserved **frescoes**★★★ were painted by the Piedmontese artist Giovanni Canavesio between 1472-92; in late Gothic style, they form a veritable catechism in pictures. The 500 figures illustrate the artist's great mastery of movement and expression. The walls of the nave are covered with scenes from Christ's Passion (including an extraordinary depiction of the Death of Judas) while the west wall is occupied by a vast fresco of the Last Judgement.

The Death of Judas,
Chapelle of Notre-Dame-des-Fontaines

The triumphal arch at the entrance to the choir is the work of another artist from Piedmont, Giovanni Baleisoni; his treatment of scenes from the Life of the Virgin and the childhood of Jesus is altogether more delicate.

The Practical Information section at the end of the guide lists :
– information about travel, motoring, accommodation, recreation
– local or national organisations providing additional information
– calendar of events
– admission times and charges for the sights described in the guide

SARLAT-LA-CANÉDA★★★

Population 9 909
Map p 8 – Michelin map 75 fold 17 or 235 fold 6 – Green Guide Dordogne
Town plan in the current Michelin Red Guide France

Sarlat is the capital of the Périgord Noir (Black Périgord) country, the well-treed agricultural region bounded by the Dordogne and Vézère rivers. The town grew up around the Benedictine abbey founded in the middle of the 9C, from whose rule the townspeople managed to free themselves in 1299.

The wealth of the surrounding countryside poured into the town, enabling it to support a prosperous population of merchants, clerics and lawyers, among them Étienne de la Boétie (1530-63), friend of Montaigne, philosopher, and one of the first translators of Classical Greek literature into French.

Sarlat reached its peak during the 13C and 14C. During the Hundred Years War, many of its houses were neglected and required major restoration once peace returned; cumulative extensions over the course of the centuries have left a number of them with Renaissance upper stories built over a medieval ground floor, the whole topped by roofs laden with classical details.

The town has long played host to busy fairs and markets, and such traditional activity still takes place every Saturday, when the produce of the season is bought and sold, poultry, cereals, horses, nuts, geese, foie gras, truffles...

★★★ **Old Sarlat** – A conservation programme begun in 1964 has safeguarded Sarlat's exceptional townscape. In the 19C, the ruler-straight Rue de la République was driven ruthlessly through the irregular network of medieval streets, dividing the popular west from the more refined east. But there are houses of great charm all over the town, many with attractive courtyards. Most are ashlar-built from the fine golden limestone of the area, and this stone is used for the roofs too. Unlike the slates or schists of other regions, it is cut in thick slabs, and the roof-beams consequently have a heavy load to carry. The tiler often had to distort the profile of the roof, which however has the advantage of leaving lots of small openings to improve the ventilation of the timber structure below. The finest houses include: **Maison de la Boétie★**, a Renaissance building of 1525; the **Hôtel de Malleville★** consisting of three medieval dwellings knocked into one another in the 16C; the **Hôtel de Plamon★**, every storey of which was built in a different century, and the Présidial, which was once the seat of the royal court of justice. The 12C Lantern of the Dead was probably used as a funerary chapel.

► ► **Place des Oies★** – Rue des Consuls★.

Meauxsoone/PIX

Maison de La Boétie, Sarlat

SARTÈNE★★

Population 3 525
Map p 10 – Michelin map 90 fold 18 – Green Guide Corse (in French)

The writer Prosper Mérimée thought Sartène, 305m – 1 000ft above the Bay of Valinco, the "most Corsican of Corsican towns".

The area around has been occupied by man for more than 5 000 years and there are abundant traces (dolmens and menhirs) from the time of the megalith builders, notably at Cauria and Palaggiu. The warlike Torreans too *(p 155)* left their mark in a number of places like Alo Bisucce, Cucuruzzu and in particular Filitosa. Corsica's medieval history is based to a great extent on the chronicles of Giovanni della Grossa (1388-1464), who was born and who died at Grossa *(12km – 7 miles west of Sartène)*. In his early days he was a determined opponent of the Genoese, but later he allied himself to their cause, taking part in many of the decisive events in the island's history. Finally he became a lawyer and recorded his stirring times in writing.

Between the 16C and the 18C, Sartène suffered at the hands of pirates from the Barbary coast, so much so that it was deserted by part of its population.

Place de la Libération – The shady square is the focus of local life.

It is overlooked by the **Église Ste-Marie**, built in granite. To the left of the main entrance are the chains and the heavy cross of oak borne by Catenacciu, the anonymous red-robed penitential figure at the centre of the nocturnal procession on Good Friday. This procession is probably the island's most ancient ceremony.

★★ **Old Town** – Go through the arch of the Town Hall (Hôtel de ville) and take the street opposite (Rue des Frères-Bartoli). The narrow stone-flagged alleyways, occasionally stepped or vaulted, are lined by tall granite-built houses with a fortress-like air. The **Santa Anna★★** part of the town has a particularly characteristic townscape of this kind.

⊙ ► ► Musée de préhistoire corse.

SAUMUR★★

Population 30 301
Map p 5 – Map 64 fold 12 or 232 fold 33 – Green Guide Châteaux of the Loire
Town plan in the current Michelin Red Guide France

Dominated by its château on a chalky spur overlooking the meeting-point of the Thouet with the Loire, Saumur is famous for its wines and the French army's prestigious cavalry school.

The town owed its early prosperity to the wooden bridge which crossed the Loire via two islands (the Île d'Offrand and the Île Millocheau, now joined together). It formed the only crossing point over the river between Tours and Ponts-de-Cé downstream from Angers at the time of pilgrimages to Santiago de Compostela. In the 13C, the monks from the Abbey of St Florent undertook to replace the original structure by one of stone, constructed at the rate of one arch a year. Though often carried away by floods, this bridge was always rebuilt.

Like all the towns along the great river (Decize, Nevers, La Charité, Cosne, Gien, Orléans, Blois...), Saumur's site was chosen, regardless of orientation, on whichever bank offered the better protection from high waters. The attractive old houses facing the Loire have walls of pale tufa and steeply-pitched slate roofs.

Saumur's long association with the horse began in 1763, when the crack corps known as the Carabiniers Regiment was sent here, under the command of Louis XV's brother ("Monsieur"). It was a time when the refinement of riding technique which had begun under de Pluvinel (Louis XIII's Master of the Horse) had become fashionable among the aristocracy. The National Equitation Centre (École Nationale d'Équitation) was founded in 1972, incorporating the famous **Cadre Noir** (Black Squad) which had consisted originally solely of army instructors. This aspect of the town's identity is evoked in the museum in the Château and in the **Musée de la Cavalerie★** ⊙ which has displays on post-18C military history and on the development of horsemanship. In addition, there is a **Musée des Blindés★** ⊙, with displays of armoured vehicles both French and foreign from 1918 onwards.

★★ **Château** ⊙ – In the 14C, the château was rebuilt on the foundations of the medieval fortress originally erected by Philippe Auguste and Louis IX. As a consequence, it has a somewhat irregular layout. In the 15C, with the return of more peaceful times following the end of the Hundred Years War, Good King René *(qv)* endowed his "castle of love" with sumptuous decorative detail in late Gothic style. The château is shown in this state, albeit in a somewhat idealised landscape, in one of the miniatures from the *Très Riches Heures du Duc de Berry (p 102)*. In the late 16C, at the time of the Wars of Religion, the place was refortified, as Saumur was one of the strongholds of French Protestantism. There are two museums in the château, the **Musée du Cheval★** with fascinating collections of riding equipment and a number of pictures (including work by Stubbs), and the **Musée des Arts décoratifs★★**, which has a fine display of works of art from the Middle Ages and Renaissance, including a collection of faience and French porcelain from the 17C and 18C.

The Practical Information section at the end of the guide lists :
- *information about travel, motoring, accommodation, recreation*
- *local or national organisations providing additional information*
- *calendar of events*
- *admission times and charges for the sights described in the guide*

SAVERNE★

Population 10 278
Map p 7 – Michelin map 57 fold 18 or 87 fold 14 or 242 fold 19
Green Guide Alsace et Lorraine (in French)
Town plan in the current Michelin Red Guide France

The town has given its name to one of the main routes through the Vosges uplands, the Saverne Gap (Col de Saverne). To the west is the plateau of Lorraine, to the east steep wooded slopes dropping down to the lowlands of the Rhine valley and the other towns of Alsace.

★ **Château** – This splendid red sandstone palace replaced the old residence of the prince-bishops of Strasbourg which was burnt down in 1779. It was rebuilt by the high-living Cardinal de Rohan who endowed it with a monumental Louis XVI **façade★★** giving on to the park. It has a central peristyle with eight massive Corinthian columns; to either side extend long wings with fluted pilasters supporting an attic floor and a roof balustrade, while at each end stands a projecting corner pavilion.

► ► Saverne: Old houses★.

EXCURSION

★★ Église de Marmoutier – *6km – 4 miles south*. This former abbey church was built around 1150-1160. Its fine **west front★★** in the red sandstone of the region is in Romanesque style incorporating Carolingian and Rhineland influences.
The façade is articulated by horizontal bands carried on low arches and by flattened buttresses, giving a highly compartmentalised effect. The central bell-tower is set back somewhat and flanked by two octagonal corner towers. The overall impression is one of unalterable solidity, barely relieved by minor decorative touches like the foliage scrolls on the austere capitals in the porch.

SEDAN

Population 21 667
Map p 7 – Michelin map 53 fold 19 or 241 fold 10
Guide Champagne (in French)
Town plan in the current Michelin Red Guide France

The ruler of Sedan, Count de la Marck, built a fortress on a rocky outcrop here in 1424. His descendants served a variety of overlords, the Holy Roman Emperor, the King of France... without however neglecting the proper interests of their town. In the 16C, Sedan turned Protestant; a military academy was founded in the town which was attended in his youth by Turenne (Henri de la Tour d'Auvergne). This great soldier was born in the castle here in 1611: of serious and scrupulous character, he became progressively more adventurous as his experience broadened. In an age still preoccupied with the techniques of the siege, he advocated more mobile ways of making war. In the course of the Thirty Years War, he showed almost incredible bravery, beating the impetuous Condé at Bléneau and opening the gates of Paris to Louis XIV in 1652. The victories won by him at Arras and in the sand-dunes near Dunkirk brought Spain to the negotiating table and led to the Treaty of the Pyrenees. In 1675, he was slain by a cannon ball. His funeral elegy, composed on the same lines as that of the Grand Condé, was given by Bossuet.

The end of the Second Empire – On 1 September 1870, the French army executed a bold manœuvre designed to relieve General Bazaine besieged in Metz. But the attack failed, and the troops fell back on Sedan and its fortifications. On 2 September, the ailing Napoleon III met Bismarck, who had him escorted to the château at Bellevue. It was here that the Emperor's plenipotentiary was forced to sign the humiliating surrender of the French forces to the future Kaiser William I. Napoleon himself was taken to Kassel, then eventually to exile in England.

★ Château fort ⊘ – With a total area of 35ha – 86 acres, this was the most extensive stronghold in 15C Europe. Built on a rocky spur, its 30m – 100ft high walls had bastions added to them in the 16C. At the beginning of the 17C, it was extended and given extra height by Turenne's father. The timber construction inside the Great Tower (Grosse Tour) is a remarkable piece of 15C master carpentry. The castle's apartments are laid out on seven floors. In the south wing is a museum.

SENLIS★★

Population 14 439
Map p 6 – Michelin map 86 fold 11 or 195 folds 8, 9
Green Guide Flanders, Picardy and the Paris Region
Town plan in the current Michelin Red Guide France

At the centre of a rich agricultural region, Senlis was already a prosperous place in Gallo-Roman times. Later, the Merovingian rulers made it their place of residence, followed by the Carolingian kings; eventually Senlis became a royal domain, the kernel of the Île-de-France, itself the core of the future kingdom of France. The old part of the town, to the south of the cathedral, is sited on the Gallo-Roman settlement which preceded it; it has a number of old dwellings in the characteristic style of the Valois area, built of brick and soft limestone. Many of the streets are still paved with big flagstones.

★★ Cathédrale Notre-Dame – Begun in 1153 with the support of Louis VII, it is one of the first churches in the Île-de-France to be built in Transitional style. The choir was completed in 1180 and the west front ten years later. Of this first building a few features survive. They include the choir and the insensitively restored west front, as well as three bays of square plan on either side of the transept; these have sexpartite vaults held up by columns alternating with piers of massive proportions; the elevation here includes a gallery on the Norman model.

Around 1240, the building of a false transept involved the loss of four columns and the shifting of two piers to the centre of the nave, thereby breaking the continuity of the pattern previously established. At the same time, the south tower was given its spire.

The Flamboyant Gothic appearance of the cathedral is the result of the restoration undertaken between 1513-60, following a great fire in 1504. The transept and its arms were rebuilt, as were the upper parts of the elevation; the roof was given extra height, the new vaults being supported on flying buttresses. The base of the building was extended by adding a second run of aisles with complex lierne and tierceron vaulting. Pierre Chambiges, the son of Martin Chambiges who had worked at Sens, Beauvais and Troyes, was in charge of building the south doorway; whether because of tradition or out of respect for his father, he continued to work in the Flamboyant style (with luxuriant sculpted ornamentation, mouldings, balustrades and galleries). He also added features of Early Renaissance type like basket-handle arches and cable-moulding.

The tall **spire**★★ of the south tower soars 78m – 256ft heavenwards, its verticality emphasised by the gables which have the additional function of converting the square plan to the octagonal and of keeping the whole composition in a state of equilibrium. The rigorous geometry of the design is relieved by the crockets and by the dormers and gables which set a trend all over the Valois area until the 16C.

Cathedral spire, Senlis

Ⓥ ►► Old streets★; Chapelle royale St-Frambourg★ – Fondation Cziffra.

SENS★★

Population 27 082
Map p 6 – Michelin map 61 fold 14 or 237 fold 45 – Green Guide Burgundy Jura
Town plan in the current Michelin Red Guide France

In Gallo-Roman times, Sens was the capital of the province of Senonia. Later, at a time when Paris was little more than an overgrown village, the city was extended outwards to new limits still marked by the line of today's boulevards. Its central position in relation to Burgundy, Champagne and the Île-de-France gave it an administrative and ecclesiastical importance lasting for centuries; for a long time it was the Bishop of Sens who crowned French kings, and the bishopric of Paris was subordinate to the archbishopric of Sens until 1627.

★★ **Cathédrale St-Étienne** – In its general conception this is the very first of France's great Gothic cathedrals, its foundations laid in the years 1128-30, though most building took place between 1140 and 1168.

The influence of the Romanesque can still be discerned in a number of features like the slightly pointed "Burgundian" arches of the nave, a series of twin openings at tribune level with a false gallery, as yet no triforium, and, in the side-chapels, a combination of rounded and pointed arches. But it is the Gothic which is decisive. There is use throughout of quadripartite vaulting; the choir has sexpartite vaults of square plan resting on massive pillars alternating with slender columns and the ambulatory has pointed arches, still awkwardly asymmetrical.

Following the collapse of the south tower of the west front in 1268, the building was restored and altered, with the probable addition of flying buttresses. In the 13C and 14C, the clerestorey windows were given extra height, then, in the 15C and 16C, the transepts were built in Flamboyant style.

Outside, the decorative features include the pier of the central portal, the famous statue of St Stephen (in style intermediate between the Schools of Chartres and Amiens), and the Flamboyant gable of the north portal, the work of Martin Chambiges.

Inside, the eye is drawn to the **stained glass**★★; this is of 12C date in the ambulatory and north side of the choir, while the Jesse Tree and St Nicholas in the south transept and the rose window of the north transept are all Renaissance works by master-glaziers from Troyes. The ambulatory, the chapels opening off it, and the choir all have very fine grilles of wrought and gilded ironwork (18C).

Ⓥ ►► Museum, treasury and the Palais Synodal.

Prieuré de SERRABONE★★

Map p 9 – Michelin map 86 fold 18 or 235 fold 52 or 240 fold 41
Green Guide Pyrenees-Languedoc-Tarn Gorges

In its remote and stony setting among the austere Aspres mountains, the former priory contains some of the finest Romanesque sculpture in Roussillon.
The schist-built structure sits well in this wild landscape, its severity relieved somewhat by the use of delicate pink marble.

The chapel **tribune**★★ ⊙ of about 1080, originally intended to serve as the choir, was moved to the centre of the nave at the beginning of the 19C. It is an unusual feature to have survived and has wonderful decoration in low relief as well as exceptionally richly carved capitals. The latter show traces of oriental or Lombard influence, for example in the symbolic treatment of the lions and in the integration of the figures of animals in the total composition. A delightful south-facing **gallery**★ (Promenoir des Chanoines) overlooks the ravine far below.

SISTERON★★

Population 6 594
Map p 10 – Michelin map 81 folds 5, 6 or 245 fold 20
Green Guide Alpes du Sud (in French)
Town plan in the current Michelin Red Guide France

Sisteron lies between the Laragne valley to the north and the valley of the middle Durance to the south. As well as marking the historic boundary between Dauphiné and Provence, this is also the northern limit of the cultivation of the olive.

★ **Citadelle** ⊙ – Major restoration had to be carried out following the heavy bombing carried out by the Americans on 15 August 1944. Of the 12C fortress little remains other than the keep and the sentry walk since the defences were virtually rebuilt in the 16C by Jean Évrard, Henri IV's military engineer and predecessor of Vauban. The important N85 highway tunnels its way through the rock on which the citadel is built. From the Guérite du Diable there is an impresssive view over the **site**★★ of Sisteron. The limestone beds were dramatically folded to form the Baume Rock (Rocher de Baume), which the ice of Quaternary times then refashioned into a glacial bar.

⊙ ►► Église Notre-Dame★.

EXCURSION

★★ **Signal de Lure** – *27km – 17 miles southwest*. The Lure mountains are a bleak limestone range, an extension eastwards of Mount Ventoux, with the same friable rock which quickly breaks down into a mass of debris and the same pattern of vegetation; on the south-facing slopes, garrigue and lavender and evergreen oaks; on the northern flank of the mountains, beeches, firs and larches and patches of grazing. From the summit there is a vast panoramic **view** stretching as far as the Mediterranean, the Vercors Massif and Mount Ventoux.

SOLIGNAC★

Population 1 345
Map p 8 – Map 72 fold 17 or 239 fold 13 – Green Guide Berry Limousin (in French)

Before becoming trusted advisor to the Frankish king Dagobert, the legendary figure of St Eligius (St Eloi) had been a goldsmith, learning the intricacies of the art at Limoges. In the year 632, he founded an abbey here in the valley of the Briance by the side of the old Roman road linking Limoges with Périgueux.

★★ **Église Abbatiale** ⊙ – Rebuilt around 1175, the building shows Limoges influence in its use of granite and in certain characteristic mouldings, but its domes are based on the ones at Souillac in Quercy erected 35 years previously. The abbey's outside appearance is strikingly robust; the elevations of north wall and apse are particularly harmonious. From the steps of the porch there is a fine general view of the beautifully proportioned **interior**★★; the overall impression is one of great purity and simplicity, a result of the architect's careful control of the layout and his use of materials of high quality. The multiple domes are supported by great pointed arches and pendentives; as well as being among the last of their kind to be built in Aquitaine, they are some of the finest examples to be seen in the region.

There are many other features of interest in the abbey; the first bay of the lateral inspection gallery has capitals of archaic design, while there is an extraordinarily deformed dome over the choir and one of ovoid shape covering the north transept. One of the crossing pillars is painted with an impressive portrait of St Christopher.

SOUILLAC★

Population 3 459
Map p 9 – Michelin map 75 fold 18 or 235 fold 6 or 239 fold 38 – Green Guide Dordogne

Souillac evolved originally as a river port at the upper limit of navigation on the Dordogne and its present role as a market town goes back to this time too. The town spread out on the alluvial plain of an old meander around a Benedictine abbey whose golden age was in the 12C, after which decline set in, hastened by the troubled times of the Hundred Years War and the Wars of Religion.

Ancienne église abbatiale – The model for the church was Cahors Cathedral, but at Souillac the architect improved on the original by making his pillars much less massive and giving extra height to the main arches. The latter are cleverly integrated with the transverse arches to form the square base on which four pendentives and a cornice of corbels support the slender arch-stones of the three domes.

The discreet elegance of the exterior of the Romanesque east end of the church finds its counterpart inside in the harmonious arrangement of the chapels opening off the hemicycle of the choir.

The west front was mutilated by the Huguenots in 1573; the fragments of the **former portal★** have been rearranged on the inside of the doorway. The right engaged pillar which was once the central pillar of the doorway is richly decorated; on the right are the forms of concupiscence associated with the different stages of life, in the middle, their effects (monsters devouring each other), and, on the left, the remission of sin by the sacrifice of Isaac, with Abraham's hand held back by the messenger of God.

To the left of this pillar is the fine low relief figure of **Isiah★★** – its affinities with the depiction of Jeremiah at Moissac are obvious; there is the same expressiveness and virtuosity, but the sculptor has moved beyond the conventional approach of his model.

⊘ ►► Musée National de l'automate et de la robotique★.

STRASBOURG★★★

Conurbation 388 483
Map p 7 – Michelin map 62 fold 10 or 87 or fold 45 or 242 folds 20, 24
Green Guide Alsace et Lorraine (in French)
Town plan in the current Michelin Red Guide France

Strasbourg's name comes from the German meaning "city of the roads", and the place is indeed a meeting point for the highways, railways and waterways linking the Mediterranean with the Rhineland, Central Europe, the North Sea and the Baltic via the Belfort Gap and the Swabian Basin.

Since 1949, Strasbourg has been the seat of the Council of Europe.

On 14 February in the year 842 the **Strasbourg Oaths** were sworn by two of the sons of Louis the Pious (himself the son of Charlemagne). One year before the Treaty of Verdun, the brothers Charles and Louis undertook to be loyal to one another in their attempt to frustrate the ambitions of their elder brother Lothair. Protocol demanded that each declare the oath in a language comprehensible to his brother's entourage; thus it was that the text read out by Louis the German is considered to be the oldest such document in a Romance language, the first written example of the language which has evolved into modern French. The same can be said for the German text.

Some Strasbourg figures – Strasbourg remained a free city within the Holy Roman Empire even after the virtual incorporation of the rest of Alsace into France by the Peace of Westphalia in 1648, but eventually submitted to annexation by Louis XIV in 1681.

Among the many great people born here were:

François Kellermann (1735-1820), the hero of Valmy, acting under the orders of Dumouriez, then the commander responsible for putting down the Lyons rising of 1793, finally a supporter of the Bourbon Restoration and a member of parliament;

Frédéric de Dietrich (1748-93), *see p 248; the Marseillaise;*

Sébastien Érard (1752-1831), famous maker of grand pianos and harps;

Jean-Baptiste Kléber, *p 249;*

Jean-Pierre Clause (1757-1800), celebrated chef, cook to the Marshal de Contades and the populariser of *pâté de foie gras;*

Gustave Doré (1832-83), the caricaturist and illustrator;

Charles de Foucauld (1858-1916), who began his career as an army officer, but subsequently became a missionary in Algeria and wrote a pioneering work on Morocco, a then unknown country. He later became a Benedictine monk, living as a hermit in the remote Hoggar mountains of southern Algeria; here he collected Touareg poetry and wrote the first French-Tamahag dictionary before dying at the hands of assassins;

Petite France quarter, Strasbourg

Jean Arp (1887-1966), one of the great postwar generation of artists, who moved from Surrealism to Abstraction then to even more revolutionary forms of expression.

The Marseillaise – On 24 April 1792, Frédéric de Dietrich, Strasbourg's first constitutional mayor, threw a farewell celebration for the volunteers of the Army of the Rhine. The conversation turned to the need for a marching song to match the troops' enthusiasm. Dietrich asked **Rouget de Lisle** *(qv)* to compose "something worth singing"; de Lisle set to, working through the night with pen and violin. By the morning he had finished; with Dietrich's niece accompanying him on the piano, he sang his "marching song for the Army of the Rhine". Not long after, it was adopted by the Federates of Marseilles, and ever since has been known as the Marseillaise.

★★ **Cathédrale Notre-Dame** (**KZ**) – In 1176, the cathedral was rebuilt in red Vosges sandstone on a site above flood level but nevertheless using bundles of oak piles as a foundation (these were recently reinforced with concrete).

Externally, this is still a Romanesque building as far as choir, transept and lantern **tower** ⊙ are concerned. The famous Gothic **spire**★★★ is an architectural masterpiece, its verticality emphasized by its forward position immediately over the west front. An unmistakable landmark, visible over much of the Alsace plain, it rises to a height of 142m – 466ft. The openwork octagon supporting it was erected between 1399-1419 by a Swabian architect and given an extra 7m – 23ft in height during the course of construction for reasons of prestige. Its final stage was designed and built between 1420-39 by a Cologne architect, using techniques from the previous century; it is particularly notable for the projecting structures carrying the external staircases.

The High Gothic **west front**★★★ was the work of Erwin von Steinbach. It is decorated with a wealth of sculpture (statues and low-reliefs of many different periods) especially in the **central portal** with its double gable and delicate lancets masking part of the rose window. The three lower levels of the tympanum have particularly fine 13C work, including depictions of the Entry into Jerusalem, scenes of the Passion and Resurrection, and the Death of Judas; in the arching can be seen the Creation, the story of Abraham, the Apostles, the Evangelists and the Martyrs.

In the **south doorway** is a famous portrayal of the Seducer about to succeed in tempting the most daring of the Foolish Virgins (she is undoing her dress). The statues of the Church and Synagogue (copies) on the south side of the cathedral are equally celebrated.

Inside, the nave elevation is a straightforward example of the High Gothic style of the 14C, with an openwork triforium and wide aisles lit by elegant window-openings.

STRASBOURG

C Hôtel de la chambre du Commerce F Pharmacie du Cerf H Hôtel de ville M¹ Musée de l'Œuvre Notre-Dame

In the south transept is the 13C **Angel Pillar★★** or **Last Judgement**; its delicate statuary, on three levels, raises Gothic art to a peak of perfection. **Stained-glass windows★★★** from the 12C, 13C, and 14C are remarkable.

The **Astronomical Clock★** ⊘ nearby, dating from 1838, continues to draw crowds with its automata ringing out the quarter-hours (the figure of Death has the privilege of sounding the hours) and the crowd of figures brought out to mark midday (12.30).

★★★ **Musée de l'Œuvre Notre-Dame** ⊘ – Housed in a number of old dwellings just to the south, this museum greatly enhances the visitor's appreciation of the cathedral. Its great treasure is the famous **Head of Christ★** from Wissembourg in northern Alsace. In addition, there is the oldest stained glass in existence and above all, many of the cathedral's original statues, including the Church and the Synagogue, the Wise and Foolish Virgins. The architect's drawings of the west front and the spire are here too.

★ **Palais des Rohan** (KZ) ⊘ – This was the residence of the Prince-Bishops of Strasbourg, among their number Armand, who built the place, and high-living Louis, who was involved in the affair of Marie-Antoinette's necklace.

The palace was built between 1732-42 to the plans drawn up by Robert de Cotte, a quarter-century after the de Rohans' Parisian mansion had been completed; its architecture reflects the more relaxed style ushered in by the reign of Louis XV. It is a fine building in the classical manner, with a curving entrance colonnade ornamented with statues and trophies, a main courtyard defined by balustraded galleries, a façade with dressings of pale limestone, a fine entablature, and mansard roofs lit by bull's-eye windows.

The Prince-Bishops' state rooms are considered to be among the finest French interiors of the 18C.

The building's most elegant façade is the one overlooking the River Ill; it has tall Corinthian columns, a dome and a balustraded terrace.

★★ **Musées** ⊘ – The palace houses museums with rich collections.

The **Musée des Arts décoratif** includes the **State Apartments** and tells the story of the city's crafts and craftsmen. It has one of the finest **ceramic collections★★** in France, particularly rich in Strasbourg and Niderwiller faience and porcelain.

The **Musée des Beaux-Arts** is known for its Italian paintings (Primitives and Renaissance), its Spanish works (Zurbaran, Murillo and Goya) and 15-17C

M² Musée historique   M³ Musée Alsacien   M⁴ Musée d'Art Moderne   Q Maison Kammerzell   Y Maison de Pasteur

Netherlandish Old Masters. On no account should the visitor miss Nicolas de Largillière's 1703 portrait of *La Belle Strasbourgeoise*, the elegant, black-robed beauty.

The **Musée archéologique** covers the period between the Quaternary era and the end of the first millennium AD. There are displays on prehistory, extinct animals, ceramics, and on Roman and Merovingian times.

★★★ **Old Strasbourg** (JKZ) – Two parts of the old city evoke the delightful spectacle of a bygone Alsace of timber-framed houses with the whole array of traditional features, wooden galleries, loggias on brackets, windows with tiny panes of coloured glass, as well as the overhanging upper stories which continued to be built here in the post-1681 years even though they had been banned in France proper. Each house can be enjoyed for its own sake; together, they compose the most ravishing of townscapes.

★★★ **Cathedral quarter** (KZ) – Two especially attractive buildings give on to the **Place de la Cathédrale**★; at the corner with the Rue Mercière there is the Pharmarcie du Cerf (**F**) of 1268, supposedly the oldest pharmacy in France, and, on the north corner is the **Kammerzell House**★ of the same date with frescoes and wooden sculptures. Other streets and squares, like the Place du Marché-aux-cochons-de-lait (Sucking-Pig Market Square), Rue Mercière and Rue des Cordiers, complete the pleasure of a stroll.

★★ **Petite France** (HZ) ⊘ – This is the city's well-preserved historic core. It owes its name to a former French hospital and was once the abode of fishermen, tanners and millers. The arms of the Ill were provided with locks giving shipping from the Rhine access to the back door of virtually every shop. With its gabled Renaissance houses reflected in the green waters of the river, it forms a charming urban scene, notably in the **Rue du Bain-aux-Plantes**★★.

Place Kléber (JY) – This is the city's most famous square, named after Jean Kléber (1753-1800), the hero of the battles of Mainz (1793), Fleurus and Maastricht, who was assassinated in the course of Napoleon's campaign in Egypt.

⊘ ►► Cour du Corbeau★; Covered Bridges★; View★★ from the Barrage Vauban; Musée Alsacien **M³**; Musée Historique **M²**; Église St-Thomas – mausoleum of Marshal de Saxe★★; Orangerie★; Palais de l'Europe★.

SUC-AU-MAY★★★

Map p 9 – Map 72 fold 19 or 239 fold 27 – Green Guide Berry Limousin (in French)

Suc-au-May (908m – 2 979ft high) rises from the Monedières range overlooking the Limousin plateau, a bleak landscape of scattered hamlets with solid granite-walled and slate-roofed houses and endless expanses of heather and bracken.

In fine weather, there is a vast **panorama**★★★ taking in the mountains of the Massif Central to the east. The regular outline and apparent horizontality of the landscape seems to disprove any notion that these ancient crystalline rocks were significantly affected by the dramatic earth-movements of Tertiary times. Nevertheless, a gradual slope runs from southeast to northwest, a result of the uplifting of the Massif Central by the terrific pressure exerted during the formation of the Alps. The measure of the slope is nicely expressed in the descending order of altitude of summits, starting with Mount Pilat at 1 432m – 4 698ft and continuing via the Forez uplands (1 360m – 4 462ft), the Livradois (1 000m – 3 281ft), the base of the more recent Monts Dômes (873m – 2 864ft), the Monts Blond (515m – 1 690ft) and ending with St-Michel-Mont-Mercure in the Vendée at 285m – 935ft.

To the northeast, forming a foreground to all this immensity, extends the **Plateau de Millevaches**, the most typical stretch of these harsh Limousin uplands, known collectively as La Montagne ("The Mountain").

SURGÈRES

Population 6 049
Map p 8 – Map 71 fold 3 or 233 fold 15 – Green Guide Atlantic Coast

Surgères evolved around a fortified settlement (remains of which can be seen in the public gardens) of which there remains the Romanesque **Église Notre-Dame**★; the building has a west front characteristic of the region (rebuilt in the 19C) as well as a pyramidal colonnaded tower.

In 1578, the poet **Ronsard** published his *Amours d'Hélène (Loves of Helen)*. 54 years old, disappointed in love, he had retired to the St-Gilles priory at Montoire in order to write this collection of sonnets. They celebrated the dominion exercised over his heart by Hélène de Surgères, Catherine de Medici's lady-in-waiting, who had remained untouched by the dissolute life of the royal household.

Charentes Butter – In 1872, the Charente *département* was still an important wine-producing area and good-quality spirits were manufactured in the distilleries at Surgères. A number of old buildings still have sculptures recalling these activities. But phylloxera struck, annihilating the vines and ruining the producers.

Prisoners of war returning after 1870 had told local people about the cooperative methods used by farmers in the Swiss Jura to manufacture and market cheese; they were also aware that butter could be produced using industrial methods, and furthermore, a cooperative bakery had been operating locally since 1867.

Eugène Biraud was a land owner from **Chaillé** *(4km – 2 1/2 miles northeast)*, well aware that salvation lay in innovation. On 13 January 1888, together with 12 of his neighbours, he founded the first dairy cooperative based on the three principles of: pooling of raw materials, industrial methods of production, and collective marketing techniques. A few days later, the cooperative sent off its first consignment of butter to Paris. Success came well up to expectations, and similar cooperatives began to spread in the limestone plains of Poitou and the Aunis country. Surgères has become the area's main centre for the production of butter, as well as the seat of France's National Dairy College.

Gorges du TARN★★★

Map p 9 – Michelin map 80 folds 4, 5, 6, 14 or 240 folds 6, 10
Green Guide Pyrenees-Languedoc-Tarn Gorges

The deep gorges cut by the Tarn through the harsh limestone plateaux *(causses)* to the south of the Massif Central make up one of France's most spectacular natural landscapes. The source of the Tarn lies high (1 575m – 5 167ft) in the granitic uplands of Mount Lozère; tumbling torrent-like down the slopes of the Cévennes, the river then enters the most spectacular section of its course at Florac.

FROM FLORAC TO MILLAU *83km – 52 miles – allow about four hours*

The river flows through a deep canyon, joined by side valleys like those of the Jonte and the Dourbie. Escape from the valley bottom is by means of roads which twist and turn up the precipitous slopes to join the roughly-planed surface of the Méjean *causse;* its porous limestone is deeply fissured and hollowed out to form the caves for which the region is famous.

Most visitors come here when the summer sun is beating down, but the scene should also be appreciated in the kindlier conditions of spring and autumn, when the mantle of vegetation is better able to assert itself and local life is flourishing. Nor should the spectacle of winter be missed, when every feature has its frosty outline. Above the river's pebbly bed are piled up the successive beds of limestone, some of them 50m – 165ft thick, evidence of the huge scale of the sedimentation which took place over almost inconceivably long stretches of time during the Secondary era. Rocky debris from the mountains fringing the warm and shallow seas of these remote times was washed down to mingle with the remains of corals and crustaceans, spongy tissues and the skeletons of fish; subjected to the heat generated by their own increasing weight, these accumulations slowly built up to form this massive addition to the Earth's crust which extends all around the southern fringe of the Massif Central, here reaching an astonishing thickness of some 600m – 2 000ft. Some idea of the great force of the Alpine uplift can be gained when it is realised that the earth movements of the time raised this great plinth of stone 1 000m – 3 300ft above its original level. At the same time faulting and fracturing occurred in a number of places (as is proved by the non-conformity of the strata on opposite sides of the river), thus opening the way (south of Ste-Énimie and between the Cirque des Baumes and Le Rozier) to the formation of today's gorges.

No trace of the underground realm of chasms (**Aven Armand★★★**) and caverns is visible at the surface; those who venture into this unsuspected world are rewarded by the extraordinary spectacle presented by the dissolution of the limestone, and by the strange forms of the stalactites and stalagmites.

In contrast to the gorges of the Verdon and the Ardèche, one never inhabited, the other depopulated, the hostile landscape here has been humanised by centuries of stubborn human effort. Thus there are villages on the flatter patches of cultivable land which occur on the valley bottom and sides (Ste-Énimie, La Malène, Les Vignes...) and the castles of lords and robber-barons on the more easily-defended sites overlooking the river. On the plateau above are isolated farms based on the better soils of the little depressions known as dolinas; the drystone walls once made by piling up the boulders collected laboriously from the fields are now supplemented by electric fences, and the thoughtless forest clearance of the 19C is being made good by the planting of Austrian pines.

★★ **Les Détroits** (The Straits) – This is the narrowest part of the valley, hemmed in by plunging cliffs of coloured limestone.

★★★ **Cirque des Baumes** – Below Les Détroits, the gorge widens, forming this magnificent natural amphitheatre.

Rocher de Cinglegros – This huge detached rock rears up over the Lafont Farm (Mas de Lafont) on the left bank of the river.

★★★ **Le Point Sublime** – *Adds 26km – 16 miles to the journey between La Malène and Les Vignes.* This splendid viewpoint above the Cirque des Baumes overlooks both canyon and *causse.*

★★ **Roc des Hourtous** – *Adds 25km – 16 miles to the journey between La Malène and Les Vignes.* Dramatic vista downstream towards Les Détroits and the Cirque des Baumes as well as wide views over the *causse.*

Carcanague – Obeliiane/IMAGES PHOTOTHÈQUE

Tarn-Schlucht

Abbaye du THORONET★★

Map p 11 – Michelin map 84 fold 6 or 114 fold 21 or 245 fold 34
Green Guide French Riviera

Of the "three Cistercian sisters of Provence" (the others being Silvacane and Sénanque), Le Thoronet ⊘ is the earliest; it was founded in 1136, when St Bernard was still alive. It is one of the most characteristic of Cistercian abbeys, as well as one of the most austere.

Its plain architecture is unrelieved by decoration, save in the chapter house, where two roughly-sculpted capitals relieve the prevailing rigour.
The **abbey church★** *(1 hour)* has a simple beauty. Built from 1160 onwards, it has remarkable stonework which was cut and assembled without the use of mortar (notably in the oven-vaulted apse).
The **cloisters★** of about 1175 have kept their four barrel-vaulted walks; the change of level is more obvious here than in the church and is still causing problems of subsidence.

TOUL★

Population 17 752
Map p 7 – Michelin map 62 fold 4 or 242 fold 17
Green Guide Alsace et Lorraine (in French)
Town plan in the current Michelin Red Guide France

For many years from the 11C onwards, Toul was ruled by its bishops, whose interests frequently failed to coincide with those of their subjects. Together with Metz and Verdun, the city was one of the three Imperial Bishoprics which were annexed by Henri II in 1552 and were finally recognised as belonging to the French crown by the Peace of Westphalia in 1648.
Vauban came here at the end of the 17C to redesign the fortifications, the Metz Gate in particular. After the loss of France's eastern provinces in 1871, Toul became part of the defensive system created in the early days of the Third Republic by General Séré de Rivières; this was based on huge half-buried polygonal forts like the one at Villey-le-Sec *(7km – 4 miles east)* which was intended to secure the strategically vital Toul Gap.

★★ **Cathédrale St-Étienne** – 1221-1496. The influence of the very Early Gothic architecture of the neighbouring province of Champagne (Notre-Dame-en-Vaux Church and Châlons-sur-Marne Cathedral) makes itself felt in the cathedral's very simple elevation (consisting only of main arches and clerestorey), in its east end (a straightforward apse with tall 13C windows), and in the inspection gallery running round the aisles at the base of the windows. The highly pointed arches of the first five bays of the nave are in the High Gothic style of the 14C.
The **west front★★**, almost overloaded with architectural ornament, lost its statuary at the time of the French Revolution. A number of features like the tympanums with window openings are characteristic of the architecture of the late 15C, while the triangular gable is of earlier date. The other gables are later and herald the awakening Renaissance, as do the upper parts of the façade and the little central lantern.

⊘ ►► Église St-Gengoult★ – Cloisters★★; Musée municipal★.

TOULON★★

Conurbation 437 553
Map p 10 – Map 84 fold 15 or 114 fold 45 or 245 fold 46
Green Guide French Riviera
Town plan in the current Michelin Red Guide France

Backed by high hills whose summits are crowned by forts, Toulon is France's second most important naval base.

The siege of 1793 – In 1793, an anti-revolutionary uprising had gained control of the whole of Corsica, pitting the monarchist Paoli *(qv)* against the loyalist Napoleon Bonaparte. Paoli enjoyed British support, and the warships of the Royal Navy controlled the waters between the island and the Toulon anchorage. The city had remained faithful to the monarchy, in whose cause it had welcomed an Anglo-Spanish fleet into its fine harbour.
The Revolutionary government in Paris, threatened as it was by both internal and external enemies, had to take action. On 15 December, its troops attacked. The British were in possession of strongpoints on the St-Mandrier peninsula and between La Seyne and Fort Balaguier (known as Little Gibraltar). The French infantry blockaded the city on the east while the artillery threatened it from the

northwest. Captain Bonaparte (who had left Corsica in June) took bold advantage of the situation, redeploying his guns in order to subject the British positions to direct fire. Little Gibraltar fell, and on the night of the 18 December, the British evacuated their troops, taking part of the population with them.

Repression was harsh; however Napoleon intervened and the Revolutionary government's threat to raze the city to the ground was not carried out.

★★ **Roadstead** - Construction of Toulon's Old Port (Vieille darse) began under Henri IV. Richelieu appreciated the strategic advantages of the roadstead and ordered the building of the first naval installations. In the reign of Louis XIV, the base was extended and the New Port (Darse Neuve) laid out by Vauban. In the 19C, the Mourillon extension and the Castigneau basin were built, completing the naval base which had become the home port of the French Mediterranean Fleet.

Beyond the harbour lies the magnificent Outer Roadstead (Grande Rade), approached via the Inner Roads (Petite Rade), guarded to the north by the Royal Tower (Tour Royale) and the main jetty, to the south by Vieille Point; it is here that the naval base, with all its installations and repair yards is located. The still considerable remains of the French fleet had anchored here after the disaster of Mers-el-Kébir in 1940, when the Royal Navy had turned its guns on the ships of its defeated ally in order to prevent them falling into German hands. The same danger threatened in July 1942; in response to the Allied landings in North Africa, the Germans had swiftly overrun the hitherto unoccupied part of France. Caught by surprise and unable to escape, 60 warships scuttled themselves, only a few submarines managing to make their way to the open sea.

Atlante by Pierre Puget, Toulon

D'après photo J. Guillard/SCOPE

★ **Port** ⓥ - To the west of the Quai de Stalingrad (landing stage for boat-trips ⓥ) is the Navy Museum. Once the entrance to the old Arsenal, its doorway is a Louis XV masterpiece; it is flanked by sculptures of Mars and Bellona and has marble columns with Doric capitals framing tableaux of maritime motifs. The balcony of the former Town Hall (Hôtel de ville) is supported by two splendidly muscular **atlantes★**, the work of Pierre Puget.

★★★ **Mont Faron** - This is the easternmost of the limestone ranges which were raised up in Provence on the fringe of the great earth movements associated with the formation of the Alps in Tertiary times.

★ **Musée-Mémorial du Débarquement** ⓥ - From the Beaumont Tower (507m - 1 663ft) there are fine views inland over the extensive forests of maritime pine, as well as a magnificent seaward **panorama★★★** over the Hyères Islands, the Toulon roadstead and the whole of the coast between Sanary and Bandol. The diorama explains the course of the landings which took place on the night of 14-15 August 1944 and of the subsequent liberation of the coast between Antheor and Marseilles. This second front supplemented the one already opened up by the Normandy landings, and forced the Wehrmacht to beat a rapid retreat to avoid being cut off.

ⓥ ►► Mount Faron corniche road★★; Musée de la Marine★; Old Toulon★.

TOULOUSE★★★

Conurbation 608 430
Map p 9 - Michelin map 82 fold 8 or 235 fold 30
Green Guide Pyrenees-Languedoc-Tarn Gorges
Town plan in the current Michelin Red Guide France

Toulouse is contemporary France's sixth largest urban centre. The city has long been the focus of very diverse influences; it is linked with the Mediterranean via the low Lauraguais Pass and with the Atlantic via the Garonne, while the valleys running down from the Pyrenees keep it in touch with Spain. Many of the great movements of population which have taken place since Roman times have consequently left their mark in this area.

The city was the capital of the Visigothic kingdom, and enjoyed considerable prosperity between the 9C and 13C under the Raymond dynasty whose court was considered to be one of the most cultured in Europe. Alas! the Albigensian crisis of the 13C put an end to the power of these rulers, giving the Capetian kings the chance to push their frontier southwards into Languedoc.

TOULOUSE

In 1323, Europe's oldest literary society was founded here to further the cause of the language of southern France (Langue d'Oc). Later, in the 16C, the city flourished again because of a boom in what at the time was the most widely-cultivated of all dye plants, woad, which yielded a blue-black colour.

The epic of the air – As early as 1917, strategic industries like aircraft manufacturing were being set up in southwestern France, as far away as possible from the country's vulnerable eastern border. In the interwar period, Toulouse became the starting-point of France's first scheduled air service.

Clément Ader (1841-1925) – Born at nearby Muret. This pioneer experimented with a balloon at Toulouse in 1870 and also designed a dirigible. On 9 October 1890, he succeeded in flying a short distance in a heavier-than-air machine.

Pierre Latécoère (1883-1943) – Built aircraft for the French army during the First World War. On Christmas Day 1918, assisted by Cornemont, he carried out a test flight to investigate the possibilities of a link with Barcelona.

Didier Daurat (1891-1969) – With a great talent for leadership, he became director of the airline set up by Latécoère, then ran Aéropostale, and finally headed Air France. On 10 March 1919, he inaugurated the first air mail service to link Toulouse and Casablanca (though the official opening was not until 1 September).

TOULOUSE

C	Hôtel de Fumel
D	Basilique N.-D.-de-la-Daurade
E	Hôtel Béringuier-Maynier
L	Tour Pierre Séguy
M¹	Musée du Vieux-Toulouse
R	Tour de Sarta

Émile Dewoitine (1892-1979) – Founder of Toulouse's aviation industry and builder of the Dewoitine 520 fighter plane.

Antoine de Saint-Exupéry (1900-44) – A pilot on the Toulouse-Casablanca route, he was responsible for investigating the Dakar link which was eventually inaugurated on 1 June 1925. He also flew extensively in South America and was the author of internationally acclaimed works like *Night Flight* and the *Little Prince.*

Jean Mermoz (1901-1935) – Pioneered the trans-Andean route between Rio and Santiago. In 1930, he set up the first airmail route between France and South America. He died aboard his seaplane *Croix-du-Sud.*

Henri Guillaumet (1902-1940) – Helped Latécoère set up the trans-Andean route and completed a total of 393 flights over this formidable mountain barrier.

21 April 1949 – Jean Gonord piloted the Leduc 010 on its maiden flight. The plane's ram jet, designed by René Leduc, was the precursor of the engines powering the high-speed aircraft of later decades.

27 May 1955 – Maiden flight of the Caravelle, piloted by P. Nadot. This was one of the world's first jet airliners, second only to the ill-starred British Comet.

2 March 1969 – André Turcat took off in the supersonic Anglo-French Concorde with its distinctive tapering fuselage designed by Servanty.

A BRICK-BUILT CITY

In the Early Middle Ages, Toulouse was one of France's most important centres of cultural and artistic activity. Today, little remains of this distant period other than the great St-Sernin Church and the Romanesque sculptures in the Augustinians' Museum.

The city's medieval growth could not be catered for by building in stone, the nearest quarries being 80km – 50 miles distant. The problem was solved by using the Garonne clays to manufacture the bricks which are such a characteristic feature of the Toulouse townscape. Robust, cheap, easy to use, but perhaps less decorative than stone, brick added a further layer of austerity to that wished for by the mendicant orders who were so influential here.

★★★ **Basilique St-Sernin** (DX) – The great church was built to honour the memory of the Gaulish martyr St Sernin (or Saturninus). A first phase of construction lasting from around 1080-1118 was in a mixture of brick and stone, a second phase in brick alone.

St-Sernin was one of a number of major Romanesque pilgrimage churches on the route to Compostela like Cluny, St-Martin at Tours, St-Martial at Limoges, St-Hilaire-le-Grand at Poitiers, St-Remi at Rheims and Santiago de Compostela itself, which, often provided with five aisles to accommodate the throngs of pilgrims, form a distinct grouping; it was on these great institutions that the medieval Papacy relied for the consolidation of its temporal power, the Reconquest of Spain from the Moors and the extirpation of the Cathar heresy. These churches also played a role in the realisation of Capetian designs on Languedoc.

St-Sernin's octagonal belltower is particularly characteristic of the area, with five levels of twin arches built in brick, the upper two of which are provided with little pediments.

★★ **Les Jacobins** (DY) ⊘ – This was the first church of the Preaching Friars, an order founded at **Fanjeaux** *(20km – 12 miles south of Castelnaudary)* in 1215 by St Dominic, and intended by him to help in the fight against the Cathar heresy. To the poverty demanded by St Francis of his followers, Dominic added a solidly-based knowledge of theology and a training in eloquence which enabled his disciples to overcome their opponents in argument and spread true doctrine.

Vault of the Église des Jacobins, Toulouse

H. Champollion/OUEST-FRANCE

The church is the key building in the evolution from 1230 onwards of Southern French Gothic as influenced by the mendicant orders.

The first rectangular-shaped church, built between 1230-35, was enlarged in the middle of the century, then again between 1275-92 in order to accommodate the growing fraternity. This was the point at which major changes were made in the apse and elevation of the nave. The size of the edifice, combined with the impossibility of providing it with external support (because of ownership and circulation problems), ruled out the construction of a single nave, and the building's original division into two parts had to be retained. Decisive in the choice of roofing method was the recent destruction in a fire of the Order's timber-roofed church at Bayonne; thus it was that the architect here resorted to the expedient of a marvellous ribbed vault and the "palm-tree" of the chancel with its splendid array of 22 radiating arches. All this in 1292, 170 years before the great pointed vaults of the Late Gothic.

The tower dates from 1298, several years later than the upper stages of the tower of St-Sernin; with its great height, octagonal plan, pedimented arches and rhomboid openings, it became the model for the towers of the major churches of Southern France (just as the gable-wall of the adjoining Church of Notre-Dame-du-Taur formed the prototype for many village churches).

★ **Capitole** (DY H) – This is Toulouse's City Hall, its name being derived from the "capitouls" or consuls who administered the city when it was ruled by the Raymonds. With its Ionic pilasters and alternating use of brick and stone, it is a fine example of the urban architecture of the 18C.

★ **Cathédrale St-Étienne** (EY) – There is a fascinating contrast here between the nave completed in 1212, a vast hall in the Mediterranean tradition designed to accommodate large numbers of people, and the chancel, begun 60 years later on the pattern of the Gothic churches of Northern France. The architect of this later addition was Jean Deschamps, who took it upon himself to propagate this style throughout Languedoc once it had become part of the Capetian realm. The nave and chancel are not aligned on the same axis and hardly seem to form part of a whole. The original plan had envisaged a more or less total reconstruction, but in the event the old nave was retained, and the link between it and the chancel cleverly improvised by some architectural virtuosity in what should have been the north transept.

★★ **Musée des Augustins** (DEY) ⊘ – The museum is housed in the former convent; in the chapter house there is a famous Pietà.

The superb collection of **Romanesque sculpture**★★★ (mostly 12C), much of it in grey Pyrenean marble, comes for the greater part from the cloisters of St-Sernin and St Stephen's, and from Notre-Dame-de-la-Daurade. The influence of Moissac (qv) is evident (La Daurade was a priory attached to the abbey there), as is that of Chartres and St-Denis, where Gilbertus, the sculptor responsible for the cloisters of St Stephen's, may well have worked.

⊘ ►► Hôtel d'Assezat★ (DY); Musée St-Raymond★★ – archaeology; Musée d'Histoire naturelle★★; Musée Paul-Dupuy★ (EZ) – applied arts from medieval times to the present.

Le TOUQUET★★★

Population 5 596
Map p 6 – Michelin map 51 fold 11 or 236 fold 11
Green Guide Flanders, Picardy and the Paris Region
Town plan in the current Michelin Red Guide France

Le Touquet was simply the name given to a stretch of uninhabited sand-dunes at the mouth of the River Canche, when, in 1837, the area was purchased by a speculator who planted it up with maritime pines and later, in 1876, divided it into residential plots. At the beginning of the 20C, a British company, the "Le Touquet Syndicate" moved in and built the first of many exclusive holiday dwellings. By 1912 the place had developed to such an extent and become so fashionable among the leisured classes, not only of England but also of Paris, that it took on the name of **Le Touquet Paris Plage**.

Today, the "Pearl of the Opal Coast" is not only a favoured resort for the well-to-do families of France's industrial North, but also enjoys an international reputation, with its range of facilities, which include casinos and a hydrotherapy centre as well as golf, tennis, riding, land-yachting...

The town is divided into two; there is the well-treed residential area with its luxurious villas, some of them modern, but many in that hybrid style known as "Anglo-Norman", then there is the resort itself, stretching out along the magnificent beach of fine sand. The town centre is laid out on a grid pattern and the main shopping streets are Rue St-Jean and Rue de Paris.

TOURNUS★

Population 6 568
Map p 10 – Michelin map 69 fold 20 or 242 folds 39, 40
Green Guide Burgundy Jura
Town plan in the current Michelin Red Guide France

Originally founded by the Aidui tribe, Tournus became a Gallo-Roman settlement on a river-terrace on the right bank of the Saône, then later an important stopping-place for river traffic.

The sanctuaries erected over the tomb of St Valerian from Merovingian times onwards made it one of the earliest centres of monasticism in France. In the 9C, monks from Noirmoutier fled here from the Vikings, bringing with them the relics of St Philibert. The place's wealth excited the envy of the Hungarian hordes, who sacked it in 937.

★★ **Église St-Philibert** – The reconstruction of the church was begun 25 years after the Hungarian raid. A number of features date from this period, including the **crypt**★, where the persistence of Carolingian tradition can be seen in the layout of the chapels and the barrel vault of the ambulatory, as well as the narthex, whose enormous circular abacus pillars are one of the great achievements of this early phase of the Romanesque. The west front dates from the 10C-11C; it was built like a castle keep, down to having loophole slits (the machicolations are a 19C addition).

At the beginning of the 11C, after a fire in 1006, work was started on the nave. The splendid cylindrical pillars are almost unique in the history of medieval architecture, and the early 12C vault is highly original too; its five transversal barrel vaults offered a number of structural advantages by eliminating lateral thrusts, allowing longitudinal pressures to cancel each other out, and making use of narthex and transept for support as well. In view of this, it is surprising that it remained an isolated example, with no imitators.

The rapid development of the Romanesque style can be traced in both transept and choir, the latter with a barrel vault on divergent transverse arches.

TOURS★★

Conurbation 271 927
Map p 5 – Michelin map 64 fold 15 or 232 folds 35, 36 or 238 fold 13
Green Guide Châteaux of the Loire – Town plan in the current Michelin Red Guide France

Built in white tufa and roofed in slate, the old dwellings of Tours fill the isthmus between the Loire and its tributary the Cher. The place originated in Gaulish times, becoming an important centre of trade and administration under the Romans. The peaceful atmosphere of the Loire valley with its exceptionally clear light may be responsible in part for the many great figures associated with the city in one way or another. They include:

St Gatien, the first bishop of Tours (3C), who helped convert Gaul to Christianity;

St Martin (316-97), whose veneration by the common people made the "city of St Martin" into a place of pilgrimage as well as an important crossroads;

Gregory of Tours (6C), the chronicler of Merovingian times;

Alcuin of York (late 8C), who helped implement Charlemagne's revival of intellectual life and who founded an illustrious school of calligraphy;

Jean Fouquet (1420-81), Charles VII's portrait-painter;

Louis XI (1423-83), responsible for introducing silk and velvet manufacture to the city;

Jean Bourdichon (1457-1521), miniaturist and portrait-painter in the reign of Charles VIII, who decorated the field of the Cloth of Gold for François I;

Jean Clouet (1485-1541), François I's court painter;

Pierre Ronsard (1524-85), the highly individualistic poet who passed his last 20 years as Prior of nearby St Cosmas';

Anatole France (1844-1924), the somewhat sceptical but nevertheless optimistic humanist who stayed at La Béchellerie and St-Cyr-sur-Loire;

Henri Bergson (1859-1941), the philosopher of the prewar years whose work was devoted to bridging the gap between metaphysics and science and who stayed at La Gaudinière.

Ronsard

315

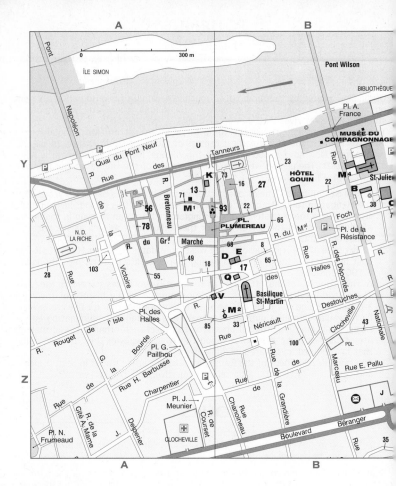

★★ Old Tours (ABY) – The city long prided itself on its craftsmen, and even at the end of the 19C there were still three guilds jealously guarding their traditions. The **Musée du Compagnonage** ⊘ contains many fine examples of the work of master craftsmen like roofers and slaters, blacksmiths and locksmiths, saddlers and carpenters...

★ Château (CY) – This is a heterogenous collection of buildings ranging in date from the 4C to the 19C. The lower parts of the wall on the west side go back to Roman times and here too is the 11C residence of the Counts of Anjou; the Guise Tower (Tour de Guise) with its machicolations and pepper-pot roof is of the 13C-15C, while the dormer-windowed Governor's Lodging (Logis du Gouverneur) is 15C and other additions were made as recently as the 17C-19C.

★★ Cathédrale St-Gatien – Following a fire, the cathedral was rebuilt from 1235 onwards. The work lasted all of 250 years; the choir dates from the reign of Louis IX and the nave from the age of Charles VII and Duke John of Brittany. The latter was probably responsible for commissioning a master-glazier from Rennes to make one of the cathedral's stained glass windows. The west front was completed under Louis XI and Charles VIII; in Flamboyant style, it has an openwork tympanum and triangular gable, while the design of the lantern crowning the twin towers is characteristic of the Early Renaissance.

The stained glass ranges in date from the 13C (high windows in the chancel) via the 14C (transept rose-windows) to the 15C (rose-window of the west front). In the south transept chapel is the tomb of the children of Charles VIII; mounted on a base carved by Geronimo di Fiesole, it is the work of the sculpture workshop founded by Michel Colombe. The choir is lit by a rare 18C chandelier.

★ La Psalette ⊘ – This is the name given to the cathedral cloisters where canons and choir-master used to meet. The tiny Archive Room (Salle des Archives) of 1520 and the vaulted Library (Librairie) are reached by means of a spiral staircase, Gothic in structure but Renaissance in the way in which it is detailed.

★ Place Plumereau (ABY) – This busy square is located at the old "meeting of the ways"; it is bordered by fine 15C residences built of stone and timber. On the corner with the Rue du Change and the Rue de la Monnaie is a carved corner post with a somewhat mutilated depiction of the Circumcision.

316

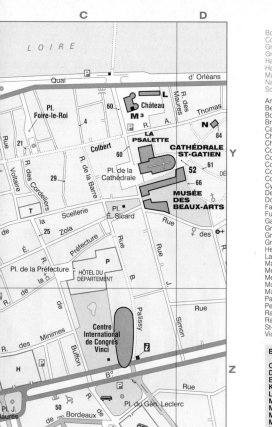

★★ Musée des Beaux-Arts (CDY) ⓥ – In the former Bishops' Palace (17C-18C), its rooms are decorated with Louis XVI panelling and silk hangings made locally. It houses works of art from the châteaux at Richelieu and Chanteloup (now demolished) as well as from the great abbeys of Touraine. The collection of paintings consists mostly of French works of the 19C-20C, but there are also two outstanding Mantegnas, a Resurrection and Christ in the Garden of Olives (late 15C).

★ Prieuré de St-Cosme ⓥ – 3km – 2 miles southwest on the south bank of the river. Leave Tours by the Pont Wilson.
Now in ruins, this is the priory to which Ronsard retired (p 308). He lived and died in the Prior's Lodging (Logis du Prieur), a charming little 15C dwelling, and is buried in the church.

Château de Plessis-lès-Tours ⓥ – 3km – 2 miles southwest after crossing the Pont Wilson.
This modest brick building is all that remains of the substantial château built here by Louis XI and where he spent much of his time.
The room in which he died still has the linenfold panelling much favoured in the 15C.
This Louis was a restless monarch, more of a politician than a military man; he succeeded in imposing his authority on the country and in bringing the Hundred Years War to an end, after which he turned his attention to restoring France's devastated economy.
He incorporated into his kingdom not only the Duchy of Burgundy, but also the Somme towns, Artois and the Franche-Comté (all in 1477), followed by Maine and Anjou in 1481 and Provence in 1486. Conscious of the importance of monarchical prestige, he feigned good health in his declining years in spite of serious illness.

ⓥ ►► Rue Briçonnet★; Place Grégoire-de-Tours★; Hôtel Gouin★ – Musée de la Société archéologique de Touraine★; Historial de Touraine★ (in the castle) **M³**; tropical aquarium; Jardin de Beaune-Semblançay★ **B**; Musée des équipages militaires et du train★.

TRÉGUIER★★

Population 2 799
Map p 4 – Michelin map 59 fold 2 or 230 fold 7 – Green Guide Brittany

Tréguier is a little medieval city, overlooking the wide estuary of the Jaudy and Guindy rivers, one of the drowned valleys known as *abers (qv)* which are so characteristic of the Breton coast.

The place was converted to Christianity in the 6C by St Tugdual, a monk of Welsh origin, and soon became the seat of a bishop. The most popular Breton saint, the ecclesiastical judge Monsieur **Saint-Ives** (1253-1303), lived here; he was often depicted in the act of even-handedly dispensing justice between rich and poor alike and hence became the patron saint of well-versed lawyers.

The town and its surroundings were no strangers to misfortune. In 1345-47 the area was devastated by the English allies of Jean de Montfort in retribution for having supported Jeanne de Penthièvre in the War of the Breton Succession *(qv)*. In 1592 it was pillaged by the Catholic Leaguers for having taken the part of Henri IV, then punished again in 1789 for its opposition to the taxes and clerical reforms introduced at the time of the French Revolution.

The timber-framed **house** ⊙ where the writer **Ernest Renan** (1823-92) was born is devoted to his memory, and his statue stands in the Place du Martray.

The cloisters, Tréguier

★★ **Cathédrale St-Tugdual** – Begun in 1339, this is one of the finest buildings of its kind in Brittany, Anglo-Norman in style in spite of the use of the local granite. The exterior is notable for its Romanesque Hastings Tower (Tour d'Hastings) and the balustrades adorning the slate roofs, as well as for the two porches on the south side; the larger one with its statues of the Apostles is known as the People's Porch (Porche du Peuple), the other with its much eroded statuary is the Bell Porch (Porche des Cloches).

Within, the Lanceolate version of the Gothic survives in the three-storeyed elevation. A frieze sculpted in white tufa runs underneath the blind triforium, while in the south transept there is a graceful **window**★ with a depiction of the **Mystic Vine**★ symbolising the Church in Brittany. In the ambulatory is a 13C wooden figure of Christ, and the nave has a copy of the tomb of St Ives built by Duke John V.

The **cloisters**★ (1458) ⊙ are among the few to survive in Brittany. Timber-roofed and with a carved frieze, it has 48 elegant arches giving on to a hydrangea-planted courtyard.

Forêt de TRONÇAIS★★★

Map p 9 – Michelin map 69 fold 12 or 238 folds 32, 43, 44
Green Guide Auvergne-Rhône Valley

This splendid forest, "one of the finest in France, indeed in Europe" (J.L. Reed), lies at the southeastern end of the great plains of central France, bounded by the rivers Allier and Cher.

Today's forest covers a total area of 10 954ha – 27 067 acres. It passed into the hands of the French Crown when François I put an end to the independence of the Bourbonnais in 1527. A steady process of deterioration set in which was reversed by the great Colbert in 1670; anxious to maintain the supply of ship timber for the expanding French navy, he instituted measures for the conservation and renewal of the woodland. However, in 1788 an iron foundry was opened, and to satisfy its demands for charcoal, two-thirds of the area was converted from high forest to a coppice regime, thereby destroying much of the resource slowly built up over the preceding century.

In 1832 a new policy of conservation was adopted, and since 1928 six blocks of high forest totalling 650ha – 1 606 acres have been managed on a long rotation of 225 years.

The forest consists largely of sessile oak. The finest stands are called the **Hauts-Massifs**★★★; here there are a number of exceptional individuals with their own names, some of them more than 300 years old.

To the east of the Gardien clearing are the Carré, Émile-Guillaumin and Charles-Louis-Philippe oaks, and to the west of the Buffévent clearing in the Richebout block other venerable trees bearing the names Jacques-Chevalier, de la Sentinelle and des Jumeaux.

The Tronçais region straddles the boundary between the north and south of France. To the north is the country of *langue d'oil*, four-wheeled carts, and slate or flat-tiled roofs, to the south *langue d'oc*, carts with only two wheels, and roofs covered with pantiles in the Roman fashion.

⊘ ►► Western forest blocks★ *(Séries de l'Ouest)* – Colbert Stand★ *(Futaie Colbert)* – St-Bonnet★, Pirot★ and Saloup★ Ponds *(Étangs de St-Bonnet, de Pirot, de Saloup)*.

TROYES★★

Conurbation 122 763
Map p 6 – Michelin map 61 folds 16, 17 or 241 fold 37
Green Guide Champagne (in French)
Town plan in the current Michelin Red Guide France

Troyes shares with Rheims the distinction of being one of the capitals of the province of Champagne, though the city looks southeast towards Burgundy and the Langres plateau rather than northwards to the Ardennes. The town developed in the Seine valley on the great trade route between Italy and the cities of Flanders; in the Middle Ages it was host to two huge annual fairs, each lasting for three whole months, and attracting merchants and craftsmen from all over Europe. But by the end of the 14C the pattern of commercial exchanges had changed, and these great gatherings fell into decline.

A number of important figures were either born in Troyes or worked here. They include:

Saint Loup (383-478) who was born at Toul. An associate of Saint Germanus of Auxerre, he founded an abbey and became Bishop of Troyes, saving the city from Attila's assault;

Christian of Troyes (1135-83), author of verse-chronicles and of romances celebrating courtly love;

Jean Juvénal des Ursins (1350-1431), the magistrate who conducted on behalf of Charles VI the negotiations with John the Fearless which led to the signing of the Treaty of Arras (1414), which it was hoped, would put an end to the war between Armagnacs and Burgundians;

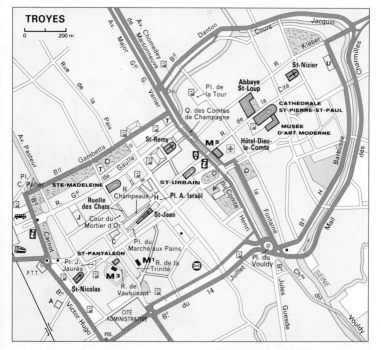

M¹ Maison de l'Outil
et de la Pensée ouvrière

M³ Hôtel de Vauluisant
M⁵ Pharmacie de l'Hôtel-Dieu

Pierre Mignard (1612-95) the painter, a master of colour, who portrayed Mazarin, Mme de Sévigné, Turenne, Colbert. He also designed the dome of the Church of Notre-Dame-du-Val-de-Grâce in Paris *(p 193);*

François Girardon (1628-1715) the sculptor, famous for the tomb he designed for Richelieu *(qv)* and for his contribution to the statuary in the gardens at Versailles. The Treaty of Troyes giving Henry V of England sovereignty over France was signed on 21 May 1420 by Charles VI the Mad, the possibility of the "so-called" Dauphin Charles VII succeeding to the throne being excluded because of the notorious misconduct of Isabel of Bavaria.

Troyes has long been France's most important centre of hosiery manufacture. The industry was introduced here at the very beginning of the 16C, followed by cloth-making, dyeing, paper-making...and prosperity. The city's wealth enabled it to overcome the great fire of 1524; houses and churches were quickly rebuilt in a style showing both the Italianate influence of the artists who came here from Fontaine-bleau around 1540 as well as the persistence of local, medieval traditions.

In an area lacking suitable stone there is nevertheless fine sculpture, especially the work of Jean Gailde and Jacques Julyot. Early sculpture reflects troubled times, as in the *St Martha* by the Master of Chaource in the city's St Mary Magdalen Church (Église Ste-Madeleine). Later work, like the *Virgin with the Grape* in St Urban's Church (Église St-Urbain) is more refined, while finally the Italian Il Fiorentino introduces a note of southern gracefulness. Stained glass was made here too, eventually becoming a kind of painting on glass, with the artist using and reusing for economy's sake the same cartoons for different projects. Advances were made in graphic skills, with elaborate designs like Jesse Trees divided into several parts, or involving a variety of closely juxtaposed scenes explained by means of a written commentary (the ancestor perhaps of the strip cartoon). Grisaille work can be seen in St Pantaleon's Church (Église St-Pantaléon) and the green glass made in the province is famous.

The hosiery industry – From 1505 onward the hosiers of Troyes were making hats and bonnets and knitting socks and stockings. They acquired guild status in 1554. In 1746, looms were installed in the city's Trinity Hospital in order to give employment to destitute children. Troyes is still France's hosiery capital, with some 300 different enterprises at work.

In the 16C **Hôtel de Vauluisant★** (**M³**) is a **Musée de la bonneterie** ⊙ with exhibits depicting the industry's evolution, including historic looms and other machinery and a variety of products, some of which go back to the 18C.

★★ **Old Troyes** – The outline of the old part of the city bears a curious resemblance to a champagne cork, with the area around the cathedral forming the head. The majority of the old houses are timber-framed, with vertical members held together by horizontal beams rather than by timbers set obliquely or in the form of a St Andrew's cross as elsewhere in France. The most elegant infill is the characteristic local chequer-board pattern made from brick, slate or chalk rather than the cob or daub commonly employed.

The streets with the best examples of such houses are Rue Champeaux, Ruelle des Chats, Rue de Vauluisant as well as the Cour du Mortier d'Or.

The **Maison de l'Outil et de la Pensée ouvrière** ⊙ is housed in the Hôtel du Mauroy (**M'**), a fine architectural setting for the fascinating range of objects displayed. The dignity of labour is celebrated here in the subtle but never gratuitous diversity of forms no less than in the individual character and highly specialised function of each object. Though some are conventionally beautiful or pleasingly ornamented, one is more touched in the end by the way in which tools like hammers have been shaped over time by the hand that has used them as well as by the material they have been in contact with.

La Maison du Boulanger and the
Tourelle de l'Orfèvre, Troyes

Église Ste-Madeleine ⊙ is Troyes' oldest place of worship. Much rebuilt in the 16C, it is famous for the **rood-screen**★★ made by Jean Gailde; this has scalloped ogee arches with no intermediate supports, fine glass (the Passion, the Creation, a Jesse Tree), as well as a statue of **St Martha**★ of striking gravity.

★★ **Cathédrale St-Pierre et St-Paul** – The cathedral was begun in 1208. Work on the vast edifice continued into the 16C, enabling the regional Gothic style to be traced over the whole period of its evolution. The chancel is remarkable for its three-storeyed elevation, carried out entirely in openwork, a pioneering achievement on this scale.

It was completed in 1228, followed by the transepts in 1300 and the vaulting of the nave in 1497.

In 1506 the architect Martin Chambiges came to Troyes, having already worked at Sens. He was responsible for the design of the elaborate west front in the Flamboyant style, worked on until 1556 by his son Pierre, his son-in-law and his grandson Jean Bailly.

The **stained glass windows**★★ of the cathedral cover a total area of 1 500m² – about 16 000sq ft. One of the supreme achievements of this art form, they transform the building into a cage of glass.

Most periods are represented, the 13C by the large-scale figures in the choir and the scenes of the *Passion* in the east window; the 14C by the transept clerestory windows; the end of the 15C by the Jesse Tree with its fine figures and foliage (upper part of the glass in the sixth bay on the south side of the nave); the 16C by the great western rose window with the celestial court painted by Jean Soudain in 1546 and the 17C by Linard Gontier's *Mystic Wine-Press* of 1626 in which the Church reasserts itself at the time of the Counter-Reformation.

★★ **Musée d'Art moderne** ⊙ – This is the collection built up since 1939 by Pierre and Denise Lévy, noted hosiery manufacturers. It comprises thousands of items dating from 1850 to 1950, many of them donated to the State and now on display in the former Bishops' Palace.

Lévy was on good terms with many artists, visiting their studios and becoming firm friends with some of the great figures of our age. Particularly well represented here are the **Fauves**, who, together with Braque, Dufy, Matisse and Van Dongen "made colour roar". Derain too, one of the first to appreciate the art of Africa, is very much present, as is Maurice Marinot, a local artist and glass-maker.

⊙ ►► Basilique St-Urbain★; Église St-Pantaléon★; Musée St-Loup – Fine art and archeology★; Pharmacie★ de l'Hôtel Dieu **M⁵**.

VAISON-LA-ROMAINE★★

Population 5 663
Map p 10 – Michelin map 81 folds 2 or 245 fold 17 or 246 fold 9
Green Guide Provence
Town plan in the current Michelin Red Guide France

Founded 60 years before Caesar's conquest of Gaul, Vaison-La-Romaine still evokes the life of a Gallo-Roman city.

Before the legions came, the place had been the capital of a Celtic tribe, the Vocontii. Under Roman rule it became the seat of great landed proprietors, a flourishing city possibly as large as Arles or Fréjus, one of the centres of Transalpine Gaul and subsequently of Narbonensis. It fell into ruin at the time of the barbarian invasions.

★★ **Ruines romaines** ⊙ – The layout of modern Vaison has allowed two parts of the Roman city to be excavated.

The **La Villasse quarter** lies to the southwest of the Avenue Général-de-Gaulle on either side of a paved central street; there are shops, houses and a basilica. The Dolphin House (Maison du Dauphin) dating from 30 BC is particularly interesting, as is the House of the Silver Bust (Maison du Buste-d'argent).

The **Puymin quarter** lies to the east of the avenue. Here there is the House of the Messii (Maison des Messii) with its atrium, peristyle and baths, as well as the Roman Theatre.

The latter structure *(approached via a tunnel)* dates from the time of the Emperor Augustus; the pits containing the machinery and curtain have been well preserved and the tiers of seating were reconstructed in 1932 by the then Inspector-General of Historical Monuments, Jules Formigé, though it is left to the visitor's imagination to visualise what the stage wall (like the one at Orange) must have looked like.

⊙ ►► Musée archéologique Théo-Desplans★; Ancienne cathédrale Notre-Dame – High Altar★, cloisters★ – Chapelle de St-Quenin.

Château de VALENÇAY★★

Map p 5 – Michelin map 64 fold 18 or 238 fold 16
Green Guide Châteaux of the Loire

The medieval **castle** ⊘ which once stood here was rebuilt by Jacques d'Étampes from 1540 onwards. Even more than at Azay-le-Rideau 22 years previously, the defensive features of the traditional castle are used here in a purely decorative way; there are harmless turrets, an entrance pavilion disguised as a keep, sham machicolations and a sentry-walk held up on brackets rather than on corbels as hitherto.

The Italian influence of the Early Renaissance is well represented too, in a number of distinctive features like the steeply-pitched roofs with their dormer-windows and chimneys treated as miniature classical temples, the balustraded entablature, the windows separated by pilasters and tableaux in stone, and the superimposed Orders arranged according to the Vitruvian canon (published a few years previously, in 1521).

The west wing was added in the 17C and altered in the 18C.

In 1803, the estate was acquired by **Charles-Maurice de Talleyrand-Périgord** (1754-1838), paid for almost entirely by Napoleon, at the time still First Consul.

> For almost a quarter of a century, the château served as a glittering background to the masterly manœuvres in international diplomacy conducted by its illustrious owner, who held high offices of state from the time of Louis XVI to the Restoration.
>
> Inside the château are fine furnishings of the Régence and Empire periods, including 18C Savonnerie carpets, the round table from the Congress of Vienna (in fact it came from the Kaunitz Palace, the French Embassy at the time of the Congress), and a portrait by Élisabeth Vigée-Lebrun of Talleyrand's wife, the Princess of Benevento.

VANNES★★

Pop 45 644
Map p 4 – Michelin map 63 fold 3 or 230 folds 36, 37 – Green Guide Brittany
Town plan in the current Michelin Red Guide France

Vannes lies at the highest point to which tides flow at the head of the Morbihan Gulf. In pre-Roman times, it was the capital of the Veneti, a tribe of Central European origin, some of whose number had settled in the Veneto in northeastern Italy. One of Gaul's most powerful peoples, they were intrepid sailors, crossing the seas to trade with the inhabitants of the British Isles. They nevertheless suffered a terrible defeat at sea in 56 BC at the hands of the Romans, losing 200 ships in a single day. Immobilised by a dead calm and lacking any form of long-range weaponry, their navy was an easy prey for the Roman galleys with their battering rams, grappling irons and tough mariners ready to storm aboard. This was a triumph for Caesar, earning him the loyalty of the legions and ensuring his popularity in both Senate and Forum. Brittany's fate was to become a backwater for a very long time indeed.

Ramparts and wash-houses, Vannes

In the 9C, Vannes was the place where Breton unity was sealed. **Nominoé** had already been made a count by Charlemagne; in 826, he was raised to the rank of duke by Louis the Pious, mindful of the advantage to himself of giving the province to a Breton rather than to a Frank.

Ten years later, Nominoé made Vannes his capital; in 850, he put an end to his tutelage to Charles the Bald by seizing the eastern and southern marches of Brittany from the Franks, going on to push back the Normans, then taking measures to reduce the influence of the high clergy.

★★ **Old Vannes** – Surrounded by **ramparts★**, the area around the cathedral, the successor to a much more ancient place of worship, still has the air of a medieval town. Among the old half-timbered houses built over a granite ground floor with pillars, arcades, and lintels is a 14C market hall known as **La Cohue★**. Its upper floor served as the ducal law-court right up until 1796, the ground floor as a market until 1840.

There are fine houses bordering **Place Henri IV★** and in the adjoining streets. Note the timber cross-braces, corbelling, granite pilasters and 16C slate-hung gables.

★ **Cathédrale St-Pierre** – Of robust granite construction, it has a north aisle with a balustraded terrace and sharply-pointed granite gables in Breton Flamboyant style separating the chapels.

Inside, the 15C nave is covered by a heavy ribbed vault of the 18C, concealing the original timber roof.

⊙ ►► Vannes : Ramparts★; Musée archéologique; Aquarium océanographique et tropical; Cairn de Gavrinis.

EXCURSIONS

★★ **Golfe du Morbihan** – This little inland sea was formed when the land sank and the sea level rose as a result of the melting of the great Quaternary glaciers, drowning the valleys occupied by the Vannes and Auray rivers. The indented coastline and the play of the tides around the countless islands make this one of Brittany's most fascinating maritime landscapes.

★ **Château de Suscinio** ⊙ – This was once the summer residence of the Dukes of Brittany. There is a rare 13C decorated tiled floor (accessible via a spiral staircase with 94 steps). The massive buildings lining the courtyard are now partly ruined. A gun-emplacement at the foot of the northwest tower may well date from the time of the War of the Breton Succession.

Port-Navalo – The little port and seaside resort guards the entrance to the Gulf. There are fine views.

★★ **Locmariaquer Megaliths** ⊙ – This group of megaliths is an important part of a programme of conservation and restoration of megalithic sites. Three megaliths can be found on this site: the **Grand Menhir brisé** (probably broken on purpose into five pieces, after it had served as a landmark for sailors); the **Table des Marchands** (a recently restored dolmen as well as the tumulus underneath) and the **Tumulus d'Er-Grah** (where excavations are presently underway).

★ **Presqu'île de Quiberon** – Quiberon used to be an island, but over the years sand has accumulated north of Penthièvre Fort to form an isthmus linking it to the mainland. The peninsula's rocky and windswept western shore is known as the **Côte Sauvage** (Wild Coast), but to the east are sheltered sandy beaches. The ferries for **Belle-Île★★** leave from Quiberon harbour.

Massif de la VANOISE★★★

Michelin map 74 folds 17, 18 and 19 and 77 folds 7, 8 and 9
or 844 folds 20, 21, 31, 32, 33
Green Guide Alpes du Nord (in French)

This famous massif lies between the valleys of the Arc and the Isère. It was proclaimed a national park in 1963 and consists of two concentric areas. The outer zone (1 450km² – 560sq miles) includes some of the largest skiing resorts in the world (Courchevel, Méribel, Les Menuires-Val Thorens, known as the Three Valleys). The central zone (530km² – 205sq miles), accessible to ramblers, is a remarkable natural site subject to strict regulations. La Vanoise Massif, which is dotted with charming villages and lovely forests, remains nonetheless a high mountain area: 107 summits exceed 3 000m – 9 900ft and the glaciers cover a total surface of 88km² – 34sq miles. The massif is noted for the extreme diversity of its fauna (marmots, ibices, chamois) and flora (around 2 000 species). Some of the more attractive sites are listed below. Visitors are advised to wear sturdy walking shoes.

★★ **Val-d'Isère** – *See Main Resorts in Introduction.* A prestigious meeting-place for winter sports enthusiasts, this resort commands an impressive view broken by a series of high peaks (Grande Sassière, Grande Motte).

Lac Blanc and the Col de Soufre

★★★ **Rocher de Bellevarde** – *Access by cable railway.* Splendid views of the Tarentaise and the Mont-Blanc.

★★ **Refuge de Prariond** – *2 hours Rtn on foot.* A pleasant walk with varied landscapes (gorges, rock faces).

★★ **Réserve naturelle de la Grande Sassière** – A superb backdrop of lakes and glaciers frame Tignes Dam. The park boasts a wealth of animals and plant species which may be easily approached. From the Saut car park, one may reach **Lac de la Sassière**★★ *(1 hour on foot)* and the **Glacier de Rhême-Golette**★★ *(2 ½ hours)*, at an altitude of around 3 000m – 9 900ft.

★★★ **Tignes** – Alt. 2 100m – 6 890ft. The resort was built around Tignes Lake in a **site**★★ dominated by the breathtaking view of the Grande Motte Glacier (3 656m – 12 052ft). We strongly advise the following route to confirmed ramblers who do not balk at 5 to 6 hours' walking: **Col du Palet**★★, **Pointe du Chardonnet**★★★ (very steep slope) or the **Col de la Croix des Frêtes**★★, the **Lac du Grattaleu**★, **col de Tourne**★.

★ **Peisey-Nancroix** – This village, nestling in the lush **Vallée de Ponturin**★, traditionally opens onto the park and is linked to the skiing area of Les Arcs.

★★ **Lac de la Plagne** – *4 hours Rtn on foot.* A beautiful route in a delightful, flowery setting, at the foot of the Bellecôte summit (3 417m – 11 269ft).

★ **Pralognon** – Alt. 1 400m – 4 600ft. One of the main stopping-places for ramblers in La Vanoise Massif.

★★ **Col de la Vanoise** – Alt. 2 517m – 8 260ft. *4 hours Rtn.* Views of the Grande Casse (3 855m – 12 705ft).

★★★ **Col d'Aussois** – Alt. 3 015m – 9 950ft. *Ascent 5 hours.* Sweeping panorama. *These two passes may also be reached from Termignon and Aussois en Maurienne.*

★★ **La Saulire** – Alt. 2 738m – 7 986ft. *Access by cablecar.* View of La Vanoise Massif and the Oisans.

★ **Réserve naturelle de Tuéda** – A beautiful forest planted with Cembro pines at the edge of Tuéda Lake.

★★★ **Cime de Caron** – Alt. 3 198m – 10 550ft. *2 ½ hours Rtn by cablecar and cable railway.* Breathtaking panorama of the Ecrins, the Tarentaise and Mont-Blanc.

The chapter on art and architecture in this guide gives
an outline of artistic achievement in the country
providing the context of the buildings and works of art
described in the Sights section
This chapter may also provide ideas for touring
It is advisable to read it at leisure

Château de VAUX-LE-VICOMTE★★★

Map p 6 – Michelin map 196 folds 33, 34
Green Guide Flanders, Picardy and the Paris Region

The splendid château built by **Nicolas Fouquet** lies at the heart of French Brie, a countryside of vast arable fields relieved by the occasional copse or spinney.

Fouquet had been Superintendent of Finances since the days of Mazarin; his vast fortune was founded on the dangerous habit of confusing the credit of the state with his own. In 1656, he decided upon the construction of Vaux, the palace which was to symbolise his success. As architect, he chose Louis Le Vau, already familiar with Maisons-Lafitte, as interior decorator, Charles Lebrun, assisted by Girardon and de Legendre, as landscaper, André Le Nôtre, as major-domo, the famous chef Vatel, as poet-in-residence, La Fontaine.

By 1661, Vaux looked as it does today. A connoisseur, a man of lavish tastes, but sadly lacking in political judgement, Fouquet had counted on being appointed in Mazarin's place right up to the moment when Louis XIV decided to take power into his own hands. Furthermore, he had alienated Colbert, and, even worse, had made advances to one of the King's favourites, Mlle de La Vallière.

By May, the decision to place him under arrest had been taken. On 17 August, the unwitting Fouquet threw the most sumptuous of festivities among the Baroque splendours of Vaux. Hoping to impress the young Louis, he only succeeded in offending his monarch more deeply by the unparalleled extravagance of the proceedings. Dinner was presented on a solid gold service, at a time when the royal silverware had been melted down to repay some of the expenses of the Thirty Years War!

On 10 September, Fouquet was arrested at Nantes, put under lock and key, his property confiscated, and his brilliant team of designers put to work on Versailles.

Vaux-le-Vicomte

MICHELIN

Le Vau's **château** ⓥ is the definitive masterpiece of the early Louis XIV style. It is majestic in its impact, with lateral pavilions fully integrated into the composition as a whole, high roofs graced by numerous chimneys, and a raised ground floor commanding the extensive gardens. It is to be understood as the central feature of a grandiose designed landscape, an archetype of immense influence over the whole of Europe in the course of the following century and a half.

Lebrun's talent is here made manifest in all its richness and diversity. He began work in 1659, but the central rotunda in the Grand Salon with its 16 caryatids remained unfinished; his King's Bedroom (Chambre du Roi) anticipates the splendour of the Royal Apartments at Versailles.

In the **gardens★★★**, Le Nôtre showed himself to be the master of perspective, with terraces, urns, clipped box hedging, water features and orange trees (later removed to Versailles) all contributing to the overall scheme.

At Vaux, the essentially decorative preoccupations of early classicism (as at Villandry) are left behind, and Baroque virtuosity is tempered by a sense of majesty. The three main bodies of water, the moats, the twin canals in the centre of the composition and the Grand Canal, all reveal themselves unexpectedly in a most dramatic fashion.

From the final circular basin known appropriately as la Gerbe, there is a fine view back over this wonderfully harmonious composition of building and landscape.

ⓥ ►► Musée des Équipages★.

Mont VENTOUX***

Map p 10 – Michelin map 81 fold 3 or 245 fold 17 or 246 fold 10
Green Guide Provence

Though hardly the equal of the soaring peaks of the High Alps, Mount Ventoux enjoys an isolated position far from any rival summit, making it a commanding presence in this part of Provence, visible over vast distances especially when topped in winter with a sparkling coat of snow. It is the most spectacular of the limestone uplands constituting the Southern Alps, one of the series of great synclinal folds running from Apt in the south to Nyons in the north which recall in the simplicity of their structure the ridge and valley morphology of the Jura *(p 132)*.

The massif is served by a scenic route 67km – 42 miles long between Vaison band Carpentras; its upper section is blocked by snow from 15 November to 15 March ⊙. The road was used for motor-racing until 1973, and the ascent is a major challenge in those years when it features as part of the Tour de France.

★★ **Vaison-la-Romaine** – *See VAISON-LA-ROMAINE.*

Shortly after leaving the little town of Malaucène, the road passes close to the Le Groseau Vauclusian Spring (Source vauclusienne du Groseau) which emerges from several fissures at the foot of an escarpment. Forests of fir follow, interspersed with grazing land, and the view then opens out over the Toulourenc valley where the folds of friable limestone have been buried beneath deep accumulations of scree. Mount Serein (1 428m – 4 685ft) appears, followed by the Dentelles de Montmirail and the Baronies Massif.

★★★ **Summit** – 1 909m – 6 263ft. The top of the mountain consists of a vast field of white shingle from which protrudes an array of masts and instruments, air force radar equipment, a TV transmitter, a weather station... Mount Ventoux, the Windy One, is so named because of the mistral which blasts it with a force unequalled elsewhere. On average, the temperature here is 11 °C-52° F lower than in the valley. The flora includes specimens of polar vegetation such as the Spitzbergen saxifrage and the Icelandic poppy.

In the early morning and late afternoon, as well as in autumn, the vast **panorama**★★★ extends from the Écrins Massif to the northeast to the Cévennes and the shore of the Mediterranean.

Below the resort of Chalet-Reynard on the descent southward are fine stands of Aleppo and Austrian black pine and Atlantic cedar, as well as beeches and oaks. Finally, beyond St-Estève, vines and fruit-trees make their appearance.

Massif du VERCORS***

Map p 10 – Michelin map 77 folds 3, 4, 12, 13, 14 or 244 folds 27, 28, 37, 38, 39
Green Guide Alpes du Nord (in French)

The Vercors is the most extensive of the Pre-Alpine massifs. Protected by sheer cliffs of Urgonian limestone, it is a natural citadel, inside which grow fine forests of beech and conifers interspersed with lush pasturelands. In places, the immensely thick limestone has been cut into by the rivers to form deep and spectacular gorges. In 1944, the Vercors saw one of the French Resistance's most tragic episodes. Since the previous year, a number of clandestine military formations had been taking to the forests of the area in order to organise its defences. They were joined in the spring of 1944 by several thousand more, as well as by young people evading the German labour draft. In June of that year, the Wehrmacht stepped up its assault on the Resistance's positions, determined to secure its communications in the face of Allied progress up the Italian peninsula and the impending break-out from Normandy. The maquisards fought off a number of attacks, but the enemy returned with reinforcements on 19 July and brought in parachute troops on 21 July. With many of their number lost, the surviving members of the Resistance were given the order to disperse on 23 July. 700 of the inhabitants and defenders of the Vercors had died, several of its villages lay in ruins.

Just to the north of the rebuilt village of Vassieux-en-Vercors is a cemetery with the graves of some of those who died in the course of that terrible summer.

★★★ **Gorges de la Bourne** – The lack of a road through the gorge meant that for many years the Lans area led its own life, orientated towards Grenoble rather than to the rest of the massif. The unusually regular walls of the gorge open out progressively downstream; its entrance is marked by the old cloth town of Pont-en-Royans with its houses clinging picturesquely to the rock face.

★★★ **Combe Laval** – One of the finest sights in the Vercors. The road clings dizzily to a vast limestone wall rising 600m – some 2 000ft above the upper valley of the Cholet.

★★★ **Grands Goulets** – An epic piece of construction dating from 1851, the narrow road was hewn directly into the rock. From its upper section it is possible to see the river beginning the process of eroding an as yet intact geological formation. The village of Les Barraques-en-Vercors was destroyed by enemy action in January 1944.

★★ **Col de Rousset** – *Go as far as the southern entrance to the disused tunnel.* The pass marks the climatic as well as the morphological boundary between the northern and southern Alps. There are spectacular views, not only of the road twisting its way downwards, but also of the great limestone walls protecting the Vercors, of the Die valley 960m – 3 150ft below and of a succession of bare ridges extending into the far distance.

Grand Canyon du VERDON★★★

Map p 10 – Michelin map 81 fold 17 or 84 folds 6 and 7 or 114 folds 7 to 10 or 245 folds 34, 35 – Green Guide Alpes du Sud (in French)

A tributary of the Durance with its source high up at the Allos Pass, the Verdon has cut Europe's most spectacular canyon through the Castellane Pre-Alps; here is one of the continent's wildest landscapes, a place which has resisted all human attempts to tame it.

Grand Canyon – The canyon extends 26km – 16 miles from the meeting-point of the Verdon with the Jabron in the east to where it flows into Ste-Croix Lake in the west at the Galetas bridge. In places the river has followed fault-lines in the domed structures formed in the Jurassic limestone; elsewhere the phenomenon of antecedence is evident, where it has cut down through the rock along the line of its original course, a result of the uplifting of the area during the Alpine-building period.

The boundaries of the successive beds of limestone are picked out by the growth of box and evergreen oak.

The opposite rims of the canyon are between 200-1 500m (about 650-5 000ft) apart. Its depth varies from 250-600m (about 800-2 000ft), while the width of its floor ranges from 8-90m (about 25-300ft). The dizzy height of the canyon's walls impresses on one the sheer scale of the Jurassic sedimentation, in terms of both time and the quantity of material deposited.

Grand Canyon du Verdon

J. Sierpinski/SCOPE

★★ **La Corniche Sublime** (South bank scenic route) – The steep and twisting *(20km – 12 mile)* road was engineered so as to open up the most spectacular views. They include: the **Balcons de la Mescla★★★** overlooking the swirling waters where the Verdon is joined by the Artuby; the **pont de l'Artuby★** linking sheer walls of rock; the Fayet tunnels above the Étroit des Cavaliers (Knights' Narrows), and the **Falaise des Cavaliers★** (Knights' Cliff) 300m – 1 000ft high.

★★ **La route des Crêtes** (North bank scenic route) – The road *(23km – 14 miles long)* links a series of viewpoints overlooking the most spectacular section of the canyon. Further to the east, the viewpoint known as the **Point Sublime★★★** dominates the downstream section of the canyon and the impressive narrows called the **Couloir de Samson★★★**.

★ **Castellane** – *See ROUTE NAPOLÉON.*

★★ **Moustiers-Ste-Marie** – The small town is the centre for the Valensole plateau, a depression filled with material brought down by the Verdon. It has an extraordinary **site★★** at the foot of a cleft in limestone cliff, across which a knight returning from the Crusades stretched the chain which can still be seen today. The church has a **tower★** with arcading in Lombard style. Faience was introduced here in 1679; the most sought-after pieces are those where the decoration was fired at high temperatures *(see Limoges)* and which have charming hunting scenes executed in blue monochrome.

VERDUN★★

Population 20 733
Map p 7 – Michelin map 57 fold 11 or 241 fold 23
Green Guide Alsace et Lorraine (in French)
Town plan in the current Michelin Red Guide France

The Gauls were the first to build a fortress here on the left bank of the Meuse. They were followed by the Romans, but Verdun entered the mainstream of history with the signing of the **Treaty of Verdun** in 843. By its terms, Charlemagne's realm was divided up among his grandsons, contrary to their father's wish for its preservation as a single unit. The Emperor, Lothair, received the central zone (Northern Italy, Provence, the Rhineland and the Low Countries), Louis, the Germanic countries, and Charles the Bald, Gaul. At the time, this signified little more than a convenient distribution of the different parts of an estate, but the + repercussions have been felt throughout the centuries to the extent that the treaty has been referred to as "the most significant in all the continent's history".

Louis the German, however, was dissatisfied with his portion; of an expansionist bent and dreaming of more clement skies, he launched what might be considered the first of all Franco-German wars in 858, following the death of Lothair. Charles was only able to resist the attack thanks to the support of the clergy led by the Bishop of Rheims.

★ **Ville haute** – The seat of a bishop, the fortified upper town rises in stages from the banks of the Meuse. It was besieged by the Duke of Brunswick on 31 August 1792, underwent an occupation of several weeks, but was then relieved following the victory at Valmy. It was besieged again in 1870 at the start of the Franco-Prussian War, then occupied for three years. In the First World War, Verdun was the scene of some of the bloodiest fighting of the Western Front, in a battle that lasted 18 months. The city's historic buildings include **Cathédrale Notre-Dame★**, laid out like the great Romanesque basilicas of the Rhineland, and the **Palais épiscopal★** constructed by Robert de Cotte in the 18C.

Ⓥ ►► Underground Citadel *(Citadelle souterraine)*.

VERDUN Haut lieu du souvenir★★★

The name of Verdun is indissolubly linked to the decisive struggle on which the outcome of the Great War turned. The gaze of the world was fixed for a year and a half on the paroxysm of violence endured by both sides, in a battle which brought forth the uttermost in steadfastness and courage. At the outbreak of war in August 1914, Verdun lay a mere 40km – 25 miles from the Franco-German frontier, though the **Schlieffen Plan** *(qv)* did not anticipate any significant military activity in this area. However, following the battle of the Marne and the ensuing stalemate of trench warfare, the German High Command decided on an attack on Verdun in order to take the French right wing from the rear and sow panic and confusion.

The 21 February 1916 dawned bright but numbingly cold; a devastating bombardment preceded the Germans' frontal assault on the French lines; the attack was contained for a while by the bravery of a Colonel Driant and his Chasseurs, but within four days Douaumont Fort had fallen. This was the moment at which General Pétain took effective charge of the battle; by the time of his replacement

Casemate

in April 1917, it was clear that the German attempt to break the staying power of the French army had failed. Verdun, the hinge of the whole Western Front, could not be taken.

The Germans now attempted to close the jaws of the trap in a series of battles which raged throughout March and April in the Argonne, around Les Éparges, and, closer to Verdun, on Hill 304 and the other eminence known chillingly as the Mort-Homme (Dead Man's Hill). This phase is known as the "Battle of the Wings". There then followed a battle of attrition, intended to "bleed the French white". But on 11 July, the final German offensive ground to a halt in front of the Souville fort, a mere 5km – 3 miles from the city, and the Crown Prince's troops were given orders to assume a defensive posture.

The French counter-offensive began in October 1916. By 20 August 1917, the Hell of Verdun, which had cost the lives of over 700 000 men, was over.

Battlefields *10km – 6 miles northeast of Verdun*

La Cote 304 – The hill was first attacked by the Germans on 20 March 1916 but held out for three months. It was retaken by the French on 24 August.

Douaumont – The 15 000 war graves overlooked by the memorial tower, the cloisters and the underground **ossuary** make this the most moving of all the battlefield sites.

With its subterranean passages, casemates, and its defences bearing for all time the scars inflicted by both French and German shells, the **Fort de Douaumont** ⊙ had only been occupied as from 5 August 1915 by a skeleton force of French Territorial gunners; it fell, almost by accident, to a small party of Germans on 25 February 1916, and was only retaken, at great cost, on 24 October.

Les Éparges – This long spur extends outwards from the Meuse Heights to dominate the Woëvre plain. It fell to the German attackers on 21 September 1914 and became the scene of some particularly bloody mine warfare. It was retaken on 10 April 1915. There is still evidence of the conflict in the shape of gaping craters opened up by the sappers' mines. The visitor should also see the monument and viewing table at "Point X" at the far extremity of the spur, as well as "Point C", and the Trottoir Cemetery (Cimetière du Trottoir).

Fleury-devant-Douaumont – Fleury was taken by the Germans on 23 June and retaken by the French on 18 August 1916. Where the village once stood are now only pine trees and a number of mounds. There is a modern chapel, dedicated to Notre-Dame of Europe.

Butte de Montfaucon – This rounded hillock was occupied by the Germans in 1914 and only retaken on 28 September 1918 by American troops who stormed its slopes in the face of determined opposition.

Le Mort-Homme – A key location in the Battle of the Wings. The German assault on it was launched from the Montfaucon heights; the fight went on throughout March and April, but the top of the hill only fell on 23 May. It was an empty victory, for further advance proved impossible, and the hill fell to the French again on 30 August 1917. Though the Germans may have reached the summit, "they did not pass".

Tranchée des Baïonnettes – A batallion of men from Brittany and the Vendée was buried alive here as they waited with fixed bayonets for a ferocious bombardment to end.

Fort de Vaux ⊙ – Taken by the Germans on 7 June 1916 and recaptured on 2 November.

Château de VERSAILLES★★★

Map p 6 – Michelin map 101 folds 22, 23
Green Guide Flanders, Picardy and the Paris Region
Conurbation plan in the current Michelin Red Guide France

Versailles is the creation of the French monarchy at the moment of its greatest splendour. Consisting of the **château** ⊙, the **gardens** ⊙, and the **Trianons** ⊙, it is a wonderfully harmonious composition of building and landscape, the definitive monument of French classicism.

In the words of Pierre Gaxotte, "Versailles taught Europe the art of living, good manners and well-bred behaviour, wit, love of truth, tolerance, human values, a love of beauty and of work well-done, the secret of being rather than merely seeming, and a concern that all should shine".

For further explanations on the following table see page 334.

MONARCHS – COURT – GOVERNMENT

LOUIS XIII – Born 1601 – Marries Anne of Austria in 1615

LOUIS XIV – Born 1638 – Marries Maria-Theresa in 1660

The Peace of Westphalia puts an end to the Thirty Years War, giving France most of Alsace and establishing French as the language of diplomacy. **1648**

The Treaty of the Pyrenees puts an end to hostilities with Spain, giving France Roussillon, the Cerdagne and Artois. **1659**

On the death of Mazarin, Louis decides to take the government into his own hands – Arrest of Fouquet – Colbert appointed Superintendent of Finance – Persecution of the Protestants. **1661**

The Port-Royal controversy. **1664**

The War of Devolution, fought in support of Louis' claim to the Spanish Netherlands, is ended in 1668 by the Treaty of Aix-la-Chapelle (Aachen); the southern part of today's Belgium (Wallonie) becomes part of France. **1667**

The Court resides at Paris (pp 220 and 229)

War with Holland ended by the Peace of Nijmegen **1672**

Conquest of the Franche-Comté **1674**

R.M.N.

Louis XIV by Lebrun

On 6 May, the Royal Court and the Government move into Versailles. **1682**

Maria Theresa dies on 30 July. "The only time she ever upset me" was Louis' comment. She had only used her splendid bedroom for just over a year. The King now moves out of the North Wing of the palace and into the Marble Court. **1683**

Revocation of the Edict of Nantes – Audience with the Doge of Genoa. **1685**

Reception of the Siamese Ambassadors – War of the League of Augsburg terminated by the Treaty of Ryswick (Rijswijk). **1686**

War of the Spanish Succession; the French victory over the Dutch and Austrians led to the Peace of Utrecht in 1713 and the final definition of France's northern frontier. **1701**

Suppression of the *camisard* revolt *(p 62)*. **1702**

Reception of the Persian Ambassadors – On 1 September, Louis XIV dies. **1715**

LOUIS XV – Born 1710 – Marries Maria Leszczinska in 1725

Philippe d'Orléans rules as Regent from 1715-23. Court and Government move from Versailles to Paris between 1715-22.

Birth of the Dauphin, father of Louis XVI. **1729**

War of the Polish Succession (fought in Italy), ended by the Treaty of Vienna in 1738.

1733

ARTISTS AND THEIR MASTERPIECES

1610-43

1624   Louis XIII has a modest hunting lodge built in this game-rich area.
1631   Philibert Le Roy designs the first château, built of brick, stone and slate.

1643-1715

1661   Le Brun is made responsible for the interior, supervising a gifted team of painters, sculptors, carvers and interior decorators.
1664   A great May festival is organised, called *"Pleasures of the Enchanted Island"*, featuring three acts of Molière's *Tartuffe*.
1666   The gardens'splendid fountains are inaugurated.
1667   The Grand Canal is dug.

1668   Le Vau extends the palace by encasing it in an "envelope" of stone; he builds the six rooms making up the Grand Apartment and lays out a spacious terrace overlooking the gardens.The **Grands Appartements**★★★ comprise the King's Suite on the north and the Queen's Suite to the south, facing the sun. Le Vau restores the **cour de Marbre**★★, built in brick with stone dressings and reserved for the King's private use; it has fine raised paving in black and white marble, façades graced by 40 busts (some of them by Coysevox), mansard roofs decorated with urns, and a colonnaded portico supporting the wrought-iron balcony of the King's Bedchamber.
The **Gardens**★★★ are laid out by Le Nôtre. They are a masterpiece of the French landscape style, going beyond the evocation of the idea of majesty (as at Vaux-le-Vicomte) to celebrate the supreme authority of the monarch by the systematic use of Classical symbolism. Among the 200 statues of this open-air sculpture museum are Keller's bronzes in the Water Gardens (Parterres d'eau), the Latona Basin (Bassin de Latone), Louis XIV's recommended starting point for a tour of his domain, Tuby's splendid *Apollo* in his chariot, low reliefs by Girardon... On 18 July, a Grand Royal Entertainment is held in the gardens.
1671   Le Brun undertakes the decoration of the State Apartments; his use of the choicest materials is characteristic of the early Louis XIV style. Portraits are painted by Rigaud and Van Loo.
1672   Boulle delivers the first items of his furniture featuring showy marquetry of tortoiseshell and brass.
1674   Lavish summer festivals are held. Le Brun designs 24 statues for the gardens. On 18 August, Racine presents the premiere of his *Iphigenia* in an open-air theatre close to the Orangerie.
1678   Lulli presents his *Alceste* in the Marble Court. Desjardins, Le Hongre and the Marsy brothers work on the Diana Fountain (Fontaine de Diane). Jules Hardouin-Mansart, a nephew by marriage of François Mansart, adds to the palace in the late Louis XIV style, giving it a grand first floor over the raised ground floor, columns to break up the monotony of horizontal lines, fine windows and roof sculptures. He completes the **Galerie des Glaces**★★★ begun by Le Brun, and built over Le Vau's terrace; this splendid reception room lies between the War Salon and the Peace Salon; its mirrors catch the rays of the setting sun. Its decoration was completed in 1687.
1680   The King's Kitchen Garden (Potager du Roi) is laid out by La Quintinie.

1683   The King's favourite musician, La Lande, composes divertimenti and ballets. The sculptor Puget carves his *Milo of Crotona* followed by his *Perseus* and *Andromeda*.

1684   Jules Hardouin-Mansart designs the Orangerie.

1688   Jules Hardouin-Mansart builds the Grand Trianon (or Marble Trianon) with its peristyle by Robert de Cotte and Empire and Restoration furniture.
1699   The Royal Chapel is built by Hardouin-Mansart (completed in 1710 by Robert de Cotte and decorated by Van Cleve and Claude Lorrain, with frescoes by Coustou and Coypel).
1701   The King's Suite is designed by Hardouin-Mansart; the room is laid out around the axis formed by the course of the sun (shown today with its summer furnishings of 1723).
1712   Hercules' Salon, on the site of the former chapel, is begun. Completed in 1736, it has a ceiling by Lemoyne.

1715-74

1729   The Queen's Bedchamber is redecorated, and finally completed by Boucher.

1738   The private suites are redecorated.
1739   The cabinet-maker Gaudreau produces a splendid medal cabinet.

War of the Austrian Succession (Peace of Aix-la-Chapelle in 1748). **1740**

The Dauphin is married to Marie-Josèphe de Saxe, the Spanish Infanta. **1745**

The Seven Years War (ended by the Peace of Paris in 1763). **1756**
Attempted assassination of Louis XV by Damiens. **1757**

Louis XV dies of smallpox. **1774**
The Genevan banker, Necker, is appointed Controller-Ge ne ra l. **1776**

LOUIS XVI - Born 1754 – Marries Marie-Antoinette in 1770

The independence of the United States is confirmed by the Treaty of Versailles
on 3 September. **1783**
The Affair of the Queen's Necklace: Cardinal Rohan arrested. **1785**

The formal session of the States-General opens in the town on 5 May. **1789**
The Real Tennis-Court Oath is sworn on 20 June.
14 July: the Fall of the Bastille.
27 August: Declaration of the Rights of Man.
6 October: the mob force the royal family to return to Paris.

REVOLUTION – EMPIRE – RESTORATION – REPUBLIC

10 August: fall of the monarchy. **1792**
21 January: Louis XVI guillotined on Place de la Concorde. **1793**

18 January: the German Empire is proclaimed in the Hall of Mirrors. **1871**
The National Assembly meets in the Opera.
The Wallon Amendment forms the basis for the establishment of the Third Republic. **1875**
28 June: the Treaty of Versailles terminates the First World War. **1919**

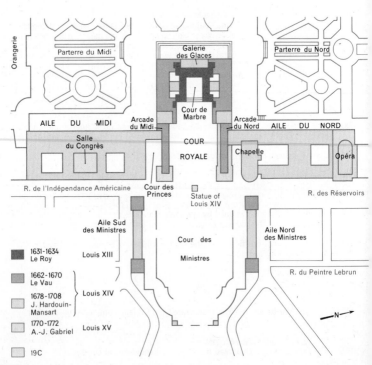

1742 Nattier is appointed court portrait-painter.

1754 Passement makes his astronomical clock with its bronze figures by Caffieri.
1755 Ange-Jacques Gabriel designs the cabinet room of the Council of Ministers.

1762 Ange-Jacques Gabriel starts work on the "Petit Trianon (woodwork by Guibert)".
1768 Ange-Jacques Gabriel builds the Royal Opera with its splendid auditorium; Pajou's decorative scheme anticipates the Louis XVI style.
1769 The celebrated roll-top desk for the King's Corner Room (Cabinet de travail du roi) is completed; it is a masterpiece of French cabinet-ma ki ng by Oeben and Riesener.

1774-93

1774 Ange-Jacques Gabriel completes the Petit Trianon and, together with the sculptor Rousseau, creates the King's Library (Bibliothèque du roi).
1775 Coustou's statues are placed in the Queen's Grove (Bosquet de la Reine).

1783 The Hamlet (Hameau) is laid out in the gardens of the Petit Trianon – the Queen's Private Suite (Cabinet intérieur de la reine) is decorated by Mique.

1787 Portrait of Marie-Antoinette with her children by Mme Vigée-Lebrun.

FROM 1790 TO TODAY

1791 The Fête de la Fédération is celebrated with gusto in Paris, Louis XVI swearing loyalty to the Revolutionary Constitution.

1810 The painter David finishes his sketch depicting the Real Tennis-Court Oath.
1833 The Apartments are demolished (with the exception of the central section of the first floor) in order to house a museum.
1837 The palace becomes a museum of the history of France.

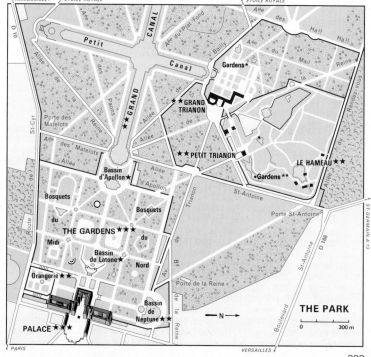

Versailles by night

Full appreciation of Versailles demands a knowledge of Classical mythology and its symbols, the château and its gardens being in effect a temple dedicated to worship of the Sun God.

The table on the previous pages draws attention to key events and major artistic achievements in the creation of the palace and its setting, a process extending over more than 150 years.

External events are indicated in red.

⊘ Visitors whose time is limited should concentrate on the items in bold type which are starred.

The enjoyment of even the shortest of visits will be greatly enhanced if the Michelin Green Guide Flanders, Picardy and the Paris Region (in English) is used.

VÉZELAY★★

Population 571
Map p 6 – Michelin map 65 fold 15 or 238 fold 23 – Green Guide Burgundy Jura

The picturesque village of Vézelay is built along the ridge of a rocky spur among the northern foothills of the Morvan countryside. Its fame is due to its wonderful basilica.

The Celts were the first to settle this hilltop site. In 878 an abbey was founded here, and in 1050 it was dedicated to Mary Magdalen. The place soon became one of France's great pilgrimage destinations and a sanctuary was built. It suffered destruction by fire more than once. It was here that St Bernard preached the Second Crusade in 1146.

In 1279, however, the monks of St-Maximin in Provence discovered the bones of Mary Magdalen in a cave; the certification of the relics as authentic led to the decline of Vézelay as a place of pilgrimage; it was pillaged by the Huguenots, razed at the time of the French Revolution and given its coup de grâce by lightning.

In 1840, Prosper Mérimée, who was in charge of the national survey of the country's heritage, came to Vézelay; recognising the value and significance of the ruin, he appointed the young Viollet-le-Duc as architect in charge of its restoration.

★★★ **Basilique Ste-Madeleine** ⊘ – First built between 1096 and 1104 and restored following the fire of 1120. The principal external features are the fine Romanesque body of the church (to which flying buttresses were added in the 13C), St Antony's Tower, and a particularly harmonious chevet with radiating chapels. From the terrace, there is a fine **view**★ over the valley of the River Cure. In the dimly-lit narthex (1140-60) is the marvellous **tympanum**★★★ of the central doorway. Dating from around 1125 (and thus preceding the one at Autun), it shows Christ blessing the twelve Apostles before sending them out into the world. Proportion is used to reinforce the meaning of the composition; of superhuman size, the figure of Christ is shown with hands extended outwards, passing on to the disciples something of His divine power, while the extraordinary length of His legs seems to elevate Him beyond all earthly contingencies. In contrast, the figures of the Apostles and the heathen are of much more modest dimensions. The sculptor's great talent is made manifest in his treatment of the Apostles and of the fantastic figures in the lintel, and in his depiction of the signs of the Zodiac and labours of the month, as well as in his masterly handling of the folds of clothes (notably Christ's robes).

The Romanesque nave of ten bays, rebuilt between 1120-35, is unusually large and exceptionally well-lit. Here in Burgundy it stands out by virtue of a number of features, including semi-circular arches, the lack of tribunes or false triforium, the boldly-patterned stonework, the pillars with engaged columns (rather than pilasters), and especially the use, even in the nave, of ribbed vaults. The greatest contribution to the basilica's decoration is made by the many **capitals**★★★ adorning the pillars; these were sculpted from 1106 onwards, and depict Biblical scenes, the lives of the saints, moralising subjects and weird beasts, all with a verve and dynamism which anticipates subsequent work at Autun. The magnificent Gothic choir (1185-1215) seems to have been influenced by the great new churches of the North of France.

VICHY★★★

Population 27 714
Map p 9 – Map 73 fold 5 or 239 fold 8 – Green Guide Auvergne-Rhône Valley
Town plan in the current Michelin Red Guide France

Pleasantly sited in the Allier valley, and well endowed with lush parks and luxurious thermal establishments *(p 52)*, Vichy is a famous spa town. The virtues of the waters drew visitors here in Roman times and in the 17C, while it is primarily due to Napoleon III that the place owes its reputation as a luxury health resort. In medieval times, the river crossing was commanded by a castle. Later, the town grew during the reign of Henri IV. More recently, Vichy gave its name to the government of the French State, the regime led by Marshal Pétain which ruled the country under close German supervision from 12 July 1940 until 20 August 1944.

The florid spa architecture of the second half of the 19C is well represented by a number of constructions such as the Grand Casino of 1865, the Napoleon Gallery (Galerie Napoléon) of 1857, the covered galleries bordering the park (Parc des Sources) which formed part of the 1889 Paris Universal Exhibition before being re-erected here, and the Grand Baths (Grand établissement thermal) of 1900.

VIENNE★★

Population 29 449
Map p 10 – Michelin map 74 folds 11, 12 or 88 folds 19, 20 or 246 fold 16
Green Guide Auvergne-Rhône Valley
Town plan in the current Michelin Red Guide France

Vienne is favoured with a sunny **site**★ on the east bank of the Rhône. The town overlooks the bend formed by the river as it makes its way through the crystalline rocks marking the last outposts of the Massif Central.
Originally the capital of the Allobroges tribe, Vienne came under Roman rule 60 years before Caesar's conquest of Gaul. In the 3C and 4C, the city was the centre of the vast province known as the Viennoise stretching from Lake Geneva to the mouth of the Rhône. Great public buildings were erected at the foot of Mount Pipet, opposite **St-Romain-en-Gal**, the **Gallo-Roman city**★ with its houses and shops. In the 5C, Vienne became the capital of the Burgundians who ruled over the east bank of the Rhône before being chased away by the Franks in 532. Ruled subsequently by its archbishops, the city became the object of the rivalry between the Kingdom of France and the Holy Roman Empire until its final incorporation into France at the same time as the Dauphiné, in 1349.

★★ **Temple d'Auguste et de Livie** – This Classical temple was first built in the reign of Emperor Augustus shortly before the beginning of the Christian era; it seems likely that it was then reconstructed, somewhat carelessly, under Claudius, about 50 years later. At the time it would have dominated the Forum to the east. Its good state of preservation is due to its successive reuse as a public building of some kind (Church, Jacobin club, tribunal, museum, library), and subsequently to its restoration by Prosper Mérimée in 1850.
It is identifiable as Roman work by the way in which its 16 Corinthian columns rise from a podium rather than directly from the ground in the Greek manner. In the pediment are traces of a bronze inscription to the glory of Augustus and Livia.

★★ **Cathédrale St-Maurice** – The present building was begun around 1230 by the architect Guillaume de l'Œuvre who redesigned the 11C chevet, giving it additional height and providing it with a ribbed vault. There followed major modifications to the seven Romanesque bays of the nave (identifiable by their fluted pilasters) with the provision of columns, a triforium and clerestory windows, making possible the construction of the choir vault at the same height. Finally, in the 14C, the final four bays of the nave were built, together with the west front and its portals.
Only 35 years after its completion, the cathedral suffered much mutilation during the Wars of Religion. It underwent extensive restoration in the 19C (vaults, arching of the portals, rose window). But much remains to be admired inside, including the fine Renaissance window in the south aisle *(to the right*

of the choir), the 13C low-relief between the sixth and seventh chapel in the north aisle depicting Herod and the Magi, and the rare 11C Bishop's Throne *(in the apse behind the high altar)*.

The inner niches contain episodes from the life of Christ; in the equivalent central niche is a depiction of the corresponding Old Testament event, while the outer niche portrays the Prophet who foretold the episode; thus in the third level on the right can be seen (reading from inside to outside), firstly Christ's descent into Hell, then Lot leaving Sodom in flames, and finally the Prophet Hosea.

⊙ ►► Théâtre romain★; Église St-André-le-Bas★; Cloître de St-André-le-Bas★; Ancienne église St-Pierre★; Musée Lapidaire★.

Jardins et Château de VILLANDRY★★★

Map p 5 – Map 64 fold 14 or 232 fold 35 – Green Guide Châteaux of the Loire

In 1536, Jean Le Breton, who had been France's ambassador in Italy, rebuilt the **château**★★ ⊙ here on the foundations of an earlier one. The new building had a number of features which made it unusual in Touraine: ditches and canals, an esplanade and a terrace, rectangular pavilions in place of round towers, and, above all, its gardens.

The interior is distinguished by Louis XV panelling in the Great Salon and Dining Room, by the fine ramped staircase in wrought iron, and by a surprising 13C Mudejar ceiling from Spain, brought here by Joachim de Carvallo.

★★★ **Gardens** ⊙ – In 1906, Dr Carvallo, founder of the French Historic Houses Association (Demeure Historique), bought the Villandry estate and began to restore the gardens. The plan of the gardens shows both the influence of the agricultural writer **Olivier de Serres** and the synthesis of the monastery garden with the Italian garden proposed by Jacques II Androuet Du Cerceau.

Gardens, Château de Villandry

Covering a total area of 7ha – 17 acres, the gardens have many fascinating features. There are three terraces one above the other, separated by shady avenues of limes and vines; the highest is the water garden with its mirror-like stretch of water, then comes an ornamental garden with box clipped into patterns symbolising the varieties of love: tragic (sword and dagger blades), fickle (butterflies and fans), tender (masks and hearts), and passionate (broken hearts). Finally there is a kitchen garden with 85 000 plants contained in clipped box beds. The use of the humblest of vegetables (cabbage, celery...), chosen for their culinary value, symbolism, therapeutic value or colour, is here raised to an art form of great delicacy and seasonal interest.

The Practical Information section at the end of the guide lists :
- *information about travel, motoring, accommodation, recreation*
- *local or national organisations providing additional information*
- *calendar of events*
- *admission times and charges for the sights described in the guide*

VILLEFRANCHE-DE-ROUERGUE★

Population 12 291
Map p 5 – Michelin map 79 fold 20 or 235 fold 15
Green Guide Pyrenees-Languedoc-Tarn Gorges

Villefranche was once a staging-post on the Roman road from Rodez to Cahors. In 1252, Alphonse de Poitiers, brother of Louis IX, founded a bastide here. The little fortified settlement became a market town, linking the wheatlands on the Quercy *causse* to the west with the rye-growing areas to the east; the yield of the infertile plateaux was increased by the application of lime, made possible after the building of the railway at the beginning of the 20C.

★ **Bastide** – The old town on the north bank of the River Aveyron has kept many of the typical features of a planned urban foundation of the 13C. Its cobbled streets, connected by narrow alleyways, are laid out on a grid pattern, and there is a central square (**Place Notre-Dame★**) with covered walks, dominated by a large metal figure of Christ. The tall, severe houses are characteristic of the Rouergue area; a number of them have high open balconies with provision for drying grain. The President Raynal House (Maison du Président Raynal) with its 15C façade is particularly striking, and the Dardennes House (Maison Dardennes) has a fine galleried courtyard.
There is a **fortified church★** (Église Notre-Dame) with splendid ironwork around the font.

★ **Chartreuse St-Sauveur** ⊙ – Built in 1461 in an unusually pure Gothic style. The little cloisters are a monastic masterpiece of Flamboyant architecture.

VILLEQUIER★

Population 822
Map p 5 – Michelin map 52 fold 13 or 54 fold 3 or 231 fold 21
Green Guide Normandy

On the banks of the Lower Seine, Villequier is the point at which ships change the pilot who has brought them through the channels of the estuary for the one who will take them up the river to Rouen. It is also a key site in the literary history of France, and the Vacquerie House is now the **Musée Victor-Hugo★** ⊙. As well as commemorating this Grand Old Man of literature (and in particular, his ties with Normandy), the museum evokes his relationship with his companion Juliette Drouet and the short life of his beloved daughter Léopoldine.

"At Villequier" – In September 1843, Victor Hugo (1802-85) is at the height of his literary fame; at his fine home in Place des Vosges in Paris (also a museum), he learns of the death in an accident of his 19-year-old daughter, Léopoldine, married only seven months previously to Charles Vacquerie.
Under the impact of this terrible blow, Hugo stopped writing for a whole year; then, on 4 September 1844, at a single sitting, he composed the poem *"At Villequier"* (*À Villequier*), later included in his volume of poems entitled *Les Contemplations*, dedicated to the memory of his daughter. Critics have seen in these elegaic lines some of the finest verse in the French language.

Col de VIZZAVONA

Map p 10 – Michelin map 90 northeast of fold 6 – Green Guide Corse (in French)

The Ajaccio-Bastia road is the main route to cross Corsica's mountainous backbone; it climbs up the valley of the Gravona to this pass (Col de Vizzavona) at 1 163m – 3 816ft, then descends into the basin of the Tavignano, the stream which waters the Aléria plain on the east side of the island. With its immensely tall Corsican pines and graceful beech trees, the Vizzavona forest has a park-like character.
The pass is overlooked to the north by the ruins of a Genoese fort, confirmation of the long history and strategic importance of the route; opposite, from near the transmitter, there is a fine **view★** over the Gravona valley.
For 44 years, the "king of the maquis", the celebrated bandit Antoine Bellacoscia, had evaded the law, aided by the local population; on 25 June 1892, at the age of 75, he ceremoniously gave himself up at the little station of the metre-gauge railway 4km – 2 1/2 miles north of the pass.

YVETOT

Population 10 807

Map p 5 – 52 fold 13 or 231 fold 22 – Green Guide Normandy – Town plan in the current Michelin Red Guide France

Yvetot is an important market-town serving the Caux country, a bare chalk plateau of fertile silty soils, relieved in places by woodland growing on damp patches of clay-with-flints.

4km – 2 1/2 miles south *(on the right of the road, just before Touffreville-la-Corbeline)* is a **farmstead★** with many traditional features typical of the Caux area. The buildings are laid out in the middle of a grazed orchard shaded by apple-trees, while the whole area is defined by a high hedge-bank planted with beech-trees. The farmyard itself is dominated by the family dwelling with fine dovecots of wattle construction whose rendering is reinforced with a mixture of pebbles and bricks.

Église St-Pierre – This is a modern building of circular shape. It has splendid **stained-glass windows★★**, the work of Max Ingrand. The liturgical role of light is expressed in a number of ways, by the play of colour, by the arrangement of the figures of the saints and by the design of the various scenes.

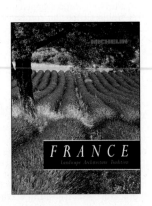

Recapture the atmosphere, sights, sounds and gastronomic sensations of your French holiday in this superb book « France ». Evocative photographs and a lyrical turn of phrase celebrate the unique character and flavour of each French region.

Practical
Information

Planning your trip

Passport – Visitors entering France must be in possession if a valid national passport. Citizens of one of the European Union countries only need a national identity card. In case of loss or theft report to the embassy or consulate and the local police.

Visa – No **entry visa** is required for American and Canadian citizens as long as their stay in France does not exceed 3 months. Australians and New Zealanders must apply for one at the nearest French consulate. For other countries, check with a French consulate or travel agent.
US citizens should obtain the booklet **Your Trip Abroad** (US\$ 1.25), which provides useful information on visa requirements, customs regulations, medical care, etc. for international travellers. Contact the Superintendent of Documents, PO Box 371954, Pittsburgh, PA 15250-7954, ☎ 202-512-1800.

Customs – Apply to the Customs Office (UK) for a leaflet entitled **A Guide for Travellers** on customs regulations and the full range of duty-free allowances. The US Customs Service, PO Box 7407, Washington, DC 20044, ☎ 202-927-5580, offers a free publication **Know Before You Go** for US citizens. There are no customs formalities for holidaymakers bringing caravans into France for a stay of less than 6 months. No customs document is necessary for pleasure boats and outboard motors for a stay of less than 6 months, but the registration certificate should be kept on board.

French Tourist Offices – For information, brochures, maps and assistance in planning a trip to France travellers should contact the official tourist office in their own country:

Australia-New Zealand
Sydney – BNP Building, 12 Castlereagh Street, Sydney, New South Wales 2000.
☎ (61) 2-231-5244
Fax (61) 2-221-86-82

Canada
Toronto – 30 St Patrick's St, Suite 700, Toronto,
ONT M5T 3A3.
☎ 416-593-4723.
Montreal – 1981 Av McGill College, Suite 490,
Montreal, PQ H3A 2W9.
☎ 514-288-4264.
Fax 514-845-48-68

Eire
Dublin – 35 Lower Abbey St, Dublin 1
☎ (1) 703 4046
Fax (1) 874 7324

United Kingdom
London – 178 Piccadilly, London W1.
☎ (0891) 244 123
Fax (0171) 493 6594

United States
France On Call Hotline: 900-990-0040 (US\$0.50/min)
for information on hotels, restaurants and transportation.
East Coast: New York – 444 Madison Avenue, NY, NY 10022.
☎ 212-838-7800.
Fax 212-838-7855
Mid-West: Chicago – 676 North Michigan Avenue, Suite 3360, Chicago, IL 60611-2819.
☎ 312-751-7800.
Fax 312-337-6339
West Coast: Los Angeles – 9454 Wilshire Boulevard, Suite 715, Beverly Hills, CA 90212-2967.
☎ 310-271-2693.
Fax 310-276-2835.

When to go – To give the visitor a general idea of the weather in France, here is a temperature chart which covers the entire country.
Spring, Summer and Autumn are the best seasons to visit France but there is a region for every season. The Summer period can be beautiful but attracts crowds so it would be wiser to travel either in June or September when French children are still at school.

Temperature chart throughout France

	Jan	Feb	Mar	Apr	May	Jun	Jul	Aug	Sep	Oct	Nov	Dec
Bordeaux	9 / 1	10 / 2	15 / 4	17 / 9	20 / 12	23 / 13	25 / 13	25 / 13	23 / 12	18 / 8	12 / 4	8 / 2
Brest	8 / 4	9 / 3	11 / 4	13 / 7	15 / 8	18 / 11	19 / 12	20 / 13	18 / 11	15 / 8	11 / 6	9 / 4
Clermont	7 / -1	8 / -1	13 / 2	16 / 5	19 / 7	23 / 11	25 / 13	25 / 12	22 / 10	16 / 6	11 / 3	7 / 0
Grenoble	5 / -3	8 / -2	13 / 2	16 / 5	20 / 8	23 / 12	26 / 14	26 / 13	23 / 11	16 / 6	10 / 3	6 / -1
Lille	5 / 0	6 / 0	10 / 2	13 / 4	17 / 7	20 / 10	22 / 12	22 / 12	19 / 10	14 / 7	9 / 3	6 / 1
Nice	12 / 4	13 / 4	14 / 5	17 / 9	20 / 12	23 / 16	26 / 18	26 / 18	24 / 16	20 / 12	16 / 8	13 / 5
Paris	7 / 1	7 / 1	12 / 3	15 / 6	19 / 9	22 / 12	24 / 14	24 / 14	21 / 11	15 / 8	10 / 4	6 / 2
Perpignan	12 / 3	13 / 4	16 / 7	18 / 9	21 / 12	25 / 16	28 / 19	28 / 18	25 / 16	20 / 12	15 / 8	12 / 5
Strasbourg	3 / -2	5 / -1	11 / 1	15 / 4	19 / 6	23 / 11	24 / 13	25 / 13	20 / 10	14 / 5	8 / 2	4 / -1

Maximum temperatures in red; minimum temperatures in black.

Time – France is one hour ahead of Greenwich Mean Time (GMT), except between the end of September and the end of October, when it is the same.
When it is **noon in France**, it is

- 11am in London
- 11am in Dublin
- 6am in New York
- 3am in Los Angeles
- 7pm in Perth
- 9pm in Sydney
- 11pm in Auckland

In France "am" and "pm" are not used but the 24-hour clock is widely applied.

Getting there

By air – The various national and other independent airlines operate services to **Paris** (Roissy-Charles de Gaulle and Orly airports), **Bordeaux, Lyon, Mulhouse, Toulouse, Marseille, Nice, Montpellier, Perpignan**. North American airlines usually operate flights to Paris. However Delta Airlines also operates a daily direct flight from New York to Nice. Regional airports are widely connected to both Parisian airports.
There are also package tour flights with a rail or coach link-up as well as Fly-Drive schemes. Information, brochures and timetables are available from the airlines or travel agents.

By rail – British Rail and French Railways (SNCF) operate a daily service via the Channel Tunnel on Eurostar in 3 hours between **London** (Waterloo International Station) and **Paris** (Gare du Nord). Fast inter-city service from **Paris** to most towns throughout France run several times a day. For further information, contact the SNCF or your travel agent.
There are rail passes offering unlimited travel and group travel tickets offering services for parties. **Eurailpass, Flexipass** and **Saver Pass** are options available in the US for travel in Europe and must be purchased in the US – ☎ 212-308-3103

(information) and 1-800-223-636 (reservations). In the UK information and booking from French Railways, 179 Piccadilly, London, W1. ☎ (0891) 515 477 and from main British Rail Travel Centres and travel agencies.

Tickets bought in France must be validated (composter) by using the orange automatic date-stamping machines at the platform entrance.

You can always buy the **Thomas Cook European Rail** Timetable which gives all the different timetables throughout France and useful information on trains.

By coach - Regular coach services between London and many towns throughout the country:

Eurolines (London), 52 Grosvenor Gardens, Victoria, London, SW1, OAU ☎ (0171) 730 8235/8111.

Eurolines (Paris), 28 avenue du Général de Gaulle, 93170 Bagnolet, ☎ 01 49 72 51 51.

By car - Drivers from the British Isles can easily travel to France. Numerous **cross-Channel services** (passenger and car-ferries, hovercraft, SeaCat and via the Channel Tunnel operate accross the English Channel and St George's Channel). For details contact travel agencies or:

P&O European Ferries, Channel House, Channel View Road, Dover, Kent CT17 9TJ. ☎ (0990) 980 980.

Stena Line, Charter House, Park Street, Ashford, Kent TN24 8EX. ☎ (01233) 647 047.

Hoverspeed, International Hoverport, Marine Parade, Dover, Kent CT17 9TG. ☎ (01304) 240 241.

Sally Line, 81 Piccadilly, London W 1V 9HF. ☎ (0171) 409 2240.

Brittany Ferries, Millbay Docks, Plymouth, Devon PL1 3EW. ☎ (0990) 360 360.

Irish Ferries, 24 Merrion Row, Dublin 2. ☎ (3531) 661 0511.

Le Shuttle-Eurotunnel, ☎ (0990) 35 35 35.

To choose the most suitable route between one of the ports along the north coast of France and your destination, use the Michelin Motoring Atlas France, Michelin map 911 (which gives travel times and mileages) or Michelin maps from the 1:200 000 series (yellow cover).

Getting around

Motoring in France

Documents - Nationals of the EU require a valid national **driving licence**. Nationals of non EU countries should obtain an **international driving licence** (obtainable in the US from the American Automobile Association, cost for members: US$10, for non-members US$22). For the vehicle it is necessary to have the registration papers (log-book) and a nationality plate of the approved size.

Insurance - Certain UK motoring organisations (AA, RAC) offer accident insurance and breakdown service schemes for members. Europ-Assistance (252 High St, Croyden CRO 1NF) has special policies for motorists. Members of the American Automobile Association should obtain the free brochure **Offices To Serve You Abroad.**

Highway code - The minimum driving age is 18 years old. Traffic drives on the right. It is compulsory for the front-seat passengers to wear **seat belts** and it also compulsory for the back-seat passengers when the car is fitted with them at the back. Full or dipped headlights must be switched on in poor visibility and at night; use side lights only when the vehicle is stationary.

In the case of a **break-down** a red warning triangle or hazard warning lights are obligatory. Drivers should watch out for unfamiliar road signs and take great care on the road. In built-up areas **priority** must be ceded to vehicles coming from the right. However, traffic on main roads outside built-up areas (indicated by a yellow diamond sign) and on round-abouts has priority. Vehicles must stop when the lights turn red at road junctions and may filter to the right only where indicated by a flashing amber arrow.

The regulations on **drinking and driving** (limited to 0.50 g/litre) and **speeding** are strictly enforced - usually by an on-the-spot fine and/or confiscation of the vehicle.

Speed limits - Although liable to modification these are as follows:
- toll motorways *(péage)* 130kph-80mph (110kph-68mph when raining);
- dual carriage roads and motorways without tolls 110kph-68mph (100kph-62mph when raining);
- other roads 90kph-56mph (80kph-50mph when raining) and in towns 50kph-31mph;
- outside lane on motorways during daylight, on level ground and with good visibility - minimum speed limit of 80kph-50mph.

Parking regulations - In town there are zones where parking is either restricted or subject to a fee; tickets should be obtained from the ticket machines (*horodateurs* - small change necessary) and displayed inside the windscreen on the driver's side; failure to display may result in a heavy fine or even the offending vehicle being towed away. In some towns you can find blue parking zones *(zone bleue)* which are signalized by a blue line on the pavement or a blue signpost with a P and a small square underneath. In this particular case you have to display a "time disc" (a cardboard disc with different times) which will allow you to stay for 1 1/2 hours (2 1/2 hours over lunchtime) free. You can buy these "time discs" in supermarkets or petrol stations (ask for a *disque de stationnement*).

Route planning - For 24-hour road traffic information dial 01 56 96 33 33 or consult Minitel 3615 Code Route (1.29F/min).
The road network is excellent and includes many motorways. The roads are very busy during the holiday period (particularly weekends in July and August) and to avoid traffic congestion it is advisable to follow the recommended secondary routes (Bison Futé-itinéraires bis).

Tolls - In France, most motorway sections are subject to a toll *(péage)*. This can be expensive especially if you drive south. You can pay with cash or by credit card (Visa, Mastercard).

Car rental - There are car rental agencies at airports, railway stations and in all large towns throughout France. European cars usually have manual transmission, but automatic cars are available on demand. (advance reservation recommanded). It is relatively expensive to hire a car in France; Americans in particular will notice the difference and should consider booking a car from home before leaving or taking advantage of fly-drive schemes.
Central Reservation in France: Avis: 01 46 10 60 60
                                      Eurodollar: 01 49 58 44 44
                                      Hertz: 01 47 88 51 51
                                      Europcar: 01 30 43 82 82
                                      Budget: 01 46 86 65 65

Petrol - In France you will find 4 different types of petrol (US: gas):
super leaded *(super)*
super unleaded 98 *(sans plomb 98)*
super unleaded 95 *(sans plomb 95)*
diesel *(diesel/gazole)*
Petrol is more expensive in France compared to the United States and even the United Kingdom.

Tourist Information

Local Tourist Offices - To find all the addresses of local tourist offices throughout France, contact the **Fédération Nationale des Comités Départementaux de Tourisme**, 280 boulevard St-Germain, 75007 Paris. ☎ 01 44 11 10 20.

Tourism for the Disabled - Some of the sights described in this guide are accessible to handicapped people and are indicated in the Admission Times and Charges section with the symbol &. The **Michelin Red Guide France** and **Michelin Guide Camping Caravaning France** indicate hotels and camp sites with facilities suitable for physically handicapped people. You can also consult the Minitel service 3615 HANDITEL (1.01F/min) where you will find useful information, or contact the local handicapped people's information office: Association des Paralysés de France (APF), 9 boulevard Blanqui 75013 Paris, ☎ 01 45 81 30 63.

Accommodation

Places to stay - The **Michelin Red Guide France**, lists a selection of hotels and restaurants. Loisirs Accueil is an officially-backed booking service that has offices in most French *départements*. For information contact Réservation **Loisirs Accueil**, 280 boulevard St-Germain, 75007 Paris. ☎ 01 44 11 10 44:
The brochure **Logis et Auberge de France** is available from the different French Tourist Offices (see list p. 340).

Rural accommodation - The **Maison des Gîtes de France** has a list of self-catering accommodation where you can stay in France. This usually takes the form of a cottage or apartment decorated in the local style where you will be able to make yourself at home. Gîtes de France have offices in:

London: 178 Piccadilly, London W1. ☎ (0891) 244 123.
Paris: 35 rue Godot-de-Mauroy, 75009 Paris.
☎ 01 49 70 75 75.

Bed and Breakfast – Gîtes de France (see above) publishes a booklet on bed and breakfast accommodation (chambres d'hôtes) which include a room and breakfast at a reasonable price.
You can also contact two **associations** which offer you addresses throughout France:
Café-Couette, Central Reservation, 8 rue de l'Isly, 75008 Paris.
☎ 01 42 94 92 00 Fax 01 42 94 93 12 or minitel 3615 CAFECOUETTE (2.23F/min).
Bed & Breakfast (France), International Reservations Centre, PO Box 66, Henley-on-Thames, Oxon, RG9 1XS, ☎ (01491) 578 803, Fax (01491) 410 806.

Youth Hostels – There are two main youth hostel associations (auberges de la jeunesse) in France.

Paris: Ligue Française pour les Auberges de la Jeunesse, 38 boulevard Raspail,
75007 Paris. ☎ 01 45 48 69 84, Fax 01 45 44 57 47.
Fédération Unie des Auberges de Jeunesse, 27 Rue Pajol, 75018 Paris,
☎ 01 44 89 87 27, Fax 01 44 89 87 10, Minitel 3615 code FUAJ (1.01F/min).
Holders of an international Youth Hostel Federation card should contact the International Federation or the French Youth Hostels Association to book a bed. Hostelling International / American Youth Hostel Association in the US (☎ 202-783-6161) offers a publication **International Hostel Guide for Europe** (US$13.95) – also available to non-members.

Camping – There are numerous officially graded sites with varying standards of facilities throughout the country. The **Michelin Guide Caravaning France** lists a selection of camp sites. An international Camping Carnet for caravans is useful but not compulsory; it may be obtained from motoring organisations or the Camping and Caravanning Club (Greenfield House, Westwood Way, Coventry CV4 8JH, ☎ (01203) 694 995.

Basic information

Electricity – The electric current is 220 volts. Circular two pin plugs are the rule. You should buy adaptors before leaving home. They are on sale at most airports.

Medical treatment – First aid, medical advice and chemist's night service rota are available from chemists/drugstores (*pharmacie* identified by a green cross sign). It is advisable to take out comprehensive insurance cover as tourists undergoing medical treatment in French hospitals or clinics have to pay for it themselves. Nationals of non-EU countries should check with their insurance companies about policy limitations. Reimbursement can then be negotiated with the insurance company according to the policy held. All prescription drugs should be clearly labelled; it is recommended to carry a copy of the prescription. American Express offers its cardholders only a service, "Global Assist", for any medical, legal or personal emergency: ☎ 01 47 16 25 29.
British and Irish citizens should apply to the Department of Health and Social Security for **Form E111**, which entitles the holder to urgent treatment for accident or unexpected illness in EU countries. A refund of part of the costs of treatment can be obtained on application in person or by post to the local Social Security offices *(Caisse Primaire d'Assurance Maladie)*.

Tipping – Since a service charge is automatically included in the price of meals and accommodation in France, it is not necessary to tip in restaurants and hotels. However taxi drivers, bellboys, doormen, filling station attendants or anybody who has been of assistance are usually tipped at the customer's discretion. Most French people give an extra tip in restaurants and café's (about 50 centimes for a drink and several francs for a meal). There is no tipping in theatres.

Currency – There are no restrictions on the amount of currency visitors can take into France. Visitors wishing to export currency in foreign banknotes in excess of the given allocation from France should complete a currency declaration form on arrival.

Coins and notes - *See illustration on page 348.* The unit of currency in France is the French Franc (F), subdivided into 100 centimes. French coins come in the following values:

5, 10, 20, 50 centimes (all gold coloured except the 50 centime coin which is silver) 1, 2, 5, 10, 20 francs (all silver except the 10 and 20 franc coins which are silver with a gold band).

French notes are available for the values 50, 100, 200 and 500 francs (the old 20 franc note is being phased out).

Banks - Banks are generally open from 9am to noon and from 2pm to 4pm and are closed on Monday or Saturday (except if market day). Banks close early on the day before a bank holiday. A passport is necessary for identification when cashing cheques (travellers' or ordinary) in banks. Commission charges vary and hotels usually charge more than banks for cashing cheques for non-residents.

Most banks have **cash dispensers** (ATM) that accept international credit cards. These are easily recognizable by the CB logo. American Express cards can only be used in dispensers operated by the Credit Lyonnais bank or by American Express.

Credit cards - American Express, Visa, Mastercard-Eurocard and Diners Club are widely accepted in shops, hotels, restaurants and petrol stations. In case your card is lost or stolen call the following 24-hour hotlines:

American Express 01 47 77 72 00
Visa 01 42 77 11 90
Mastercard/Eurocard 01 45 67 84 84
Diners Club 01 47 62 75 50

You must also report any loss or theft to the local police who will issue you with a certificate (useful proof to show the credit card company).

Post - Main post offices open Monday to Friday from 8am to 7pm, Saturday from 8am to noon. Smaller branch post offices can close at lunchtime between noon and 2pm and can also close at 4pm.

Postage via airmail to: UK: letter (20 g) 3.00 F
North America: letter (20g) or postcard 4.30F; aerogramme 5F
Australia and New Zealand: letter (20 g) or postcard 5.10F

Stamps are also available from newsagents and bureaux de tabac. Stamp collectors should ask for *timbres de collection* in any post office.

Public Holidays - The following are days when museums and other monuments may be closed or may vary their hours of admission:

1 January	New Year's Day
	Easter Sunday and Monday *(Pâques)*
1 May	May Day
8 May	V E Day
	Whit Sunday and Monday *(Pentecôte)*
	Ascension Day *(Ascension)*
14 July	France's National Day (Bastille Day)
15 August	Assumption
1 November	All Saints' Day *(Toussaint)*
11 November	Armistice
25 December	Christmas Day

Local Radios - These usually give frequent updates on traffic, local demonstrations, etc. as well as information on local cultural events. To find the local stations, ask at the Tourist Office or in the local newspapers.

Embassies and Consulates

Australia:	Embassy	4 Rue Jean-Rey, 75015 Paris, ☎ 01 40 59 33 00 Fax 01 40 59 33 10
Canada:	Embassy	35 Avenue Montaigne, 75008 Paris, ☎ 01 44 43 29 00 Fax 01 44 43 29 99
Eire:	Embassy	4 Rue Rude, 75016 Paris, ☎ 01 44 17 67 00 Fax 01 45 00 84 17

New Zealand:	Embassy	7 ter Rue Léonard-de-Vinci, 75016 Paris,
		☏ 01 45 00 24 11
		Fax 01 45 01 26 39
UK:	Embassy	35 Rue du Faubourg St-Honoré, 75008 Paris,
		☏ 01 42 66 91 42
		Fax 01 42 66 95 90
	Consulate	16 Rue d'Anjou, 75008 Paris,
		☏ 01 42 66 06 68 (visas)
		9 Avenue Hoche, 75008 Paris,
		☏ 01 42 66 38 10
USA:	Embassy	2 Avenue Gabriel, 75008 Paris,
		☏ 01 43 12 22 22
		Fax 01 42 66 97 83
	Consulate	2 Rue St-Florentin, 75001 Paris,
		☏ 01 44 29 40 00

Telephoning

Public Telephone – Most public phones in France use pre-paid phone cards *(télécartes)*. Some telephone booths accept credit cards (Visa, Mastercard/Euro-card; minimum monthly charge 20F). *Télécartes* (50 or 120 units) can be bought in post offices, branches of France Télécom, *bureaux de tabac* (authorised cigarette sales point) and newsagents, and can be used to make calls in France and abroad. Calls can be received at phone boxes where the blue bell sign is shown.

National calls – When calling within France you only have to dial the 10 digit correspondent's number. There are no area codes. After a few initial short pips, the French ringing tone is a series of long tones and the engaged (busy) tone is a series of short beeps.

International calls – To call a correspondent in France, dial the country code (33) + the 9 last digits (drop the first 0) of the correspondent's number. When calling abroad from France dial 00, then dial the country code, followed by the area code and number of your correspondent. For international inquiries dial 00 33 12 + country code (be prepared to wait for up to an hour).

To use your personal calling card dial: AT&T: 00-0011
                                             MCI: 00-0019
                                           BT: 00-0044
                                         Mercury: 00-00944

Rates from a public phone (1995):
Between France and the UK: 2.97F/min (2.23F/min reduced rate)
Between France and the USA: 4.45F/min (3.46F/min reduced rate)
Between France and Canada: 4.45F/min (3.46F/min reduced rate)
Between France and Australia: 8.65F/min (6.92F/min reduced rate)
Reduced rates to the UK: from 9.30pm to 8am Monday to Friday; from 2pm Saturday all day Sunday and public holidays.
Reduced rates to the US and Canada: the lowest rates apply from 2am to noon all week.
Reduced rates to Australia: from 9.30pm to 8am from Monday to Saturday and all day Sunday.

International dialling codes:
Australia: 61
Canada: 1
Eire: 353
New Zealand: 64
United Kingdom: 44
United States: 1

Toll-free numbers: In France numbers beginning with 0800 are toll-free.

Emergency numbers: Police: 17
Fire *(Pompiers)*: 18
Ambulance *(SAMU)*: 15

Minitel – France Telecom has a modern interactive communication service called Minitel, similar to the teletex system, offering a range of services from directory inquiries (free of charge up to 3 min) to 3614, 3615, 3616 and 3617 prefixed numbers (fee charged between 0.37F and 5.57F/min). These small computer-like machines can be found in some post offices, hotels and France Telecom agencies and in most French homes.

Listed below are some of the telematic services offered:

3615 TCAMP (1.01F/min)	camping information
3615 METEO (1.29F/min)	weather report
3615 HORAV (1.29F/min)	general airline information and flight schedules from and to Paris
3614 BBC (0.37F/min)	BBC news
3615 MICHELIN (1.29FF/min)	Michelin tourist and route information
3617 MICHELIN (5.57F/min)	Michelin tourist and route information sent by fax

> For information in English dial 0800 201 202.
> Directory inquiries in English on minitel: 3614 ED (0.37F/min)

Shopping

Opening hours – Department stores are open Monday to Saturday, 9am to 6.30pm-7.30pm. Smaller, more specialised shops may close during the lunch hour. Food stores (grocers, wine merchants and bakeries) are open from 7am to 6.30pm-7.30pm. Some open on Sunday mornings. Many food stores close between noon and 2pm and on Mondays. Hypermarkets are usually open until 9pm-10pm.

What to buy – There are so many things to bring back that to list them all would be impossible. However a *Food and Drink map* in the introduction will give you a good idea of what to bring back.
Travellers to America cannot bring back food and plant products, especially cheeses and fruit. Americans are allowed to bring back home, tax-free, up to US$400 worth of goods, Canadians up to CND$300, British up to £136, Australians up to AUS$400 and New Zealanders up to NZ$700.

Markets – When travelling around France make sure you have a look around the different local markets – an important domestic institution – or the various agricultural fairs which are held regularly throughout the year.

VAT Refund – In France a sales tax (*TVA* or VAT) is added to the various products you buy. For non-Europeans, this tax can be refunded as long as you have bought more than 2.800F of goods at the same time and in the same shop. This fixed amount may vary so it is wiser to check with the VAT-refund counter *(service de détaxe)*.

Telephone codes...
As from mid-October 1996,
all French telephone numbers must have ten digits.
Before the old 8-digit number insert:
01 for Paris and the Paris region.
02 for northwest France.
03 for northeast France.
04 for southeast France.
05 for southeast France.

Conversion tables

Weights and measures

| 1 kilogram (kg) | 2.2 pounds (lb) | 2.2 pounds |
| 1 ton (tn) | 2.2 tons | 2.2 tons |

to convert kilograms to pounds, multiply by 2.2

| 1 litre (l) | 1.7 pints (pt) | 2.1 pints |
| 1 litre | 0.22 gallon (gal) | 0.26 gallon |

to convert litres to gallons, multiply by 0.26 (US) or 0.22 (UK)

| 1 hectare (ha) | 2.47 acres (a) | 2.47 acres |
| 1 square kilometre (km²) | 0.39 square miles (sq mi) | 0.39 square miles |

to convert hectares to acres, multiply by 2.4

1 centimetre (cm)	0.3937 inches (in)	0.3937 inches
1 metre (m)	3.2 feet (ft) - 39.3 inches - 1.09 yards (yd)
1 kilometre (km)	0.6214 miles (mi)	0.6214 miles

to convert metres to feet, multiply by 3.28 . kilometres to miles, multiply by 0.6

Clothing

Women							Men
	35	4	2½	40	7½	7	
	36	5	3½	41	8½	8	
	37	6	4½	42	9½	9	
Shoes	38	7	5½	43	10½	10	**Shoes**
	39	8	6½	44	11½	11	
	40	9	7½	45	12½	12	
	41	10	8½	46	13½	13	
	36	4	8	46	36	36	
	38	6	10	48	38	38	
Dresses &	40	8	12	50	40	40	**Suits**
Suits	42	12	14	52	42	42	
	44	14	16	54	44	44	
	46	16	18	56	46	48	
	36	08	30	37	14½	14,5	
	38	10	32	38	15	15	
Blouses &	40	12	14	39	15½	15½	**Shirts**
sweaters	42	14	36	40	15¾	15¾	
	44	16	38	41	16	16	
	46	18	40	42	16½	16½	

As sizes often vary depending on the designer, it is best to try on the articles before purchasing.

Speed

kph	10	30	50	70	80	90	100	110	120	130
mph	6	19	31	43	50	56	62	69	75	80

Temperature

Celsius (°C)	0°	5°	10°	15°	20°	25°	30°	40°	60°	80°	100°
Fahrenheit (°F)	32°	40°	50°	60°	70°	75°	85°	105°	140°	175°	212°

to convert: °F = (°C × 1.8) + 32   °C = 0.55 × (°F -32)

Coins and notes

500 Francs featuring
the scientists
Pierre and Marie Curie
(1858-1906), (1867-1934)

200 Francs featuring
the philosopher
Ch. de Montesquieu
(1689-1755)

100 Francs featuring
the Romantic painter
Eugène Delacroix
(1798-1863)

50 Francs featuring
the pilot and writer
Antoine de Saint-Exupéry
(1900-1944)

20 Francs

10 Francs

5 Francs

2 Francs

1 Franc

50 Centimes

20 Centimes

10 Centimes

5 Centimes

Good food

France is the land of good food and good living and it has a host of regional specialities. In addition to the map of regional dishes and major vineyards in the Introduction, and the **Michelin Guide to Hotels and Restaurants** in France, here are a few more examples of traditional fare.

Garbure

Soups and consommés: the best-known are cream of asparagus, leek and potato, onion, lobster, *garbure* (a thick soup with cabbage popular in south-western France), and *cotriade* (Breton fish soup), all of which are served at the start of a meal.

Hors d'œuvres: There are countless ways to begin a meal and French chefs have boundless imagination in this respect. The following, though, deserve a special mention: *salade niçoise* (tomatoes, anchovies, onions, olives), *salade lyonnaise* (using various meats with seasoning and a blend of oil, vinegar and shallots), and *salade cauchoise* (celery, potatoes and ham). Another good start to a meal is a *flamiche* (a leek quiche that is a speciality of Picardy), or a *ficelle* (a ham pancake with a mushroom sauce). *Tapénade* is one of the traditional dishes of Provence (black olive puree into which are blended capers, anchovies and tuna fish). Or you may prefer quiche lorraine (made with ham or bacon and cream) or *pissaladière* (provençal quiche with onions, tomatoes, and anchovies).

No mention of starters would be complete without seafood and shellfish, such as oysters from Belon, Cancale or Marennes, shrimps, prawns and clams.

Main courses: there are two main "families" of main course – fish or meat accompanied by all sorts of vegetables depending on the season, or served with a *gratin dauphinois* (potatoes, eggs and milk), not to be confused with *gratin savoyard* (potatoes, eggs and stock). *Bouillabaisse* is the famous stew from Marseille made with three types of fish (scorpion fish, red gurnard and conger eel) seasoned with saffron, thyme, garlic, bay, sage and fennel. *Brandade* is a creamy blend of mashed cod with olive oil, milk, and a few cloves of garlic; it is a speciality of Nîmes. In Brittany, what better than lobster *à l'armoricaine*, mussels in cream, shad or pike with Nantes-style "white butter sauce", worthy rivals of Dieppe-style sole or the

Bouillabaisse

shrimps and cockles of Honfleur in Normandy, and of the bass grilled with fennel or baked over a fire of vine shoots, a dish that is popular in Provence and on the Riviera.

There are so many regional dishes that we can do no more than provide a glimpse of the delights in store.

The best-known meat dishes include Strasbourg sauerkraut (cabbage, potatoes, pork, sausages, and ham), Toulouse or Castelnaudary *cassoulet* (bean stew with pieces of goose or duck and pork-meat products), Caen-style tripe, Rouen duck *(canard au sang)*, Burgundy *meurette* (wine sauce) that is as good an accompaniment for poached eggs as for brains or beef – cooked Burgundy-style of course! Also well worth a mention are Auvergne *potée* (cabbage, piece of pork, bacon, and turnips) or its cousin from Franche-Comté (cabbage, Morteau or Montbéliard sausage), Chaudes-Aigues *aligot* (a creamy blend of fresh *tomme* cheese and mashed potato seasoned with garlic), *tripoux* from Aurillac, Basque-style chicken (with tomatoes and pimentoes), rabbit *chasseur* and rabbit *forestier* (with mushrooms and diced bacon).

Ch. Fleurent/TOP

Cheese

There is such a wide range of cheeses in France that it is difficult to know them all so it is worth defining the main "families".

I – Soft cheeses

a) Cheese with surface mould (Brie de Meaux, Camembert, Chaource etc.)

b) Cheese with washed rind (Livarot, Reblochon, Munster, Vacherin etc.)

c) Cheese with natural rind (Tomme de Romans, Cendres de Bourgogne, Brie de Melun etc.)

II – Hard pressed non-boiled cheeses

(Cantal, Fourme de Laguiole, Gapron d'Auvergne etc.)

III – Hard pressed boiled cheeses

(Emmental de Savoie, Comté de Franche-Comté, Beaufort de Savoie, and Beaufort de Dauphiné etc.)

IV – Blue cheeses

a) Blue cheeses with natural crust (Bleu de Bresse, Bleu de Corse, Fourme de Montbrison etc.)

b) Scraped blue cheeses (Roquefort, Bleu d'Auvergne, Bleu des Causses etc.).

V – Finally, there are processed cheeses such as Crème de Gruyère, spreads with walnuts or grapes and a whole range of cheese spreads.

Fruit and desserts

There are innumerable "desserts" to round off a meal. Apart from the baskets of fruit, strawberries and cream or strawberries in red wine, fruit salads and macedoines using all the orchard fruits, there are apple, pear, and peach compotes, and all sorts of cakes e.g. tarte Tatin (a caramelised tart cooked with the filling underneath), Grenoble walnut cake, Breton *far* (a baked custard dessert), spice bread in the Gâtinais region, *clafoutis* (a blend of milk and eggs mixed with fruit and baked in the oven), and *kougelhopf* from Alsace baked in the form of a ring and served as a dessert or as an afternoon snack. Not to mention all the creme caramels, baked cream desserts, and soft meringues with custard sauce *(île flottante)* that are found in nearly every region of France.

Recreation

Information and brochures outlining the sporting and outdoor facilities available may be obtained from the French Government Tourist Office or from the organisations listed below.

Wine Tours – In the various regions wine tours which take in the main wine-producing areas and cellars are signposted. For information apply to the Tourist Information Centre.

Buying your own wine directly from the grower can be an adventurous and satisfying holiday occupation. Signs announce farmgate sales *(vins-vente directe)* or wine tasting and sales *(dégustation vente).*

Crafts – Many arts and crafts studios (weaving, wrought-iron, pottery) on the coast and inland are open to visitors in summer. For courses apply to the Tourist Information Centre.

Cycling Holidays – The Fédération Française de Cyclotourisme: 8 Rue Jean-Marie-Jégo, 75013 Paris, ☎ 01 45 80 30 21 supplies itineraries covering most of France, mentioning mileage, difficult routes and sights to see.

You can also contact the Fédération française de cyclisme, 5, rue de Rome, 93561 Rosny-sous-Bois cedex ☎ 01 49 35 69 00.

Lists of hire cycle businesses are available from the Tourist Information Centres. The main railway stations also hire out cycles which can be returned at a different station.

Rambling – Short, medium and long distance footpath Topo-Guides are published by the Fédération Française de la Randonnée Pédestre – Comité National des Sentiers de Grande Randonnée. These give detailed maps of the paths and offer valuable information to the rambler and are on sale at the Information Centre: 64 Rue de Gergovie, 75014 Paris. ☎ 01 45 45 31 02; or by mail order from McCarta, 15 Highbury Place, London N5 1QP, ☎ (0171) 354 1616.

Fishing – Current brochures: folding map *Fishing in France* (Pêche en France) published and distributed by the Conseil Supérieur de la Pêche, 134 Avenue de Malakoff, 75016 Paris, ☎ 01 45 02 20 20; also available from the departmental fishing organisations.

For information about regulations contact the Tourist Information Centres or the offices of the Water and Forest Authority (Eaux et Forêts).

Cruising – Two publishers produce collections of guides to cruising on French canals. Both series include numerous maps and useful information and are provided with English translations. The publishers are: Grafocarte, 125, rue J.-J. Rousseau, 92130 Issy-les-Moulineaux ☎ 01 41 09 19 00.

Guides Vagnon, Les Éditions du Plaisancier, 100 Avenue du Général-Leclerc, 69641 Caluire Cedex. ☎ 04 78 23 31 14.

Sailing – Many resorts have sailing clubs offering courses. In season it is possible to hire boats with or without crew; apply to the Fédération Française de Voile: 55 Avenue Kléber, 75016 Paris. ☎ 01 44 05 81 00.

Canoeing – Apply to Fédération Française de Canoe-Kayak, 87 Quai de la Marne, 94340 Joinville-le-Pont. ☎ 01 45 11 08 50. A guide is published annually indicating schools and places where canoeing may be practised.

Motor boating and water-skiing – Enquire at the local Tourist Information Centre or at the resort. Anyone who intends to drive a powered boat (6hp – 50hp) within five nautical miles of a French harbour must qualify for a sea certificate *(carte mer)*. Beyond the 5-mile limit an additional sea permit *(permis mer)* is required. Yachts and boats with engines of less than 6hp are exempt.

Scuba-diving – Apply to the Fédération Française d'Études et de Sports Sous-Marins, 24, quai de Rive Neuve, 13007 Marseille. ☎ 04 91 33 99 31.

Wind surfing – The sport which is subject to certain regulations is permitted on lakes and in sports and leisure centres. Apply to sailing clubs. Boards may be hired on all major beaches.

Riding and Pony Trekking – Apply to the Fédération des Randonneurs Équestres, 16 Rue des Apennins, 75017 Paris, ☎ 42 26 23 23. The Association Nationale de Tourisme Équestre (ANTE) Parc de l'île Saint-Germain, 170, quai Stalingrad, 92130 Issy-les-Moulineaux ☎ 01 46 48 83 93 publishes an annual handbook covering the whole of France.

Hunting – For all enquiries apply to **"Saint-Hubert"** – **"Club de France"**, 10 Rue de Lisbonne, 75008 Paris, ☎ 01 45 22 38 90.

Golf – For location, addresses and telephone numbers of golf courses in France, consult the map *Golfs, les Parcours français*, published by Edition Plein Sud based on **Michelin maps.** You can also contact the Fédération Française de Golf, 69 Avenue Victor-Hugo, 75016 Paris, ☎ 01 44 17 63 00.

Skiing – For all enquiries contact the Club Alpin Français, 24 Avenue de Laumière, 75019 Paris. ☎ 01 53 72 88 00.

Mountaineering – Excursions with qualified instructors are organised by sections of the Club Alpin Français (apply to the above address for information on regional sections) or by local guides. For information apply to the Tourist Information Centres or to the Fédération Française de la Montagne et de l'Escalade, 8, quai de la Marne, 75019 Paris. ☎ 01 40 18 75 50.

Speleology – Apply to the Speleology sections of the Club Alpin Français (see under Skiing and Mountaineering).

Gliding – Apply to the Fédération Française de Vol à voile, 29 Rue de Sèvres, 75006 Paris. ☎ 01 45 44 04 78.

3615 MICHELIN on the Minitel saves time and trouble
by calculating journey times, mileage and the most direct
route to your destination.
For further information on Minitel see telephoning
in the Practical Information section.
Have a good trip!

Calendar of events

This list includes a selection of festivals and events likely to be of interest to the visitor, further details of which can be obtained from the telephone numbers shown after the name of the town (Michelin map reference given if the town is not in guide).

Religious and civic festivals

Late February

Nice	04 93 87 16 28	Carnival
Chalons-sur-Saône	03 85 48 39 79	Carnival, Winter Fur and Pelt Fair
Le Touquet	02 21 99 05 43	Motorbike Race along the beach

Maundy Thursday

Le Puy-en-Velay	04 71 09 38 41	White Penitents Procession
Sauges (76 16)	04 71 77 84 46	White Penitents Procession (at night-fall)

Good Friday

Arles-sur-Tech (86 18)	04 68 39 11 99	Black Penitents Procession
Burzet (76 18)	04 75 94 41 03	The Passion re-enacted
Collioure (86 20)	04 68 82 15 47	Penitents Procession
Perpignan	04 68 66 30 30	Black Penitents Procession
Roquebrune-Cap-Martin	04 93 35 62 87	Procession of the Entombment of Christ
Sartène	04 95 77 05 11	U Catenacciu Procession

Easter Sunday

St-Benoit-sur-Loire	02 38 35 72 43	Easter Service

Easter Monday

Cassel (51 4)	03 28 42 40 13	Carnival of the Giants Reuze-Papa and Reuze-Maman

April

Chartres	02 37 21 54 03	Students' Pilgrimage

Mid-April

Gérardmer	03 29 63 00 80	Flower Festival

Early May

Orléans	02 38 79 23 86	Joan of Arc Festival

Mid May

St-Tropez	04 94 97 45 21	Procession in honour of St-Tropez (Bravade)
Tréguier	02 96 92 30 19	Pardon of St-Ives
Mont-St-Michel	02 33 60 14 30	Feast of St-Michael in Spring

Late May

Rouen	02 35 74 41 77	Joan of Arc Festival
Les Stes-Maries-de-la-Mer	04 90 47 82 55	Gypsy Pilgrimage

Whit

Honfleur	02 31 89 23 30	Seamen's Festival

Early June

Pomarez (78 7)	05 58 89 33 32	Running of the Cows
La Rochelle	05 46 44 62 44	International Regatta
Utah Beach-Omaha Beach	02 33 41 31 18	Commemoration of the D-Day Landings (American sector)
Gold-Juno-Sword	02 31 86 53 30	Commemoration of the D-Day Landings (Anglo-Canadian sector). The two events are combined every five years

Mid-June

Chambord	02 47 55 09 16	Game Fair
Le Mans	03 43 40 24 24	24 hour car race

Illuminations, Chambord

E. Streichan/PIX

Son et Lumiere performances in the Loire Valley

Amboise	02 47 57 14 47	*"At The Court of King François"*
Azay-le-Rideau	02 47 45 42 04	*"The Imaginary World of Azay-le-Château"*
Blois	02 54 78 72 76	*"The Story of Blois"*
Chambord	02 54 20 34 86	*"Days through the Centuries"*
Chenonceau	02 47 23 90 07	*"The Ladies of Chenonceau"*
Cheverny	02 54 42 69 03	*"The River Loire down the ages"*
Loches	02 47 59 07 98	*"The Strange Story of Bélisane"*
Le Lude	02 43 94 60 09	*"Spectacular Historical Events"*
Valencay	02 54 00 04 42	*"Esclarmonde"*

You are advised to book accommodation well in advance at festival times, even out of season.

Cultural Festivals

The following list includes some of the more important annual festivals of this type with an indication of their length and nature.

Aix-en-Provence	04 42 17 34 00	*July*	International music Festival
Albi	05 63 54 22 30	*June July*	Theatre Music
Arles	04 90 96 76 06	*2nd fortnight July*	International Photo Festival
Avignon	04 90 82 67 08	*2nd fortnight July*	Dramatic art
Belfort	03 84 54 24 24	*late November*	Cinema
Bellac (72 7)	05 55 68 10 44	*late June/ early July*	Drama, music
Besançon	03 81 80 73 26	*September*	Classical music
Beziers (83 15)	04 67 36 73 73	*1st fortnight in July*	Classical music
Bordeaux	05 56 48 58 54	*1st fortnight in May*	Music
Bourges	02 48 70 61 11	*late April/ early May*	Music Festival
Cannes	04 42 66 92 20	*May*	International Film Festival
Carcassonne	04 68 25 33 13	*July*	Theatre, music and dance
Carpentras	04 90 63 46 35	*mid-July/ early August*	Music and dance
La Chaise-Dieu	04 71 00 01 16	*late August/ early September*	French religious music
Chartres	02 37 21 54 03	*July and August*	Religious music
Chaumont-sur-Loire	02 54 20 99 22	*mid-June/ mid-October*	International Garden Festival
Deauville	02 31 88 21 43	*1st fortnight in September*	American film Festival
Divonne	04 50 40 34 16	*2nd fortnight in June*	Chamber music
Entrecasteaux (84 6)	04 94 04 42 86	*2nd fortnight in August*	Chamber music
Évian	04 50 75 04 26	*mid-May*	Music
Gannat	04 70 90 12 67	*2nd fortnight in July*	International folk music
Juan-les-Pins	04 93 33 95 64	*2nd fortnight in July*	World Jazz Festival
Lannion (58 7)	02 96 37 07 35	*mid-July/ late August*	Organ and choral music
Lille	03 20 52 74 23	*October-November*	Dance and theatre
Lorient	02 97 21 24 29	*early August*	Celtic festival
Lyon	04 72 40 26 26	*2nd fortnight in September*	even years: dance uneven years: music and contemporary art

Montauban	05 63 63 60 60	*early August*	Choreography
Nantes	02 40 47 04 51	*early July*	Folkways
Orange	04 90 34 24 24	*2nd fortnight in July*	Music and opera
Pau	05 59 27 85 80	*mid-June/mid-July*	Theatre, music and dance
Prades (86 17) .	04 68 96 33 07	*late July/ mid-August*	Chamber music (Festival Pablo Casals)
Le Puy-en-Velay .	04 71 09 38 41	*mid-September*	Renaissance Festival
Quimper	02 98 55 53 53	*4th Sunday in July*	Cornouaille Festival
Rennes	02 99 30 38 01	*early July*	Theatre, music, dance and poetry
St-Céré (75 19) .	05 65 38 29 08	*mid-July/ late August*	Music
St-Donat-sur-l'Herbasse (77 2)	04 75 45 10 29	*late July/ early August*	Bach Festival
St-Guilhem-le-Desert	04 67 63 14 99	*July/August*	Baroque Music
St-Malo	02 99 40 42 50	*late October*	Comics Festival
St-Remy-de-Provence	04 90 92 16 31	*mid-July/ mid-September*	Organ music
Salon-de-Provence (84 2) .	04 90 42 12 12	*July*	Jazz/Rock
Sarlat	05 53 31 10 83	*late July/ early August*	Theatre
Sceaux (101 25)	01 46 60 07 79	*mid-July/ late September*	Classical and chamber music
Toulouse	05 61 11 02 22	*late June/ late August*	Classical, Jazz and Folk Music
Vaison-la-Romaine	04 90 36 12 92	*July and August*	Theatre and dance-Folklore
Vannes	02 97 47 24 34	*15 August*	Arvor Festival (folk music)
Versailles	01 39 50 36 22	*May to October every Sunday*	Fountain display with music
	01 39 50 36 22	*2 weekends in July 2 weekends in September*	Illuminations of the Neptune Basin, fireworks display and fountain display with music

Some books to read

Copies of titles mentioned below may be obtained through public libraries.
France Today by J. Ardagh *(Penguin 1990)*
The French by T. Zeldin *(Collins Harvill 1988)*
The Identity of France 1. History and Environment by F. Braudel *(Fontana 1989)*
A Traveller's History of France by R. Cole *(Windrush 1988)*
French and English by R. Faber *(Faber 1975)*
Britain and France: Ten Centuries by D. Johnson F. Bedarida and F. Crouzet *(Dawson 1980)*
The Lives of the Kings and Queens of France by the Duc de Castries *(Weidenfeld 1979)*
Searching for the New France by J. Hollifield and G. Ross *(Routledge)*
The Lost World of the Impressionists by A. Bellony-Rewald *(Galley 1976)*
French Architecture by P. Lavedan *(Penguin 1956)*
The Wine Lover's Guide to France by M. Busselle *(Pavilion, Michael Joseph 1986)*
The Food Lover's Guide to France by P. Wells *(Eyre and Spottiswoode)*
The Wines and Winelands of France – Geological Journeys by L. Pomerol *(Edition du BRGM)*

A few films

Alps: *La Route Napoléon* (1953) by J. Delannoy (several villages in the Alpes-de-Haute-Provence).

Alsace-Lorraine: *La Grande Illusion* (1937) by Jean Renoir (Château du Haut-Kœnigsbourg, Colmar and around Neuf-Brisach).

Atlantic Coast: *Moderato Cantabile* (1960) by P. Brook (Blaye, Gironde).

Berry: *Tous les Matins du Monde* (1992) by A. Corneau (Château de Bodeau near Rougnat).

Brittany: *Les Vacances de Monsieur Hulot* – **Monsieur Hulot's Holidays** (1951) by J. Tati (St-Marc-sur-Mer, Dol, Dinan).

Burgundy-Jura: *Mayerling* (1968) by T. Young (Pontarlier).

Champagne: *Camille Claudel* (1988) by B. Nuytten (Villeneuve-sur-Fere); *Au Revoir les Enfants* (1988) by L. Malle (Provins).

Châteaux of the Loire: *La Règle du Jeu* (1939) by C. Renoir (Château de la Ferté-St-Aubin, Lamotte-Beuvron, around Brinon-sur-Sauldre).

Corsica: *Napoléon* (1927) by A. Gance (Ajaccio, Grotte de Casone, Pointe des Sanguinaires).

Dordogne-Périgord-Quercy: *Les Misérables* (1935) by R. Boleshawski (Sarlat, Montpazier).

Flanders: *Germinal* (1993) by C. Berri (Oignies, Astres).

French Riviera: *To Catch a Thief* (1956) by A. Hitchcock (Monaco).

Ile-de-France: *La Guerre des Boutons* (1961) by Y. Robert (Rambouillet); *La Haine* (1995) by M. Kassovitz (Paris Suburbs).

Normandy: *Les Parapluies de Cherbourg* (1963) by J. Demy (Cherbourg).

Paris: *Zazie dans le Métro* (1960) by L. Malle; *Le Ballon Rouge* – **Red Balloon** (1955) by A. Lamorisse.

Provence: *Marius* (1931) by Pagnol (Marseille); *Crin Blanc* (1953) by A. Lamorisse (Camargue); *La Gloire de mon Père* and *Le Château de ma Mère* (1990) by Y. Robert (Marseille, Allauch, Grambois).

Pyrenees-Languedoc-Tarn Gorges: *37°2 au Matin* – **Betty Blue** (1986) by J. J. Beineix (Gruissan, Marvejols).

Rhône Valley: *L'Horloger de Saint-Paul* (1973) by B. Tavernier (Lyon).

Raimu and Fernandel in the "Well-Digger's Daughter"

Admission times and charges

The information that follows applies to individual adults with no reduction. Special conditions for admission times and prices for groups are available. Since admission charges increase with the cost of living and times change frequently for many sights, the following entries are given for guidance only. In cases where we were unable to obtain recent information, the entries from the earlier edition of the guide were included. These appear in italics.

Religious buildings do not admit visitors during services. Certain churches and most chapels are often closed. Admission times are mentioned if the interior is of special interest. In cases where the visitor must be accompanied by the person in charge of the key, a donation or an offering is recommended.

In certain towns, guided tours of the entire area or for sites of historical interest are organised during the tourist season. These tours are mentioned in the town's heading along with the admission times and charges. For towns of special historical and artistic interest, symbolized by ▲, *tours are organized by guide-lecturers licensed by the Caisse Nationale des Monuments Historiques et des Sites.*

When the sights include facilities designed for handicapped people, the heading is followed by the ♿ *symbol.*

A

ABBEVILLE   🛈 1, place Amiral-Courbet - 80100 - ☎ 03 22 24 27 92

Château de Bagatelle – Guided tours (30min) daily from the 1st weekend in July to the 1st weekend in September 2pm to 6pm; the rest of the year by appointment; closed Tuesday. 32F; ☎ 03 22 24 02 69.

Musée Boucher-de-Perthes – Open daily (except Tuesday); admission free; ☎ 03 22 24 08 49

AIGUES-MORTES   🛈 porte de la Gardette - 30220 - ☎ 04 66 53 73 00

Tour de Constance and ramparts – Reception area at the base of the tower. Open 1 June to 31 August 9.30am to 7pm; the rest of the year 9.30am to 12.30pm and 2pm to 4.30pm; closed 1 January, 1 May, 1 and 11 November and 25 December; 28F. ☎ 04 66 53 61 55.

AIX-EN-PROVENCE   🛈 2 place du Général-de-Gaulle - 13100 - ☎ 04 42 16 11 61

Guided tours of the town ▲ – Contact the tourist information office.

Cathédrale and Romanesque Cloisters – To see the Triptych of the Burning Bush and the sculpted doorway panels, apply to the caretaker's lodge to the right of the west door; closed Sunday; ☎ 04 42 21 10 51.

Musée Granet – Open 10am to noon and 2pm to 6pm; closed Tuesday and most holidays; 18F; ☎ 04 42 38 14 70.

Eglise Ste-Marie-Madeleine – Open during the week only 9.30am to 11.30am.

Muséum d'Histoire naturelle – Open 10am to noon and 2pm to 6pm; closed 1 January, 1 May, 25 and 26 December; 14F; ☎ 04 42 26 23 67.

Eglise St-Jean-de-Malte – Open 9am to noon and 3.30pm to 7pm; closed Wednesday morning; ☎ 04 42 38 25 70.

Fondation Vasarely – Open daily 1 July to 30 September from 10am to 7pm; the rest of the year 10am to 1pm and 2pm to 6pm; closed Tuesday; 35F; ☎ 04 42 20 01 09.

Musée des Tapisseries – Open daily 10am to noon and 2pm to 5pm; closed Tuesday; 14F; ☎ 04 42 21 05 78.

AJACCIO

Musée napoléonien – Open all year round 9am to noon and 2pm to 5.30pm; closed Saturday, Sunday and holidays. The Grand Salon is sometimes closed during official functions at the town hall; 5F; ☎ 04 95 21 48 17.

Musée Fesch – 🚻 Open from mid-June to mid-September 10am to 12.30 pm and 3pm to 7pm; in July and August, also open Friday from 9pm to midnight; the rest of the year 9.30am to noon and 2.15pm to 6pm; closed Sunday and Monday as well as 1 May, Easter, Ascension, Pentecost, 1 November and Christmas; 25F; ☎ 04 95 21 48 17.

Maison Bonaparte – Open daily from 1 May to 30 September 9am to noon and 2pm to 6pm; the rest of the year 10am to noon and 2pm to 5pm; closed Sunday afternoon and Monday morning as well as 1 May; 20F.

ALBI

Choir of the cathédrale Ste-Cécile – For guided tours, contact the tourist information office; access to choir 3F.

Palais de la Berbie (Toulouse-Lautrec Museum) – Open from 1 June to 30 September 9am to noon and 2pm to 6pm, in April and May 10am to noon and 2pm to 6pm, the rest of the year daily 10am to noon and 2pm to 5pm; closed Tuesday and 1 January, 1 May, 1 November and 25 December; 20F; ☎ 05 63 54 14 09.

ALÉRIA

Musée Jérôme-Carcopino – Open from 16 May to 30 September 8am to noon and 2pm to 7pm; the rest of the year closed at 5pm (visitors are no longer admitted 30min prior to closing time); closed Sunday from November to beginning April and 1 January, 1 May, 1 and 11 November and 25 December; 10F; ☎ 04 95 57 00 92.

Excavation site – Same admission times and charges as the museum; the ticket is included in the museum admission fee.

AMBOISE

Château – Guided tour or unaccompanied visit (45min) from 1 July to 31 August 9am to 8pm; from 1 April to 30 June and from 1 September to 31 October 9am to 6.30pm; the rest of the year 9am to noon and 2pm to 5pm; closed 1 January and 25 December; 33F; ☎ 02 47 57 00 98.

Clos-Lucé, residence of Leonardo da Vinci – 🚻 Open from 23 March to 12 November as well as during holidays 9am to 7pm (8pm in July and August); the rest of the year, 9am to 6pm; closed in January and 25 December; 35F; ☎ 02 47 57 62 88.

AMIENS

Guided tour of the town 🄰 – Contact the tourist information office.

Musée de Picardie – Open 10am to 12.30pm and 2pm to 6pm; closed Monday and certain holidays; 20F; ☎ 03 22 91 36 44.

Hortillonnages – Boat trip (1 hour) from 1 April to 31 October daily from 2pm on. Enquire at 54, bd. Beauvillé; 28F; ☎ 03 22 92 12 18.

Château ANCY-LE-FRANC

Guided tour (45min) daily from 1 May to 15 September at 10am, 11am, 2pm, 3pm, 4pm, 5pm and 6pm; last tour at 5pm the rest of the year; closed 15 November to 25 March; 42F; ☎ 03 86 75 14 63.

LES ANDELYS

Château-Gaillard – Guided tour or unaccompanied visit (45min) from mid-March to mid-November 9am to noon and 2pm to 7pm; open the rest of the year during the weekend, holidays and school holidays at the same times; closed all day Tuesday and Wednesday mornings; 17F; ☎ 02 32 54 04 16 or 02 32 54 41 93.

Château and Chapelle ANET

Guided tour (45min) daily from 1 April to 31 October 2.30pm to 6.30pm, Sunday and holidays 10am to 11.30am and 2.30pm to 6pm; the rest of the year, open Saturday 2pm to 5pm, Sunday and holidays 10am to 11.30am and 2.30pm to 6.30pm; 36F; ☎ 02 37 41 90 07.

ANGERS

An annual pass for a fixed price (valid until 31 December of the current year) provides access to the château, the galerie David d'Angers, the logis Barrault, the Hôtel Pincé and the Musée Jean-Lurçat.

Guided tour of the town ▲ – 15 June to 15 September, daily except Sunday (different times: 2pm, 5pm or 9pm depending on the day); the rest of the year a theme tour one Saturday or Sunday per month. Contact the tourist information office, which publishes a programme of lecture-tours by theme.

Château – Guided tour (1 hour) or unaccompanied visit from 1 June to 15 September 9am to 7pm; from Palm Sunday to 31 May 9am to 12.30pm and 2pm to 6.30pm; the rest of the year, 9.30am to 12.30pm and 2pm to 6pm; closed 1 January, 1 May, 1 and 11 November and 25 December; 32F; ☎ 02 41 87 43 47.

Musée Jean-Lurçat – ♿ Open from 15 June to 15 September 9.30am to 7pm; the rest of the year from 10am to noon and 2pm to 6pm; closed Monday, 1 January, 1 May, 8 May, 14 July, 1 and 11 November and 25 December; 20F; ☎ 02 41 88 64 65.

Galerie David d'Angers – Open from 15 June to 15 September 9.30am to 7pm; the rest of the year 10am to noon and 2pm to 6pm; closed Monday from 16 September to 14 June, 1 January, 1 May, 8 May, 14 July, 1 and 11 November and 25 December; 10F; ☎ 02 41 88 64 65.

Hôtel Pincé – Same admission times and charges as for the Galerie David d'Angers; 10F; ☎ 02 41 88 64 65.

Eglise St-Serge – Closed Sunday morning. Guided tour (30min), Sunday 2.30pm to 6pm in July and August (except 15 August); ☎ 02 41 43 66 76.

ANGOULÊME
🛈 2, place St-Pierre – 16000 – ☎ 05 45 95 16 84

Guided tour of the town ▲ – Contact the tourist information office.

C.N.B.D.I.: Musée et Médiathèque – Free or guided tour (2 hours) daily (except Monday) 10am to 7pm; on the weekend and holidays 2pm to 7pm; closed 1 January, 1 May and 25 December; 30F; ☎ 05 45 38 65 65.

ANNECY
🛈 Centre Bonlieu, 1 rue J. Jaurès – 74000 – ☎ 04 50 45 00 33

Guided tour of the town ▲ – Contact the tourist information office.

Palais de l'îsle – Same admission times and charges as for the château.

Lake – Various boat trips are available from beginning April to the end of September. Length: 1 hour 30min. Door-to-door omnibus: 63F. Cruise with a stop at Doussard: 67F (children under 12: 56F). For times and reservations ☎ 04 50 51 08 40.

Château – Open daily from 10am to noon and from 2pm to 6pm; from June to end September, also open between noon and 2pm; closed Tuesday (except from mid-June to mid-September) and holidays; 30F; ☎ 04 50 33 87 31.

ANTIBES
🛈 11, place du général de Gaulle – 06200 – ☎ 04 92 90 53 00.

Château Grimaldi: Musée Picasso – Open from mid-June to mid-September from 10am to 6pm; the rest of the year, closed from noon to 2pm; closed Monday and public holidays and from 1 November to 10 December; 20F; ☎ 04 92 90 54 20.

ARBOIS
🛈 hôtel de ville – 39600 – ☎ 03 84 37 47 37

Maison de Pasteur – Guided tour (45min) from 1 June to 30 September at 9.30am, 10.30am, 11.30am, 1.45pm, 2.45pm, 3.45pm, and 4.45pm; the rest of the year at 10am, 11am, 2pm, 3pm and 4pm (except Thursday); closed 1 January, 14 February, 14 July, 15 August, 1 November and 14 December; 30F; ☎ 03 84 66 11 72.

ARCACHON
🛈 Esplanade Georges-Pompidou B.P. 42 – 33311 Cedex – ☎ 05 56 83 01 69

Bassin (bay) – U.B.A.(Union des Bateliers Arcachonnais) boats offer, in season, the Archachon-Cap Ferret crossing round trip (45F), a guided tour of oyster beds (50F), a tour of the Banc d'Arguin reserve (65F), fishing expeditions (65F), a tour of the littoral (70F); all year round, a tour of the Ile aux Oiseaux (65F); embarkation: Jetée Thiers and Jetée d'Eyrac (Arcachon), jetée Bélisaire (at Cap Ferret); for information, ☎ 05 56 54 60 32/83 01.

ARC-ET-SENANS

Saline royale – Open from 1 July to 31 August 9am to 7pm; from 1 April to 30 June and from 1 September to 1 November 9am to noon and 2pm to 6pm; 2 November to 31 December and from 1 January to 31 March 10pm to noon and 2pm to 5pm; 29F; ☎ 03 81 54 45 45.

ARLES ⓘ 35, Place de la République - 13200 - ☎ 04 90 18 41 20

A pass provides access to all the Arles sights: 55F. It can be purchased at any of the sights.

Guided tour of the town - Contact the tourist information office.

Théâtre antique - Open from 1 April to 30 September 9am to 7pm, the rest of the year 10am to 4.30pm; 15F.

Arènes, théâtre antique - Open from 1 April to 30 September 9am to 7pm, the rest of the year 10am to 4.30pm; closed 1 January, 1 November and 25 December; 15F.

Saline royale, Arc-et-Senans

Cryptoporticus - Open from 1 April to 30 September 9am to 7pm, the rest of the year 10am to 4.30pm; 12F.

Eglise St-Trophime: cloisters - Open from 1 April to 30 September 9am to 7pm, the rest of the year 10am to 4.30pm; 15F or 20F (during special exhibitions).

Museon Arlaten - Open 9am to noon and 2pm to 7.30pm (6pm in April, May, September and October, 5 pm the rest of the year); closed Monday from October to June as well as 1 January, 1 November and 25 December; 15F; ☎ 04 90 96 08 23.

Musée Réattu - Open from 1 April to 30 September 9am to noon and 2pm to 7pm, the rest of the year 10am to noon and 2pm to 4.30pm; 15F; a pass includes the visit to the Commanderie Ste-Luce; ☎ 04 90 49 37 58.

Palais Constantin - Open from 1 April to 30 September 9am to noon and 2pm to 7pm, the rest of the year 10am to noon and 2pm to 4.30pm; 12F.

Les Alyscamps - Open from 1 April to 30 September 9am to 7pm, the rest of the year 10am to 4.30pm; 12F.

ARRAS   ⓘ Hôtel de Ville, Place des Héros - 62000 - ☎ 03 21 51 26 95.

Guided tour of the town 🅰 - Contact the tourist information office.

Hôtel de ville - Open (lift) during the week 10am to noon and 2pm to 6pm; Sundays and public holidays 10am to noon and 3pm to 6pm; 10am to 6pm in July and August; closed 1 January and 25 December; ☎ 03 21 51 26 95.

Beffroi (bell tower) - Open during the week 10am to noon and 2pm to 6pm; Sundays and public holidays 10am to noon and 3pm (2.30pm in July and August) to 6.30pm; closed 1 January and 25 December; 13F; ☎ 03 21 51 26 95.

Musée des Beaux-Arts - Open during the week (except Tuesday) 10am to noon and 2pm to 6pm (5pm from 15 October to 31 March); Saturday 10am to noon and 2pm to 6pm; Sunday 10am to noon and 3pm to 6pm; closed 1 May; 14F; admission free the first Wednesday and the first Sunday of each month; ☎ 03 21 71 26 43.

AUBUSSON   ⓘ Rue Vieille - 23200 - ☎ 05 55 66 32 12.

Musée départemental de la Tapisserie - 🅰 Open daily (except Tuesday) from mid-June to mid-September 9am to 12.30pm and 2pm to 6.30pm; from mid-September to mid-June 9.30am to noon and 2pm to 6pm; closed 1 January and 25 December; 18F (summer), 12 F (the rest of the year); ☎ 05 55 66 33 06.

Exhibitions of tapestries and carpets - Open daily from July to September 2pm to 6pm; daily from November to June (except Sunday and Monday) 10am to noon and 2pm to 6pm; closed in October; admission free; ☎ 05 55 66 18 08.

AUCH   ⓘ 1, rue Dessoles - 32000 - ☎ 05 62 05 22 89

Choir-stalls - Open from 1 April to 30 September 8.30am to noon and 2pm to 6pm; the rest of the year 9.30 to noon and 2pm to 5pm; 6F.

Cathédrale Ste-Marie – Closed during the lunch hour. A recorded commentary in the entrance hall explains the building's characteristics. To visit the ambulatory and stained-glass windows, recording machines are available for 10F. An identity card must be left at the reception.

AUTUN
🛈 3, av. Charles de Gaulle - 71400 - ☎ 03 85 86 30 00

Guided Tour of the town 🖪 – Contact the tourist information office.

Cathédrale St-Lazare – Free tour possible daily from 8am to 7pm.

Musée Rolin – Open daily (except Tuesday) from 1 April to 30 September 9.30am to noon and 1.30pm to 6pm; in November and December and from 1 January to 31 March 10am to noon and 2pm to 4pm (5pm in October); out of season on Sunday open 2.30pm to 5pm only; closed for public holidays; 16F; ☎ 03 85 52 09 76.

AUXERRE
🛈 1, quai de la République - 89000 - ☎ 03 86 52 06 19

Abbaye St-Germain: abbey crypt – Open from 1 June to 31 October 10am to 6.30pm; for the rest of the year, 10am to noon and 2pm to 5.30pm; closed Tuesday, 1 January, Easter Monday and Pentecost, 1 and 8 May, 1 and 11 November, 25 December; 20F (ticket may also be used for the Musée Leblanc-Duvernoy); admission free on Wednesday; ☎ 03 86 51 09 74.

Cathédrale St-Étienne: treasury and crypt – Open daily (except Sunday morning) 9am to noon and 2pm to 6pm. In July and August closes at 7pm and an organ concert is held from 2pm to 3pm. Sound and light show from 1 July to 30 September 10pm to 11.15pm daily (25F); ☎ 03 86 52 23 29.

AVEN ARMAND

Guided tour (1 hour) from 1 June to 31 August from 9am to 7pm; from 15 March to 31 May as well as in September from 9am to noon and from 1.30pm to 6pm; from 1 October to 3 November, from 9am to noon and from 1.30pm to 5pm; 40F, children 20F; for a ticket that may also be used to visit Montpellier-le-Vieux: 50F, children 25F; ☎ 04 66 45 61 31.

AVIGNON
🛈 41 cours Jean-Jaurès - 84000 - ☎ 04 90 82 65 11

Guided tour of the town 🖪 – Contact the tourist information office.

Palais des Papes – Open 1 April to 2 November from 9am to 7pm (8pm from 21 August to 30 September); the rest of the year from 9am to 12.45pm and 2pm to 6pm; for the guided tour (1 hour 30min), request times and charges; last admission 45min before closing time; closed 1 January and 25 December; no guided tours 1 May; 42F or 53F (guided tour); ☎ 04 90 27 50 74.

Pont St-Bénézet – Open from 1 April to 30 September from 9am to 6.30pm; the rest of the year 9am to 1pm and 2pm to 5pm (except Monday); closed 1 January, 1 May, 14 July and 25 December; 10F or 28F with a multi-media show held in the Espace St-Bénézet next door; ☎ 04 90 85 60 16 (Avignon bridge) or ☎ 04 90 82 56 96 (multi-media show).

Musée du Petit Palais – Open daily (except Tuesday) in July and August 10.30am to 6pm, the rest of the year 9.30am to noon and 2pm to 6pm; closed 1 January, 1 May, 14 July, 1 November and 25 December; 18F, free admission on Sunday from 1 October to 1 March; ☎ 04 90 86 44 58.

Cathédrale N.-D-des-Doms – Treasure open 9am to noon and 2pm to 7pm from Easter to All Saints Day.

Musée Calvet – Closed for restoration and reorganization of the collections.

Musée Louis-Vouland – Open daily (except Monday) from 1 June to 30 September 10am to noon and 2pm to 6pm; the rest of the year 2pm to 6pm; closed Sunday and during public holidays; 20F; ☎ 04 90 86 03 79.

Musée lapidaire – Open 10am to noon and 2pm to 6pm; closed Tuesday; ☎ 04 90 86 33 84.

AZAY-LE-RIDEAU

Château – Free tour or guided tour (1 hour) from 1 July to 31 August 9am to 7pm; from 1 April to 30 June and in September 9.30am to 6pm; the rest of the year 9.30am to 12.30pm and 2pm to 5.30pm; closed 1 January, 1 May, 1 and 11 November and 25 December; 32F; ☎ 02 47 45 26 61.

B

BARBIZON

Auberge du père Ganne – Open daily (except Tuesday) from 1 April to 30 September 10am to 12.30pm and 2pm to 6pm Monday to Friday; 10am to 6pm on the weekend and public holidays; closes at 5pm the rest of the year; 25F; ☎ 03 60 66 22 27.

Musée de l'école de Barbizon – Open from Monday to Friday 10am to 12.30pm and 2pm to 5.30pm, on the weekend and public holidays 10am to 5.30pm; closed Tuesday; 20F: ☎ 03 60 66 22 38.

BARCELONNETTE
🚹 Place Fréderic-Mistral - 04400 - ☎ 04 92 81 04 71

Villa de la Sapinière, musée de la vallée – Open from the beginning of July to the beginning of September daily 10am to noon and 3pm to 7pm, the rest of the year on Wednesday, Thursday and Saturday 3pm to 6pm; closed 1 January and 25 December 18F; ☎ 04 92 81 27 15.

Les BAUX-DE-PROVENCE
🚹 30 Grande Rue - 13520 - ☎ 04 90 54 34 39

Château (Musée d'Histoire des Baux) – Open from 1 March to 1 November 8am to 7.30pm (9pm in summer); the rest of the year 9am to 6pm; 32F, with access to the citadel; ☎ 04 90 54 55 56.

Cathédrale d'image – Open from February to September 10am to 7pm, from October to November 10am to 6pm, in January and December from 1.30pm to 5.30pm; closed from mid-November to beginning December and during the second half of January; 40F; children 25F; ☎ 04 90 54 38 65.

Musée Yves-Brayer – Open daily (except Tuesday from 1 October to 31 March) 10am to 12.30pm and 2pm to 5.30pm; closed from beginning January to mid-February; 20F; ☎ 04 90 54 36 99.

BAYEUX
🚹 Pont St-Jean - 14403 - ☎ 02 31 92 16 26

A pass may be purchased for 50F that provides access to all four museums (Bayeux tapestry, Musée mémorial 1944, Musée Baron-Gérard, musée d'Art religieux).

Tapisserie de la Reine Mathilde – Open from 1 May to 16 September and during Easter and Ascension weekends 9am to 7pm; the rest of the year 9am to 12.30pm and 2pm to 6.30pm (6pm from 16 October to 15 March); closed 25 and 26 (morning) December, 1 and 2 January (morning); 33F; ☎ 02 31 92 05 48.

Musée mémorial de la Bataille de Normandie – 1944 – &. Open in June, July and August 9am to 7pm; from 16 March to 31 May and from 1 September to 15 October 9.30pm to 12.30pm and 2pm to 6.30pm; the rest of the year 10am to 12.30pm and 2pm to 6pm; 28F; children 12F; ☎ 02 31 92 93 41.

Musée Baron Gérard – Open from 1 June to 15 September 9am to 7pm; from 16 September to 31 May 10am to 12.30pm and 2pm to 6pm; closed 25 December and 1 January; 19F; ☎ 02 31 92 14 21.

BAYONNE
🚹 1 place de la Liberté - 64100 - ☎ 05 59 46 01 46

Guided tour of the town 🅰 – Contact the tourist information office.

Musée Bonnat – Open daily (except Tuesday) 10am to noon and 2.30pm to 6.30pm (20.30pm on Fridays); closed for public holidays; 15F; ☎ 05 59 59 08 52.

Musée Basque – Closed for restoration; ☎ 05 59 59 08 98.

BEAULIEU-SUR-DORDOGNE
🚹 6 place Marbot - 19120 - ☎ 05 55 91 09 94

Église St-Pierre: treasury – For a guided tour on Tuesday during the summer, contact the tourist information office.

BEAUNE
🚹 rue de l'Hôtel de Ville - 21200 - ☎ 03 80 26 21 30

Guided tour of the city 🅰 – Contact the tourist information office.

Hôtel-Dieu – Open daily from 8 April to 19 November 9am to 6.30pm, the rest of the year 9am to 11.30am and 2pm to 5.30pm; 29F; ☎ 03 80 24 45 00.

Musée du vin de Bourgogne – Open daily 9.30am to 5.30pm; closed Tuesday from 1 December to 30 March as well as 1 January and 25 December; 20F; ☎ 03 80 22 08 19.

BEAUVAIS
🚹 1, rue Beauregard - 60000 - ☎ 03 44 45 08 18

Guided tour of the city 🅰 – Contact the tourist information office.

Cathédrale St-Pierre: astronomical clock – Guided tour (25min) at 10.40am (except Sunday from 11 May to 1 November), 2.40pm, 3.40pm, and 4.40pm; 22F; ☎ 03 44 48 11 60.

Musée départemental de l'Oise – Open daily (except Tuesday) 10am to noon and 2pm to 6pm; closed 1 January, Easter Monday and Whitsun, 1 May and 25 December; 16F, free on Wednesday; ☎ 03 44 48 48 88.

Abbaye du BEC-HELLOUIN

Open daily except for Tuesday. For guided tours (45min), from 1 June to 30 September, starting 10am, 11am, 3pm, 4pm and 5pm (on Saturdays the 5pm tour is not held); Sundays and public holidays the tours begin at noon; from 1 October to end May tours at 11am, 3.15pm and 4.30pm during the week and at noon, 3pm and 4pm on Sunday; 21F; ☎ 02 32 44 86 09; concerts are held several times per year. Contact the abbey for information.

BELFORT   🖪 Place de la Commune - 90000 - ☎ 03 84 28 12 23

Le Lion – Open daily from July to end September 8am to 7pm; in May and June 8am to noon and 2pm to 7pm (6pm in April and October); from 1 November to 31 March 10am to noon (8am during the weekend and public holidays) and 2pm to 5pm; 3F; ☎ 03 84 28 52 96.

Le Camp Retranché – Guided tour (1 hour) from June to September. Out of season, by appointment on Saturday and Sunday if weather permits; closed 1 January, 1 November and 25 December; 10F; ☎ 03 84 28 52 96.

BELLE-ÎLE   🖪 Quai Bonnelle, le Palais - 56360 - ☎ 02 97 31 81 93

Cars, bicycles, tandems and small motorcycles may be rented at the Palais.

Citadelle le Vauban – ♿ Open from 1 July to 31 August 9am to 7pm; from 1 April to 30 June and from 1 September to 31 October 9am to 6pm; the rest of the year 9.30am to noon and 2pm to 5pm; 28F; ☎ 02 97 31 84 17.

BESANÇON   🖪 place de l'Armée Française - 25000 - ☎ 03 81 80 92 55

Guided tour of the city 🅰 – Contact the tourist information office.

Horloge astronomique – Guided tour (30min) at 9.50am, 10.50am, 11.50am, 2.50pm, 3.50pm, 4.50pm and 5.50pm; closed Tuesday and Wednesday from 1 October to 31 March, on Tuesday only from 1 April to 30 September, and on 1 January, 1 May, 1 and 11 November, 25 December, and the month of January; 14F; ☎ 03 81 81 12 76.

Musée des Beaux-Arts – Open 9.30am to noon and 2pm to 6pm; closed on Tuesday, 1 January, 1 May, 1 November and 25 December; 21F; free admission on Sunday and holidays; ☎ 03 81 81 44 47.

Musée de la Citadelle – Open from 1 April to 30 September 9.15am to 6.15pm; the rest of the year 9.45am to 4.45pm; closed 1 January and 25 December; 40F (ticket valid for all four museums in the citadel); ☎ 03 81 65 07 50.

Musée comtois, musée agraire – Same admission times and charges as the citadel; closed on Tuesdays.

Musée d'Histoire naturelle – Same admission times and charges as the citadel; closed on Tuesday (except for the zoo and the aquarium).

Musée de la Résistance et de la Déportation, musée d'Histoire naturelle – Same admission times and charges as the citadel; closed on Tuesdays.

Bibliothèque municipale – Guided tour (1 hour) daily (except Sunday) 9am to noon and 1.30pm to 6pm (2pm during school vacations); closed 1 to 8 July; admission free; ☎ 03 81 81 20 89.

Grottes de BÉTHARRAM

Guided tour (1hour 30min) from Palm Sunday to mid-October 8.30am to noon and 1.30pm to 5.30pm; in July and August, due to the large numbers of tourists, it is advised to take the tour in the morning; 48F; children under 10, 24F; ☎ 05 62 41 80 04.

BEYNAC-ET-CAZENAC   🖪 La Balme - 24200 - ☎ 05 53 29 43 08

Château – Free tour (from noon to 2pm) or guided tour (50min) daily from March to November 10am to 6pm; from December to February 1pm to 6pm; 30F; ☎ 05 53 29 50 40.

BITCHE   🖪 Hôtel de Ville - Porte de Strasbourg - 57230 - ☎ 03 87 06 16 16

Citadelle – Tour (with infrared earphones, 2 hours) daily from 1 March to 15 November 9am to 5pm (6pm in July and August); adults 35F, children 20F; Tourist information office ☎ 03 87 06 16 16.

BITCHE

Fort du Simserhof – Guided tour (1 hour 40min) by written request – contact the tourist information office for the Bitche region, B.P. 47, 57232 Bitche Cedex, ☏ 03 87 06 16 16; closed Monday; adults 35F, children 20F; wear warm clothing.

BLOIS
🖪 pavillon Anne-de-Bretagne, 3 avenue J-Laigret – 41000 – ☏ 02 54 74 06 49

Guided tour of the city 🔺 – Contact the tourist information office. ☏ 02 54 78 16 06.

Château – Free or guided tours (1 hour) from 15 March to 15 October daily from 9am to 6.30pm (8pm from 15 June to 31 August); the rest of the year from 9am to 12.30pm and from 2pm to 5.30pm; closed 1 January and 25 December; 32 F (the ticket provides access to the Cloître St-Saturnin and the archeological museum); ☏ 02 54 74 16 06.

Hôtel d'Alluye: galleries – Tour by appointment, call ☏ 02 54 56 38 00.

Château de BONAGUIL

Guided tour (1 hour 30min) daily from June to August 10am to 5.30pm; during school holidays from February to May and from September to November 10.30am to noon and 2.30 to 4.30; closed in December and January; 25F: ☏ 05 53 71 39 75.

BONIFACIO
🖪 Place de l'Europe – 20169 – ☏ 04 95 73 11 88

Église Saint-Dominique – Guided tour (30min) from 1 July to 31 August; 10F; at other times, contact the tourist information office.

BORDEAUX
🖪 12 cours du XXX juillet – 33080 – ☏ 05 56 00 66 00
🖪 gare St-Jean (arrival platform) – 33000 – ☏ 05 56 91 64 70
🖪 Bordeaux-Mérignac airport (arrival hall) – 33700 – ☏ 05 56 34 39 39

Guided tour of the city 🔺 – Guided tours by theme and by district are organised by the tourist information office. They also offer tours of the vineyards. Contact one of the reception areas mentioned above.

Basilique St-Michel – Open from 8.30am to 6pm, Sunday until 11am.

Grand Théâtre – Guided tour (1 hour) depending on rehearsal schedule; 25F; ☏ 05 56 44 28 41.

Musée des Beaux-Arts – Open daily (except Tuesday) 10am to 6pm; closed for public holidays; 18F; admission free on Wednesday; ☏ 05 56 10 16 93.

Musée d'Aquitaine – ♿ Open daily (except Monday) 10am to 6pm; closed for public holidays; 18F; admission free on Wednesday; bookstore; ☏ 05 56 01 51 00.

Musée d'Art contemporain (Entrepôt Lainé) – Open daily noon to 7pm (10pm on Wednesday); closed Monday, 1 January, 1 May and 25 December; 30F – the ticket also provides access to the "Arc en rêve" architecture centre; admission free between noon and 2pm; the bookstore and the library are open daily (except Monday) from noon to 7pm; the café on the terrace is open during the same times as the museum; ☏ 05 56 44 16 35.

Croiseur Colbert – Open from 1 April to 30 September 10am to 6pm (7pm on Saturday, Sunday and holidays); the rest of the year, daily (except Monday) during the week 2pm to 6pm, Saturday, Sunday and holidays 10am to 7pm; closed 1 January and 25 December; 42F; ☏ 05 56 44 96 11.

Village des BORIES

Tour from 9am to sunset; 25F; ☏ 04 90 72 03 48.

Musée des Tumulus de BOUGON

♿ Free or guided tour (2 hours) daily (except Wednesday morning) during July and August 10am to 7pm (8pm during the weekend and holidays); the rest of the year 10am to 6pm; closed 25 December and in January; 25F; ☏ 05 49 05 12 13.

BOULOGNE-SUR-MER
🖪 quai de la Poste – 62200 – ☏ 03 21 31 68 38

Guided tour of the town 🔺 – Contact Mme Soubit at the Château-Musée.

Basilique Notre-Dame: the crypt and the treasury – Open daily (except Monday) 2pm to 5pm; 10F; ☏ 03 21 92 43 54.

Colonne de la Grande Armée – Open from April to September 9am to noon and from 2pm to 7pm (6pm on Monday); the rest of the year 9am to noon and 2pm to 5pm; closed Tuesday and Wednesday; 20F; ☏ 03 21 80 43 69.

Musée Château – Open from 15 May to 15 September 9.30am to 12.30pm and 1.30pm to 6.15pm (Sunday 9.30am to 12.30pm and 2.30pm to 6.15pm); the rest of the year 10am to 12.30pm and 2pm to 5pm (Sunday 10am to 12.30pm and 2.30pm to 5.30pm). Closed Tuesday and 1 January, 1 May and 25 December; 20F; ☎ 03 21 10 02 20.

Nausicaa – ⅙ Open from 1 June to 14 September 10am to 8pm; the rest of the year 10am to 6pm during the week, until 7pm on Saturday, Sunday and holidays and during school holidays of Zone B; adults 50F, children 35F; ☎ 03 21 30 98 98.

BOURG-EN-BRESSE 🖰 6, Av. Alsace-Lorraine – 01005 – ☎ 04 74 22 49 40

Guided tour of the city 🄰 – Contact the tourist information office.

Église de Brou – Open from 1 April to 30 September 9am to 12.30pm and 2pm to 6.30pm; the rest of the year 9am to 12pm and 2pm to 5pm; closed 1 January, 1 May, 1 and 11 November, 25 December; ☎ 04 74 22 26 55.

Musée – Open from 1 April to 30 September 9am to 12.30 pm and 2pm to 7pm; the rest of the year 9am to noon and 2pm to 5pm; closed 1 January, 1 May, 1 and 11 November and 25 December; 12F; ☎ 04 74 45 39 00.

BOURGES 🖰 21 rue Victor-Hugo (near the cathedral) B.P. 145 – 18003 – ☎ 02 48 24 75 33

Guided tour of the city 🄰 – Contact the tourist information office.

Cathédrale St-Étienne: Tour of the north tower of the cathedral – Open daily from 8am to 6pm; lighting of the nave 10F (under the organ-case to the left); ☎ 02 48 65 49 44.

Crypt – Guided tour (35min) daily (except Sunday morning) from April to October 9am to noon and 2pm to 6pm (5pm from November to March); closed 1 January, 1 May, 1 and 11 November, 25 December; 27F (ticket includes climbing the north tower).

Palais Jacques-Cœur – Guided tour (45min) daily from April to October 9am to noon and 2pm to 6pm; from November to March 9am to noon and 2pm to 5pm; closed 1 January, 1 May, 1 and 11 November, 25 December; 27F; ☎ 02 48 24 06 87.

Musée du Berry (Hôtel Cujas) – Free or guided tour (1 hour 30min) daily (except Tuesday and Sunday morning) 10am to noon and 2pm to 6pm; closed 1 January, 1 May, 1 and 11 November, 25 December; 18F (admission free on Wednesday); ☎ 02 48 57 81 15.

Musée des Arts décoratifs (Hôtel Lallemant) – Free or guided tour (1 hour) daily (except Monday and Sunday morning) 10am to noon and 2pm to 6pm; closed 1 January, 1 May, 1 and 11 November, 25 December; 18F (admission free on Sunday); ☎ 02 48 57 81 17.

Musée Maurice-Éstève (Hôtel des Échevins) – Free or guided tour (1 hour) daily (except for Tuesday and Sunday morning) 10am to noon and

Hurdy-gurdy player

2pm to 6pm; 18F (free on Sunday); closed 1 January, 1 May, 1 and 11 November, 25 December; ☎ 48 24 75 38.

BRANTÔME 🖰 Pavillon Renaissance – 24310 – ☎ 05 53 05 80 52

Bell-tower – Guided tour (1 hour) daily (except Sunday morning) in July and August 10am to 7pm; daily (except Tuesday and Sunday morning) from April to June 10am to noon and 2pm to 6pm; 20F; ☎ 05 53 05 80 63.

Château de la BRÈDE

Guided tour (30min) daily (except Tuesday) from 1 July to 1 October 2pm to 6pm; Saturday, Sunday and holidays 2pm to 6pm from beginning April to end of June; from beginning October to 11 November on Saturday, Sunday and holidays only 2pm to 5.30pm; closed 12 November to 31 March; 30F.

BREST

🛈 Place de la Liberté - 29200 - ☎ 02 98 44 24 96

Musée des Beaux-Arts – Open 10am to 11.45am and 2pm to 6pm; closed Sunday morning, Tuesday and holidays; admission free; ☎ 02 98 44 66 27.

Oceanopolis – ♿ Open all year round daily 9.30am to 7pm (6pm from 1 October to 14 April during the week); closed Monday morning off-season (except for short school holidays); 50F from 15 June to 30 September; 47F the rest of the year; ☎ 02 98 34 40 40.

BRIANÇON

🛈 la Citadelle - 05100 - ☎ 04 92 21 08 50

The tourist information office in Briançon offers a pass that includes the Porte Pignerol, exhibitions in the Chapelle des Récollets and the Eglise des Cordeliers, the château fort and the fort des Salettes; ☎ 04 92 21 08 50.

Guided tour of the city 🅰 – Contact the "Animation du patrimoine" centre, Porte Pignerol; ☎ 04 92 21 08 50.

Citadelle – Guided tour (45mn) of the upper part of the fortress only from 3 July to 27 August 10am to noon and 1.30pm to 6pm; closed the rest of the year; 15 F. ☎ 04 92 20 29 49.

C

CAEN

🛈 Hôtel d'Escoville, place St-Pierre - 14300 - ☎ 02 31 27 14 14

Guided tour of the city 🅰 – In July and August tours on foot or by a small train are offered daily at 2.45pm; from 1 July to 31 August on Tuesday (Mathilde) and Friday (Guillaume), evening tour at 9.30pm; Monday and Thursday, lecture-tours. Contact the tourist information office.

Musée des Beaux-Arts – ♿ Free or guided tour (1 hour) all year from 10am to 6pm; closed Tuesday, 1 January, Easter Sunday, 1 May, Ascension, 11 November and 25 December; 25F, free on Wednesday; ☎ 02 31 85 28 63.

Musée de Normandie – Open 1 April to 30 September daily 10am to 12.30pm and 1.30pm to 6pm; Saturday, Sunday and Monday 9.30am to 12.30pm and 2pm to 6pm; the rest of the year 9.30am to 12.30pm and 2pm to 6pm; closed Tuesday as well as 1 January, 1 November and 25 December; 10F; admission free on Wednesday; ☎ 02 31 86 06 24.

Mémorial: un musée pour la Paix – ♿ Open from beginning July to 31 August 9am to 9pm; the rest of the year 9am to 7pm (6pm during winter); closed from 1-15 January as well as 19 March and 25 December; last admission 1 hour 15min before closing time; 61F; Research and Documentation Centre, playground, money exchange; ☎ 02 31 06 06 44.

Église de la Trinité – Open daily 9am to 6pm, except during church services; ☎ 02 31 95 21 49.

CAHORS

🛈 Place Aristide Briand - 46000 - ☎ 05 65 35 09 56

Guided tour of the city 🅰 – Contact the tourist information office.

Pont Valentré – Open daily during July and August 10 am to noon and 2.30pm to 6pm; 12F; ☎ 05 65 35 09 56.

CALAIS

🛈 12, boulevard Clemenceau - 65100 - ☎ 03 21 96 62 40

Musée des Beaux Arts et de la Dentelle – ♿ Open daily 10am to noon and 2pm to 5.30pm; closed Tuesdays and 1 January, 1 May, 14 July, 15 August, 1 November and 25 December; 15F; admission free on Wednesday; ☎ 03 21 46 62 00, ext. 6317.

La CAMARGUE

Musée Camarguais – Open in July and August, 9.15am to 6.45pm; from 1 April to 30 June and in September, 9.15am to 5.45pm; the rest of the year, 10.15am to 4.45pm; closed Tuesday from 1 October to 31 March and 1 January, 1 May and 25 December; 25F; ☎ 04 90 97 10 82.

Centre d'information de Camargue – Free admission to the exhibition hall, to the panoramic hall and the information bank, daily from 1 April to 30 September 9am to 6pm; the rest of the year daily (except Friday) 9.30am to 5pm; closed 1 January, 1 May and 25 December; for films shown on the first floor, a contribution of 5F is requested per person and per film; information leaflets available in the center; ☎ 04 90 97 86 32.

CAMBRAI

🛈 48, rue de Noyon - 59400 - ☎ 03 27 78 26 90

Guided tour of the city 🅰 – Contact the tourist information office.

Église de la CANONICA

Restoration work in progress; to visit apply to the mairie in Lucciana; ☎ 04 95 36 00 47.

CARCASSONNE   🖪 15 bd Camille-Pelletan - 11000 - ☎ 04 68 25 07 04

Château Comtal – Open in July and August 9am to 7.30pm; from June to September 9am to 7pm; in April and May 9.30am to 12.30pm and 2pm to 6pm; in October 10am to noon and 2pm to 6pm; the rest of the year 10am to noon and 2pm to 5pm; closed 1 January, 1 May, 1 and 11 November, 25 December; tickets are no longer sold 30min prior to closing time; 27F; ☎ 04 68 72 63 81.

CARNAC   🖪 Avenue des Druides - 56340 - ☎ 02 97 52 13 52

Musée de Préhistoire J.-Miln-Z.-Le-Rouzic – ♿ Open 1 July to 31 August 10am to 6.30pm; from 2 January to 30 June and from 1 September to 31 December 10am to noon and 2pm to 5pm (6pm in June and September); closed Wednesday as well as 1 January, 1 May and 25 December; 32F; ☎ 02 97 52 22 04.

Tumulus St-Michel – Guided tour (15min) from 1 July to 31 August 9.30am to 7.30pm; from 16-30 June and 1-15 September 10am to 6pm; from 20 April to 15 June and from 16-30 September 10am to noon and 3pm to 6pm; closed 1 May; 6F50; ☎ 02 97 52 06 86.

CARPENTRAS   🖪 170 allée Jean-Jaurès - 84200 - ☎ 04 90 63 00 78

Guided tour of the city 🖾 – Contact the tourist information office.

CASTRES   🖪 3 rue Milhau Ducommun - 81100 - ☎ 05 63 35 26 26
🖪 33 place Soult (15 May-15 September) - 81100 - ☎ 05 63 51 20 37

Musée Goya – Open daily in July and August 9am (10am on Sunday and holidays) to noon and 2pm to 6pm; from 1 April to 30 June and from 1-21 September daily except Monday at the same times; daily except Monday the rest of the year 9am (10am on Sunday and holidays) to noon and 2pm to 5pm; closed 1 January, 1 May, 1 November and 25 December; 20F in July and August, otherwise 15F; ☎ 05 63 71 59 30.

La CHAISE-DIEU

Abbaye – Open daily from 1 June to 30 September 9am to noon and 2pm to 7pm; from 1 October to 31 May, tour 10am to noon and 2pm to 5pm; ☎ 04 71 00 06 06 (Abbaye reception area).

CHÂLONS-EN-CHAMPAGNE   🖪 3, Quai des Arts - 51000 - ☎ 03 26 65 17 89

Guided tour of the city 🖾 – Contact the tourist information office.

Église Notre-Dame-en-Vaux – Closed Sunday except for services.

Musée du cloître de Notre-Dame-en-Vaux – Open daily (except Tuesday) 10am to noon and 2pm to 6pm (5pm from 1 October to 31 March from Monday to Friday); closed 1 January, 1 May, 1 and 11 November and 25 December; 21F; ☎ 03 26 64 03 87.

CHALON-SUR-SAÔNE   🖪 Boulevard de la République - 71100 - ☎ 03 85 48 37 97

Guided tour of the city 🖾 – Contact the tourist information office.

Musée Nicéphore Niepce – Open daily (except Tuesday) in July and August 10am to 6pm; the rest of the year 9.30am to 11.30am and 2.30pm to 5.30pm; closed for public holidays; 10F (admission free on Wednesday); ☎ 03 85 48 41 98.

Musée Denon – Open daily 9.30am to noon and 2pm to 5.30pm; closed Tuesday and holidays; 10F (free on Wednesday); ☎ 03 85 48 01 70 (ext. 4237).

CHAMBÉRY   🖪 24, bd. de la Colonne - 73000 - ☎ 04 79 33 42 47

Guided tour of the town 🖾 – Contact the tourist information office. Departure from the guide office, place du château.

Château – Guided tour (1 hour 30min): in July and August, daily (except Sunday morning) at 10.30am, 2.30pm, 3.30pm, 4.30pm and 5.30pm; in May, June and September, daily at 2.30pm and 4pm; in April and October, Saturday, Sunday and holidays at 2.30pm and 4pm; the rest of the year, Saturday, Sunday and holidays at 2.30pm (except 25 December and 1 January); tours start from the Treasury Tower; 25F; ☎ 04 79 33 42 47.

Les Charmettes – Open 10am to noon and 2pm to 6pm (4.30pm from 1 October to 31 March); closed Tuesday and holidays; 10F; ticket also provides access to the Musée Savoisien and the Musée des Beaux-Arts; 20F; ☎ 04 79 33 39 44.

Musée Savoisien – Open from 10am to noon and from 2pm to 6pm (except Tuesday and holidays); 20F; ticket can include other sights (see Les Charmettes); ☎ 04 79 33 44 48.

Château de CHAMBORD

Open in July and August 9.30am to 7.15pm; from 16-30 June and 1-10 September, 9.30am to 6.15pm; the rest of the year 9.30am to 12.15pm and 2pm to 6.15pm (5.15pm from 2 January to 31 March and from 1 October to 31 December). Last admission 30min before closing time; closed 1 January, 1 May, 1 and 11 November, 25 December; 35F; ☎ 02 54 20 31 32 or 02 54 50 40 18; lecture-tours by appointment.

CHAMONIX-MONT-BLANC ▐ Place Triangle de l'Amitié - 74400 - ☎ 04 50 53 00 24

Téléphérique de l'Aiguille du Midi – The trip is divided into two sections: Chamonix – Plan de l'aiguille and Plan de l'aiguille – Aiguille du Midi; departure every 30min, from 8am to 3.45pm; in July and August from 6am to 5pm; closed from mid-November to 10 December; length of round trip with a panoramic stop: 1 hour 30min; price for both sections round-trip: 170F, 180F in July and August; ☎ 04 50 53 30 80.

Télécabine de la Vallée Blanche – This cablecar service connects the Aiguille du Midi with the Pointe Helbronner and provides a connection to Italy. When weather conditions permit, the cablecar runs from 9am to 3pm in April, May, June and September; from 8am to 4.30pm in July and August; duration of round-trip with panoramic stop: 3 hours; round-trip price from Chamonix: 244F, 264F in July and August (half-price for children under 12); ☎ 04 50 53 30 80.

Télécabine et Téléphérique du Brévent – Runs all year except from mid-May to mid-June and beginning October to mid-January; length of the Chamonix-Planpraz trip by cablecar: 10min; Planpraz-Brévent by cable railway: 10min; 74F round trip; ☎ 04 50 53 13 18.

Téléphérique des Praz à la Flégère – Runs during the summer season from mid-June to mid-August 8am to 12.30pm and 1.30pm to 4.30pm (no pause at noon in July and August); length of trip: 12min; summer rate 95F round trip; La Fléchère: 50F round trip; ☎ 04 50 53 18 58.

CHAMPIGNY-SUR-VEUDE

Sainte-Chapelle – Open 1 April to 1 October 10am to noon and 2pm to 6pm; closed Tuesday; 16F; ☎ 02 47 95 71 46.

Château de CHAMPS

Open from 1 April to 30 September 10am to noon and 1.30pm to 5.30pm (6pm on Saturday, Sunday and holidays); the rest of the year open 10am to noon and 1.30pm to 4.30pm; closed Tuesday, 1 January, 1 May, 1 and 11 November and 25 December; 27F; ☎ 03 60 05 24 43.

Château de CHANTILLY

Château – Open daily from 1 March to 31 October (except Tuesday) 10am to 6pm; the rest of the year 10.30am to 12.45pm and 2pm to 5pm; 37F; ☎ 01 44 57 08 00.

Musée vivant du Cheval et du Poney – Open from 1 April to 31 October 10.30am to 5.30pm (6pm on Saturday, Sunday and holidays); from 1 November to 31 March 2pm to 4.30pm (10.30am to 5.30pm Saturday, Sunday and holidays); closed 1 January, 25 December, Tuesday (except in May and June) and Tuesday morning in July and August; 45F (50F on the weekend); ☎ 01 44 57 13 13.

Jardin anglais – ♿ Open daily from 1 March to 31 October 10am to 6pm; the rest of the year 10.30am to 12.45pm and 2pm to 5pm; 17F; ☎ 01 44 57 08 00.

Jardin anglais – Same admission times and charges as the park.

CHARTRES ▐ Place de la Cathédrale - 28000 - ☎ 02 37 21 50 00

Musée des Beaux-Arts – Open daily from 1 April to 31 October 10am to 6pm; from 1 November to 31 March 10am to noon and 2pm to 6pm (2pm to 5pm only on Sunday); closed 1 January, 1 and 8 May, 1 and 11 November and 25 December; 10F; ☎ 02 37 36 41 39.

Cathédrale Notre-Dame: inspection gallery – Open from 1 April to 30 September 9.30am to 11.30pm and 2pm to 5.30pm (5.15 on Saturday); March and October 10am to 11.30pm and 2pm to 4.30pm; from 1 November to 28 February 10am to 11.30am and 2pm to 4pm; closed 1 January, 1 May, 1 and 11 November and 25 December; 14F; ☎ 02 37 36 08 80.

CHÂTILLON-SUR-SEINE

The treasure of Vix – Open 16 June to 15 September 9am to noon and 1.30pm to 6pm; 1 April to 15 June and 16 September to 15 November 9am to noon and 2pm to 6pm; 16 November to 31 March 10am to noon and 2pm to 5pm; closed Tuesday from 16 September to 15 June, 1 January, 1 May and 25 December; 25F; ☎ 03 80 91 24 67.

Château de CHAVANIAC-LAFAYETTE

Guided tour (1 hour) from April to mid-November 9am to 11.30am and 2pm to 6pm; the rest of the year by appointment; 25F (château and park); 10F (park is free); ☎ 04 71 77 50 32.

Château de CHENONCEAU

Open daily from 16 March to 15 September 9.30am to 7pm; in the off-season the château closes at 6.30pm, then at 6pm, and during the winter at 5.30pm, 5pm or 4.30pm depending on the period; 40F; restaurant at the château. In July and August: boat trips on the Cher river, small electric train, outdoor playground for children (from April to October); ☎ 02 47 23 90 07.

CHERBOURG   🛈 2, quai Alexandre III - 50100 - ☎ 02 33 93 52 02

Musée de la Libération - Open from 1 April to 30 September 10am to 6pm daily; the rest of the year from 9.30am to noon and from 2pm to 5.30pm, except Monday; 20F; ☎ 02 33 20 14 12.

Château de CHEVERNY

May be visited all year, from 1 June to 15 September 9.15am to 6.45pm; the rest of the year 9.30am (9.15 in April and May) to noon and 2.15pm to 6.30pm (6pm from 16-30 September, 5.30pm in March and October); guided tour with written request to Château de Cheverny, 41700 Cheverny. Visitors can watch the dogs being fed from 1 April to 15 September at 5pm except Saturday, Sunday and holidays; the rest of the year at 3pm, except Tuesday, Saturday, Sunday and holidays; 31F; ☎ 02 54 79 96 29.

CHINON   🛈 12, rue Voltaire - 37500 - ☎ 02 47 93 17 85

A small tourist train gives a guided tour (40min) with historical comments; daily from 1 July to 31 August; Easter Saturday and Sunday to 30 June and 1 September to 30 September; tour starts every 45min between 2.30pm and 7pm at the Hôtel de ville; 22F, children 18F; ☎ 02 47 22 51 91.

Château - Open daily from 15 March to 30 September 9am to 6pm (7pm in July and August); October 9am to 5pm; the rest of the year 9am to noon and 2pm to 5pm; closed Wednesday in January and December, 1 January and 25 December; 23F; ☎ 02 47 93 13 45.

Grotte de CLAMOUSE

Guided tour (45min) in July and August 10am to 8pm (last tour at 7pm); the rest of the year noon to 6pm (last tour at 5pm); 40F, children 19F; bar open all year, snack bar open in July and August only; ☎ 04 67 57 71 05.

CLERMONT-FERRAND   🛈 69, boulevard Gergovia - 63038 - ☎ 04 73 93 30 20

Guided tour of the town 🅰 - Contact the tourist information office.

Cathédrale N.-D.-de-l'Assomption - Free tour daily 8am to noon and 2pm to 6pm during the week; Sundays 3pm to 6.30pm.

Musée des Beaux-Arts - ♿ Open daily (except Monday) from 10am to 6pm; closed 1 January, 1 May, 1 November and 25 December; 21F; ☎ 04 73 23 08 49.

CLUNY   🛈 6, rue Mercière - 71250 - ☎ 03 85 59 05 34

Abbaye - Free or guided tour (1 hour 15min) from 1 April to 30 June 9.30am to noon and 2pm to 6pm; July, August and September 9am to 7pm; in October 9.30am to noon and 2pm to 5pm; from 1 November to 31 March 10.30am to 11.30am and 2pm to 4pm; closed 1 January, 1 May, 1 and 11 November and 25 December; 26F; ☎ 03 85 59 12 79.

PARIS-BORDEAUX 1895   1ᵉ VOITURE sur PNEUS MICHELIN

MICHELIN

Musée Ochier - Open daily from 1 July to 23 September 9am to 7pm; 1 April to 30 June and 24-30 September 9.30am to noon and 2pm to 6pm (5pm in October); in November 10am to noon and 2pm to 4pm; from 1 December to 15 February 10am to 11.30am and 2pm to 4pm; from 16 February to 25 March 10am to noon and 2pm to 4.30pm; closed 1 January, 1 May, 1 and 11 November, 25 December; 14F; ☎ 03 85 59 23 97.

COGNAC

🛈 16, rue du 14-juillet - 16100 - ☎ 05 45 82 10 71

Musée municipal – Open daily (except Tuesday) from June to September 10am to noon and 2pm to 6pm; the rest of the year 2pm to 5.30pm; closed 1 January, 1 and 8 May, 14 July, 15 August, 1 and 11 November, 25 December; 12F; ☎ 05 45 32 07 25.

COLMAR

🛈 4 rue Unterlinden - 68000 - ☎ 03 89 20 68 92

Musée d'Unterlinden – Open 1 April to 31 October 9am to 6pm; 1 November to 31 March except Tuesday 9am to noon and 2pm to 5pm; closed 1 January, 1 May, 1 November, 25 December; 28F; ☎ 03 89 20 15 50.

Église des Dominicains – Open end March to end December 10am to 6pm; 8F; ☎ 03 89 41 27 20.

Eglise St-Matthieu – Open during spring school holidays, May public holidays, daily from 15 June to 15 October 10am to noon and 3pm to 5pm; ☎ 03 89 41 44 96.

COLOMBEY-LES-DEUX-ÉGLISES

La Boisserie – Open daily (except Tuesday) from 10am to noon and 2pm to 5pm; closed 25 December and in January; 18F; ☎ 03 25 01 52 52.

COMPIÈGNE

🛈 place de l'Hôtel-de-Ville - 60200 - ☎ 03 44 40 01 00

Guided tour of the town 🄰 – Contact the tourist information office.

Palace:

Historic apartments – Guided tour (45min) or a guide (1 hour 30min) daily (except Tuesday) from 1 April to 30 September 9.15am to 6.15pm (no tickets sold after 5.30pm); the rest of the year 9.15am to 4.30pm (no tickets sold after 3.15pm); closed 1 January, 1 May, and 25 December; 31F; ☎ 03 44 38 47 02.

Musée de la Voiture – Same admission times as the historic apartments; guided tour (45min) or a guide (1 hour 30min); 22F; ☎ 03 44 38 47 02.

Musée de la Figurine Historique – Open 9am to noon and 2pm to 6pm (5pm from November to February); closed Sunday morning, Monday and 1 January, 1 May, 14 July, 1 November and 25 December; 12F; ☎ 03 44 40 72 55.

Musée Vivenel – Open daily (except Monday all day and Sunday morning) 9am to noon and 2m to 6pm (5pm from November to February); closed 1 January, 1 May, 14 July, 1 November and 25 December; 12F; ☎ 03 44 20 26 04.

Forêt de COMPIÈGNE

Wagon du maréchal Foch – Open daily (except Tuesday) from 1 April to 14 October 9am to 12.15pm and 2pm to 6.15pm; from 15 October to 31 March 9am to 11.45pm and 2pm to 5.15pm; closed 1 January and 25 December; 10F; ☎ 03 44 85 14 18.

CONCARNEAU

🛈 Quai d'Aiguillon - 29900 - ☎ 02 98 97 01 44

Ramparts – Open 15 June to 15 September 10am to 9.30pm; from Easter to 14 June 10am to 6.30pm; from 16 September to Easter 10am to 5pm; 5 F June to September, admission free the rest of the year; access to the ramparts may be forbidden in adverse weather conditions and during the festival of the Blue Nets; ☎ 02 98 50 56 55.

Musée de la Pêche – 🕭 Open 15 June to 15 September 9.30am to 7pm; the rest of the year 9.30am to 12.30pm and 2.30pm to 6pm; 30F; ☎ 02 98 97 10 20.

CONQUES

🛈 12 320 ☎ 05 65 72 85 00

Treasury – Open in July and August 9am to 7pm; the rest of the year 9am to noon (11am Sunday and holidays) and 2pm to 6pm; closed 1 January; 28F; combined ticket includes tour of the Trésor II; ☎ 05 65 72 85 00.

Château de CORMATIN

🕭 Guided tour (45min) daily 10am to noon and 2pm to 6.30pm from Easter to All Saints Day; closing time at 5pm in October and November; closed from 11 November to Easter and Monday in May (except the 1st); 30F; ☎ 03 85 50 16 55.

CORTE

🛈 avenue du Général-de-Gaulle - 20250 - ☎ 04 95 46 01 76
🛈 Citadelle - ☎ 04 95 46 24 70

Citadel – Open beginning May to end October 9am to 7pm; 20F; guided tours (45min) are organised starting June to end September every hour; to visit the citadel in the winter, contact Mme Depoorter, Citadelle, Bureau Municipal du Tourisme; ☎ 04 95 46 24 20 or 04 95 61 01 62.

COUPVRAY

Maison natale de Louis-Braille – Open May to October 10am to noon and 2pm to 5pm; the rest of the year 2pm to 5pm; closed Tuesday; ☎ 01 60 04 82 80.

La COUVERTOIRADE

Ramparts – Open 9.30am to 6.30pm from 1 June to 31 August; from 1 March to 31 May and from 1 September to 11 November 10am to noon and 2pm to 5.30pm; closed 12 November to 28 February; 15F; ☎ 05 65 62 25 81 or 05 65 62 11 62.

Fortified church – Open March to November 9am to 6pm and for two weeks over Christmas and New Year; if closed, contact the mairie or Mlle Christiane Pinet, weaver, or Mlle Josy Prucel or M. Izombard, rural policeman.

CREVECŒUR-EN-AUGE

Château-musée Schlumberger – Free or guided tour (30min) in July and August daily 11am to 7pm; in April, May, June, and September, open from 11am to 6pm; closed Tuesday as well as from 1 October to 31 March; 26F; ☎ 02 31 63 02 45.

D

Grotte des DEMOISELLES

Guided tour in July and August 9am to 7pm; from 1 April to 30 June and in September 9am to noon and 2pm to 7pm; the rest of the year 9.30am to noon and 2pm to 5pm; closed 1 January and 25 December; 36F, children 18F; ☎ 04 67 73 70 02.

DIEPPE
🛈 quai du Carénage - BP 152 - 76204 - ☎ 02 35 84 11 77

Guided tour of the town ◭ – Open 15 July to 10 September Tuesday, Thursday and Saturday at 2.30pm. Contact "Dieppe, ville d'art et d'Histoire", Hôtel de Ville, B.P. 226 - 76203 Dieppe-Cedex; ☎ 02 35 40 18 57.

Museum – Open daily from 1 June to 30 September 10am to noon and 2pm to 6pm; from 1 October to 31 May 10am to noon and 2pm to 5pm during the week, 6pm on Sunday; closed Tuesday and 1 January, 1 May, 1 November and 25 December; 13F; ☎ 02 35 84 19 76.

Cité de la Mer – ♿ Open daily from 1 April to 30 September 10am to 12.30pm and 2pm to 7pm; the rest of the year 10am to noon and 2pm to 6pm; closed Monday morning and from 24 December to 3 January; 25F; ☎ 02 35 06 93 20.

DIJON
🛈 34 rue des forges - 21022 - ☎ 03 80 44 11 44

Guided tour of the town ◭ – Contact the tourist information office.

Musée des Beaux-Arts – Open daily (except Tuesday) 10am to 6pm; the Modern Art section is closed between noon and 1.30pm; closed 1 January, 1 and 8 May, 14 July, 1 and 11 November, 25 December; 15F (free on Sunday); ☎ 03 80 74 52 70.

Anciennne Chartreuse de Champmol – ♿ Puits de Moïse and chapel door can be visited free of charge daily all year round 8.30am to 7pm; free; ☎ 03 80 42 48 48.

Crypte of the Cathédrale St-Bénigne – Open 9am to 7pm (6pm from 15 November to 28 February); 4F; ☎ 03 80 30 14 90.

Musée archéologique – Open daily (except Tuesday and holidays) 9.30am to 6pm from 1 June to 30 September; the rest of the year 9am to noon and 2pm to 6pm; 11F (free on Sunday); ☎ 03 80 30 88 54.

DINAN
🛈 6, rue de l'Horloge - 22100 - ☎ 02 96 39 75 40

Guided tour of the town ◭ – In July and August, tours on specific themes at 10am, general guided tours at 3pm; contact the tourist information office.

Château – Open from 1 June to 15 October 10am to 6.30pm; from 16 March to 31 May and from 16 October to 15 November 10am to noon and 2pm to 6pm except Tuesday; from 16 November to 31 December and from 7 February to 15 March 1.30pm to 5.30pm except Tuesday; closed January and the first week in February; 20F; ☎ 02 96 39 45 20.

DISNEYLAND PARIS

Open all year from 1 April to 23 June 10am to 6pm during the week and 10am to 8pm Saturday and certain holidays; from 24 June to 3 September daily 9am to 11pm; from 10 September to 31 October 10am to 6pm during the week and 10am to 8pm on Saturday only; outside of these periods, call ☎ 01 64 74 30 00. For guided tours: contact City Hall on the Town Square in Main Street, U.S.A: 50F (adults) and 35F (children). Parking: cars 40F, motorcycles 20F. Euro Disneyland Passport in the high season: 1 day: 195 F (adults) and 150F (children 3 to 11 years of age); 2 days: 370F (adults) and 285F (children); 3 days: 505F (adults) and 390F (children). Off-season: 1 day: 150F (adults) and 120F (children); 2 days: 285F (adults) and 230F (children); 3 days: 390F (adults) and 310F (children). Two and three-day passports can be used non-consecutively. For information, consult the Minitel 3615 Disneyland or telephone ☎ (1) 01 60 30 60 30.

DOMRÉMY-LA-PUCELLE

Maison natale de Jeanne-d'Arc – Open from 1 April to 30 September 9am to 12.30pm and 2pm to 7pm; the rest of the year 9.30am to noon and 2pm to 5pm; closed Tuesday from 1 October to 31 March and 1 January and 25 December; 6F; ☎ 03 29 06 95 86.

LE DORAT   🛈 place de la Collégiale - 87210 - ☎ 05 55 60 76 81 or 05 55 60 74 20

Crypt of the Collégiale St-Pierre – Guided tour from April to September 9am to 6pm; from October to March 9am to 5pm.

DOUAI   🛈 70, place d'Armes - 59500 - ☎ 03 27 88 26 79

Guided tour of the town 🅰 – Contact the tourist information office.

Musée de l'Ancienne Chartreuse – Open daily (except Tuesday) from 10am to noon and 2pm to 5pm (3pm to 6pm Sunday and holidays); closed 1 January, 1 May, Ascension Day, 14 July, 15 August, 1 and 11 November, 25 December; 12F; ☎ 03 27 87 17 82.

Beffroi – Guided tour (1 hour) in July and August daily at 10am, 11am, 2pm (except for Sunday), 3pm, 4pm and 5pm; the rest of the year Sundays and holidays at 10am, 11am, 3pm, 4pm and 5pm; closed 1 January and 25 December; 10F; ☎ 03 27 88 26 79.

DOUARNENEZ   🛈 Rue Docteur-Mevel - 29100 - ☎ 02 98 92 13 35

Port-Musée – Open 1 May to 30 September (in season) from 10am to 7pm (6pm the rest of the year); closed 1 January, 1 May and 25 December, as well as from 10 January to 10 February; 50F (in season), 40F (off season); ☎ 02 98 92 65 20.

Fort de DOUAUMONT

Open 1 May to 10 September 9am to 6.30pm; in May 9.30am to 6pm; from 13 February to 31 March 10am to noon and 2pm to 4.30pm; from 11 September to 29 December 9.30am to noon and 1pm to 5.30pm; from 2 January to 12 February 11am to 3pm; closed 1 January and 25 December; 15F; ☎ 03 29 88 32 88.

DUNKERQUE   🛈 rue de l'Amiral-Ronarc'h - 59240 - ☎ 03 28 66 79 21

Musée d'Art Contemporain – Open daily (except Tuesday) 10am to noon and 2pm to 6pm; closed for public holidays; 20F (ticket is also valid for the Musée des Beaux-Arts), admission free on Sunday; ☎ 03 28 59 21 65.

Musée des Beaux-Arts – Open daily (except Tuesday) from 10am to noon and 2pm to 6pm; closed for public holidays; 20F (ticket is also valid for the Musée d'Art Contemporain), admission free on Sunday; ☎ 03 28 59 21 65.

E

Château d'ÉCOUEN

Musée de la Renaissance – Open daily (except Tuesday) from 9.45am to 12.30am and 2pm to 5.15pm; guided tour (1 hour 30min) Saturday and Sunday at 3.30pm and by appointment other days; closed 1 January, 1 May and 25 December; 22F; ☎ 02 39 90 04 04.

EMBRUN   🛈 Place Général Dosse - 05200 - ☎ 04 92 43 72 72

Cathédrale N.-D.-du-Réal – Closed Wednesday during the school holidays and during services.

ÉVREUX

1, place du Général-de-Gaulle - 27000 - ☎ 02 32 24 04 43

Musée Municipal – ♿ Open 1 April to 30 September from 10am to noon and from 2pm to 6pm (Sunday from 2pm to 6pm); the rest of the year closing time at 5pm; admission free; ☎ 02 32 31 52 29.

Les EYZIES-DE-TAYAC

Place de la Mairie - 24620 - ☎ 05 53 06 97 05

Grotte de Font de Gaume – As visits are limited to a certain number daily in season, a reservation is necessary and costs between 10F and 80F for groups of 1 to 10 people or more; guided tour (40min) daily (except Tuesday) from 1 April to 30 September 9am to noon and 2pm to 6pm, in October and March 9.30am to noon and 2pm to 5.30pm, from 2 November to 28 February 10am to noon and 2pm to 5pm; last visit 1 hour before closing; closed 1 January, 1 May, 1 and 11 November, 25 December; 31F; ☎ 05 53 06 90 80.

Grotte des Combarelles – Same admission charges as for the Grotte de Font-de-Gaume (by appointment in season); guided tour (45min) daily (except Wednesday) 1 April to 30 September 9am to noon and 2pm to 6pm; from 2 November to 28 February 10am to noon and 2pm to 5pm; in October and March 9.30am to noon and 2pm to 5.30pm; last visit 1 hour before closing; closed 1 January, 1 May, 1 and 11 November, 25 December; 31F; ☎ 05 53 06 90 80.

Gisement de Laugerie-Haute – ♿ Guided tour (40min); same admission times and charges as for the Grotte de Font-de-Gaume (by appointment); 20F; ☎ 05 53 06 90 80.

Poisson shelter – Same admission charges and times as for the Grotte de Font-de-Gaume (by appointment); guided tour (45min) daily (except Tuesday during the winter); closed 1 May, 1 and 11 November, 25 December and 1 January; 20F; ☎ 05 53 06 90 80.

Grotte du Grand-Roc – Guided tour (30min) daily from June to mid-September 9am to 7pm (last tour at 6.30); from April to May and from mid-September to mid-November 9.30am to 6.30pm (last tour at 6pm); from February to March and from mid-November to December 10am to 5pm; closed in January; 35F; ☎ 05 53 06 92 70.

F

FÉCAMP

113, rue Alexandre-le-Grand B.P. 112 - 76400 - ☎ 02 35 28 51 01

Guided tour of the town ⚑ – Tours organized in July and August certain days of the week. Contact the Service Animation du Patrimoine, 113, rue Alexandre Le Grand, 76400 Fécamp.

Palais Bénédictine – Open daily from 28 May to 3 September 9.30am to 6pm; from 18 March to 24 May and from 4 September to 12 November 10am to noon and 2pm to 5.30pm; the rest of the year, one tour at 10.30am and another at 3.30pm; closed 1 January and 25 December; 25F; ☎ 02 35 10 26 10.

Musée Centre des Arts – Open 10am to noon and 2pm to 5.30pm; closed Tuesday and 1 January, 1 May and 25 December; 20F (ticket may also be used for the Musée des Terre-Neuvas); ☎ 02 35 28 31 99.

Musée des Terre Neuvas et de la Grande Pêche – ♿ Open 8am to noon and 2pm to 5.30pm (6.30pm in July and August); closed Tuesday (except in July and August) and 1 January, 1 May, and 25 December; 20F; (ticket may also be used for the Musée Centre-des-Arts); ☎ 02 35 28 31 99.

FIGEAC

Hôtel de la Monnaie, Place Vival - 46102 - ☎ 05 65 34 06 25

Guided tour of the old town ⚑ – Wednesday and Saturday at 5pm from 1 May to 3 July, daily in July and August from at 10.30am and 5pm; in September daily at 5pm; contact the tourist information office.

Hôtel de la Monnaie – Open daily in July and August 10am to 12.30pm and 2.30pm to 7pm; from 1 April to 30 June and from 1 September to 30 October 10am to noon and 2.30pm to 6pm; the rest of the year 11am to noon and 2.30pm to 5.30pm; closed 25 December, 1 January, 1 May and 11 November; 10F; ☎ 05 65 34 06 25.

Musée Champollion – Open daily from 1 March to 31 October, 10am to noon and 2.30pm to 6.30pm; the rest of the year from 2pm to 6pm; closed Monday (except July and August, Easter and Whitsun) and 1 January, 1 May and 25 December; 20F; ☎ 05 65 34 66 18.

FILITOSA

Station préhistorique – Open March to 31 October 8.30am to 1 hour before sunset continuously; 22F; the best time to visit is in the middle of the day, as the light is better for seeing details of the sculptures and engravings; the rest of the year, contact ☎ 04 95 74 00 91.

FOIX

🖪 45 cours G.-Fauré – 09000 – ☎ 05 61 65 12 12

Château – Open daily all year round; in July and August 9.45am to 6.30pm; in June and September 9.45am to noon and 2pm to 6pm; the rest of the year 10.30am to noon and 2pm to 5.30pm; closed Mondays and Tuesdays from November to April, 1 January and 25 December; 25F; ☎ *05 61 65 56 05.*

FONTAINEBLEAU

🖪 31 place Napoléon Bonaparte – 77300 – ☎ 01 64 22 25 68

Appartements des Reines Mères et du Pape – Closed for restoration.

Appartement intérieur de l'Empereur – Open starting 18 October 1995; same admission times and charge as for the Grands Appartements.

Galerie de Diane – Same admission times and charges as for the Grands Appartements;

Palace: Ensemble des Grands Appartements – ⅙ Open daily (except Tuesday) in June 9.30am to 5pm; in July and August 9.30am to 6pm; in September and October 9.30am to 5pm; from November to May 9.30am to 12.30pm and 2pm to 5pm; closed 1 January, 1 May and 25 December; 31F (reduced price on Sunday); ☎ 01 60 71 50 70.

Palace: Petits appartements and Galerie des Cerfs – Guided tour (45min) Monday and holidays 9.30am to 12.30pm and 2pm to 5pm; closed 1 January, 1 May and 25 December; 15F; ☎ 01 60 71 50 70.

Palace: Musée Napoléon – Same admission times and charges as for the Grands Appartements.

Abbaye de FONTENAY

Open daily, July and August 9am to 1pm and 2pm to 6pm; the rest of the year 9am to 12noon and 2pm to 6pm, guided tours (1 hour) from mid-March to mid-November, 39F; ☎ 03 80 92 15 00.

FONTEVRAUD-L'ABBAYE

Abbaye – The various buildings are in the process of extensive restoration which will last for several years. Free or guided tour (1 hour) from 1 June to the 3rd Sunday in September from 9am to 7pm; the rest of the year 9.30am to 12.30pm and 2pm to 6pm; closed 1 January, 1 and 11 November, 25 December; 27F; ☎ 02 41 51 71 45.

Abbaye de FONTFROIDE

⅙ Visit 9.30am to 6.30 every half-hour; from 1 March to 9 July and from 1 September to 31 October 10am to noon and 2pm to 5pm every 45min; the rest of the year 10am to noon and 2pm to 6pm every hour; 32F; ☎ 04 68 45 11 08.

FOUGÈRES

🖪 1, place A.-Briand – 35300 – ☎ 02 99 94 12 20

Guided tour of the town 🅰 – Contact the Service du Patrimoine at the Hôtel de ville, B.P. 111, 35301 Fougères cedex; ☎ 02 99 94 88 67.

Château – Free or guided tour (1 hour) from 15 June to 15 September 9am to 7pm; from 1 April to 14 June and 16-30 September 9am to noon and 2pm to 6pm; the rest of the year 10am to noon and 2pm to 5pm; closed 25 December and in January; 21F for guided tour, 26F lecture-tour; ☎ 02 99 99 79 59.

Cap FRÉHEL

Parking – June to September: 5F per vehicle.

Le FUTUROSCOPE

⅙ Open daily from July to beginning September 9am to 11pm; on the weekend and holidays from April to June and from beginning September to 11 November 9am to 11pm; from April to June and from end October to beginning November 9am to 7pm; from beginning September to end October and beginning November to March 9am to 6pm; 145F (2 days 260F), children 110F (2 days 195F) ☎ 05 49 49 30 20; information by Minitel, 3615 code FUTUROSCOPE.

G

GABARIT

Viaduc de Gabarit – A boat restaurant trip (3 hours 15min) from May to September; starting at 165F; contact the Gabarit Hôtel, ☎ 04 71 23 42 75. Boat trip on the Lac de retenue de Grandval beginning May to end September daily; 45min; 38F; towards the Château d'Alleuze: in July and August at 3.30pm; 2 hours; 52F; towards the Gorges de la Truyère: in July and August at 4pm; 45min; 40F.

Cairn de GAVRINIS

Access by boat from the port of Larmor-Baden (embarkation at Penn-Lannic), leaving every 30min (no more than 20 people); 55F round trip; guided tour (30min) from beginning June to end September daily 10am to noon and 2pm to 6pm; in April and May, Saturday, Sunday and holidays 10am to noon and 2pm to 6pm, during the week 2pm to 6pm only; in March and October, daily 3pm to 6pm; 30F. It is advised to reserve a ticket, especially during the high season; ☎ 02 97 57 19 38.

GERMIGNY-DES-PRÉS

Eglise – Guided tour by appointment: ☎ 02 38 58 27 30 or 02 38 58 27 03.

GORDES ▯ place du Château - 84220
- ☎ 04 90 72 02 75

Château and Musée Didactique Vasarely – Open daily (except Tuesday) 10am to noon and 2pm to 6pm; 35F; ☎ 04 90 72 02 89.

GRASSE ▯ Palais des Congrès, 22, cours Cresp - 06130 - ☎ 04 93 36 66 66

Guided tour of the town 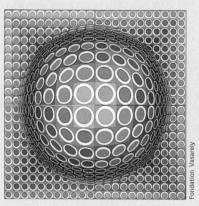 – Contact the tourist information office.

Villa-musée Fragonard – Same admission charges and times as the Musée d'Art et d'Histoire de Provence.

Musée international de la Parfumerie – Open from 1 June to end September 10am to 7pm; the rest of the year 10am to noon and 2pm to 5pm; closed Mondays and Tuesdays in winter; closed public holidays; 15F; ☎ 04 93 36 01 61.

Heet, by Vasarely

GRENOBLE ▯ 14, rue de la République - 38000 - ☎ 04 76 42 41 41

Guided tour of the town 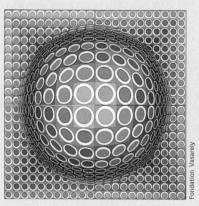 – Contact the tourist information office.

Fort de la Bastille: cablecar – Runs daily 10am to 6pm (starting at 11am on Monday); closed the first 3 weeks of January; from April to October until midnight except Sundays in September and October (7.30pm); length of trip 7min; 32F return ticket; ☎ 04 76 44 33 65.

Église St-Laurent – Open 10am to noon and 2pm to 6pm; closed Tuesday and 1 January, 1 May and 25 December; 15F; ☎ 04 76 44 78 68.

Musée de Grenoble – ♿ Open daily 11am to 7pm (10pm on Wednesday); closed Tuesday, and 1 January, 1 May and 25 Dcember; 25F; ☎ 04 76 63 44 44.

Musée dauphinois – Open 9am to noon and 2pm to 6pm; closed Tuesday and 1 January, 1 May and 25 December; 15F; ☎ 04 76 85 19 00.

GRIGNAN ▯ Grande Rue - 26230 - ☎ 04 75 46 56 75

Château – Guided tour (1 hour) in July and August 9.30am to 11.30am and 2pm to 6pm; the rest of the year daily (except Tuesday from 1 November to 31 March); closed 1 January and 25 December; 25F, 8F (exterior only); ☎ 04 75 46 51 56.

Château de GROS-BOIS

Guided tour (45min) from 15 March to 15 December 2pm to 5pm Sunday and holidays; closed the rest of the year, 1 January and 25 December; 15F; ☎ 05 45 69 03 47.

GUISE

Château – Guided tour (1 hour) 9am to noon and 2pm to 6pm (5pm in winter); closed 20 December to 6 January; 25F; ☎ 03 23 61 11 76.

H

Abbaye d'HAMBYE

♿ Open 1 February to 15 December from 10am to noon and 2pm to 6pm; closed Tuesday and from 16 December to 31 January; 20F; ☎ 02 33 61 76 92.

Abbaye royale de HAUTECOMBE

Tour with recorded lecture (30min) 10am to 11.30am and 2pm to 5.25pm; Sunday 10.30am to noon and 2pm to 5pm; closed Tuesday; donation is recommended; ☎ 04 79 54 26 12.

Château de HAUTEFORT

Guided tour (45min) daily in July and August 9.30am to 12.45pm and 2pm to 7pm; from April to June and September to mid-October 10am to noon and 2pm to 6pm; from February to March and mid-October to mid-November 2pm to 6pm; Sunday from 2pm to 6pm the second two weeks of January and from mid-November to mid-December; 28F; ☎ 05 53 50 51 23 or 05 53 50 59 46.

Château du HAUT-KŒNIGSBOURG

Open 1 June to 30 September 9am to 6pm; the rest of the year 9am to noon and 1pm to 5pm (6pm in April and May, 4pm from 1 November to 28 February); closed 1 January, 1 May, 1 and 11 November, 25 December and beginning January to beginning February (excpet during school holidays); 35F (10F for children 12-17 years old); ☎ 03 88 92 11 46.

Le HAVRE
🛈 Forum de l'Hôtel-de-Ville - 76059 - ☎ 02 35 21 22 88

Musée des Beaux-Arts André-Malraux – Same admission times and charges as the Musée l'Ancien Havre; 10F.

HONFLEUR
🛈 Place Arthur-Boudin - 14600 - ☎ 02 31 89 23 30

Guided tour of the town 🅰 – Open in July, August and September Tuesday and Thursday at 10am, Monday, Wednesday, Friday and Saturday at 3pm; in March, April, May, June, and September, each Saturday at 3pm; contact the tourist information office.

Musée Eugène Boudin – Open 15 March to 30 September 10am to noon and 2pm to 6pm; from 1 October to 14 March, during the week from 2.30pm to 5pm and the weekend 10am to noon and 2.30pm to 5pm; closed Tuesday and from 1 January to 15 February; 18F (in winter), 20F (in summer); ☎ 02 31 89 54 00.

Église Sainte-Catherine: bell-tower – The ticket for the Musée Eugène-Boudin provides access to the Ste-Catherine bell-tower, with the same admission times.

Les HOUCHES
🛈 74310 - ☎ 04 50 55 50 62

Téléphérique de Bellevue – Runs from December to end April and beginning June to mid-September; length of trip 4min; 43 F round trip; ☎ 04 50 54 40 32.

I

ISSOIRE
🛈 Place Général-de-Gaulle - 63500 - ☎ 04 73 89 15 90

Ancienne abbatiale St-Austremoine: Last Judgement – Open daily 8am to 7pm; a guided tour is offered free of charge by Mr. Raoul Ollier in July and August on Tuesday and Friday at 5pm (tour starts at the church chevet).

J

JOSSELIN
🛈 Place de la Congrégation - 56120 - ☎ 02 97 22 36 43

Château – Guided tour (45min) daily in July and August 10am to 6pm; in June and September 2pm to 6pm; in April, May and October, Wednesday, Saturday, Sunday, public and school holidays 2pm to 6pm; 29F; one ticket for both the château and the Musée des poupées; 51F, children 41F; ☎ 02 97 22 36 45.

Abbaye de JUMIÈGES

Église Notre-Dame – Free or guided tour (45min) from mid-June to mid-September 9am to 6.30pm; the rest of the year 10am (9am in April, May, mid-September and October) at noon and 2pm to 6pm (5pm in April, May, mid-September and October); closed 1 January, 1 May, 1 and 11 November, 25 December; 27F; ☎ 02 35 37 24 02.

K

KAYSERSBERG

Musée Albert-Schweitzer – Open during Spring school holidays and from 2 May to 31 October daily 9am to noon and 2pm to 6pm; 10F; ☎ 03 89 47 36 55.

L

LANGEAIS

Château – Free or guided tour (1 hour) from 15 July to 31 August 9am to 9pm; from 15 March to 14 July and from 1 September to 30 September 9am to 6.30pm; 1 October to 2 November 9am to 12.30pm and 2pm to 6.30pm; the rest of the year from 9am to noon and 2pm to 5pm; 35F; ☎ 02 47 96 72 60.

LAON   🛈 place du Parvis-de-la-Cathédrale - 02000 - ☎ 03 23 20 28 62

Guided tour of the town – Contact the tourist information office.

Musée – Open daily (except Tuesday) 10am to noon and 2pm to 6pm (5pm from October to March); closed 1 January, 1 May, 14 July and 25 December; 11F; admission free on Sunday during winter; ☎ 03 23 20 19 87.

Chapelle des Templiers – Open daily (except Tuesday) from 8am to 6pm (5pm from 1 October to 31 March); closed 1 January, 1 May, 14 July and 25 December; admission free.

Église St-Martin – Guided tour from 1 May to 30 September on weekends, in July and August daily; contact the tourist information office.

Château de LAPALISSE

Guided tour (45min) daily (except Tuesday) from April to beginning November 9am to noon and 2pm to 6pm; 25F; ☎ 04 70 99 08 51 or 04 70 55 01 12.

Grotte de LASCAUX II

Guided tour (40min) daily in July and August 9.30am to 7.30pm; from 7 February to end June and from 1 September to end December 10am to noon and 2pm to 5.30pm; closed Monday (except public holidays and in July and August), in January, 25 December and 1 May. During the summer, tickets are sold at Montignac under the arcades of the Point-Information; ticket sales begin at 9am and end once 2,000 have been sold, which happens quickly. The ticket for Lascaux I also provides access to the park and the musée du Thot (45F); ☎ 05 53 51 95 03.

LAVAUDIEU

Cloître – Guided tour (30min) daily from 16 June to 15 September 10am to noon and 2pm to 6pm; from Easter to 15 June and from 16 September to 31 October, open daily except Tuesday 10am to noon and 2pm to 4.30pm; 20F; ☎ 04 71 76 45 89.

Iles de LÉRINS

Access – Regular ferry service daily starting from Cannes: Compagnie Esterel Chanteclair, Ile Ste-Marguerite: 40F; Ile-St-Honorat: 45F; both islands, 60F; ☎ 04 93 39 11 82; in season, boat trips (1 hour 30min) on the Nautilus, with a view of the sea bottom; 70F; ☎ 04 93 99 62 01.

Centre historique minier de LEWARDE

Partial guided tour (mine tour: 2 hours) 10am to 5pm (4pm from 1 November to 31 March); closed 1 January, 1 May, 1 November and 25 December and from 15-31 January; in the main season: adults 60F, children 7-17 30F; off-season: adults 52F, children 26F; ☎ 03 27 98 03 89.

LILLE   🛈 Palais Rihour - 59000 - ☎ 03 20 30 81 00

Guided tour of the city – Contact the tourist information office.

Comtesse Hospice – Open daily (except Tuesday) from 10am to 11.45am and from 2pm to 5.15pm; closed 1 January, 1 May, 14 July, 1 November, 25 December, Monday of Lille festivals and Sunday and Monday of the Grande Braderie; 15F; ☎ 03 20 49 50 90.

Citadelle – Guided tour (1 hour) from April to October on Sunday at 3pm and 4.30pm; tour starts at the citadelle; in season, we recommend you register in advance with the tourist information office; 35F; ☎ 03 20 30 81 00.

Musée des Beaux-Arts – Planned to re-open in 1996; for information call ☎ 03 20 57 01 84.

LIMOGES
🛈 Boulevard de Fleurus - 87000 - ☎ 05 55 34 46 87

Musée municipal de l'Evêché – Open daily from July to September 10am to 11.45am and 2pm to 6pm; daily in June (except Tuesday) 10am to 11.45am and 2pm to 6pm (5pm from October to May); closed 1 January, 1 May, 1 and 11 November, 25 December; ☎ 05 55 34 44 09.

Musée Adrien-Dubouché – Free or guided tour (1 hour 15min) daily (except Tuesday) in July and August 10am to 5.15pm; the rest of the year 10am to noon and 1.30pm to 5.15pm; closed 1 January, 1 May and 25 December; 20F; ☎ 05 55 77 45 58.

LISIEUX
🛈 11, rue d'Alençon - 14100 - ☎ 02 31 62 08 41

Les Buissonnets – Open from Palm Sunday to 1 October 9am to noon and 2pm to 6pm (5.30pm in May and June); from 2 October to Palm Sunday 10am to noon and 2pm to 4pm (5pm in October and November); closed in January; admission free; ☎ 02 31 31 49 71.

Carmelite Chapel – Open from Easter to October daily 8.30am to noon and 1.30pm to 7pm, the rest of the year 9am to noon and 2pm to 5pm; admission free; ☎ 02 31 31 49 71.

Manoir de Coupesarte – Exterior only, all year 8am to 9pm; donation recommended.

LOCHES
🛈 place Wermelskirchen - 37600 - ☎ 02 47 59 07 98

Guided tour of the town – Open by appointment only. Contact the tourist pavilion.

Château – Open daily 1 July to 31 August 9am to 6pm; from 15 March to 30 June and from 1 September to 30 September 9am to noon and 2pm to 6pm; from 1 February to 14 March and from 1 October to 30 November 9am to noon and 2pm to 5pm; closed Wednesday (except in July and August) as well as during January and December; 18F; ☎ 02 47 59 01 32.

Keep – Guided tour (45min) from July to 15 September 9am to 7pm; from 15 March to 30 June and 16 to 30 September 9.30am to 13pm and 2.30pm to 7pm; from the rest of the year 9.30am to 1pm and 2.30pm to 6pm; 20F for the donjon only, 26F for a ticket that provides access to the Logis Royaux in the château; ☎ 02 47 59 07 86.

LOCMARIAQUER
🛈 Place de la Mairie - 56740 - ☎ 02 97 57 33 05

Ensemble mégalithique – Guided tour (45min) from 1 June to 30 September 10am to 7pm; from end March to 31 May and from 1 October to 31 October 10am to 1pm and 2pm to 5pm or 6pm; 25F; ☎ Sagemor 02 97 57 37 59.

LOCRONAN
🛈 Place de la Mairie - 29180 - ☎ 02 98 91 70 14

Conservatoire de l'Affiche en Bretagne – Open from 1 July to 1 October 10am to 1pm and 2pm to 6pm (6.30pm Saturday and Sunday); from 25 February to 28 May 10am to noon and 2pm to 6pm; 20F; ☎ 02 98 51 80 59.

LOURDES
🛈 place Peyramale - 65100 - ☎ 05 62 42 77 40

Château – Open from 1 April to 30 September 9am to noon and 2pm to 7pm; the rest of the year 9am to noon and 2pm to 6pm (5pm on Friday); last admission 1 hour before closing time; closed Tuesdays and public holidays from 15 October to 31 March; 26F; ☎ 05 62 94 02 04.

LUNÉVILLE

Château: musée – Open daily (except Tuesday) from 10am to noon and 2pm to 6pm (5pm from 1 October to 31 March); closed 1 January, Shrove Monday and 25 December; 10F; ☎ 03 83 76 23 57.

LYON
🛈 Place Bellecour et Place St Jean - 69000 - ☎ 04 78 42 25 75

A day-pass provides access for a reduced price to all the city museums of Lyon: Musée des Beaux-Arts, Musée de l'hôtel de Gadagne, Musée d'art contemporain, Musée de l'Imprimerie et de la Banque, Centre d'Histoire de la Résistance et de la Déportation and the Musée Henri-Malartre at La Rochetaillée.

Guided tours of the town 🅰 – These tours are organised by the Lyon tourist information bureau. The tours include the Traboules of the Croix-Rousse (2 hours), or Old Lyon (2 hours). Contact the tourist information office, place Bellecour, open all day from Monday to Saturday and Avenue A. Max daily; ☎ 04 78 42 25 75.

Musée de la Civilisation Gallo-romaine – ♿ Open 9.30am to noon and 2pm to 6pm; closed Monday, Tuesday and holidays; 20F; ☎ 04 78 25 94 68.

Primatiale St-Jean – Closes at 5pm Saturday and Sunday; closed in the afternoon on public holidays.

Le Guignol of Lyon – Marionnette shows are held from 1 September to 11 July. Children's shows are given Wednesday and Sunday at 3pm; adults 35F to 95F; children starting at 25F; reservations: ☎ 04 78 28 92 57.

9C-10C ivory casket,
Treasury, Primatiale St-Jean

Musée de l'Imprimerie et de la Banque – Open 9.30am to noon and 2pm to 6pm, and on Fridays also from noon to 2pm; closed Mondays, Tuesdays and holidays; 20F; ☎ 04 78 37 65 98.

Musée des Beaux-Arts – Open 10.30am to 6pm; closed Mondays, Tuesdays, 1 January, 1 and 8 May, Ascension Day, 14 July, 15 August, 1 and 11 November and 25 December; 20F; ☎ 04 78 28 07 66.

Musée historique des Tissus – Open daily 10am to 5.30pm; closed Monday and holidays; 26F (ticket provides access to the Musée des Arts Décoratifs); free on Wednesday for individual tourists; ☎ 04 78 37 15 05.

Musée des Arts décoratifs – Open 10am to noon and 2pm to 5.30pm; closed Monday and all public holidays; 26F (ticket provides access to the Musée historique des tissus); for guided tour, call ☎ 04 78 37 14 05.

Musée Guimet d'Histoire naturelle – Open Wednesday to Friday 1.30pm to 5.30pm; closed during holidays; 20F (40F if exhibits); ☎ 04 78 93 22 33.

Musée des Hospices civils – Open Monday to Friday 1.30pm to 5.30pm; closed during holidays; 10F; ☎ 04 78 41 30 42.

Église St-Nizier – Closed Monday morning; open at 3pm.

M

Le MAINE-GIRAUD

Open daily 9am to noon and 2pm to 6pm; admission free; ☎ 05 45 64 04 49.

Château de MAISONS-LAFFITTE

Open from 1 April to 15 October daily from 10am to noon and 1.30pm to 6pm (5pm the rest of the year); lecture-tour the 1st Sunday of the month at 3pm; closed 1 January, 1 May, 1 and 11 November and 25 December; 27F; ☎ 01 39 62 01 49.

LE MANS   🖪 Hôtel des Ursulines, rue de l'Etoile - 72000 - ☎ 02 43 28 17 22

Guided tour of the town 🅰 – Daily in July and August at 3pm; tour starts at the cathedral. Contact the tourist information office.

Queen Berengaria's House – Guided tour (1 hour 15min) 9am (10am Sundays) to room and 2pm to 6pm. Closed bank holidays; 14F (free Sundays); combined ticket with the Musée de Tessé. 22F. ☎ 02 43 47 38 51.

Musée de l'automobile – ♿ Open daily from 1 June to 30 September 10am to 7pm; from 15 February to 31 May and from 1 October to 31 October 10am to 6pm except Tuesday; from 2 January to 16 February on the weekend 10am to 6pm; 25 December and 1 January open 3pm to 6pm; 35F; ☎ 02 43 72 72 24.

Musée de Tessé – ♿ Same admission times and charges as the Musée de la Reine Berengère. Admission free on Sunday; ☎ 02 43 47 38 51.

MARNAY

Musée Maurice-Dufresne – ♿ Open from 1 May to 31 October 9.15am to 7pm (6pm the rest of the year). Closed in January and February; 48F; ☎ 02 47 45 36 18.

MARQUÈZE

Marquèze – Can only be reached by the "petit train des résiniers" leaving from the gare de Sabres daily 10.10am to 12.10pm and 2pm to 5.20pm, in April, May, and October, during the week at 3pm, on Saturday 2pm to 5.20pm; on Sunday and public holidays 10.10am to 12.10pm and 2pm to 5.20pm; closed from 2 November to 31 March; free or guided tour (1 hour); 45F, children 25F; the restaurant is open daily in season, weekends only out of season; picnic areas, drinks for sale; ☎ 05 58 07 52 70.

MARSEILLE   🖪 4, La Canebière – 13001 – ☎ 04 91 13 89 00

Guided tour of the town 🄰 – Contact the tourist information office.

Basilique St-Victor: crypt – For a guided tour (10F), enquire at ☎ 04 91 33 25 86.

Musée des Docks romains – Open daily (except Monday) from 1 June to 30 September 11am to 6pm; the rest of the year 10am to 5pm; closed for holidays; 10F; ☎ 04 91 56 28 38 (ext. 399).

Centre de la Vieille Charité – Open 1 June to 30 September 11am to 6pm; the rest of the year from 10am to 5pm; closed Monday and holidays; opening of the "Roquepertuse et les Celto-Ligures" section not certain; opening of the "Art Populaire du Mexique" section planned during 1996; Musée d'Archéologie méditerranéenne: 10F; musée des Arts Africains, Océaniens et Amérindiens: 10F; temporary exhibits: 20F; combined ticked for museum and exhibition: 25F; ☎ 04 91 56 28 38.

Musée du Vieux Marseille – Open from 1 July to 30 September 11am to 6pm; the rest of the year 10am to 5pm; closed Monday and holidays; 10F; ☎ 04 91 55 10 19.

Ancienne cathédrale de la Major – Temporarily closed to the public.

Musée Cantini – Open from 1 June to 30 September 11am to 6pm; the rest of the year, 10am to 5pm; closed Monday; 10F, admission free on Sunday morning; ☎ 04 91 54 77 75.

Château Borély – Closed for restoration.

Musée Grobet-Labadié – Open 1 June to 30 September 11am to 6pm; the rest of the year 10am to 5pm; closed Monday and holidays; 10F; admission free on Sunday morning; ☎ 04 91 62 21 17.

Musée des Beaux-Arts – Open 1 June to 30 September 11am to 6pm; the rest of the year 10am to 5pm; closed Monday; free Sunday morning; ☎ 04 91 62 21 17.

Visit of the modern port – During the afternoon on Sunday and holidays only, the Digue du Large is accessible to tourists by the door no2 (Arenc). During working days, guided tours of the port are organised; contact the Port Autonome de Marseille, Service Communication et Relations publiques, section Visites, 23, place de la Joliette, BP 1965, 13226 Marseille Cedex 02 one month before the desired date; ☎ 04 91 39 47 24.

Château d'If – Boat trip (1 hour 30min, including a tour of the château): embarkation on the quai des Belges in the Vieux Port de Marseille. Departure every hour in summer, every hour and 30 min in winter; 40F. The times of château tours are organised according to boat times: from 1 April to 30 September 9am to 7pm; the rest of the year 9.15am to 7.15pm; 21F. Groupement des Armateurs Côtiers Marseillais, 1 quai des Belges – 13001 Marseille; ☎ 04 91 55 50 09. This company also organises regular ferry services to the islands of Frioul; price for the islands of If and Frioul: 60F.

Aven de MARZAL

Guided tour (1 hour) from 1 April to 31 October, from 11am to 5.30pm; in March and November, Sundays and holidays 11am, 2pm and 3.30pm; closed the rest of the year; 35F; ☎ 04 75 04 12 45.

Zoo préhistorique – Open 1 April to 31 October 10am to noon and 2pm to 6pm; in March and November, Sunday and holidays only; 32F.

Grotte du MAS-D'AZIL

Cave – Guided tour (40min) from 10am to noon and 2pm to 6pm from 1 June to 30 September, during the week from 1 April to 30 June 2pm to 6pm (in addition, 10am to noon on Sunday and holidays); in March and from 1 October to 30 November Sunday and holidays only 2pm to 6pm; closed beginning December to end February; 20F for a ticket that includes a visit to the museum; ☎ 05 61 69 97 71.

Le MAS SOUBEYRAN

Musée du Désert – Open from 1 July to the 1st Sunday in September 9.30am to 6.30pm; from 1 March to 30 June and beginning September to 30 November 9.30am to noon and 2.30pm to 6pm; closed 1 December to 28 February; 20F; ☎ 04 66 85 02 72.

MEAUX
🆔 2, rue Notre-Dame – 77100 – ☎ 01 64 33 02 26

Guided tour of the town 🅰 – Contact the tourist information office.

Musée Bossuet – Open daily (except Tuesday) 10am to noon and 2pm to 6pm; closed 1 January, 1 May and 25 December; 15F (free on Wednesday); ☎ 01 64 34 84 45.

Château de MEILLANT

Guided tour (40min) daily in spring and summer 9am to 11.45am and 2pm to 6.45pm; in autumn and winter 9am to 11.45am and 2pm to nightfall; closed 15 December to 31 January; 40F; ☎ 02 48 63 30 58 or 02 48 63 32 05.

MENTON
🆔 Palais de l'Europe – 06500 – ☎ 04 93 57 57 00
🆔 maison du patrimoine, 5 rue Ciapetta – 06500 – ☎ 04 93 10 33 66

Guided tour of the town 🅰 – Every Tuesday afternoon. Contact the Maison du patrimoine.

Hôtel de ville – The Salle de mariages Jean Cocteau is open from 8.30am to noon and 1.30pm to 4.45pm all year from Monday to Friday; 5F; ☎ 04 93 10 50 29.

Église St-Michel – Open noon to 3pm; ☎ 04 93 35 81 63.

Musée du palais Carnolès – Open daily 10am to noon and 2pm to 6pm; closed Tuesday and public holidays. ☎ 04 93 35 49 71.

METZ
🆔 place d'Armes – 57000 – ☎ 03 87 55 53 76

Cathédrale St-Étienne – Open May through September during the week from 9am to 6.30pm, Sunday noon to 6.30pm; the rest of the year during the week 9am to noon and 2pm to 6pm, Sunday 2pm to 6pm; closed 1 May and 15 August; 12F; ☎ 03 87 75 54 61.

La Cour d'Or, Musées – Oepn 10am to noon and 2pm to 6pm; closed 1 January, Holy Friday, 1 May, 1 and 11 November and 25 December; 20F, free on Wednesday and Sunday mornings; ☎ 03 87 75 10 18.

Eglise St-Pierre-aux-Nonnains – Open April through September daily except Monday 2pm to 6pm ("Metz, Lumières d'Histoire" show at 6pm); from October to March Saturday and Sunday 2pm to 5pm ("Metz, Lumières d'Histoire" show at 5pm); 10F; Information at the Arsenal ☎ 03 87 39 92 00.

Pic du MIDI DE BIGORRE

Toll road – From the col du Tourmalet to the hôtel-refuge des Laquets (parking); hikers 6F; vehicles (adult passengers 23F, children 6 to 12 years, 10F); for information contact Heliotour; ☎ 05 62 91 90 33 (in season) or ☎ 05 62 95 41 14 (out of season).

Observatory – Guided tour (45min) from 1 July to 15 September, from 8am to 6pm; 12F, children 7F.

MILLAU
🆔 Avenue Alfred-Merle, B.P. 331 – 12103 – ☎ 05 65 60 02 42

Fouilles de la Graufesenque ♿ – Open 9am to noon and 2pm to 6.30pm; closed 1 January, 1 May, 1 and 11 November, 25 December; 21F; ☎ 05 65 60 11 37.

Archaelogical Museum – Open 10am to noon and 2pm to 6pm; closed Sunday from 1 October to 31 March and 1 January, 1 May and 11 November, 25 December; 22F; ☎ 05 65 59 01 08.

Principauté de MONACO
🆔 2, boulevard des Moulins – ☎ [00-377] 93 16 61 66

Musée océanographique – Open in July and August 9am to 9pm; in September, October and from March to June 10am to 6pm; from November to end February 10am to 6pm; closed Sunday afternoon following Ascension Day; 60F; ☎ [00-377] 93 15 36 00.

Palais du Prince – Open daily 9.30am to 6.30pm; closed 1 November to 31 May; 30F; ☎ [00-377] 93 25 18 31.

Jardin exotique – Open mid-May to mid-September 9am to 7pm, the rest of the year 9am to 6pm; closed 19 November and 25 December; 36F for a ticket that also provides access to the grotte de l'Observatoire and the musée d'Anthropologie préhistorique; ☎ [00-377] 93 30 33 65.

Principauté de MONACO

Grotte de l'Observatoire – Same admission charges and times as for the Musée d'Anthropologie préhistorique.

Musée d'Anthropologie préhistorique – Open from May to end August 9am to 7pm; the rest of the year 9am to 6pm; 36F (includes a visit to the Jardin exotique and the grotte de l'Observatoire); ☎ [00-377] 93 15 80 06.

Musée napoléonien – Open June to September 9.30am to 6.30pm; in October 10am to 5pm; from December to May 10.30am to 12.30pm and 2pm to 5pm; closed Monday from December to end May, 25 December and 1 January, and the entire month of November; 20F; (40F for a ticket that also provides access to the Palais du Prince). ☎ [00-377] 93 25 18 31.

Musée des Poupées et Automates – Open from Easter to beginning September 10am to 6.30pm; the rest of the year 10am to 12.15pm and 2.30pm to 6.30pm; closed 1 January, 1 May, Ascension Day, 19 November, 25 December and the four days of the Monaco automobile races; 26F; ☎ [00-377] 93 30 91 26.

Château de MONTAIGNE

Guided tour (30min) daily (except Monday and Tuesday) from 18 February to 6 January 9am to noon and 2pm to 7pm; 16F; ☎ 05 53 58 63 93.

MONTAUBAN
🛈 Ancien collège pl. Prax – 82000 – ☎ 05 63 63 60 60

Musée Ingres – Open in July and August 9.30am to noon and 1.30pm to 6pm; open daily (except Monday) from Palm Sunday to end June and from 1 September to the 2nd Sunday in October 10am to noon and 2pm to 6pm; open daily (except for Sunday morning and Monday) the rest of the year 10am to noon and 2pm to 6pm; closed for holidays; 15F, 20F (if exhibit); ☎ 05 63 22 12 91.

MONTBÉLIARD
🛈 rue Henri-Mouhot – 25200 – ☎ 03 81 94 45 60

Musée Peugeot in Sochaux – ♿ Open daily 10am to 6pm; 30F; ☎ 03 81 94 48 21.

MONT-LOUIS

Solar oven – Guided tour (30min) daily 10am to 12.30am and 2pm to 6pm; 25F; ☎ 04 68 04 14 89.

MONTPELLIER
🛈 "Le Triangle" – Passage du Tourisme – 34000 – ☎ 04 67 58 67 58

Musée Atger – Free or guided tour (1 hour) 1.30pm to 4.30pm; closed Saturday, Sunday, holidays, the month of August, and during Christmas school holidays; ☎ 04 67 66 27 77.

Musée Fabre – Open 9am to 5.30pm (5pm Saturday and Sunday); closed Monday and certain holidays; 20F; ☎ 04 67 14 83 00.

Chaos de MONTPELLIER-LE-VIEUX

Open daily from 15 March to 3 November 9am to 7pm; the rest of the year by appointment only; 25F, children 10F; for the "petit train", 15F return ticket, 10F one-way, children 10F return ticket, 5F one-way.

Le MONT-ST-MICHEL
🛈 Corps-de-Garde-des-Bourgeois – 50116 – ☎ 02 33 60 14 30

Abbey – Guided tour (1 hour) from 2 May to 30 September 9.30am to 6pm; the rest of the year, 9.30am to 4pm (4.30pm during school holidays); closed 1 January, 1 May, 1 and 11 November and 25 December; 36F; lecture-tours (2 hours) in season; information at the abbey, out of season Wednesday, Saturday and Sunday at 10.30am and 2.30pm; 56F; ☎ 02 33 60 14 14.

MONTSÉGUR

Château – Open in July and August 9am to 7pm; only to groups of at least 15 people and by appointment from 1 April to 30 June and in September 9am to 7pm; in February, March, October and November 10am to 6pm; closed from 1 December to 11 February; 20F for a ticket that provides access to the Musée archéologique. ☎ 05 61 01 06 94.

Musée archéologique – Open daily from 1 April to 30 September 10am to 1pm and 2pm to 7pm; 11am to 5pm in October, November, February and March; closed in December and January; 20F combined ticket for visit of castle. ☎ 05 61 01 06 94.

MORGAT

Les Grandes Grottes – From 1 May to 30 September, boat trip (45min). Departure all day according to tides. Motorboats at the port; ☎ 02 98 27 09 54.

MOULINS
🚉 Place de l'Hôtel-de-Ville - 03000 - ☎ 04 70 44 14 14

Musée d'art et d'archéologie - Free or guided tour (1 hour) daily (except Tuesday) from 10am to noon and 2pm to 6pm; closed 1 January and 25 December; 10F: ☎ 04 70 20 48 47.

Mausolée du duc de Montmorency - Guided tour (30min) in July and August 9am to 11.30am and 3pm to 6pm; the rest of the year 9am to 11.30am and 2pm to 5pm (during this time, contact the tourist information office); closed Sunday, 14 July and 15 August; 10F in July and August; ☎ 04 70 44 14 14.

MOZAC

Eglise - Open daily (except Saturday afternoon and Sunday morning) from 9am to 7pm in summer (5pm in winter).

MULHOUSE
🚉 9 avenue Foch - 68100 - ☎ 03 89 45 68 31

Musée national de l'Automobile - ♿ Open daily (except Tuesday from 1 October to 30 April) 10am to 5.30pm; closed 1 January and 25 December; 56F: ☎ 03 89 42 29 17.

Musée français du Chemin de Fer - ♿ Open 9am to 6pm (5pm from 1 October to 30 March); closed 1 January, 25 and 26 December; 43F, children 20F; ☎ 03 89 42 25 67.

Musée de l'Impression sur Étoffes - Closed for restoration; expected to re-open in October 1996.

Musée Historique - Open daily (except Tuesday) from 10am to noon and 2pm to 6pm (5pm from 1 October to 14 June); closed 1 January, Holy Friday, Easter Monday and Whitsun, 1 May, 14 July, 1 and 11 November, 25 and 26 December; 20F (free the 1st Sunday of each month); ☎ 03 89 45 43 20.

Musée français du Chemin de Fer

Temple St-Étienne - ♿ Open from 2 May to 30 September 10am to noon and 2pm to 6pm (5pm on Saturday); closed Tuesday, Sunday morning, holidays except for 15 August; free admission; ☎ 03 89 46 58 25.

Parc zoologique et botanique - ♿ Open May to August 8am to 7pm; in April and september 9am to 6pm; in March, October and November 9am to 5pm; in December, January and February 10am to 4pm; adults 40F, children 20F; ☎ 03 89 44 17 44.

Château de MUROL
🚉 Rue Jassaguer - 63790 - ☎ 04 73 88 62 62

Free tour daily from 11 April to 30 September 10am to 6pm and only Saturday from 9 July to 12 September; tour with costumes daily except Saturday from 9 July to 12 September, and by appointment outside this period; Free tour: 20F; costume-tour: 40F; ☎ 04 73 88 67 11 (Compagnons de Gabriel).

N

NANCY
🚉 14 place Stanislas - 54000 - 03 83 35 22 41

Guided tour of the city 🅰 - Contact the tourist information office.

Palais Ducal - Open daily, except Tuesday, May to September 10am to 6pm; the rest of the year 10am to 12noon and 2pm to 5pm (6pm Sundays and holidays); closed 1 January, Easter, 1 May, 14 July, 1 November, 25 December; 20F. ☎ 03 83 32 18 74.

Musée Historique lorrain - Open daily (except Tuesday) from beginning May to end September 10am to 6pm; the rest of the year 10am to noon and 2pm to 5pm (6pm on Sunday and holidays); closed 1 January, Easter, 1 May, 14 July, 1 November and 25 December; 20F; ☎ 03 83 32 18 74.

Eglise and Couvent des Cordeliers - Open daily (except Tuesday) from May to end September 10am to 6pm; the rest of the year 10am to noon and 2pm to 5pm (6pm Sundays and holidays); closed 1 January, Easter, 1 May, 14 July, 1 November and 25 December; 20F; ☎ 03 83 32 18 74.

Musée français du chemin de fer, Mulhouse

NANCY

Musée des Beaux-Arts – Open daily (except Tuesday) 10.30am to 6pm, Monday 2pm to 6pm; closed 1 January, 1 May, 1 November and 25 December; 20F; ☎ 03 83 85 30 72 extn. 2804.

Musée de l'École de Nancy – Open daily (except Tuesday) 10am to noon and 2pm to 6pm (5pm from 1 October to 31 March); closed 1 January, Easter, 1 May, 1 November and 25 December; 20F; guided tour (1 hour) Sunday at 3.30pm, 12 F extra; ☎ 03 83 40 14 86.

NANTES
🛈 Place du Commerce - 44000 - ☎ 02 40 47 04 51

Guided tour of the town ⛰ – In July, August and September, many walks and tours on specific themes daily; contact the tourist information office.

Château des ducs de Bretagne – Free or guided tour (1 hour) every day from 1 July to 31 August 10am to 7pm for the château, 10am to noon and 2pm to 7pm for the museums; the rest of the year 10am to noon and 2pm to 6pm for the château and museums; the museums are closed Tuesday as well as 1 January, 1 May, 1 and 11 November and 25 December; 10F; ☎ 02 40 41 56 56.

Cathédrale St.-Pierre-et-St.-Paul – Tour of the crypts 10am to 12.30pm and 2pm to 5pm, except Tuesday and during religious services; ☎ 02 40 14 23 00. For guided tours of the cathedral, contact the tourist information office.

Musée des Beaux-Arts – ♿ Open daily except Tuesday 10am (11am on Sunday) to 6pm (9pm on Friday); closed for all holidays; 30F (admission free on Sunday); ☎ 02 40 41 65 65 and 02 40 41 65 50.

Muséum d'Histoire naturelle – Open 10am to noon and 2pm to 6pm; closed Sunday morning, Monday and holidays; 20F (admission free on Sunday), 30F during temporary exhibitions; ☎ 02 40 41 67 67.

Palais Dobrée – Open 10am to noon and 1.30pm to 5.30pm; closed Monday and all holidays; 20F (ticket also provides access to the Manoir de la Touche and the Musée archéologique); ☎ 02 40 71 03 50.

Musée Jules-Verne – Open 10am to noon and 2pm to 5pm; closed Sunday morning, Tuesday and all holidays; 8F; ☎ 02 40 69 72 52.

Musée archéologique – Open 10am to noon and 1.30pm to 5.30pm; closed Monday and holidays; 20F (ticket also provides access to the Manoir de la Touche and the Palais Dobrée); ☎ 02 40 71 03 50.

NARBONNE
🛈 Place R.-Salengro - 11100 - ☎ 04 68 65 15 60

Guided tour of the town ⛰ – Information, reservations: Ville de Narbonne, Service Culture Communication, B.P. 823 – 11108 Narbonne Cedex; ☎ 04 68 90 30 66.

Cathédrale St-Just – Guided tour (1 hour) daily except Sunday and holidays during the summer 9.30am to noon and 2pm to 5.30pm; in the autumn, 2.30pm to 4.30pm, by appointment in winter; ☎ 04 68 32 09 52.

Treasury – Open daily (except Sunday) from 1 May to 31 October 2.30pm to 4.30pm; by appointment only the rest of the year; closed 15 August; 10F; ☎ 04 68 33 70 18.

Palais des Archevêques – Guided tour daily from 15 June to 30 September at 10am, 2pm and 4pm; the rest of the year by request for groups of at least 5 people; tour starts at the reception of the Hôtel de ville (ground floor hall of the donjon Gilles Aycelin); 25F; request information at the Service Culture Communication, B.P. 823 – 11108 Narbonne Cedex; ☎ 04 68 90 30 66.

Donjon Gilles Aycelin – Guided tour by request to the Service Culture Communication; ☎ 04 68 90 30 66.

Musée archéologique, musée d'Art, Horreum – Free or guided tour (☎ 04 68 90 30 54) from 2 May to 30 September 9.30am to 12.15pm and 2pm to 6pm; the rest of the year open daily (except Monday) 10am to noon and 2pm to 5pm; closed 1 January, 1 May, 14 July, 1 November and 25 December; 10F; ☎ 04 68 90 30 54.

Musée lapidaire – Free or guided tour (☎ 04 68 90 30 66) from 1 July to 31 August 9.30am to 12.15pm and 2pm to 6pm; closed 14 July; 10F.

Basilique St-Paul-St-Serge – Open during the week 9am to noon and 2pm to 6pm.

NEVERS
🛈 31 rue Pierre Bérégovoy - 58000 - ☎ 03 86 59 07 03

Guided tour of the town ⛰– Contact the tourist information office.

Municipal Museum – Open daily (except Tuesday) from 1 May to 30 September 10am to 6.30pm; the rest of the year from 10am to noon and 2pm to 5.30pm; 10F; ☎ 03 86 68 45 62.

St-Gildard convent – ♿ Open daily from 1 April to 31 October 7am to 12.30pm and 1.30pm to 7.30pm; the rest of the year from 7.30am to noon and 2pm to 7pm; admission free; ☎ 03 86 57 79 99.

Cathédrale St-Cyr-et-Ste-Juliette – Open Tuesday to Friday in July, August and September 9.30am to noon and 2pm to 6pm; guided tour by appointment: request Mlle S. Morlé ☎ 03 86 59 06 74.

Grotte de NIAUX

Reservation necessary; guided tour (1 hour 15min) every 45min from 1 July to 30 September 8.30 to 11.30 and 1.30 to 5.15; the rest of the year at 11am, 3pm and 4.30pm; closed 1 January and 25 December; 50F; ☎ 05 61 05 88 37.

NICE

🅱 Avenue Thiers – 06000 – ☎ 04 93 87 07 07
🅱 2, rue Massenet – 06000 – ☎ 04 93 87 60 60

Château lift – Runs daily in January, February, March, October and November 10am to 6pm; April, May and September 9am to 7pm; June, July and August until 8am; 3F one-way ticket; 4.40 F return ticket; ☎ 04 93 85 62 33.

Ride in tourist train – Runs all year from 10am to 7pm; length of trip: 40min; closed from 15 November to 15 January; 25F; ☎ 04 93 18 81 58.

Cimiez: Gallo-Roman archaeological site – Visit from May to September 10am to noon and 2pm to 6pm; October to April 10am to noon and 2pm to 5pm; closed Monday and Sunday morning and 1 January, Easter 1 May, 25 January and all November; admission free; ☎ 04 93 81 59 57.

Musée Matisse – Open 1 April to 30 September 11am to 7pm; the rest of the year 10am to 5pm; closed Tuesday; 25F; ☎ 04 93 81 08 08.

Musée Marc-Chagall – ♿ Open from July to September 10am to 7pm; the rest of the year 10am to 12.30pm and 2pm to 5.30pm; closed Tuesday and 1 January, 1 May and 25 December; 27F (when temporary exhibitions, 35F); ☎ 04 93 81 75 75.

Musée des Beaux-Arts – Open from beginning May to end September 10am to noon and 3pm to 6pm; the rest of the year 10am to noon and 2pm to 5pm; closed Monday and 1 January, Easter, 1 May, and 25 December; admission free; ☎ 04 93 44 50 72.

Musée d'Art moderne et d'art contemporain – Open 11am to 6pm; 10pm on Friday; closed Tuesday and holidays; 25F; ☎ 04 93 62 61 62.

Musée Masséna – Same admission times and charges as the Musée des Beaux-Arts; closed for the month of November; admission free; ☎ 04 93 88 11 34.

Musée d'Art naïf Jakovsky – Open from May to September 10am to noon and 2pm to 6pm; the rest of the year, 10am to noon and 2pm to 5pm; closed Tuesday, 1 January, Easter, 1 May and 25 December; admission free; ☎ 04 93 71 78 33.

Chapelle de la Miséricorde – Lecture-tours only, Tuesday and Sunday at 3pm; lecture-tour starts from the palais Lascaris; ☎ 04 93 62 18 12.

Eglise St-Martin-St-Augustin – Open 9am to 11.30am and 2pm to 5pm; closed Monday and Sunday afternoon.

NÎMES

🅱 6 rue Auguste – 30000 Nîmes – ☎ 04 66 67 29 11

Guided tour of the town 🅰 – Contact the tourist information office.

Arènes – Open in the summer 9am to 6.30pm; in the winter 9am to noon and 2pm to 5pm. For further information on admission times, contact the tourist information office. From October to end April, the tours are always guided tours; during shows, corridas and the Feria de Nîmes, the amphitheatre are closed, as well as 1 January, 1 May and 25 December; 22F; ☎ 04 66 67 29 11.

Maison Carrée – Open in the summer 9am to 7pm; in winter 9am to noon and 2pm to 6pm; closed 1 January, 1 May and 25 December; ☎ 04 66 67 29 11.

Musée d'Archéologie – Open daily (except Monday) 11am to 6pm; closed 1 January, 1 May, 1 and 11 November, and 25 December; 22F; ☎ 04 66 67 25 57.

Musée des Beaux-Arts – ♿ Open daily (except Monday) from 11am to 6pm; closed 1 January, 1 May, 1 and 11 November, 25 December; 22F; book shop; ☎ 04 66 67 38 21.

Musée du Vieux Nîmes – Open daily (except Monday) from 11am to 6pm; 22F; ☎ 04 66 36 00 64.

Carré d'Art – ♿ Open in the summer 10am to 7pm; the rest of the year 10am to 6pm; closed Monday as well as 1 January, 1 May and 25 December; Centre de Documentation, ☎ 04 66 76 35 89; 22F; ☎ 04 66 76 35 70.

NOHANT

Château – Guided tour (1 hour) daily in July and August 9am to 7pm; from April to June and September to mid-October 9am to 12.15pm and 2pm to 6.30pm; same hours the rest of the year but closing time at 4.30pm; closed 1 January, 1 May, 1 and 11 November, 25 December; 27F; ☎ 02 54 31 06 04.

Abbaye de NOIRLAC

Free or guided tour (40min) daily in July and August 9.45am to 6.30pm; from April to June 9.45am to noon and 1.45pm to 6.30pm (5pm on concert nights); 1 October to 31 March 9.45am to noon and 1.45pm to 5pm; access closed 30min in the morning and 1 hour in the afternoon prior to closing time; closed Tuesday in October, November, December, January and the 1 January and 25 December; 25F; ☎ 02 48 96 23 64.

Chapelle N.-D.-des-FONTAINES

Open from Easter to All Saints Day 8am to 7pm; the rest of the year ask at the local cafés and restaurants who will provide the key in exchange for an identify card.

ORADOUR-SUR-GLANE   🛈 place du Champ de foire - 87520 - ☎ 05 55 03 13 73

Village – ♿ Free or guided tour (15min) daily 9am to noon and 2pm to 5pm; admission free; ☎ 05 55 03 13 73 (tourist information office).

ORANGE   🛈 cours Aristide-Briand - 84104 - ☎ 04 90 34 70 88

Guided tour of the town – Contact the tourist information office.

Théâtre antique – ♿ General view of the interior, but no access to the tiered seats; open from 1 April to 30 September 9am to 6.30pm; the rest of the year 9am to noon and 1.30pm to 5pm; closed 1 January and 25 December; 25F also provides access to the Musée municipal; ☎ 04 90 34 70 88.

Aven d'ORGNAC

Guided tour (1 hour) in July and August 9.30am to 6pm; from 1 April to 30 June and September 9.30am to noon and 2pm to 6pm; from 1 October to 15 November 9.30am to noon and 2pm to 5pm; closed from mid-November to end February; 36F or 47F for a combined ticket that includes a visit to the museum; ☎ 04 75 38 62 51.

ORLÉANS   🛈 place Albert-Ier - 45000 - ☎ 02 38 53 05 95

A 45min tour in a small train runs through the heart of the town; departure at the place Sainte-Croix in front of the cathedral, daily from 1 July to 31 August at 2.30pm, 3.45pm, 4.45pm and 6pm; from 28 May to 30 June and from 1 to 4 September the 6pm tour is cancelled; 25F; information at the tourist information office.

Guided tour of the town – Tour available from May to September on Wednesday and Saturday at 2.30 starting at the tourist information office. Many tours on specific themes are organized as well; contact the tourist information office.

Musée des Beaux-Arts – Open 10am to noon and 2pm to 6pm; closed Tuesday, 1 January, 1 and 8 May, 1 November and 25 December; 17F; ☎ 02 38 53 39 22.

Musée historique – Same admission times and charges as for the Musée des Beaux-Arts; closed Tuesday; 12F; ☎ 02 38 53 39 22.

Parc floral de la Source – ♿ Free or guided tour (1 hour) from 16 June to 31 August from 9am to 8pm; from 1 April to 15 June and from 1 September to 15 November from 9am to 6pm; the rest of the year 2pm to 5pm; 20F; closed Friday; 20F; 35F includes a visit to the butterfly house; ☎ 02 38 49 30 00.

Musée des Sciences naturelles – ♿ Open from 2pm to 6pm; closed Saturday as well as 1 January, 1 May, 14 July, 1 November, and 25 December; 20F; ☎ 02 38 54 61 05.

Crypt and Treasury of the Cathédrale Ste-Croix – Guided tour (45min) from 15 June to 15 September 3pm to 6.30pm; closed Friday; ☎ 02 38 66 64 17 (M. Grandet).

OTTMARSHEIM

Centrale hydro-électrique – Guided tour (2 hours) from Monday to Thursday 8am to noon and 2pm to 4.30pm, Friday 8am to noon; for groups of 10 or more (minimum age: 12 years) by written request three weeks in advance to E.D.F., Département technique, 83 rue Koechlin, 68060 Mulhouse Cedex; ☎ 03 89 32 48 23; individual tourists can join already planned tours.

Île d'OUESSANT

Can be reached by boat starting at Brest (see the Red Michelin Guide France). The boat lands at Stiff. A bus service (from June to September) or taxis (off season) goes to Lampaul. Bicycles may be rented at Stiff during school holidays and at Lampaul all year round. Information: Service maritime départemental ☎ 02 98 80 27 68. Access by air from Brest-Guipavas; information: ☎ 02 98 84 64 87.

Rocks on Ouessant

Centre d'interprétation des Phares et Balises – Open daily from 1 June to 30 September and during school holidays 10.30am to 6.30pm; the rest of the year from 2pm (1pm in April and May) to 6.30pm (4pm from 1 October to 31 March); closed Monday outside of school holiday periods, 1 January and 25 December; 25F; ☎ 02 98 48 80 70.

Phare du Stiff – The lighthouse has been automatic since September 1993, and lighthouse keepers from Créac'h lighthouse now organise guided tours. Guided tour (30min) from 1 May to 30 September 11m to 12.30pm and 2pm to 5pm except Sunday; the rest of the year by appointment; ☎ 02 98 48 80 21.

P

Gouffre de PADIRAC

Guided tour (1 hour 30min) daily in August 8am to 7pm; during the second two weeks of July, 8.30am to 6.30pm; from April to mid-July and September to the second Sunday in October 9am to noon and 2pm to 6pm; 41F; ☎ 05 65 33 64 56.

PARIS

Musée de l'Armée – Open 10am to 5.30pm (4.30pm from 1 October to 31 March); 35F; ☎ 01 44 42 37 67; closed 1 January, 1 May, 1 November and 25 December; the ticket is valid for two consecutive days to allow a complete tour of the Musée de l'Armée, the Eglise du Dôme, the Galerie des plans-reliefs and films. On the eastern side of the ground floor, documentaries, newsreels and films are shown on the two World Wars.

Eglise du Dôme – Same admission times and charges as the Musée de l'Armée (except during services); the church remains open from 1 June to 31 August until 7pm; ☎ 01 44 42 38 42.

L'Arc de Triomphe – Open daily from 1 April to 30 September 9.30am to 6.30pm; from 1 October to 31 March 10am to 5pm; 31F; ☎ 01 43 80 31 31.

Tour Eiffel – Access to all three floors daily from 1 July to 3 September 9am to midnight; the rest of the year 9.30am to 11pm; 1st floor lift: 20F; 2nd floor: 38F; 3rd floor: 55; 1st and 2nd floor: 12F; ☎ 01 44 11 23 23.

Palais de Justice – The Palais is open from 8am to 6pm except Sunday and holidays; common law or summary hearings can be attended. The Galerie des Bustes and the Tribunal pour Enfants are closed to the public; ☎ 01 44 32 67 19.

La Conciergerie - Open daily from 1 April to 30 September, except for holidays, 9.30 am to 6pm; from 1 October to 31 March 10am to 5pm; 25F; ☎ 01 43 54 30 06.

Panthéon - Open daily except for holidays (crypt; view of the nave, which is closed to the public) from 1 April to 30 September 9.30am to 5.45pm; from 1 October to 31 March 10am to 4.45pm; 26F; ☎ 01 43 54 34 51; fax 01 44 61 20 36.

Opéra Garnier (Bibliothèque-Musée) - Open daily from 10am to 4.30pm; closed 1 January and 1 May; 30F; ☎ 01 40 01 22 63.

La Sainte-Chapelle - Open daily except for holidays from 1 April to 30 September 9.30am to 1pm and 2pm to 6pm; from 1-31 October and from 1 February to 31 March 10am to 1pm and 2pm to 5pm; from 1 November to 31 January 10am to 1pm and 2pm to 4pm; ☎ 01 42 65 35 80.

Musée national du Moyen Âge et des Thermes de Cluny - Open daily (except Tuesday) 9.15am to 5.45pm; closed 1 January, 1 May, 1 November and 25 December; 27F; ☎ 01 46 34 45 17.

Palais de la Découverte - Open daily (except Monday) 9.30am to 6pm; Sunday and holidays 10am to 7pm; 22F; ☎ 01 40 74 80 00; Minitel 3615 DECOUVERTE.

Centre Georges-Pompidou - Open from noon (10am Saturday, Sunday and holidays) to 10pm; closed Tuesday and 1 May; 35F (Musée national d'art moderne), 45F (Grande Galerie), 60F (day-pass which provides access to the Musée national d'art moderne, all exhibits and guided tours, especially the "visite-découverte"); all tickets are purchased on the ground-floor; ☎ 01 44 78 12 33.

Orangerie - Open daily (except Tuesday) from 9.45am to 5.15pm; closed 1 January, 1 May and 25 December; 27F; ☎ 01 42 97 48 16.

Musée du Louvre - You may also refer to the *Visit Paris* section. ᘒ Open daily except Tuesday 9am to 6pm; Monday (Richelieu wing) and Wednesday (the entire museum) open until 10pm. The exhibit rooms begin closing 30min prior to closing time. The medieval section of the Louvre and the historical rooms of the museum are open from 9am to 10pm; bookstores, restaurants and cafés from 9.30am to 10pm; temporary exhibits under the pyramid are open 10am to 10pm; 40F, 20F after 3pm and Sunday, free for children under 18. Tickets are valid all day even if you leave the museum. Ticket sales stop at 5.15pm and 9.15pm. The *carte Musée et Monuments* is a pass that is valid for 1, 3 or 5 days for 65 museums and monuments and sold at the pay desk. The *carte Fidélité* gives free access to temporary exhibits under the Pyramid, reduced rates for the auditorium, lecture tours and workshops; the *carte des Amis du Louvre* (valid for 1 year; may be purchased at the desk of the Amis du Louvre near the Chalcography section between the Pyramid and the upside-down smaller pyramid) provides free access to the museum and the temporary exhibits, as well as reductions in many other exhibits around the city. General pre-recorded information by phone ☎ 01 40 20 51 51; reception ☎ 01 40 20 53 17; Minitel 3615 LOUVRE.

Musée d'Orsay - See also the information on the Musée d'Orsay in the *Visit Paris* section. ᘒ Open 10am (9am Sunday and from 20 June to 20 September) to 6pm (9.45pm Thursday; ticket office closes at 5.15pm and 9.15pm); closed Monday and 1 January, 1 May, and 25 December; 35F; ☎ 01 45 49 11 11 (general pre-recorded information).

La Cité des Sciences et de l'Industrie - ᘒ Open daily 10am to 6pm (Mediathèque 10am to 8pm, admission free); closed Monday, 1 May and 25 December; 45F (a *Cité-Pass* also includes a visit

View of Les Invalides and Place de la Concorde

to the Argonaute submarine); ☎ 01 36 68 20 30 (pre-recorded message) or 01 40 05 70 00, fax 01 40 05 82 35; Cité des enfants 20F; combined ticket (Cité-Géode) 85F; also available are double combined tickets for Cité-Cinaxe or triple tickets Cité-Géode-Cinaxe. Consult the Minitel 3615 VILLETTE.

La Géode – Performances every hour from Tuesday to Sunday 10am to 9pm; closed Monday except for holidays; request information; 55F; Reservation at ☎ 01 36 68 29 30; general information ☎ 01 40 03 75 03.

La Grande Arche – Open 9am to 7pm (6pm from 1 October to 31 March); 40F; ☎ 01 49 07 27 57.

Musée National des Techniques – Closed for restoration until 1997. The Lavoisier laboratory is open daily 10am to 5.30pm; closed Monday and holidays; ☎ 01 40 27 23 31.

PAU
🛈 place Royale - 64000 - ☎ 05 59 27 27 08.

Château – Guided tour (1 hour) of the apartments 9.30am to 11.45am and 2pm to 5.15pm; closed 1 January, 1 May and 25 December; 27F; ☎ 05 59 82 38 19.

Musée des Beaux-Arts – Open daily (except Tuesday) 10am to noon and 2pm to 6pm; closed 1 January, Whit Monday, 14 July, 1 November and 25 December; 10F; ☎ 05 59 27 33 02.

Centre de Préhistoire du PECH MERLE

Guided tour (1 hour 30min) daily from April to September 9.30am to noon and 1.30pm to 5.30pm; in October and November, 9.30am to noon and 1.30am to 4.45pm; please note: only 700 visitors per day are allowed in the cave; 42F; ☎ 05 65 31 27 05 (cave) or 05 65 31 27 61 (Town hall).

PÉRIGUEUX
🛈 Rd Point Tour Mataguerre, 26 Place Francheville - 24000
🛈 ☎ 05 53 53 10 63

Guided tour of the town 🅰– Contact the tourist information office.

Eglise St-Étienne-de-la-Cité – Free tour daily (except Sunday afternoon) 7am to 6.45pm.

Cathédrale St-Front – Free tour daily 8.30am to 7.30pm; guided tour by request ☎ 05 53 53 23 62.

Musée du Périgord – Open daily (except Tuesday) from April to September 10am to noon and 2pm to 6pm; from October to March 10am to noon and 2pm to 5pm; closed for holidays; 12F; ☎ 05 53 53 16 42.

PÉROUGES
🛈 01800 - ☎ 04 74 61 00 88

Musée du Vieux-Pérouges – Open daily from Easter to end October 10am to noon and 2pm to 6pm; the rest of the year open on Saturday and Sunday only; closed in January; 15F, the ticket provides access to the Maison des Princes de Savoie (art exhibits) and to the hortulus; ☎ 04 74 61 00 88.

PERPIGNAN
🛈 Palais des Congrès, pl A.-Lanoux - 66000 - ☎ 04 68 66 30 30

Palais des rois de Majorque – Open from 1 June to 30 September 10am to 6pm, the res of the year 9am to 5pm; last admission 45min before closing time; closed 1 January, 1 May, 1 November and 25 December; 20F; ☎ 04 68 34 48 29.

Castillet (Casa Pairal) – Open daily (except Tuesday) from 15 June to 15 September 9.30am to 7pm (6pm on Sunday); the rest of the year 9am to 6pm ((5pm on Sunday); closed for holidays; admission free; ☎ 04 68 35 42 05.

Château de PEYREPERTUSE

Open daily all year round; Wear good walking shoes; 10F; ☎ 04 68 45 40 55.

PIERREFONDS

Château – Tour (1 hour guided tour Sunday) from 1 May to 31 August 10am to 6pm (7pm Sunday); in March, April, September and October during the week from 10am to 12.30pm and 2pm to 6pm, Sunday 10am to 6pm; from 1 November to 28 February during the week 10am to noon and 2pm to 5pm, Sunday 10am to 5.30pm; last admission 45min before closing time; closed 1 January, 1 May, 1 and 11 November and 25 December; 27F; ☎ 03 44 42 80 77.

Haras du PIN

Guided tour daily from 1 April to 9 September 9.30am to 6pm; from 15 July to 15 September the "Jeudis du Pin" on Thursday present a lecture on harnessing and studs of different races (1 hour) in the Cour d'honneur at 3pm (you should arrive at 2.30pm); the rest of the year during the week open 2pm to 4pm, Sunday and holidays 9.30pm to 5.30pm; 25F; ☎ 02 33 36 68 68.

POITIERS

🏛 8, rue des Grandes-Ecoles - 86000 - ☏ 05 49 41 21 24

Guided tour of the town 🄰 – Contact the tourist information office.

Baptistère St-Jean – Open daily in July and August 10.30am to 12.30pm and 3pm to 6pm; daily (except Tuesday) at the same times from April to June and from September to beginning November; from beginning November to March 2.30pm to 4.30pm; closed 1 January, 1 May and 25 December; 4F.

Palais de Justice – Open daily (except on the weekend and holidays) from 8am to 6pm.

Musée Ste-Croix – Free or guided tour on Saturday (1 hour 15min) daily (except Monday) 10am to noon and 1pm to 5pm (2pm to 6pm on the weekend and holidays); 15F; ☏ 05 49 41 09 53.

POLIGNAC

Château – Guided tour (1 hour) in July and August 10am to noon and 2pm to 7pm; free tour from Easter to end June and in September (closes at 5.30pm); 6F.

PONT-DU-GARD

Parking place: right bank 12F; left bank 18F.

Abbaye de PORT-ROYAL-DES-CHAMPS

Musée national des Granges – Open daily (except Tuesday) 10am to noon and 2pm to 6pm (5.30pm from 15 October to 1 March); closed 1 January and 25 December; 15F (10F on Sunday); ☏ 01 30 43 73 05.

PRAFRANCE

Bambouseraie – ♿ Open from 1 April to 26 September 9.30am to 7pm; in March from 9.30am to 6pm; from 27 September to 31 December, check times; closed Monday and Tuesday in November and December, and during the months of January and February; 28F; children 16F; ☏ 04 66 61 70 47.

PROVINS

🏛 Chemin de Villecran - BP 44 - 77160 - ☏ 01 64 60 26 26

Guided tour of the town A – Contact the tourist information office.

Tour de César – Open daily from Easter to All Saints' Day 10.30am to 6pm; the rest of the year 10.30am to 5pm; 15F; ☏ 01 64 60 26 26.

Le PUY DU FOU

Ecomusée de la Vendée – Open from 1 May to 30 September 10am to 6.30pm; from 1 October to 30 April 10am to 11.30pm and 2pm to 5.30pm; closed Monday, 1 January and 25 December; 12F; ☏ 02 51 57 60 60; Minitel: 3615 code PUY DU FOU.

Cinéscénie – Son et Lumière performance from early June to early September. Fridays and Saturdays only; reservations. ☏ 02 51 64 11 11. Minitel 3615 code PUY DU FOU.

"Son et lumière" show, Le Puy du Fou

Le PUY-EN-VELAY

🛈 Place Breuil - 43000 - ☎ 04 71 09 38 41

Guided tour of the town 🅰– Contact the tourist information office.

Musée Crozatier – Open 10am to noon and 2pm to 6pm; from October to end April, closes at 4pm and on Sunday mornings; closed Tuesday all year, 1 January, 1 November, and 25 December; 12F; ☎ 04 71 09 38 90.

Rocher Corneille – Open mid-March to end April 9am to 6pm; from May to end September, 9am to 7pm; the rest of the year 10am to 5pm; closed in December and January, and Tuesday from November to mid-March; 10F; ☎ 04 71 04 11 33.

Cathédrale Notre-Dame – Open 9am to 6pm in season (off season, closed from noon to 2pm);
Guided tour – Contact the sacristy or the Rector (Recteur); ☎ 04 71 05 44 93

Cloisters – Free or guided tour (45min) from beginning April to end September 9.30am to 12.30pm and 2pm to 6pm; the rest of the year, 9.30am to noon and 2pm to 4.30pm (open from noon to 2pm Sunday and holidays); closed 1 January, 1 May, 1 and 11 November, 25 December; 16F; ☎ 04 71 05 45 52.

Chapelle St-Michel-d'-Aiguilhe – Open mid-June to mid-September 9am to 7pm; from mid-March to mid-June and mid-September to 12 November 10am to noon and 2am to 6pm (5pm in March and starting 15 September); during Christmas school holidays and in February, 2pm to 4pm; closed the rest of the year as well as 1 January and 25 December; 5F; ☎ 04 71 02 71 32.

Q

QUIMPER

🛈 Place de la résistance - 29000 - ☎ 02 98 53 04 05

Guided tour of the town 🅰 – Tour daily from June to September. Contact the tourist information office.

Musée des Beaux-Arts – ♿ Free or guided tour (1 hour 30min) daily from 1 July to 31 August 10am to 7pm; the rest of the year 10am to noon and 2pm to 6pm, closed Tuesday, Sunday morning (from 1 October to 31 March) and 1 January, 1 May, 1 and 11 November and 25 December; 25F; ☎ 02 98 95 45 20.

Musée départemental breton – ♿ Open daily from 1 June to 30 September 9am to 6pm; the rest of the year 9am to noon and 2pm to 5pm; closed Sunday morning and Monday from October to May; 20F (off-season), 25F (June to September); ☎ 02 98 95 21 60.

Musée de la faïence – Open 18 April to 28 October 10am to 6pm; closed Sunday and holidays; 26F; guided tour by appointment; ☎ 02 98 90 12 72.

R

RAMBOUILLET

🛈 Hôtel de Ville - 78120 - ☎ 01 34 83 21 21

Château – Guided tour (30min) all year 10am to 11.30am and 2pm to 5.30pm (4.30pm from 1 October to 31 March). Closed Tuesday, 1 January, 1 May, 1 and 11 November, 25 December and during presidential visits; 27F; ☎ 01 34 83 02 49.

Parc – Open daily from 1 May to 31 August 6.30am to 7.30pm; from 1 February to 30 April and 1 September to 31 October 7am to 6pm; the rest of the year 8am to 5pm; closed during presidential visits; admission free; ☎ 01 34 83 02 49.

Laiterie de la Reine et Chaumière des Coquillages – Guided tour (45min) from 10am to 11.30am and 2pm to 5.30pm (3.30pm from 1 October to 31 March); closed Monday and Tuesday, 1 January, 1 May, 1 and 11 November and 25 December; 14F; free 16 and 17 September; ☎ 01 34 83 02 49.

REIMS

🛈 2, rue Guillaume de Machault - 51100 - ☎ 03 26 77 45 25

Guided tour of the town 🅰 – Contact the tourist information office.

Palais du Tau – Open 16 March to 30 June and 1 September to 14 November 9.30am to 12.30pm and 2pm to 6pm; in July and August 9.30am to 6.30pm; from 15 November to 15 March 10am to noon and 2pm to 5pm (6pm Saturday and Sunday); closed 1 January, 1 May, 1 and 11 November and 25 December; 27F; ☎ 03 26 47 81 79.

REIMS

Musée St-Remi – Open 2pm to 6pm (6.45pm Saturday and Sunday); closed 1 January, 1 May, 14 July, 1 and 11 November and 25 December; 10F; ☏ 03 26 85 23 36.

Musée-hôtel Le Vergeur – Guided tour (1 hour 15min) daily (except Monday) 2pm to 6pm; closed 1 January, 1 May, 14 July, 1 and 11 November and 25 December and from 24 December to 2 January; 20F; ☏ 03 26 47 20 75.

Veuve Clicquot-Ponsardin – Guided tour (1 hour 30min) from 1 March to 31 October except Sunday by appointment a few days in advance; contact Mme Danielle Brissaud; ☏ 03 26 89 54 41.

Mumm – Guided tour (1 hour) in season 9am to 11am and 2pm to 5pm; off season, Saturday, Sunday, and holidays 2pm to 5pm; closed 1 January and 25 December; 20F; ☏ 03 26 49 59 70.

Piper Heidsieck – Tour of the cellars in a vehicle (20min) 9am to 11.45am and 2pm to 5.15pm; closed Tuesday and Wednesday from 1 December to 28 February, 1 January and 25 December; 20F; ☏ 03 26 84 43 44.

Pommery – Guided tour (1 hour) from 1 April to 31 October 11am to 5pm; the rest of the year from Monday to Friday by appointment; closed from end December to beginning January; ☏ 03 26 61 62 56.

Ruinart – Guided tour by appointment only from Monday to Friday; contact the Service Relations Publiques, 4 rue des Crayères, 51053 Reims; ☏ 03 26 85 40 29.

Taittinger – Guided tour (about 45min) during the week 9.30am to noon and 2pm to 4.30pm; Saturday, Sunday and holidays 9am to 11am and 2pm to 5pm; closed Saturday, Sunday and holidays from 1 December to 28 February; 18F; ☏ 03 26 85 45 35.

Musée des Beaux-Arts – Open daily (except Tuesday) 10am to noon and 2pm to 6pm; closed 1 January, 1 May, 14 July, 1 and 11 November and 25 December; 10F; ☏ 03 26 47 28 44.

Chapelle Foujita – Open daily from 15 April to 31 October (except Wednesday) 2pm to 6pm; 10F, free on Saturday; ☏ 03 26 47 28 44.

Centre historique de l'automobile française – Open daily from March to November (except Tuesday) 10am to noon and 2pm to 7pm; the rest of the year on Saturday, Sunday and holidays 10am to noon and 2pm to 7pm; during the week by appointment; 30F; ☏ 03 26 82 83 84.

RENNES

🛈 pont de Nemours – 35005 – ☏ 02 99 79 01 98
🛈 SNCF Railway station ☏ 02 99 53 23 23

Guided tour of the city 🅰 – Daily in July and August; check with the tourist information office with the "Rennes Ville d'Art et d'Histoire" department.

Palais de Justice – Closed due to the fire that damaged the Palais de Justice (Parlement de Bretagne) during the night of 4 February 1994.

Cathédrale St-Pierre – Open daily 9am to noon and 2pm to 6pm; ☏ 02 99 30 12 03.

Musée des Beaux-Arts – ♿ Open 10am to noon and 2pm to 6pm; closed Tuesday and all holidays; 15F; ☏ 02 99 28 55 85.

Écomusée du pays de Rennes – Open Monday through Friday 9am to noon and 2pm to 6pm; Saturday and Sunday 2pm to 6pm (7pm on Sunday); closed Tuesday, from 16-31 January and all holidays; 25F, children 13F; ☏ 02 99 51 38 15.

La RHUNE

Access via rack-railway starting from the Col de St-Ignace; from 1 July to 30 September, leaves daily at 10am and 3pm and every 35 min starting at 9am if there are too many people; during spring holidays, leaves daily at 10am and 3pm; in May and June and from 1 October to 15 November, Saturday, Sunday and holidays only for groups of at least 40; leaves at 10am and 3pm; one-way 30F (children 20F); return ticket 45F (children 30F); ☏ 05 59 54 20 26.

RICHELIEU
🖪 6, Grande-Rue - 37120 - ☎ 02 47 58 13 62

Musée de l'hôtel de ville – Guided tour (30min) 10am to noon and 2pm to 6pm (4pm from 1 September to 30 June); closed Tuesday all year and Saturday, Sunday and holidays from September to June; 7F; ☎ 02 47 58 10 13.

Train trips – Runs Saturday, Sunday and holidays from end May to beginning September; departures from 9.45am to 3.45pm; 78F (1st class), 58F (2nd class) for a return ticket Richelieu-Chinon (diesel, autorail or steam); ☎ 02 47 58 12 97.

RIOM
🖪 16, rue du Commerce - 63200 - ☎ 04 73 38 59 45

Guided tour of the town 🅰 – Contact the tourist information office.

Sainte-Chapelle – Guided tour daily (except on the weekend) from mid-July to mid-August 10am to noon (last entry at 11.30am); same admission times during the last two weeks in July and the last two weeks of August but from 2.30pm to 5.30pm (last admission at 5pm); from Wednesday to Friday in June 3pm to 5pm (last entry 4.30pm) (open exceptionally for the festival of St-Amable); in September, from Wednesday to Friday 2.30pm to 5.30pm (last entry at 5pm); in May, Wednesday 3pm to 5pm (last entry at 4.30pm); the rest of the year by appointment; closed 14 July and 15 August; 15F; ☎ tourist information office.

Musée régional d'Auvergne – Open daily (except Tuesday) from June to September and during school vacations 10am to noon and 2.30p to 6pm; open daily (except Monday and Tuesday) October to May 10am to noon and 2pm to 5.30; closed for holidays and during the Foires des Cendres et de la St-Amable; 18F (admission free on Wednesday); ☎ 04 73 38 17 31.

Musée Mandet – Open daily (except Tuesday) from June to September and during school vacations 10am to noon and 2.30pm to 6pm; daily (except Monday and Tuesday) from October to May 10am to noon and 2pm to 5.30pm; closed for holidays and during the Foires des Cendres et de la St-Amable; 18F (admission free on Wednesday); ☎ 04 73 38 18 53.

RIQUEWIHR
🖪 2 rue de la 1re Armée - 68340 - ☎ 03 89 47 80 80

Musée du Dolder – Open from Good Friday to end October Saturday, Sunday and holidays 9.15am to noon and 1.30pm to 6.15pm, daily during school vacations; 10F.

RIXHEIM

Musée du Papier peint – Open 10am (9 am from 1 June to 30 September) to noon and 2pm to 6pm; closed Tuesdays from 1 October to 31 May and 1 January, Good Friday, 1 May, 25 December; 30F; ☎ 03 89 64 24 56.

ROCAMADOUR
🖪 Hôtel de ville - 46500 - ☎ 05 65 33 62 59

Hôtel de ville – Free tour daily in July and August 10am to 8pm; from April to June and in September 10am to noon and 2pm to 7pm; from October to mid-November 10am to noon and 2pm to 6pm; from mid-November to March 2.30pm to 5.30pm; closed 1 January and 25 December; 7F; ☎ 05 65 33 74 13.

Musée trésor Francis-Poulenc – ♿ Free or guided tour (1 hour) daily from June to September 9am to 7pm; 15F; ☎ 05 65 33 23 23.

ROCHEFORT
🖪 Avenue Sadi-Carnot - 17300 - ☎ 05 46 99 08 60

Guided tour of the town 🅰 – Contact the tourist information office.

Maison de Pierre Loti – Guided tour (50min) daily (except Sunday morning) from July to September at 10am, 10.30am, 11am, 2pm, 2.30pm, 3pm, 3.30pm, 4pm, 4.30pm, and 5pm; daily (except Tuesday and Sunday morning) from October to June at 10am, 11am, 2pm, 3pm and 4pm; closed holidays and from mid-December to mid-January; 40F; ☎ 05 46 99 16 88.

Musée Naval – Free or guided tour by previous appointment (1 hour 15min) daily (except Tuesday) 10am to noon and 2pm to 6pm; closed on holidays (except Easter and Pentecost Day) and from mid-October to mid-November; 26F; ☎ 05 46 99 86 57.

Musée d'Art et d'Histoire de la ville – Free or guided tour (from April to October) daily in July and August 1.30pm to 7pm; daily (except Sunday and Monday) from September to June 1.30pm to 5.30pm; closed holidays; 10F; ☎ 05 46 99 83 99.

La ROCHEFOUCAULD
🖪 Halle aux grains, place de Gourville - 16110 - ☎ 05 45 63 07 45

Château – Free or guided tour (2 hours) from May to September 10am to 7pm; from October to April 2pm to 7pm Sunday and holidays; 35F; ☎ 05 45 62 07 42.

La ROCHELLE 🖪 Quartier du Gabut, place de la Petite-Sirène - 17000 - ☎ 05 46 41 14 68

Tour St-Nicolas – Open daily from mid-June to mid-September 9.30am to 7pm; from April to mid-June and the second fortnight in September 9.30am to 12.30pm and 2pm to 6.30pm; daily (except Monday) from October to March 9.30am to 12.30pm and 2pm to 5pm; closed 1 January, 1 May, 1 and 11 November; 25 December; 21F; ☎ 05 46 41 74 13.

Tour de la Lanterne – Open daily from mid-June to mid-September 9.30am to 7pm; from April to mid-June and the second half of September 9.30am to 12.30pm and 2pm to 6.30pm; daily (except Monday) from October to March 9.30am to 12.30pm and 2pm to 5pm; closed 1 January, 1 May, 1 and 11 November; 25 December; 21F; ☎ 05 46 41 56 04.

Siege of La Rochelle by Henri Motte

Muséum d'Histoire naturelle – Open daily (except Monday 10am to 12.30pm and 1.30pm to 5.30pm (2pm to 6pm on the weekend); closed for holidays; 16F; ☎ 05 46 41 18 25.

Musée du Nouveau-Monde – Open daily (except Tuesday) 10.30am to 12.30pm and 1.30pm to 6pm; Sunday and holidays from 3pm to 6pm; closed 1 January, 1 May, 1 November and 25 December; 16F; ☎ 05 46 41 46 50.

Musée des Beaux-Arts – Open daily (except Tuesday) from 3pm to 6pm; closed 1 January, 1 May, 1 November and 25 December; 16F; ☎ 05 46 41 64 65.

Musée d'Orbigny – Open daily (except Tuesday and Sunday morning) 10am to noon and 2pm to 6pm; closed 1 January, 1 May, 1 November and 25 December; 16F; ☎ 46 41 18 83.

ROCHETAILLÉE-SUR-SAÔNE

Musée Henri-Malartre – Open 9am to 6pm (7pm in June, July and August); last admission 1 hour before closing time; closed 1 January and 25 December; 20F; ☎ 04 78 22 18 80.

RODEZ
🖪 Place Foch - 12005 - ☎ 05 65 68 02 27

Musée Fenaille – Closed for restoration.

RONCHAMP

Chapelle de Notre-Dame-du-Haut – Open daily from March to November 9am to 7pm; closes at 4pm the rest of the year; ☎ 03 84 20 65 13.

ROQUEBRUNE-CAP-MARTIN 🖪 20, avenue Paul-Doumer - 06190 - ☎ 04 93 35 62 87

Donjon – Open 10am to 12pm and 2pm to 5.30pm, closes at 7pm during the summer, closed Friday in the winter, 1 May and 13 November to 14 December; 10F; ☎ 04 93 35 07 22.

ROUEN
🖪 25, place de la Cathédrale - 76000 - ☎ 02 32 08 32 40

Guided tour of the town 🅰 – Open daily from 8 July to 3 September at 10am and 3pm; from 15 April to 2 July Saturday, Sunday and holidays at 10am and 3pm; contact the tourist information office.

Cathédrale Notre-Dame – Guided tour (45min) from Easter to 10 September from Monday to Saturday at 10am, 11am, 2pm, 3pm, 4pm and 5pm; on Sunday tours are offered only in the afternoon; the rest of the year, tours Saturday and Sunday afternoon until 4pm; 14F; ☎ 02 35 89 73 78.

Eglise St-Ouen – Open daily 15 March to 31 October, except Tuesday, 10am to 12.30pm and 2pm to 6pm; from 1 November to 15 December and from 16 January to 15 March, Saturday, Sunday and Wednesday from 10am to noon and 2pm to 4.30pm; closed from 16 December to 15 January; ☎ 02 35 08 13 90.

Musée des Beaux-Arts – Open 10am to 6pm; closed on Tuesday and 1 January, 1 and 8 May, Ascension Day, 14 July, 15 August, 1 and 11 November, and 25 December; 20F; ☎ 02 35 71 28 40.

Musée de la Céramique – Free or guided tour (1 hour 30min); same admission times as for the Musée des Beaux-Arts; 13F; ☎ 02 35 07 31 74.

Palais de Justice – Contact the tourist information office, place de la Cathédrale.

Musée Le Secq des Tournelles – Same times as for the Musée des Beaux Arts; guided tour (1 hour) by appointment at ☎ 02 35 52 00 62; closed Tuesdays and all public holidays; 13F; ☎ 02 35 88 42 92.

Musée des Antiquités de la Seine-Maritime – Free or guided tour (1 hour 30min) all year 10am to 12.30pm and 1.30pm to 5.30pm; closed Tuesday, Sunday morning and holidays; 20F; ☎ 02 35 98 55 10.

Eglise St-Godard – Tour during the week only 9am to noon and 2pm to 6pm; ☎ 02 35 71 47 12.

Serres dans le Jardin des Plantes – Open 1 April to 30 September 8am to 7pm; the rest of the year closes at 5.30pm or 6pm; the greenhouses are open 8am to 11.30am and 1.30 to 4.30pm; admission free; ☎ 02 35 72 36 36.

Abbaye de ROYAUMONT

Open daily 10am to 6pm (5.30pm from 1 November to 28 February); guided tours offered in the afternoon on Saturday, Sunday and holidays; 22F; ☎ 01 30 35 88 90.

RUEIL-MALMAISON

Musée – Open daily (except Tuesday) 10am to noon and 1.30pm to 5pm (4.30pm from 1 October to 31 March); Saturday and Sunday, guided tour (1 hour); closed 25 December and 1 January; 27F (admission free for children); ☎ 01 41 29 05 57.

Château de Bois-Préau – Open 1 April to 30 September 10.30am to 12.30 pm and 2pm to 5.30pm (5pm from 1 October to 31 March); closed the same days as the museum; 12F, free under 18; ☎ 01 47 49 20 07.

S

ST-BARTHÉLÉMY-D'ANJOU

Château de Pignerolle (musée européen de la Communication) – ♿ Free or guided tour (2 hours) from 1 July to 1 November 10am to 12.30pm and 2.30pm to 6.30pm; from 1 April to 30 June, same times, but closed on Tuesday; the rest of the year Saturday afternoon and Sunday; closed for Christmas; 50F; ☎ 02 41 93 38 38.

ST-BENOÎT-SUR-LOIRE

Basilica – Free or guided tour (1 hour) from Easter to end October at varying hours, displayed at the entrance; no tour Sunday morning or during Holy Week; 15F; ☎ 02 38 35 72 43.

ST-BERTRAND-DE-COMMINGES

Cathédrale Ste-Marie-de-Comminges – The cathedral and the cloisters are open from 1 April to 31 October 9am to noon and 2pm to 6pm; the rest of the year (except Sunday morning) 10am to noon and 2pm to 5pm; guided tours by appointment: ☎ 05 61 89 04 91.

ST-CLAUDE
🛈 6, rue du Marché - BP 94 - 39200 - ☎ 03 84 45 34 24

Cathédrale St-Pierre – Open daily 9am to noon and 2pm to 6pm; guided tour in July and August; ☎ 03 84 45 48 53.

Cathédrale ST-DENIS

Cathédrale – Open daily from 1 April to 30 September 10am to 7pm; the rest of the year 10am to 5pm; closed 1 January, 1 May, 1 and 11 November, 25 December; 27F; ☎ 01 48 09 83 54.

ST-ÉMILION
🛈 Place des Créneaux - 33330 - ☎ 05 57 24 72 03

Church – Guided tour (45min - starts from the tourist information office, Salle du Doyenne) daily at 10am, 10.45am, 11.30am, 2pm, 2.45pm, 3.30pm, 4.15pm, 5pm (and 5.45pm from 1 April to 31 October); closed 1st week of January and 24, 25 and 31 December; 33F; ☎ 57 24 72 03.

ST-GERMAIN-EN-LAYE
🛈 38, rue du Pain - 78100 - ☎ 01 34 51 05 12

Guided tour of the town 🅰 – Contact the tourist information office.

Musée des Antiquités nationales – Open all year from 9am to 5.15pm; guided tour Saturday, Sunday, Wednesday and during school holidays; closed Tuesday; 22F; ☎ 01 34 51 53 65.

Musée du Prieuré – Open all year 10am to 6.30pm (5.30pm from Wednesday to Friday); closed Monday, Tuesday, 1 January, 1 May and 25 December; 25F; ☎ 01 39 73 77 87.

ST-GERVAIS-LES-BAINS
🛈 115, avenue du Mont-Paccard - 74170 - ☎ 04 50 78 22 43

Tramway du Mont-Blanc – From St-Gervais to the Col de Voza (1800m) the tramway runs all year except in May; time round trip 2 hours; 80F; from St-Gervais to the Nid d'Aigle (2400m); runs from mid-June to September; time round trip 2 hours 30min; 129F; for exact times, call ☎ 04 50 47 51 83.

ST-JEAN-DE-LUZ
🛈 place Maréchal-Foch - 65400 - ☎ 05 59 26 03 16

Maison Louis XIV – Guided tour (30min) daily (except Sunday morning) in July and August 10.30am to noon and 2.30pm to 6.30pm; in June and September, 10.30am to noon and 2.30pm to 5.30pm; prices not received; ☎ 05 59 26 01 56.

ST-MALO
🛈 Esplanae St-Vincent - 35400 - ☎ 02 99 56 64 48

Guided tour of the town 🅰 – Contact the Musée d'Histoire de la ville in the Grand donjon of the château; ☎ 02 99 40 71 57.

Musée d'Histoire de la ville et d'Ethnolographie du pays malovin – Open 10am to noon and 2pm to 6pm; closed Monday from 2 November to 31 March and 1 January, 1 May, 1 November and 25 December; 20F; ☎ 02 99 40 71 57.

Quic-en-Groigne Tower – Guided tour (45min) from Palm Sunday to end September daily 9.30am to noon and 2pm to 5.45pm; 19F; ☎ 02 99 40 80 26.

Fort National – Guided tour (30min) daily from 15 June to 15 September as well as Saturday, Sunday and the holidays for Easter, Whitsun, Christmas and New Year's Day; times vary following low tide; closed during high tide; 12F; ☎ 02 99 46 91 25.

ST-NECTAIRE
🛈 Mairie - 63710 - ☎ 04 73 88 50 86

Church – Open daily (except Tuesday and Sunday morning) from June to September 10am to 11.30am and 2pm to 5.30pm; the rest of the year enquire; closed from December to March; ☎ 04 73 88 50 67.

ST-NICOLAS-DE-PORT

Basilique – Guided tour available (1 hour) of the chapelle des Fonts, the treasury, the crypt and the sacristy from beginning July to the 1st Sunday of September, Sunday and holidays 2am to 6pm; 20F; the towers 10F; ☎ 03 83 46 81 50.

ST-OMER
🛈 boulevard Pierre-Guillain - 62500 - ☎ 03 21 98 08 51

Musée de l'hôtel Sandelin – Open 10am to noon and 2pm to 6pm (5pm Thursday and Friday); closed Monday, Tuesday and certain holidays; 15F (for 20 F the ticket also provides access to the Musée Henri-Dupuis); ☎ 03 21 38 00 94.

ST-POL-DE-LÉON

Chapelle du Kreisker – Open daily from June to September 9am to noon and 2pm to 6pm; ☎ 02 98 69 11 79.

ST-QUENTIN
🛈 14, rue de la Sellerie - 02100 - ☎ 03 23 67 05 00

Guided tour of the town 🅰 – Contact the tourist information office.

Musée Antoine-Lécuyer – Open daily (except all day Tuesday and Sunday morning) from 10am to noon and 2pm to 5pm (6pm Saturday and Sunday); closed 1 January, 1 May, 14 July, 1 November, 25 December; 8.60F; ☎ 03 23 64 06 66.

ST-RÉMY-DE-PROVENCE
🛈 place Jean-Jaurès - 13210 - ☎ 04 90 92 05 22

Ruines de Glanum - ♿ Open 1 April to 30 September 9am to 7pm; the rest of the year, 9am to noon and 2pm to 5pm; closed 1 January, 1 May, 1 and 11 November, 25 December; 32F; ☎ 04 90 92 23 79.

ST-RIQUIER

Abbey Church - Open mid-February to end November from Wednesday to Sunday 2pm to 6pm; the rest of the year by appointment; 5F.

Trésorerie - Open daily 1 May to 30 September 9.30am to noon and 2pm to 6pm; from 11 February to 30 April and 1 October to 30 November daily 2pm to 6pm as well as Saturday and Sunday 9.30am to noon; admission free; ☎ 03 22 28 20 20.

ST-SAVIN

Abbey Church - Free or guided tour (1 hour 15min) daily in July and August 9.30am to 7pm; from May to June and in September 9.30am to 12.30pm and 1.30pm to 6.30pm; the second fifteen days of April 2pm to 6pm; the second fifteen days of December 2pm to 5pm; from mid-February to mid-April and from October to mid-December on weekends and holidays 2pm to 6pm; closed from January to mid-February, 14 May and 25 December; 15F (free tour); 20 F (guided tour); ☎ 05 49 48 66 22.

ST-THÉGONNEC

Funérary chapel - Open daily in summer; admission free.

ST-TROPEZ
🛈 quai Jean-Jaurès - 83990 - ☎ 04 94 97 45 21

Musée de l'Annonciade - Open from 1 October to end May 10am to noon and 2pm to 6pm; from June to September 10am to noon and 4pm to 8pm; closed Tuesday, in November, 1 January, Ascension Day, 1 May and Christmas; 25F; ☎ 04 94 97 04 01.

A game of *pétanque*, St-Tropez

SAINTES
🛈 Villa Musso, 62 Cours national - 17100 - ☎ 05 46 74 23 82

Guided tour of the town 🅰 - Contact the tourist information office.

Musée des Beaux-Arts - Open daily (except Tuesday and Sunday morning) from May to September 10am to noon and 2pm to 6pm; from October to April 10am to noon and 2pm to 5pm; closed 1 January, 1 May, 1 November and 25 December; 10F (in summer); admission free the rest of the year; ☎ 05 46 93 03 94.

Abbaye aux Dames - Free or guided tour (1 hour 30min) daily from June to September 10am to 12.30pm and 2pm to 7pm; from October to May, Wednesday and Saturday at the same times, the rest of the week 2pm to 7pm; closed from 24 December to beginning January; 20F (free tour), 25F (guided tour); ☎ 05 46 97 48 48 or Minitel code ABBAYEDAMES

Fort de SALSES

Open all year daily 9.30am to 12.30pm and 2pm to 6pm; closed 1 January, 1 May, 1 and 11 November, 25 December; 36F; ☎ 04 68 38 60 13.

SAN MICHELE DE MURATO

Church – Open Monday through Friday from July to end September, 8am to noon and 2pm to 6pm; the rest of the year, enquire at the Mairie de Murato.

SARLAT-LA-CANÉDA ⬛ Hôtel de Vienne Place de la Liberté - 24203 - ☎ 05 53 59 27 67

Guided tour of the town ▲ – Contact the tourist information office.

SARTÈNE ⬛ 6 rue Borgo - 20100 - ☎ 04 95 77 15 40

Musée de préhistoire corse – Open mid-June to mid-September 10am to noon and 2pm to 6pm; the rest of the year, closes at 5pm; closed Sunday all year and Saturday off-season; in season, open during public holidays; 10F; ☎ 04 95 77 01 09.

SAUMUR ⬛ place Bilange - BP 241 - 49400 - ☎ 02 41 40 20 60

Musée de l'École de Cavalerie – Open Tuesday, Wednesday, Thursday and Sunday from 9am to noon and 2pm to 5pm, Saturday from 2pm to 5pm; closed 1 January and 25 December; admission free; ☎ 02 41 83 93 06.

Musée des Blindés – ♿ Open 9am to noon and 2pm to 6pm; closed 1 January and 25 December; 20F; ☎ 02 41 53 06 99.

Le Château et ses musées – Free tour for the Musée du Cheval, guided tour (1 hour) for the Musée des Arts décoratifs; from 1 June to 30 September; 9am to 6pm; from 1 October to 31 May (except Tuesday) 9.30am to noon and 2pm to 5.30pm; special walks (every evening) and evening tours Wednesday and Saturday from 8.30pm to 10.30pm; closed 1 January and 25 December; 33F; ☎ 02 41 51 30 46.

SEDAN ⬛ 41, place du Château-Fort - 08202 Cedex - ☎ 03 24 27 73 73

Château fort – Both self-guided tour and guided tour (1 hour) from 15 March to 15 September 10am to 6pm; the rest of the year 1.30pm to 5.30pm (guided tour at 2pm, 3.15pm, and 4.30pm); closed 1 January and 25 December; 30F; ☎ 24 27 73 73; evening tours by torchlight from mid-June to end September Friday, Saturday and Sunday at dusk; 40F.

Abbaye de SÉNANQUE

Open from 1 March to 31 October 10am to noon and 2pm to 6pm; the rest of the year 2pm to 5pm; closed on Sunday mornings and religious holidays as well as Good Friday and 25 December; 18F; ☎ 04 90 72 05 72.

SENLIS ⬛ place du Parvis Notre-Dame - 60300 - ☎ 03 44 53 06 40

Guided tour of the town ▲ – Contact the tourist information office.

Chapelle royale St-Frambourg – Open from April to October Saturday, Sunday and holidays from 3pm to 6.30pm; Sunday only the rest of the year from 3pm to 5pm; 20F; ☎ 03 44 53 44 52.

SENS ⬛ place Jean-Jaurès - 89100 - ☎ 03 86 65 19 49

Museum, treasury and the Palais Synodal – ♿ Open daily from 1 June to 30 September 10am to noon and 2pm to 6pm; the rest of the year, open Monday, Thursday and Friday from 2pm to 6pm, Wednesday, Saturday, Sunday and holidays 10am to noon and 2pm to 6pm; 18F (admission free on Wednesday); ☎ 03 86 64 15 27.

SERRABONE

Prieuré – Open April to October 10am to 6pm, the rest of the year 10am to 5pm; closed public holidays; 10F; ☎ 04 68 84 09 30.

SÈVRES

Musée National de Céramique – ♿ Open all year from 10am to 5pm; closed Tuesday, 1 January, Easter Monday and Whitsun, 1 May, 1 November and 25 December; 20F; ☎ 01 41 14 04 20.

SÉVRIER

Musée de la Cloche – Open 10am to noon and 2.30pm to 5.30pm (6.30pm from June to end August); closed Sunday morning, Monday and 1 January, Easter, and 25 December; 20F; ☎ 04 50 52 47 11; guided tour of the foundry from June to September: 30 F (including a visit to the museum).

SISTERON

🆔 04200 - ☎ 04 92 61 12 03

Citadelle - Open 15 March to 1 November 9am to 5.30pm; from 1 June to 1 September 8.30pm to 7.30pm; closed the rest of the year; 15F; ☎ 04 92 61 27 57.

Eglise Notre-Dame - *Closed Sunday afternoon from All Saints Day to Easter.*

SOISSONS

🆔 Cour St-Jean-des-Vignes - 02200 - ☎ 03 23 53 17 37

Guided tour of the town 🅰 - Contact the tourist information office.

SOLIGNAC

🆔 place Dubreuil - 87110 - ☎ 05 55 00 42 31

Eglise abbatiale - Open daily (except during services) from 8am to 7pm in summer; 9am to 5pm in winter; tour with pre-recorded lecture on walkman (rented at the Syndicat d'initiative 10F); ☎ 05 55 00 42 31 (Syndicat d'initiative) or 05 55 00 50 28 (presbytry).

SOSPEL

🆔 Pont-Vieux - 06380 - ☎ 04 93 04 15 80

Fort St-Roch - Guided tour (1 hour) in July and August 2pm to 6pm daily; from beginning April to end June and in Spetember, open Saturday and Sunday from 2pm to 6pm; closed Monday; 20F; ☎ 04 93 04 00 09 and 04 93 04 00 70.

SOUILLAC

🆔 Bd. Louis-Jean-Malvy - 46200 - ☎ 05 65 37 81 56

Musée national de l'automate et de la robotique - ♿ Open daily in July and August 10am to 7pm; in June and September 10am to noon and 3pm to 6pm; daily from April to May and in October (except Monday) 10am to noon and 3pm to 6pm; daily (except Monday and Tuesday) from November to March 2pm to 5pm; 25F; ☎ 05 65 37 07 07.

STRASBOURG

🆔 17 place de la cathédrale - 67200 - ☎ 03 88 52 28 28

Guided tour of the town 🅰 - Contact the tourist information center.

Cathédrale Notre-Dame: tower - Ascent to the tower in July and August 8.30am to 7pm; from 1 April to 30 June and in September 9am to 6.30pm; in March and October 9am to 7.30pm; from 1 November to 28 February 9am to 4.30pm; enquire at the bottom of the tower, place du Château; 12F; ☎ 03 88 32 59 00, ext. 241.

Cathédrale: astronomical clock - Tour (20min) at 12.30pm; 5F; can be closed during exceptionally long services or concert rehearsals; ☎ 03 88 52 28 28.

Musée de l'Oeuvre Notre-Dame - Open daily (except Monday) 10am to noon and 1.30pm to 6pm; Sunday from 10am to 5pm; closed 1 January, Good Friday, 1 May, 1 and 11 November and 25 December; 15F; ☎ 03 88 52 50 00.

Musées du Palais Rohan - Open daily (except Tuesday) 10am to noon and 1.30pm to 6pm, Sunday 10am to 5pm; closed 1 January, Good Friday, 1 May, 1 and 11 November and 25 December (closed during certain public holidays, enquire); 15F per museum; ☎ 03 88 52 50 00.

Boad trips on the Ill River - Embarkation at the Palais Rohan; departure end March to end October every 30min 9.30am to 9pm; from beginning January to end March and in November and December departure at 10.30am, 1pm, 2.30pm and 4pm; closed 25 December; adults 37F, children 19.50F; from 1 May to 1 October, "Evening cruise" on the floodlit Ill at 9.30pm and 10pm; adults 39F, children 20.50F; for information ☎ 03 88 32 75 25.

Barrage Vauban - Tour and ascent to the panoramic terrace from 9am to 8pm;

Musée alsacien - Open daily (except Tuesday) 10am to noon and 1.30pm to 6pm, Sunday 10am to 5pm; closed 1 January, Good Friday, 1 May, 1 and 11 November and 25 December; 15F; ☎ 03 88 52 50 00.

Musée d'Art moderne - Open daily (except Tuesday) from 10am to noon and 1.30pm to 6pm, Sunday 10am to 5pm; closed 1 January, Good Friday, 1 May, 1 and 11 November and 25 December; 15F; ☎ 03 88 52 50 00.

Musée historique - Closed for renovation; reopening planned for end 1997.

Château de SUSCINIO

Open from 1 June to 30 September 10am to 7pm; from 1 April to 31 May daily 10am to noon and 2pm to 7pm; the rest of the year Thursday, Saturday, Sunday and holidays from 10am to noon and 2pm to 5pm; Monday, Wednesday and Friday from 2pm to 5pm; closed Tuesday and from 20 December to 10 January; 20F; ☎ Sagemor 02 97 41 91 91.

T

Abbaye de THORONET

Open from October to March 9.30am to 12.30pm and 2pm to 5pm, from April to September from 9am to 7pm during the week (closed noon to 2pm Sundays and holidays); closed 1 January, 1 May, 1 and 11 November and 25 December; guided tour 1 hour 27F; ☎ 04 94 73 87 13.

TOUL
🚩 Parvis de la Cathédrale - 54203 - ☎ 03 83 64 11 69

Eglise St-Gengoult – Contact the tourist information office.

Musée municipal – Open daily (except Tuesday) from 1 April to 31 October 10am to noon and 2pm to 6pm; the rest of the year from 2pm to 6pm only; closed 1 January, Easter Sunday, 1 May, 1 November and 25 December; 16F; ☎ 03 83 64 13 38.

TOULON
🚩 Place des Riaux - 83000 - ☎ 04 94 18 53 00

Le port – From mid-June to end September, a warship, anchored in the port, may be visited Saturday, Sunday and certain holidays. Contact the boatmen, quai de Cronstadt.

Boat trips – Embarkation at quai Cronstadt in front of the statue of Cuverville. Guided tours (50min) to the Rade de Toulon from mid-April to end October, morning and afternoon; the rest of the year, only the afternoon; 40F; departure daily from mid-June to mid-September for the Ile de Porquerolles, from May to September a tour of the Iles d'Hyères, or the Calanques de Cassis; information and reservations at S.N.R.T.M., 1247 route du Faron, 83200 Toulon; ☎ 04 94 62 41 14.

Mémorial du Débarquement – Open 1 April to 31 October 9.30am to 11.30am and 2.30pm to 5.30pm; from November to April 9.30am to 11.30am and 2.30pm to 4.30pm; closed Monday; 20F; ☎ 04 94 88 08 09.

Musée de la Marine – Open daily 10am to noon and 1.30pm to 6pm (7pm in July and August); closed Tuesday and holidays except at Easter, at Pentecost and in July and August; 24F; ☎ 04 94 02 02 01.

TOULOUSE
🚩 Donjon du Capitole - 31000 - ☎ 05 61 11 02 22

Guided tour of the town – Contact the tourist information office.

Les Jacobins – Open from 1 July to 15 September weekly 10am to 6.30pm, Sunday and holidays 2.30pm to 6.30pm; the rest of the year 10am to noon and 2.30pm to 6pm, Sunday and holidays 2.30pm to 6pm; 10F; ☎ 05 61 22 21 92.

Musée des Augustins – Open from 1 June to 30 September 10am to 6pm (5pm the rest of the year); open in the evening on Wednesday until 10pm in summer and 9pm in Winter; closed public holidays; 10F.

Hôtel d'Assezat – Open daily (except Tuesday) from 1 June to 30 September 10am to 6pm; the rest of the year 10am (11am on Sunday) to 5pm (6pm on Sunday); 25F; ☎ 05 61 12 06 89.

The arcades on Place de la Capitole, Toulouse

Musée St-Raymond – The museum is presently closed for refurbishment until spring 97.

Muséum d'Histoire Naturelle – Open daily from 1 June to 30 September (except Tuesday) 10am to 6pm; the rest of the year 10am to 5pm; closed holidays; 10F; ☎ 05 61 52 00 14.

Musée Paul-Dupuy – ♿ Open daily from 1 June to 30 September 10am to 6pm; the rest of the year daily 10am and 5pm; closed Tuesday mornings and holidays; 10F (20F during exhibitions); ☎ 05 61 22 21 75.

Château de TOURNOËL

Open daily from Easter to 30 September 9am to noon and 2pm to 7pm; from 1-31 October, open 9am to noon and 2pm to 6.30pm; closed Tuesday; from 1 November to Easter, opening is not certain; 18F; ☎ 04 73 33 53 06.

TOURS

🛈 78, rue Bernard-Palissy - 37000 - ☎ 02 47 70 37 37

A multi-tour pass is for sale at the tourist information office and at all the municipal museums for 50F. It provides access once to each museum, and is valid 1 year from the date of purchase. It also is valid for a lecture tour (on foot, 2 hours 30min).

Guided tour of the town 🅰 – There are two possible tours. The first, a *general* guided tour (Cathedral quarter and Plumereau quarter, with no interior visits) on Monday, Wednesday, Thursday, Friday and Sunday, and lecture tours Tuesday and Saturday which are described in a special schedule distributed by the tourist information office. These tours on foot are given by the interpreter-guides of Touraine. Contact the Direction départementale du tourisme.

Musée du Compagnonage – ♿ Open 16 June to 15 September 9am to 6.30pm; the rest of the year, 9am to noon and 2pm to 6pm (5pm from 16 September to 31 March); closed Tuesday off-season and 1 January, 1 May, 14 July, 1 and 11 November and 25 December; 20F; ☎ 02 47 61 07 93.

La Psalette – Guided tour (30min) from 9am to noon and 2pm to 6pm (5pm from 1 October to 31 May); closed 1 January, 1 May, 1 and 11 November, 25 December; no tours during services; 14F.

Musée des Beaux-Arts – ♿ Open 9am to 12.45pm and 2pm to 6pm; closed Tuesday, 1 January, 1 May, 14 July, 1 and 11 November and 25 December; 30F; ☎ 02 47 05 68 73.

Prieuré de St-Cosme – Open 1 June to 30 September 9am to 7pm; the rest of the year 9am to noon and 2pm to 6pm (5pm from beginning February to mid-March and from 1 October to 30 November); closed Monday off-season, and in December and January; 21F; ☎ 02 47 37 32 70.

Château de Plessis-lès-Tours – Guided tour (45min) from 10am to noon and 2pm to 6pm (5pm from 1 October to 31 March); closed Tuesday, all of January and 1 May, 14 July, 1 and 11 November and 25 December; 10F; ☎ 02 47 37 22 80.

Hôtel Gouin – Free or guided tour (1 hour) from 1 July to 31 August from 10am to 7pm; from 15 March to 30 June and the month of September 10am to 12.30pm and 2pm to 6.30pm; from 1 February to 14 March and in October and November from 10am to 12.30pm and 2pm to 5.30pm, except Friday; closed in December and January; 18F; ☎ 02 47 66 22 32.

Historial de Touraine – Open 1 July to 31 August from 9am to 6.30pm; from 16 March to 30 June and from 1 September to 31 October 9am to noon and 2pm to 6pm; the rest of the year from 2pm to 5.30pm; 33F; ☎ 02 47 61 02 95.

Tropical aquarium – ♿ Open 1 July to 31 August daily 9.30am to 7.30pm; from 1 April to 30 June and 1 September to 15 November 9.30am to noon and 2pm to 6.30pm; closed Sunday morning; the rest of the year, 2pm to 6.30pm; 28F; ☎ 02 47 64 29 52.

Musée des équipages militaires et du train – Free or guided tour (1 hour) 10am to noon and 1.30pm to 5.30pm (Sunday from 1am to 5pm); closed Saturday, Sunday and holidays; admission free; ☎ 02 47 77 20 35.

TRÉGUIER

🛈 Hôtel-de-ville - 22220 - ☎ 02 96 92 30 19

House of Ernest Renan – Open from 1 April to 30 September daily except Tuesday and Wednesday 10am to noon and 2pm to 6pm; closed 1 May; 14F; ☎ 02 96 92 45 63.

Cathédrale St-Tugdual: cloisters – Open daily 1 July to 31 August 9am to 6.30pm (Sunday 12.30pm to 6.30pm); from 15 April to 30 June and September 10am to noon and 2pm to 6pm (Sunday 2pm to 6pm); closed for religious services; 14F.

Forêt de TRONÇAIS

Guided tours of the forest are organized for one or two months each summer starting from the Rond du Vieux Morat; contact the Office National des Forêts, at Moulins. For information on tourist activities, contact the Association du Pays de Tronçais at Cérilly; ☎ 04 70 67 55 89.

TROYES

🛈 16, Bd Carnot - 10014 - ☎ 03 25 73 00 36

Guided tour of the town 🅰 – Contact the tourist information office.

Hôtel de Vauluisant – Open daily 10am to noon and 2pm to 6pm; closed Tuesday and holidays; 20F; a ticket for 4 museums is available for 40F; admission free on Wednesday; ☎ 03 25 76 21 60.

TROYES

Maison de l'Outil et de la Pensée ouvrière – Open 9am (10am on Saturday, Sunday and holidays) to 1pm and 2pm to 6.30pm; 30F; ☎ 03 25 73 28 26.

Eglise Ste-Madeleine – Open in August 10.30am to 7pm; from 1-15 September 10.30am to 5pm; the rest of the year, 10am to noon and 2pm to 4pm.

Musée d'Art moderne – ♿ Open daily (except Tuesday) 11am to 6pm; closed holidays; 20F, admission free on Wednesday; ☎ 03 25 76 26 80.

Eglise St-Pantaléon – Open 1 May to 31 December daily except Sunday morning 10am to noon and 2pm to 4pm; in summer open longer; check with the tourist information office; ☎ 03 25 73 00 36.

Musée St-Loup – Open daily (except Tuesday) 10am to noon and 2pm to 6pm; closed holidays; 20F (40F for a ticket that provides access to 4 museums); admission free on Wednesday; ☎ 03 25 76 21 60.

Pharmacie de l'Hôtel-Dieu – Open daily (except Tuesday) 10am to noon and 2pm to 6pm; closed for holidays; 10F (40F for a ticket that provides access to 4 museums); free on Wednesday; ☎ 03 25 76 21 60.

U

UNGERSHEIM

Écomusée d'Alsace – Open in July and August 9am to 7pm; in April, May, June, and September 9.30am to 6pm; in March and October 10pm to 5pm; the rest of the year 11.30am to 4.30pm; adults 65F (high season), 44F (mid-season), 30F (off season); children 30F (high season), 25F (mid-season), 15F (off season); ☎ 03 89 74 44 74.

UTAH BEACH

Musée du Débarquement – ♿ Free or guided tour (45min) from 1 June to 30 September 9.30am to 7pm; 1 April to 31 May and 1 October to 15 November 9.30am to 12.30pm and 2pm to 6pm; 25F; ☎ 02 33 71 53 35.

V

VAISON-LA-ROMAINE   🛈 place du Chanoine-Sautel – 84110 – ☎ 04 90 36 02 11

Guided tour of the town 🅰 – Contact the tourist information office.

Ruines romaines (Puymin, Villasse) – Free or guided tour (1 hour) from 1 June to 31 August 9am to 12.30pm and 2pm to 6.45pm; from 1 March to 31 May and from 1 September to 31 October 9.30am to noon and 2pm to 5.45pm; the rest of the year 10am to noon and 2pm to 4.30pm; closed 1 January and 25 December; 35F for a combined ticket that provides access to all the city monuments; ☎ 04 90 36 02 11.

Musée archéologique Théo-Desplans – Open from 1 June to 31 August 10am to 1pm and 2.30pm to 7pm; from 1 March to 31 May and 1 September to 31 October 10am to 1pm and 2.30pm to 6pm; the rest of the year daily (except Tuesday morning) 10am to noon and 2pm to 4.30pm; closed 1 January and 25 December; 35F for a combined ticket that provides access to all city monuments; ☎ 04 90 36 02 11.

VALCABRÈRE

Basilique St-Just – Open daily from Easter to All Saints Day and during local school holidays 10am to noon and 2pm to 7pm; the rest of the year only on the weekend at the same times; ☎ 05 61 95 44 44 or ☎ 05 61 88 35 82.

Château de VALENÇAY

Guided tour (45min) daily from June to September 9am to 6pm (last admission at 5.15pm); from March through May and October to end November 9am to noon and 2pm to 6pm (last entrance at 11.15am and 5.15pm); closed from December to February; 40F (the ticket includes a visit of the Parc and the Musée de l'Automobile du Centre); ☎ 02 54 00 10 66.

VANNES   🛈 1, rue Thiers – 56000 – ☎ 02 97 47 24 34

Guided tour of the town 🅰 – Contact the Animation du Patrimoine, Place St-Pierre. ☎ 02 97 47 35 86.

Musée archéologique – Open 1 April to 30 October 9.30am to noon and 2pm to 6pm; the rest of the year 2pm to 6pm; closed Sunday; 20F; ☎ 02 97 42 59 80.

Aquarium océanographique et tropical – &. Open 1 June to 31 August 9am to 7pm; the rest of the year 9am to noon and 1.30pm to 6.30pm; 46F, children 26F; ☎ 02 97 63 74 84.

Château de VAUX-LE-VICOMTE

Open daily from 1 May to 15 October 10am to 6pm (closed from 1pm to 2pm on Saturday); in April and from 16-31 October 10am to 1pm and 2pm to 6pm (10am to 6pm Sundays and holidays); from 1-11 November 11am to 5pm; from 1 May to 15 October candlelight evenings 8.30pm to 11pm on Saturday; 56F (château, gardens and Musée des équipages); 75F (candlelight evening); ☎ 01 64 14 41 90.

Gardens – Open from 1 April to 31 October 10am to 6pm and from 1-11 November 11am to 5pm; from 1 May to 15 October 10am to 11pm on Saturday (candlelight tour); 30F and 45F (candlelight tour); ☎ 01 64 14 41 90.

Musée des Équipages – &. Open daily from 1 April to 31 October 10am to 6pm; from 1-11 November 11am to 5pm; from 1 May to 14 October 10am to 11pm on Saturday; 30F (museum and garden); 45F (candlelight evening); ☎ 01 64 14 41 90.

Mont VENTOUX

Road conditions – For information on the snow conditions on the roads of the Ventoux massif (risk of closed roads between November and May) call Mont Serein at ☎ 04 90 60 72 75 or Carpentras at ☎ 04 90 67 20 88.

VERDUN
🛈 place de la Nation - 55016 - ☎ 03 29 86 14 18

La Citadelle souterraine – Open in July and August 9am to 7pm, in April, May and June 9am to 5.30pm, in September 9am to 1pm and 2pm to 6pm; from 1 October to 12 December 9am to noon and 2pm to 7pm, from 15 February to 31 March 9.30am to noon and 2pm to 4.30pm; the rest of the year 2pm to 4pm; closed 1 January and 25 December; 30F; ☎ 03 29 86 62 02.

Fort de Vaux – Open from 1 May to 10 September 9am to 6.30pm, in May 9.30am to 6pm; from 13 February to 31 March 10am to noon and 2pm to 4.30pm; from 11 September to 29 December 9.30am to noon and 1pm to 5.30pm; from 2 January to 12 February 11am to 3pm; closed 1 January and 25 December; 15F; ☎ 03 29 88 32 88.

VERSAILLES
🛈 7, rue des Réservoirs - ☎ 01 39 50 36 22

Guided tour of the town 🅰 – Contact the tourist information office.

Château – Daily (except Monday); a reservation must be made on site the same day; Admission C or D; lecture-tour 1 hour: 25F, 1 hour 30min: 37F, 2 hours: 50F; ☎ 01 30 84 76 20.

Chapelle et Grands Appartements – Open daily (except Monday) from 2 May to 30 September 9am to 6pm; the rest of the year 9am to 5pm; 42F; ☎ 01 30 84 76 20.

Grand Trianon – Open daily (except Monday) from 2 May to 30 September 10am to 6pm; the rest of the year 10am to noon and 2pm to 5pm Tuesday through Friday, 10am to 5pm Saturday and Sunday; 29F (ticket also valid for the Petit Trianon); ☎ 01 30 84 76 20.

VÉZELAY

Basilique Ste-Madeleine – Open daily (closed Sunday until 1pm); guided tour by written request to the Service des visites, place de la Basilique, 89450 Vézelay or by fax 03 86 33 36 93; ☎ 03 86 33 24 36.

VIEIL-ARMAND

Monument national du Vieil-Armand – Open daily from 1 April to 1 November 8.30am to noon and 2pm to 6.30pm; 5F; for further details contact the Tourist office of Cernay, ☎ 03 89 75 50 35.

VIENNE
🛈 cours Brillet - 38200 - ☎ 04 74 85 12 62

Guided tour of the town 🅰 – Contact the tourist information office.

Eglise St-André-le-Bas – To visit the church, request the key from the caretaker of the Cloître de St-André; closed Tuesday (and also Monday in winter).

Eglise St-André-le-Bas, cloître, ancienne Eglise St-Pierre – Open daily 1 April to 15 October (except Tuesday) 9.30am to 1pm and 2pm to 6pm (from 1 May to 31 August the Théâtre romain is open on Tuesdays); the rest of the year from Wednesday to Saturday 10am to noon and 2pm to 5pm, Sunday 2pm to 6pm only; closed 1 January, 1 May, 1-11 November, 25 December; 8F for each monument (for a pass giving access to all the sights and monuments): 21F; ☎ 04 74 85 50 42; guided tour by request: contact the tourist information office.

Château de VILLANDRY

Château – Free or guided tour (45min) from 1 June to 31 August 9am to 6.30pm; from mid-March to 31 May and from 1 September to 11 November 9am to 5pm; château and garden 41F; ☎ 02 47 50 02 09.

Gardens – Open from 1 June to 31 August 8.30am to 8pm; from 1 April to 31 May and from 1 to 30 September 9am to 7pm; the rest of the year 9am to dusk; 27F; ☎ 02 47 50 02 09.

VILLEFRANCE-DE-ROUERGUE 🛈 Promenade Guiraudet - 12200 - ☎ 05 65 45 13 18.

Chartreuse St-Sauveur – Guided tour (1 hour) from 1 July to 20 September 10am to noon and 2pm to 6.30pm; 20F; ☎ 05 65 45 13 18.

VILLENEUVE-LÈS-AVIGNON 🛈 1 place Charles-David - 30400 - ☎ 04 90 25 61 33.

Guided tour of the town A – Contact the tourist information office.

Chartreuse du Val de Bénédiction – Open from 1 April to 30 September 9am to 6.30pm; the rest of the year 9.30am to 5.30pm; last admission 30min before closing; closed 1 January, 1 May, 1 and 11 November, 25 December; 27F; ☎ 04 90 15 24 24.

VILLEQUIER

Musée Victor Hugo – Free or guided tour (1 hour 30min) 10am to 12.30pm and 2pm to 6.30pm; the rest of the year closed at 6pm; closed Tuesday, 1 January, 1 May and 25 December; 20F; ☎ 02 35 56 78 31.

VITRÉ
🛈 Promenade St-Yves - 35500 - ☎ 02 99 75 04 46

Guided tour of the town A – Open daily in July and August; contact the tourist information office.

Château de VINCENNES

Guided tour daily from 10am to 5.45pm; 10am to 4.15pm 1 October to 31 March; long tour (1 hour 15min) 32F; Short tour (45min) 22F. The keep is presently closed for restoration. ☎ 01 48 08 31 20.

Telephone codes...
As from mid-October 1996,
all French telephone numbers must have ten digits.
Before the old 8-digit number insert:
> *01 for Paris and the Paris region.*
> *02 for northwest France.*
> *03 for northeast France.*
> *04 for southeast France.*
> *05 for southeast France.*

Index

Mont-St-Michel — Towns, sights and tourist regions.
Toulouse-Lautrec, Henri de — People, historical events and subjects.

Isolated sights (caves, châteaux, dams, abbeys etc.) are listed under their proper name.

French World Heritage sites are <u>underlined in blue</u>.

C

Notes

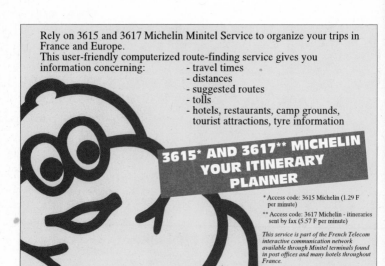

Rely on 3615 and 3617 Michelin Minitel Service to organize your trips in France and Europe.
This user-friendly computerized route-finding service gives you information concerning:
- travel times
- distances
- suggested routes
- tolls
- hotels, restaurants, camp grounds, tourist attractions, tyre information

3615* AND 3617** MICHELIN YOUR ITINERARY PLANNER

* Access code: 3615 Michelin (1.29 F per minute)

** Access code: 3617 Michelin - itineraries sent by fax (5.57 F per minute)

This service is part of the French Telecom interactive communication network available through Minitel terminals found in post offices and many hotels throughout France.

MANUFACTURE FRANÇAISE DES PNEUMATIQUES MICHELIN

Société en commandite par actions au capital de 2 000 000 000 de francs

Place des Carmes-Déchaux – 63 Clermont-Ferrand (France)

R.C.S. Clermont-Fd B 855 200 507

© Michelin et Cie, Propriétaires-Éditeurs 1996

Dépôt légal avril 1996 – ISBN 2-06-149103-0 – ISSN 0293-9436

Printed in the EU 05-97/1

Photocomposition : MAURY Imprimeur S.A., Malesherbes

Impression et brochage : CASTERMAN Imprimeur, Tournai

Cover illustration by Nathalie BENAVIDES/Jean-Luc ROYER

Travelling companions

Michelin *Tourist Guides* and detailed *Maps* are designed to be used together

MICHELIN®

Drop in

and get
to know more
about Michelin!

Discover
the world of Michelin...
Tyres, Tourist Guides
and the Michelin Man:
the entire illustrious story
told through a series
of innovative exhibits
and multimedia displays.

Bibendum
(a.k.a. The Michelin Man)...
The "Bibendum by Michelin"
shop offers a wealth of objects
and souvenirs representing
nearly a century of Bibendum
memorabilia.

Travel...
Michelin's comprehensive collection
of maps and travel guides
opens up worlds to you.